ORIENTATION

It takes only an image or two to evoke Washington, DC: the tiered dome of the **Capitol**, the tall white needle of the **Washington Monument**, or the Romanesque elegance of the **White House**. It's no wonder that first-time visitors to the city feel a sense of déjà vu: They've seen many of the sites countless times on TV, in editorial page cartoons, and in the movies.

Images of the capital possess a certain importance and formality: Imposing structures and institutions house a workforce with a single mind-set—the governing of a nation. Along with this mission goes plenty of pomp—monuments, memorials, museums, and statuary. **The Mall** with its powerhouse sites—the **National Gallery of Art** and the ever-popular **National Air and Space Museum**—is certainly not to be missed. After all, it's also home to the cherished **Lincoln Memorial** and the poignant **Vietnam Veterans Memorial**, both deeply meaningful to our nation's history.

But after making the requisite pilgrimages, the visitor won't be long in discovering the "other Washington," a city of human scale. By law the skyline is low-level, to emphasize the Capitol and the memorials, and many of the city's neighborhoods reveal shady, quiet streets, lined with charming town houses—perfect for a stroll in spring or fall.

It also has more green space than you'd imagine possible in a city, from the remarkably pristine **Rock Creek Park** to the Mall, America's "backyard" and the scene of many political demonstrations and holiday celebrations. Transport yourself with a stroll through the lush, formal gardens of **Dumbarton Oaks**; a wonderland of terraces, pools, and arbors, it's DC's best-kept secret. On weekends at **Capitol Hill's Eastern Market**, congressional representatives, TV newscasters, and other familiar faces may appear amid the crowd of regular city dwellers, here sampling a farmers' market chock-full of produce, picking over handmade crafts, or haggling with flea-market merchants.

In terms of nightlife, it's true that Washington isn't as hot as its northern neighbor, New York City. But DC's nightlife has plenty to offer—from ethnic food sampling and barhopping in funky, mobbed **Adams Morgan**, to a performance in the **Kennedy Center's** elegant **Opera House**, to late-night coffee at Dupont Circle's venerable **Kramerbooks** (open 24 hours on weekends). Or maybe Georgetown's **Blues Alley** is your preference, with the hottest jazz headliners around.

And don't confine your sense of Washington inside its famous **Beltway**. The nearby

Courtesy of the Washington, DC, Convention and Visitors Association

How to Read This Guide

ACCESS® WASHINGTON, DC is arranged by neighborhood so you can see at a glance where you are and what is around you. The numbers next to the entries in the following chapters correspond to the numbers on the maps. The text is color-coded according to the kind of place described:

Restaurants/Clubs: Red

Hotels: Purple | **Shops: Orange**

🍃 **Outdoors/Parks: Green** | **Sights/Culture: Blue**

♿ Wheelchair accessible

WHEELCHAIR ACCESSIBILITY

An establishment (except a restaurant) is considered wheelchair accessible when a person in a wheelchair can easily enter a building (i.e., no steps, a ramp, a wide-enough door) without assistance. Restaurants are deemed wheelchair accessible only if the above applies and if the rest rooms are on the same floor as the dining area and their entrances and stalls are wide enough to accommodate a wheelchair.

RATING THE RESTAURANTS AND HOTELS

The restaurant star ratings take into account the quality, service, atmosphere, and uniqueness of the restaurant. An expensive restaurant doesn't necessarily ensure an enjoyable evening; a small, relatively unknown spot could have good food, professional service, and a lovely atmosphere. Therefore, on a purely subjective basis, stars are used to judge the overall dining value (see the star ratings below). Keep in mind that chefs and owners often change, which sometimes drastically affects the quality of a restaurant. The ratings in this guidebook are based on information available at press time.

The price ratings, as categorized at right, apply to restaurants and hotels. These figures describe general price-range relationships among other restaurants and hotels in the area. The restaurant price ratings are based on the average cost of an entrée for one person, excluding tax and tip. Hotel price ratings reflect the base price of a standard room for two people for 1 night during the peak season.

RESTAURANTS

★	Good
★★	Very Good
★★★	Excellent
★★★★	Extraordinary Experience
$	The Price Is Right (less than $12)
$$	Reasonable ($13–$20)
$$$	Expensive ($21–$30)
$$$$	Big Bucks ($31 and up)

HOTELS

$	The Price Is Right (less than $100)
$$	Reasonable ($100–$150)
$$$	Expensive ($150–$200)
$$$$	Big Bucks ($200 and up)

MAP KEY

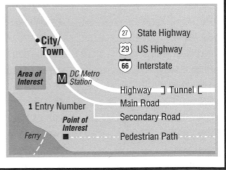

suburbs in **Maryland** and **Virginia** have their own rich history and other surprises too, like a burgeoning collection of first-rate ethnic restaurants—especially those serving Southeast Asian cuisines. They're also homes to some of the area's well-known sights and attractions, like Arlington National Cemetery and Mount Vernon.

Although politics is the local sport, most Washingtonians do not live and die by which party is in power, and the viciousness that characterizes political rhetoric is remarkably absent in the District's citizenry. Just stop and ask someone for directions, and you're likely to get a detailed and friendly response. Summing up DC and its environs with a single image—no matter how powerful—could hardly do the area justice. The Capitol, the Washington Monument, and the White House are only just the beginning. The Washington described between these covers offers something for every taste—regardless of political stripe.

Area code 202 unless otherwise noted.

Getting to DC Airports

Ronald Reagan National Airport (DCA)

Handling domestic and commuter flights, this is the most convenient airport to Downtown DC, just 3.5 miles or a 25-minute cab ride away. In 1997, a more efficient complex housing **Terminals B** and **C** opened next to what is now called **Terminal A**. The new layout has alleviated much of the former traffic and congestion problems, as well as added a pleasant, light-filled waiting area with shops, fast-food establishments, and a few restaurants. For general information, call 703/417.8000 or visit the web site at www.metwashairports.com/national.

AIRPORT SERVICES

Airport Emergencies...............................703/419.3972

Business Service Center 703/417.3200

Information 703/417.8000

Interpreters 703/419.3972

Lost and Found 703/417.0673

Parking ....703/417.7275; recording, 703/417.4311

Police 703/417.8560

Travelers' Aid................703/417.3972, 703/417.3974

AIRLINES

Air Canada 888/247.2262

AirTran 800/AIRTRAN

Alaska Airlines.......................................800/252.7522

America West Airlines 800/235.9292

American Airlines...................................800/433.7300

American Trans Air.................................800/435.9282

Continental Airlines 800/523.3273

Delta Airlines...800/221.1212

Frontier Airlines 800/432.1359

Midwest Airlines 800/452.2022

Northwest Airlines 800/225.2525

Spirit Airlines...800/772.7117

United Airlines.......................................800/864.8331

US Airways/US Airways Shuttle 800/428.4322

In the late 1890s, luxury apartments rented for $35 to $50 a month in DC's most fashionable buildings. Current lessees have to shell out upward of $2,000 per month.

It is a popular delusion that the government wastes vast amounts of money through inefficiency and sloth. Enormous effort and elaborate planning are required to waste this much money.

—P.J. O'Rourke ,
Parliament of Whores

Getting to and from Ronald Reagan National Airport (DCA)

BY BUS

The **Metrobus** (637.7000) stop is at the base of the **National Airport Metro** station. Buses travel to areas not served by Metrorail.

BY CAR

As you leave the airport, you'll face a tangle of roads; if you're headed for DC, take care to follow the frequently appearing signs marked "Exit to Washington." This will put you on the George Washington Memorial Parkway heading north. Take the exit for **Interstate 395** north (it comes up quickly) to the 14th Street Bridge, which will lead you into the downtown area.

If you're going to Foggy Bottom/West End or Georgetown, stay on the parkway and follow the signs for Arlington Memorial Bridge, which will take you to the Lincoln Memorial. Bear left at the memorial and you'll be in Foggy Bottom; keep going and you'll arrive in Georgetown.

Each terminal at the airport has its own parking area, with pedestrian bridges connecting two garages to Terminals B and C. A third garage sits across the traffic circle from Terminal A; airport shuttle buses serve it as well as the more far-flung (and cheaper) satellite lots. For parking and shuttle bus information, call 703/417.7275 or 703/417.4311.

RENTAL CARS

The following rental car companies operate at the airport:

Alamo (off airport)........703/684.0086, 800/832.7933

Avis..800/331.1212

Budget 703/920.3360, 800/527.0700

Dollar 800/800.4000

Enterprise (off airport)..703/553.7744, 800/736.8222

Hertz 703/419.6300, 800/654.3131

National 800/227.7368

Thrifty (off airport) 703/658.2200, 800/367.2277

BY LIMOUSINE

Private vendors operate limousine service from National. A one-way trip to Downtown DC starts at approximately $50.

BY TAXI

There are several taxi stands in the traffic circle in front of Terminal A. At Terminals B and C, the taxi stands are located just outside the baggage-claim area on the lower level. Dispatchers are on duty at all stands. Expect to pay $12-$18 for a trip to Downtown DC, which should take 25 minutes during non–rush hours.

BY TRAIN

The Metrorail (637.7000) is without a doubt the cheapest way to get to or from National Airport. The

National Airport Metro station (on the **Yellow** and **Blue** lines) offers trains to Downtown DC; service begins at 5:30AM on weekdays and 7AM on weekends and runs until approximately midnight weekdays, 3AM weekends. Terminals B and C are connected to the Metro station by covered pedestrian walkways.

Washington–Dulles International Airport (IAD)

Eero Saarinen's expressive design for the main terminal epitomizes the joy of flight: This was the first airport (completed in 1962) designed for the jet age, and its airy main terminal is still spectacular. Saarinen's other idea, mobile lounges designed to carry passengers to airplanes, has been altered somewhat by the surge in traffic. Now, most airlines use the lounges to carry passengers to midfield terminals, where they board through conventional gates. Long-range plans call for replacing the lounges with underground people movers.

International arrivals, customs, baggage claim, ground transportation, a bank, a post office, and 24-hour car rentals are on the ground floor. You also will find information and foreign language assistance services, duty-free gift shops, ATMs, retail stores, and restaurants throughout the airport. For general information, call 703/572.2700 or check online at www.metwashairports.com.

Airport Services

Airport Emergencies	703/572.2952
Information	703/572.2700
International Visitors' Information	703/572.2536
Lost and Found	703/661.6211
Parking	703/572.4500, 703/572.4580
Police	703/572.2952
Travelers' Aid	703/572.8296

Airlines

Aeroflot	888/686.4949
Air Canada	888/247.2262
Air France	800/237.2747
AirTran	800/247.8726
	(AIRTRAN)
Alaska Airlines	800/252.7522
Alitalia	800/223.5730
American Airlines	800/433.7308
ANA	800/235.9262
Austrian Airlines	800/843.0002
British Airways	800/247.9297
	(AIRWAYS)
British Midland Airways	800/788.0555
BWIA International Airways	800/538.2942
Continental Airlines	800/523.3273
Delta Airlines	800/221.1212
Ethiopian Airlines	800/445.2733

Frontier Airlines	800/432.1359
Grupo Taca	800/400.8222
	(400.TACA)
JetBlue	800/538.2583
Korean Air	800/438.5000
Lufthansa	800/645.3880
Northwest Airlines/ KLM Royal Dutch Airlines	800/225.2525
SAS	800/221.2350
Ted	800/225.5833
United Airlines	800/864.8331
US Airways	800/428.4322
Virgin Atlantic	800/821.5438

Getting to and from Washington–Dulles International Airport (IAD)

By Bus

Washington Flyer (888/WASHFLY, www.washfly.com) offers nonstop bus service between **Dulles** and the **West Falls Church Metro** station (on the **Orange** line). Buses leave **Dulles** approximately every 30 minutes beginning at 5:45AM weekdays, 7:45AM weekends and holidays. The last bus leaves the West Falls Church station at 10:45PM daily. Cost is $8 one way, $14 round trip. Buy tickets at Dulles's **Ground Transportation Centers** by Door 4 on the arrivals level. If departing from West Falls Church station, purchase tickets on arrival at Dulles. **SuperShuttle** (800/258.3826; www.supershuttle.com) travels between the airport and local homes, businesses, and hotels. The SuperShuttle boarding area is located on the airport's lower level, outside at curb 1D or 1E. A uniformed company representative assists with baggage and boarding. After midnight, call 703/416.7884 for service. Prices vary depending on distance traveled.

By Car

To get to Downtown DC from the airport, take the **Dulles Access Road** going east (and avoid the **Dulles Toll Road**, a parallel road for local traffic) and watch for the signs connecting you to either **Interstate 66** or Interstate 495 (the Beltway). I-66 will take you over the **Theodore Roosevelt Memorial Bridge** and into Downtown DC in about 45 minutes. It is the more direct route into town; however, during the morning rush hour (6-9:30AM) you must have at least two occupants in your car to use this road. If you take the Beltway, head north and take the George Washington Memorial Parkway exit, which follows the **Potomac River** (the views are spectacular). Follow the parkway to any of the four major bridges into town: the **Key** (into Georgetown), the Roosevelt Memorial or Arlington Memorial (into **Foggy Bottom**, just west of Downtown), or the **14th Street** (into the Mall and Downtown).

For those who are driving to the airport, short- and long-term parking lots are located just outside the terminal; other long-term lots (with cheaper rates) are a free shuttle bus ride away. Check with the airport's parking information line (703/572.4500).

Rental Cars

The following rental car companies have 24-hour counters at the airport:

Alamo 703/684.0086, 800/823.7933

Avis.......................................800/331.1212

Budget 703/920.3360, 800/527.0700

Dollar 800/800.4000

Enterprise 703/478.2300, 800/736.8222

Hertz 703/471.6020, 800/654.3131

National 703/419.1032, 800/227.7368

Thrifty 703/684.2054, 800/367.2277

By Limousine

Private vendors offer limo service from the airport to area locations. Prices start at $50 for Downtown DC and suburban Maryland destinations.

By Taxi

A **Washington Flyer** taxi (703/661.6655) dispatcher is on duty at the airport 24 hours a day at the east and west ramps on Main Terminal's lower level. The cabs accept most major credit cards and are metered. Expect to pay $50-$58 for a trip to Downtown Washington.

Baltimore–Washington International Airport (BWI)

Located 10 miles south of Baltimore and 32 miles north of Washington, **BWI** used to be called **Friendship International** (and still is by some old-timers). The main terminal is a two-level building with access roadways on each level. The bi-level design separates arriving and departing passengers. You can walk directly from individual airline entrances to ticket counters no more than 50 feet away. From there, all departure gates are easily accessible.

Arriving passengers go directly to the lower level, where they find the baggage-claim areas, customs, car rentals, and ground transportation. Airport services include the usual complement of bars, restaurants, and a duty-free shop. For general nonflight airport information, call 800/IFLYBWI or check online at www.bwiairport.com.

Airport Services

Airport Emergencies................................410/859.7040

Business Service Center 410/859.4466

Currency Exchange 410/859.4466

Poet Walt Whitman was an unorthodox Civil War nurse. He had little formal medical training but would go from bed to bed dispensing cheer, an orange, a cigar, letter-writing paper, and stamps—and a generous dose of his large personality. A wartime correspondent wrote, "His presence seemed to light up the place as it might be lighted by the presence of the God of love."

Customs 410/859.3337

Information 410/859.7111

Interpreters 410/859.7111

Lost and Found 410/859.7387

Parking 800/468.6294

Police 410/859.7040

Travelers' Aid 410/859.7207

Airlines

Aer Lingus 800/474.7424

Air Canada 888/247.2262

Air Jamaica 800/523.5585

AirTran..800/247.8726
(AIRTRAN)

American Airlines....................................800/433.7300

British Airways..800/247.9297
(AIRWAYS)

Continental Airlines 800/523.3273

Delta Airlines...800/221.1212

Frontier Airlines 800/432.1359

Icelandair 800/223.5500

Northwest Airlines 800/225.2525

Pan Am 800/359.7262

Midwest Airlines 800/452.2022

Southwest Airlines..................................800/435.9792

United Airlines...800/864.8331

US Airways 800/428.4322

USA 3000 ....877/872.3000

Getting to and from Baltimore–Washington International Airport (BWI)

By Bus and Van

The **BWI Express Metro bus** (*B30*) runs daily between the **Greenbelt Metro** station (on the **Green** line) and the airport at intervals of about 40 minutes. The first bus leaves the station at 6:10AM weekdays, 8:45AM weekends, with the last bus leaving the airport at 10:30PM daily. The **SuperShuttle** (800/258.3826; www.supershuttle.com) travels between the airport and local homes, businesses, and hotels. Between the hours of 6AM and 2AM, service can be arranged at the **Ground Transportation Desk** on the lower level. During other times, call 888/826.2700 to arrange for transportation. Prices vary depending on distance traveled.

By Car

The drive between Downtown DC and BWI is about 45 minutes, except during rush hour, when the trip can take at least a half hour longer. The most direct route to DC from BWI is to take **Interstate 195** north from the airport to the **Baltimore–Washington Parkway** (less than a mile) and proceed south. The BW Parkway ends just outside the District's limits; from there, **New York**

Avenue leads into the Downtown area. An alternate route is to take I-195 north to **Interstate 95** (about 6 miles) and proceed south to the **Capital Beltway** (where I-95 continues). Continue to the BW Parkway heading south, or go west on the Beltway (**Interstate 495**) and get off at any number of major exits (**Georgia** or **Connecticut Avenues, Rockville Pike/Wisconsin Avenue**) heading south to DC.

For those driving to the airport, a large parking garage is located close to the one and only terminal; satellite lots (which are cheaper) are a short shuttle bus ride away. For more information on parking options, call 800/468.6294.

RENTAL CARS

The following rental car companies have counters at a new facility connected to the airport by a shuttle:

Alamo 410/859.8092, 800/832.7933

Avis..............................410/859.1680, 800/331.1212

Budget 410/859.0850, 800/527.0700

Dollar 410/859.5600, 800/800.4000

Enterprise 800/736.8222

Hertz 410/850.7400, 800/654.3131

National 410/859.8860, 800/328.4567

Thrifty 410/850.7139, 800/367.2277

BY LIMOUSINE

Private Car RMA Worldwide (301/231.6555; 800/878.7743) offers limo and sedan service from the airport to any location. Make reservations ahead of time or visit the company's counter on the airport's lower level on arrival. The service charges approximately $100 one way between BWI and Downtown DC.

BY TAXI

Taxi service is available from the airport to Baltimore and Washington. A dispatcher is always on duty; call 410/859.1100. For a 45-minute non-rush hour ride to Downtown Washington, expect to pay upward of $60.

BY TRAIN

BWI's **Rail Station** (410/672.6169) is located 2 miles from the airport. **Amtrak** trains pass through on their way to such Northeast Corridor cities as Philadelphia, New York, and Boston; they stop at this station several times a day. One-way fare from the airport to DC's **Union Station** is $24 ($21.60 with AAA discount). A free shuttle bus travels to and from the rail station every 10 minutes during the day, every 20 minutes during overnight hours. The **MARC train**'s (800/325.7245) **Penn line** runs between Union Station, BWI Airport, and Baltimore's Penn Station Monday through Friday. Fares vary on the basis of points of departure and destination.

BUS STATION (LONG-DISTANCE)

The only bus station in the DC area is the **Greyhound Station** (1005 First Street NE, at K Street; 289.5146; www.greyhound.com) three blocks north of Union Station, just north of Capitol Hill. A taxi stand is right at the main entrance. The station is open 24 hours a day. For Greyhound schedules and fares, call 800/229.9424.

TRAIN STATION (LONG-DISTANCE)

Washington's Union Station (50 Massachusetts Avenue NE, at First Street; 371.9441) is one of the city's architectural jewels. Constructed in 1908, its soaring spaces are pretty much intact, thanks to a major restoration in the 1980s. (For a more detailed description of the building, see the "Capitol Hill" chapter.) The station is conveniently located just north of the Capitol (you'll see that familiar dome as you come out of the station's main doors). Most of the trains serve the eastern seaboard, especially the Northeast Corridor (from Washington up to Boston). But there is service to the Midwest and connecting trains to other points. The station's offices are open from 5AM to midnight, although the building is open 24 hours a day. A Metrorail station is on the lower level, and a taxi stand is at the main entrance, where a dispatcher will guide you to a cab. For information on Amtrak schedules and fares, call 800/872.7245.

Getting Around DC

BICYCLES

Biking around DC can be thrilling—and dangerous. A ride along the bike paths of Rock Creek Park is glorious. But maneuvering around DC's angled streets and traffic circles, with confused tourists and reckless diplomats, is daunting even for residents. If you'd like to rent a bike, try Georgetown's **Thompson Boat Center** (333.9543; www.thompsonboatcenter.com) and **Revolution Cycles** (965.3601; www.revolutioncycles.com). **Bike the Sites** (842.BIKE; www.bikethesites.com) offers 3-hour tours of DC, with bike and helmet rentals.

BY BUS

More than 1,500 Metrobuses thread their way along some 400 routes in the DC area at speeds seldom exceeding 35 miles per hour. Many routes are designed to supplement and extend the reach of the rail system, but in some areas the bus is the sole source of public transportation. Buses are the only public transportation available to Georgetown, for example. Even-numbered 30 buses (30, 32, 34, 36) connect Georgetown to Downtown DC and **Upper Northwest**.

Bus-to-bus transfers are free within DC, with some surcharges on routes to the suburbs; get a transfer from the driver as you enter. The fare is $1.25 for regular routes, $3 for express routes; exact change is required, and dollar bills are accepted. For more information, call the **Washington Metropolitan Area Transit Authority** (962.1234; www.wmata.com).

BY CAR

DC is a somewhat bewildering place to navigate. The National Park Service's highway signs—easily read at horse-and-buggy speed—are often illegible to a harried motorist trying to find the right lane on the Rock Creek Parkway.

CAPITAL CELEBRATIONS

Washingtonians love a parade—or a street fair or festival or any excuse to party and, not incidentally, be given a day off from work. (After all, this is the only place in America where workers get a holiday every fourth 20 January—Inauguration Day.) Planning a trip to Washington on any major holiday guarantees you can get in on the fun. Read on for details on those celebrations and a few others throughout the year. Admission to all events is free unless otherwise noted.

January

Inauguration Day As mentioned, every 4 years on 20 January, a new term of office begins for a US president and the city is packed with well-wishers from the winning party. Private parties are the order of the day, but there are usually public events on the Mall, and you can stand along **Pennsylvania Avenue** and watch the president lead an impressive parade of bands from just about every state.

Martin Luther King Jr.'s Birthday The civil rights leader's birthday is celebrated in mid-January, with tributes to Dr. King at the Lincoln Memorial.

February

Chinese New Year Parade Washington has a tiny **Chinatown**, but that doesn't dampen the enthusiasm or turnout for this annual affair, complete with colorful dancing dragons and street-level fireworks. Call 789.7000 for the exact date.

Washington's Birthday Parade On the Saturday closest to 22 February, **Old Town Alexandria** throws a big party for our nation's first chief executive, whose **Mount Vernon** home is just down the road. Locals turn out in colonial costume, bands play, and there are even a few floats, though this will never be mistaken for the Tournament of Roses parade. Call 703/838.4200 for schedule of events.

Abraham Lincoln's Birthday is celebrated at his memorial with a reading of the Gettysburg Address.

March

Smithsonian Kite Festival On the last Saturday of March, the skies around the **Washington Monument** are filled with colorful, high-flying contraptions of paper and light wood. Competitions in design, performance, and other categories are held, but winning is secondary to the exhilaration of being outdoors on an early spring day. For more information, call 357.3030.

April

Cherry Blossom Festival Spring officially kicks off with this festival, which seems to grow larger every year. The blossoms usually bloom the first week of April, with 2 weeks of celebration offering a wide variety of events.

Concerts and a big parade (usually the first Saturday of April) are the highlights. Call 547.1500 or check the web site www.nationalcherryblossomfestival.org for a schedule of events.

White House Easter Egg Roll Celebrated since 1878 on the Monday after Easter, this event invites children aged 3 through 6, accompanied by an adult, to assemble on the **South Lawn** of the **White House**. Participation is limited, but a larger party also takes place across the street on the **Ellipse**. For more information, call 456.7041.

Filmfest DC For 2 weeks during spring, Washington turns into a modest approximation of Cannes, with screenings of films from a variety of countries, as well as parties and receptions—all open to the public. Events are held at several commercial theaters and a few of the not-for-profit venues like the museum theaters. Admission is charged. Call 628.FILM or see www.filmfestdc.org for more information.

May

Memorial Day ceremonies Arlington National Cemetery (703/607.8000), the **Vietnam Veterans Memorial** (634.1568), and the **US Navy Memorial** (737.2300) are the sites for solemn ceremonies to honor the nation's war dead. Call for ceremony schedules.

Taste of DC During Memorial Day weekend, Pennsylvania Avenue is closed to cars and open to booths with samplings of many of the area's best restaurants. Live entertainment adds to the fun. This is a great way to decide where you want to eat during your visit. For more information, call 789.7000.

June

Smithsonian Folklife Festival For the last weekend in June and first in July, the **Smithsonian**'s museums put on the summer's best show. The **Mall** becomes home to craftspeople, musicians, and, perhaps most important, cooks serving American or foreign cuisines. Each year focuses on different regions of the US or the world. Call 275.1150 or check www.folklife.si.edu for more information.

Capital Pride Festival Each June this annual event celebrates gay and lesbian life with a parade and street fair featuring vendors, dancers, and musicians. For more information, contact the Whitman-Walker Clinic, which sponsors the event, at 797.3510, or the web site at www.capitalpride.org.

During the third week of June, restaurants compete to test their barbecue talents in the **Safeway Annual National Capital Barbecue Battle** on Pennsylvania Avenue. For more information, call 301/860.0630 or visit the web site at www.barbecuebattle.com.

Then, in late June, the colorful **Caribbean Carnival** is held. For more information on this event, call 726.2204 or visit the web site at www.dccaribbeancarnival.com.

July

Fourth of July celebration A huge **Independence Day** parade kicks off Washington's biggest party. In the early evening the **National Symphony Orchestra** presents a free concert on the **West Lawn** of the **Capitol**. Get there early with your blanket and picnic supplies. Finally, there's the mammoth fireworks display centered at the Washington Monument, visible from many areas of the city. For more information, call 789.7000.

Bastille Day On 14 July French Independence Day is celebrated with a race featuring waiters and waitresses carrying trays of Champagne along 12 blocks of Pennsylvania Avenue. Live entertainment and food keep the celebration going into the night. For more information, call 789.7000.

August

Maryland State Fair Maryland's own piece of Americana doesn't change much from year to year, and most people like it that way. The fair is held late in the month at the **Maryland Fairgrounds**, north of Baltimore. Admission is charged. Call 410/252.0200 for exact dates.

September

National Symphony Orchestra Concert On Sunday of **Labor Day** weekend, the end of summer is marked by this big outdoor concert, held on the West Lawn of the Capitol. Crowds are more modest and temperatures more reasonable than at the Fourth of July affair. For more information, call 800/444.1324 or check out www.kennedy-center.org/nso.

Adams Morgan Festival This weekend event in September is the urban equivalent of a state fair, with games, music, crafts, and plenty of food in Washington's most ethnically diverse neighborhood. Call 328.9451 or 332.4935 for a schedule of events.

Black Family Reunion Celebration is held in early September. More information is available at 737.0120 or www.ncnw.org.

The Kennedy Center Prelude Festival provides a 2-week review of the upcoming season. Call 800/444.1324 or visit www.kennedy-center.org/prelude for more details.

The Kalorama House and Embassy Tour is given in mid-September. More details are available at 387.4062 or www.woodrowwilsonhouse.org. This event is a unique opportunity to see the interiors of selected houses and mansions.

October

Marine Corps Marathon The marines only run the race, they don't run in it. On a crisp fall Sunday in late October, you get to cheer on some of the country's best long-distance runners—and take some inspiration for your own fitness regimen. Call 800/786.8762 for the exact date.

Halloween in Georgetown Not a scheduled event—more of a happening on the 31st. Thousands of people congregate at **Wisconsin Avenue Northwest** and **M Street** to parade their costumes, which are often of a political bent.

In the middle of October, the **Reel Affirmation Film Festival** offers gay and lesbian–orientated films. Call 986.1119 or visit their web site at www.reelaffirmations.org.

November

Veterans Day On 11 November wreaths are laid at the **Tomb of the Unknowns** (703/607.8000) and ceremonies are held at the Vietnam Veterans Memorial (634.1568), as thousands of vets come to Washington to honor their fallen comrades. Call for ceremony schedules.

December

Scottish Christmas Walk On the first weekend of the month, Alexandria's annual parade and festival honors Celtic traditions. Crafts and food will get you in the holiday mood. For more information, call 703/838.4200.

The Pageant of Peace Also early in the month, the lighting of the National Christmas Tree on the Ellipse, with music and caroling, is the official kickoff for the holiday season. See www.pageantofpeace.org for the exact date and more details.

New Year's Eve celebrations As part of a growing trend, many cities in the Washington–Baltimore area are holding no-alcohol family-oriented festivals featuring music, dance, and other performances. Among the participating communities is Alexandria. Call 703/838.4200 for more information.

Unfortunately, you'll probably have ample time to read the signs, as the highways are crowded. The Beltway (I-95 and I-495) loops around the city's Downtown area and connects it to the suburbs. The few bridges over the Potomac (the **American Legion Memorial** and the **Woodrow Wilson Memorial Bridges** on the Beltway; the Roosevelt Bridge on I-66; the Key and Arlington Memorial Bridges; and the popular 14th Street Bridge) quickly become rush-hour bottlenecks. Radio traffic reports on **WTOP** (1500 AM) are helpful.

In an attempt to handle Washington rush hours, certain traffic adjustments have been made. For example, some major thoroughfares, such as Connecticut Avenue, switch the direction of several lanes to match the traffic flow. I-66 is restricted to car pools with two or more people inbound during morning rush hour and outbound in the evening; I-395 has restricted car pool lanes during rush hours.

In addition to traffic woes, DC drivers have another worry: diplomats. Washingtonians have long cringed at the vehicular mayhem caused by some members of the diplomatic corps, who take advantage of the diplomatic immunity that protects them from criminal prosecution and civil suits resulting from an accident. Concern over these reckless drivers who refuse to heed parking regulations or speed limits has resulted in a law granting victims of diplomatic drivers some financial compensation in lieu of insurance payments. The State Department issues red-white-and-blue license plates to the diplomatic corps. You'd be wise to give them a wide berth.

Parking

Be forewarned that the DC government is singularly efficient in its parking enforcement. Metered street parking generally runs for a 2-hour maximum at a quarter for each 15 minutes; carry lots of quarters and return to the car on time. Expired meters incur a hefty ticket, and cars left in rush-hour zones are swiftly towed at painful cost. The DC police have also instituted strict weekend parking regulations in Georgetown in an effort to reduce congestion. Obey the special signs or risk having your car impounded. All spaces for the disabled are monitored; if your car doesn't have a handicap license plate, don't try it. Your best bet is to leave your car in one of the Downtown parking garages, which are plentiful but expensive, and use the Metro to get around from there. Given the high cost of tickets and towing, the garages could almost turn out to be a bargain.

Subways

The steadily expanding Metrorail system—part subway, part surface transit—comprises five color-coded lines that snake from the suburbs through Downtown DC and back (see map on page 254). Thanks to built-in quality-control features by designer **Harry Weese**, travel by Metrorail is clean, comfortable, and usually very safe. More than 500,000 passengers use the system on an average day. Hours of operation are M-Th, 5:30AM-midnight; F, 5:30AM-3AM; Sa, 7AM-3AM; Su, 7AM-midnight. If you're going to be using the Metro near closing time, check the "last train" posting at the station kiosk. Station entrances are marked by a tall, dark

brown pylon with a large letter *M* displayed on all four sides. Brightly colored stripes beneath the logo indicate which lines serve that particular station. In addition to the color of the line, it is essential to know that train's last stop; trains on the same line may have different end points. The front of each train is clearly marked.

The fare you pay depends on where you get on and off and what time of day you travel. From opening until 9:30AM and between 3-7PM and until 2AM fares range from $1.35 minimum to $3.90 maximum. At other times there is a $1.35 minimum, $1.85 mid range, and $2.35 maximum. A fare card is a good way to handle the cumbersome price hierarchy. You can get fare cards from vending machines in values of $1.35 to $45, and online in values of $10, $15, and $20. A 1-day pass is available for $6.50 and is good for travel on weekdays after 9:30AM and all day on weekends. You can get it at the sales office at the Metro Center station.

Special discount fares for senior citizens and the disabled are also available. (Although Metrorail is accessible to the disabled, its elevators are sometimes hard to find and are often being repaired.) Subway-to-bus transfers are available from machines inside your station of origin, but there are no bus-to-subway transfers.

Don't be daunted; once you figure out how to use it, the subway is very convenient to most of the places you'll want to visit. If you have questions, go to Metro Center, the main transfer point on the Blue, Red, and Orange lines. An agent at one of the station windows at the **12th and F Streets** exit can help you, or call 637.7000 for information about routes, fares (including disabled, student, and senior citizen), and parking and how to get schedules by mail. Other help lines: on-call service for the disabled (962.1825); TDD for the hearing-impaired (638.3780); lost and found (962.1195); transit police (962.2121).

By Taxi

DC's taxi system is somewhat of a local embarrassment. Cabs are often dilapidated, and drivers are often rude, unscrupulous, and ignorant of the city's geography. The situation could be improved if Congress would legislate meters, and if the District would do something about the lax regulation of the taxi system. On the other hand, DC cabs are cheap and plentiful compared with those in other cities. There are about 8,000 cabs, so hailing one is rarely a problem.

DC cab fares are based on a zone system (the District is divided into eight zones), with an additional charge for each zone traversed. A surcharge is added onto the fare for additional passengers and during evening rush hours. Fare information, along with zone maps, should be displayed in each cab (be sure to specify which quadrant of the city you want). Copies of the zone maps can be found online at www.dctaxi.dc.gov. Unfortunately, this confusing system, in combination with the low fares, encourages drivers to overcharge. Caveat emptor: Drivers are allowed to pick up multiple fares as long as they take the original rider no more than five blocks out of the way of the original destination—great if it's a rainy day and you're the second or third fare; not so great if you're in a hurry. Fares from DC to the airports are based on mileage.

Two large DC cab companies are **Yellow Cab** (546.7900; www.dcyellowcab.com) and **Diamond** (387.6200), which have radio-dispatch cabs. Maryland and Virginia cabs use meters; they can take you in and out of DC, but not between spots within DC itself.

TOURS

For a walking tour of Washington, contact **Anecdotal History Tours of Washington, DC** (301/294.9514; www.dcsightseeing.com), Tour DC (301/588.8999; www.tourdc.com), **Washington Walks** (484.1565; www.washingtonwalks.com), or **Cultural Tourism DC** (828.9522; www.culturaltourismdc.org). **Washington Photo Safari Tours** offer tips on the best spots for photo taking (877/512.5969; www.washingtonphotosafari.com). If you'd rather ride, the **Martz Gold Line/Gray Line** (301/386.8300; www.graylinedc.com) offers a variety of tours on large air-conditioned buses or red trolleys. Roll by the major sites with **Old Town Trolley Tours of Washington** (832.9800; www.oldtowntrolley.com) or **Tourmobile** (554.5100; www.tourmobile.com). **DC Ducks** (832.9800) lets you cruise both the streets and the Potomac—without leaving your seat—in a World War II amphibious vehicle. They operate between April and October. For a cruise on the Potomac, contact **Dandy Cruise Ships** (703/683.6076; www.dandydinnerboat.com), which offer lunch and dinner cruises daily year-round; **Odyssey Cruises**, 888/741.0281 or www.odysseycruises.com, which offer very attractive lunch and dinner cruises in their distinctive low and flat vessels; or **Spirit Cruises** (866/211.3811; www.spiritcruises.com), for lunch and dinner cruises as well as trips to Mount Vernon. If you'd like to try cycling around DC, **Bike the Sites** (842.BIKE; www.bikethesites.com) offers several tours geared to different abilities. Fun, educational itineraries can be custom-designed for your family by the **Children's Concierge** (877/888.5462; www.childrensconcierge.com). Outside the city, **Watermark Cruises** (410/268.7600; www.watermarkcruises.com) offers tours of Annapolis and Baltimore.

WALKING

There's an easy and inexpensive way to see Washington: on foot. Walking around the Mall on a lovely day is a pleasure few other cities can offer; so many attractions are near one another, and the broad lawn and shady trees provide a buffer to all that concrete and marble. A number of neighborhoods—Georgetown, Adams Morgan, Capitol Hill, Foggy Bottom—were made for strolling, with their fine architecture and plentiful diversions, restaurants, and shops. When walking in unfamiliar areas, however, don't wander too far from popular attractions, and exercise extra caution at night.

FYI

ACCOMMODATIONS

DC's many hotel rooms are at times occupied by almost as many visitors as conventioneers. In early spring,

around the time the cherry blossoms appear, rooms can be hard to come by, unless you're willing to settle for modest lodgings in areas less convenient to attractions. For help finding the right hotel, contact **Washington D.C. Accommodations** (800/503.3330; www.dcaccommodations.com) or **Capitol Reservations** (800/847.4832; www.capitolreservations.com). For information about bed-and-breakfast accommodations, contact the **Bed & Breakfast Accommodations, Ltd.** (P.O. Box 12011, Washington, DC 20005; 877/893.3233; www.bedandbreakfastdc.com).

CLIMATE

DC is a temperate city, except during the summers, when the heat and humidity can wilt even the hardiest soul. Thunderstorms are frequent during the summer, and about 18 inches of snow falls during an average winter—just enough to send Washington drivers into a tizzy. Spring and fall are the best times to visit; during these seasons a sweater or jacket should be just right.

MONTHS	AVERAGE TEMPERATURE (°F)
December-February	37
March-May	57
June-August	78
September-November	60

DRINKING

The legal drinking age in DC, Maryland, and Virginia is 21. Bars in the District can serve liquor until 2AM Monday through Thursday and Sunday, and until 3AM Friday and Saturday. Retail liquor store prices are generally cheapest within DC. Beer is sold in liquor stores, supermarkets with liquor departments, and the occasional market. Liquor stores close on Sunday.

MONEY

Banks are generally open Monday through Friday from 9AM to 3PM, with longer hours on Friday. Weekend hours are rare. Cash machines are plentiful and can be found not only at banks but also in public places like **Smithsonian** museums, supermarkets, and some Metrorail stations. **Thomas Cook Foreign Exchange** exchanges foreign currency, as do several major banks. Traveler's checks are available at most local banks.

PERSONAL SAFETY

The city's reputation for street crime is in some ways well earned, but most of the personal crime takes place in neighborhoods far away from the tourist attractions, although recently there has been a rise in crimes in more popular parts of DC. Wherever you go, it's important to stay alert. Pickpockets are not unusual on crowded Metro trains, and muggers can lurk in the shadows on lonely side streets. The Metrorail system has an exemplary safety record, with a strong police presence and attendants at each station to assist you. Metrobuses are not as well monitored. Car break-ins are not uncommon, so don't leave any possessions visible in your car when you park it. You can hail cabs in the more populous areas, or ask your hotel's concierge or a restaurant maître d' to call a cab.

PUBLICATIONS

The *Washington Post* is the region's major daily; the *Washington Times* offers a conservative slant. The free weekly *City Paper* is particularly good for tracking the local entertainment scene, as is the *Post*'s "Weekend" section, published every Friday. *Washingtonian Magazine* is a monthly lifestyle magazine with information on dining, shopping, travel, and local personalities. *The Hill* and *Roll Call* provide the lowdown on the doings on Capitol Hill. The *Current* newspapers, with weekly editions for Northwest, Georgetown, and Rock Creek, cover music, lectures, and shops in their respective areas. The *Washington Blade* is a weekly newspaper covering local and national gay community news plus arts and entertainment. *Where Magazine* is distributed in local hotels and provides visitor information.

RADIO STATIONS

Station formats can change with the seasons; don't be surprised if what you hear is not what you expected.

ON THE DIAL	CALL LETTERS	FORMAT
AM:		
570	WTNT	Talk
630	WMAL	News/talk/sports
1260	WWRC	News
1500	WTOP	News radio
FM:		
88.5	WAMU	News/talk/music (NPR)
89.3	WPFW	Jazz/community radio
90.9	WETA	Classical (NPR)
93.9	WKYS	Urban contemporary
94.7	WARW	Classic rock
95.5	WPGC	Urban contemporary
96.3	WHUR	Urban adult
97.1	WASH	Soft rock
98.7	WMZQ	Country
99.1	WHFS	Alternative
99.5	WHIT	Top 40
101.1	WWDC	Rock
103.5	WGMS	Classical
104.1	WWZZ	Top 40
107.3	WRQX	Adult contemporary

The Marine Band, which made its debut at the White House in 1801, is the oldest military band in the United States.

An existing set of George Washington's false teeth is made of rhinoceros ivory and sealing wax, jointed by spiral springs.

RESTAURANTS

Because you'll be vying for a table with Washington's ever-burgeoning dining-out population, it's wise to make reservations. Dress at most restaurants is relaxed, but it never hurts to double-check; for example, summer attire such as shorts and sandals may not pass muster. A few restaurants in the Foggy Bottom area (near the Kennedy Center) and Downtown (near the **Shakespeare Theatre**) offer menus for pre-theater diners, and some of the city's tonier spots offer prix-fixe menus; ask about special menus when making reservations. Regarding late-night meals: In this hardworking town, most people hit the sack early (even on weekends), so you may have to look around for restaurants that stay open late; these are likeliest to be in Georgetown and Adams Morgan.

SHOPPING

Downtown used to be the place to shop in Washington, and there is still some good shopping at the **Shops at National Place** (F Street NW, between 13th and 14th Streets), but more fertile fields lie along lower Connecticut Avenue (between K Street and Florida Avenue), in Georgetown (along Wisconsin Avenue and M Street), and in Adams Morgan (along 18th Street and Columbia Road). Upper **Wisconsin Avenue**, near the Maryland line, is home to two city malls: **Mazza Gallerie** and **Chevy Chase Pavilion**, catering to shoppers with deeper pockets. The best place to shop ethnic, especially Latin, Caribbean, and African, is in Adams Morgan. And don't forget the Smithsonian shops, all of which offer good selections of souvenirs and one-of-a-kind gifts adapted from the museums' collections.

SMOKING

It is illegal to smoke on public transportation, in theaters, outside of designated smoking areas in restaurants, and in most shops.

STREET PLAN

DC is a rectangle bordered on the southwest by the Potomac River and the other three sides by the state of Maryland. Within the city are four quadrants: Northwest (largest, most of Downtown), Northeast (mostly residential), Southwest (smallest, government buildings, the Potomac waterfront), and Southeast (Capitol Hill and residential). The Capitol is at the "center" of the city, and the quadrants are determined in relation to it. Not all the quadrants are the same size, so some have many fewer streets than others. The directions in which they branch off determine the street names; for example, there are four **First Streets** in Washington: NW, NE, SW, and SE.

Within the quadrants, streets form a grid: Those running north–south are numbered and east–west streets are lettered—up to W but not including J. Avenues—many named for states such as Pennsylvania, Connecticut, and New York—run on diagonals through the grid. Avenues intersect with other avenues at traffic circles.

Phone Book

EMERGENCIES

AAA Emergency Road Service 703/222.5000
Ambulance/Fire/Police..911
Auto Impound 727.5000
Auto Theft...311
Locksmith (AAA 24-hour) 415.0484
Pharmacy (24-hour) 785.1466
Poison Control Center............................800/222.1222
Police (nonemergency) 311

HOSPITALS

George Washington University........................715.4000
Georgetown University....................................444.2000

Sibley Memorial Hospital 537.4000
Washington Hospital Center 877.7000

VISITORS' INFORMATION

American Youth Hostels 783.4943
Amtrak Railroad Service 800/872.7245
Better Business Bureau..................................393.8000
Disabled Visitors' Information 301/528.8664
Greyhound Bus.....................................800/231.2222
Metro Transit (Washington
Metropolitan Area Transit Authority)...............637.7000
US Passport Office 647.0518
Weather 936.1212

(**Dupont Circle**, where Massachusetts, Connecticut, and New Hampshire Avenues intersect, is the best known.)

TAXES

In DC, the hotel tax is 14.5%, the meal tax is 10%, and the sales tax is 5.75%. In Maryland and Virginia, taxes vary by city/county.

TICKETS

Most theaters in the Washington area sell advance tickets over the phone, charged to your credit card for a small fee. When you call, ask about student and senior citizen discounts. **Ticketmaster** (432.7328) has a monopoly on many big-event tickets, although tickets for sellout events such as **Washington Redskins** games are often available at hefty markups through classified ads in the *Washington Post* as well as through other ticket brokers. For tickets to **Orioles** games, try the **Orioles Team Store** (925 17th Street NW, between I and K Streets; 296.2473). No telephone charges are accepted. Ticketsnationwide.com (8630 Fenton Street, Suite 707, Silver Spring, MD; 800/666.6849; www.ticketdoor.com) sells tickets to concert, theater, and sporting events. **Ticket Finders** (7833 Walker Drive, off Greenbelt Road, Suite 510, Greenbelt, MD; 800/356.7983; www.ticketfinders.com) specializes in tickets for sellout events, including concerts and Redskins games; cost rises with the popularity of the event. Located in Penn Quarter, **TicketPlace** (407 Seventh Street NW, between D and E Streets; TIC-KETS and www.ticketplace.com) sells half-price tickets the day of the show for local theaters, including the **Arena Stage**, Kennedy Center, and **Warner** and **National Theatres**. **Top Centre Ticket Service** (11781 Lee Jackson Highway, Suite 270, Fairfax, VA; 800/673.8422; www.topcentre.com) sells tickets for

Redskins games and other sporting events, concerts, and theatrical performances. A service charge is added. **Washington Performing Arts Society** (2000 L Street NW, at 20th Street; 833.9800; www.wpas.org), the city's largest nonprofit arts organization, sponsors concerts at the Kennedy Center, **Dance Place**, and **Lisner Auditorium**, with offerings ranging from foreign orchestras (**Warsaw Philharmonic**, **Vienna Symphony Orchestra**) to folk music, dance, jazz, and gospel. If all else fails, ask your hotel's concierge, who may have his or her own resources.

TIME ZONE

Washington is in the Eastern Time Zone, same as New York City, and 3 hours ahead of California.

TIPPING

A 15% tip is standard in restaurants; the meal tax is 10%, so increase the tax by half, unless you feel like being generous. Taxi drivers are also tipped 15% of the fare. Hotel and station porters generally expect $1 per bag; maids should get at least $2 a day, depending on the size and accoutrements of the room.

VISITORS' INFORMATION CENTER

The **Washington, DC Convention and Tourism Corporation** provides visitor information via a toll-free number (800/422.8644) and a web site (www.washington.org). The **DC Chamber of Commerce** operates a visitors' center at the Ronald Reagan Building at the International Trade Center (1300 Pennsylvania Avenue NW, 866/324.7386; www.dcchamber.org), offering hotel, dining, and tour information. The center is open Monday through Saturday during the spring and summer, weekdays only during the fall and winter.

Capitol Hill/
Northeast/
Southeast

DOWNTOWN

Florida Ave. NE

4th St.
5th St.
6th St.

1

2

West Virginia Ave. NE
Queen St. NE
Oates St. NE
Trinidad Ave.
Neal St.
Morse St.
Montello Ave. NE

M St. NE

4

L St. NE

K St. NE

I St. NE

7th St. NE
8th St. NE

H St. NE

3rd St. NE

NORTHEAST

G St. NE

5th St. NW
4th St. NW
3rd St. NW
2nd St. NW
1st St. NW

New Jersey Ave. NW

N Capital St.

1st St. NE

M Judiciary Sq

Louisiana Ave.

Delaware Ave.

5 6
M
Union Station

F St. NE

E St. NE

7

8

9

10

Maryland Ave. NE

D St. NE

C St. NE

Massachusetts Ave. NE

Tennessee Ave. NE

Pennsylvania Ave. NW

11

Constitution Ave. NE

Spring 12 Grotto

13

14

The Mall

Maryland Ave. SW

15 Union Square

Canal St. SW

16

17 A St. NE

E Capitol St.

20

21

A St. SE

18 Lincoln Park

CAPITOL HILL

North Carolina Ave. SE

9th St. SE
10th St. SE
11th St. SE
12th St. SE
13th St. SE

14th St. SE

Kentucky Ave.

Independence Ave. SE

1st St. SE
2nd St. SE

22

23

24

25

26

27

Federal Center SW
M

4th St. SW

SOUTHWEST

Delaware Ave. SW

S Capitol St.

Capitol South
M D St. SE

29

28

4th St. SE
5th St. SE
6th St. SE

C St. SE

South Carolina Ave. SE

Pennsylvania Ave. SE

Potomac Ave
M

E St. SE

F St. SE

Virginia Ave

7th St. SE

M Eastern Market

30

31

32

G St. SE

34 35

SOUTHEAST

Potomac Ave.

New Jersey Ave. SE

395

Southeast Fwy.

I St. SE

M Waterfront

K St. SE

L St. SE

M St. SW

N St. SW

O St. SW

P St. SW

Half St.

36

M Navy Yard

M St. SE

37

Marine Corps Museum

Navy Museum

U.S.S. Barry

Anacostia Bridge

11th Street Bridge

1st St. SW

Potomac Ave. SE

Anacostia River

Frederick Douglass Memorial Bridge

U.S. Naval Reservation

Ridge Pl. SE

S St. SE

Good Hope Rd.

Martin Luther King Jr. Ave. SE

U St. SE
V St. SE
W St. SE
13th St.
14th St.

M Anacostia

39

40

N

km
mi
1/4
1/2
1/2
1

CAPITOL HILL/NORTHEAST/SOUTHEAST

Although Capitol Hill may not lie in the exact geographic center of Washington, it is, nonetheless, the heart of the city. Whether you're involved in government or not, there is a permeating sense that much of what happens in this town either starts or concludes on "the Hill." Appropriately, the directionals at the end of every DC street name give its relation to this country's seat of democracy with its familiar dome.

In 1791, when **Pierre Charles L'Enfant**, the Frenchman hired to design a capital city on the banks of the **Potomac**, spied the grassy rise, it was called **Jenkins Hill**. L'Enfant had already chosen a site a few miles to the west for the presidential residence, so this "pedestal waiting for a monument" would be the home of what he modestly called "the congressional building."

Ten years later, as the building, now known as the **Capitol**, was under construction, Secretary of the Treasury Albert Gallatin described the neighborhood around the Capitol as containing "seven or eight boarding houses, one tailor, one shoemaker, one printer, a washing woman, a grocery shop, a pamphlets and stationery store, and an oyster house," and considered it "far from being pleasant or even convenient."

More than 200 years later, Capitol Hill, the area that fans out eastward from the Capitol, and the adjoining neighborhoods to the north and south have become quite pleasant, with a few more merchants and places to eat and stay than in Gallatin's day; and thanks to the **Metro** subway system, it is easily accessible.

Currently, Capitol Hill is swarming with construction equipment as the **Capitol Visitor Center** takes shape. When it opens, it will provide visitors to the Capitol with a variety of amenities, within a secure public environment. This underground center, at nearly 600,000 square feet, will be located on the east side of the Capitol. When completed, the entire **East Front Plaza** will be restored to its original historic plan.

Surrounding the Capitol are several other buildings, familiar perhaps more by name than by sight. To the immediate south sit three huge House office buildings (the **Rayburn**, **Longworth**, and **Cannon**); to the north, three more office buildings for the Senate (the **Russell**, **Dirksen**, and **Hart**). To the east are the **Library of Congress**, whose ever-expanding collections have filled three buildings, and the **Supreme Court**, the final arbiter of legal disputes. To the north is the splendid **Union Station**, a train station that's filled to the brim with shops and eateries.

Beyond these impressive structures lies the "real Hill," a quiet residential neighborhood of neatly maintained row houses, most dating from the turn of the 19th century, some back even further. **Pennsylvania Avenue**, which extends southeast from the Capitol, is the Hill's main street, home to many businesses and restaurants (but, alas, no oyster house). At the heart of the Hill is the **Eastern Market** on **Seventh Street Southeast**. The lone survivor of the city's three major food markets from the late 19th and early 20th centuries, the market offers farmers' produce, crafts, and delicious crab cakes; it also serves as a weekend gathering place—and Flea Market—for residents to catch up with one another after a week of political posturing. Capitol Hill's boundaries depend on who does the mapping—real-estate folks, mindful of the cachet the Hill's name holds, throw the net farthest into Northeast and Southeast territory.

Northeast is home to two universities and a college—including **Gallaudet University**, a leader in educating the deaf since 1864, and **Catholic University of America**, since 1887 a bastion of Catholic higher learning. On the grounds of Catholic University sits the impressive **National Shrine of the Immaculate Conception**. **Trinity College** has been offering women a liberal arts education for about a century. Northeast also boasts two glorious refuges, the **US National Arboretum** and the **Kenilworth Aquatic Gardens.** Southeast is divided by the slow-moving waters of the **Anacostia River.** On the Capitol Hill side are blocks of residences and two military facilities, the tidy **Marine Corps Barracks** complex and the sprawling **Washington Navy Yard.** Across the river lies **Anacostia,** a neighborhood whose hills afford some of the best views of the city. Isolated and more self-contained than any other Washington neighborhood, Anacostia boasts two of the city's most important cultural institutions of African-American history: the recently refurbished **Anacostia Museum,** located in what was once known as Uniontown, a community settled after the Civil War by freed slaves; and **Cedar Hill,** the home of Frederick Douglass, onetime slave and eloquent leader of the abolitionist movement. Douglass's home has been restored by the National Park Service and is now a National Historic Site and museum.

1 UNION MARKET (FLORIDA AVENUE FARMERS MARKET)

Open year-round, this shoppers' mecca comprises several wholesale warehouses that carry fresh meats, eggs, and fish, plus choice fruits and vegetables. Ethnic foods predominate. Several vendors prepare sandwiches, baked goods, and more for takeout. ♦ M-Sa. Florida Ave NE (between Fourth and Fifth Sts). &. Metro: Union Station

2 GALLAUDET UNIVERSITY

Edward Miner Gallaudet, son of Thomas Hopkins Gallaudet, founder of the first permanent school for deaf students in the US, helped establish this beautiful Gothic-style campus as a higher-learning institution for the deaf. Chartered in 1864 by Abraham Lincoln, the world's only accredited liberal arts college for the hearing-impaired enrolls about 2,000 students. Its formal Victorian stone structures are laced with points and arches, and the grounds reflect the master touch of landscape architect Frederick Law Olmsted. Arrange tours of the campus through the **Visitors' Center.** ♦ 800 Florida Ave NE (between West Virginia Ave and Sixth St). Main number, 651.5000; Visitors' Center, 651.5050 (voice and TTY). &. www.gallaudet.edu. Metro: Union Station

3 US NATIONAL ARBORETUM

Few locals seem aware of this 446-acre plot of garden and woodland (see arboretum map, p. 20) overlooking the **Anacostia River,** which is practically deserted except for the few weeks in spring when the azaleas (and tourists) run wild. So much the better for the cognoscenti, because this semisecret garden is a lovely place.

Established by Congress in 1927 as a research institution, the arboretum harbors such rare plants as the dove tree and Oconee bells, as well as thousands of azaleas, ornamental crab apples, cherries, and dogwoods. During Washington's languorous spring, each week brings a new cascade of color and fragrance. Amid all this life rises an incongruous stand of Corinthian columns, salvaged from a renovation of the **Capitol** and erected here in the late 1980s. Also on the vast grounds is the **Herbarium,** filled with a "library" of more than 650,000 dried plants.

Perhaps the arboretum's most prestigious feature is the **National Bonsai and Penjing Museum,** valued at more than $5 million (and protected by an elaborate alarm system). A gift from the people of Japan, the plants are housed in pavilions near the **National Herb Garden.** Artfully stunted in shallow pots, the 150 or so trees, representing a wide variety of species, stand no more than 2 feet high.

The arboretum's peak season is the spring. In winter, the austere scene is populated mainly by dwarf and slow-growing conifers assembled on a hill. The arboretum regularly presents special demonstrations, films, and flower shows. From mid-April to mid-October, 40-minute tram tours of the grounds are offered weekends and holidays. Arrange group tours for 10 or more by calling at least 3 weeks in advance. ♦ Free. Fee for tram tours. Daily, 8AM-5PM. Bonsai collection: daily, 10AM-3:30PM. Entrances at 3501 New York Ave NE (between South Dakota Ave and Bladensburg Rd) and 24th and R Sts NE (east of Bladensburg Rd). 245.2726. www.usna.usda.gov

4 TRINITY COLLEGE

Founded in 1897 by the Sisters of Notre Dame, this liberal arts college for women has

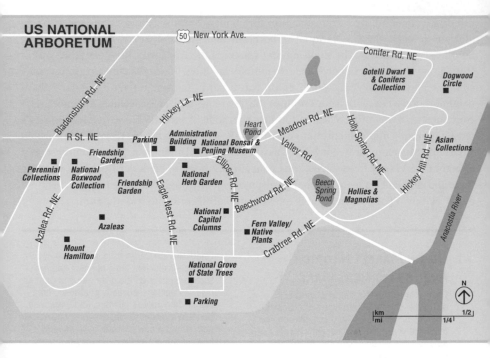

US NATIONAL ARBORETUM

about 1,500 registered students. A strong continuing-education program for working women is included in the curriculum. The granite **Main Hall** is a Northeast landmark with its marble parquet and stained glass, culminating in a four-story atrium. ♦ 125 Michigan Ave NE (between Franklin and Fourth Sts). 884.9000. www.trinitydc.edu. &. Metro: Brookland/CUA

Within Trinity College:

NOTRE DAME CHAPEL

Inside the college's Byzantine house of worship, find a 75-foot-tall mosaic dome by Bancel LaFarge. ♦ By appointment only. 884.9000

4 CATHOLIC UNIVERSITY OF AMERICA

Past and future meet at this century-old coeducational institution, founded by the Catholic bishops of the US. While some students pursue the university's highly respected traditional ecclesiastical curriculum, others work with researchers in biomedical engineering, physics, and biochemistry. The university's

School of Philosophy is renowned too. The **Hartke Theatre** stages productions from Greek and Shakespearean dramas to opera and American musicals. Guided campus tours can be arranged by appointment; call 319.5305. ♦ 620 Michigan Ave NE (between John McCormack and Harewood Rds). 319.5000. &. www.cua.edu. Metro: Brookland/CUA

Within Catholic University of America:

THE BASILICA OF THE NATIONAL SHRINE OF THE IMMACULATE CONCEPTION

The key word here is *huge*: The church is about 460 feet long, 160 feet wide, and 329 feet high and can hold about 6,000 people. This magnificent edifice attests to the Catholic devotion to the Virgin Mary. In 1913 the rector of Washington's **Catholic University of America** obtained papal sanction for a new monument dedicated to the "Patroness of the US" (as she was decreed by Pope Pius IX in 1847), and construction began in 1920. Completed in 1959, the largest Catholic church in the Americas (and the eighth largest in the world) is a modern cruciform giant with both Byzantine and Romanesque elements. More than sixty chapels contain bright mosaic altars portraying interpretations of the Virgin from all around the world. Light streams through 200 stained-glass windows to wash over an immense mosaic shrine whose construction depleted an entire Italian

Abraham Lincoln lived in Mrs. Spriggs's boarding house on Capitol Hill while he was a member of Congress. From his window he could see slaves being bought and sold in an active slave market on Capitol Hill. The site is now the Library of Congress.

quarry. Home to the largest collection of contemporary ecclesiastical art in the US, the shrine also displays artifacts like the coronation tiara of Pope Paul VI. Because every parish in the US contributed to the building fund, the shrine belongs to every American Catholic. With this in mind, the church administration actively encourages pilgrimages, and Communion is celebrated daily. There is also a gift shop, bookstore, and cafeteria. ◆ Free. Daily, 7AM-6PM Nov-Mar; 7AM-7PM Apr-Oct. Tours (usually given on the hour) daily, 9AM-3:30PM. 400 Michigan Ave NE (at Harewood Rd). 526.8300. &. www.nationalshrine.com

4 POPE JOHN PAUL II CULTURAL CENTER

Opened in 2001, this high-tech museum of faith features interactive galleries (bell ringing, stained-glass window making), exhibits of Vatican art, and displays of papal memorabilia. It also serves as a research facility. ◆ Free (suggested donation). Tu-Sa, 10AM-5PM; Su, noon-5PM. 3900 Harewood Rd NE (at Michigan Ave). 635.5400. &. www.jp2cc.org. Metro: Brookland/CUA

4 DANCE PLACE

The area's largest producer of contemporary and avant-garde dance puts on performances by national and international troupes such as **Jane Franklin Dance**, **Step Afrika!**, and **Liz Lerman Dance Exchange**. Ongoing modern and West African dance classes are offered, and a **DanceAfrican Festival** takes place in June. The theater seats about 170 people, and the box office opens 1 hour before showtime; call to reserve seats in advance. ◆ Box office: M, 2PM-5PM; Tu-F, noon-5PM; Sa, 10AM-3PM. 3225 Eighth St NE (between Franklin and Monroe Sts). 269.1600. &. www.danceplace.org. Metro: Brookland/CUA

4 COLONEL BROOKS' TAVERN

★$ It's tough to find a restaurant in the largely residential Brookland area, so this casual, reliable place is something of an oasis. Good burgers, sandwiches, egg dishes, and desserts round out the seasonal menu. Customers can complement their meals with dark or light ales from a list of about 15 drafts. Local Dixieland bands take the stage on Tuesday nights. ◆ American ◆ M-Sa, lunch and dinner; Su, brunch and dinner. 901 Monroe St NE (at Ninth St). 529.4002. &. Metro: Brookland/CUA

4 FRANCISCAN MONASTERY

Officially the Commissariat of the Holy Land for the United States, this monastery provides a fascinating glimpse of cloistered life. The enterprising mendicants here, who belong to the Order of the Friars Minor, raise funds to preserve shrines in the Holy Land; closer to home, they also maintain the beautiful grounds surrounding the monastery. A 45-minute tour of the rose garden and the early–Italian Renaissance church, completed in 1899, includes faithful replicas of several Holy Land shrines. Also on the tour (the only way to see it) is a small, authentic reproduction of a Roman catacomb beneath the church illustrating the plight of early Christian worshipers. ◆ Tours: on the hour M-Sa, 10AM-3PM; Su, 1PM-3PM. 1400 Quincy St NE (at 14th St). 526.6800. www.myfranciscan.com. Metro: Brookland/CUA

5 NATIONAL POSTAL MUSEUM

Opened in 1993, the Smithsonian's museum devoted to philatelic history is housed in the City Post Office Building, which served as Washington's main post office between 1914 and 1986. Designed in 1914 by **Graham and Burnham** to complement nearby **Union Station**, this smaller, less opulent Beaux Arts building is rendered in white Italian marble and trimmed with an Ionic colonnade. There's still a working post office on the first floor, and the lobby's marble and fixtures are restored to gleaming brilliance. On the lower atrium level is the world's largest collection of stamps and other philatelic items, drawn from the Smithsonian's **National Museum of American History**. Exhibits trace the history of postal collection, sorting, and delivery. The **Library Research Center**, open by appointment Monday through Friday, and the educational **Discovery Center**, with activity kits and games, is not always open; call ahead for schedule information. ◆ Free. Museum: daily, 10AM-5:30PM. Post office: M-F, 7AM-midnight; Sa, Su, 7AM-8PM. 2 Massachusetts Ave NE (at N Capitol St). 633.5555. &. www.si.edu/postal. Metro: Union Station

5 CAPITOL CITY BREWING COMPANY

★$$ Located in the former City Post Office, this brewpub serves housemade ales, porter, and kolsch, along with seasonal brews. The menu features hearty sandwiches and entrées, from meat loaf to salmon. ◆ American ◆ Daily, lunch and dinner. 2 Massachusetts Ave NE (at N Capitol St). 842.BEER. www.capcitybrew.com. Metro: Union Station. &. Also at 1100 New York Ave NW (at 11th St). 628.2222. &. Metro: Metro Center; and at 2700 S Quincy St, Arlington, Virginia. 703/578.3888

Restaurants/Clubs: Red | Hotels: Purple | Shops: Orange | Outdoors/Parks: Green | Sights/Culture: Blue

6 UNION STATION

Architect **Daniel Burnham**'s magnificent Beaux Arts monument to the optimism of the early 1900s is back on track, after a bumpy ride through the latter part of the century. The restoration of the station, along with the opening of stores and eateries within the building, has also pumped economic life into the surrounding area. The 1908 white granite railroad terminal, based on the Arch of Rome (outside) and the Baths of Caracalla and Diocletian (inside), originally had its own bowling alley, mortuary, icehouse, and Turkish baths. In 1937, at its apogee, as many as 42,000 travelers passed through the concourse daily.

With the decline of rail travel, however, the station fell into disrepair. In 1976 railroad operations were moved to a squalid temporary terminal behind the station, and the original vaulted waiting room was converted to a short-lived bicentennial visitors' center. Further decay ensued—a leaking roof caused huge chunks of plaster to fall from the ceiling, water pipes burst repeatedly, and toadstools sprang from the muddy floor. A public–private partnership eventually came to the building's rescue during the 1980s. After a $160 million renovation, the building's 1988 reopening resurrected the grandeur Burnham had intended. The original walls, columns, and windows were restored, and much of the space is now given over to office and retail use. A large portion of the painting, stenciling, and restoration of the moldings and scagliola (imitation marble) is the work of master craftsman **John Barianos**, whose artistry can also be seen at the **Willard Inter-Continental Hotel**, in Downtown DC, and at the **Capitol**.

The **Main Hall**, with a majestic 96-foot-high barrel-vaulted coffered ceiling, contains a newsstand, a concierge station, and several cafés and restaurants, including **B. Smith's**, model Barbara Smith's Southern-flavored spot (see below), and **America** (see opposite). The **West Hall** and the two-level **Station Concourse** behind the **Main Hall** contain dozens of shops, among them **Ann Taylor**, **The Body Shop**, **Nine West**, **Godiva Chocolatier**, and **Victoria's Secret**. The **East Hall** offers kiosks selling unusual jewelry and crafts. The **Train Concourse**, just north of the **Station Concourse**, provides access to **Amtrak** trains and connects the station to the 1,400-space parking garage behind it. (The first 2 hours of parking cost $1 with validation.) Travelers will find an entrance to the **Metro** on the lower-level **Metro Concourse**, where about 25 international fast-food shops and a nine-screen movie theater complex are dramatically positioned among 25-foot-deep piers and arches. Just outside the main entrance is a statue of Columbus and a reproduction of the Freedom Bell, surrounded by a half circle of 55 flags—one for each state and the five territories of American Samoa, Guam, the Northern Mariana Islands, Puerto Rico, and the US Virgin Islands. ♦ Station: daily, 24 hours. Stores: M-Sa, 10AM-9PM; Su, noon-6PM. Restaurants: hours vary. 50 Massachusetts Ave NE (at First St). 371.9441. ♿. www.unionstationdc.com. Metro: Union Station

Within Union Station:

B. SMITH'S

★★$$$ Model, TV personality, and author Barbara Smith opened this restaurant in 1994, occupying Union Station's former Presidential Suite. Beneath 30-foot ceilings, diners choose from a menu of Cajun, Creole, and Southern cuisine. The restaurant features live jazz Friday and Saturday evenings and during Sunday brunch. ♦ Southern ♦ M-Sa, lunch and dinner; Su, brunch and dinner. 50 Massachusetts Ave NE, street level. 289.6188. www.bsmith.com

AMERICA

★$$ A real Yank extravaganza, this restaurant offers indoor and outdoor seating and a menu with specialties from virtually every state in the union. Some popular dishes: New Orleans fried oyster po'boy and blue-corn enchiladas with Gulf shrimp and chili sauce. Finish up with Death by Chocolate if you think you can survive the dense, five-layer concoction of semisweet and bittersweet chocolate. ♦ American ♦ Daily, lunch and dinner. Street level. 682.9555. ♿

7 THE MONOCLE

★★$$ Traditionally an after-work watering hole for Senate-side power-brokers, this spot also serves good pasta, steaks, and seafood. The place is particularly pleasant when Congress is not in session. ♦ American ♦ M-F, lunch and dinner. Reservations recommended. 107 D St NE (between First and Second Sts). 546.4488. www.themonocle.com. Metro: Union Station

8 UNION PUB

★$ Replacing the Red River Grill, this large pub offers several different bars and numerous TVs showing sports of all kinds. There are daily specials such as Half Price Mondays, Ladies' Night Tuesdays, Margarita Thursdays, and drink specials on Friday. An outdoor patio is a popular place during the summer. ◆ American ◆ Daily, lunch and dinner. 201 Massachusetts Ave NE (between Second and Third Sts). 546.7200. www.unionpubdc.com. Metro: Union Station

8 LOUNGE 201

★$ Lobbyists, congressional staffers, the occasional senator, and Capitol Hill residents congregate at this stylish spot to sip both trendy flavored martinis and cool-again classic cocktails like Side Cars and Gibsons. There are also two pool tables, as well as a menu of appetizers, salads, and sandwiches. ◆ M-F, 4PM-2AM; Sa, Su, private events only. 201 Massachusetts Ave NE (at 2nd St). 544.5201. www.lounge201.com. Metro: Union Station

9 TWO QUAIL

★★$$ Creative but uneven New American cuisine is served in three intimate rooms, all quirkily furnished with a collection of mismatched chairs and silverware. Capitol Hill locals come here when looking for a romantic dinner. The standout on the seasonal menu is, not surprisingly, the restaurant's namesake, stuffed with raspberries, brie, and French bread. ◆ Nouvelle American ◆ M-F, lunch and dinner; Sa, Su, dinner. Reservations recommended. 320 Massachusetts Ave NE (between Third and Fourth Sts). 543.8030. www.twoquail.com. Metro: Union Station

9 CAFE BERLIN

★★$$ Dine inside or out on stick-to-your-ribs dishes such as sauerbraten with potato dumplings and red cabbage, or beef goulash with spaetzle. Good choices on the huge dessert menu are apple strudel, Black Forest cake, and linzer torte. ◆ German ◆ M-Sa, lunch and dinner; Su, dinner. Reservations recommended. 322 Massachusetts Ave NE (between Third and Fourth Sts). 543.7656. www.cafeberlindc.com. Metro: Union Station

10 THE WHITE TIGER

★★★$$ Occupying a neat corner location with an outside terrace, this restaurant sets fine standards for Indian cuisine in this part of town. All the traditional favorites are on the menu, including lamb, chicken, beef, and seafood, supported by a good selection of *biryani* (rice) *anaj* (bread). There's a good selection of vegetarian dishes too. The weekday lunch buffet and Sunday brunch are a good value. ◆ Indian ◆ Daily, lunch and dinner. 301 Massachusetts Ave NE (between Third and Fourth Sts). 546.5900. www.whitetigerdc.com. Metro: Union Station

11 SEWALL-BELMONT HOUSE

The National Women's Party bought the house in 1929 for its headquarters, eventually converting it into a museum of American women's political achievements. Its displays commemorate the work of Alice Paul, author of the original Equal Rights Amendment. Exhibits trace the history of the women's movement from its bid for suffrage to the present.

Robert Sewall built this house in 1800 but the next year rented it to Albert Gallatin, secretary of the Treasury under both Jefferson and Madison. Gallatin is purported to have worked out the details of the Louisiana Purchase here. The British burned parts of the house in 1813, and numerous remodelings reflect Federal, Queen Anne, Georgian, and classical influences. ◆ Donation. Tu-F, 11AM-3PM; Sa, noon-4PM. 144 Constitution Ave NE (at Second St). 546.1210. www.sewallbelmont.org. Metros: Capitol South, Union Station

12 THE SUMMER HOUSE

Visit this cool and quiet hideaway on a hot summer day. Frederick Law Olmsted—best known as the creator of New York's Central Park—designed the redbrick structure during the 1870s as part of a plan to improve the **Capitol**'s grounds. ◆ Constitution Ave NW (between New Jersey Ave and First St). Metros: Union Station, Capitol South

13 PEACE MONUMENT

Franklin Simmons designed this marble memorial erected in 1877 to commemorate sailors slain in the Civil War. Neptune, Mars, Victory, and Peace comfort America as she weeps on the shoulder of History. Inscribed in America's book: "They died that their country might live." ◆ Pennsylvania Ave NW and Union Sq. Metros: Federal Center SW, Judiciary Sq

14 GENERAL ULYSSES S. GRANT MEMORIAL

Henry Shrady's statuary in Union Square, at 252 feet by 70 feet, is one of the world's largest equestrian monuments. At the center is a 17-foot bronze of Grant. To the north is the Cavalry Group; seven mounted men prepare to charge as their officer brandishes a sword, his mouth wide open as he shouts the advance. To the south of Grant's statue is the Artillery Group. Three horses, one with a rider, pull a cart holding a cannon and three soldiers, each of whom reveals a different face of battle: One is ready, another frightened, a third weary to the bone.

Restaurants/Clubs: Red | Hotels: Purple | Shops: Orange | Outdoors/Parks: Green | Sights/Culture: Blue

Shrady was only 31 years old and largely unknown when a jury of the most respected sculptors of his day—among them Augustus Saint-Gaudens and Daniel Chester French—commissioned him for this work. It was dedicated in 1922, though he died before it was completed. The 6-acre Reflecting Pool at the foot of the memorial reflects the entire Capitol dome. ♦ Union Sq (between Maryland Ave SW and Pennsylvania Ave NW). Metros: Federal Center SW, Judiciary Sq

15 CAPITOL

George Washington officiated when the building's cornerstone was laid in 1793, but it was not until 22 November 1800 that the House and Senate moved in and officially called the first joint session of Congress to order. **Dr. William Thornton**'s building at that time was a three-story square construction. By 1807 a similar edifice had been built for the House of Representatives, with a wooden walkway linking the two buildings. British troops invaded Washington on 24 August 1814 and convened a session of their own in the Senate building. They decided that day to burn the building down along with other federal structures; only a sudden summer rainstorm spared the building from total destruction. Five years later, it was repaired, and Congress returned home. What you see today (see the illustration below) is an outgrowth of that 1819 restoration. (Incidentally, by law no structure in DC can be higher than the Capitol.)

Most official visitors enter the building via the **East Front**, where every 4 years on 20 January—with rare exceptions, such as Ronald Reagan's two inaugurations—a presidential inauguration ceremony takes place. As you go up the steps toward the magnificent bronze **Columbus Doors**, pity the poor souls standing here for 1½ hours while William Henry

Harrison delivered the longest inaugural speech on record in a drizzly downpour; he died of pneumonia 1 month later. Here too, Franklin D. Roosevelt reassured an economically depressed nation, by declaring that "the only thing we have to fear is fear itself." From the steps of the **East Portico** John F. Kennedy uttered the famous words "Ask not what your country can do for you; ask what you can do for your country."

A small wooden dome sheathed in copper once crowned the **Capitol**, but in the 1850s Congress decided it was badly proportioned to the expanded building. A much bigger one, designed by **Thomas U. Walter**, was commissioned and was to be raised, topped with a sculpture, with the engineering expertise of General Montgomery C. Meigs. But erratic financing followed by the Civil War slowed construction. When the secretary of war wanted to divert the iron and manpower involved to the war effort, it seemed likely that the project would be scrapped.

At the time, Washington was a shambles, and morale was low. The Capitol building was doing double duty as a field hospital. Abraham Lincoln appraised the situation and, ignoring criticism, decided construction must go on "as a symbol that our nation will go on." And so, while doctors and chaplains ministered to the wounded, builders hammered overhead. Late in 1863, amid tremendous fanfare, the 19.5-foot statue of *Freedom* was raised to the top of the 9-million-pound cast-iron dome. From a distance, the figure resembles a Native American: She wears a helmet rimmed by stars and finished with a crest featuring an eagle's head, feathers, and talons and is positioned so that she never faces the setting sun.

Much of the artwork in the **Rotunda** and throughout the Capitol is a testament to one man, Constantino Brumidi. A political refugee

Capitol Building

COURTESY OF THE BUREAU OF ENGRAVING AND PRINTING

from Italy, he spent 25 years (1855–1880) painting the Capitol's interior as a way of thanking his adoptive homeland. Brumidi created the fresco *The Apotheosis of Washington* in the center of the dome, which depicts George Washington ascending to power surrounded by female figures representing Liberty, Victory/Fame, and the original 13 states. He began painting the massive frieze around the Rotunda—a portrayal of 400 years of American history—but, tragically, he nearly fell off his scaffolding and died a few months later. Fellow Italian Filippo Costaggini continued the work; it was finally completed in 1953 by Allyn Cox. Four of the eight large oil paintings lining the Rotunda's walls are the work of John Trumball, an aide to then-general George Washington. Trumball had witnessed each of the Revolutionary War scenes he depicted. When water leaked into the Rotunda during a thunderstorm in 1990, it became clear that the dome needed renovating. Several years and temporary fixes later, the first stage of a major overhaul, begun in January 1999, is near completion. The next stage will begin after construction of a new Capitol Visitors' Center is complete.

In 1864, each state was asked to contribute statues of its two most celebrated citizens for exhibition in the Capitol. Thirty-eight figures, including likenesses of such people as Robert E. Lee (Virginia) and Brigham Young (Utah), are displayed in **National Statuary Hall**, south of the Rotunda. (Because Statuary Hall became too crowded, 59 other statues donated by the states were moved to various locations throughout the Capitol.) Three states have yet to send their second statue. The House of Representatives met here until 1857. Many politicians probably took advantage of an acoustical phenomenon of Statuary Hall's design: It seems that at certain spots in the hall you can clearly hear conversations that are taking place across the room, while those standing in between hear nothing. In 1848 John Quincy Adams suffered a fatal stroke in this chamber, and a small gold star on the floor designates where the sixth president fell to the ground.

Public areas outside of the Rotunda include the **Crypt** and the **Old Supreme Court Chamber**. If you're not on the official Capitol tour but wish to sit in the **Visitors' Galleries** in either the **Senate Chamber** or the **House Chamber**, stop by the office of your senator or representative (depending on which chamber you wish to observe) and pick up a gallery pass. If you don't know your representative's name or office location, call the Capitol switchboard (224.3121). Foreign visitors may obtain gallery passes from the **South Visitor Screening Facility** located to the south of the Capitol. Space is reserved in each gallery for visitors with disabilities. An American flag flying over the chamber (south is the House; north, the Senate) means that that legislative body is in session, and a lantern glowing from the Capitol dome signals that at least one of the chambers is at work. To find out what's on the day's agenda, check the *Washington Post*'s daily "Today in Congress" column. The action on Capitol Hill intensifies during December, when elected officials tie up loose ends so they can go home for the holidays. If you want to see Congress in action, this is the time. Although a visit to the chamber galleries is pro forma, those seeking drama during the rest of the year should observe at least one committee meeting. Schedules are also listed in the *Washington Post*. If it's an open meeting, you're free to show up—get there 15 to 30 minutes early.

The Senate cafeteria, on the first floor, is open to the public between 7:30AM and 3:30PM (you may see some familiar faces). The famous Senate bean soup has been served daily since 1901. During the summer, the Capitol's **West Terrace** hosts free concerts, beginning at 8PM: Monday, **US Navy Band**; Tuesday, **US Air Force Band**; Wednesday, **US Marine Band**; Friday, **US Army Band**. Special concerts take place on Memorial Day weekend, the Fourth of July, and Labor Day weekend. At all times, the West Terrace affords an outstanding view of the city and a close-up of the original sandstone **West Front**, which was handsomely restored. When the House or Senate is in night session, that wing remains open.

Tours of the Capitol are given Monday through Saturday between 9AM and 4:30PM; they last 30 minutes. Beginning at 9AM, free, timed, same-day tour tickets are given out on a first-come, first-served basis at the **Capitol Guide Service kiosk** located southwest of the Capitol near the intersection of First Street SW and Independence Avenue. It is advisable to call the Capitol Guide Recorded Information number (225.6827) to check on the latest status of visits. Ticket holders then proceed to the South Visitor Screening Facility, and from there to the Capitol tour. Write your senator or representative in advance to arrange a VIP tour. The address for senators is United States Senate, Washington, DC 20510; for representatives, it's United States House of Representatives, Washington, DC 20515. ♦ M-Sa. East Front entrance at Capitol Plaza (between New Jersey Ave SE and Delaware Ave NE). 225.6827. www.aoc.gov. ♿. Metros: Capitol South, Union Station

16 SUPREME COURT

Armed only with the US Constitution and a carefully delineated authority, the highest court in the land steers the direction of American society perhaps more than any other single power. Thus, anyone who comes to Washington to explore the federal government will find a session at the **Supreme Court Building** one of the city's most rewarding experiences. The nine justices—that number varied until 1869—are called into session the first Monday in October. They hear cases for 2 weeks, then retire to formulate their decisions for another 2 weeks, continuing this pattern through April. The court's hearings during in-session weeks are open to the public (Monday through Wednesday) on a first-come, first-served basis. Call 479.3030 for more information, as days and times change. There are two lines: a "three-minute line," which admits people for 3 minutes only; and a "regular line," which allows visitors to sit through an entire argument. The *Washington Post* reports the cases due for review on in-session days. If possible, visit on Monday, because, following discussion, the court takes the bench every Monday (usually until 4 July) to hand down orders and opinions. When the Supreme Court is not sitting, courtroom lectures are given Monday through Friday every hour on the half hour, between 9:30AM and 3:30PM. In addition, a 24-minute film features the chief justice and others on the bench explaining the history and day-to-day workings of the court.

The Supreme Court began hearing cases in 1790, but the tribunal so lacked prestige that its first chief justice, John Jay, resigned to become governor of New York. Almost 150 years passed before the court was deemed worthy of its own home, a dazzling white neoclassical edifice it occupied in 1935. Designed by **Cass Gilbert**, the marble building is fronted with bronze doors that weigh 13,000 pounds each; they depict the history of the legal system from ancient times to the present.

On a less historic note, the Supreme Court Building happens to have one of the government's best cafeterias. ♦ Free. Court: M-F, 9AM-4:30PM. Cafeteria: M-F, 7:30-10:30AM, 11:30AM-2PM. 1 First St NE (between E Capitol St and Maryland Ave). 479.3030. www.supremecourtus.gov. ⅃. Metros: Capitol South, Union Station

17 FREDERICK DOUGLASS MUSEUM AND HALL OF FAME FOR CARING AMERICANS

Located in the restored Capitol Hill home of abolitionist, publisher, and orator Frederick Douglass, this museum houses a permanent collection of Douglass memorabilia and a memorial dedicated to those who have spent their lives in service to others. ♦ Free. M, W, F, noon-2PM by appointment. 320 A St NE (between Third and Fourth Sts). 547.4273. www.caringinstitute.org. Metros: Capitol South, Union Station

18 LINCOLN PARK

Two of the city's finest and most affecting statues grace this compact urban park, the site of the Lincoln Hospital during the Civil War. The 1876 *Emancipation Monument*, sculpted by Thomas Ball and funded by former slaves, depicts a life-size Abraham Lincoln holding the Emancipation Proclamation. At Lincoln's feet, a slave is rising, his chains finally broken. Ball is said to have modeled the man's face after a photo of Archer Alexander, the last person to be taken under the Fugitive Slave Act. The heartening sculpture of black educator-activist Mary McLeod Bethune portrays the former adviser to Franklin D. Roosevelt passing her legacy to two children. It reads in part, "I leave you a thirst for

Supreme Court

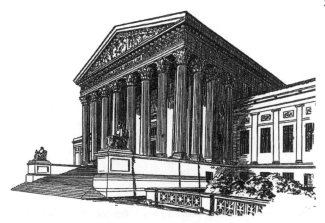

education. I leave you a respect for the use of power. I leave you faith. I leave you racial dignity. I leave you a desire to live harmoniously with your fellow man." ◆ E Capitol St (between 11th and 13th Sts). Metro: Eastern Market

19 RFK STADIUM/DC ARMORY

Two impressive structures—**RFK Stadium** and the **DC Armory**—compose this huge concert, trade-show, and sports complex controlled by the **DC Sports & Entertainment Commission**. The circular, five-tier amphitheater seats 56,000. Various athletic events, rock concerts, and even religious convocations alternately fill the arena. Though **Redskins** fans now watch their team at **FedEx Field** (see page 176) in Landover, Maryland, it is now the temporary home of the Washington Nationals, who play in the National League of Major League Baseball, and the **DC United** professional soccer team still draws its share of spirited fans here.

Next to RFK Stadium is the DC Armory, a domed structure whose two levels comprise a total of about 120,000 square feet of space. The adaptable main hall hosts events as diverse as the circus, inaugural balls, and car shows. ◆ 22nd and E Capitol Sts SE. Information, 547.9077; www.dcsec.com. Tickets, 432.7328. ⅙. Metro: Stadium/Armory

Within RFK Stadium:

FARMERS MARKET

Local farmers set up shop in the parking lot north of the stadium to sell their fresh produce, cheese, and bread. The DC government sponsors the market. ◆ Tu, Th, Sa, 7AM-4PM May-Dec; Th, Sa only Jan-Apr. Parking Lot 6 (off Benning Rd NE). ⅙

20 FOLGER SHAKESPEARE LIBRARY

Established in 1932 by Henry Clay Folger, a Standard Oil executive and Shakespeare maven, the library contains the world's largest collection of plays and poetry by the Bard, including 79 copies of the 1623 First Folio, the original printed collection of Shakespeare's plays, and the only surviving copy of the *Titus Andronicus* quarto. Selected works from the collection are displayed in the gallery.

The building, one of **Paul Philippe Cret**'s finest designs, reconciles a neoclassical exterior (its nine bas-reliefs depict Shakespearean scenes) with an Elizabethan interior. The late-1970s additions are tasteful and well done. The museum shop sells all kinds of souvenirs sporting Shakespeare's image and his words. A full-scale model of an Elizabethan theater, with seating for 250, is home to plays, musical performances,

readings, and lectures. It also used to be the home of the **Shakespeare Theatre**, which has since moved to Seventh Street NW. An open house celebrating the Bard's birthday takes place here every April. ◆ Free. M-Sa, 10AM-4PM. Tours: M-F, 11AM; Sa, 11AM and 1PM; group tours by appointment. Garden tours third Sa of the month, 10AM and 11AM, Apr-Oct. 201 E Capitol St SE (between Second and Third Sts). 544.4600. www.folger.edu. ⅙. Metros: Capitol South, Union Station

21 LIBRARY OF CONGRESS

Ensconced within this institution is the largest library collection in the world, with some 120 million items (and growing). Among its treasures are Jefferson's first draft of the Declaration of Independence, Pierre L'Enfant's original design for Washington, and one of three perfect Gutenberg Bibles (ca. 1456) in existence. Other holdings include rare books, photographs, films, sheet music, maps, and one of the world's largest collections of comic books.

Funded in 1800 with a mere $5,000, the collection began as a single reference room for Congress in the US Capitol. When the British burned the Capitol down in 1814 (using the library's books as kindling), Thomas Jefferson sold his fine private collection to the government as a replacement. The **Jefferson Building**, constructed in 1897 by **Smithmeyer and Pelz**, is an ornate Italian Renaissance–Beaux Arts confection originally criticized for being too over-the-top. Most striking is the **Main Reading Room**, which is crowned by a soaring, domed octagon in three colors of veined marble. At the entrance, the **Great Hall** is magnificently outfitted with marble columns, arches, mosaics, and paintings. Roland Hinton Perry's whimsical fountain, ***The Court of Neptune***, bubbles next to the building's front steps. Twice in the past 60 years, the library has been expanded: first the white Georgia marble **John Adams Building**, developed in 1939 by **Pierson and Wilson** (2 Second St, between Independence Ave SE and E Capitol St), which focuses on science, technology, and business; then the six-story, 46-acre **James Madison Memorial Building** (101 Independence Ave SE), which houses part of the library's collection of more than 13 million photos and prints, including Mathew Brady's Civil War photographs. The Madison Building (designed in 1980 by **DeWitt, Poor, and Shelton**) contains the nation's largest film archive, while its jewel-like **Mary Pickford Theater** screens classics at no charge; call 707.5677 for the schedule.

Specialized collections include the **Manuscript Division**, which contains 23

THE SECRET SERVICE

Secret Service agents always surround the president of the United States. They are the discreet men in black who are sworn to protect the president and his or her family, to literally throw themselves in front of an assassin's bullet.

But protecting the first family was not the original mission of the Secret Service. Immediately after the Civil War, the US confronted a currency crisis: Between a third and a half of all its circulating paper money was counterfeit. Enter the Secret Service, created under the Department of the Treasury, whose special task became combating the production of funny money. Within a decade, counterfeiting was severely curtailed (but has yet to be completely eliminated).

Soon the agency broadened its purpose to investigate other government problems: the Teapot Dome scandals, the Ku Klux Klan, land fraud, and espionage cases. Beginning in 1894, Secret Service agents began guarding President Grover Cleveland on a part-time basis. Then the 1901 assassination of William McKinley, the third president to be assassinated in less than 50 years (Lincoln and Garfield had preceded him), forced the issue of full-time presidential protection. Congress mandated that responsibility be turned over to the Secret Service in 1906. By 1917 three or four men were assigned to the **White House**, whereas the majority of agents still served the Treasury's anticounterfeiting force. Though the number of agents guarding the president today has increased, the Secret Service won't reveal any figures.

In 1930, after an unknown intruder managed to walk into the presidential dining room undetected, the White House police were placed under the supervision of the Secret Service. Two decades later, officer Leslie Coffelt was shot and killed by Puerto Rican nationalists while protecting President Harry S. Truman at **Blair House**. Spurred into action by that attack, Congress enacted legislation that permanently authorized the Secret Service to protect the president, his immediate family, and the vice president. After the assassination of John F. Kennedy in 1963, Congress passed a special act authorizing 2 years of Secret Service protection for Jacqueline Kennedy and her two children. Then in 1965 that protection was extended to all former presidents and first ladies for life and to children up to the age of 16 (but not first pets: Spotty and Barney are on their own when the Bushes leave the White House). Interestingly, the widow of a president loses her protection if she remarries.

As a result of Robert F. Kennedy's assassination in 1968, Congress authorized protection of major presidential and vice-presidential candidates. "Major" candidates are those who have qualified for federal campaign matching funds of at least $100,000, have received at least $2 million in contributions, and score at least 5% of the vote in major polls and 10% in consecutive primaries. The campaign trail—with multiple stops and staff intent on exposing their candidate to as many voters as possible—can be especially grueling for agents. Twenty-hour days are not unusual. During the 1976 campaign for the Democratic nomination, presidential hopeful Mo Udall and his wife, Ella, showed their appreciation by sharing a nightcap with their Secret Service agents at the end of each day.

On 5 September 1975, President Gerald Ford escaped harm when a Secret Service agent grabbed a pistol aimed at him by Lynette (Squeaky) Fromme, a Charles Manson follower, in Sacramento. Less than 3 weeks later, agents again came to Ford's rescue when political activist Sara Jane Moore fired a revolver, unsuccessfully, at the president. Ronald Reagan was the only president to be hit by a bullet and survive. John Hinckley got off six bullets on 30 March 1981, wounding Reagan in the chest and disabling press secretary Jim Brady before Secret Service agents were able to push them into the limousine and rush to **George Washington University Hospital** (where the emergency unit has since been renamed the Ronald Reagan Emergency Room).

Today the agency (www.ustreas.gov/usss) has approximately 5,000 employees, about 2,100 of whom are special agents assigned to investigative and protective services. Their recruits hail from many areas of expertise: forensics, psychology, intelligence, and communications, to name a few. Among the various divisions are a bicycle unit that patrols the White House grounds and a K-9 unit. Founded in the 1970s, the K-9 division originally used German shepherds but has since switched to Belgian Malinois (from Holland), a breed known for their stamina and adaptability to new environments. At night, the dogs go home with their handlers as part of the family.

Agents protect not only the president and vice president but also the Treasury, embassies, visiting heads of state, and diplomats. They may also be called on to guard an item of importance—which have included the Gutenberg Bible, the *Mona Lisa*, the Declaration of Independence, and the US Constitution. The Secret Service will not discuss its methods, other than to say that it works in concert with other public service personnel, including fire and rescue divisions and branches of the law enforcement community.

groups of presidential papers; the **Local History and Genealogy Division**, where family records may be researched; extensive Asian and European collections; and the **National Library Service for the Blind and Physically Handicapped**.

Concerts are offered in various locations year-round; call 707.5502 for the schedule. Fortunate visitors will catch the **Juilliard String Quartet** playing the library's collection of fine stringed instruments. Between October and May, literary events are held in the Madison Building and feature noted poets and authors; call 707.5394 for more information.

The Library of Congress is open to all researchers over 18 years of age (younger visitors are welcome to see the hallway displays but are not allowed in the reading rooms). A 12-minute orientation film runs four times an hour in a theater off the Jefferson Building's visitors' center Monday through Saturday, between 10AM and 5:15PM. The Jefferson Building offers free guided tours Monday through Friday at 10:30AM, 11:30AM, 1:30PM, 2:30PM, and 3:30PM and Saturday at 10:30AM, 11:30AM, 1:30PM, and 2:30PM. For these tours, visitors should enter through the West Front entrance (across from the **Capitol**). For more information, call 707.5458. A gift shop in the Jefferson Building sells books, cards, and crafts. ♦ Free. M-Sa, 10AM-5:30PM. Jefferson Bldg, First St SE (between Independence Ave and E Capitol St). 707.5000; reference, 707.5522; reading room, 707.6400. www.loc.gov. ᷄. Metro: Capitol South

Within the Library of Congress:

MADISON BUILDING CAFETERIA

★$ On the sixth floor of the **Madison Building** is one of the Hill's best restaurant bargains, with high-quality soups, salads, sandwiches, and heavier entrées served in an attractive dining room commanding a panoramic view of the city. ♦ American ♦ No credit cards accepted. M-F, breakfast and lunch. 707.5000

22 LE BON CAFÉ

★★$ The tables are set too close together, but the fresh sandwiches and pastries, best followed up with a bowl of frothy cappuccino, outweigh this café's inconveniences. For that extra soupçon of European flavor, outside

seating is available when weather permits. Place your order at the counter; there's no table service. ♦ French ♦ Daily, breakfast and lunch. 210 Second St SE (between C St and Pennsylvania Ave). 547.7200. Metro: Capitol South

22 TROVER SHOP

A pleasant place to browse, this two-floor shop has a comprehensive selection of political books, best-sellers, and classics, as well as a number of out-of-town newspapers. Cigar connoisseurs can select from an abundance of stogies. ♦ M-F, 7AM-8PM; Sa, 7AM-7PM; Su, 7AM-3PM. 221 Pennsylvania Ave SE (between Second and Third Sts). 547.BOOK. ᷄. www.trover.com. Metro: Capitol South

22 SONOMA RESTAURANT AND WINE BAR

★★★$$ This neighborhood restaurant and bar uses the best local produce that can be found. The cuisine is New American with an Italian influence and offers four groups of foods: cheeses and charcuterie, handmade pasta and pizza, wood-grilled meats and fish, and organic salads and other produce. Many of the offerings are small plates served family-style, but they can be doubled in size if you so choose. The wine list features 200 American and Italian vintages, with about 40 available by the glass in the wine bar. ♦ New American ♦ M-F, lunch; M-Su, dinner. 223 Pennsylvania Ave SE (between Second and Third Sts). 544.8088. www.sonomadc.com. Metro: Capitol South

22 CAPITOL LOUNGE

Often billed as a cigar and martini lounge, this casual spot is really more of a sports bar. Sports fans come here to catch everything from English premier-league soccer matches to college and NFL football games. ♦ M-Th, dinner; F, lunch and dinner; Sa, Su, brunch and dinner. 229 Pennsylvania Ave SE (between Second and Third Sts). 547.2098. Metro: Capitol South

23 CAPITOL HILL SUITES

$$ A former apartment building on a quiet residential block just two blocks from the **Capitol**, this recently renovated hotel offers 152 suites—some for nonsmokers, some with fully equipped kitchens. Continental breakfast adds to the appeal; there's no restaurant. ♦ 200 C St SE (at Second St). 543.6000, 800/424.9165. ᷄. www.capitolhillsuites.com. Metro: Capitol South

24 TAVERNA THE GREEK ISLANDS

★★$$ Try the moussaka (a layered casserole of ground meat, sliced eggplant, and béchamel sauce), lamb pie, stuffed grape leaves, kabobs, and other specialties, as well as one of several varieties of Greek wine. ◆ Greek ◆ M-Sa, lunch and dinner. 305 Pennsylvania Ave SE (between Third and Fourth Sts). 547.8360. Metro: Capitol South

24 POUR HOUSE/POLITIKI

★ Steelers fans, unite! The recently renovated Pour House offers a slice of Pittsburgh in our nation's capital, with pierogies, hand-cut fries, Iron City beer, and, of course, Steelers games on TV. Downstairs, the mood changes dramatically in Politiki, the city's very own tiki bar complete with palm trees, murals, and tropical drinks like mai tais and scorpion bowls. ◆ Pour House: M-Th, 4PM-close; F, 3PM-close; Sa, Su, 10AM-close. Politiki: M-Sa, 5:30PM-close. 319 Pennsylvania Ave SE (between Third and Fourth Sts). 546.1001. www.pennavepourhouse-dc.com. Metro: Capitol South

24 HAWK "N" DOVE

★★$ This brick-walled pub is a very typical Capitol Hill meeting place for young staffers. The six rooms provide plenty of privacy and the fare is strictly pub variety. Drink specials are on hand all week from 1PM to close, while Thursdays are intern nights. ◆ American ◆ Daily. 329 Pennsylvania Ave SE (between Third and Fourth Sts). 543.3300. Metro: Capitol South

25 EASTERN MARKET

Inside the **Adolph Cluss**-designed structure (1873), greengrocers and butchers offer the freshest food money can buy—they'll even handpick each item and wrap it as if they were serving royalty. The prices they charge, however, may seem like a king's ransom. Saturday mornings are the most energetic, as Capitol Hill residents crowd the market and craftspeople take over the north sidewalk plaza. Farmers from West Virginia, Pennsylvania, Virginia, and Maryland sell produce, cider, flowers, and baked goods. On Sundays, the food stalls are replaced by an ad hoc flea market selling knickknacks and old furniture. ◆ Tu-Sa, 7AM-6PM; Su, 9AM-4PM. 225 Seventh St SE (between C St and North Carolina Ave). www.easternmarketdc.com. ⅂. Metro: Eastern Market

Within Eastern Market:

MARKET LUNCH

★★$ The name may say "lunch," but lines snake out the door Saturday mornings for breakfast, and with good reason. On the other hand, lunch has its benefits too—namely, fabulous crab cakes, served on homemade bread with coleslaw and hot sauce. Stop in during the week, when it's less crowded. ◆ American ◆ No credit cards

accepted. Tu-Sa, breakfast and lunch; Su, lunch. 547.8444. ⅂

26 PREGO DELI

★$ The overstuffed sandwiches at this Italian deli run by a Korean and staffed by African-Americans and Latinos make for a delicious defense of multiculturalism. A fine selection of wines, cheeses, and gourmet foods is also available. ◆ Deli ◆ Daily, lunch and dinner. 210 Seventh St SE (between C St and North Carolina Ave). 547.8686. Metro: Eastern Market

26 TUNNICLIFF'S TAVERN

★$$ Scenes of the old **Eastern Market** are etched on the glass dividers decorating this place. The Cajun specialties, fresh fish, and steaks can be savored outdoors in warm weather. ◆ American ◆ M-F, lunch and dinner; Sa, Su, brunch and dinner. Reservations recommended. 222 Seventh St SE (between C St and North Carolina Ave). 544.5680. Metro: Eastern Market

27 THE VILLAGE

Around the corner from **Eastern Market**, this wonderful gift shop carries ornaments, cards, clothing, pottery, and more from South America, Asia, and India. ◆ Tu-F, 11AM-6PM; Sa, 10AM-6PM; Su, noon-4PM. 705 North Carolina Ave SE (between Independence Ave and Seventh St). 546.3040. Metro: Eastern Market

28 THE FAIRY GODMOTHER

Books, toys, and music crowd this microscopic shop, where European toys, audio tapes, and a special bilingual section make this spot a charming alternative to Toys "Я" Us. ◆ M-Sa, 10AM-5PM. 319 Seventh St SE (between Pennsylvania Ave and C St). 547.5474. Metro: Eastern Market

28 BREAD & CHOCOLATE

★★$ After a whirl through **Eastern Market**, this spot is the perfect place to stop for an espresso and some biscotti. Scrumptious offerings, such as omelets, quiche, and specialty sandwiches, are sure to tempt. In warm months, you can dine alfresco and soak up the Capitol Hill scene. ◆ Café ◆ Su, 8AM-6PM; M-Sa, 7AM-7PM. 666

Pennsylvania Ave SE (at Seventh St). 547.2875. Metro: Eastern Market

29 BULLFEATHERS

★$$ Congressional staffers throng here for the happy hour. Otherwise, this Victorian-style pub is a relatively calm place to come for hearty American fare, including burgers—(half-price on Monday), crab cakes, and steaks. At brunch there's a full bar, featuring Bloody Marys that you can fix yourself. ♦ American ♦ M-F, lunch and dinner; Sa, brunch and dinner. Reservations recommended. 410 First St SE (between North Carolina Ave and D St). 543.5005. www.bullfeatherscapitolhill.com. &. Metro: Capitol South

30 CHRIST CHURCH, WASHINGTON PARISH

This Gothic Revival Episcopal church designed by **Robert Alexander** witnessed the burning of Washington during the War of 1812 and served as a lookout post for Union soldiers during the Civil War. Completed in 1806, it's probably the oldest ecclesiastical edifice in the District. Over the years, the congregation has included many of Washington's leading citizens, among them presidents Thomas Jefferson and John Quincy Adams and composer John Philip Sousa. ♦ Tours by appointment only. 620 G St SE (between Sixth and Seventh Sts). 547.9300. &. www.washingtonparish.org. Metro: Eastern Market

31 BANANA CAFÉ

★$$ The kitchen offers a variety of Cuban, Puerto Rican, and other Latin-influenced dishes. Upstairs, a piano bar provides lots of fun. ♦ Latin ♦ M-Sa, lunch and dinner; Su, brunch and dinner. 500 Eighth St SE (at E St). 543.5906. &. Metro: Eastern Market

32 NEWMAN GALLERY & CUSTOM FRAMES

This shop offers rotating exhibits of original work by local and international artists. ♦ Tu-Sa, 10AM-6PM. 513 11th St SE (between G and E Sts). 544.7577. www.gallerynewman.com. Metro: Eastern Market

33 HISTORIC CONGRESSIONAL CEMETERY

"Being interred beneath these grounds adds a new terror to death" is how one US senator described the oppressive solemnity of this final resting place, reserved for members of Congress—including 19 senators and 71 representatives—and other prominent citizens. The process of filling the burial reservations of Washington's eminent started in 1807. Seventy years later, Washington architects **William Thornton** and **Robert Mills**, a Choctaw chief, and John Philip Sousa were among the last to find their places under **Benjamin Latrobe**'s stern, predesigned gravestones. Also laid to rest here were J. Edgar Hoover and photographer Mathew Brady. The gatekeeper will provide information and memorial maps. ♦ Free. Daily, during daylight hours. Office open M, W, F, 10AM-2PM; Sa, 9AM-1PM. 1801 E St SE (at 18th St). 543.0539. &. www.congressionalcemetery.org. Metro: Potomac Ave

34 ALVEAR STUDIO

At this worldly shop, find furnishings, lamps, mirrors, and folk art from Mexico, Italy, and other countries. Ask the staff about personal shopping services and design consultations. ♦ Tu-Th, Sa, 11AM-7PM; F, 11AM-8PM; Su, noon-5PM. 705 Eighth St SE (between I and G Sts). 546.8434. www.alvearstudio.com. Metro: Eastern Market

35 MARINE CORPS BARRACKS

America's first marine post is still home to the "Eighth and Eye" marines. The **Commandant's House**, with its classical overtones and bay windows, is the only original building standing on the grounds. The Marine Corps holds parades in the barracks courtyard on Fridays at 8:45PM during the summer. It's a great spectacle, even for those not wild about rifle drills and precision marching. Reservations are required. (If you can't get in, a shorter sunset version of the parade takes place Tuesday evenings at 7PM during the summer on the grounds of the **Iwo Jima Memorial** in Arlington.) ♦ Eighth St SE (between I and G Sts). 433.6060. www.mcu.usmc.mil. &. Metro: Eastern Market

36 NATION

Formerly the Capitol Ballroom, this multilevel spot for live music and dancing boasts one of the area's most impressive sound and light systems. Terraces, balconies, and a VIP area provide lots of choices when it comes to taking in the action. A huge dance floor offers plenty of space for grooving, whereas an outdoor patio provides a place to cool down. ♦ Admission for live shows. Call for show times. 1015 Half St SE (between L and K Sts). Information, 554.1500; tickets, 432.7328. Metro: Navy Yard

37 WASHINGTON NAVY YARD

Kids of all ages play and learn in this historic precinct, which served as the **Naval Gun Factory** during the 19th century. Distinguished architect-engineer **Benjamin Latrobe**

Restaurants/Clubs: Red | Hotels: Purple | Shops: Orange | Outdoors/Parks: Green | Sights/Culture: Blue

came up with the original plan; although various refurbishings have eroded signs of his influence, the main gates still evoke his style. (Some speculate that he designed the Commandant's House as well.) Splendid officers' mansions once lined the waterfront here; now the functional factory and ware-house buildings stand in their place.

The **Navy Museum** illuminates a more-than-200-year history of naval weapons, famous ships, and battle scenes, from the US Revolutionary War through Desert Storm. Its exhibitions are designed for the young and energetic: Gun turrets revolve, periscopes rise, and ships stand at the ready for boarding by boisterous young admirals. Claustrophobes should avoid the authentic submarine room and content themselves with the large dioramas depicting heroes damning the torpedoes and going full speed ahead. A decommissioned Vietnam-era destroyer, the *USS Barry*, can also be toured. High-tech fans will want to seek out the inertial guidance systems; fashion followers will want to check out the display of World War II uniforms by naval couturier Captain Guy Molyneux.

♦ Free. M-F, 9AM-4PM; Sa, Su, 10AM-5PM, reservations 24 hours in advance. Ninth and M Sts SE. 433.6897; www.history.navy.mil. &. Metro: Navy Yard

38 ANACOSTIA PARK

Extending 8 miles along the Anacostia River, these 1,200-plus acres qualify more as a natural preserve than as a conventional park, with mostly fertile marshland and small, sunny glades hidden in the forests. In the northeast are **Kenilworth Aquatic Gardens** (see below); adjacent to the gardens are approximately 70 acres of wetlands inhabited by songbirds and wading birds, such as green and great blue herons. During the winter migrating season, hordes of ducks and geese also congregate in the park. You can walk almost anywhere, except to the river's upper reaches, where its natural wild state renders the area inaccessible. A multipurpose pavilion at the south end of the park offers environmental-education programs, community exhibitions, and a roller-skating rink. ♦ Kenilworth and Pennsylvania Ave SE. 426.6905. www.nps.gov/anac. Metro: Anacostia

Within Anacostia Park:

KENILWORTH PARK AND AQUATIC GARDENS

Acres of water-loving flora and fauna are hidden within this seldom-visited marshland in the northeastern part of **Anacostia Park**. Civil War veteran W.B. Shaw began the gardens' evolution in 1882 with a few water lilies from Maine. Native willow oaks, red maples, and magnolias sheltered the ponds, which attracted a variety of water dwellers. Today, birds, frogs, turtles, and butterflies populate the gardens, whereas beaver, wren, and salamanders inhabit the 77-acre **Kenilworth Marsh**. Visit early in the morning, because many of the night-blooming lotuses close during harsh daylight. Group tours are possible with advance notice. ♦ Free. Daily, 7AM-4PM. 1650 Anacostia Ave NE (between Douglas and Quarles Sts). 426.6905. www.nps.gov/kepa

39 FREDERICK DOUGLASS NATIONAL HISTORIC SITE (CEDAR HILL)

Abolitionist and statesman Frederick Douglass resided at this simple white Victorian house from 1877 until his death in 1895. Douglass, who was born a slave on a Maryland plantation in 1817, escaped at the age of 21 and eventu-ally became an adviser to four presidents and an eloquent spokesman for the antislavery movement. During the Civil War, Douglass coun-seled President Abraham Lincoln and supported postwar constitutional amendments that gave blacks citizenship and the right to vote.

Cedar Hill, built in 1854, rests on a hilltop. Its large, airy porch, punctuated by Doric columns, offers breathtaking vistas of the **Capitol** and its vicinity. Much restored to its original appearance, Douglass's home holds furniture and several gifts from Lincoln and other contemporaries, including Harriet Beecher Stowe and William Lloyd Garrison. One remarkable feature is the self-taught philosopher's personal library, containing more than 1,200 volumes.

The **Visitors' Center**, which contains Ed Dwight's life-size statue of Douglass, is located at the bottom of the grounds so as not to obstruct the view from the house. An accurate and affecting picture of Douglass's work is captured in a short film, shown every hour on the hour. Tours are given on the half hour, and group tours can be arranged by calling in advance. Limited parking is provided. ♦ Admission. 9AM-4PM 16 Oct-14 Apr; 9AM-5PM 15 Apr-15 Oct. 1411 W St SE (between 14th and 16th Sts). 426.5961. &. www.nps.gov/frdo. Metro: Anacostia

40 ANACOSTIA MUSEUM

Founded in 1967 as a branch of the **Smithso-nian Institution**, this recently renovated museum displays exhibits on African-American history and culture. There are also art displays and, at times, educational lectures, films, and concerts, as well as demonstrations of black music and dance. On the grounds is a picnic area with tables and grills. Groups of 15 or more may arrange tours by calling in advance. ♦ Free. Daily, 10AM-5PM. 1901 Fort Pl SE (at Erie St). 633.4820. &. www.si.edu/anacostia. Metro: Anacostia

WASHINGTON BETWEEN THE COVERS

Washington has been the scene of so much history that many books, whether political tomes or novels, are bound to include it as a backdrop at some point. The following volumes put the city and its machinations front and center:

Democracy, by Henry Adams (New American Library, 1983) This descendant of two presidents carved his own niche as a historian and man of letters. Written in 1880, his scathing novel of the scandal-ridden Grant administration is a cautionary tale that too many politicians have since ignored.

Dupont Circle, by Paul Kafka-Gibbons (Houghton Mifflin, 2001) This novel explores love and marriage among the wealthy Allard family, with action taking place in **Dupont Circle** town houses, the **DC Court of Appeals**, and other locations around town.

Her, by Laura Zigman (Knopf, 2002) The author's third novel looks at Washington through the eyes of displaced New Yorker Elise and her fiancé, Donald. **Chevy Chase** clothing boutique **Relish** and its owner are said to have served as inspiration for the novel's shop Embellish.

Lost in the City: Stories, by Edward P. Jones (Morrow, 1992) A collection of stories about the "others" of Washington, the African-American residents whose lives are rarely affected by the doings at either end of **Pennsylvania Avenue**. Jones writes with humor and compassion about lives often torn, and occasionally enriched, by the day-to-day struggles of urban life.

The Man Who Loved Children, by Christina Stead (Holt, Rinehart & Winston, 1940) Australian novelist Stead spent enough time in Washington in the late 1930s to write this brilliantly perceptive tale of a domestic situation that appears idyllic at first glance, then gradually reveals itself to be dark and, finally, tragically flawed. Samuel Clemens Pollit, the easygoing protagonist who tends his brood in a rambling house north of Georgetown, is a fine literary creation.

The Patron Saint of Unmarried Women, by Karl Ackerman (St. Martin's Press, 1994) This wry and funny first novel captures Washington as hometown. Jack Townsend, a landscape architect, and his girlfriend, artist Nina Lawrence, lead readers away from Washington's monuments and into the city's funkier neighborhoods.

Primary Colors, by Anonymous (Random House, 1996) *Newsweek* columnist Joe Klein got himself in hot water when he was revealed to be the author of this best-selling novel about a Southern governor who runs for

president. The unflattering and thinly veiled portrait is reputedly based on Clinton's rise to power.

Reveille in Washington: 1860–1865, by Margaret Leech (Carroll and Graf, 1991) Written in 1942, this engaging history of Washington during the Civil War reminds us that the capital of the United States was south of the Mason-Dixon Line and only 120 miles north of Richmond, the capital of the Confederacy. Mixed loyalties and intrigue abound, and the towering presence of Lincoln hovers over all.

Strange and Fascinating Facts About Washington, DC, by Fred L. Worth (Random House, 1988) Just what the title says: plenty of trivia, but also lots of substantial information about nearly every aspect of life in DC.

Twilight at Mac's Place, by Ross Thomas (Mysterious Press, 1990) A former CIA man, Thomas writes some of the most literate cloak-and-dagger fiction around. A number of his thrillers are set in Washington; this one revolves around the intrigue at a **Dupont Circle** bar.

Waking the Dead, by Scott Spencer (Knopf, 1986) Neither a horror story nor a religious tract, this is the tale of a thirtysomething Congressional wannabe. The Washington scenes capture the city well, which isn't surprising, because the author is a DC native.

Washington: A History of the Capital, 1800–1950, by Constance McLaughlin Green (Princeton University Press, 1961–1963) Originally published in two volumes (the first won a Pulitzer Prize), this magisterial look at the city's first 150 years also manages to be readable and entertaining. A one-volume edition is available in paperback.

Washington, D.C., by Gore Vidal (Little, Brown, 1967) No novelist of the past 30 years has written so well about Washington's recent and more distant past. This novel, which Vidal started when John F. Kennedy was still alive and finished when the Vietnam War was in full swing, reflects his growing disillusionment with the political process. Also recommended are Vidal's **Burr** (Random House, 1973) and **Lincoln** (Random House, 1984).

Washington Itself, by E.J. Applewhite (Knopf, 1981) The longtime Washington resident and former CIA executive offers what he calls an "informal guide" to Washington, with an emphasis on architectural details of the city's many historic buildings. The author isn't always impressed with what may appear to some as grand designs, but that's part of the informative and engaging charm. The line drawings are lovingly rendered by Fred H. Greenberg.

Restaurants/Clubs: Red | Hotels: Purple | Shops: Orange | Outdoors/Parks: Green | Sights/Culture: Blue

The Mall/
Southwest

Farragut West M

McPherson Sq M

1

2

3

W Executive Ave.

E Executive Ave.

New York Ave. NW

E St. NW ←

E St. NW →

Virginia Ave.

FOGGY BOTTOM

C St. NW

23rd St. NW

21st St. NW

20th St. NW

19th St. NW

18th St. NW

17th St. NW

15th St. NW

1

4
Ellipse

Ellipse Rd. NW

14th St. NW

5
*Constitution
Gardens*

Vietnam
Veterans
Memorial

10

Reflecting Pool   12

11

13

14

27

Independence Ave. SW

28

Kutz Memorial
Bridge

29

Maine Ave. SW

26
West
Potomac
Park

■ *Japanese
Lantern*

R. Wallenberg Pl. SW

30

31
Tidal Basin

W Basin Dr. SW

Ohio Dr. SW

■ Franklin
D. Roosevelt
Memorial

37

E Basin Dr. SW

1

395

Potomac River

38

1

26 *East
Potomac
Park*

ARLINGTON

Lady Bird
Johnson
Park

14th Street
Bridges

Buckeye Dr. SW

(George Mason
Memorial Bridge)

Ohio Dr. SW

(Rochambeau
Memorial Bridge)

N

1
395

km
mi
1/4   1/2   1
1/2

It is a view even the most jaded Washingtonian never tires of: From the west side of the **Capitol** is a rectangular carpet of green lawn flanked by small groves of trees and a collection of impressive—if somewhat mismatched—buildings, each no more than four stories high. In the distance, a spiky obelisk rises from the green expanse, and beyond, a long, narrow pool leads to a columned Greek temple.

This is the Great American Mall—no, not an indoor shopping extravaganza, but our National Backyard. Those buildings are the major **Smithsonian** museums, the obelisk is the **Washington Monument**, and the temple is the **Lincoln Memorial**. To the north of the Washington Monument is another, smaller, grassy expanse, the **Ellipse**, and north of that, the **White House**. South of the Monument is the stately **Jefferson Memorial** and the poignant **Holocaust Memorial Museum**.

The **Mall** and its environs are the magnetic center of Washington, drawing millions of visitors every year, as well as throngs of proud locals. The pope said Mass here, Martin Luther King delivered a historic speech at the Lincoln Memorial, and countless political demonstrations have engulfed this legendary lawn. Every summer the Smithsonian hosts an outdoor bash, the Smithsonian Folklife Festival, when the Mall is transformed into fairgrounds, with dancing, live music, and food booths that hawk the cuisine of various states or countries. On the Fourth of July, the Mall is the scene of a daylong birthday blast, culminating in a mammoth fireworks display. With all this activity, it's a wonder that by summer's end there's any grass left. But every fall the National Park Service dutifully reseeds the bare patches, and each spring the green carpet rolls out again.

Tucked between the Mall and the **Potomac River** is Washington's smallest quadrant: Southwest. Unlike the rest of the city, its buildings seem to have been almost wholly created within the last 30 years. During the 19th century, when its waterfront location was prime real estate for Washington's commercial interests, Southwest was an important business center. The 20th century brought a slow and painful decline to the area, but in the 1960s, Southwest became a testing ground for urban renewal, and now its waterfront is dotted with restaurants and also boasts a popular fish market. Farther inland are the nationally acclaimed **Arena Stage**, the **L'Enfant Plaza** complex, and a mélange of row houses, apartment high-rises, and federal buildings.

---

1 EISENHOWER EXECUTIVE OFFICE BUILDING

Originally designed to house the State, War, and Navy Departments, this outrageous French Second Empire building was so hated by the time of its completion in 1888 that no one wanted to pay architect **Alfred B. Mullett**. At the same time, nobody could justify the cost of demolishing the structure, which has 4.5-foot-thick granite walls and an iron door and window frames, trimming, and baseboards, all cast in an on-site foundry. Newly restored, the building is used for senior-level **White House** offices. Particularly notable are the stained-glass rotundas over the cantilevered staircases; the **State Department Library**, with four cast-iron balconies and Minton tile floors; and the **Indian Treaty Room**, with marble wall panels and elaborate ironwork. The **War Department Library**, now the **White House Law Library**, features eclectic cast iron, including Moorish, Gothic, classical, and Baroque designs plated with bronze and brass. ♦ As of press time, tours of the building have been suspended indefinitely. Call ahead to see if the 90-minute Saturday-morning tours have been reinstated. Pennsylvania Ave NW and 17th St. 395.5895. &. Metros: Farragut West, Farragut North

2 TREASURY BUILDING

After months of congressional foot-dragging, Andrew Jackson impatiently chose this site for the new Treasury Building (two previous incarnations burned down in 1814—thanks to the British—and in 1833), even though the exquisite Greek Revival building raised here blocks **Pierre Charles L'Enfant's** intended view of the **Capitol** from the **White House**. The building, which took more than 30 years to complete (in part because of the Civil War), still houses the administrative offices of the Treasury Department; the interior has been restored to its former glory. The **East Wing**, designed by **Robert Mills**, was completed in 1842; the other wings were designed by **Thomas U. Walter**, with supervising architects **Ammi Young**, **Isaiah Rogers**, and **Alfred B. Mullett**. An impressive statue of Alexander Hamilton, the first secretary of the Treasury, adorns the garden. ♦ As of press time, tours of the building had been suspended indefinitely. Call ahead to see if the free Saturday-morning tours have been reinstated. Pennsylvania Ave NW and 15th St. 622.0896. www.ustreas.gov. ♿. Metro: McPherson Square

3 WHITE HOUSE

When John Adams arrived at his new home on 1 November 1800, he found a shantytown of workers' shacks just outside the front door and unplastered walls inside. Not a single room was finished. The central staircase was a pile of timbers on the floor, and only with flames blazing in 13 fireplaces could Adams fend off the damp chill. That night, in a letter to his wife, Abigail, the nation's second president and the executive mansion's first tenant wrote, "I pray Heaven to bestow the best of blessings on this house and all that shall hereafter inhabit it. May none but honest and wise men ever rule under this roof."

Since that inauspicious first day, 42 presidents and their families have called the White House home. The only US president not to list 1600 Pennsylvania Avenue as his address was George Washington, who served his term in Philadelphia while the capital city was under construction. It was Washington, however, who selected the location of the "President's House," or the "President's Palace," as it was often called. When he staked out the site in 1791, the city was a flat, unpopulated woodland with one distinguishable rise in elevation, which would later become **Capitol Hill**. Washington declared that the executive mansion should be built 1 mile west of the hill, to secure a commanding view of the Potomac and, beyond that, Alexandria.

James Hoban, the original architect, was Irish, and despite many alterations over the years, the house today remains as crisp, elegant, and white as fine Irish linen. Thomas Jefferson, who lost the original design competition (he submitted it under a pseudonym), used his clout as the third president to tinker with the Georgian country-house design. Then, during the War of 1812, the British took its remodeling into their own vengeful hands by setting fire to the White House—a severe thunderstorm saved it from total destruction. The building's exterior was first painted white to cover the charring. It isn't known who coined the term *White House*, but Theodore Roosevelt officially named it such in 1901, well after the moniker had become commonplace. Hoban was enlisted to help with reconstruction after the fire. Other alterations have included the front portico, which was added in 1829; the wings, which **McKim, Mead, and White** designed in 1902; and such modern amenities as running water (in 1833), gas (in 1848), bathrooms (in 1878), and electricity (in 1890). The house was remodeled in 1902, in conjunction with the wing additions. Then from 1948 to 1952, after it was discovered to be structurally unsound, the whole house was taken apart: The stone framing was replaced with steel and the original panelings and decorations were removed, restored, and reconstructed. The White House now contains 132 rooms.

Through the years, the mansion has witnessed 1 presidential wedding (Grover Cleveland and Frances Folsom), 6 first-family weddings, 11 births, 7 presidential funerals, at least 39 redecorations—and numerous scandals. Because it was designed to serve not only as the home but also as the office of the president, the two functions frequently got crossed. In 1902 the second floor was at last set aside for the exclusive use of the president's family, but as late as 1962 the first family's meals were still being served on the nonprivate first floor, because the second floor had no kitchen.

When Jacqueline Kennedy, wife of the thirty-fifth president, arrived at the White House in 1961, she found the interior décor to be a mishmash of at least 34 individual tastes, with few historically accurate (or original) objects left. Deciding that "everything in the White House must have a reason for being there," the first lady spearheaded an extensive restoration project aimed at returning to the White House furnishings and possessions used during previous administrations. Significant artifacts were scattered around the globe but could be retrieved. (After all, early in the 20th century, the descendant of a British soldier had graciously returned James

---

Restaurants/Clubs: Red | Hotels: Purple | Shops: Orange | Outdoors/Parks: Green | Sights/Culture: Blue

Madison's medicine box, purloined during the fire in 1814.) Under Jackie's direction, people from all over the world pitched in. Thanks to these efforts and those of subsequent administrations, which have continued the project, today's White House is as much a museum of priceless American antiques as it is a home and an office.

On a tour (see below for tour information) visitors get a look at a handful of the mansion's 132 rooms. The white-and-gold **East Room**, where legend has it that Abigail Adams hung her laundry to dry and where Theodore Roosevelt's children roller-skated, is now used for receptions, press conferences, concerts, and dances. On the east wall is Gilbert Stuart's famous painting of George Washington, rescued by Dolley Madison when the British invaded the city in 1814. Seven presidents who died in office, including Lincoln and Kennedy, have lain in state in this room. Connecting doors lead from the East Room through the small reception chamber known as the **Green Room**, which has walls lined with green silk. This room is often the setting for presidential photo ops with foreign heads of state. The oval-shaped **Blue Room**, which Grover Cleveland used as a wedding chapel in 1886, is where the White House Christmas tree stands during the holidays. Just off the Blue Room is the **Red Room**, where Dolley Madison held her legendary Wednesday-night parties. The final tour stop is the **State Dining Room**. Note the inscription on the marble mantel: It's John Adams's White House prayer.

Each December, you can take a candlelight tour of the White House in all its Christmas glory. In the spring and fall, an afternoon **Garden Tour** opens the usually off-limits White House grounds to the public. And on Easter Monday, the traditional **Easter Egg Roll** takes place. (After the events of 11 September 2001, the White House has held limited public events. Call 456.7041 for up-to-the-minute information as well as ticketing procedures where applicable.)

As of press time, public tours of the White House are available for groups of 10 or more people. Requests must be submitted through one's Member of Congress and are accepted up to six months in advance. The free self-guided tours are offered Tuesday through Saturday from 7:30AM to 12:30PM (excluding federal holidays). They're scheduled on a first-come, first-served basis approximately one month in advance of the requested date. If you can't take a tour, the next best thing is a visit to the **White House Visitors' Center** (E Street NW, between 14th and 15th Sts, 208.1631; Metro: Federal Triangle). Open daily between 7:30AM and 4PM, the center contains a museum devoted to the White House and often hosts special exhibits.

Incidents at the White House during the early 1990s—one involving a suicidal pilot who crashed his light plane at the base of the Executive Mansion on the **South Lawn**, another in which a man sprayed the **North Lawn** with bullets—prompted a serious security review by the Secret Service. The April 1995 bombing in Oklahoma City further exacerbated fears of terrorist acts against government buildings. In May 1995, President Bill Clinton approved a plan to close Pennsylvania Avenue NW from 15th to 17th Streets to vehicular traffic. It has remained closed ever since, and recent security enhancements and a beautification project led to the installation of trees. A short section of E Street NW—along the southwest perimeter of the grounds—is also closed to vehicles. In addition, be aware of recently mandated one-way streets to the north of the White House and limited on-street parking to the south along 15th and 17th Streets. ◆ Free. White House: Tu-Sa, 10AM-noon. Signed tours for the hearing-impaired may be arranged through your representative or senator. 1600 Pennsylvania Ave NW (between 15th and 17th Sts). Tours and events, 456.7041 (recording); visitors' center, 208.1631. www.whitehouse.gov. &. Metro: McPherson Square

At the White House:

WHITE HOUSE GROUNDS

The 18 acres known as the **President's Park** contain more than 80 varieties of trees planted over the years by almost every presidential family. A seedling from John Quincy Adams's home in Massachusetts is now the giant American elm on the Center Oval. Andrew Jackson brought a magnolia from Tennessee as a memorial to his wife. The other magnolia, near the east entrance to the **White House**, was planted by Warren Harding in remembrance of animals killed during World War I. More recent trees include the Gerald Ford family's white pine, a giant sequoia set by Richard Nixon in the Center Oval, and little Amy Carter's tree house, built on poles and shielded by a magnificent silver Atlas cedar.

Perhaps the most famous part of the park is Ellen Wilson's rose garden, planted in 1913 and redesigned by Mrs. Paul Mellon at the request of John F. Kennedy in 1962. This rendition of an 18th-century garden also includes osmanthus and boxwood hedges, tulips, narcissus, chrysanthemums, and heliotrope.

The grounds are closed to visitors except during the White House garden tours and the annual **Easter Egg Roll**, the biggest and best-attended—and least formal—party the White House throws. Because grass stains

White House

COURTESY OF THE BUREAU OF ENGRAVING AND PRINTING

are almost inevitable, jeans and sneakers are just fine. All children 6 years old and younger (and accompanied by an adult) are welcome.

The Easter Egg Roll's history, according to the White House, is as follows: More than 100 years ago, egg rolling was very big with the kids of DC, and their favorite spot was the gentle slope of the **Capitol** lawn. But enthusiastic egg rolling tore up the grounds in 1876, leading Congress to pass the Turf Protection Law, which prohibited the lawn from being used for such activities. No egg rolling took place the next year because of rain. But in 1878, one of two things is said to have happened: Either hordes of kids, angered to learn they would not be allowed at the Capitol, stormed the gates of the White House and demanded to be let in, or President Rutherford Hayes, aware of the situation, invited the young egg rollers to the White House grounds. Regardless of the true version of events, the first official White House Easter Egg Roll took place in 1878.

During World War II, Franklin D. Roosevelt called the event off, and it remained suspended for 12 years, long after the war's end. Traditionally, the first lady hosts the event, and it was Mamie Eisenhower who decided that happy times warranted a comeback of the festive event. After more than a decade, no one knew quite what to expect. Yards of storm fencing were put up to protect flower beds and the president's putting green; rest rooms and drinking fountains were hastily erected. When the great day arrived, the lawn was mobbed. Kids threw more eggs than they rolled, and the Eisenhower children retreated speedily to the White House. Secret Service agents had to rescue the president, who was holding his baby granddaughter. Although the lawn

became a matted mess of eggs, jelly beans, and marshmallows, the event was declared a huge success. These days, after so many years of experience, it has rarely taken more than an afternoon to return the lawn to its tidy state.

All egg rolling currently takes place in eight well-marked lanes, but real eggs and long-handled spoons are still used. Each recipient gets two eggs—one for practice. The Reagan administration added another spin to the festivities: All participants are awarded wooden eggs inscribed with the White House insignia as a prize. In addition, executive staffers send out thousands of eggs to politicians, athletes, and entertainers to be autographed and returned; these become treasures in the **Easter Egg Hunt**, which takes place at the same time as the egg roll in an enclosure at the side of the White House. Twenty-five young egg hunters at a time search this area. The White House has also begun sending eggs to respected American artists and foreign embassies for special decoration. Easter visitors can view the finished results, which are often quite wonderful, in a display case on the lawn.

4 ELLIPSE

The 52-acre oval yard south of the **White House** is best known as the site of the National Christmas Tree, which the president lights each December. Carolers and other yuletide celebrants fill the area with pageantry throughout the holiday season. In 1998 a menorah was added to the decorations, in honor of Hanukkah. During the rest of the year, vendors, chess players, softball players, and strollers enliven the park on sunny days. On the southeast and southwest corners of the Ellipse are the two curious Bulfinch Gate-

---

Restaurants/Clubs: Red | Hotels: Purple | Shops: Orange | Outdoors/Parks: Green | Sights/Culture: Blue

houses. In the early 1800s Charles Bulfinch was directed to enclose the Ellipse, and these are the only remains of the fence he built. Also, just across from the southwest corner is the old Lockkeeper's House. At one time a branch of the C&O Canal passed through here and this house, probably dating from around 1833, was near Lock B. ♦ Bounded by 15th and 17th Sts NW and by Constitution Ave and E St. ㅂ. Metros: Federal Triangle, Farragut North

5 Constitution Gardens

℗ This park is located between the **Washington Monument** and the **Lincoln Memorial**, where temporary Navy Department buildings from World War I stood until 1971, when President Richard Nixon had them demolished to make way for the gardens. **Skidmore, Owings & Merrill** originally designed a 50-acre park, but the recessionary budget cuts of the 1970s marred the plan. Though some find the results disappointing, this spot is a lovely, little-known haven in the midst of the bustling tourist sites. Walking paths and bike trails surround the 7.5-acre lake and its landscaped island, where you can examine Joseph E. Brown's memorial to the 56 signers of the Declaration of Independence. More than 5,000 trees create their own islands of shade. ♦ Daily. Free. Just south of Constitution Ave NW. 426.6841. ㅂ. www.nps.gov/coga. Metro: Foggy Bottom/GWU

5 Vietnam Veterans Memorial

In 1980, Congress authorized the construction of a memorial to the veterans of the Vietnam War on this plot near the **Lincoln Memorial**. After a national design competition with 1,421 entries, Congress unanimously chose a design by Maya Ying Lin, then a 21-year-old architecture student at Yale University. She conceived of the monument's polished black granite walls as a park within a park, a quiet place. The walls point to the **Washington Monument** and the Lincoln Memorial, and the 58,235 names of those killed in the war are inscribed in chronological order of the date of death, beginning at the walls' intersection, the memorial's deepest point. In a very real sense, the names become the memorial.

Lin's unconventional design stirred a storm of controversy. A flagpole and a more traditional bronze statue of three soldiers, by Washington sculptor Frederick Hart, were added nearby to mollify critics. The **Women's Memorial**, Glenna Goodacre's bronze sculpture of three uniformed women tending a wounded male soldier, honors the estimated 10,000 women who served in the war. However, Lin's work has transcended the initial criticism. Her Vietnam memorial is one of the nation's most moving public monuments. Veterans' groups

maintain vigils here, and those who lost loved ones leave flowers, medals, letters, and other tokens of remembrance. Volunteers are available to help find names, and a guard is on duty between 8AM and 11:45PM. ♦ 426.6481. ㅂ. www.nps.gov/vive

6 The National Museum of American History

The museum will be closed for renovations until summer 2008. Updates are available on their web site or via a free monthly e-mail newsletter.

Celebrating the country's scientific, technological, political, and cultural heritage, this collection functions as the "attic" of America, storing all the outdated contraptions that remind us who we once were and how we've changed. In 1858, the US Patent Office transferred its overcrowded cabinet of curiosities to the Smithsonian. To this base was added a windfall of exhibitions from the Philadelphia Centennial Exposition in 1876. Today, behind its pink Tennessee marble exterior, the 750,000-square-foot museum shelters agricultural machinery from a time when farming was strictly a family business, a 1913 Ford Model T, an Oscar the Grouch puppet, and a 280-ton steam locomotive.

Among the many displays you'll find a Foucault pendulum, which demonstrates the earth's rotation; a 200-year-old log house; inaugural gowns and other memorabilia from US first ladies; Native American pottery; and the **Ceremonial Court**, a re-creation of the **White House**'s **Cross Hall** that displays Thomas Jefferson's writing desk, White House china, and other presidential items. In the **Star-Spangled Banner Lab**, visitors can watch conservators at work on restoring the original flag that Francis Scott Key saw "by the dawn's early light" still flying over Fort McHenry in 1814.

The American Presidency explores the duties, ceremony, and history surrounding the job of chief executive. The **Museum Shop** features books, CDs, and items related to the museum's exhibits. ♦ Free. Daily, 10AM-5:30PM. Tours: Tu-F, 10:15AM and 1PM; Sa, 10:15AM. Constitution Ave NW (between 12th and 14th Sts). 633.1000. www.americanhistory.si.edu. ㅂ. Metros: Federal Triangle, Smithsonian

7 National Museum of Natural History

This treasure chest of natural science displays dioramas, re-creations, prototypes, and artifacts used to study evolution, cultures, dinosaurs, fossils, amphibians, reptiles, birds, sea organisms, mammals, insects, plants, rocks, minerals, and meteorites—in short, the entire planet (see floor plan opposite). There's too much here to digest in one visit, but some of the highlights are a 7-foot-long, 1-ton triceratops skull that greets you at the museum's entrance; a 13-foot-tall African bush elephant, the largest known specimen of the largest land animal of modern times; a 3.4-billion-year-old stromatolite; dinosaur skeletons; and one of Easter Island's famous stone heads. Press onward, even if your senses are overloaded, because there is also a life-size model of a 92-foot-long whale; a giant squid; the new **Kenneth E. Behring Family Hall of Mammals**; and, in the renovated **Janet Annenberg Hooker Hall of Geology, Gems, and Minerals**, more than 1,000 precious and semiprecious stones—the star of which is the legendary Hope Diamond, a 45-carat dazzler. Another must-see is the **O. Orkin Insect Zoo**, which features thousands of live bugs. Volunteers display these remarkable creatures. Even after you've taken an exhaustive (and exhausting) tour, the vast majority of the museum's 125 million objects remain stored unseen behind the scenes, where the museum's scientists have their laboratories. Free lectures or films are sometimes offered on Friday at noon. And there are two cafés and several museum shops. ♦ Free. Daily, 10AM-5:30PM, extended hours to 7:30PM in the summer. Tours: M-F, 10:30AM and 1:30PM; no tours July and Aug. Passes for Discovery Room available at the door. Constitution Ave NW (between Ninth and 12th Sts). Mall entrance: Madison Dr NW (between Ninth and 12th Sts). Information, 633.1000; reservations for groups of six or more, 357.2747. ♿. www.mnh.si.edu. Metros: Federal Triangle, Smithsonian

7 BUTTERFLY HABITAT GARDEN

Squeezed into a small rectangular area between the busy underpass and the museum is the delightful Butterfly Habitat Garden. Featuring four habitats—Wetlands, Meadows, Woodland, and Backyard—it explains that over 700 of this Lepidoptera species exist in the

US, with 80 of these making their homes in DC. In fact, this is just one of the six little garden areas spread around the Smithsonian museums. They make very pleasant places to rest and take a little break between the interesting, but arduous, explorations of the museums.

8 NATIONAL GALLERY OF ART SCULPTURE GARDEN ICE-SKATING RINK

Occupying a 6.1-acre site, and set around a large central fountain that, for winter fun, becomes an ice-skating rink, the garden is planted with all kinds of shrubs and flowering trees that form a background for primarily American 20th-century sculpture ranging from 42 inches to nearly 20 feet

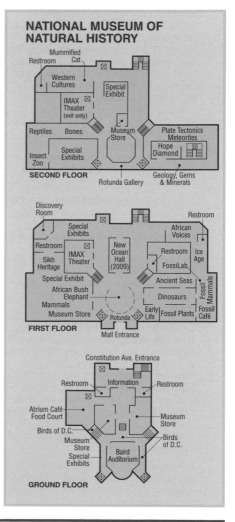

NATIONAL MUSEUM OF NATURAL HISTORY

SECOND FLOOR

Mummified Cat — Restroom

Western Cultures

IMAX Theater (exit only)

Special Exhibit

Reptiles — Bones — Museum Store — Plate Tectonics Meteorites

Insect Zoo — Special Exhibits — Hope Diamond

Rotunda Gallery — Geology, Gems & Minerals

FIRST FLOOR

Discovery Room — Restroom

Special Exhibits — African Voices

Restroom — Sikh Heritage — IMAX Theater — New Ocean Hall (2009) — Restroom FossiLab — Ice Age

Special Exhibit — Ancient Seas

African Bush Elephant — Dinosaurs — Fossil Mammals

Mammals — Museum Store — Rotunda — Early Life — Fossil Plants — Fossil Café

Mall Entrance

GROUND FLOOR

Constitution Ave. Entrance

Restroom — Information — Restroom

Atrium Café Food Court

Birds of D.C.

Museum Store — Museum Store — Birds of D.C.

Special Exhibits — Baird Auditorium

It's quite a foot-slog to get around all the city's museums—especially in the hot and humid summer conditions prevalent in DC. So, just take the *Circulator* bus that, for $1, allows you to hop on and off at leisure and explore all these fantastic museums and memorials.

Restaurants/Clubs: Red | Hotels: Purple | Shops: Orange | Outdoors/Parks: Green | Sights/Culture: Blue

high. The **Pavilion Café** is a great place for a break, and there is jazz in the garden on some summer evenings. ♦ M-Sa, 10AM-5PM; Su, 11AM-6PM; extended summer hours. Constitution Ave NW (between Seventh and Ninth Sts). 737.4215. &. Metro: Archives/Navy Memorial

9 NATIONAL GALLERY OF ART

Here is one of the world's most exceptional collections of European and American painting, sculpture, and graphic art dating from the Middle Ages to the present. (Its core collection was a gift to the United States by Andrew Mellon, banker and onetime secretary of the Treasury.) The gallery's **West Building**, designed in 1941 by **John Russell Pope**, houses pre-20th-century art by Titian, Rembrandt, El Greco, Rubens, Van Eyck, Fragonard, Renoir, Monet, Whistler, Gainsborough, and Cézanne. Included here are Botticelli's priceless *The Adoration of the Magi* and Raphael's *The Alba Madonna*. The *Ginevra de' Benci* by Leonardo da Vinci is the Italian master's only painting outside Europe. Grand spaces inside the simple neoclassical exterior (a Pope characteristic) set the stage for the art; the pantheon-like rotunda, with marble trim from quarries in the US and abroad, is particularly majestic. The outdoor **Sculpture Garden** (at Seventh St), with an elegant fountain and winter ice-skating rink, features 17 works by such celebrated artists as Roy Lichtenstein, Claes Oldenburg, and Louise Bourgeois.

Across the **National Gallery Plaza**, connected by an underground concourse, is the **East Building**, built in 1978 by **I.M. Pei and Partners**, where you will find distinguished 20th-century artworks such as Alexander Calder's last major mobile, *Untitled*, and Joan Miró's dramatic tapestry, *Woman*. Henry Moore's ever-changing sculpture *Knife Edge Mirror Two Piece* is stationed outside at the entrance portico.

Considered one of the best modern buildings in the city, the East Building's two triangles fit together to fill the oddly shaped site, leaving only a narrow green belt around the perimeter. Pei designed the new gallery to blend with the mathematical harmonies of the older one—height, color, even the size of the marble blocks reflect the example of the West Building. The interior spaces are strong and dramatic, and the roofline is a wonderland of frames and towers.

In recent years, the National Gallery has hosted several prestigious shows, including Vermeer and Van Gogh. Free advance tickets may be required for some shows (the 1998 Van Gogh exhibition had people lined up as early as 6AM for same-day tickets). Beware of hucksters selling tickets outside of the gallery

(for $20 and up); often counterfeit, these tickets will not be honored.

Sunday lectures, given in the East Building auditorium at 2PM, feature art historians discussing their own research or works in the museum's collection. Free Sunday-evening concerts, performed by the **National Gallery Orchestra** or guest artists, begin at 7PM (seating begins at 6PM) in the **West Garden Court** of the West Building (October–June). During July and August, jazz concerts are held in the **Sculpture Garden**. **Gallery Talks** examine one type of painting or a special exhibition or a particular work in depth. Check the **Information Desk** for a schedule of upcoming talks. Introductory tours of the East and West Buildings are given several times a day; call for times. Tours in foreign languages or for groups of 15 or more can be arranged (842.6247).

Art documentaries and an adventurous program of feature films are screened, free of charge, in the 460-seat theater in the East Building. For inexpensive postcards or poster reproductions of works by artists from da Vinci to Picasso, the **National Gallery Sales Shops** are incomparable. An excellent collection of art books is available at both the shop in the West Building and the one near the **Cascade Café** in the underground passageway between the West and East Buildings. ♦ Free. M-Sa, 10AM-5PM; Su, 11AM-6PM. West Bldg: Constitution Ave NW (between Fourth and Seventh Sts). East Bldg: Constitution Ave (between Third and Fourth Sts). 737.4215. &. www.nga.gov. Metros: Archives/Navy Memorial, Judiciary Sq

10 LINCOLN MEMORIAL

This structure (see page 44), so perfectly etched on Washington's landscape—not to mention the penny and the $5 bill—was built only after much debate over its shape and location. Among the early design proposals were an obelisk, a pyramid, and—sponsored by car and real-estate interests—a 72-mile-long memorial parkway between Gettysburg and Washington. The flea-ridden, swampy site eventually chosen had to be drained and filled before construction could begin in 1914. And yet a better choice now seems unimaginable. **Henry Bacon**'s classical memorial anchors the east–west axis of the **Mall**. A larger-than-life Lincoln gazes over the **Reflecting Pool** toward the **Washington Monument** and the **Capitol**. To the rear, an imaginary line connects the man who preserved the union with Robert E. Lee's final resting place in **Arlington National Cemetery**. The memorial is essentially a Greek-style temple ("Coolly cribbed from the Parthenon," reported one critic) with a Roman-style attic or roof. The entrance is on the broad side

NATIONAL GALLERY OF ART

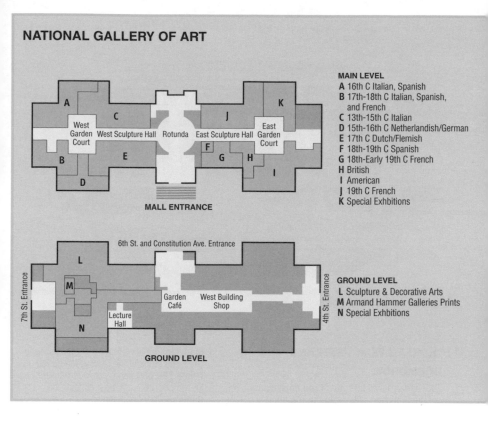

MAIN LEVEL
A 16th C Italian, Spanish
B 17th-18th C Italian, Spanish, and French
C 13th-15th C Italian
D 15th-16th C Netherlandish/German
E 17th C Dutch/Flemish
F 18th-19th C Spanish
G 18th-Early 19th C French
H British
I American
J 19th C French
K Special Exhbitions

GROUND LEVEL
L Sculpture & Decorative Arts
M Armand Hammer Galleries Prints
N Special Exhbitions

facing the Mall rather than on one of the narrow ends, as would have been typical in antiquity.

Thirty-six Doric columns rim the building; they tilt inward so as not to create the optical illusion of a bulging top. Above the colonnade is a frieze inscribed with the names and admission dates of the 36 states in the Union at the time of Lincoln's death. (The date for Ohio is off by 1 year.) Higher on the attic frieze are the names of the 48 states in the union at the time of the memorial's dedication in 1922.

Daniel Chester French's statue, often called "The Brooding Lincoln," looms from the center of the memorial. French designed the statue but only supervised the carving. The Piccirilli Brothers executed it in 4 years, using 28 blocks of white Georgia marble. The sixteenth president leans back in a monumental throne adorned with fasces, the Roman symbol of the authority of the state. From heel to head, the seated statue measures 19 feet, and if this stone exaggeration of our tallest president were to stand, it would tower above the crowd at a height of 28 feet.

Carved on the south wall is the Gettysburg Address, and on the north, Lincoln's second inaugural address. Above the texts are huge (12 feet high, 600 feet long) murals by Jules Guerin; one depicts the Angel of Truth liberating a slave; the other, the unity of North and South.

When the memorial was dedicated, one of the speakers was Dr. Robert Moton, the black president of Tuskegee Institute. Ironically, on Moton's arrival, a Marine Corps usher escorted him from the dais to the all-black section, separated from the memorial and the rest of the audience by a roadway. In the years since, the memorial has become a powerful symbol of the struggle for racial equality. In 1939, when the Daughters of the American Revolution refused to allow a concert by Marian Anderson at Constitution Hall, Anderson sang instead before 75,000 people from the steps of the memorial.

A magnificent sight at all times, the Lincoln Memorial is most impressive at dawn and dusk. ♦ Daily, 24 hours. Ranger on duty 8AM-11:45PM. 23rd St (between Independence Ave SW and Constitution Ave NW). 426.6841. ♿ www.nps.gov/linc. Metro: Foggy Bottom/GWU

Restaurants/Clubs: Red | Hotels: Purple | Shops: Orange | Outdoors/Parks: Green | Sights/Culture: Blue

Lincoln Memorial

COURTESY OF THE BUREAU OF ENGRAVING AND PRINTING

11 KOREAN WAR VETERANS MEMORIAL

Opened in July 1995, the 42nd anniversary of the armistice, this tribute to the men and women who served in the "forgotten war" is located on the south side of the **Reflecting Pool**, complementing the **Vietnam Veterans Memorial** on the north side. The **Cooper-Lecky Architects'** design consists of two intersecting components: the triangular *Field of Service* and the circular *Pool of Remembrance*. Scattered on the field are statues, sculpted by Frank Gaylord, of 19 servicemen clad in foul-weather ponchos. Walkways lead pedestrians along two sides of the triangle to a point that intersects with the pool. Bordering one walkway is a granite wall with photographic images of the war taken from the National Archives. ◆ Daily, 24 hours. Ranger on duty 8AM-11:45PM. North of Independence Ave SW. 426.6841. &. www.nps.gov/kowa. Metros: Foggy Bottom/GWU, Smithsonian

12 REFLECTING POOL

The glassy surface of this shallow, rectangular pool mirrors both the **Washington Monument** and the **Lincoln Memorial**. The pool, a third of a mile long by 180 feet wide and 3 feet deep, is bordered by tree-lined pedestrian paths—usually a peaceful oasis in this fast-paced city. However, many celebrations and demonstrations held here have disrupted the tranquil setting. The 1963 Civil Rights March on Washington climaxed with Martin Luther King Jr. giving his "I Have a Dream" speech (from the steps of the Lincoln Memorial) before 250,000 people crowded around, and in, the pool. ◆ &. Metros: Foggy Bottom/GWU, Smithsonian

13 NATIONAL WORLD WAR II MEMORIAL

Located just west of the Washington Monument, this long-awaited site designed by Friedrich St. Florian serves as the first national memorial honoring those who served during World War II. It was dedicated with much fanfare during Memorial Day Weekend 2004; folks like President George W. Bush, Bob Dole, and Tom Hanks spoke during the opening ceremonies. Though the memorial's importance isn't disputed, many local activists did find fault with the location of the display, fearing disruption of the landscape between the **Lincoln Memorial** and the **Washington Monument**. But that hasn't stopped visitors from flocking to the site, where arches mark the north and south ends of the memorial plaza and 56 granite pillars represent each US state and territory during World War II. Twenty-four bronze bas-relief panels depict America's war years at home and overseas. The historic **Rainbow Pool** was restored during the memorial's construction, and its fountains now symbolize the joy of the Allied victory. ◆ Free. Accessible 24 hours daily. 17th St NW (between Independence and Constitution Aves). 426.6841. &. www.nps.gov/nwwm. Metro: Smithsonian

PENNSYLVANIA AVENUE

As John F. Kennedy's inaugural motorcade rolled down Pennsylvania Avenue from the **White House** to the **Capitol**, the president-elect took in "America's Main Street." He viewed an avenue in economic shambles with tacky souvenir shops and cheap restaurants. The once grand **Willard Hotel** was tattered; peep shows, pawn shops, and liquor stores had turned the avenue into a seedy strip. Supposedly, JFK declared, "It's a disgrace—fix it."

From Kennedy's orders grew a comprehensive redevelopment plan for Pennsylvania Avenue—although things did not improve immediately. Kennedy's assassination, the riots of 1968, and the building of the FBI headquarters (an architectural monstrosity that even J. Edgar Hoover called the ugliest building he'd ever seen) set planning back a decade.

In 1974 the **Pennsylvania Avenue Development Corporation** (**PADC**), established by Congress under President Richard Nixon, issued its first report proposing parks, restored historic buildings, and revitalized commercial space. Today, though some elements of the PADC's original proposal were changed, the plan's revitalizing spirit has persevered to create a grand Pennsylvania Avenue forged from the old and the new.

The Willard Hotel (1401 Pennsylvania Avenue NW, at 14th Street; 628.9100), which closed in 1968, was reopened in 1986, meticulously restored. Both the **National Theatre** (1321 Pennsylvania Avenue NW, between 13th and 14th Streets; 628.6161) and the **Warner Theatre** (13th and E Streets NW; 783.4000) are running full entertainment schedules. The old **Apex Liquor Store** at Pennsylvania Avenue and Seventh Street Northwest, with the often-photographed Temperance Fountain out front, has been restored and now houses the National Council of Negro Women.

New construction has added 20th-century architecture to the avenue. **I.M. Pei** perfectly suited the **East Wing** of the **National Gallery of Art** (Fourth Street NW, between Madison Drive and Constitution Avenue; 737.4215) to its triangular site. Nearby, the Canadian government built a new chancery (501 Pennsylvania Avenue NW, between Constitution Avenue and Sixth Street), designed by award-winning architect Arthur Erickson, where an old, nondescript library once stood. And most welcome to pedestrians are two parks— **Freedom Plaza** and **Pershing Park**—both near the White House.

Pierre L'Enfant, Washington's first city planner, envisioned Pennsylvania Avenue as a grand ceremonial boulevard, linking the Capitol and the presidential "palace." More than 200 years later, the avenue appears closer than ever to that goal.

14 WASHINGTON MONUMENT

The simple yet grand presence of this monument (pictured page 46) is, at 555 feet, the tallest structure in DC. It was the tallest in the world when it opened to the public in 1888. The Washington National Monument Society, which launched a nationwide competition to select a landmark for the capital, didn't favor **Pierre Charles L'Enfant**'s original idea of an equestrian statue of Washington that would have stood on the current site of the **Jefferson Pier**. Instead it preferred **Robert Mills**'s richly decorated obelisk, designed to rise like a giant birthday candle from behind a Greek-style circular temple that was to hold the tombs of Revolutionary War heroes. Plans also included a massive marble statue of Washington driving a quadriga (a Roman chariot pulled by four horses) in front of the monument. Lack of money and public support for these frills led to the establishment of the simple gleaming tower—a familiar symbol of Washington the city as well as Washington the man.

Funds for the monument initially came from private groups that solicited $1 apiece from citizens across the nation. Construction proceeded smoothly for 7 years—until a single block of marble was donated by Pope Pius IX. This infuriated the antipapist Know-Nothing Party, members of which allegedly stole the "pope's stone" and sabotaged further fundraising for the monument. Then the Civil War broke out, and the project was abandoned for more than a decade.

In 1876—after the war and the US Centennial Exposition—public interest returned and construction was turned over to the Army Corps of Engineers. They strengthened the foundation

Why is the Washington Monument a monument, and everything else a memorial?

Memorials are planned and dedicated after the death of the individual concerned. As Washington was still alive when this was initially planned—although work didn't begin on it until after his death in 1848—it is a monument to him and not a memorial.

Restaurants/Clubs: Red | Hotels: Purple | Shops: Orange | Outdoors/Parks: Green | Sights/Culture: Blue

(although it still sinks a quarter inch every 30 years) and redesigned the monument, much improving the original proportions. A slight change of color in the stone marks the point at which construction resumed. In 1884, the obelisk was capped with a 9-inch tip made of solid aluminum (an exotic material at the time) and wired with 144 platinum lightning conductors. The government picked up the more than $1 million tab. In 2002, a much-needed $8 million restoration of the monument was completed.

Tickets are required to tour the monument. Reserved tickets may be obtained for a $1.50 fee by calling 800/967.2283 or by visiting www.reservations.nps.gov. Free same-day tickets are given out on a first-come, first-served basis at a kiosk on the monument grounds at 15th Street and Madison Drive beginning at 8:30AM; tickets usually run out early. ♦ Free. Daily, 9AM-4:45PM. West of 15th St. 426.6841. www.nps.gov/wash. &. Metro: Smithsonian

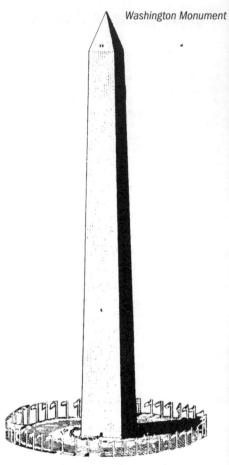

Washington Monument

COURTESY OF THE BUREAU OF ENGRAVING AND PRINTING

15 FREER GALLERY OF ART

A 4-year renovation (1989–1993) of this Italian Renaissance building, which originally opened in 1923, not only retained but heightened its charm. An elegant little theater was added, display cases were dramatically lit, explanatory texts were expanded, and the entrance was cleared of an intrusive gift shop. Housed within is an eclectic collection of Asian art and late 19th- and early 20th-century American art showing a Far Eastern influence. The late Charles Lang Freer, a wealthy Detroit businessman, began collecting Eastern art on the advice of a close friend, artist James McNeill Whistler. The flamboyant **Peacock Room**, decorated by Whistler, is a highlight of the collection. ♦ Free. Daily, 10AM-5:30PM. Tours: M, Tu, Th-Su, 12:15PM. Jefferson Dr SW (between Seventh and 12th Sts). 633.4880. &. www.asia.si.edu. Metro: Smithsonian

16 SMITHSONIAN INSTITUTION BUILDING

Popularly known as the "Castle" because of its marvelous spires, towers, turrets, and crenellated parapets, this was the **Smithsonian's** first building. Designed by **James Renwick** and completed in 1855, it is composed of red sandstone from Seneca Creek, Maryland, and widely recognized as one of the finest Gothic Revival buildings in America. The Smithsonian's administrative offices and the **Smithsonian Information Center** occupy the Castle. Also within is the **Crypt Room**, housing the tomb of the Smithsonian's British benefactor, James Smithson. It was his $500,000 bequest to the United States in 1838 that established the

Smithsonian Institution. ♦ Free. Daily, 8:30AM-5:30PM. 1000 Jefferson Dr SW (between Seventh and 12th Sts). 633.1000. &. www.si.edu. Metro: Smithsonian

17 ARTS & INDUSTRIES BUILDING

This 19th-century building was originally constructed to house items that had been displayed at Philadelphia's Centennial Exposition in 1876. Designed in a High Victorian style by the Washington architectural firm of **Cluss and Schulze**, it opened in 1881 in time for President James A. Garfield's inaugural ball. The building is an elaborate polychrome-brick affair with giant industrial trusses, meandering iron balconies, and a fountain in the rotunda. It typically houses a rotating schedule of special exhibits; however, as of press time, the building was closed for a multiyear renovation. ♦ Free. 900 Jefferson Dr SW (between Seventh and 12th Sts). 633.1000. &. www.si.edu/ai. Metro: Smithsonian

18 ENID A. HAUPT GARDEN

Conceived by **Smithsonian Institution** Director Emeritus S. Dillon Ripley in 1987, the garden, comprising more than 4 acres, is sandwiched between the **Smithsonian Institution**, the **Sackler Gallery**, and the **National Museum of African Art**. It's named after Enid Annenberg Haupt of New York, who contributed more than $3 million toward its establishment. The central Victorian parterre is a retreat from the museum bustle, with antique wrought-iron park benches and beds of bright flowers that form patterns modeled after the garden designed for Philadelphia's 1876 Centennial Exposition. The main entrance, in front of the parterre, is known as the **Renwick Gates**, after Smithsonian architect **James Renwick**, who sketched a carriage gate in 1849 that was never built. The entrance's four stone pillars are made from the same red Seneca sandstone that was used to build the Smithsonian Institution building. Two minigardens, one on either side of the parterre, reflect the styles of the museums below. The **Island Garden** near the Sackler Gallery features two 9-foot-tall pink granite "moon gates," one on either side of a pool paved with half-round pieces of granite and shaded by two weeping cherry trees. The **Fountain Garden** near the National Museum of African Art is designed to be a haven on hot days, with a waterfall and thornless hawthorns. ◆ Daily, 6:30 AM-dusk. Independence Ave SW (between Seventh and 12th Sts). 🌀. Metro: Smithsonian

18 THE QUADRANGLE

Pressed for more exhibition and office space, the Smithsonian Institution slipped a three-story complex below the **Enid A. Haupt Garden** (see above). Within this space, which is 96% belowground, are the **Smithsonian Associates**. Also below ground level is the **National Museum of African Art** pavilion, whose domed roofs recall the arch motif of the **Freer**, and the **Arthur M. Sackler Gallery** pavilion, its pyramidal silhouette echoing the roof lines of the **Arts & Industries Building**. ◆ Independence Ave SW (between Seventh and 12th Sts). 🌀. Metro: Smithsonian

Within the Quadrangle:

NATIONAL MUSEUM OF AFRICAN ART

The only museum in the US dedicated to the collection and conservation of African art was founded by Warren Robbins in 1964 as a private institution in a series of connected row houses on **Capitol Hill** (one of which belonged to Frederick Douglass). It became a branch of the Smithsonian in 1979.

The collection demonstrates how the continent's hundreds of distinct cultures weave art into daily life, expressing religious beliefs and practices not only in masks and figures created for ceremonial purposes but also in everyday objects, such as splendid sculptures, textiles, building tools, and household utensils. Most are made from impermanent organic materials, such as wood; therefore, the bulk of the collected works date back only to the late 19th and 20th centuries.

Permanent collections include masks and sculpture, contemporary works, ceramics, and art from the royal court of Benin. The museum also offers a variety of children's programs, workshops, lectures, films, and musical performances throughout the year. ◆ Free. Museum: daily, 10AM-5:30PM. Library: by appointment. Tours: M-F, 1:30PM; Sa, Su, 11AM, 1PM. 633.4600. 🌀. www.nmafa.si.edu

ARTHUR M. SACKLER GALLERY

The museum's two floors of belowground galleries give the **Smithsonian** its first real opportunity to showcase its extensive collection of Asian art. Dr. Arthur M. Sackler, a New York research physician, donated some 1,000 masterworks to found this collection. He also gave $4 million toward the construction of the museum. On display are ancient Chinese jade and bronzes, South Asian sculpture, paintings from Iran and India, Chinese Ming dynasty furniture, and Near Eastern works in silver, gold, bronze, and lesser minerals.

The second-level library houses more than 80,000 volumes and more than 11,000 images. There are often free events, including concerts, films, and dance presentations. ◆ Free. Galleries: daily, 10AM-5:30PM. Library: M-F, 10AM-5PM. Tours: M, Tu, Th-Su, 12:15PM. 633.4880. 🌀. www.asia.si.edu

19 HIRSHHORN MUSEUM AND SCULPTURE GARDEN

For the modern art enthusiast, this is the stuff of which dreams are made. The museum is, in fact, the realized dream of American

Anacostia, established in 1854, started off as Uniontown. So many towns were named Uniontown after the Civil War that in 1886 the area was rechristened Anacostia, for the river that flows nearby.

Restaurants/Clubs: **Red** | Hotels: **Purple** | Shops: **Orange** | Outdoors/Parks: **Green** | Sights/Culture: **Blue**

immigrant and self-made millionaire Joseph Hirshhorn. The industrialist spent more than 40 years indulging his love of art and championing many yet-to-be-discovered American artists at a time when most Americans still looked to Europe for artistic legitimacy.

At its premiere, the Hirshhorn collection consisted of 6,000 pieces, including some 2,000 sculptures, and was estimated to be worth at least $50 million. Under the **Smithsonian**'s guidance, the collection has grown and now boasts sculptures by Auguste Rodin, Constantin Brancusi, David Smith, Alexander Calder, and Henry Moore. The museum's 19th- and 20th-century paintings are by Winslow Homer, Willem de Kooning, Jean Dubuffet, Josef Albers, Georgia O'Keeffe, Andy Warhol, Anselm Kiefer, and Jackson Pollock, to name just a few of the notables. The Hirshhorn also mounts several major loan exhibitions each year, concentrating on an artist, medium, style, or theme.

Gordon Bunshaft/Skidmore, Owings & Merrill's controversial doughnut-shaped building (the circular forms look concentric, but they're very slightly off center) aims to maximize wall space while minimizing sun damage to the art. Accordingly, there are no exterior windows, but the third-floor balcony offers a great view.

Spend a moment in the sunken garden across from the museum: The terraces, reflecting pool, and works by master sculptors make it one of the city's most evocative settings. A rewarding stop in the sculpture garden is Rodin's *Burghers of Calais*. This haunting piece dramatizes the moment when the town fathers of Calais, France, gave themselves up to British invaders so that their town might be saved. The six proud, anguished men wear nooses around their necks as they prepare to hand over the keys to the city.

On certain Thursday and Friday evenings at 8:00, the Hirshhorn shows independently produced film shorts or documentaries (free showings held between September and June). Special tour arrangements can be made by calling in advance. ♦ Free. Daily, 10AM–5:30PM. Tours of permanent collection: 1 Sept-31 May, M-F, 10:30AM and noon; Sa, Su, noon and 2PM; 1 June-31 Aug, M-F, noon; Sa, Su, noon and 2PM. Outdoor cafeteria open for lunch during summer only. Independence Ave SW and Seventh St. Information, 633.1000; special tours, film and lecture schedule, 633.1618. &. www.hirshhorn.si.edu. Metro: L'Enfant Plaza

20 NATIONAL AIR AND SPACE MUSEUM

This is rightfully one of the world's most popular museums (see floor plan opposite). Its exhibition areas overflow with reminders of the finest

hours of aviation and space flight: the Wright Brothers' 1903 Flyer; Robert Goddard's early rockets; Charles Lindbergh's *Spirit of St. Louis*; Amelia Earhart's Lockheed Vega; Chuck Yeager's Bell X-1; the Apollo 11 command module *Columbia*; and, as a fanciful tribute, the original model of the *USS Enterprise* from the *Star Trek* TV series. The "How Things Fly" exhibit incorporates a supersonic wind tunnel, a floor-to-ceiling sliding barometer, and Boeing 757 fuselage section—all to help visitors understand gravity, thrust, and forward motion. Other exhibits include a touchable moon rock, flight simulators that allow visitors to "fly" aircraft on display, and a walk through Skylab. Tours are given daily at 10:30AM and 1PM.

One of the museum's highlights is the **Lockheed Martin IMAX Theater**, with a five-story-high screen. An ever-changing film schedule has included the classic *To Fly!*, *Cosmic Voyage*, *Mission to Mir*, and *Everest*. The IMAX experience can be so realistic that some viewers may feel a little motion sickness, especially during *To Fly!*. Tickets may be purchased at the box office up to 2 weeks before the show, and they often sell out during the tourist season.

The new **Wright Place Food Court** offers burgers and fries from McDonald's, home-style meals from Boston Market, and pizza from Donato's Pizzeria. A three-level gift shop, the Smithsonian's largest, features books, models, kites, posters, and other items for the aviation enthusiast. ♦ Free. Daily, 10AM–5:30PM. Independence Ave SW (between Fourth and Seventh Sts). 633.1000. &. www.nasm.si.edu. Metro: L'Enfant Plaza

21 NATIONAL MUSEUM OF THE AMERICAN INDIAN

Opened in September 2004, this museum, nearly 15 years in the making, explores the history of America's native people. Located just east of the **Air and Space Museum**, it occupies a curvilinear building made of various-sized pieces of golden-hued Kasota limestone, which gives the structure the appearance of a mass carved by wind and water. In keeping with Native American traditions, the building faces the rising sun. Inside, exhibits display 200 artworks by Allan Houser and George Morrison and approximately 8,000 objects, everything from weavings and dolls to peace medals and a 20-foot totem pole. Also on site: a boat-building demonstration area and a 120-seat theater that presents a 13-minute multimedia show complete with a simulated campfire. Though admission to the museum is free, timed passes are required. Same-day passes are distributed at the museum's east entrance beginning at 10AM. Advance passes are available (for a small fee) by calling 866/400.6624 or by

NATIONAL AIR AND SPACE MUSEUM

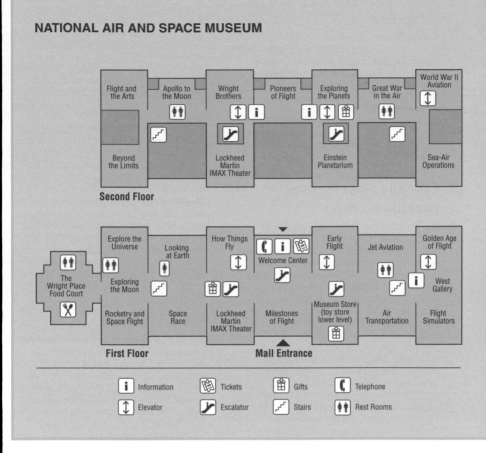

visiting www.americanindian.si.edu or www.tickets.com. ♦ Free. Daily, 10AM-5:30PM. 4th St and Independence Ave SW. 633.1000. &. www.americanindian.si.edu. Metro: L'Enfant Plaza

22 US BOTANIC GARDEN

This cast-iron-and-glass Victorian nursery—a 19th-century style epitomized by the Syon and Kew gardens in England—recently underwent an extensive renovation. The gardens house ferns, succulents, cacti, orchids, palms, cycads, and other botanical collections, some of which get transplanted to congressional offices. Group tours are available; call for information. ♦ Free. Daily, 10AM-5PM.
First St SW (between C St and Maryland Ave). 225.8333. &. www.usbg.gov. Metros: Federal Center SW, Capitol South

23 BARTHOLDI FOUNTAIN

This 40-ton cast-iron extravaganza by Frédéric-Auguste Bartholdi, creator of the

Statue of Liberty, was a prizewinner at the 1876 Centennial Exposition in Philadelphia. Three nymphs hold up a basin, rimmed with fanciful lamps that were originally gas operated but, nowadays, are run by electricity. This was one of the first public displays of electric illumination. ♦ Independence Ave SW and First St. &. Metros: Federal Center SW, Capitol South

24 VOICE OF AMERICA (VOA)

This government-run broadcasting service reaches an audience of 87 million over the radio, satellite TV, and the Internet. VOA announcers broadcast in 44 languages: You may hear programs in Swahili, Urdu, or Albanian, depending on the time of day. Forty-five-minute tours explain the role of the VOA and its parent organization, the US Information Agency. ♦ Free. Tours: M-F, 10:30AM, 1:30PM, 2:30PM. Reservations required; groups limited to 25. C St SW (between Third and Fourth Sts). 619.3919. &. www.voa.gov. Metro: Federal Center SW

Restaurants/Clubs: Red | Hotels: Purple | Shops: Orange | Outdoors/Parks: Green | Sights/Culture: Blue

25 HUBERT H. HUMPHREY BUILDING

Marcel Breuer's bold design for the headquarters of the Department of Health and Human Services is often compared favorably to his nearby **Housing and Urban Development (HUD)** building (see page 53). The carbon monoxide funnels for I-395 (which runs under Capitol Hill) are incorporated into the structure, so the building sometimes appears to smoke. The building is not open to the public. ♦ 200 Independence Ave SW (between Washington Ave and Third St). Metro: Federal Center SW

26 EAST AND WEST POTOMAC PARK/HAINS POINT

East Potomac Park is the island created by the Washington Channel; West Potomac Park encompasses the area between the **Tidal Basin** and the **Lincoln Memorial**. Together, these parks cover 700 acres at the west end of the **Mall**. Scattered with monuments, pools, and trees, they offer some of the city's best views. Come during cherry blossom time and enjoy almost 2,000 pink double-blossomed trees in bloom, generally 2 weeks later than those at the Tidal Basin. (Take the 14th Street Bridge and head south on Ohio Drive to the park.) Visitors can play golf at the public course, ride along the bike paths, paddle a boat, savor a picnic, or just enjoy the sunshine. At Hains Point, the peninsula's southern tip, check out *The Awakening*, Seward Johnson's unusual 1980 aluminum sculpture—a gigantic figure rising out of the ground as if coming to life. ♦ Ohio Dr SW (south of Independence Ave). Information, 426.6841; tennis and golf information, 554.7660. &. Metro: Smithsonian

Within East and West Potomac Park:

FRANKLIN DELANO ROOSEVELT MEMORIAL

Designed by architect **Lawrence Halprin**, this long-overdue tribute to the president who led America through the Great Depres-

> The impressive Franklin D. Roosevelt Memorial is not what the former president had in mind. According to Supreme Court Justice Felix Frankfurter, Roosevelt told him, "I am likely to shuffle off long before you kick the bucket. If they are to put any memorial to me, I should like it to be placed in the center of that green plot in front of the Archives Building. I should like it to consist of a block about the size of this." He pointed to his desk.
> —Douglas E. Evelyn and Paul Dickson, *On This Spot*

sion and all but the last months of World War II opened in May 1997. It features four outdoor "rooms" (one for each of Franklin Delano Roosevelt's terms in office), covering 7.5 acres. Incorporating fountains and gardens, it's very different in concept from the self-contained memorials to Lincoln and Jefferson. Studded with bronze sculptures reflecting periods of FDR's presidency, this memorial goes beyond the celebration of one man and also honors the institution of the presidency, the human struggles of the Great Depression, the US's emergence as a world power, and First Lady Eleanor Roosevelt. When the memorial was dedicated, there wasn't any kind of portrayal of FDR in a wheelchair, in keeping with his reluctance to be photographed in it. But disabled activists successfully lobbied to get a statue added, and several years later, a depiction of FDR sitting in a wheelchair was dedicated. Interestingly, it was the first memorial in Washington, DC, that was designed to be wheelchair accessible. ♦ Daily, 24 hours. Ranger on duty 8AM-11:45PM. 426.6841. &. www.nps.gov/frde

27 SYLVAN THEATER

Weather permitting, this outdoor theater with a huge lawn regularly presents musicals, Shakespearean plays, and concerts. Thousands of people flock to the small stage on hot summer evenings; the first to arrive claim the best spots by spreading picnic blankets or unfolding their own lawn chairs up front. Military and big band concerts are usually held throughout the summer. ♦ Free. 15th St SW and Independence Ave. 426.6841. &. Metro: Smithsonian

28 UNITED STATES HOLOCAUST MEMORIAL MUSEUM

Opened in 1993, this museum has established itself as one of the most moving memorials in Washington, if not the world. It tells the story of the millions of Jews, Gypsies, and other "undesirables" who were executed by the Nazis between 1933 and 1945. Give yourself ample time to experience this museum. **James Ingo Freed**, of **Pei Cobb Freed & Partners**, designed the building, and his intelligence and creativity show in every detail, from interior lights that resemble watchtower spotlights to exits that look like prison doors. Through strange angles, slanted walls, and out-of-kilter staircases, the structure intimates that visitors are entering a world where sanity no longer prevails. The exhibits here build on one another, augmenting viewers' feelings of shock and horror and creating an unforgettable experience.

At the beginning of the tour visitors receive a card containing information about a particular

Dramatic DC

Although it could be said that DC's best drama unfolds on the congressional floor, Washington also has its share of legitimate theater. Home to the first lady of theater Helen Hayes, opera diva Denyce Graves, and film star Sandra Bullock, Washington nurtures a proud tradition of performing arts.

The **John F. Kennedy Center for the Performing Arts** (see page 60), an imposing monumental white structure that glistens over the **Potomac**, opened in 1971 and now attracts over 20 million visitors a year. Most come to tour the building, walking through the flag-adorned **Hall of States** or **Hall of Nations** and on to the **Grand Foyer**, a room 630 feet long and 60 feet high. Worth admiring are Robert Berks's enormous bust of President Kennedy, the 18 crystal chandeliers, and the view of the Potomac and Downtown from floor-to-ceiling windows. Performances here include everything from the ballet and Broadway shows to comedy revue and college theater festivals held in one of the center's five stages: the **Opera House, Eisenhower Theater, Concert Hall, Theater Lab,** and **Terrace Theater.** Ticket prices run the gamut—from $10 for a senior/student concert ticket to $250 for a box seat at the opera. Standing-room tickets are sometimes available on a limited basis. Free events are shown nightly at 6PM on the **Millennium Stage.**

Arena Stage (see page 54), the first not-for-profit theater in the US, opened in 1950 under the direction of Zelda Fichandler. Now in Southwest DC near the waterfront, the complex houses three theaters: the 800-seat **Fichandler Theater** (in the round), the **Kreeger,** and smallest of the three, the **Old Vat Room.** James Earl Jones and Jane Alexander got their starts here; both Kevin Kline and Stacey Keach have made frequent appearances. Each season showcases old standbys as well as "unjustly neglected works" and productions by new playwrights from around the world.

Both the **National Theatre** (see page 93), a block from the **Willard Hotel,** and the **Warner Theatre** (see page 93) book Broadway blockbusters. The National, Washington's oldest theater in continuous operation, opened in 1835, weathered five fires, was rebuilt, and was later renovated in 1984. Free performances for children are shown on most Saturday mornings. **Ford's Theatre** (see page 93), where President Abraham Lincoln was shot, produces plays in an intimate setting. Closed after the assassination, the theater was later leased by the government. Then in 1964 a careful renovation began, including restoration of the presidential box; the stage reopened on 13 February 1968.

Each season the well-established **Shakespeare Theatre's** (see page 96) repertory company presents three Shakespearean plays as well as two works by the Bard's contemporaries or playwrights he influenced. Under the direction of Michael Kahn, the company performs in a well-designed, 451-seat space—which also attracts such guest artists as Harry Hamlin, Patrick Stewart, Dixie Carter, and Kelly McGillis. Every June the company offers 2 weeks of the free Shakespeare in the Park at **Carter Barron Amphitheatre** (see page 154) in **Rock Creek Park.**

For a cutting-edge alternative to traditional Shakespeare, the **Washington Shakespeare Company** (Clark Street Playhouse, 601 S Clark Street; at Old Jefferson Davis Highway, Arlington; 703/418.4808) presents audacious adaptations of the Bard as well as contemporary theater. In *The Winter's Tale*—one of Shakespeare's "problem" plays—the innovative company staged Bohemia as a 1950s beach party, complete with Autolycus dressed as Elvis Presley.

Since 1979, the **Studio Theatre** (see page 108) has put on contemporary works by such playwrights as August Wilson, A.R. Gurney, and Alfred Uhry. An extensive renovation has given the space a sleek, modern design that now houses two 200-seat theaters. More avant-garde contemporary works are performed by the **Woolly Mammoth Theatre Company** at its own theater, which opened in 2005 at 7th and D Streets NW 289.2443).

The latest Spanish-language performances by new playwrights, as well as concerts and classical works, can be seen at the **Gala Hispanic Theatre** (see page 77). Simultaneous English translation is available through earphones.

If you're still begging for more, try **Discovery Theater** for children's plays, musicals, and puppet shows, and try the many university theaters that present a wide range of theater, music, and opera. Check local newspapers—especially the *Washington Post's* Friday edition and the *City Paper*—for listings.

Restaurants/Clubs: Red | Hotels: Purple | Shops: Orange | Outdoors/Parks: Green | Sights/Culture: Blue

Holocaust witness, thus allowing them to establish a bond with an individual from history. This helps most people feel the impact of a tragedy that affected millions. Be sure to save time (and energy) for the last exhibit—*Testimony*, an hour-long film—presented in a stark, open auditorium. Haunting accounts of the Holocaust are delivered by several of its survivors—a heart-wrenching yet inspiring experience. At the end of your tour, stop in the calmingly spare **Hall of Remembrance** to absorb all you've encountered. A computer learning center also provides electronic databases for those who want to conduct additional research.

No passes are needed to enter the building or to view the museum's special exhibits. However, owing to the volume of visitors, timed tickets are required for the permanent exhibition *The Holocaust*. Tickets may be obtained from **Tickets.com** by calling 800/400.9373 or by visiting www.tickets.com, but they will levy a service charge. A limited number of same-day tickets are available at the museum beginning at 10AM; get here early. ♦ Free, with ticket. Daily 10AM-5:30PM; Tu and Th, April to mid-June, 10AM-7:50PM. 100 Raoul Wallenberg Pl SW (at Independence Ave). 488.0400. ఈ. www.ushmm.org. Metro: Smithsonian

29 DEPARTMENT OF AGRICULTURE

This was the first building erected by the McMillan Commission, which was charged at the turn of the 19th century with resurrecting **Pierre Charles L'Enfant**'s plan for a gracious, ceremonial capital city. ♦ Independence Ave SW and 14th St. ఈ. Metro: Smithsonian

30 BUREAU OF ENGRAVING AND PRINTING

Once every fiscal year the Federal Reserve puts in an order at the **Bureau of Engraving and Printing**. The order is for a great deal of paper money—so much, in fact, that the presses must roll 24 hours a day all year to print it. In 2003, the bureau printed 3,699,200,000 notes in $1 denominations. To put this into perspective, if you had that much money and spent it at the reasonable rate of $1 per second, it would take you about 117 years to go broke. Of all the notes printed each year, 95% are used to replace notes already in circulation and nearly half are $1 bills.

Aside from a whole lot of bucks, the bureau prints Federal Reserve notes, Treasury securities, invitations to the White House, and postage stamps (though that won't be the case for much longer) every year. In the past it has turned out food stamps, and during the oil embargo of 1973, it had an order—never filled—to print coupons for gas rationing.

Watching crisp sheets of money roll off the presses is great fun for kids and fuels the

fantasies of adults. The bureau offers a free tour, which begins with a short video on the history of the bureau. Visitors then proceed to the gallery, which offers an excellent view of large sheets of money being printed, checked, overprinted with the treasury seal, cut, stacked, and bundled for shipment. The tour ends at the **Visitors' Center**, where presidential portraits and commemorative coins are displayed and sold. Additional exhibitions further explain the engraving process and the activities of the bureau. Buy a small bag of shredded money or a sheet of uncut currency for a unique souvenir.

Tickets are required March to August only. From September to February no tickets required. Free same-day tickets can be picked up at the ticket booth, located on the 15th Street side of the building (at Raoul Wallenberg Place), beginning at 8AM; tickets usually run out quickly. ♦ Free. Tours: M-F, 9-10:45AM and 12:30-2PM; extended hours May-Aug, 5-7PM. Visitors' Center: M-F, 8:30AM-3PM. 14th St SW (between Maine and Independence Aves). 874.2330. ఈ. www.moneyfactory.com. Metro: Smithsonian

31 TIDAL BASIN

Come here to picnic, jog, read, or enjoy the view. On the east side are gardens of seasonal flowers—especially brilliant in spring, when the tulips appear—and a concession stand that sells hot dogs and burgers and rents the little blue paddleboats that skim the lake ($8 per hour for a 2-passenger boat and $16 per hour for a 4-passenger boat; daily mid-March to Labor Day and Wednesday through Sunday until Columbus Day, weather permitting). Near East Basin Drive is the **Japanese Pagoda**, and near the Kutz Memorial Bridge is the **Japanese Lantern**. This park and breeze-swept lake will take your breath away when the 1,678 surrounding cherry trees bloom (sometime between mid-March and mid-April, depending on the weather). The best way to experience blossom time is on foot. In fact, driving can be a miserable experience, with traffic jams and honking horns. Use public transportation to reach the **Mall**, then walk through the lovely park, where the crowds attract vendors and street performers. Other places to see Japanese cherry trees are the **Washington Monument** grounds (see page 45) and **East and West Potomac Park** (see page 50). The basin was created in 1897 to collect water from the Potomac and empty it into the Washington Channel, possibly because the river is an estuary and rises with the tide. ♦ Boat house/concession: daily, 10AM-6PM Apr-Oct. 479.2426. ఈ. Metro: Smithsonian

32 MANDARIN ORIENTAL, WASHINGTON, DC

$$$$ One of DC's newest hotels, and one of its most luxurious, the Mandarin Oriental enjoys

excellent views of the southwest waterfront and the city's monuments and memorials. Sixteen different types of rooms and suites are available, all of which have been designed according to the principles of feng shui. All feature handmade silk tapestries above the beds, reproductions of artworks from the **Smithsonian Institution**'s collections, flat-screen TVs, high-speed Internet access, and bathrooms decked out with Chinese marble. Amenities include twice-daily housekeeping, 24-hour room and valet service, concierge services, and a 14,000-square-foot spa, gym, and indoor pool. Eric Ziebold, former chef de cuisine at the French Laundry, oversees the action at **CityZen**, which serves modern American cuisine plus more than 800 kinds of wine. **Café MoZU**, open for breakfast, lunch, and dinner, boasts an Asian-inspired menu; the **Empress Lounge** offers martinis and cocktails, an extensive selection of champagnes by the glass, and sakes and cognacs served by the bottle. ◆ 1330 Maryland Ave SW (at Maine Ave). 554.8588, 888/888.1778; fax 554.8999. ♿ www.mandarin-oriental.com. Metro: L'Enfant Plaza

33 L'ENFANT PLAZA

Acres of red granite were intended to be the soil of a garden of urban delights watered by a splashing fountain, but so far nothing has taken root. All the shopping action is below plaza level in the **L'Enfant Plaza Promenade** (see opposite). One of the few highlights is the US Postal Service's **Philatelic Sales Center**, on the ground floor of the **West Building**; another is the yellow glow of the plaza's trademark globe lamps. ◆ L'Enfant Promenade (between Frontage Rd and D St). ♿ Metro: L'Enfant Plaza

On L'Enfant Plaza:

L'ENFANT PLAZA HOTEL

$$$$ Both sightseers and conventioneers appreciate this four-star quality hostelry with 370 spacious, contemporary rooms and suites. **Club 480** offers such VIP perks as express check-in and check-out, concierge service, a meeting parlor, and even fresh fruit, cheese, and Godiva chocolates waiting in your suite. Dining options include the brasserie **American Grill** and the **Old Dominion Brew Pub**, which offers casual fare and microbrews. There's also a state-of-the-art health club and rooftop swimming pool to help burn off those calories. Conference rooms, audiovisual services, and catering are among the special business amenities. Children under 18 stay free with an adult, and young ones receive "welcome bags" that include items like crayons and toys. Ask about weekend

specials. ◆ 480 L'Enfant Plaza. 484.1000; fax 646.4456. www.lenfantplazahotel.com. ♿. Metro: L'Enfant Plaza

33 L'ENFANT PLAZA PROMENADE

One flight below the hotel lobby is an underground mall with more than 50 shops (from **Hallmark Cards** to **RadioShack**) and services (dry cleaners, beauty salons, post office, bank, and florist), as well as a number of fast-food stands. ◆ L'Enfant Promenade (between Frontage Rd and D St). Metro: L'Enfant Plaza

Within L'Enfant Plaza Promenade:

REPRINT BOOK SHOP

The best reason by far to visit **L'Enfant Plaza**, this store is one of the shopping center's originals (it opened in 1968), and it's still going strong with an excellent selection of general interest titles; special emphasis is on fiction and African-American studies. Note the weekday-only hours. ◆ M-F, 7:30AM-6PM. 554.5070

34 DEPARTMENT OF HOUSING AND URBAN DEVELOPMENT (HUD)

The grid pattern in the exterior's beige concrete walls is relentless, despite an open ground floor. **Marcel Breuer**'s unusual double-Y layout (also used in his design for the NATO building in Paris) improves circulation within the building and helps minimize the alienation evoked by endless miles of office corridors. The building is not open to the public. ◆ 451 Seventh St SW (between I-395 and D St SW). ♿. Metro: L'Enfant Plaza

35 DEPARTMENT OF TRANSPORTATION (NASSIF BUILDING)

Edward Durell Stone's insistent vertical lines and thin slab roof are rendered here in Carrara marble. The building is not open to the public. ◆ 400 Seventh St SW (at D St). Metro: L'Enfant Plaza

36 MARKET INN

★$$$ Settle into the music-filled dining room, or opt for a quiet, dimly lit booth in the bar. Then choose from a huge selection of fresh seafood, homemade soups, and other entrées. This is a favorite gathering spot for Washington old-timers, having originally opened in 1959. ◆ Seafood ◆ M-F, lunch and dinner; Sa, dinner; Su, brunch and dinner. Reservations recommended. 200 E St SW (at Second St). 554.2100. ♿. www.marketinnrestaurant.com. Metro: Federal Center SW

Restaurants/Clubs: Red | Hotels: Purple | Shops: Orange | Outdoors/Parks: Green | Sights/Culture: Blue

37 JEFFERSON MEMORIAL

John Russell Pope's monument is a fitting tribute to a man who was an accomplished architect as well as a powerful and thoughtful statesman. Essentially an adaptation of the Roman Pantheon favored by Jefferson, the memorial recalls the third president's own designs for his home, **Monticello**, and for the rotunda of the **University of Virginia**. The circular building is rimmed by 54 Ionic columns and is fronted, on the side facing the **Mall**, with a classical portico and a pediment supported by even more columns. Three other entrances bring light and air into the gracefully proportioned chamber.

Like so much of the Mall, this site was under brackish water until the commencement of an 8-year dredging project. The reclaimed land couldn't support the memorial, whose every column weighs 45 tons, without a specially prepared foundation. Concrete-filled steel cylinders were driven 135 feet into the earth before reaching bedrock.

The interior of the coffered dome is of Indiana limestone. The walls are of white Georgia marble and the floors of pink-and-gray Tennessee marble. Standing in this grand setting is a majestic 19-foot-high statue of Jefferson—who stood 6 feet 2 inches in life. He wears knee breeches, a waistcoat, and a fur-collared greatcoat like the one that the Polish patriot Thaddeus Kosciuszko gave him. Rudolph Evans's design was chosen from more than 100 submissions. During dedication ceremonies, officiated by Franklin D. Roosevelt in 1943, a plaster model represented the sculpture. It couldn't be cast in bronze until several years later when the wartime ban on the use of domestic metal was lifted.

The offerings at any local postcard stand will prove that the Jefferson Memorial is one of the most popular attractions in this monumental city. But at the time of its construction, the memorial was denounced as being too sweet and feminine. Its low circular shape prompted one critic to rename the memorial "Jefferson's muffin." Some parking is available near the memorial. ♦ Daily, 24 hours. Ranger on duty 8AM-11:45PM. Rotunda open and lighted through the night. E Basin Dr SW (between Maine Ave and Ohio Dr). 426.6841. ♿ www.nps.gov/thje. Metro: Smithsonian

38 GEORGE MASON MEMORIAL

In 1989, an effort began to create a memorial to George Mason, the Virginia statesman considered the Father of the Bill of Rights, on the **National Mall**. In 2002, that memorial was finally dedicated, thanks to the board of regents of Gunston Hall Plantation (George Mason's Virginia home), which was instrumental in bringing the project to fruition. Located near the **Tidal Basin** and **Jefferson Memorial**, a statue of Mason sits beneath a curving arbor, flanked by walls inscribed with his words. In front of the statue, find a peaceful garden. ♦ Daily, 24 hours. Ohio Dr SW. 426.6841. www.nps.gov/gemm. Metro: Smithsonian

39 THE MAINE AVENUE FISH MARKET

Locals swear by the freshly caught and reasonably priced bounty trucked to this market from the Chesapeake Bay and the lower Potomac and Delaware Rivers. The market brings you the daily catches of more than a dozen fish peddlers, who set up shop along the Potomac's edge, some off the back of their boats, selling bushels of blue crabs, rockfish, oysters, shrimp—almost anything edible that swims in the region's waters. ♦ Daily. Maine Ave SW (between Ninth and 12th Sts). Metros: L'Enfant Plaza, Waterfront

40 PHILLIPS FLAGSHIP

★★★$$ This is not only the largest restaurant in the DC metropolitan area (seating 1,200 inside, with room for 300 more outside), it is also an institution in this city and the one where you can have the most fun. The range of fish and seafood cannot be beaten anywhere, and this is reflected not just on the traditional menu but also on the famous Watermen's Harvest Buffet that features over 50 delightful choices. There is also a sushi bar. This restaurant is packed after church on Sundays with people dressed in their finest outfits. ♦ Seafood ♦ Daily, 24 hours; brunch on weekends. 900 Water Street SW. 488.8515. www.phillipsseafood.com. Metros: L'Enfant Plaza, Waterfront

41 CHANNEL INN

$$ This waterside hotel is set among the strip of restaurants along the Washington Channel. All rooms have balconies. The inn's **Pier 7 Restaurant** specializes in seafood, including Maryland crab dishes. The inn has an outdoor swimming pool, and live jazz is offered six nights a week in the **Engine Room Lounge**. Children under 13 stay free. ♦ 650 Water St SW (off Maine Ave). 554.2400, 800/368.5668; fax 863.1164. ♿ www.channelinn.com. Metro: Waterfront

42 ARENA STAGE

From its first production in 1950 in a former burlesque house, the **Arena** has grown into one of the nation's best regional theaters.

Under artistic director Molly Smith, an emphasis has been placed on American playwrights. Three spaces showcase a variety of productions: the **Fichandler**, a theater-in-the-round; the **Kreeger**, a proscenium theater; and the **Old Vat Room**, a cabaret-style theater, where recent offerings have included **Mrs. Bob Cratchit's Wild Christmas Binge.** ◆ Box office: daily. 1101 Sixth St SW (at Maine Ave). Information, 554.9066; box office, 488.3300. ♿ www.arenastage.org. Metro: Waterfront

43 THE *ODYSSEY*

This mammoth cruise ship offers a different view of Washington and neighboring Virginia as it glides up and down the Potomac River. This sleek craft boasts glass ceilings over the dining areas and plenty of outdoor deck space for strolling. There's live jazz during all cruises and dancing during dinner cruises. ◆ M-F, lunch and dinner; Sa, Su, brunch and dinner. Jacket recommended for dinner. Gangplank Marina, Sixth and Water Sts SW. 888/741.0281. ♿ www.odysseycruises.com. Metro: Waterfront

43 SPIRIT CRUISES

The 600-passenger *Spirit of Washington* offers lunch and dinner cruises along the Potomac River, with indoor and outdoor seating, a live musical revue, and dancing. The 350-passenger *Potomac Spirit* travels to George Washington's **Mount Vernon**, where visitors take a 3-hour tour of the estate before reboarding the ship. ◆ Pier 4, Sixth and Water Sts SW. 866/211.3811. ♿. www.spiritcruises.com. Metro: Waterfront

44 THOMAS LAW HOUSE

This classic three-story Federal-style house was built by **William Lovering** in 1796. Once the home of George Washington's granddaughter, it is not currently open to the public. ◆ 1252 Sixth St SW. Metro: Waterfront

45 WHEAT ROW

Located in the shadow of the successful Harbour Square apartment complex urban renewal project, **William Lovering**'s Federal-era structures on **Wheat Row** are believed to be the first rowhouses built in DC. ◆ 1315-21 Fourth St SW (between P and N Sts). Metro: Waterfront

46 *TITANIC* MEMORIAL

Located in a park near the **Washington Channel**, just a slip of land, this memorial was sculpted by Gertrude Vanderbilt Whitney in memory of the men who died (many of whom gave up their places in the lifeboats) when the famous ocean liner sank. The granite figure stands with arms outstretched in the shape of a cross. The sculptor's own brother went down in 1915 when the Kaiser's navy sank the *Lusitania*. ◆ Fourth and P Sts SW. ♿. Metro: Waterfront

47 FORT LESLEY J. MCNAIR

Over the years, the name and function of this strategic military post have changed. In 1791, **Pierre Charles L'Enfant** intended it to be the main fortification point of the capital. As the **Washington Arsenal**, the fort was a major distribution center for government hand weapons and cannons in the early 1800s. In 1814, after setting fire to the **White House**, **Capitol**, and other federal buildings, the British invaded the fort, only to lose 40 of their own men when a supply of gunpowder accidentally exploded. Discouraged, the British left the ruined fort. In succeeding years, the US continued to store and also produce weapons at the arsenal. By the time of the Civil War, the fort contained more than 800 cannons, 50,000 rifles, and hundreds of gun carriages. One more explosion finally convinced the government that the arsenal was unsafe: In 1864, an ignited rocket in a row of fireworks killed or maimed more than 100 women who were making rifle cartridges in the laboratory.

The fort served as a warehouse and a hospital until the **Army War College** was built on the mile-long peninsula. Later merged with the **Industrial College of the Armed Forces**, the college is still housed in its original, disciplined Beaux Arts structure under the name of the **National Defense University**. The **Inter-American Defense College** and the headquarters of the US Army Military District of Washington are nearby; the Romanesque barracks and more sumptuous officers' quarters add a graceful note to the military primness. Soldiers' old quarters have been preserved, making the beautiful grounds well worth a visit. ◆ P and Fourth Sts SW. 703/545.6700. ♿. Metro: Waterfront

---

Wedged between Downtown and Georgetown are the revitalized neighborhoods of West End and Foggy Bottom. With the exception of the higher ground to the east, which is the site of one of DC's oldest residential enclaves and the **Octagon House** (where the Madisons lived after the British burned the **White House** in 1814), these once-swampy areas seemed almost an afterthought for Washington planners. During the last century and partway into this one, West End (north of **K Street**) was full of warehouses, whereas Foggy Bottom (south of K Street) contained a glass factory, a brewery, and a giant gasworks. The industrial fumes and smoke, along with the fog drifting off the **Potomac**, contributed to the neighborhood's name. From an industrial zone, the area deteriorated into one of DC's worst slums, which later became first on the city's list for urban renewal.

The turning point for DC's westernmost neighborhoods came in the 1950s, when the **State Department** established residence in a sprawling modern building along the west end of **Constitution Avenue**, and at long last the mist began to lift on development in Foggy Bottom. **George Washington University**, a longtime tenant, soon launched an ambitious expansion program, and in the 1960s, the brewery building was razed and the **John F. Kennedy Center for the Performing Arts** took its place. This was followed by the construction of the luxurious **Watergate** complex of office space, condominiums, upscale shops, and a posh hotel. Not surprisingly, the value of historic row houses on the adjacent streets skyrocketed.

Foggy Bottom's modest size and the variety of its attractions—from the **Corcoran Gallery of Art** to the bustling campus of George Washington University—make it one of the most attractive areas of Washington for strolling. And it's also convenient to the West End, which caught Foggy Bottom's revival bug in the 1970s and 1980s. Gone are the warehouses of old, and in their place are some of the city's most interesting attractions and plenty of fine dining to sustain you along the way.

WEST END

1 1250 24TH STREET NORTHWEST

If you're in the neighborhood, walk by **Don Hisaga**'s elegant office building, designed within preexisting walls. There's a recessed bow front, fully glazed behind a white grid; inside, walkways lead around a sparkling, leafy atrium. ♦ Between M and N Sts. Metro: Foggy Bottom/GWU

1 AGUA ARDIENTE

★★$ Earth tones and Latin American–style décor set the scene at this restaurant/ lounge that offers an absolutely authentic selection of excellently prepared Spanish cuisine and tapas including Tortilla España and paella. The spot's name means "fire

water," which is also a Sambuca-style liquor that serves as the signature drink. ♦ Latin ♦ M-F, lunch and dinner, bar till 2AM; Sa, Su, dinner, bar till 3AM. 1250 24th St NW (between M and N Sts). 833.8500. www.latinconcepts.com. Metro: Foggy Bottom

2 EMBASSY SUITES HOTEL

$$$ All 318 suites overlook a soaring interior courtyard, picturesque with a garden atrium and grand, soothing fountains. Service is foremost here: Guests can partake of a complimentary breakfast and happy hour, concierge assistance, and room service until 11PM, as well as a pool, sauna, and exercise room. Children under 18 stay free. ♦ 1250 22nd St NW (between M and N Sts). 857.3388, 800/362.2779; fax 785.2411. ♿. www.embassysuites.com. Metros: Foggy Bottom/GWU, Dupont Circle

3 THE FAIRMONT WASHINGTON, DC

$$$$ This 10-story, 415-room hotel designed by **Vlastimil Koubek** has something of a Hollywood pedigree. Film crews for *Nixon* and *Contact* stayed here, and the hotel appeared in *Enemy of the State*. Rooms are described as "residential" with a mix of contemporary and period styles. Amenities include two restaurants (try the **Colonnade**'s popular Sunday brunch), concierge service, 24-hour room service, and a state-of-the-art health club offering a pool, a squash/racquetball court, aerobics classes, and dry and wet saunas. Facing an interior garden, a set of glazed arches contains the **Lobby Lounge** and the **Bistro** restaurant, serving casually upscale pub fare. It's a civilized, airy retreat for a light lunch or drinks. ♦ 2401 M St NW (at 24th St). 429.2400, 866/540.4505; fax 457.5010. ♿ www.fairmont.com. Metro: Foggy Bottom/GWU

4 PARK HYATT WASHINGTON

$$$$ The Hyatt completed a $24 million renovation in 2006. It offers 215 newly designed large rooms and public spaces combining classic modernism with a traditional American style by **Tony Chi.** The bedrooms feature down duvets and a sitting area with a large flat-screen TV. Round-the-clock room service, a 24-hour fitness area, and an indoor pool are some of the additional amenities. The **Blue Duck Tavern** has a lively neighborhood bar environment. The Hyatt's tea cellar has more than 50 rare and vintage teas from Japan, Sri Lanka, China, and the Himalayas. The tea cellar is open from 6:30AM until 1:30AM. ♦ 1201 24th St NW (at M St). 789.1234; fax 419.6795. ♿ www.parkwashington.hyatt.com. Metro: Foggy Bottom/GWU

5 ASIA NORA

★★$$$ Nora Pouillon, the namesake of **Restaurant Nora** in Dupont Circle, runs this jazzy postmodern joint. Although sometimes

> The Corcoran Gallery of Art's symbol—immense Canova lions, one alert and one asleep, that grace the gallery's steps—were originally bought in Italy for the K Street home of businessman Benjamin Holladay. The Corcoran purchased the lions in 1888 at an estate auction held after Holladay's death.

noisy and cramped, it's always fun. Organic ingredients star in Pouillon's Asian fusion dishes like tamari-bourbon marinated pork tenderloin and roasted wild king salmon with steamed Maine mussels. ♦ Asian ♦ M-Sa, dinner. Reservations recommended. 2213 M St NW (between 22nd and 23rd Sts). 797.4860. www.noras.com. Metro: Foggy Bottom/GWU

6 WASHINGTON MARRIOTT

$$$$ Yet another deluxe choice in this hotel-heavy neighborhood, this 418-room hostelry offers amenities such as an indoor pool, a health club with sauna and whirlpool, concierge, room service, and the **Atrium Restaurant** and **Court Lounge**. ♦ 1221 22nd St NW (between M and N Sts). 872.1500, 800/228.9290; fax 872.1424. ♿ www.marriott.com. Metro: Foggy Bottom/GWU

7 MEIWAH

★★★$$$ This is a bright and airy restaurant offering an exceptional array of Chinese delicacies. Their excellent take-out service is free within a limited area with a minimum order of $15. ♦ Chinese ♦ Daily, lunch and dinner. 1200 New Hampshire Ave NW. 833.2888. www.meiwahrestaurant.com. Also at 4457 Willard Ave, Chevy Chase, Maryland

7 GRILLFISH

★★★$$ Whether you are eating inside or outside on the terrace, you will find this an informal, friendly restaurant with a fine array of fresh fish and seafood at very acceptable prices. They offer selections of pasta and a few meat dishes for non-seafood lovers. ♦ Seafood ♦ M-F, lunch; daily, dinner. 1200 New Hampshire Ave NW. 331.7310. www.grillfishdc.com

WESTIN
HOTELS & RESORTS

8 THE WESTIN GRAND

$$$$ Experience Old World elegance in a setting of modern luxury. Amenities include all-marble bathrooms with extra-deep tubs, in-room minibars, concierge and room services, a fitness center, an outdoor pool, and the **M Street Grille** and **Café on M** restaurants. Some suites have dining rooms. This 263-room hotel was designed in 1984 by **Skidmore, Owings & Merrill**, with the interior by Charles Pfister. Children under 18 stay free. ♦ 2350 M St NW (between 23rd and 24th Sts). 429.0100, 800/848.0016; fax 429.9759. ♿ Metro: Foggy Bottom/GWU

9 THE RITZ-CARLTON, WASHINGTON, DC

$$$$ This 300-room luxury property offers rooms—and a variety of suites—with accents like marble tubs and goose-down pillows. The ninth-floor club-level rooms have access to a private lounge with a fireplace and five daily food and drink presentations. Amenities include 24-hour room service and access to the swanky **Sports Club/LA** (where celebs often work out)—for a $16-per-day fee. ♦ 1150 22nd St NW (between L and M Sts). 835.0500; fax 835.1588. Metro: Foggy Bottom/GWU

Within the Ritz-Carlton:

THE GRILL

★★$$$$ Dale Chihuly sculptures decorate this spot where the cooking action takes place in a see-in kitchen. House specialties include crab cakes, porcini-crusted sea bass, and seared duck breast. Afternoon tea is served Fridays between 2PM and 5PM, and Saturdays and Sundays between 1PM and 3:30PM. ♦ American ♦ M-Sa, breakfast, lunch, and dinner; Su, brunch and dinner. 974.5566. &

10 M STREET HOTEL

$$$ Formerly known as the Wyndham City Center, it is currently owned by Marriott, who promise a thorough 6-month renovation ending with a completely new hotel early in 2007, when it will become part of the Renaissance collection. It promises to be stylish, large, and centrally located, with many facilities. ♦ 1143 New Hampshire Ave NW. 775.0800; fax 331.9491. Metro: Foggy Bottom/GWU

Within the M Street Hotel:

SHULA'S STEAK HOUSE

★★$$$ Former Miami Dolphins coach Don Shula brings NFL-sized 48-oz steaks to DC with this carnivore-friendly spot in the West End that is themed after the Miami Dolphins' perfect season in 1972. Free valet parking is available. ♦ Steak house ♦ Daily, breakfast, lunch, and dinner. 828.7762

11 MARCEL'S

★★★★$$$ Opened in 1999, the restaurant was honored with a DiRoNA (Distinguished Restaurants of North America) Award in 2002 for its French-Flemish fare like *boudin blanc*. There's live jazz most nights, and there is a complimentary shuttle to the **Kennedy Center**. ♦ French ♦ Daily, dinner. Reservations recommended. 2401 Pennsylvania Ave NW (at 24th St). 296.1166. www.marcelsdc.com. &. Metro: Foggy Bottom/GWU

12 THE MELROSE

$$$$ Formerly a Wyndham, this completely renovated 240-room hotel is convenient to Georgetown and the **Kennedy Center**. Guests can dine at the **Landmark Restaurant**, relax at the **Library Bar**, or watch in-house movies. Rooms feature original artwork commissioned for the hotel, and amenities include a new fitness center and high-speed Internet access. Children under 12 stay free. ♦ 2430 Pennsylvania Ave NW (between 24th and 25th Sts). 955.6400, 800/MELROSE; fax 955.5765. &. www.melrosehotel.com. &. Metro: Foggy Bottom/GWU

13 CIRCLE BISTRO

★★$$ Formerly the beloved West End Cafe, this space has been stylishly redone by architectural firm **Adamstein & Demetriou**. In addition to the main dining room, there is a lounge with bar, a carryover from the space's previous incarnation. The three-course pretheater special is a steal. ♦ American/French ♦ Daily, breakfast, lunch, and dinner. Reservations recommended. 1 Washington Cir NW (at New Hampshire Ave). 293.5390. www.circlebistro.com. Metro: Foggy Bottom/GWU

FOGGY BOTTOM

14 RIVER INN

$$$ A small, all-suite boutique hotel with views of the Potomac River, this inn is within walking distance of the **Kennedy Center**, Georgetown, and the State Department. The elegant rooms with full kitchens offer complimentary high-speed Internet access. Amenities include an exercise facility, same-day valet/dry cleaning service, and valet parking. ♦ 924 25th St NW (between I and K Sts). 337.7600, 888/874.0100; fax 337.6520. &. www.theriverinn.com. Metro: Foggy Bottom/GWU

Within the River Inn:

DISH

★$$ This cozy and attractive restaurant features a gas fireplace and a famous 8-foot photo of a reclining Weimaraner. The food—of the upscale comfort variety—has made it a favorite of West End diners. Perfect for pre- or post–Kennedy Center dining or Sunday brunch. ♦ American ♦ M-F, breakfast, lunch, and dinner; Sa, Su, breakfast and dinner. Reservations recommended. 338.8707. &. www.dishdc.com

15 GEORGE WASHINGTON UNIVERSITY INN

$$ This 95-room hotel recently underwent a major renovation. Rooms now boast Williamsburg-inspired décor, high-speed Internet access, refrigerators, and microwaves. Some suites have full kitchens. Amenities include underground valet parking, nightly turndown service, and same-day dry cleaning service. ♦ 824 New Hampshire Ave NW (between H and I Sts). 337.6620, 800/426.4455; fax 298.7499. &. www.gwuinn.com. Metro: Foggy Bottom/GWU

Within the George Washington University Inn:

NOTTI BIANCHI

***$$$ This very attractive small restaurant has all the ambience of an Italian trattoria, and a cuisine to match. Expect a full range of antipasti, salads, pastas, and meat and fish including dishes such as *garganelli*—little sausage meatballs, broccoli rabe, and roasted red pepper purée, and crispy skin sablefish with carmelized artichoke hearts, trio of onions, and whole-grain mustard. Cell phones are not allowed, since they interfere with the making of the risotto! ♦ Italian ♦ M-F, lunch and dinner; M-Sa, dinner. 298.8085. &

16 DOUBLETREE GUEST SUITES

$$$ Each of the 103 one-bedroom suites and 2 two-bedroom suites features a traditional-style living room, spacious bedroom, large closets, and a fully equipped kitchen. Amenities include room service (there's no restaurant on the premises), self-service and valet-service laundry, a rooftop pool, and access to nearby health clubs. Children under 18 stay free. ♦ 801 New Hampshire Ave NW (at H St). 785.2000, 800/222.TREE; fax 785.9485. www.doubletree.com. Metro: Foggy Bottom/GWU

17 WATERGATE COMPLEX

This waterfront complex includes apartments with sweeping curves and toothy balustrades. On the lower level of the apartment complex, find shops and services, including a barber shop, a supermarket, a pharmacy, a post office, a salon, and a florist. The outwardly unremarkable office building is where the bungled burglary of the Democratic Party's National Headquarters, which led to President Richard Nixon's resignation, took place. ♦ New Hampshire and Virginia Aves NW. Metro: Foggy Bottom/GWU

Within the Watergate Complex:

WATERGATE SHOPS

One of Washington's more prestigious shopping arcades, a half-dozen boutiques circle the exterior of the **Watergate 600 Office Building**, carrying pricey designer fashions. Among the shops are **Valentino**, **Yves Saint Laurent**, **Saks Jandel**, and **Vera Wang**. ♦ M-Sa. &

WATERGATE PASTRY

Founded in 1966, the bakery here is noted for its numerous oven-fresh delicacies, including a variety of mousse cakes, French pastries, and memorable wedding and birthday cakes with unusual fillings. There are also 25 flavors of homemade chocolate, including rum, almond, honey, and orange. ♦ M-F, 8AM-7PM; Sa, 8AM-5PM; Su, 10AM-2PM. 2534 Virginia Ave NW. 342.1777. &. www.watergatepastries.com

18 THE JOHN F. KENNEDY CENTER FOR THE PERFORMING ARTS

When **Edward Durell Stone**'s **Kennedy Center** (acoustically designed by Dr. Cyril Harris) opened in 1971, Washington began to draw the liveliest of national and international arts. More than 30 years later, the center is host to millions of people each year.

The dramatic **Grand Foyer** lines the riverside wall of the center and houses Robert Berks's 8-foot bronze bust of President John F. Kennedy. The interior space of the foyer is 60 feet high, with more floor area than two football fields, and is furnished with gifts from nations around the world. Separating the center's performance spaces spatially and acoustically are the **Hall of States**, a gallery containing the flags of each American state, territory, and the District of Columbia, and the **Hall of Nations**, displaying flags of every nation recognized by the US. Walk-in tours of the center are given Monday through Friday between 10AM and 5PM and Saturday and Sunday between 10AM and 1PM; meet in the parking plaza of Level A.

Performances range from huge, long-running theatrical extravaganzas to hundreds of free shows; from the 2,500-voice audience participatory *Messiah* Sing-Along to small Friday-evening jazz recitals in the Grand Foyer. The center's own programs account for the

PEDAL POWER

Washington is a bike-friendly city. No American metropolis can rival European capitals like Amsterdam or Copenhagen, where bikes are a mode of transportation, not just recreation. But with 670 miles of paved, off-road multi-use trails, Washington residents and tourists can go most places on two wheels. Cyclists and their bikes are even allowed on **Metrorail** during off-peak hours and weekends.

A few essentials are needed before cyclists take off on a tour of the capital. First, of course, is a bike. Rentals are available from **Thompson Boat Center** (2900 Virginia Avenue NW, at Rock Creek Parkway; 333.9543) and **Fletcher's Boat House** (4940 Canal Road NW, just north of Reservoir Road; 244.0461) to name a couple (see page 9 for other shops). Be sure to rent—and use—a helmet and a strong U-lock.

A good bike map is also a must. An excellent compact guide, small enough to tuck into a back pocket, is Michael Leccese's *Short Bike Rides: Washington, DC* (Globe Pequot Press, 1998). Leccese's snappy prose suggests a variety of rides, many not too strenuous, and the maps are easy to follow. Remember too that you're riding in a city, sharing roads with sometimes aggressive drivers. Even off-road lanes are not exclusively for

cyclists; joggers, walkers, in-line skaters, and skateboarders also use the space.

The best rides for tourists are the well-traveled routes along the **Potomac** and the **Mall**. Highly recommended is the 13-mile loop (which takes about 90 minutes at a moderate rate) that starts at Thompson Boat Center, meanders along the river, circles the major monuments, and then retraces your path to Thompson's. For families, this route has several advantages: It's scenic, well-traveled, and relatively flat, and there are rest rooms and snack bars at the monuments.

If you would rather have a guided tour, **Bike the Sites** (842.BIKE; www.bikethesites.com) leads groups around the Mall and on the **Mount Vernon Trail** (an 18.5-mile path that starts at Thompson Boat Center, crosses the Potomac, and runs along the Virginia side of the river through **Old Town Alexandria** to **Mount Vernon**). Bike rentals are included in the price. The **Washington Area Bicyclist Association** (518.0524; www.waba.org) offers information on trails and paths, riding clubs, and special events.

majority of performances, but local performing arts groups—the **Washington Performing Arts Society**, the **Washington Opera**, and the **Choral Arts Society of Washington**, to name a few—use hall space to present their own production seasons. Amplifying headsets are available for hearing-impaired persons (a driver's license or major credit card is held as collateral; check at the usher's desk 1 hour before curtain time). ◆ Free. Daily, 10AM-midnight (on performance days). Tours: M-F, 10AM-5PM; Sa, Su, 10AM-1PM. Tour reservations required for groups of 20 or more. 2700 F St NW (between New Hampshire Ave NW and Rock Creek Pkwy). General information and tickets, 467.4600, 800/444.1324; tour services, 416.8340; hearing-impaired (TTY), 416.8524. &. www.kennedy-center.org. Metro: Foggy Bottom/GWU

Within the Kennedy Center:

CONCERT HALL

The 2,442-seat gold-white theater, illuminated by Hadelands crystal Norwegian chandeliers and with a 4,144-pipe organ, presents symphonies, choral groups, and other musical performances. Conductor

Leonard Slatkin, the **National Symphony Orchestra**'s music director, has hosted such guest artists as cellist Yo-Yo Ma, violinist Itzhak Perlman, and soprano Jessye Norman. For information about the 2007 season, call 467.4600, or visit the web site at www.kennedy-center.org.

OPERA HOUSE

Three levels of seating face a gold-and-red Japanese-silk stage curtain. Plays, dance performances, operas, and music programs take place here. DC scored a major coup in 1995 when Placido Domingo became artistic director of the **Washington Opera**. He has widened the repertoire to include lesser-known works, as well as Latin American operas. He also performs and conducts on occasion. For information about the 2007 season, call 467.4600, or visit the web site at www.kennedy-center.org.

EISENHOWER THEATER

Small-scale musicals, dramas, and dance programs fill this 1,100-seat theater. For information about the 2007 season, call 467.4600, or visit the web site at www.kennedy-center.org.

Restaurants/Clubs: Red | **Hotels: Purple** | **Shops: Orange** | **Outdoors/Parks: Green** | **Sights/Culture: Blue**

TERRACE THEATER

This 513-seat theater hosts chamber music, jazz performances, and some dramatic productions. For information about the 2007 season, call 467.4600, or visit the web site at www.kennedy-center.org.

THEATER LAB

This black-box space with padded balconies was originally intended to house experimental works. Today the 400-seat theater, the center's smallest, hosts young people's shows as well as the long-running comedy whodunit *Shear Madness*, which lets the audience play armchair detective.

GRAND FOYER

Home to the **Millennium Stage** since 1997, this unconventional theater space presents free performances daily at 6PM. Acts range from gospel ensembles and classical pianists to Klezmer groups and Latino folk musicians. At 60 by 630 feet, it is one of the largest rooms in the world, and the Washington Monument could lay sideways in it with room to spare. Robert Berks's famous bust of JFK adorns the center of the room.

ROOF TERRACE RESTAURANT AND BAR

★★$$$ American regional cuisine, such as Maryland crab cakes and Colorado rack of lamb, is served in opulent surroundings. But at this recently remodeled restaurant, the atmosphere and Potomac River views are the real stars. ◆ American ◆ M-Sa, dinner; Su, brunch and dinner; hours may vary with theater schedules. Reservations recommended. 416.8555. &

KC CAFE

★$ This newly renovated self-serve spot features a broad menu of salads, sandwiches, and entrées. The dining room offers a great view of the Potomac and the city, but beware the crush before and after shows. ◆ American ◆ W-Su, lunch and dinner; M, Tu, dinner. 416.8560. &

19 2000 PENNSYLVANIA AVENUE

The renovation by **Hellmuth, Obata & Kassabaum** of the **Lion's Row** town houses in 1983 won kudos for retaining the original brick façade. Within the building is a minimall that includes a coffee bar and a newsstand with out-of-town and foreign newspapers. ◆ 2000 Pennsylvania Ave (at 20th St). &. Metro: Foggy Bottom/GWU

Within 2000 Pennsylvania Avenue:

KINKEAD'S

★★★★$$$ Robert Kinkead—honored with the prestigious James Beard Foundation Mid-Atlantic Chef of the Year Award in 1995 and the DiRoNA (Distinguished Restaurants of North America) Award from 1996 to 2001—has gained a huge following at this two-level bistro specializing in seafood dishes. Downstairs is dominated by a huge and (in the evening) noisy bar; upstairs is more formal and more serene. Wherever you're sitting, start your meal off with a crab cake or chowder, and then move on to the seared sea scallops or the pepita-crusted salmon. The crème brûlée is a must for dessert. ◆ American ◆ M-F, lunch; daily, dinner. Reservations suggested. 296.7700. &. www.kinkead.com

LINDY'S BON APPÉTIT

★$ Come here for hamburgers—22 charbroiled varieties—as well as hot dogs, pizza, fries, and sandwiches. This agreeably funky take-out place, popular with several generations of George Washington University students, also offers a few outdoor tables. Enter outdoors on I Street. ◆ American ◆ M-F, breakfast, lunch, and dinner; Sa, Su, lunch and dinner. 452.0055

ONE STOP NEWS

This interesting shop, located inside the urban mall and just off Pennsylvania Avenue, is one of the few places in DC that sell international newspapers, along with a very wide selection of domestic newspapers and magazines. ◆ M-F, 7:30AM-9PM; Sa, 8AM-8PM; Su, 9AM-7PM. 872.1577

20 GEORGE WASHINGTON UNIVERSITY

With hopes of establishing a national university, the first president of the United States bequeathed his stock in the Potomac Company (the precursor of the company that built the C&O Canal) as an endowment. But members of Congress could not agree on the federal government's role in such an institution, and the Potomac Company went under, so the endowment was useless. Finally, in 1821, the Baptist church raised funds to create the nonsectarian **Columbian College**, which, less than 100 years later, was renamed **George Washington University**. Although it has a popular undergraduate program, GW (as the school is called around town) is probably better known for its fine schools of law and medicine, as well as the highly respected **George Washington University Medical Center**. GW is one of the city's largest land-

GET THEE TO THE GREENERY

"The city of Washington has never had the praise it deserves from those of us who do not give ourselves altogether to city life. Unlike New York, it makes room for nature in its midst and seems to welcome it." Louis J. Halle wrote these words several decades ago in his classic book *Spring in Washington* (Johns Hopkins University Press, second edition, 1988).

Surprisingly, despite Washington's staggering growth in the last half century, Halle's words still ring true. Flying into any of DC's airports, travelers are impressed by the overwhelming green space of the city. Parks and other outdoor spaces are the best place to enjoy a lovely spring, summer, or fall day in Washington. They offer a respite from noise, hustle, and people—and refresh you for more adventures in the urban jungle.

With the possible exception of Paris and London, no national capital is as devoted to trees as Washington. The first citywide tree planting on record was Thomas Jefferson's promenade of Lombardy poplars from the **White House** to the **Capitol**. But it wasn't until the late 1800s that serious landscape design took hold in the capital. Local politician Alexander "Boss" Shepherd planted 60,000 trees, which along with other civil improvements ran the city coffers $10 million into debt. DC's most famous trees were a gift from Japan in 1912. Today hundreds of Japanese cherry trees flower in the spring around the **Tidal Basin**, causing 2 weeks of downtown gridlock (so come at dawn for the best viewing). Lady Bird Johnson's national beautification program planted thousands of trees, especially along the **Potomac**. Today Washington is home to over 300 varieties of trees—from Europe, Africa, Asia, and America—which are best described in Melanie Choukas-Bradley and Polly Alexander's *City of Trees—The Complete Field Guide to the Trees of Washington, DC* (Johns Hopkins University Press, second edition, 1987). So much greenery makes bird-watching very popular in DC. For information on walks and the best viewing spots, contact the **Wild Bird Center** (301/229.9585), the **Audubon Naturalist Society** (301/652.9188), or **DC Audubon Society** (547.2355).

Aside from **Rock Creek Park**, whose charms and facilities are trumpeted everywhere, hikers will find trails and plenty of wildlife—especially deer, raccoons, and possum—in many parts of the city. West of Rock Creek lies another slice of nonurbanized land, **Glover Archbold Park**. Most of this tract was given to the public in 1924 by Charles C. Glover and Anne Archbold, Washingtonians who intended the park to be a bird sanctuary and nature refuge for wildlife as well as people. There are occasional picnic tables, but the grounds, which wind for about 3 miles between Georgetown and Upper Northwest, are intentionally unkempt. A nature trail bordering a small stream runs the length of the park.

Theodore Roosevelt Island Park (703/289.2500), a 91-acre island in the middle of the **Potomac River**, is a fitting tribute to the twenty-sixth president, who was the nation's first "environmental" chief executive. His love of the outdoors, nurtured by his adventures on the frontier, is reflected in the island's wild state; among the only nods to civilization are the 18-foot-tall statue of Teddy, four granite tablets inscribed with some of his epigrams, and a modest nature trail for hikers. In the 18th century the island was owned by a banker who used it for a summer home and raised sheep there. In 1932 the Theodore Roosevelt Memorial Association purchased the land. Access to the island, which is open daily dawn to dusk, is via the northbound lanes of the **George Washington Memorial Parkway**, a pedestrian causeway connected to Lee Highway in Arlington, Virginia, or by rental canoe from **Thompson Boat Center** (333.9543) on the DC side of the river.

More challenging hikes are through **Great Falls Park** (9200 Old Dominion Drive, at Georgetown Pike, McLean; 703/285.2965) on the Virginia side of the Potomac. Trails are well marked, but warnings must be taken seriously. Every year people drown in the dangerous river currents. Children must be especially cautious. From the Beltway, take Exit 44 to Route 193; the park entrance is about 5 miles west.

holders, and therein lies much of its prestige. When the school settled here in 1912 (its third site), it wisely engulfed many of the neighborhood's fine old homes, converting them into offices and dormitories. Now 20 full blocks of central Washington are owned by the university, making it a one-institution urban renewal force. ♦ 2121 I St NW (between 21st and 22nd Sts). 994.4949. ☐. www.gwu.edu. Metro: Foggy Bottom/GWU

Within George Washington University:

LISNER AUDITORIUM OF GEORGE WASHINGTON UNIVERSITY

A classic modern structure built during the 1940s, this theater is home to the **Christmas Revels**, who put on different shows each year, and the **Dimock Gallery** (994.1525), which

---

Restaurants/Clubs: Red | **Hotels: Purple** | **Shops: Orange** | **Outdoors/Parks: Green** | **Sights/Culture: Blue**

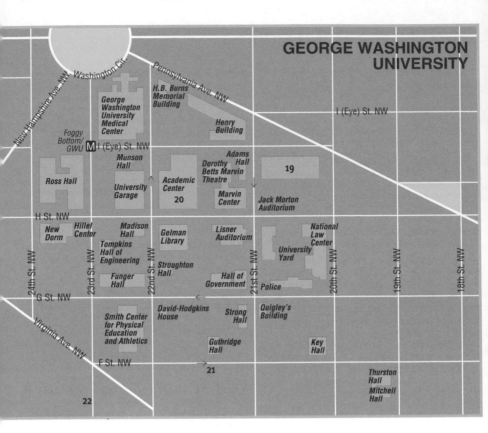

GEORGE WASHINGTON UNIVERSITY

exhibits works by university students and faculty as well as by locally prominent artists; exhibitions change six to eight times a year. On permanent display in the auditorium is an abstract mural by Augustus Tack, painted on the stage fire curtain. Independent production companies such as the **Washington Performing Arts Society** put on most of the performances here, but occasionally the university presents rock concerts, comedy shows, and other artistic events. The box office opens about 1 hour before performances to offer last-minute tickets (cash and check only). Check local newspapers for event listings. The theater seats 1,500. ♦ 730 21st St NW (at H St). 994.6800. www.gwu.edu/~lisner

In *Domestic Manners of the Americans*, Mrs. Trollope (mother of Anthony) wrote in 1831, "I was delighted with the whole aspect of Washington: light, cheerful and airy, it reminded me of our fashionable watering places. . . . The total absence of all sights, sounds, or smells of commerce adds greatly to its charm."

Frank Lloyd Wright called the Corcoran Gallery of Art "the best designed building in Washington."

21 GARDEN CAFE

★★$$ Located in the unremarkable **State Plaza Hotel**, this spot—gracefully renovated in 2006—has become a favorite of both **George Washington University** students and **State Department** employees for its contemporary dishes and solid service. A secluded courtyard is just the place for romantic dining. ♦ American ♦ Daily, breakfast, lunch, and dinner. 2116 F St NW (between 21st and 22nd Sts). 861.0331. Metro: Foggy Bottom/GWU

22 MAGIC GOURD

★$ Convenient to **George Washington University** and the **State Department** is this Chinese restaurant with a broad menu of Szechuan, Hunan, and Cantonese favorites. Try the hot-and-sour soup or firecracker shrimp. ♦ Chinese ♦ M-F, lunch and dinner; Sa, Su, dinner. Columbia Plaza, 528 23rd St NW (between E St and Virginia Ave). 466.3995. ₺. Metro: Foggy Bottom/GWU

23 WINDER BUILDING

Built in 1848 by **William H. Winder**, this five-story office building was the city's first

THE BEST

Carla Cohen

Politics & Prose Bookstore and Coffeehouse

First, it's very important to plan your trip at the best time. Contrary to conventional wisdom, do not come to Washington during cherry blossom time, when it's crowded. Instead, if you come in the spring, come the third week in April when dogwoods and azaleas are in bloom (and tulips and jonquils, and sometimes even lilacs). The best time to visit Washington is in autumn, October and November. It rarely gets cold before the end of November, and the leaves are often still on the trees for the first week or so. The air is cool and relatively dry compared with spring, meaning it's fun to walk outside.

- Start your tour by **Tourmobile** (operated under the aegis of the **National Park Service**) at **Union Station**. There are not as many trains as when I was a child, and there are no long comfy wooden benches in the waiting room. However, the fun food downstairs and the chic shops more than compensate. And the **Daniel Burnham** building, now nearly 100 years old, is shown to its best advantage. It's still a thrill to stand in that gorgeous waiting room, and it's even more of a thrill to walk out to the **Capitol** dome, right in front of you. Climb on the bus and take off for . . .

- The **Mall**: Not only are there a series of wonderful sites to visit on the Mall, but also, you need some tips within the buildings. Stop first at the **National Gallery** and, no matter what exhibit is in the **East Wing** (the triangular **I.M. Pei** building), be sure that you allow time for the quiet comfort of the older **John Russell Pope** building, which is really quite grand. I particularly like the Flemish and Dutch galleries, but each period has some remarkable works. And, I want to underline, you are likely to have the rooms to yourself.

If you can get tickets to the **Holocaust Museum**, I recommend that you allow time for the movie at the end, which is said to be 24 hours of interviews with survivors. It is good to know, at the end of this searing experience, that some fortunate people did survive and make a good life. Their personal recollections are extraordinarily powerful.

As you continue on the bus up to **Capitol Hill**, I highly recommend a stop at the **Library of**

Congress Reading Room. The Capitol is a grand building, and the view from the west balcony is a lovely one. The grounds, designed by Frederick Law Olmstead, are gracious and make a great picnic place.

- Slightly off the Mall, a short ride on the elegant **Metro** train, is the **National Building Museum**. Once the **Pension Building**, this handsome building was converted into a museum of architecture, but it's the building itself that's worth the visit. Close by is **Chinatown**, so you can get a good lunch.

- **Georgetown** is worth visiting for **Dumbarton Oaks**. This garden is unique: The grounds are beautiful, and fun for adults and children, with intricate landscaping and beautiful garden "rooms." It's only open in the afternoons, but do plan your schedule to go one day. The 17th- and 18th-century houses and narrow streets in Georgetown are attractive, but stay away from the major thoroughfares, which are choked with teenyboppers. The shops are merely dull branches of chains.

- Do *not* go to the **Kennedy Center**, unless there is a special concert or play you want to see. It is embarrassingly run down from the numbers of people who pass through. It's hard to get to, there's no parking, and the food is laughable.

- **Rock Creek Park** and the **National Zoo** are special. The zoo is terrifically well maintained and stocked. The park runs through the city and is used by residents of all classes. I love the area around **Old Pierce Mill** about 1 mile north of the zoo on **Beach Drive** (the road that runs through the park). There you can visit the mill and the art barn, and picnic and stroll.

- Try to take a nighttime tour of the city. The monuments are particularly beautiful at night: **Lincoln** and **Jefferson**, the **Reflecting Pool**.

- Hang around **Dupont Circle** and on **18th Street** in **Adams Morgan** for a variety of restaurants and a variety of people of all colors and classes. Don't worry about crime. Enjoy the urban experience.

- Come uptown and see some more of the grand neighborhoods. When you get to the 5000 block of **Connecticut Avenue**, stop at **Politics & Prose Bookstore and Coffeehouse**, and we'll give you more tips.

CHILD'S PLAY

1. Watch giant pandas Tian Tian and Mei Xiang and their new baby, Tai Shan, munch on bamboo, and young elephant Kandula—now 4 years old, 6 feet 5 inches tall, and 3,835 pounds—play with zookeepers at the **National Zoo**.

2. Make friends with a computer, learn Morse code, and simulate driving a city bus at the **Capital Children's Museum** near **Union Station**.

3. Pet the animals at **Oxon Hill Farm**, a working replica of a turn-of-the-19th-century farm in suburban Maryland, and at the **Claude Moore Colonial Farm**, an 18th-century farm with a one-room log cabin in Northern Virginia.

4. Pedal a paddleboat past the **Jefferson Memorial** on the **Tidal Basin**.

5. Ride the antique carousel in front of the **Arts & Industries Building** on the **Mall**.

6. Observe daily feedings of sharks, alligators, or piranhas at the **National Aquarium**.

7. Watch a live theatrical performance at the **Discovery Theater** in the **Ripley Center** on the Mall.

8. Hike through the wilds of **Rock Creek Park** with a trained naturalist or go in-line skating or bike riding on the park's **Beach Drive** (car-free on weekends).

9. Check out creepy-crawly things from the world of nature at the **O. Orkin Insect Zoo** at the **National Museum of Natural History** on the Mall.

10. Take a ride on the European and American trolleys at the **National Capital Trolley Museum**, in suburban Maryland.

high-rise. It was also the first building in the area to use structural cast iron and central heating. The main offices of the US Trade Representative are inside; the building is not open to the public. ♦ 600 17th St NW (between F and G Sts). Metro: Farragut W

24 AMERICAN INSTITUTE OF ARCHITECTS BOOKSTORE

Just behind the **Octagon Museum** and across the street from the **Corcoran Gallery**, this store has all kinds of books relating to architecture—on history, construction, design, and graphics—as well as children's books, T-shirts, and mugs. It even sells ties with architectural themes. ♦ M-F, 9AM-5PM. 1735 New York Ave NW (between 17th and 18th Sts). 626.7475. ♿ www.aia.org/books. Metro: Farragut W

25 OCTAGON MUSEUM

The museum is closed for renovations for the foreseeable future. However, group tours of 10 to 25 people may be arranged by calling 202/638.3221. Built in 1799–1801 as a town house for Colonel John Tayloe III and designed by **Dr. William Thornton**, the Federal-style Octagon contains a small museum dedicated to architecture and design. The building was spared by the British-ignited fires that swept through the **White House** and other parts of the city in 1814, and it served as President James and First Lady Dolley Madison's home during that fall and winter. Madison signed the Treaty of Ghent here, establishing final peace with Great Britain. During several decades afterward, the building changed hands and

deteriorated, but the **American Institute of Architects** (**AIA**) saved it from neglect in 1902. A $5.5 million restoration in the early 1990s returned the house to its 1817 splendor. Original Chippendale and Federal-period furniture was placed in the high-ceilinged rooms; the cornices of the original English Coadestone mantels were restored; and the circular table believed to be the location of the treaty's signing was again set in the upstairs parlor. In 1949 the AIA moved its headquarters to a new, adjoining building. The allegedly haunted Octagon is now a registered National Historic Landmark, owned by the **American Architectural Foundation**, an offshoot of the AIA. 1799 New York Ave NW (at 18th St). 638.3221. ♿ www.octagon.org. Metro: Farragut W

26 RAWLINS PARK

Don't overlook this dainty park, where two shallow pools offer duck-watching on lazy spring days when the air is filled with the scent of tulip-tree magnolias. The park was named after President Ulysses Grant's chief of staff, John Rawlins (1831–1869), and, later, secretary of war, whose statue, after being positioned in seven other locations, finally found a home here. ♦ E St NW (between 18th and 19th Sts). ♿. Metro: Farragut W

27 CORCORAN GALLERY OF ART

In the late 1850s, banker William Wilson Corcoran commissioned architect **James Renwick** to create a suitable home for his paintings and sculptures, but the collection quickly outgrew that building (it's now the **Renwick Gallery**, just north on 17th Street).

Today's **Corcoran** is essentially Beaux Arts in design, but an American influence gives it cleaner lines and massing. Designed by **Ernest Flagg** and completed in 1897, it was **Frank Lloyd Wright**'s favorite building in Washington. The **Clark Wing** was designed by **Charles Platt** in 1925.

With an emphasis on early portraiture, primitives, the Hudson River School, American Impressionism, Abstract Expressionism, the Ashcan School, Pop, and Minimalism, the Corcoran is a celebration of American art. Though William Corcoran's collection still forms the nucleus of the museum, two substantial bequests have added a small but impressive European collection. Works by Degas, Courbet, Pissaro, Renoir, and Millet, as well as the breathtaking **Salon Doré**, a gilded 18th-century French period room, are must-sees. The impressive Evans-Tibbs collection of African-American art, which spans more than a century, was donated to the museum in 1996. Privately funded (it's not part of the Smithsonian empire), this museum has used its freedom to present some remarkable shows, including works by edgy performance artists and up-and-coming local talents, many of whom have studied or taught at the adjacent **Corcoran College of Art and Design**.

The **Frances and Armand Hammer Auditorium** offers talks by artists and art historians as well as a free jazz concert the first and third Wednesdays of the month. The Frances and Armand Hammer Musical Evening Series presents chamber music. (Past highlights include the **Tokyo String Quartet** playing on the Corcoran's prized Amati violins.) A sprawling atrium café serves lunch Wednesday through Saturday, dinner on Thursdays, and a gospel brunch each Sunday. The **Gallery Shop** sells books, posters, reprints, and gifts. ◆ Admission: W-Su, 10AM-5PM; Th, open until 9PM. Closed Thanksgiving, Christmas, and New Year's Day. 500 17th St NW (at E St). 639.1700. &. www.corcoran.org. Metro: Farragut W

28 STATE DEPARTMENT

Founded in 1789, this was the first Cabinet department created. The biggest draw for nondiplomats is the eighth-floor **Diplomatic Reception** rooms, decorated with an outstanding collection of 18th- and 19th-century American art and furniture, much of it historically significant. A mahogany writing table, said to have served for the signing of the Treaty of Paris, is here. With these surroundings, it's hard to believe you're in a modern office building, but the splendid view of the **Mall** reminds you that you're in Washington. (Visitors who expect to see diplomats in action will be disappointed; this is a fine arts attraction.) Tours fill quickly in the peak season and are by reservation only; visitors can make reservations up to 90 days in advance. ◆ Tours: M-F, 9:30AM, 10:30AM, 2:45PM. 2201 C St NW (between 21st and 23rd Sts). 647.3241. &. www.state.gov. Metro: Foggy Bottom/GWU

29 US DEPARTMENT OF THE INTERIOR MUSEUM

This gallery is as multifaceted as the department itself, encompassing exhibitions that outline the history of the National Park Service, wildlife preservation, land management, land reclamation, geological survey, and Indian affairs. On display are Indian crafts and artifacts and turn-of-the-19th-century surveying equipment used to establish western state boundary lines. ◆ Free. M-F, 8:30AM-4:30PM; third Sa of month, 1-4PM. Photo ID required for adults. 1849 C St NW (at 19th St); access for the disabled at 18th and E Sts. &. 208.4743. www.doi.gov/museum. Metro: Farragut W

At the Department of the Interior:

INDIAN CRAFT SHOP

Native American–made jewelry, baskets, rugs, Navajo and Zuni carvings, and other handicrafts are available here. ◆ M-F, 8:30AM-4:30PM; third Saturday each month, 10AM-4PM. 1849 C St NW (at 19th St), room 1023; access for the disabled at 18th and E Sts. 208.4056. &. Metro: Farragut W

30 DAR MUSEUM/MEMORIAL CONTINENTAL HALL

Members of the Daughters of the American Revolution (DAR) trace their lineages to the colonists who fought for independence. The oldest section of their headquarters building, designed by **Edward Pearce Casey**, echoes that period; the elaborate four-story Beaux Arts affair is marked by a vast porte cochere supported by enormous Ionic columns.

Within, some 31 "period rooms" commemorate various states; there's the **Tennessee Room**, featuring **White House** furnishings from the Monroe presidency; the **Oklahoma Room**, displaying 18th- and 19th-century kitchen utensils; the **Missouri Room**, with a Victorian parlor; and the **New Hampshire Attic**, with antique toys and dolls.

Restaurants/Clubs: Red | Hotels: Purple | Shops: Orange | Outdoors/Parks: Green | Sights/Culture: Blue

The excellent collection of pre-1840 American artifacts includes silver by Paul Revere. The genealogical library (which you can use for a modest charge) is one of the best in the nation. The museum also presents changing exhibits. ◆ Free. Museum: M-F, 9:30AM-4PM; Sa, 9AM-5PM. Tours: M-F, 10AM-2:30PM; Sa, 9AM-4:30PM. 1776 D St NW (at 18th St). 628.1776. ⅙. www.dar.org. Metro: Farragut W

30 DAR CONSTITUTION HALL

Architect **John Russell Pope** was a master of simple Roman forms, and this 1929 building is among his best, with its clear circulation patterns and acoustics, which Arturo Toscanini considered remarkable. The hall, which seats 3,702, reigned for many years as the city's major concert venue. Although it has been surpassed in popularity by the **Kennedy Center**, it still attracts its share of noteworthy performers. ◆ Box office open day of performance only; times vary. 1776 D St NW (at 18th St). 638.2661. ⅙. www.dar.org/conthall. Metro: Farragut W

31 AMERICAN RED CROSS HEADQUARTERS

Clara Barton organized the US branch of this international service organization in 1881. The centerpiece of its three-building headquarters is the marble palace, built in 1917 by **Trowbridge & Livingston** to commemorate the women who ministered to Civil War wounded. Historical displays fill the structure, including a collection of recruitment and public-service posters found in the **Presidential Suite**. A trio of stained-glass Tiffany windows lights the **Board of Governors Hall**, and sculptures by such artists as Hiram Powers and Felix de Weldon decorate the buildings and grounds. A new 10-story office building located across from **Red Cross Square** was completed in 2003. To the south of the headquarters, a small garden memorializes Red Cross workers killed in action. From this complex, 940 Red Cross chapters are coordinated to offer vital community services ranging from disaster relief and blood banks to children's swimming lessons. ◆ Free. Visitors' Center and museum: M-F. Tours of the museum: Tu and F at 9AM. 1730 E St NW. 639.3300. ⅙. www.redcross.org/museum. Metro: Farragut W

32 NATIONAL ACADEMY OF SCIENCES

President Abraham Lincoln signed the charter establishing the academy in 1863, to provide the government with independent, objective, and scientific advice. As the importance of science and technology grew, the institution expanded to include the **National Research Council** in 1916, the **National Academy of Engineering** in 1964, and the **Institute of Medicine** in 1970. Collectively known as the **National Academies**, these honorary societies elect new members to their ranks each year.

To accomplish its work, the institution enlists committees of the nation's top scientists, engineers, and other experts who volunteer their time to study specific issues. The resulting reports examine a range of subjects, from the social impact of AIDS to obesity to science education, nuclear waste, and more. The majority of studies are requested and funded by the federal government.

Completed in 1924, the academy building was designed in a delightfully understated Greek style by **Bertram Goodhue**. Note the six window panels: They're two stories high and tell the story of scientific progress from the Greeks to the moderns. The **Great Hall** is also worth a peek. It's an ornate cruciform chamber with a 56-foot-high central dome. In the hall a Foucault pendulum illustrates the earth spinning on its axis. The pendulum, however, is often taken down for receptions. (To ensure seeing this phenomenon, visit the **National Museum of American History**, where a pendulum swings perpetually.)

Stroll the building's pleasant grounds. And of particular interest is the **Einstein Memorial**, built in 1979 by Robert Berks, in the southwest corner. Sitting on a white granite bench, the sculpture is 21 feet tall. Children love to climb on the famed physicist's larger-than-life lap, proving the allure of Berks's grandfatherly sculpture. Next to it is a circular dais with a 28-foot diameter made from emerald-pearl granite from Larvik, Norway, embedded with over 2,700 studs that represent the location of astronomical objects on April 22, 1979, when this impressive statue was inaugurated.

The academy auditorium, built in 1970 by **Wallace K. Harrison** with an acoustical design by Dr. Cyril Harris, is one of the most acoustically perfect spaces in the city. The chamber walls are composed of a huge curving shell covered with large diamond-shaped facets joined at the edges. Fine art, photography, and other exhibitions occur on a regular basis. Free concerts are held here from fall through spring. ◆ Free. M-F, 9AM-5PM. 2100 C St

NW. 334.2436. ♿. www.nas.edu. Metro: Foggy Bottom/GWU

33 FEDERAL RESERVE

The ephemeral value of a dollar is set here by "the Fed," a quasi-public institution charged with controlling the national cash flow, setting interest rates, and regulating the pace of the economy. The Fed's board generally meets every other Monday; the meetings are sometimes open to the public. Call 452.3206 for information and the agenda of topics to be discussed. **Paul Philippe Cret** designed the 1937 Art Deco **Eccles Building**. At press time, prearranged tours that take in the boardroom and the building's architectural highlights are available for groups only. The **Federal Reserve Board Gallery** features 19th- and 20th-century painting, sculpture, and works on paper; it is currently open to the public, but reservations are required 24 hours in advance. Call 452.3778 for reservations. ♦ 20th St and Constitution Ave NW. Information, 452.3000; tour information, 452.3149. ♿. www.federalreserve.gov. Metro: Foggy Bottom/GWU

34 ORGANIZATION OF AMERICAN STATES (OAS)

Formerly called the **Pan American Union**, this coalition of the United States, Canada, and 33 Latin American and Caribbean nations was formed in 1948. Its headquarters, built in 1910 by **Albert Kelsey** and **Paul Philippe Cret**, is one of the capital's most striking Beaux Arts buildings, rendered in white Georgian marble and black Andean granite. Inside are the **Hall of Heroes**, where a collection of busts of famous heroes of the Americas is displayed, and the **Hall of the Americas**, a grand room with barrel-vaulted ceilings, three Tiffany chandeliers, and flags of the American nations, which hosts OAS diplomatic soirées and recitals by artists from the member nations. At the building's center are the **Aztec Gardens**, filled with guavas, banana trees, coffee trees, date plants, breadfruit plants, rubber trees, cocoa trees, and other exotic plants. The **Peace Tree**, planted by President William Taft in 1910, is a graft of fig and rubber trees, symbolic of the cultural roots of the American continents.

The OAS is the oldest political organization with which the US has been associated, and it hosts lectures and symposia on a variety of inter-American issues. Outside the building's entry, note the statue of Queen Isabella I, a gift from Spain in 1966 and a rare remembrance of the woman who financed Columbus's serendipitous expedition. Tours are available by reservation for organized groups only. ♦ M-F. 17th St and Constitution Ave NW. Tour information: 458.3927. ♿. Metro: Farragut W

At the Organization of American States:

ART MUSEUM OF THE AMERICAS

A statue of the Aztec god of flowers, Xochipilli, overlooks a blue-tile fountain designed by Gertrude Vanderbilt Whitney. Beyond is a small but excellent collection of modern Latin American and Caribbean works. ♦ Free. Tu-Su, 10AM-5PM. 201 18th St NW (at Virginia Ave). 458.6016. ♿. www.museum.oas.org

SIMON BOLÍVAR

Simon Bolívar (1783-1830), an aristocratic Venezuelan, became a revolutionary after studying in Spain between 1810 and 1824. He and his forces fought the Spanish and liberated what are now Venezuela, Peru, Ecuador, and Bolivia, which was named in his honor. This impressive equestrian statue of the Liberator, reaching 27 feet at the top of the raised sword, is technically the tallest in DC.

> The Watergate Apartments are a wedding cake and the Kennedy Center is the box it came in.
> —E.J. Applewhite, *Washington Itself*

Restaurants/Clubs: Red | **Hotels: Purple** | **Shops: Orange** | **Outdoors/Parks: Green** | **Sights/Culture: Blue**

69

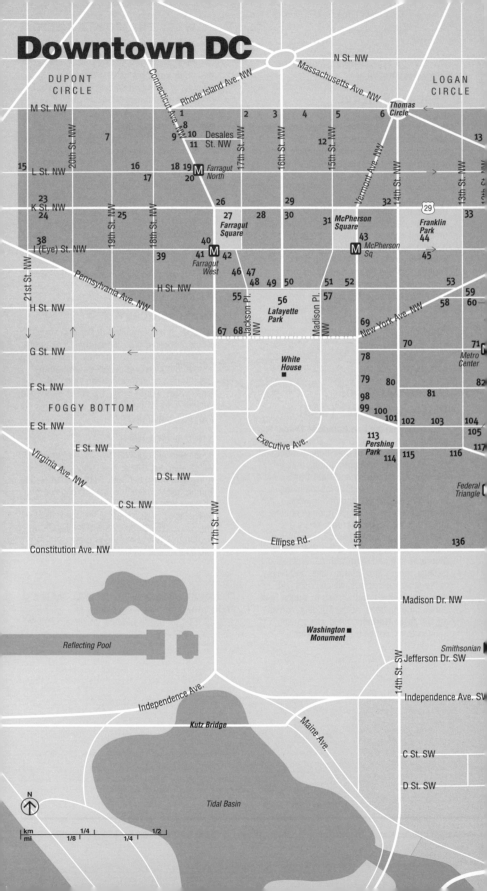

The downtown area is usually a city's main business district, and it's often where the oldest buildings and most of the shops are located. Originally, during the early 19th century, Washington's main business district was located just west of **Capitol Hill**, on and around **Seventh Street NW, Pennsylvania Avenue**, and the **Center Market**, where federal workers from nearby office buildings bought fresh meats, fish, and produce. Washington's first department stores all went up in this part of town. Hotels, serving as temporary lodgings for congressmen, also appeared.

More than a century later, during the 1950s and 1960s, a second downtown business center began emerging a little farther to the west. Boxy office buildings housing the city's burgeoning law firms sprang up along **K** and **M Streets** west of **15th Street**, and a host of restaurants and shops followed. Functional and no-nonsense, the character of this new Downtown is best reflected by the army of business suits walking purposefully along K Street.

Although few of its 19th-century buildings are standing today, Old Downtown is not dominated by boxy office buildings. From the stately Civil War **Pension Building**, which now houses the **National Building Museum**, to the restored **Seventh Street** corridor, it seems better connected to Washington's distant past than any other part of the city.

Where the two sections run together and overlap, they give Downtown something of a split personality. This duality is best appreciated east of 15th Street and **Vermont Avenue**, where old and new stand cheek by jowl: **Ford's Theatre** and the **Hard Rock Cafe**; the historic **F Street** shopping corridor and the newer **Shops at National Place**; the somewhat worn-looking **Chinatown** and the bright, refurbished Seventh Street corridor of galleries, restaurants, and clubs.

Downtown suffered a blow in 1995 when the beloved **Woodward & Lothrop** department store shuttered its doors. Subsequent plans to move the **Washington Opera** to the site were shelved when Placido Domingo opted to stay at the **Kennedy Center**. But today hip Swedish clothier H & M occupies part of the old Woodies building, and Downtown DC has received a great boost from the **Verizon Center**. Home to DC's basketball and hockey teams, the sports arena rests atop the Gallery Place/Chinatown Metro stop. The complex has energized Downtown DC, drawing back visitors who have shunned the area for years.

1 BURBERRY

This outlet of the cool-again, mad-for-plaid company offers fashions and accessories for men and women including suits, shirts, skirts, umbrellas, and, of course, trench coats. ♦ M-Sa, 9:30AM-6PM; Su, noon-5PM. 1155 Connecticut Ave NW (at M St). 463.3000. www.burberry.com. Metro: Farragut N

NATIONAL
GEOGRAPHIC
SOCIETY

2 NATIONAL GEOGRAPHIC SOCIETY

The society has been funding worldwide exploration and publishing its monthly travelogue since 1888. **Edward Durell Stone** designed this modern structure in 1964 to serve as the society's headquarters. The first of his many Washington buildings, it may also be his best—balanced and restrained. The ground floor houses the **National Geographic Museum** at **Explorers Hall**, which offers science, photography, and other exhibits as well as lectures and special programs. The well-stocked shop offers an excellent collection of National Geographic maps, atlases, videos, and lavish photography books. *Marabar*, a monumental 1984 environmental sculpture by Elyn Zimmerman, sits on the plaza between the 17th Street and M Street buildings. It consists of a dozen large pieces of granite quarried in South Dakota. Some of the surfaces have been left in their natural state, whereas others have been sheared clean and polished to reflect a small pool. **Skidmore, Owings & Merrill** designed the society's M Street building in 1984. Resembling a terraced ziggurat, it contains offices and the **Gilbert H. Grosvenor Auditorium**. ◆ M-Sa, 9AM-5PM; Su, 10AM-5PM. 17th and M Sts NW. Information, 857.7588; tours and groups, 857.7689. www.nationalgeographic.com/museum. &. Metro: Farragut N

3 HUBBARD MEMORIAL HALL

Hornblower & Marshall designed this simple, massive Italianate building in 1902, with enormous Romanesque windows lighting the second story. It was the original headquarters of the **National Geographic Society** (see page 72), which eventually outgrew the space and moved; now the society inhabits only a part of the complex, which is not open to the public. ◆ 16th and M Sts NW. Metro: Farragut N

4 METROPOLITAN A.M.E. CHURCH

The national church of African Methodism was once a stop on the Underground Railroad. Members of its congregation used to hide escaped slaves behind the structure's broad Gothic Revival façade, and funeral services for Frederick Douglass were held here. Its influential black congregation has been active in the civil rights struggle ever since. Of particular architectural interest are the 2-foot-thick brick-bearing walls on the first floor, which support the vast second-story sanctuary. ◆ 1518 M St NW (between 15th and 16th Sts). 331.1426. www.metropolitanamec.org. &. Metros: Farragut N, McPherson Sq

5 THE MADISON—A LOEWS HOTEL

$$$$ The classiest of Washington's older hotels is accustomed to dealing with the whims of visiting heads of state (every president since JFK has slept here)—it even features a top-security floor. The plush, 353-room and 42-suite hostelry includes 24-hour room service, a multilingual staff, valet parking, two restaurants, a lounge, and a fitness center. Be sure to take a peek at the gorgeous antiques in the lobby. ◆ 15th and M Sts NW. 862.1600, 800/424.8577; fax 785.1255. www.loewshotels.com. Metros: Farragut N, McPherson Sq

Within the Madison:

PALETTE

★★$$$ This sleek new spot offers art both on the plate and on the walls. The restaurant boasts a rotating collection of modern art from North, Central, and South America. The

ingredients and culinary traditions indigenous to these regions influence the menu of "21st-century American cuisine"–think roasted wild Alaskan salmon and smoked heirloom tomato risotto. A neutral color scheme prevails throughout the space, which features mahogany-accented chairs, leather and suede furnishings, slate tile, and a glass wall with geometric cutouts. ◆ American ◆ M-F, lunch and dinner; Sa, Su, dinner. 587.2700

6 WYNDHAM WASHINGTON, DC

$$$$ Formerly the **Westin Washington**, this modern luxury hotel features 400 rooms set around a soaring atrium. Amenities include 24-hour room service, complimentary weekday newspaper delivery, valet parking, two bars, and a fitness center. The elegant **Verandah Restaurant** serves breakfast, lunch, and dinner; the **Bake Shop** offers sweet tooth–satisfying treats. ◆ 1400 M St NW (at Thomas Cir). 429.1700, 800/WYNDHAM; fax 785.0786. www.wyndham.com. &. Metro: McPherson Sq

7 FAMOUS LUIGI'S

★$$ Candlelit, crowded, and casual, this is one of the most reasonable and reliable Italian restaurants in DC. The pizza is crusty, the pasta comes with a variety of sauces, and the house wine is good and cheap. ◆ Italian ◆ Daily, lunch and dinner. 1132 19th St NW (between L and M Sts). 331.7574. www.famousluigis.com. &. Metros: Farragut N, Farragut W

8 TINY JEWEL BOX

No longer so tiny, this store has expanded to offer jewelry on the street level, as well as crystal, antique silver, and charming gift items on two upper levels. ◆ M-Sa, 10AM-5:30PM. 1147 Connecticut Ave NW (between Desales and M Sts). 393.2747. www.tinyjewelbox.com. &. Metro: Farragut N

9 THE IMPROV

Tucked away in a basement, the club has established itself as a venue for first-rate comedy, featuring such stand-up artists as Jay Mohr, Jake Johannsen, and Robert Schimmel. Rob Becker's *Defending the Caveman* got its start at the Improv before it went national. Keep well away from the stage unless you're sure you can take a joke; otherwise, it could get a little hairy. ◆ Cover. Showtimes: Tu-Th, 8:30PM; F, Sa, 8PM, 10:30PM; Su, 8PM. Reservations recommended. 1140 Connecticut Ave NW (between L and M Sts). 296.7008. www.dcimprov.com. Metro: Farragut N

Restaurants/Clubs: Red | Hotels: Purple | Shops: Orange | Outdoors/Parks: Green | Sights/Culture: Blue

10 FILENE'S BASEMENT

Bargain hunters from nearby office buildings fill this place during the lunch hour on weekdays, pawing through the racks for steals on women's and men's clothing and accessories. The merchandise changes frequently, so you never know what you'll find. ◆ M-Sa, 9:30AM-8PM; Su, noon-5PM. 1133 Connecticut Ave NW (at Desales St). 872.8430. www.filenesbasement.com. Metro: Farragut N. Also at 529 14th St NW (between F St and Pennsylvania Ave). 638.4110. Metro: Metro Center; and at 5300 Wisconsin Ave NW (at Jenifer St). 966.0208. Metro: Friendship Heights

11 RENAISSANCE MAYFLOWER HOTEL

$$$$ Centrally located in the business district, the Mayflower, with 583 rooms and 74 suites, is the largest luxury hotel in DC and has served luminaries and power-brokers with style since it opened in 1925. One of the most luxurious lodgings in DC, **Warren & Wetmore**'s yellow brick-and-limestone Beaux Arts building is listed on the National Register of Historic Places. As long as a city block, the lobby is accented with Italian marble, chandeliers, and gilded ceilings. The opulent **Grand Ballroom** is one of the few left in the world, with Wedgwood-like bas-reliefs, terraces, and balconies topped by a 21-foot-high ceiling. Ask for a room with furnishings by Henredon. Some suites have wet bars. The **Café Promenade**, set in a light and airy atrium, serves Mediterranean fare daily; the two eye-catching Italianate murals date back to the hotel's opening. Reservations are recommended for breakfast, lunch, and dinner. The clubby **Town and Country Lounge** offers a buffet lunch and serves some of the best martinis in town. Valet parking, 24-hour room service, health club, concierge service, and nonsmoking rooms all help justify the price tag. ◆ 1127 Connecticut Ave NW (at Desales St). 347.3000, 800/HOTELS1; fax 776.9182. ᗖ. www.renaissancehotels.com. Metro: Farragut N

Pierre Charles L'Enfant's bill for the design of the federal city totaled $95,000; his invoice was rejected. After 8 years of silence, he finally was paid a total of $1,394.20. Unfortunately, most of the money went to his numerous creditors. When he died in 1825, he had a net worth of $45 and a remote Maryland grave marked only by a cedar tree. Recognized as a visionary 80 years after his death, he was reinterred in Arlington Cemetery.

12 THE *WASHINGTON POST*

One of the nation's most influential newspapers, it was started in 1877 and immediately began to founder. In 1933 Eugene Meyer, a Wall Street tycoon and former governor of the Federal Reserve Board, bought the paper at a bankruptcy auction. The *Post* gained recognition under Meyer and later under his son-in-law, Philip Graham, although critics accused Graham of using the paper as his own personal soapbox.

But under the leadership of former editor Ben Bradlee and the late Katharine Graham, the longtime publisher who took over after the death of her husband, Philip, the paper became a national force, ushering in a renaissance in American journalism that started with the publication of the Pentagon Papers (a classified study of US involvement in Vietnam) in 1971 and reached its apogee with the relentless investigative reporting of the Watergate scandal and its aftermath. In 1974—2 years before Robert Redford and Dustin Hoffman played *Post* reporters Woodward and Bernstein in the movie *All the President's Men*—the power of the press impressed enough young people to cause a 15% jump in journalism school enrollment over the previous year.

But it hasn't been all glory days; the paper has experienced its share of hard times too. In 1975 a journalists' strike over modernization erupted into violence. A few years later, Janet Cooke won and then returned a Pulitzer Prize for a series of articles about a child heroin addict because the subject, as it turned out, was a fictional composite, not a real person. More recently, the debut issue of a revamped Sunday magazine section drew fire from the African-American community for its emphasis on crime in the community.

Groups of up to 35 people (all must be at least 11 years old) can take a 50-minute tour of the newsroom, pressroom, and on-site museum. ◆ Tours: M, 10AM-3PM. Reservations required. 1150 15th St NW (between L and M Sts). 334.7969. Metro: McPherson Sq

13 CHURCH OF THE ASCENSION AND ST. AGNES

The exterior is a good example of High Victorian Gothic design, whereas the interior features cast-iron columns, walnut pews, a gold- and silver-leaf mural, and abstract designs in the nave windows. ◆ 1217 Massachusetts Ave NW (between 12th and 13th Sts). 347.8161. ᗖ. www.ascensionandsaintagnes.org. ᗖ. Metros: McPherson Sq, Mt. Vernon Sq/UDC

14 WASHINGTON CONVENTION CENTER

Opened in 2003, the city's new 2.3-million-square-foot convention center offers more than 700,000 square feet of exhibit space and more than 100,000 square feet of meeting space. It's the largest building in DC, as big as six football fields. Inside find one of the largest ballrooms on the East Coast, a lobby with 80-foot ceilings, state-of-the-art audio and visual systems, several food vendors, 68 public rest rooms, and a $4 million art collection that includes paintings, sculptures, and photos by local artists. In its first year of operation, the facility hosted nearly one million visitors and was named Best New Convention Center by *Meetings East* magazine. ◆ 801 Mount Vernon Pl NW (between N, Seventh, and Ninth Sts and Mount Vernon Sq). 202/249.3000. &. www.dcconvention.com. Metro: Mount Vernon Sq/Convention Center

15 GALILEO

★★★★$$$$ The food and interior couldn't be more authentic if you were dining in northern Italy. The simple white walls are hung with pretty prints and watercolors, while terra-cotta floor tiles add still more warmth. The pastas are memorable, especially the meltingly rich risotto and the *agnolotti* (half-moon-shaped ravioli) stuffed with spinach and ricotta. Homemade bread sticks and rolls accompany all the dishes. Besides the main dining room, there are private alcoves along one wall, a covered patio with outdoor tables, a private wine room, and the Laboratorio, where (for a price) diners can watch chef Roberto Donna in action. ◆ Italian ◆ M-F, lunch and dinner; Sa, Su, dinner. Reservations required. 1110 21st St NW (between L and M Sts). 293.7191. www.robertodonna.com. &. Metros: Foggy Bottom/GWU, Farragut N

16 LINCOLN SUITES

$$$ Smack in the heart of the business district and surrounded by some very good restaurants, this recently renovated 99-room hotel provides free continental breakfast, room service, kitchenettes, and free passes to a nearby health club. Children under 17 stay free with an adult. ◆ 1823 L St NW (between 18th and 19th Sts). 223.4320, 800/424.2970; fax 293.4977. www.lincolnhotels.com. &. Metros: Farragut W, Farragut N

17 BORDERS BOOKS AND MUSIC

Two sprawling floors of books and CDs, an extensive magazine stand, foreign newspapers, and an espresso bar-café with fresh baked goods make this an ideal rest stop. ◆ M-Th, 8AM-9PM; F, 8AM-10PM; Sa, 10AM-9PM; Su, 10AM-6PM. 1801 L St NW (at 18th St). 466.4999. &. Metros: Farragut W, Farragut N

18 THE GROOMING LOUNGE

Calling all metrosexuals: This stylish spa designed just for men offers massages, hot lather shaves, haircuts, and manicures. It also stocks a range of grooming products by names like Dermalogica, Molton Brown, and Jack Black. ◆ M-F, 9AM-7PM; Sa, 9AM-6PM. 1745 L St NW (between Connecticut Ave and 18th St). 466.8900. www.thegroominglounge.com. Metro: Farragut N

19 RIZIK'S

This ritzy fashion salon for women features creations by couture designers such as Carolina Herrera, Geoffrey Beene, and Louis Feraud. ◆ M-W, F, Sa, 9AM-6PM; Th, 9AM-8PM. 1100 Connecticut Ave NW (at L St). 223.4050. &. www.riziks.com. Metro: Farragut N

20 MORTON'S OF CHICAGO

★★★$$$$ A favorite of Capitol Hill power-brokers, this macho steak house makes a show of parading its raw beef before customers to demonstrate its quality and freshness. In truth, the steaks, which are shipped in from Chicago, are widely considered the best around. Be prepared, however, to pay dearly: These magnificent slabs of meat command hefty prices. ◆ Steak house ◆ M-F, lunch and dinner; Sa, Su, dinner. Reservations recommended. 1050 Connecticut Ave NW. 955.5997. www.mortons.com. Metro: Farragut N. Also at 3251 Prospect St NW (between Wisconsin Ave and Potomac St). 342.6258. &; and at 8075 Leesburg Pike (at Old Gallows Rd), Vienna, Virginia. 703/883.0800. &

21 MORRISON-CLARK HISTORIC INN

$$$$ Washington's first historic inn (it opened in 1987) occupies the former **Soldiers, Sailors, Marines, and Airmens Club**. The 54 rooms are furnished with Victorian country décor, neoclassical pieces, or French pieces. Original red-mahogany and gold-leaf pier mirrors and carved marble fireplaces decorate its bar and restaurant (see page 77). Complimentary continental breakfast, a fitness

---

Restaurants/Clubs: Red | **Hotels: Purple** | **Shops: Orange** | **Outdoors/Parks: Green** | **Sights/Culture: Blue**

A CIVIL WAR SALUTE

To protect the capital city, which straddles the line that divided North and South during the Civil War, the Union erected 68 forts and batteries. The only battle actually fought within District lines took place on 11 and 12 July 1864 at **Fort Stevens** (Piney Branch Road NW and Quackenbos Street; 895.6000), where President Lincoln came to observe; oblivious to the bullets whizzing by, he nearly lost his life. Remains of other fortifications can be found in city parks—including **Fort Reno** (near Fessenden Street NW and Reno Road; www.fortreno.com), the highest point of the city and now a site for summer concerts and soccer games, and **Battery Kemble** (Chain Bridge Road NW, between MacArthur Boulevard and Loughboro Road; 895.6000), now a favorite spot for sledding and dog-walking.

Washington's Civil War–era landmarks also include stops on the Underground Railroad. Fugitive slaves received help from Georgetown's first African-American church, **Mount Zion United Methodist Church** (1334 29th Street NW, between Dumbarton and O Streets; 234.0148). Note the tin ceiling's West African influence and the pews carved by African-American craftspeople. Just a few blocks away is **Mount Zion Cemetery** (at Q and 27th Streets NW)—the area's oldest black burial ground—which served as a hiding place for runaway slaves.

Throughout many of DC's neighborhoods, you're likely to find a Civil War hero at the center of famous circles, by a square, or in a park. **Sheridan Circle** features an impressive equestrian statue honoring General Philip H. Sheridan. The fountain gracing **Dupont Circle** is a memorial to Rear Admiral Samuel Francis du Pont, the first naval hero of the Civil War.

Not far from Thomas Circle, the **Metropolitan A.M.E. Church** (1518 M Street NW, between 15th and 16th Streets; 331.1426) served as yet another temporary safe haven for fugitives on the Underground Railroad. Farther up Vermont Avenue, at U Street, the **African-American Civil War Memorial** commemorates the sacrifices made by black soldiers who served the Union during the war.

Heading downtown, you'll find bronze horsemen honoring heroes at both **Farragut Square** (17th Street NW, between I and K Streets) and **McPherson Square** (15th Street NW, between I and K Streets). A 14-foot-tall General William Tecumseh Sherman towers over the intersection of 15th Street Northwest and Pennsylvania Avenue, where he is said to have reviewed his troops in 1865.

Those seeking memorials to our Civil War naturally start with the grand tribute to the man who sought to preserve the Union—the **Lincoln Memorial** (23rd Street, between Independence Avenue SW and Constitution Avenue NW; 426.6841). Designed by **Henry Bacon**, it was completed in 1922. Recognized around the world, Daniel Chester French's marble statue—a seated figure of President Lincoln—touches everyone with the majesty of his pose and the warmth and wisdom of his face.

Those wishing to retrace Abraham Lincoln's steps should visit the Anderson Cottage at the **US Soldiers' and Airmen's Home** (3700 N Capitol Street, between Irving Street NW and Harewood Road NW; 800/422.9988). The relatively remote site is where Lincoln wrote the last draft of the Emancipation Proclamation (in July 1862). Three years later he was shot at **Ford's Theatre** (511 10th Street NW, between E and F Streets; 426.6924) and then carried across the street to the home of William Petersen (516 10th Street NW; 426.6924). The assassination conspirators, led by John Wilkes Booth, met at Mary Surratt's boardinghouse (604 H Street NW, between Sixth and Seventh Streets), now **Wok 'n' Roll Restaurant** in the heart of Chinatown. All were caught, tried, and hung—although to this day Mrs. Surratt's guilt remains in question.

On your way to another of DC's Lincoln statues, you'll come upon a massive sculpture at the east end of the Mall—the **General Ulysses S. Grant Memorial**. The result of a design competition won by unknown New Yorker Henry Shrady, Grant is shown on horseback surrounded by artillery, infantry, and cavalry. Farther east in Lincoln Park (E Capitol Street, between 13th and 11th Streets) stands the **Emancipation Monument**, depicting Lincoln, with the Emancipation Proclamation in his hand, and a slave, newly free, his chains cast off to the side. The money necessary to erect the monument, dedicated on 14 April 1876, was contributed by freed slaves. Before that document was delivered, however, many runaway slaves were taking refuge at the **Ebenezer United Methodist Church** (Fourth and D Streets SE; 544.1415). One of these fugitives, Frederick Douglass, escaped north and started the abolitionist *North Star* newspaper. From 1877 until his death in 1895, the great orator and statesman lived at **Cedar Hill** (1411 W Street SE, between 14th and 16th Streets; 426.5961), a 15-acre estate overlooking the **Potomac**.

Farther afield, you may want to visit the home of Clara Barton (5801 Oxford Road, south of MacArthur Boulevard, Glen Echo, Maryland; 301/320.1410), supervisor of nurses during the Civil War and founder of the **US Red Cross**. Across the river in **Alexandria** is **Christ Church** (118 N Washington Street, between King and Cameron Streets, Alexandria; 703/549.1450), where Robert E. Lee was a parishioner. For 30 years General Lee and his wife, Mary Custis, lived at **Arlington House** (Arlington National Cemetery, Memorial Drive and Jefferson Davis Highway, Arlington; 703/235.1530), a Greek Revival mansion on a hilltop overlooking the cemetery, the Potomac, and DC. Northern Virginia is home to 29 other notable Civil War sites, including **Manassas** and **Forts Ward** and **C.F. Smith**. For more information, call the **Virginia Civil War Trails** project (888/CIVILWAR).

center, valet parking, and concierge service complete the picture. ♦ 1015 L St NW (between Massachusetts Ave and 11th St). 898.1200, 800/222.8474; fax 289.8576. ♿. www.morrisonclark.com. Metro: Metro Center Within the Morrison-Clark Inn:

MORRISON-CLARK RESTAURANT

★★★$$$ The Southern menu varies with the season at this pretty Victorian, where four large pier mirrors overlook marble fireplaces and circular cabbage-rose banquettes. Executive chef Richard Thompson offers seasonal menus featuring dishes like whiskey-barbecued New York steak and grilled bourbon shrimp. Be sure to save room for one of the delicious desserts. ♦ American ♦ M-F, lunch and dinner; Sa, dinner; Su, brunch and dinner. Reservations recommended. 898.1200

22 GALA HISPANIC THEATRE

Founded in 1976 to promote Hispanic culture, Gala presents plays, poetry readings, and music and dance performances. All performances are in Spanish with English translation unless otherwise noted. ♦ Shows: Th-Sa, 8PM; Su, 4PM. Warehouse Theater. 1021 Seventh St NW (between New York Ave & L St). 234.7174. www.galatheatre.org. Metro: Mt Vernon Sq

22 A.V. RISTORANTE ITALIANO

★★$$ This simple family restaurant has been serving a rich variety of Central and Southern Italian fare for about half a century. Everything from pizza to pasta to veal in all its permutations is offered here. In warm weather, dine on the outdoor patio with fountain. ♦ Italian ♦ M-F, lunch and dinner; Sa, dinner. 607 New York Ave NW (at Sixth St). 737.0550. ♿. Metro: Mt Vernon Sq/UDC

22 MARRAKESH

★$$ The exotic Moroccan setting—pillows strewn on low sofas, and waiters outfitted in traditional dress—is enhanced by the belly dancers who perform nightly. In keeping with the place's sensual nature, diners eat with their hands (which the staff washes and dries before the meal). More an event than a meal, the seven-course prix-fixe dinner lasts for several hours. Dishes include chicken with lemon and olives, lamb tajine with honey, and couscous with vegetables. Top off the experience with baklava and mint tea. ♦ Moroccan ♦ No credit cards accepted. Daily, dinner. Reservations required. 617 New York Ave NW (between Sixth and Seventh Sts). 393.9393. ♿. www.marrakeshwashington.com. Metro: Gallery Pl/Chinatown

23 THAI KINGDOM

★★$ Still the reigning favorite with many K Street office workers, this place has superb *pad thai* and vegetarian dishes. Also try the dish called Anna and the King (scallops wrapped in chicken). Because this section of K Street is deserted on weekend evenings, it's the perfect area to avoid the lines typical of Georgetown and Adams Morgan restaurants. ♦ Thai ♦ Daily, lunch and dinner. 2021 K St NW (between 20th and 21st Sts). 835.1700. ♿. Metros: Foggy Bottom/GWU, Farragut W, Farragut N

24 PRIME RIB

★★★★$$$$ The portions are large, the prime rib tops, and the atmosphere formal. Aside from the juicy, two-inch-thick signature entrée, this restaurant does a good crab cake and crab imperial (jumbo lump crabmeat tossed with seasonings and baked in a shell). Soft sounds from the glass-topped grand piano add to the pleasing ambience that includes a leopard-skin carpet, black leather chairs, and lots of flowers. Lunch is a relative bargain. ♦ American ♦ M-F, lunch and dinner; Sa, dinner. Jacket and tie required. Reservations recommended. 2020 K St NW (between 20th and 21st Sts). 466.8811. www.theprimerib.com. Metros: Foggy Bottom/GWU, Farragut W, Farragut N

24 BOMBAY PALACE

★★$$ Part of an international chain, this eatery is known for its reliable food. The tandoori chicken, barbecued in a clay oven, and the vegetable *samosas* (stuffed pastries) are among the city's best. The setting is handsome as well, with etched mirrored walls and ornate Indian prints. ♦ Indian ♦ Daily, lunch and dinner. Reservations recommended. 2020 K St NW (between 20th and 21st Sts). 331.4200. ♿. Metros: Foggy Bottom/GWU, Farragut W, Farragut N

25 INTERNATIONAL SQUARE

This minimall includes several shops and a belowground food court that offers a variety of fast-food establishments. ♦ 1850 K St NW (between 18th and 19th Sts). ♿. Metros: Farragut W, Farragut N

26 THE NEWS WORLD

Rarely can a store have been so aptly named; without doubt, this is *the* best place in Washington, DC, to obtain national and international newspapers and magazines. ♦ Daily. 1001 Connecticut Ave NW (at Farragut Square). 872.0190. Metros: Farragut W, Farragut N

Restaurants/Clubs: Red | Hotels: Purple | Shops: Orange | Outdoors/Parks: Green | Sights/Culture: Blue

27 ADMIRAL DAVID G. FARRAGUT SCULPTURE

A Civil War hero and the first admiral in the US Navy, it was Farragut (1801-1870) who said, "Damn the torpedoes, full speed ahead!" Vinnie Ream Hoxie cast this sculpture in 1881 from the metal propeller of the USS *Hartford*, Farragut's flagship. ♦ Farragut Sq, 17th and K Sts NW. Metros: Farragut W, Farragut N

28 MCCORMICK & SCHMICK'S

★★$$ The Pacific Northwest seafood power-house comes to the East Coast with a daily menu of fresh catches. Lots of dark wood and brass, as well as curtained booths, provide the right kind of atmosphere for the power brokers who lunch here. In the bar, twenty- and thirty-somethings congregate for the popular weekday happy hour menu. ♦ Seafood ♦ M-F, lunch and dinner; Sa, Su, dinner. 1652 K St NW (between 16th and 17th Sts). 861.2233. &. www.mccormickandschmicks.com. Metros: Farragut N, Farragut W. Also at 901 F St. NW, 639.9330; 7401 Woodmont Av, Bethesda, Maryland. 301/961.2626. Metro: Bethesda; 8484 Westpark Dr, McLean, Virginia. 703/848.8000; 11920 Democracy Dr, Reston, Virginia. 703/481.6600

29 CAPITAL HILTON

$$$$ Centrally located, this 544-room hotel has been extensively refurbished since it was the **Statler Hilton**. It has two unexceptional restaurants, plus a gift shop in the lobby. Ask for a corner room for extra windows and a doubly good view. Amenities include room service, a multilingual staff, babysitting, the **Capital City Club and Spa**, and concierge service. Children under 18 stay free. ♦ 1001 16th St NW (at K St). 393.1000, 800/774.1500; fax 639.5784. &. www.hilton.com. Metros: Farragut W, McPherson Sq

30 THE ST. REGIS

This grand and distinguished hotel will be closed for renovations until the fall of 2007. For progress updates and more information about the restoration, visit their web site at www.stregis.com. ♦ 923 16th St NW (at K St). 638.2626; fax 638.4231. Metro: Farragut W, McPherson Sq

31 GEORGIA BROWN'S

★★★$$ Updated Southern recipes are the specialty of this down-home restaurant with curved wood walls and an open kitchen. After a bowl of she-crab soup, try shrimp with grits, Charleston *perlau* (Carolina red rice, shrimp, and sausage), or frogmore stew (a seafood broth of shrimp, fresh fish, oysters, scallops, and clams over potatoes). In the Southern tradition, end your meal with pecan pie. This place draws a diverse clientele of young and old, black and white, famous and not-so-famous. ♦ Southern ♦ M-F, lunch and dinner; Sa, dinner; Su, brunch and dinner. 950 15th St NW (between I and K Sts). 393.4499. &. www.gbrowns.com. Metro: McPherson Sq

31 JAMES B. MCPHERSON STATUE

This is an equestrian representation of General James B. McPherson, 1828-1864, who graduated first in his class at West Point, served on Grant's staff, and was killed during the advance on Atlanta. ♦ McPherson Square

32 DC COAST

★★★$$$ The mostly seafood menu here draws inspiration from three coasts—Mid-Atlantic, Gulf, and West—and Southwestern- and Pacific Rim–style cuisine. The Art Deco–inspired décor is as memorable as the food. ♦ American ♦ Reservations recommended. M-F, lunch and dinner; Sa, dinner. 1401 K St NW (at 14th St). 216.5988. &. www.dccoast.com. Metro: McPherson Sq

33 FRANKLIN SCHOOL BUILDING

The ornate brickwork, mansard roof, and Italianate window arches of this building designed in 1868 by **Adolph Cluss** brought new prestige to public schoolhouses and influenced their design citywide. The children of presidents Andrew Johnson and Chester Arthur studied here, and Alexander Graham Bell made his first light-transmitted wireless telephone call from the building. The original bell towers, dormers, cornices, and other exterior features have since been replicated. ♦ 13th and K Sts NW. &. Metro: McPherson Sq

34 HI-WASHINGTON

$ This Hostel International facility, quite close to the new Convention Center, offers five private rooms and 270 dormitory beds and accepts Visa and MasterCard. ♦ Reservations required Mar-Oct. 1009 11th St NW. 737.2333. www.hiusa.org. Metros: Mt. Vernon Sq/UDC, Metro Center

35 HENLEY PARK HOTEL

$$$$ Fashioned after England's fine hostelries, this refurbished former apartment building, adorned with no fewer than 118 exterior gargoyles and authentic lead windows, seems truly royal. Catch an afternoon tea in the **Wilkes Room** off the hotel's parlor. Full meals can be had at the **Coeur de Lion**, which serves American cuisine infused with regional influences. The stiff tariff of this 96-room establishment is justified by such amenities as limousine service,

24-hour room service, a concierge, and a multilingual staff. ♦ 926 Massachusetts Ave NW (between Ninth and 10th Sts). 638.5200, 800/222.8474; fax 638.6740. www.henleypark.com. Metros: Mt Vernon Sq/UDC, Metro Center

36 RENAISSANCE WASHINGTON

$$$$ Near the Washington Convention Center, this 16-floor, 807-room hotel offers more than 70,000 square feet of meeting space, a large fitness center with a pool, a post office, and a 24-hour business center. On-site restaurants include **Florentine** for casual American fare and **Presidents Sports Bar** for pub fare. ♦ 999 Ninth St NW (at K St). 898.9000, 800/HOTELS-1; fax 289.0947. www.renaissancehotels.com. Metro: Mt Vernon Sq

37 CITY MUSEUM OF WASHINGTON, DC

This museum in a Beaux Arts gem (formerly the Carnegie Library and, later, part of the University of the District of Columbia) explores the capital city's history via maps, photos, paintings, artifacts, and a multimedia show. It is the only museum in DC with an interior landmark designation, and it's the only museum dedicated to telling the story of the city of DC and its people. Changing exhibits examine Washington's neighborhoods and other subjects. A state-of-the-art research library contains an extensive collection of historic materials (prints, rare publications, photographs, etc.). ♦ Admission. Tu-Su, 10AM-5PM. 801 K St NW (between Seventh and Ninth Sts). 383.1800. ૬. www.citymuseumdc.org. Metro: Mt Vernon Sq

38 HOTEL LOMBARDY

$$$ Ideally located only a few blocks from the **White House**, this classic brick-and-limestone hotel is one of Washington's best-kept secrets. Originally built in 1929 as private residences, the property's 134 guest rooms (including 28 suites) were renovated in 1994. Most feature comfortable living spaces with Oriental rugs and have kitchenettes and complimentary high-speed Internet. ♦ 2019 Pennsylvania Ave (between 20th and 21st Sts). 828.2600, 800/424.5486; fax 872.0503. www.hotellombardy.com. Metro: Foggy Bottom/GWU

Within the Hotel Lombardy:

CAFÉ LOMBARDY

★★$$$ This eatery features French-inspired continental cuisine like tournedos of beef and sautéed shrimp Provençal. Open-air dining makes this an oasis in warm weather. ♦ Continental ♦ Daily, breakfast, lunch, and dinner. 828.2600

38 ARTS CLUB OF WASHINGTON

In 1916 the onetime residence of James Monroe became the permanent home of the Arts Club, a local association open to aficionados of 19th- and 20th-century art. Spread over two floors and two buildings (the house next door to the original 1806 structure by architect **Timothy Caldwell** was annexed), rooms contain an interesting spectrum of works, much of which was done by lesser-known artists. Exhibits change every few months. The museum's donated collection of period furniture complement Caldwell's predominantly Georgian design. ♦ Free. Tu-F, 10AM-5PM; Sa, 10AM-2PM. 2017 I St NW (between 20th and 21st Sts). 331.7282. www.artsclubofwashington.org. Metro: Foggy Bottom/GWU

38 PRIMI PIATTI

★$$$ The trendy, high-style setting is balanced by simple dishes, with an emphasis on pasta, pizzas, and antipasti, as the restaurant's name suggests. But the din from the omnipresent crowd of young professionals can be deafening. ♦ Italian ♦ M-F, lunch and dinner; Sa, dinner. Reservations recommended. 2013 I St NW (between 20th and 21st Sts). 223.3600. www.primipiatti.com. ૬. Metro: Foggy Bottom/GWU

Washington's first luxury apartment building (all rentals) was built in 1879. Called Portland Flats, it was located at Thomas Circle and had a public dining room, a drugstore, and a full staff. However, few of the apartments had kitchens, as residents were expected to pay extra for their meals in the dining room.

An article in the *Washington Post* said that the FBI Building "would make a perfect stage set for a dramatization of George Orwell's *1984*."

Restaurants/Clubs: Red | Hotels: Purple | Shops: Orange | Outdoors/Parks: Green | Sights/Culture: Blue

39 TABERNA DEL ALABARDERO

★★★★$$$$ Exquisite décor—Spanish painting and tapestries, romantic lighting, and couches set around walls—as well as wonderful service and splendid Spanish cuisine can all be found here. The paella is a sure bet, as are the variety of tapas choices. It's undoubtedly the finest Spanish restaurant in DC, and part of a small but very selective chain of restaurants and hotels in Spain. ♦ Spanish ♦ M-F, lunch and dinner; Sa, dinner. Reservations recommended. 1776 I St NW (entrance on 18th St). 429.2200. www.alabardero.com. ♿. Metro: Farragut W

40 BARR BUILDING

Stanley Simmons disguised this office building—an unremarkable structure—by encrusting its façade with English High Gothic decorations. It makes a striking contrast to its more utilitarian neighbors. The building is closed to the public. ♦ 910 17th St NW (between I and K Sts). Metro: Farragut W

41 ART GALLERY GRILLE

★$ This place serves good, basic, mostly diner-style food. The portions aren't always as generous as they could be, but the bustling atmosphere provides a lively break from the business-as-usual lunch spots. ♦ American ♦ M-F, breakfast, lunch, and dinner; Sa, lunch and dinner. 1712 I St NW (between 17th and 18th Sts). 298.6658. ♿. Metro: Farragut W

42 ADC MAP AND TRAVEL CENTER

You'll always know where you're going if you come here first. This place stocks maps of every area in the world as well as travel guides. ♦ M-Th, 9AM-6:30PM; F, 9AM-5:30PM; Sa, 11AM-5PM. 1636 I St NW (between 17th St and Connecticut Ave). 628.2608. ♿. Metro: Farragut W

43 GERARD'S PLACE

★★★★$$$$ Come here for food as refreshingly simple and modest as the décor. Chef Gerard Pangaud—the youngest ever to earn two stars from the Michelin guide—excels in preparing honest, good French dishes stripped of pretentious presentations and esoteric ingredients. The menu changes often, but recommended items include roast chicken with fresh herbs stuffed under its skin, a roasted rib pork chop with dried fruit, and lamb wrapped in eggplant. The pistachio soufflé with fresh cherries is a grand finale. ♦ French ♦ M-F, lunch and dinner; Sa, dinner. Reservations recommended. 915 15th St NW (between I and K Sts). 737.4445. ♿. Metro: McPherson Sq

44 FRANKLIN PARK

One of Downtown's most spacious open spaces and its surrounding neighborhood, formerly home to an "adult" strip, has been resuscitated by nearby office building developments. Gently sloping walkways, a central fountain, lush green trees, and plenty of shaded benches make it a perfect lunch spot. ♦ Bounded by I and K Sts NW and by 13th and 14th Sts NW. Metro: McPherson Sq

45 TUSCANA WEST

★★$$ Across the street from **Franklin Park** (see above), one of Downtown's loveliest squares, is this Northern Italian restaurant, with faux-marble walls, cherrywood booths, a brick oven for pizza, and an open kitchen. It sounds terminally trendy, but good *pomodoro* (tomato) soup and a wide selection of pastas, modest prices, and attentive, enthusiastic service combine to make it a winner. The restaurant offers complimentary valet parking at dinner. ♦ Italian ♦ M-F, lunch and dinner; Sa, dinner. 1350 I St NW (between 13th and 14th Sts). 289.7300. ♿. Metro: McPherson Sq

46 EQUINOX

★★★$$$$ Acclaimed chef Todd Gray runs this critically praised restaurant near the **White House**. Seasonal menus feature contemporary American dishes (seafood, lamb, venison) that use regional ingredients. Diners can choose from a pleasant atrium or the main dining room. If you want to learn some of Gray's tips and techniques, he offers cooking classes (demonstration only) on Saturdays in Georgetown from 11:30AM to 1:30PM; they feature a wine-pairing seminar and light lunch. ♦ American ♦ M-F, lunch and dinner; Sa, Su, dinner. 818 Connecticut Ave NW (between H and I Sts). 331.8118. www.equinoxrestaurant.com

46 THE OVAL ROOM AT LAFAYETTE SQUARE

★★★$$$ Recently redone, the Oval Room is a favorite spot for politicos, lobbyists, journalists, and other members of the city's elite. A la carte and tasting menus feature seasonal American cuisine made with regional ingredients. ♦ American ♦ M-F, lunch and dinner; Sa, dinner. 800 Connecticut Ave NW (between H and I Sts). 463.8700. www.ovalroom.com

47 BOMBAY CLUB

★★★★$$$$ A favorite of the Clintons, the most elegant Indian restaurant in the city offers superb service and inspired fare from the southern India peninsula, North India, and Goa, as well as Parsis specialties. Start with an appetizer of vegetable *samosa chaat*. Move on to lamb vindaloo or *roganjosh* or mustard shrimp, or a delicate vegetable curry. There's live piano music nightly. ◆ Indian ◆ M-F, lunch and dinner; Sa, dinner; Su, brunch and dinner. Reservations recommended. 815 Connecticut Ave NW (between H and I Sts). 659.3727. www.bombayclubdc.com. &. Metro: Farragut W

48 US CHAMBER OF COMMERCE BUILDING

Another of DC's innumerable Roman temples, this structure by architect **Cass Gilbert** is trimmed with a wall of Ionic columns that harmonize with the nearby **Treasury Building**. It is closed to the public. ◆ 1615 H St NW (at Connecticut Ave). 659.6000. Metro: Farragut W

49 HAY-ADAMS HOTEL

$$$$ The former site of John Hay's and Henry Adams's homes is now one of the city's most exclusive hotels, with 145 Edwardian and Georgian rooms, including 20 suites, many of which overlook **Lafayette Park** and the **White House**—leading to the catchy catchphrase "The only thing we overlook is the White House." Amenities include full concierge service, 24-hour room service, and same-day dry cleaning and laundry service. The **Lafayette Room** offers excellent New American cuisine. ◆ One Lafayette Sq (at 16th and H Sts). 638.6600, 800/853.6807; fax 638.2716. &. www.hayadams.com. Metros: Farragut W, McPherson Sq

50 ST. JOHN'S CHURCH AND PARISH HOUSE

This Episcopalian church has been nicknamed the "Church of Presidents," because every man who has held that office—beginning with James Madison—has occupied **Pew 54** at least once since the building was completed. Architect **Benjamin Latrobe** followed a simple Greek Cross plan, to which **James Renwick** later (in 1883) added the portico, extended nave, steeple, Palladian windows, and enlarged seating. The nearby **Parish House** is a French Second Empire opus—elegant even in its scaled-down form. ◆1525 H St NW (at 16th St). 347.8766. www.stjohns-dc.org. &. Metros: Farragut W, McPherson Sq

51 SOUTHERN BUILDING

In designing this 1912 structure, architect **Daniel Burnham** reined in his characteristic flamboyance, using clean lines and balanced proportions to make it fit in gracefully with its neighbors. Architect **Moshe Safdie** raised the commercial office building to the height called for in its original specifications, because Burnham had shaved off a few floors in his execution. Although it's open to the public, there isn't much reason to go inside. ◆ 805 15th St NW (between H and I Sts). &. Metro: McPherson Sq

SOFITEL
ACCOR HOTELS & RESORTS

52 SOFITEL LAFAYETTE SQUARE

$$$$ The lobby's 17-foot-high ceilings and marble floors set an elegant tone for this new luxury hotel, with 220 rooms and 17 suites, that has a great location very close to the White House. Amenities include a fitness center and a gift shop that carries French chocolates and bath products. **Le Bar** offers a sophisticated spot for cocktails. Children 12 and under stay free with an adult. ◆ 806 15th St NW (at H St). 730.8800, 800/763.4835; fax 730.8500. www.sofitel.com. Metro: McPherson Sq

Within the Sofitel Lafayette Square:

CAFÉ 15

★★★$$$$ Three-star Michelin chef Antoine Westermann oversees the kitchen here, creating à la carte and prix-fixe menus of French cuisine. A luxurious Art Deco–inspired décor provides an excellent atmosphere for enjoying Westermann's sophisticated dishes. ◆ French ◆ Daily, breakfast, lunch, and dinner. 730.8700

Mozart CAFÉ

53 CAFÉ MOZART

★$$ Classic home cooking of Valkyrian proportions—schnitzel, sauerbraten, and sauerkraut—is the specialty here. There's a carry-out delicatessen on the premises, and free parking is available weeknights after 6PM. ◆ Austrian/German ◆ M-Sa, breakfast, lunch, and dinner; Su, brunch and dinner;

Restaurants/Clubs: Red | Hotels: Purple | Shops: Orange | Outdoors/Parks: Green | Sights/Culture: Blue

FADE TO WASHINGTON

It may not enjoy the year-round mild climate of Los Angeles or come close to having the soaring skyline of New York, but Washington has served Hollywood well as a setting (or a model) for films ranging from political thrillers to, well, political comedies.

Advise and Consent (1962) Allen Drury's hot-button novel of Capitol Hill maneuvering over a Cabinet nomination gets a respectful adaptation by director Otto Preminger. It features a superb cast, headed by Henry Fonda, Walter Pidgeon, Gene Tierney, and, in his last movie, Charles Laughton.

All the President's Men (1976) This film about the unraveling of the Watergate scandal stars Robert Redford and Dustin Hoffman as Woodward and Bernstein, Oscar-winner Jason Robards as Ben Bradlee, and Hal Holbrook as Deep Throat, the mysterious man in the parking garage. The **Main Reading Room** of the **Library of Congress** is the scene for the film's most amazing shot.

An American President (1995) Rob Reiner directed this romantic froth about a widowed president (Michael Douglas) who falls for a feisty lobbyist (Annette Bening). The **Oval Office** was uncannily replicated in the film's Hollywood set. Costars Michael J. Fox.

Being There (1980) A quiet man named Chauncy Gardener becomes the toast of Washington, dispensing simple statements that are taken as sage observations. In this masterful satire, based on Jerzy Kosinski's novel, Peter Sellers gives one of his best (and last) performances; Oscar winner Melvyn Douglas and Shirley MacLaine play his benefactors.

Born Yesterday (1950) This classic comedy about a tycoon in Washington who hires an intellectual to "educate" his ditsy mistress stars Broderick Crawford, William Holden, and the sublime Judy Holliday. The lukewarm 1993 remake features John Goodman, Don Johnson, and Melanie Griffith.

Dave (1993) Perhaps the best presidential comedy stars Kevin Kline as the president's body double. He manages to turn the **White House** upside down—and romance First Lady Sigourney Weaver—when he's "filling in." Directed by Ivan Reitman, the film also stars Charles Grodin.

The Day the Earth Stood Still (1951) One of the few 1950s sci-fi adventures that holds up as more than just kitsch, this literate and gripping story has an alien ship landing on the **Ellipse**. Its pilot, trying to convey a message of peace, is misunderstood and treated as a threat to our national security. Patricia Neal and Michael Rennie star.

Dr. Strangelove, or: How I Learned to Stop Worrying and Love the Bomb (1964) Director Stanley Kubrick's wicked satire, about a nutty general trying to launch atomic war against the Soviets, still hits the bull's-eye. Peter Sellers gives a knockout performance playing three different roles. The outstanding cast includes Sterling Hayden, George C. Scott, Keenan Wynn, and James Earl Jones.

1331 H St NW (between 13th and 14th Sts). 347.5732. &. Metros: McPherson Sq, Metro Center

54 CAPITOL CITY BREWING COMPANY

★$ The appeal of this Washington brewpub is its superfresh beer. The availability of beers changes nightly, so check the massive board to get a description of what's on tap. If you're not sure what to try, order a sampler—it's well worth the money. The food here is nothing fancy—mostly meat dishes, with a couple of fish choices thrown in—but it's generally well prepared, and the portions are generous. But be forewarned: If you're looking to have a quiet dinner, avoid the after-work rush, when lawyers, lobbyists, and other Washington types jam the place. ♦ American ♦ Daily, lunch and dinner. 1100 New York Ave NW (at 11th St). 628.2222. &. www.capcitybrew.com. Metro: Metro Center. Also at 2 Massachusetts Ave NE (at N Capitol St). 842.BEER. Metro: Union Station; and at 2700 S Quincy St, Arlington, Virginia. 703/578.3888

55 DECATUR HOUSE

Commodore Stephen Decatur, a brave and reckless naval hero (best known for having once uttered the toast "Our Country! In her intercourse with foreign nations may she always be in the right; but our country, right or wrong!"), lived in this house, which many say was built with proceeds from government-sanctioned privateering. Its simple exterior and formal interiors—especially the splendid second-floor ballroom—represent the best of the Late Federal style, as interpreted by architect **Benjamin Latrobe** in 1818. ♦ Donation. Tu-Sa, 10AM-5PM; Su, noon-4PM. 748 Jackson Pl NW (at H St). 842.0920. &. www.decaturhouse.org. Metro: Farragut W

Mary Surratt, executed for her involvement in Lincoln's assassination, ran a boardinghouse at 604 H Street Northwest, in what is now Chinatown.

Enemy of the State (1998) When attorney Robert Clayton Dean (Will Smith) unwittingly receives a tape that the National Security Agency is after, Gene Hackman's rogue surveillance expert steps in to help. Plenty of action and DC-area scenes; however, **Adams Morgan** and **Dupont Circle** are, in reality, more than a block apart.

The Exorcist (1973) The horror tale of a girl possessed, adapted from the best-selling novel, ushered in a new era in graphic special effects. Linda Blair, Ellen Burstyn, and Max von Sydow star. The house, on **Georgetown's Prospect Street**, and the adjacent stairs leading down to M Street, are still Washington's biggest movie-based tourist attractions.

A Few Good Men (1993) This court-martial drama has a young defense attorney (Tom Cruise) butting heads with the military establishment, represented by a harder-than-nails Jack Nicholson. Demi Moore and Kevin Bacon also star. Many exterior shots were filmed in Washington and suburban Virginia.

Heartburn (1986) Nora Ephron's revenge on her philandering husband, Washington journalist Carl Bernstein, was to write a thinly disguised novel about the breakup of their marriage. Meryl Streep plays Ephron opposite a randy Jack Nicholson.

In the Line of Fire (1993) This cat-and-mouse thriller stars Clint Eastwood as an aging Secret Service agent trying to erase bad memories of 1963 Dallas by trying to prevent a crazed assassin (John Malkovich) from

getting to the current president. Good rooftop chase filmed on Capitol Hill.

Independence Day (1996) This sci-fi sleeper hit the box office jackpot. A bevy of spaceships attacks the earth, blowing up the **White House** in the process. Bill Pullman portrays the president; Will Smith and Jeff Goldblum round out the cast.

The Last Detail (1973) A profane and often hilarious story of a pair of Navy "lifers" (Jack Nicholson, Otis Young) who are escorting a sad-sack seaman (Randy Quaid) from Norfolk, Virginia, to a New Hampshire prison. Their stopover in Washington is one of the film's many highlights.

Minority Report (2002) Director Steven Spielberg offers his version of DC circa 2054 in this futuristic sci-fi thriller starring Tom Cruise as a cop accused of a murder he hasn't committed yet.

Mr. Smith Goes to Washington (1939) A naïve new senator (James Stewart) stands up for honesty in a corrupt Senate. One of Frank Capra's most well-known films, it costars the one and only Jean Arthur. Though most of the Washington scenes were shot in Hollywood, Stewart's visit to the **Lincoln Memorial** was filmed on location.

No Way Out (1987) Kevin Costner stars in this sensational thriller about a naval officer caught in a compromising situation involving the dead mistress of a Cabinet official. Gene Hackman and Sean Young costar.

56 LAFAYETTE PARK

Designed by **Pierre Charles L'Enfant** as part of **President's Park**, this area was made public land by Thomas Jefferson. It was here that laborers camped and bricks were dried during **White House** construction. First called **Jackson Park**, it was renamed for Revolutionary War hero Major General Marquis de Lafayette at a reception held in 1824. At the park's center towers Clark Mills's statue of Andrew Jackson, depicted riding a spirited horse as he reviews troops before the Battle of New Orleans. In the park's corners are more statues: Major General Comte de Rochambeau, another Frenchman who distinguished himself in the Revolutionary War, stands in the southwest corner; Brigadier General Thaddeus Kosciuszko, Polish-born hero of Saratoga, stands at the northeast corner; Baron von Steuben, Prussian native and leader at Valley Forge, stands in the northwest corner; and Lafayette, pleading with the French people to

support America's revolutionary cause, stands in the southeast corner.

During the turbulent 1960s, the park was often the scene of demonstrations. Today, lunchtime brown-baggers and tourists outnumber the few dedicated protesters camped on the sidewalk, hoping to catch the president's eye. For security reasons, the Pennsylvania Avenue side of the park has been closed to vehicular traffic since 1996.
♦ Bounded by Pennsylvania Ave NW and H St and by Madison and Jackson Pls NW. Metros: McPherson Sq, Farragut W

57 DOLLEY MADISON HOUSE

Now part of the **Claims Court** complex, this was the house where the widowed former first lady lived until her death in 1849. So many power seekers and members of the social elite flocked here in the 1840s that the Lafayette Square house earned a reputation as the *real* lobby of the **White House**. Today, it's closed to the public. ♦ H St NW and Madison Pl. Metro: McPherson Sq

58 INTER-AMERICAN DEVELOPMENT BANK BUILDING

This huge structure, designed by **Skidmore, Owings & Merrill** in 1985, is a modern salute to the old office buildings surrounding it. Heavy columns, Roman barrel vaults, and a limestone façade lend it a Baroque flair, although its sheer mass (12 stories, 1.2 million square feet of space, and more than 1,200 windows) puts it squarely in the 20th century. Inside, more than a quarter acre of Greek and Italian tile paves the **Grand Court**, and a waterfall plunges down from the skylight seven stories overhead. This is turned off when an exhibit is installed in the court. Although the rest of the building is not open to the public, you're welcome to come to the atrium during business hours. The IDB Cultural Center (623.3774) hosts exhibits, concerts, and lectures. ♦ 1300 New York Ave NW (at 13th St). 623.1000. ᕷ. www.iadb.org. Metro: Metro Center

59 NATIONAL MUSEUM OF WOMEN IN THE ARTS

Collector Wilhelmina Cole Holladay founded this museum in 1981 to examine and celebrate the work of female artists; in 1987 the collection and library moved to this 1907 Renaissance Revival building, which was originally a Masonic temple. The collection contains paintings, drawings, sculpture, and other media from the 16th century to the present. International in scope, the museum displays works by Mary Cassatt, Frida Kahlo, Helen Frankenthaler, and Camille Claudel. It is the only museum in the world dedicated exclusively to recognizing the contributions of women artists. There's an excellent library devoted to women artists and a gift shop. ♦ Admission. M-Sa, 10AM-5PM; Su, noon-5PM. Group tours by appointment. 1250 New York Ave NW (at 13th St). 783.5000. ᕷ. www.nmwa.org. Metro: Metro Center

60 MARRIOTT METRO CENTER

$$$$ Located in the heart of Downtown, this 450-room and 5-suite facility offers a health club, indoor pool, high-speed Internet access, three restaurants, and 12 meeting rooms. Amenities include babysitting service, a gift shop, and concierge and room service. ♦ 775 12th NW (at H St). 737.2200, 800/228.9290; fax 347.5886. ᕷ. www.marriott.com. Metro: Metro Center

61 GRAND HYATT WASHINGTON

$$$$ This hotel offers 888 rooms, including 36 suites—three of which have saunas—all no-smoking and with oversized work desks.

Check out the hotel's 12-story atrium, which has a 7,000-square-foot lagoon, the **Grand Slam** sports bar, **Butler's Martini Lounge**, and three restaurants: **Zephyr Deli** for New York–style deli, the **Grand Cafe** coffee shop, and **Via Pacifica**, for Italian and Asian cuisine. Other amenities include parking, valet services, an indoor pool, and a fitness center. ♦ 1000 H St NW (at 10th St). 582.1234, 800/223.1234; fax 637.4781. www.hyatt.com. ᕷ. Metros: Metro Center, Gallery Pl/Chinatown

62 CHOP STICKS

★$ This basic spot offers standard Chinese fare (Hunan chicken, moo shu pork, Szechuan beef) to a local clientele. ♦ Chinese ♦ Daily, lunch and dinner. 717-719 H St NW (between Seventh and Eighth Sts). 898.1986. ᕷ. Metro: Gallery Pl/Chinatown

63 MATCHBOX

★★$$ Named the city's best new restaurant in 2004 by the Restaurant Association Metropolitan Washington, this intimate (just 15 feet wide), three-floor spot with exposed brick walls serves New York–style brick-oven pizzas, mini burgers, salads, and entrées like grilled salmon and pecan-crusted chicken breast. A bar on the street level offers a good selection of draft beers. ♦ American ♦ M-F, lunch and dinner; Sa, dinner. 713 H St NW (between Seventh and Eighth Sts). 289.4441. www.matchboxdc.com. Metro: Gallery Pl/Chinatown

63 CAPITAL Q

★$ Texas natives swear by this spot decorated with a stuffed longhorn head and autographed photos of politicians. The signature beef brisket is slow smoked for 12 hours; the pork spareribs are described as "pick'em-up-and-bite'em ribs." ♦ Barbecue ♦ M-Sa, lunch and dinner. 707 H St NW (between Seventh and Eighth Sts). 347.8396. ᕷ. www.capitalqbbq.com. Metro: Gallery Pl/Chinatown

63 RFD WASHINGTON

★★$ Advertising itself as the World of Beer in the Heart of the City, this is a beer lover's delight. It offers the largest selection of world-class beers and brewing styles in DC. Naturally, there is pub food to complement the beer. ♦ American ♦ Daily, lunch and dinner. 810 Seventh St NW. 289.2030. www.lovethebeer.com

64 TONY CHENG'S MONGOLIAN RESTAURANT

★★$$ This is fun food: Pick raw ingredients from the buffet, and the chefs will stir-fry it before your eyes on a massive Mongolian griddle. Upstairs, try **Tony Cheng's Seafood Restaurant** for fresh fish, Cantonese-style. ♦ Mongolian/Cantonese ♦ Daily, lunch and dinner. 619 H St NW (between Sixth and Seventh Sts). Ground-floor dining room, 842.8669; upstairs dining room, 371.8669. ₺. Metro: Gallery Pl/Chinatown

64 DA HUA FOOD

A one-stop shop for Asian chefs, head here for fresh meat and fish, produce, Asian spices and sauces, and cookbooks. It's short on décor but—more important—long on authentic ingredients. Check the second-floor **Saho Bazaar** for sushi plates, cookware, chopsticks, and other imported specialties. ♦ Daily, 10AM-7PM. 623 H St NW (between Sixth and Seventh Sts). 371.8888. ₺. Metro: Gallery Pl/Chinatown

65 FULL KEE

★$ This is the late-night gathering spot for chefs seeking authentic Chinese food—all for the cost of a sandwich. Bowls of broth and plates of noodles are topped with your choice of garnishes. If you can read Chinese, order one of the daily specials. ♦ Chinese ♦ No credit cards accepted. Daily, lunch and dinner. 509 H St NW (between Fifth and Sixth Sts). 371.2233. www.fullkeedc.com. Metro: Gallery Pl/ Chinatown

66 IRISH CHANNEL

★$ Talk about a melting pot. Located in Chinatown, this friendly pub serves Irish and Cajun specialties—corned beef and cabbage, fish and chips, jambalaya, and shrimp and crab étouffé. There's a seasonal outdoor patio too. ♦ Irish/Cajun ♦ M-Sa, breakfast, lunch, and dinner; Su, brunch and dinner. 500 H St NW (at Fifth St). 216.0046. www.irishchannelpub.com. Metro: Gallery Pl/Chinatown

67 RENWICK GALLERY

James Renwick designed this Second Empire mansion in 1858 to display the private art collection of banker William Wilson Corcoran (who later moved his holdings to more spacious digs at the **Corcoran Museum**). A branch of the Smithsonian Institution's **American Art Museum** (see **Donald W. Reynolds Center**, page 89), this museum focuses on American crafts and decorative art. Past shows have included Louis Comfort Tiffany masterworks, New American furniture, quilts from the antebellum South, and George Ohr pottery. Climb the large staircase to the marvelous **Grand Salon** on the second floor. Furnished

in 1870s and '80s style, the room contains overstuffed Louis XV sofas where visitors can rest and admire the 19th-century paintings and incredibly ornate moldings. The gift shop features books, and glass, fiber, ceramic, metal, and wood objects by contemporary artists. Group tours can be arranged by appointment. ♦ Free. Daily, 11:30AM-7PM. Pennsylvania Ave NW and 17th St. 633.1000. ₺. www.americanart.si.edu. Metro: Farragut W

68 BLAIR HOUSE (BLAIR-LEE HOUSES)

Built in 1824, Blair House and the adjoining Lee House are used to accommodate visiting foreign dignitaries. Harry Truman stayed here while the **White House** was being renovated. The houses are not open to the public. ♦ 1651 Pennsylvania Ave NW (between Jackson Pl and 17th St). Metro: Farragut W

69 NATIONAL SAVINGS AND TRUST COMPANY

Constructed in 1880, the remodeled **National Savings Building** is part of the Bankers' Classic Group, which includes three other Roman-temple structures: **American Security and Trust Company** (15th Street NW and Pennsylvania Avenue), **Riggs National Bank** (1503 Pennsylvania Avenue NW, at 15th Street), and the **Union Trust Building** (15th and H Streets NW). **James Windrim**'s design, which employs whimsical turrets and an unusual mixture of Victorian ornamentation, stands in direct juxtaposition to the other three, whose massive exterior columns recall the **Treasury Building**. The intention was to give Washington's financial area an imposing face, a concept fashionable among bankers of the era. You can walk into the ground-floor branch of **Crestar Bank**, if you like, to check out the impressive interior with its original marble fixtures. ♦ 15th St NW and New York Ave. Metro: McPherson Sq

70 CEIBA

★★★$$$ This new restaurant (pronounced SAY-bah)—the latest venture from the folks behind **TenPenh** and **DC Coast**—is named for an umbrella-shaped tree found in Latin America. Not surprisingly, the menu also takes its cues from that region, specifically the Yucatán, Brazil, Peru, and Cuba. Highlights include a variety of ceviches, rum-and-tamarind-glazed tuna, and Brazilian braised pork shank. The décor further adds to the Latin mood—think mosaic tile from the Yucatán and modern furniture made with

Restaurants/Clubs: Red | **Hotels: Purple** | **Shops: Orange** | **Outdoors/Parks: Green** | **Sights/Culture: Blue**

85

THE BEST

Geoffrey Dawson

Co-owner and Builder, Buffalo Billiards, Bedrock Billiards, Atomic Billiards, CarPool, Aroma Lounge

Sunset cocktails at the rooftop bar of the **Hotel Washington** (15th St and Pennsylvania Ave NW) overlooking the **White House** and the **Washington Monument**. This is a local favorite. Wait for a table by the railing; it is worth it. Great on a hot, rainy night.

Any show at the **9:30 Club** at 815 V Street NW (at Ninth St); easy access by cab, **Metro**, or car. This new venue for an old club is great. National acts (Dylan, Bodeans, Lou Reed) as well as local bands. Holds 900 people, so everyone is close to the stage.

Biking or Rollerblading on the **Crescent Trail** between **Georgetown** and **Bethesda**. This runs next to the **Potomac River** and connects two great eating and shopping areas. Smooth and well-maintained asphalt make it the best place in the area for these sports.

Canoeing and rowing at **Fletcher's Boat House** (244.0461). Fletcher's has been there forever, almost, and so have the boats. Canal access as well as to the Potomac River, where locals go to fish. 4940 Canal Road NW (just north of Reservoir Road), or take the Crescent Trail about 3 miles out of Georgetown.

Sunday runs with **Fleet Feet** (387.3888). Phil and Jan have been operating this great **Adams Morgan** runners' store for over a decade. They have a devoted local following and go for great runs on Sundays. They know everything about the running scene in DC and will be glad to share it.

Cleveland Park and the **Uptown Theater** offer lots for evening entertainment. Red line **Metro** to **Cleveland Park**. The **Uptown Theater** is among the finest in the country, old style with huge screen and balcony. Lots of restaurants and bars nearby. Really safe neighborhood.

Adams Morgan for congestion and wild nightlife. Lack of parking and lots of traffic make this a great place to walk or taxi to. Close to **Downtown** and loaded with restaurants and bars. You can't miss finding a place that fits.

Rock Creek Park. The park police close **Beach Drive** on Saturday and Sunday. This runs through the heart of the city and is a great place to run, bike, or blade. The **National Park Service** has all the info on special events. Follow **Rock Creek Parkway** north from Downtown to Beach Drive.

Brazilian woods. ♦ Latin ♦ M-F, lunch and dinner; Sa, dinner. Reservations recommended. 701 14th St NW (at G St). 393.3983. &. www.ceibarestaurant.com. Metro: Metro Center

71 HECHT'S METRO CENTER

The main store of the local chain emphasizes midpriced clothing, kitchenware, and linens, which helps explain the number of shoppers during lunch hour. ♦ Daily. 1201 G St NW (at 12th St). 628.6661. &. Metro: Metro Center

72 RUTH'S CHRIS STEAKHOUSE

★★$$$ Carnivore heaven, this dining room gives its chief rivals—**The Palm** and **Morton's of Chicago**—some serious competition. The prices here are a bit more reasonable; the atmosphere, less exclusive and clubby. ♦ Steak house ♦ Daily, dinner. 724 Ninth St NW (between G Pl and H St). 393.4488. &. www.ruthschris.com. Metro: Gallery Pl/Chinatown. Also at 1801 Connecticut Ave NW (at S St). 797.0033. &. Metro: Dupont Cir; 2231 Crystal Dr (at S 23rd St), Arlington, Virginia. 703/979.7275. &. Metro: Crystal City; 7315 Wisconsin Ave, Bethesda, Maryland. 301/652.7877. Metro: Bethesda

73 MARTIN LUTHER KING JR. LIBRARY

The main branch of Washington's public library system, completed in 1972 and designed by **Ludwig Mies van der Rohe**, is more than just a repository of books. Children's programs, author readings, classes, and exhibits all take place here. The **Washingtoniana Room** contains probably the world's largest collection of DC-related information (books, registers, photos, etc.) dating from the early 19th century, and the **Star Collection** contains masses of information from the old *Washington Star* newspaper. The building's simple, black steel-and-glass box design was one of the architect's last works and is the epitome of his style. Underground parking is available. ♦ M-Th, 9:30AM-9PM; F, Sa, 9:30AM-5:30PM. 901 G St NW (at Ninth St). 727.0321. &. www.dclibrary.org/mlk. Metros: Gallery Pl/Chinatown, Metro Center

74 ZAYTINYA

★★★$$ This Santorini-esque space with lots of buzz packs them in for hot and cold vegetable, meat, seafood, and poultry "mezzes," little dishes based on both traditional and contemporary Greek, Turkish, and Lebanese cuisine. White-and-blue walls, high ceilings, and lots of candlelight set the scene in the dining room; there's also a pleasant outdoor patio. ♦ Mediterranean ♦ M-Sa, lunch and dinner; Su, brunch and dinner. Reservations recommended for lunch. Not taken for dinner after 6:30. 701 Ninth St NW (at G St). 638.0800. &. www.zaytinya.com. Metro: Gallery Pl/Chinatown

75 BURMA RESTAURANT

★★$ Sample the cuisine of Burma—now Myanmar—including such sure bets as mango pork and tamarind fish. The vegetarian entrées and noodle dishes are superb examples of Chinatown's most exotic cuisine. ◆ Burmese ◆ M-F, lunch and dinner; Sa, Su, dinner. Reservations recommended. 740 Sixth St NW (between G and H Sts), second floor. 638.1280. Metro: Gallery Pl/Chinatown

75 CHINATOWN EXPRESS

★$ Continually rated a best bargain by *Washingtonian* magazine, this Chinatown eatery offers dishes like *lai mein*—stretched noodles and Cantonese-style roasted meats. ◆ Chinese ◆ Daily, lunch and dinner. 746 Sixth St NW (between G and H Sts). 202/638.0424. Metro: Gallery Pl/Chinatown

76 JEWISH HISTORICAL SOCIETY OF GREATER WASHINGTON

Officially named the **Lillian and Albert Small Jewish Museum**, it is set within DC's oldest synagogue, **Adas Israel**. The building—a modest, redbrick structure—is on the National Register of Historic Places. Within the museum, the society keeps records and oral histories of the community's Jewish heritage and mounts special exhibitions of Judaica. ◆ Free. Open by appointment. 701 Third St NW (at G St). 789.0900. www.jhsgw.org ◆. Metro: Judiciary Sq.

77 GOVERNMENT PRINTING OFFICE AND BOOKSTORE

A mecca for information mavens, the center publishes some 30 million volumes a year. It's one of the world's largest in-house printing operations (employing some 3,000 workers), using about 25,000 tons of paper a year. Its most important publications are the *Congressional Record* and the *Federal Register*, the government's daily trade paper. Thousands of consumer-information books and booklets are published here. Its all-time best-seller, *Infant Care*, has sold more than 17 million copies since its first printing in 1914. The bookstore stocks more than 1,500 titles and offers 12,000 more in its catalog, plus NASA and National Park Service posters, how-to books, government guides, histories, and most government publications. The main building is a massive Romanesque Revival edifice composed entirely of handmade brick. ◆ Bookstore: M-F, 8AM-4PM. 710 N Capitol St (between G and H Sts NW). 512.0132. ◆. Metro: Union Station

78 OLD EBBITT GRILL

★★$$ This bustling, circa-1856 saloon is loaded with old-time Washington charm. Since opening, it's attracted presidents, politicos, and celebs. Etched glass panels, velvet banquettes, and a mahogany bar add to the mood. Along with splendid raw oysters, the changing menu offers selections like trout Parmesan, pastas, burgers, and luscious desserts. ◆ American ◆ M-F, breakfast, lunch, and dinner; Sa, Su, brunch and dinner. Reservations recommended. 675 15th St NW (between Pennsylvania Ave and G St). 347.4800. ◆. www.ebbitt.com. Metros: McPherson Sq, Metro Center

79 METROPOLITAN SQUARE

When the façade of the **National Metropolitan Bank** was incorporated into this mixed-use office-retail complex, preservationists weren't the only ones who complained: The Secret Service said the upper floors offered a far too clear view of the **White House**. A compromise was reached; the roof deck, used during summer for social functions, cannot be used after 6PM without the Secret Service's being notified. On the 15th Street side, clear panels allow for camera shots but block the more dangerous kind. ◆ 607 15th St NW (between Pennsylvania Ave and G St). 628.0655.◆. Metros: McPherson Sq, Metro Center

80 BUTTERFIELD 9

★★★$$$ Find contemporary American dishes like prosciutto-wrapped rabbit loin and grilled lemon snapper at this glam Downtown spot with Hollywood credentials— *The Thin Man* served as the inspiration for the name, and mega-celebs Tom Cruise and Steven Spielberg have been spotted dining here. ◆ American. ◆ M-F, lunch and dinner; Sa, Su, dinner. 600 14th St NW (at F St). 289.8810. ◆. www.butterfield9.com. Metro: Metro Center

81 SHOPS AT NATIONAL PLACE

Another Downtown impulse mall, this one contains 125,000 square feet of retail shopping temptations—including the popular bargain-spot **Filene's Basement**. The terracotta tile-and-brass interior opens to the lobby of the **JW Marriott** hotel (see page 93) and extends to the **National Press Building** at the east end of the block. ◆ Stores, M-Sa, 10AM-7PM; Su, noon-5PM. F St NW (between 13th and 14th Sts). 662.1250. ◆. Metro: Metro Center

---

Restaurants/Clubs: Red | Hotels: Purple | Shops: Orange | Outdoors/Parks: Green | Sights/Culture: Blue

82 OCEANAIRE SEAFOOD ROOM

★★★$$$ Up to 30 varieties of fish are flown in daily at this elegant restaurant decorated like a 1930s ocean liner. Dishes range from grilled salmon and Maine lobsters to retro faves like clams casino and baked Alaska. Like the inspiration for its décor, the portions here are titanic. ◆ Seafood ◆ M-F, lunch and dinner; Sa, Su, dinner. 1201 F St NW (between 12th and 13th Sts). 347.2277. ᕗ. www.oceanaire.com. Metro: Metro Center

83 TOSCA

★★★$$$ Named for chef Cesare Lanfranconi's oldest daughter, this up-and-coming new restaurant focuses on contemporary Northern Italian cuisine. Try the risotto, tiramisù, or one of Lanfranconi's tasting menus. ◆ Italian ◆ Reservations recommended. M-F, lunch and dinner; Sa, Su, dinner. 1112 F St NW (between 11th and 12th Sts). 367.1990. ᕗ. www.toscadc.com. Metro: Metro Center

84 H&M

Located in part of the old Woodward & Lothrop building, this Swedish import deals in cheap chic, offering trendy fashions for men and women that won't break the bank. Come here for hip polos and sweaters for guys, jackets, skirts, and well-priced Ts for gals. The lines for dressing rooms can sometimes be long, but if you're a fashionista on a budget, it's worth waiting. ◆ M-Sa, 10AM-8PM; Su, 10AM-6PM. 1025 F St NW (at Tenth St). 347.3306. Metro: Metro Center. Also at 3222 M St NW (between Potomac St and Wisconsin Ave). 298.6792

85 ELLA'S WOOD FIRED PIZZA

★$ This casual, newish spot serves up 10-inch individual brick-oven pizzas covered in toppings ranging from prosciutto and wild mushrooms to roasted artichokes and sun-dried tomato purée. ◆ Italian ◆ Daily, lunch and dinner. 901 F St NW (entrance on Ninth St between F and G Sts). 638.3434. ᕗ. www.ellaspizza.com. Metro: Gallery Pl/Chinatown

86 McCORMICK & SCHMICK'S

★★$$ The Pacific Northwest seafood powerhouse comes to the East Coast with a daily menu of fresh catches. In what was formerly **Angelo & Maxie's**, lots of dark wood and brass set the scene for power lunches and dinners. A younger crowd gathers at the bar on weekdays during the popular happy hour (which features a $1.95 food menu). ◆ Seafood ◆ M-Sa, lunch and dinner; Su, dinner. 901 F St NW (at Ninth St). 639.9330. ᕗ. www.mccormickandschmicks.com. Metro: Gallery Pl/Chinatown. Also at 1652 K St NW (between 16th and 17th Sts). 861.2233. Metro: Farragut N; 7401 Woodmont Ave (at Montgomery Lane), Bethesda, Maryland. 301/961.2626. Metro: Bethesda; 8484 Westpark Dr (between Greensboro Dr and Leesburg Pike), McLean, Virginia. 703/848.8000; 11920 Democracy Dr (between Library and Discovery Sts), Reston, Virginia. 703/481.6600

86 PLATINUM

Located in a former bank, this high-style dance club boasts a top-notch sound and light system. A VIP room attracts occasional celebs and other high rollers. Be warned that the neighborhood is home to some aggressive panhandlers. ◆ Cover. Th-Su. 915 F St NW (between Ninth and 10th Sts). 393.3555. ᕗ. www.platinumclubdc.com. Metros: Gallery Pl/Chinatown, Metro Center

87 COURTYARD WASHINGTON CONVENTION CENTER

$$$$ Located in the former Riggs Bank building, and having just undergone a spectacular $25 million restoration, this 188-room property offers such amenities as an indoor pool, room service, in-room movies, complimentary coffee, and laundry services. ◆ 900 F St NW. 638.4600; fax 638.4601. www.marriott.com. Metro: Gallery Pl/Chinatown

Within the Courtyard Washington Convention Center:

GORDON BIERSCH

★★$$ Where bankers once counted money, German-style lagers like Marzen and Hefeweizen are now brewed according to 500-year-old purity laws. The menu offers everything from sandwiches and pizzas to pastas and steaks. ◆ American ◆ Daily, lunch and dinner. 783.5454. ᕗ. www.gordonbiersch.com. Metro: Gallery Pl/Chinatown

88 INTERNATIONAL SPY MUSEUM

One of DC's newest museums offers a highly interactive and entertaining look at the world of espionage. Visitors can test their spy skills or crawl through an air duct to listen in on conversations below. Exhibits showcase spy gadgets (bugs, cameras, a lipstick pistol, a shoe transmitter), tell the stories of famous and not-so-famous agents, and trace espionage's role throughout history. Pop culture artifacts include a James Bond Aston Martin. A fun gift shop offers everything from 007 movies to disguise kits to high-tech gadgets. Long lines can form to go into the museum; get there early or buy advance tickets at the museum or from Ticketmaster (800/551.7328). ◆ Admission. Advance ticket purchase recommended, especially for weekends and holiday periods. Daily, 800 F St NW (at Ninth St). 393.7798. ఈ. www.spymuseum.org. Metro: Gallery Pl/Chinatown

Within the International Spy Museum:

Zola

ZOLA

★★$$ Named for author (and alleged spy) Emile Zola, this stylish new spot offers dishes like caramelized lobster, New York strip, and osso buco plus an eclectic wine list. The glamorous décor includes artwork inspired by secret codes and made from materials like shredded, classified CIA documents.
◆ American ◆ M-F, lunch and dinner; Sa, Su, dinner. 654.0999. www.zoladc.com. ఈ

SPY CITY CAFÉ

★$ A good choice for a quick bite, this sleek café serves made-to-order salads, soups, sandwiches, and gourmet pizzas. ◆ American ◆ M-F, 8AM-6PM; Sa, Su, 10AM-5PM, breakfast, lunch, and dinner. 654.0999. ఈ

89 DONALD W. REYNOLDS CENTER FOR AMERICAN ART AND PORTRAITURE

During its 92-year stint as the US Patent Office, this building held archives of American ingenuity. Now the arched and pillared marble hallways that **Robert Mills** designed in the mid-1800s contain a wealth of American artistic talent. The building is a century-old replica of the Parthenon rendered in Virginia freestone. During the Civil War, it served as a temporary barracks, hospital, and morgue. Clara Barton and Walt Whitman ministered to the wounded here. After an extensive renovation, this beautiful building was reopened on schedule 1 July 2006 as the Donald W. Reynolds Center. The Center houses both the **National Portrait Gallery** and the **Smithsonian American Art Museum**.

Most visitors to the National Portrait Gallery find it both humbling and inspiring to stand face-to-face with so much greatness. The gallery is filled with images of George Washington—including the famous "Lansdowne" version—that many Americans first see on their schoolroom walls, as well as portraits of explorers, military heroes, Hollywood moguls, composers, and prizefighters. Among the colorful figures immortalized on canvas are Babe Ruth, Butch Cassidy, and the Sundance Kid. The federal government unintentionally began this collection in 1857 when it commissioned a series of presidential portraits. The permanent collection now totals 18,600 objects, including paintings, sculptures, etchings, photographs, and drawings. Works by John Singleton Copley, John Singer Sargent, Thomas Sully, Augustus Saint-Gaudens, and Charles Willson Peale, among other artists, can be found here.

The Smithsonian American Art Museum collection includes more than 39,000 pieces, including works by Edward Hopper, Andrew Wyeth, Winslow Homer, Mary Cassatt, Jacob Lawrence, and Benjamin West. There are selections of Hiram Powers's sculpture, oils by Albert Pinkham Ryder, New Deal art, and landscapes and frontier lifestyle depicted by Thomas Moran and Albert Bierstadt. The museum also has folk art, a large collection of miniatures, a 140,000-volume library, and a collection of daguerreotypes and photos dating back to 1839. A branch of the museum, the **Renwick Gallery** (see page 85), located in a separate building diagonally across from the White House, exhibits American crafts and decorative arts.
◆ Free. Daily, 11:30AM-7PM. F St NW (between Seventh and Ninth Sts). Information, 633.1000. ఈ. ww.npg.si.edu or www.americanart.si.edu. Metro: Gallery Pl/Chinatown

90 HOTEL MONACO

$$$$ In the historic building that once housed a post office and the Tariff Commission, this 183-room and very stylish boutique hotel features high-ceilinged guest rooms with Frette linens and eclectic furnishings. Amenities include a fitness center, concierge service, 24-hour room service, and complimentary Wi-Fi and evening wine receptions. ◆ 700 F St NW (at Seventh St). 628.7177, 800/649.1202; fax 628.7277. www.monaco-dc.com. Metro: Gallery Pl/Chinatown

91 ROSA MEXICANO

★★$$$ Opened in 2004, this new outpost of the New York favorite enjoys a prime spot

---

GROWING UP FIRST

By the time they are elected, most American presidents have grown families. But several of the children who have occupied the **White House** have managed to fascinate and entertain us. Here's how some of them went about doing it.

Thomas (Tad) Lincoln was only 7 when his father was elected president. Nicknamed Tadpole—and affectionately called Tad—he was the youngest of Lincoln's sons and his father's favorite. Though hampered by a speech impediment and slow to read and write, mischievous Tad was clever enough to figure out how to make all the White House bells ring at once—testing the patience of many a staff member.

Probably the most boisterous clan to occupy the Executive Manse were the **Roosevelt children**. The brood of six included **Alice**, Teddy's daughter by his first wife. Declaring herself "allergic to discipline," Alice and her teenage antics provided much fodder for the tabloids. She smoked on the White House roof, drank publicly, and was immortalized in the popular song "Alice Blue-Gown." The younger children were scarcely more manageable: **TR Junior** once fired a rifle into the ceiling of the presidential dressing room (with his father's blessing) just to make sure it worked; **Quentin**, who had a high-spirited group of friends called "the White House Gang," transported his pony, Algonquin, to his brother **Archie**'s room on the White House elevator.

Margaret Truman was hardly a child when her father was president, but she lived with her parents throughout their White House years. An only child of older parents, Margaret was doted on by her father. In her twenties she launched a singing career and gave a concert at **Constitution Hall** in 1950. A bad review by *Washington Post* critic Paul Hume prompted the president to write a stinging rebuke, part of which read: "Some day I hope to meet you. When that happens you'll need a new nose, a lot of beefsteak for black eyes, and perhaps a supporter below!" The *Post* printed Truman's letter, in full, on the front page.

When the Kennedy family moved into the White House, **John Jr.** was only a newborn and **Caroline**, 3 years old. Caroline's pony, Macaroni, roamed freely on the White House grounds, while inside she attended preschool (formed by her mother) with the children of several Kennedy friends. John Jr. delivered one of the most poignant moments at JFK's funeral when he saluted his father's casket.

Both Lyndon Johnson and Richard Nixon brought teenage daughters to the presidential mansion. **Lynda Johnson** married Charles Robb (who was later elected US senator from Virginia) in 1967, becoming the first White House bride since Woodrow Wilson's daughter, Eleanor. **Julie Nixon** married David Eisenhower, President Eisenhower's grandson, completing a family dynasty.

Amy Carter, who moved into the White House when she was 9, had three grown brothers. Her mother once said, "It is almost as though she has four fathers, and we have had to stand in line to spoil her." Known to read books during state dinners, Amy was one of the only presidential children to attend DC's public schools.

Despite the multiple scandals that plagued her father, **Chelsea Clinton** was successfully shielded from the public for much of her tenure in the White House. The Clintons were so protective of their only child that initially many Americans didn't know they had a daughter. Chelsea attended **Sidwell Friends School** in northwest Washington and, at 17, went to Stanford University. Ironically, in her sophomore year the daughter of prosecutor Kenneth Starr (who led the investigation of President Clinton) joined her at Stanford.

During their father's first term, twins **Jenna** and **Barbara Bush** tried to keep a low profile when they visited Mom and Dad in DC, although their minor brushes with the law made that tough. (They were busted for underage drinking at a U Street bar.) It's said that they don't like DC that much and prefer being deep in the heart of Texas. But they became more visible during the 2004 presidential campaign, hitting the road and making appearances in support of their dad.

---

directly across from the **Verizon Center**. Restaurant architect David Rockwell, the man behind Rosa's Lincoln Center location, also designed this 9,000-square-foot space that features 14-foot windows, a floor-to-ceiling water-wall made of blue glass tile, and a large bar and lounge area plus a separate tequila bar offering a range of tequilas and the restaurant's signature frozen pomegranate margaritas. Diners enjoy guacamole prepared tableside as well as dishes like blue corn–crusted fillet of salmon and grilled boneless beef short ribs served with a tomatillo-chipotle sauce. ♦ Mexican ♦ Daily, lunch and dinner. Reservations recommended. 575 Seventh St NW (at F St).

783.5522. &. www.rosamexicano.com/washingtondc.html. Metro: Gallery Pl/Chinatown

92 VERIZON CENTER

This sports and entertainment complex, which opened to great fanfare in 1997, is home to the **Washington Capitals** (NHL), **Wizards** (née **Bullets**; NBA), **Mystics** (WNBA), and the Georgetown **Hoyas** men's basketball team. The modern center also hosts hundreds of events, including concerts and conventions, throughout the year. With limited parking to serve the 20,000-seat arena, fans are encouraged to take the **Metro**—not only environmentally smart, the setup also seems to make for more jovial crowds arriving and leaving events. ♦ 601 F St NW (at Sixth St). Tickets 432.7328. Info: 628.3200. ຣ. www.verizoncenter.com. Metro: Gallery Pl/Chinatown

Within the Verizon Center:

MODELL'S

Stock up on Wizards, Mystics, and Capitals gear, as well as athletic equipment, at this outpost of the sporting goods chain. ♦ M-Sa, 10AM-5:30PM. 661.5252. www.modells.com

93 NATIONAL BUILDING MUSEUM (NBM)

For years, this low-budget Victorian version of the Palazzo Farnese in Italy was ridiculed as a white elephant. Its offices held 1,500 clerks processing pension payments for pre–World War I veterans and their families; during a period of 40-odd years, they doled out $8 billion. In the middle of the 20th century, the building was threatened with destruction, then happily rediscovered. In 1980 Congress created the NBM, and the Pension Building was chosen as its home. Officially opened in 1985, the museum documents and explains the US's vital building trade, from the craft of hard hats to the role of architects.

Along with exhibitions, the museum highlights controversial architectural issues with films and lectures. It has compiled an archive/data bank of thousands of models, drawings, blueprints, and other documents. The permanent exhibit *Washington: Symbol and City* explores the capital's architecture, including its monuments. Visitors are asked to choose their favorite among the designs originally submitted for the **Washington Monument**.

The building's most stunning display, though, is itself. Its central court—once the city's largest indoor space—is as long as a football field and about 15 stories high. Four tiers of balconies—some supporting ornate iron grillwork—climb its interior walls. In the center are eight Corinthian columns (among the largest in the world), measuring 75 feet high and 8 feet in diameter; each required 70,000 bricks to build.

Army Quartermaster General **Montgomery C. Meigs**, engineer of the **White House** dome, is responsible for the inspired design of this building, whose offices radiate from the central court and its balconies. One architect remarked that only a thunderstorm or an inaugural ball could fill the vast space. In fact, the inaugural celebrations of Cleveland, Harrison, FDR, Nixon, Carter, Reagan, Bush, and Clinton were held here. Hundreds of windows let in natural light and ventilation without the heat of a conventional skylight. The gift shop, perhaps the best among the city's museums, sells unique, well-designed merchandise. ♦ Free. M-Sa, 10AM-5PM; Su, 11AM-5PM. Tours: M-W, 12:30PM; Th-Su, 11:30AM, 12:30PM, and 1:30PM; groups by appointment. 401 F St NW (at Fourth St). 272.2448. ຣ. at G St entrance. www.nbm.org. Metros: Judiciary Sq, Gallery Pl/Chinatown

94 HOLY ROSARY CHURCH

Built in 1913 by early Italian immigrants, this simple Catholic church is at the heart of what used to be Washington's Little Italy. From behind the altar a massive *Madonna and Child* reaches up to the arched, coffered ceiling. Also note the jewel-like mosaic Stations of the Cross. Services are still conducted in English and Italian, and the modern **Casa Italiana**, a recent addition, accommodates post-Mass cappuccino, special functions, and a language school. ♦ 595 Third St NW (at F St). 638.0165. www.holyrosarychurchdc.org. Metro: Judiciary Sq

95 GEORGETOWN UNIVERSITY LAW CENTER

Designed at the same time (in 1971) as the **John F. Kennedy Center for the Performing Arts** and by the same architect, **Edward Durell Stone**, the law center has been widely criticized as an inhospitable mass of brick. Although it's open to the public, there isn't much of anything worth going in to see. ♦ 600 New Jersey Ave NW (at F St). 662.9000. ຣ. www.law .georgetown.edu. Metro: Union Station

96 KELLY'S IRISH TIMES

★$ Housed in what looks to be a Chinese restaurant—check out the pagoda-style roof—this boisterous pub caters to a regular crowd of **Capitol Hill** staffers and embassy employees. (Ronald Reagan used to come here on St. Patrick's Day.) Generous portions of stewed chili and fish and chips are favorites during the busy lunch hour. The jukebox plays Irish hits nonstop, from "Molly Malone" to U2 tunes. There's often live entertainment that lasts into the wee hours. ♦ Irish ♦ Daily, lunch and dinner. 14 F St NW (between N Capitol St and New Jersey Ave). 543.5433. ຣ. Metro: Union Station

97 PHOENIX PARK HOTEL

$$$$ Once small, this property with a Dublin accent and named after the famed park in Dublin attracted so many guests that an ambitious $12 million addition was constructed in 1995, adding a ballroom and meeting rooms and effectively doubling the

---

Restaurants/Clubs: Red | Hotels: Purple | Shops: Orange | Outdoors/Parks: Green | Sights/Culture: Blue

number of units to 149. Modernized deluxe rooms and suites include voice mail, in-room movies, minibars, and computer hookups. There's a health club, concierge service, and room service between 7AM and 11PM. Children under 18 stay free. The weekend rates are great. ♦ 520 N Capitol St (at F St NW). 638.6900, 800/824.5419; fax 393.3236. Ꮞ. www.phoenixparkhotel.com. Metro: Union Station

Within the Phoenix Park Hotel:

THE DUBLINER

★$ At this traditional Irish pub, pints of Guinness follow shots of Jameson and Paddy's, and each night Celtic bands encourage customer sing-alongs and plenty of blarney. ♦ Irish ♦ Daily, breakfast, lunch, and dinner. 737.3773. Ꮞ. www.dublinerdc.com

98 HOTEL WASHINGTON

$$$ This refurbished Italian Renaissance–style hotel, with 341 rooms and 26 suites, boasts of being Washington's oldest continuously operating hotel (it was built in 1918). Nearly every 20th-century US president, as well as countless national and international dignitaries, has lodged here. There are two restaurants and a workout room. No-smoking floors are available; children under 15 stay free with an adult. ♦ 515 15th St NW (between Pennsylvania Ave and G St). 638.5900; fax 638.1594. Ꮞ. www.hotelwashington.com. Metros: McPherson Sq, Metro Center

Within the Hotel Washington:

SKY TERRACE

★$ The fare is standard burgers and sandwiches, but this rooftop bar and restaurant has a panoramic view of the **White House**, **Treasury Building**, and the **Mall**, which at night may just be one of the highlights of your trip. ♦ American ♦ Daily, lunch and dinner, April-Oct. 638.5900.Ꮞ

99 THE OCCIDENTAL

★★$$$ Papered from floor to ceiling with more than 2,000 glossies of famous Washingtonians, this lively, salon-style restaurant scores with a menu that ranges from burgers to grilled swordfish and onion rings. Excellent American wines are available by the glass. ♦ American ♦ Daily, lunch and dinner. Reservations recommended. 1475 Pennsylvania Ave NW (between 14th and 15th Sts). 783.1475. Ꮞ. www.occidentaldc.com. Metros: McPherson Sq, Metro Center

100 WILLARD COLLECTION SHOPS

Rodeo Drive meets Pennsylvania Avenue at this shopping center, featuring **Chanel** and other chic shops. ♦ M-Sa. 1455 Pennsylvania Ave NW (between 14th and 15th Sts). Ꮞ. Metros: McPherson Sq, Metro Center

101 WILLARD INTER-CONTINENTAL WASHINGTON

$$$$ During its various incarnations, the Willard has served as temporary home for 10 presidents-elect, including Abraham Lincoln, Warren Harding, and Franklin Pierce, and as temporary White House for Calvin Coolidge in 1923. The term *lobbyist* was coined for the men who skulked in this lobby, waiting for a word with the powerful. During the mid-1980s, the **Oliver Carr Company**, with help from consulting architect **Vlastimil Koubek**, renovated the imposing turn-of-the-19th-century Beaux Arts marble building (drawing below), which had been abandoned in the 1960s, to its previous glory. The former front desk, now a concierge station, is a petal-shaped wonder of marble, glass, and polished wood. Highlights of the 334-rooms and 40 suites include the **Round Robin Bar**, where Henry Clay reportedly mixed DC's first mint julep; the Euro-style **Café 1401**; 24-hour room service, and twice-daily maid service. ♦ 1401 Pennsylvania Ave NW (at 14th St). 628.9100, 800/327.0200; fax 637.7326. Ꮞ. www.washington.intercontinental.com. Metro: Metro Center

Within the Willard Inter-Continental Hotel:

WILLARD ROOM

★★$$$$ Opulent Edwardian décor and secluded banquettes set the stage for formal dining on such New American dishes as roast rack of lamb, venison, and squab. The rich oak-paneled room with its elegant appointments is a consistent winner in polls about Washington's

Willard Inter-Continental Washington

best restaurant décor. ◆ American/French ◆ M-F, breakfast, lunch, and dinner; Sa, dinner. Jacket and tie recommended. Reservations suggested. 637.7440. ᏺ.

102 JW MARRIOTT

$$$$ Conveniently located between the **National Theatre** (see below); the **National Press Building**, which houses reporters' offices; and the **Shops at National Place** (see page 87), this 738-room and 34-suite hotel offers high-speed Internet connections and 32-inch HD TVs, and is the flagship of the locally based chain. Guests—many of them conventioneers—have access to no-smoking rooms, 24-hour room service, valet parking, and a health club. The stylish new **1331** offers a good selection of wines and small plates, whereas the new **Avenue Grill** serves an upscale seasonal menu of regional cuisine. ◆ 1331 Pennsylvania Ave NW (at 14th St). 393.2000, 800/228.9290; fax 626.6991. ᏺ. Metros: Metro Center, Federal Triangle

103 NATIONAL THEATRE

Established in 1835 and restored to its former glory in 1984, the 1,672-seat theater specializes in Broadway-bound productions and road shows. Recent performances have included *Mamma Mia!*, *Les Misérables*, and most recently the Tony Award–winning play *Doubt*. Its production schedule is sporadic, so call ahead for information. ◆ Box office during performance weeks: M-Sa, 10AM-9PM; Su, noon-8PM. 1321 Pennsylvania Ave NW (between 13th and 14th Sts). Information, 628.6161; Telecharge, 800/447.7400. ᏺ. www.nationaltheatre.org. Metros: Metro Center, Federal Triangle

104 WARNER THEATRE

Opened in 1924 as the **Earle**, a vaudeville house, this 2,000-seat theater later flourished as a movie house and then a concert hall. Subsequent renovations have it looking much like its former self: Crystal chandeliers hang from the gilded ceiling; the walls are done in shades of red and green, with various ornamentation. It's now used for road shows, concerts, and dance performances. David Cassidy, the musical *Fosse*, and the Washington Ballet have graced the stage in recent years. ◆ Box office: M-F, 10AM-4PM; Sa, noon-3PM. 13th and E Sts NW. 783.4000. ᏺ. www.warnertheatre.com. Metros: Metro Center, Federal Triangle

105 ESPN ZONE

★★$$ This place is rated Washington's best sports bar by AOL City Guide. It is a not-to-be-missed place for sports lovers; as it has everything they could want in the way of TV screens and videos as well as memorabilia. ◆ American ◆ Daily, lunch and dinner. 555 12th St NW. 783.3776. www.espnzone.com. Metro: Federal Triangle

106 PETERSEN HOUSE

Located across the street from **Ford's Theatre** (see below), this former boardinghouse is where Abraham Lincoln was carried after being shot on that fateful night in 1865. On view and outfitted with period furnishings are the front parlor where Mary Todd Lincoln and her son Robert Todd waited through the night, the back parlor, and the bedroom where Lincoln died the next morning. On display is Lincoln's bloodstained pillowcase. ◆ Free. Self-guided tours daily, 9AM-5PM. 516 10th St NW (between E and F Sts). 426.8630. www.nps.gov/foth. ᏺ. Metros: Gallery Pl/Chinatown, Metro Center

107 FORD'S THEATRE

Here, on 14 April 1865, during a performance of *Our American Cousin*, Abraham Lincoln was assassinated. Afterward, more than 100 years would elapse before the unlucky theater would open its doors again. A small basement contains mementos connected with both the president and his assassin, including the clothing Lincoln was wearing, the derringer pistol John Wilkes Booth used, and the diary in which he recorded his resolve to perform the deed. Upstairs, you can see the flag-draped box in which Lincoln was seated when Booth crept up behind him. The 699-seat theater, built in 1863 by **John Ford**, is now a venue for productions of contemporary plays and musicals, such as *Inherit the Wind* and *Fully Committed*. The National Park Service maintains the theater, as well as the **Petersen House**—where Lincoln died—across the street (see above). The theater offers tours daily except during matinees (on Thursday, Saturday, and Sunday) or during rehearsals, so call ahead before you go. All tours are free and self-guided. ◆ Daily. 511 10th St NW (between E and F Sts). Information, 426.6924; box office, 347.4833. ᏺ.

Restaurants/Clubs: Red | Hotels: Purple | Shops: Orange | Outdoors/Parks: Green | Sights/Culture: Blue

www.fordstheatre.org or www.nps.gov/foth. Metros: Gallery Pl/Chinatown, Metro Center

108 FEDERAL ELECTION COMMISSION (FEC)

You may have a hard time finding the agency that monitors campaign financing, and that's probably just the way most elected officials like it. The FEC doesn't get prime office space, so it's easy to walk by the agency without even noticing it. But its helpful and knowledgeable staff members make the computerized records available to the public. So stop by and get a printout of your congressperson's records and discover which political action committees are supporting his or her campaign. It's easy, and you'll probably learn more here about the way the federal government works than on a tour of the **Capitol**. ♦ M-F. 999 E St NW (at 10th St). 694.1100, 800/424.9530. www.fec.gov. Metros: Metro Center, Gallery Pl/Chinatown

109 THE DISTRICT CHOPHOUSE & BREWERY

★★$$ This brewpub serves gargantuan platters of "jock food"—porterhouse, New York strip, and filet mignon steaks—plus salads and pizzas to game-goers as well as a lively lunch crowd. ♦ American ♦ M-F, lunch and dinner; Sa, Su, dinner. 509 Seventh St NW (between E and F Sts). 347.3434. www.districtchophouse.com. Ġ. Metro: Gallery Pl/Chinatown

110 MARIAN KOSHLAND SCIENCE MUSEUM

Named for Marian Koshland (1921-1997), a member of the National Academy of Sciences who made major contributions to the fields of immunology and molecular biology, this new, interactive museum explores subjects studied by the National Academies and presents them in an easy-to-understand format. (Even so, the museum notes that it's best enjoyed by ages 13 and up.) The permanent exhibit *Wonders of Science* includes a film and infor-mation kiosks that focus on the importance of scientific research. Hands-on temporary exhibits (on view until approximately 2007) examine global warming and DNA. ♦ Admis-sion. M, W-Su, 10AM-6PM. Sixth and E Sts NW. 334.1201. Ġ. www.koshland-science-museum.org. Metro: Gallery Pl/Chinatown

111 NATIONAL LAW ENFORCEMENT OFFICERS MEMORIAL

The walled plaza, dedicated in late 1991, honors federal, state, and local law enforce-ment officers who have died in the line of duty, dating as far back as 1794. The memorial's pathways, encircling a terraced pool, are guarded on each side by majestic bronze lions. Police officers from around the country assemble here on 13 May, during National Police Week, for a somber ceremony. The **Visitors' Center**, at 605 E Street NW, features exhibits, photos, and displays of mementos left behind at the memorial. ♦ Visitors' Center: M-F, 9AM-5PM; Sa, 10AM-5PM; Su, noon-5PM. Memorial accessible 24 hours daily. E St NW (between Fourth and Fifth Sts). 737.3213. www.nleomf.com. Metro: Judiciary Sq

112 HOTEL GEORGE

$$$$ Formerly the **Hotel Bellevue**, this 139-room property is considered one of the city's first boutique hotels. Chic and elegant, the spacious guest rooms feature classic (from the 1940s on) and contemporary touches, including granite-topped desks and marble-and-black-granite bathrooms. Complimentary daily newspapers, daily shoe-shine service, and a fitness center with men's and women's steam rooms are among the amenities. The hotel also offers in-room spa treatments. New York pop artist Steve Kaufman, a former apprentice to Andy Warhol, painted the portrait of George Washington in the lobby. ♦ 15 E St NW (between N Capitol St and New Jersey Ave). 347.4200; 800/576.8331; fax 347.4213. Ġ. www.hotelgeorge.com. Metro: Union Station

Within the Hotel George:

BISTRO BIS

★★★★$$$ Rave reviews accompanied the opening of this modern bistro, where a glass-fronted balcony overlooks the zinc bar and the kitchen is visible through a wall of slightly rippled glass. Changing seasonally, the menu has a classic French accent, with such dishes as steak frites, duck confit, and seared sea scallops Provençale. Leave room for the *tarte tatin* (apple tart). ♦ French ♦ M-F, breakfast, lunch, and dinner; Sa, Su, breakfast and dinner. Reservations recommended. www.bistrobis.com. 661.2700

113 PERSHING PARK

This little swatch of turf offers a shimmering decorative pool; a thicket of trees; a skating rink in winter; and tables and chairs, a striking contrast to the stark—some might say soulless—**Freedom Plaza** (see page 95). There is also a stern statue of "Black Jack" Pershing, 1860-1948, the famed World War I general who was given the title "General of the Armies." The only other person to be so honored was George Washington, but his title was awarded posthumously. ♦ Pennsylvania Ave NW (between 14th and 15th Sts). Metros: Metro Center, Federal Triangle

114 FREEDOM PLAZA

Venturi, Rauch and Scott Brown intended the open, block-long plaza (also known as Western Plaza) to be a witty re-creation of the disrupted axis between the **Capitol** and the **White House**, but their plan was compromised when local censors eliminated its vertical elements, leaving only a broad concrete plaza. Here you will find the equestrian statue of the Polish count Kasimir Pulaski, 1748-1779, who died of his injuries in the Battle of Savannah fighting for the Revolutionary forces. Look at the impressive fountain, which is the platform from where Martin Luther King Jr departed to deliver his "I Have A Dream" speech at the Lincoln Memorial, reportedly written at the nearby Willard Hotel. The inlaid map of **Pierre Charles L'Enfant**'s city plan is worth a look too, and the plaza is used occasionally for outdoor concerts and festivals. ◆ Pennsylvania Ave NW (between 13th and 14th Sts). Metros: Federal Triangle, Metro Center

115 NATIONAL AQUARIUM

Resembling a rec room one might find in a friend's basement, this is a handy refuge from the summer heat, if not much of an aquarium. Established by the federal government in 1873 and spread out over a variety of locations, the now-centralized aquarium went private in 1982. It's the nation's oldest aquarium, and it has been showing its age for some time now: You may be disappointed by the slim pickings and lackluster maintenance. Tanks display fresh- and saltwater marine specimens. There are also slide presentations, a touch tank for children to handle live critters, daily feedings, and a gift shop. ◆ Admission. Daily, 9AM-5PM. Commerce Bldg, 14th St NW (between Constitution and Pennsylvania Aves). 482.2825. ఈ. www.nationalaquarium.com. Metro: Federal Triangle

115 JOHN A. WILSON DISTRICT BUILDING

Once reviled as a monstrosity, this overblown 1908 Beaux Arts edifice eventually won fans. The building now serves as the headquarters for much of DC's city government. It isn't open to the public. ◆ 1350 Pennsylvania Ave NW (at 14th St). Metro: Federal Triangle

116 RONALD REAGAN BUILDING & INTERNATIONAL TRADE CENTER

Designed by **James Ingo Freed**, this massive (3.1 million square feet) multi-building complex houses government employees as well as the **DC Visitors' Information Center** (866/324.7386), shops, meeting space, a food court, contemporary art, and a section of the Berlin Wall. Tours of the facility are offered Mondays, Wednesdays, and Fridays at 11AM. (Call to confirm.) During the summer, free concerts take place weekdays on the plaza. ◆ Free. Daily, 6AM-2AM. 1300 Pennsylvania Ave NW (at 13th St). 312.1300. ఈ. www.itcdc.com. Metro: Federal Triangle

117 LES HALLES

★★$$$ Inspired by Parisian brasseries, this restaurant's specialty is beef—try the *côte de boeuf* (a sumptuous prime rib for two)—but the kitchen also does justice to lamb and chicken. And pork lovers must try the rich pork loin with buttered potato purée. The large room has high tin ceilings, wood floors, burgundy leather banquettes, and plenty of greenery. Opt for terrace dining in fair weather. An upstairs area is designated for cigar smoking, but the ventilation system keeps the fumes well confined. ◆ French ◆ Daily, lunch and dinner. 1201 Pennsylvania Ave NW (at 12th St). 347.6848. www.leshalles.net. ఈ. Metros: Federal Triangle, Metro Center

118 CHAPTERS, A LITERARY BOOKSTORE

This longtime general bookstore specializes in literary criticism, literary biography, and poetry. Evening and Saturday readings attract national and local talent. ◆ M-F, 10AM-7PM; Sa, noon-7PM; Su, 2-7PM. 445 11th St NW (between Pennsylvania Ave and E St). 737.5553. ఈ. www.chaptersliterary.com. Metro: Metro Center

119 HOTEL HARRINGTON

$$ This hotel, with an excellent location close to the White House, offers 242 guest rooms in a range of sizes to suit individuals and families at very reasonable rates. Also onsite is a full-service restaurant, fast-food restaurant, pub, and gift shop. ◆ 436 11th St NW. 628.8140; fax 347.3924. www.hotel-harrington.com. Metro: Federal Triangle

120 J. EDGAR HOOVER FBI BUILDING

Within this unlovely beige concrete building, our national police force keeps track of "Most Wanted" criminals and expands the science of criminology. It was Teddy Roosevelt who created the Federal Bureau of Investigation in 1908, seeking to fight political corruption. As of press time, tours were suspended while the

---

Restaurants/Clubs: Red | Hotels: Purple | Shops: Orange | Outdoors/Parks: Green | Sights/Culture: Blue

building underwent renovation. The FBI tour is closed, and there is no date for a reopening. Please visit the web site www.fbi.gov for additional information. When tours start up again, you'll see high-tech labs and exhibits tracing the FBI's history, from the gangster era through the Cold War decade of espionage to its current, more scientific crime-fighting techniques. The tour ends with the ever-popular firearms demonstration performed by a special agent. ♦ Free. Tours M-F. Reservations recommended for large groups. 935 Pennsylvania Ave NW (between Ninth and 10th Sts). 324.3447. & www.fbi.gov. Metros: Metro Center, Gallery Pl/Chinatown, Federal Triangle, Archives/Navy Memorial

121 JALEO

★★$$ By day, this stylish tapas bar is a businessperson's lunch place and by night it's a gathering spot for the young and the hip, as well as the theater crowd. Especially good are the *gambas al ajillo* (garlic shrimp) and Spanish omelettes. The restaurant's bar is a perfect spot to nurse a beer or drink sangria. Two live dancers perform the flamenco on Wednesday nights. ♦ Spanish ♦ M-Sa, lunch and dinner; Su, brunch and dinner. 480 Seventh St NW (at E St). 628.7949. www.jaleo.com. & Metros: Archives/Navy Memorial, Gallery Pl/Chinatown

122 SHAKESPEARE THEATRE

Originally located at the **Folger Shakespeare Library** on **Capitol Hill**, the theater company moved to these larger, more modern digs in 1992, where there's not a single obstructed view in the 451-seat, horseshoe-shaped house. (The company also broke ground on a new 800-seat theater in spring 2004. It's expected to be completed in 2007.) Under director Michael Kahn, the theater has enjoyed much critical praise. A selection of Shakespearean works and classical plays are performed each season; call ahead for current offerings. ♦ Box office: M-Sa; Su, noon-6PM. 450 Seventh St NW (between D and E Sts). 547.1122. & www.shakespearetheatre.org. Metros: Archives/Navy Memorial, Gallery Pl/Chinatown

123 CAFÉ ATLÁNTICO

★★$$ This hot spot for Nuevo Latino cuisine and mojitos offers a popular Saturday Latino dim sum. Its wine list, featuring mainly South American wines, has won a *Wine Spectator* Award of Excellence. ♦ Spanish ♦ M-Sa, lunch and dinner; Su, brunch and dinner. Reservations recommended. 405 Eighth St NW (between D and E Sts). 393.0812. & Metros: Archives/Navy Memorial, Gallery Pl/Chinatown

124 406 GROUP

Located just down the street from the **Smithsonian** art museum–gallery complex, this building in the bustling Seventh Street arts corridor is a bonus for the visitor with time to spare. It contains the **Touchstone Gallery** (347.2787), an artist-owned space focusing on contemporary art. ♦ W-Su. 406 Seventh St NW (between D and E Sts). Metros: Archives/Navy Memorial, Gallery Pl/Chinatown

124 BEAD MUSEUM

Established in 1995 by the Bead Society of Greater Washington, this small museum explores the historical and cultural significance of beads, tracking their use for everything from trading to religious ceremonies. The collection spans more than 10,000 years and includes beads made from stone, glass, and other media. Special exhibits are held periodically. ♦ Free. W-Sa, 11AM-4PM; Su, 1-4PM. 400 Seventh St NW (at D St). 624.4500. www.beadmuseumdc.org. Metro: Gallery Pl/Chinatown

125 TICKETPLACE

If you're planning on catching a show while in town, check with this ticket source first. It offers half-price day-of-show and advanced tickets for productions at venues like **Arena Stage**, the **Kennedy Center**, and **Signature Theatre**. Bring your credit or debit card; TicketPlace doesn't accept cash or checks. ♦ Tu-F, 11AM-6PM; Sa, 10AM-5PM. 407 Seventh St NW (between D and E Sts). 842.5387. www.ticketplace.org. Metro: Gallery Pl/Chinatown

126 ZENITH GALLERY

Contemporary fine art, crafts, and sculpture fill this art space. The gallery offers themed group shows each year—neon, humor, new artists—as well as special exhibits. ♦ Tu-F, 11AM-6PM; Sa, noon-7PM; Su, noon-5PM. 413 Seventh St NW (between D and E Sts). 783.2963. & www.zenithgallery.com. Metros: Archives/Navy Memorial, Gallery Pl/Chinatown

127 DARLINGTON FOUNTAIN

Friends of Joseph Darlington—an esteemed member of the bar—dedicated this Art Deco sculpture to his memory after his death in

1920. The naked nymph standing beside a fawn created quite a stir among the barrister's Baptist coreligionists when it was erected. Sculptor Carl Jennewein's pointed reply was that the nymph arrived "direct from the hands of God instead of from the hands of a dressmaker." ♦ Judiciary Sq, Fifth and D Sts NW. Metro: Judiciary Sq

127 OLD CITY HALL

Built by **George Hadfield**, English architect and protégé of Benjamin West, this is one of the earliest Greek Revival buildings in the city. The east wing was completed in 1826, the west in 1849. It was DC's city hall until 1873, when the title passed from the district to the federal government. Now it houses Superior District Court offices, which are not open to the public. ♦ 451 Indiana Ave NW (at Fifth St). Metro: Judiciary Sq

128 US TAX COURT

Built in 1974 by **Victor Lundy**, this is a showpiece of engineering: Granite and bronze-tinted glass sheathe the exterior, whereas the third-floor court chambers are suspended from the ceiling by more than a hundred 3-inch-thick steel cables. The building was designed to span the nearby freeway; though that plan was abandoned, its form still reflects the original intent. Concrete and teak lend texture to the interior surfaces, which you won't be able to see unless you have a matter of unpaid back taxes to settle with Uncle Sam. ♦ Third St NW (between D and E Sts). Metro: Judiciary Sq

129 HYATT REGENCY WASHINGTON ON CAPITOL HILL

$$$$ Not in danger of being upstaged by its ponderous neighbors, this elegant hotel offers an exquisite lobby and extensive gift shop in addition to 834 rooms, a health club, an indoor pool, and a variety of restaurants and lounges in cafélike settings. Indoor parking and no-smoking floors are available. Children under 18 stay free. ♦ 400 New Jersey Ave NW (at D St). 737.1234, 800/233.1234; fax 737.5773. www.hyatt.com. &. Metro: Union Station

130 HOLIDAY INN ON THE HILL

$$ Renovated in 2003, the 343 spacious rooms here have zebrawood armoires, ergonomic desk chairs, and free high-speed Internet access. Amenities include a rooftop pool and health club. Indoor parking is available for a fee. The **Senators Grille** serves American cuisine. Children under 19 stay free; children 12 and under eat free with a paying adult (limit three children). ♦ 415 New Jersey Ave NW (between D and E Sts). 638.1616, 800/638.1116; fax 638.0707. www.hionthehilldc.com. &. Metro: Union Station

131 PAVILION AT THE OLD POST OFFICE

This Romanesque Revival chateau, which once served as the headquarters for the postmaster general, was threatened by demolition during the 1960s and '70s but was saved as a result of a fight led by the late Nancy Hanks, head of the National Endowment for the Arts from 1969 to 1977. Sponsored by the Evans Development Company and restored during the 1980s by **Arthur Cotton Moore**, it's a bold example of urban revitalization: It took the 1976 Cooperative Use Act to open up this government building to commercial use. Today, government offices occupy the upper seven floors, whereas the indoor mall below attempts to pump life into the staid, bureaucratic Federal Triangle area.

The mall's atrium is stylishly decked out with Victorian brass fittings, red-oak woodwork, and

Restaurants/Clubs: Red | **Hotels: Purple** | **Shops: Orange** | **Outdoors/Parks: Green** | **Sights/Culture: Blue**

97

frosted glass. A dozen or so specialty shops (with plenty of T-shirts and souvenirs for the kids) and a wide assortment of fast-food establishments serving pizza, curries, ice cream, and the like now fill the restaurant arcade. Free tours of the building's 315-foot-high clocktower (DC's tallest structure, after the **Washington Monument** and the **Basilica of the National Shrine of the Immaculate Conception**) leave from the stage level every 5 to 7 minutes M-F, 9AM-4:45PM; Sa, Su, 10AM-5:45PM (call to check on extended summer hours). An eastern annex containing yet more food outlets and stores opened in the early 1990s. Outside is a statue of Benjamin Franklin, 1706-1790, a man of many talents who besides being famous for his electrical experiments was the first postmaster general; he also helped negotiate the treaty ending the Revolutionary War and was the oldest man to sign the Declaration of Independence. ♦ Stores: Daily. 1100 Pennsylvania Ave NW (at 11th St). 289.4224. &. www.oldpostofficedc.com. Metro: Federal Triangle

132 TEN PENH

★★★$$$ Decorated with Asian furnishings and art (a feng shui master helped with the layout), this stylish Asian eatery near Federal Triangle inspires good press. The menu drew its inspiration from the cuisines of Thailand, the Philippines, China, and Vietnam and features dishes like curry shrimp and Chinese-style smoked lobster. The name drew its inspiration from the restaurant's location. ♦ Asian ♦ Reservations recommended. M-F, lunch and dinner; Sa, dinner. 1001 Pennsylvania Ave NW (at 10th St). 393.4500. www.tenpenh.com

133 MARKET SQUARE

This two-tower complex includes apartments, a visitors' center, restaurants, offices, shops, and an open-air park. ♦ 701-801 Pennsylvania Ave NW (between Seventh and Ninth Sts). &. Metro: Archives/Navy Memorial

Within Market Square:

NAVY MEMORIAL

Conklin Rossant's circular plaza, 100 feet in diameter, features four shimmering waterfalls and Stanley Bleifeld's **Lone Sailor**, a bronze sculpture that stands on the world's largest grid map. This is a cool place for a break. It is surrounded by fountains representing the seven seas, and in the "Blessing of the Fleet" ceremony in April, water brought back by navy vessels from those seven seas, and the five Great Lakes, refreshes the fountains. Free military band concerts take place here in the summer. The adjacent visitors' center has a small museum, a gift shop, and screenings of the 36-minute film At Sea in its theater. ♦

Daily, 9:30AM-5PM. 737.2300. &. www.lonesailor.org

701

★★$$ Contemporary American cuisine—pastas, rack of lamb, fresh fish—is served here in formal surroundings: Floor-to-ceiling windows flood the dining area; light, thick carpeting, and plush tablecloths provide hushed elegance; and widely spaced tables afford privacy. Lobbyists, lawyers, businesspeople with expense accounts, and the pre-theater crowd like its convenient location—the impressive list of caviar and wines may also have something to do with it. ♦ American ♦ M-F, lunch and dinner; Sa, Su, dinner. 393.0701. &. www.701restaurant.com

134 TEMPERANCE FOUNTAIN

In the late 19th century, eccentric California dentist Henry Cogswell used to donate these fountains—on which his name was always prominently inscribed—to any city that would accept one, hoping that pedestrians would slake their thirst with cool water rather than booze. The city long ago stopped maintaining the fountain's obsolete cooling system—which means that although the citizenry may not be dry, Cogswell's fountain is. ♦ Pennsylvania Ave NW and Seventh St. Metro: Archives/Navy Memorial

135 CAPITAL GRILLE

★★$$$$ Subdued lighting and dark wood paneling help give this classic New York–style steak house a comfortable clubby feel. "Dry-aged" steaks and fresh seafood flown in daily from New England stand out among the entrées. There is a separate smoking section, and the restaurant keeps a collection of cigars for diners who enjoy topping off their meal with a stogie. ♦ Steak house ♦ M-Sa, lunch and dinner; Su, dinner. Reservations suggested. 601 Pennsylvania Ave NW (at Sixth St). 737.6200. www.thecapitalgrille.com. &. Metro: Archives/Navy Memorial

136 DEPARTMENTAL AUDITORIUM

Arthur Brown Jr.'s dynamic sculpture in the exterior pediments hints at the opulence within. The neoclassical–Beaux Arts theater style was used liberally in movie houses nationwide at the time; this one was completed in 1935, but it's one of the few theaters where you see are the real thing. The 1,300-seat auditorium is used mainly for ceremonial events, both public and private. ♦ 1301 Constitution Ave NW (between 12th and 14th Sts). Metro: Federal Triangle

137 NATIONAL ARCHIVES

About 70 years ago—after the documents that serve as the foundation of the federal government were variously lost, mistaken for worthless paper, threatened by advancing armies, and left to crumble in dark vaults—a suitable home was finally created for the Declaration of Independence, the Bill of Rights, and the US Constitution. The archives are the nation's safe-deposit box: Treaties, photos, laws, maps, land claims, bills of sale, sound recordings, and other important documents fill 250,000 four-drawer filing cabinets.

The seemingly infinite amount of memorabilia here includes Richard Nixon's letter of resignation, the Emancipation Proclamation, the surrender documents of Japan's World War II government, a copy of the Magna Carta, and even a letter from the King of Siam to Abraham Lincoln expounding the efficiency of elephant labor. Motion pictures—300,000 reels—and literally miles of sound recordings, from FDR's "Fireside Chats" to Tokyo Rose's propaganda messages, are also on file.

The archives' main attractions, though, are the Declaration of Independence, the Constitution, and the Bill of Rights, all on permanent display in the recently renovated domed **Rotunda**, accessible via the Constitution Avenue entrance. They are sealed in helium to guard against aging, and lowered into deep vaults at night for added security. Barry Faulkner's massive murals depicting the forging of these papers encircle the display. In the **Exhibition Hall** around the Rotunda are rotating exhibitions, most of them thematic, celebrating the American genius for invention, or a single remarkable person. Many of the exhibitions rely on photographs and engravings. Spanning the history of photography, the collection includes many historical works, such as Mathew Brady's Civil War photos.

The **National Archives** is more than a museum, however: Access to important records and research assistance is offered for genealogical searches. Immigration records; ships' logs; slave transit and ownership records; treaties with Native American tribes; and volumes of information on taxes, military service, births, and deaths help families rediscover their heritage. (One story researched here was Alex Haley's *Roots*.)

The building that houses so much American minutiae has a shimmering white exterior

trimmed with Corinthian columns, evidence of architect **John Russell Pope**'s facility with classical forms. Ninety-minute behind-the-scenes tours are offered. Make reservations by calling at least 2 weeks in advance. The gift shop sells document facsimiles, cards, and books.

In 1993, the National Archives opened a branch in suburban Maryland, for public use as a research facility; at the **New Archives** (its informal name) you can listen to the legendary Watergate Tapes. Call the Washington or Maryland number with your research request, and you'll be directed to the right location. Note that researchers must be at least 14 years old; evening and weekend researchers should call ahead to ensure that the records in question will be available. ♦ Free. Rotunda and Exhibition Hall: Memorial Day weekend to Labor Day, daily 10AM-9PM; after Labor Day to March, daily 10AM-5:30PM; April to Memorial Day weekend, daily 10AM-7PM. Research areas: M-Sa. Constitution Ave NW (between Seventh and Ninth Sts). ♿. www.nara.gov. Metro: Archives/Navy Memorial. Also at 8601 Adelphi Rd (between University Blvd and Metzerott Rd), College Park, Maryland. 301/837.2000. ♿

138 MELLON FOUNTAIN

Sidney Waugh's elegant fountain comprises three concentric bronze basins; the outermost is the largest ever cast. From the center gushes a 20-foot-high plume of water. ♦ Sixth St NW (between Constitution and Pennsylvania Aves). Metro: Archives/Navy Memorial

139 CANADIAN EMBASSY

This massive marble building includes a 175-seat theater, a library, and an art gallery, plus a three-story rotunda and waterfall set in a titanic courtyard that features an echo chamber and a pond. The views of the **Capitol** and the eastern end of the **Mall** from the courtyard are worth a photo or two. ♦ Gallery: M-F; library: by appointment. 501 Pennsylvania Ave NW (between Constitution Ave and Sixth St). 682.1740. ♿. www.canadianembassy.org. Metro: Archives/Navy Memorial

---

Restaurants/Clubs: Red | Hotels: Purple | Shops: Orange | Outdoors/Parks: Green | Sights/Culture: Blue

North of Downtown DC, away from most of the monuments and museums, the glitzy stores and hip galleries, are the quiet neighborhoods of Logan Circle and Howard University. They're as rich in history as any Washington enclave, much of it preserved in their ornate mansions, apartment buildings, and churches.

The area's western border is **16th Street Northwest**, whose dramatic lineup of churches, temples, and shrines makes it a required walking tour for even the most casual admirer of architecture. Mary Henderson, wife of US Senator John Henderson, was instrumental in developing the street in the late 19th and early 20th centuries. Her crowning achievement was **Meridian Hill Park**, a gently terraced series of waterfalls and fountains.

Head east and you'll come to Logan Circle, named after notable Civil War general and Illinois senator John A. Logan. Many of the city's most elegant mansions are located in this area, where residents, eager to renovate and preserve these Victorian homes, have banded together to quell encroaching criminal activity. The nearby **14th Street** corridor, the site of riots after the assassination of Martin Luther King Jr. in 1968, has been rejuvenated after years of neglect. In the mid-1980s, the city erected the **Frank D. Reeves Municipal Center** at 14th and U **Streets**, and a group of cafés, craft shops, and clubs known as the "New U" soon sprang up around it. The Metro's **Green Line** serves the neighborhood, making it easily accessible to the rest of the city.

To the northeast is the **Howard University** campus, since 1867 a bastion of African-American higher education. The campus sits atop a hill overlooking the city and the huge **McMillan Reservoir**; the university hospital occupies the site of the old **Griffith Stadium**, home for many years to Washington's former **American League** baseball team—the **Senators**. South of Howard is LeDroit Park; in the early years of the 20th century, some of the city's leading black citizens resided in these mansions. In recognition of that fact, and of its splendid examples of Revival period design, LeDroit Park is listed on the National Register of Historic Places.

---

1 WALTER REED ARMY MEDICAL CENTER

The hospital facilities here are located within a huge seven-story square. Especially worth noting is the headquarters of the **Armed Forces Institute of Pathology**, built in the late 1940s as a prototype for the "atomic bomb–proof" buildings intended to be the standard for Downtown's architecture. But the development of the hydrogen bomb in the early 1950s rendered that vision—and this windowless building—almost immediately obsolete. ◆ 6825 16th St NW (between Aspen St and Alaska Ave). 782.3501. ⅃

On the grounds of Walter Reed Army Medical Center:

NATIONAL MUSEUM OF HEALTH AND MEDICINE

This facility was founded in 1862 to research medical conditions that arose during the Civil War. (Most soldiers died from diarrhea or dysentery.) Amputation was the most common treatment for wounds, hence the museum's grisly photographs of amputations and collection of severed limbs—not a sight for the squeamish. Also on view are the bullet that killed Lincoln, odd medical specimens like a hair ball removed from the stomach of a 12-year-old girl, and an extensive collection of microscopes. ◆ Free. Daily, 10AM–5:30PM. 6900 Georgia Ave NW (at Elder St), bldg 54. 782.2200. ⅃. www.nmhm.washingtondc.museum

2 ROCK CREEK CEMETERY

The city's oldest cemetery is filled with historic graves, including the famous *Adams Memorial*, a haunting statue of a woman sculpted in 1890 by Augustus Saint-Gaudens. Commonly called *Grief*, the memorial was commissioned by writer Henry Adams in honor of his wife, Clover, who committed

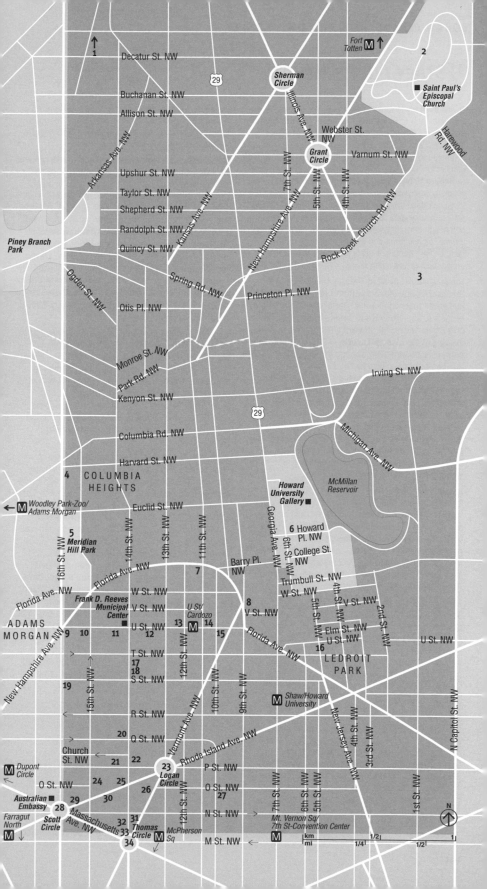

U STREET IN ITS HEYDAY

During the early to mid-1900s, the U Street corridor—an area just north of **Downtown**, bounded by **North Capitol Street** and **15th Street Northwest** and by **M Street Northwest** and **Florida Avenue Northwest**—emerged as a vibrant city neighborhood, a cultural destination, and a magnet for successful black businessmen. The proximity to **Howard University** attracted writers, artists, and scholarly types who found congenial surroundings where they could take up residence. Sadly, the riots of 1968 devastated the area, and nearly 2 decades passed before it underwent an economic revival. Today, a stroll around the neighborhood evokes memories of days gone by and, happily, reveals many new signs of the area's most recent renaissance.

The magnificent **Howard Theater** (Seventh and T Streets NW) opened in 1910 and attracted large audiences to its concert hall, renowned for its superb acoustics. After decades of deterioration, plans are now under way for the Howard's restoration. With the opening of the **Lincoln Theatre** (1215 U Street NW, between 12th and 13th Streets; 328.6000) in 1922, the area became known as "Black Broadway." The annual President's Birthday Balls were held at the Lincoln during the Roosevelt and Truman administrations. First Lady Eleanor Roosevelt once attended with Lucille Ball and Red Skelton by her side. U Street was the place to see and be seen. Thousands came to the neighborhood to hear the likes of Pearl Bailey, Ethel Waters, Nat King Cole, Lena Horne, Ella Fitzgerald, Harry Belafonte, Leontyne Price, Sarah Vaughn, and Sammy Davis Jr.

Jelly Roll Morton opened a club nearby at 1211 U Street Northwest. Duke Ellington lived one block away at 1212 T Street Northwest, and his Washingtonians performed on U Street before moving on to Harlem's Cotton Club. The first internationally acclaimed African-American opera singer, Lillian Evans Tibbs, known as Madame Evanti, lived at 1910 Vermont Avenue NW (at 10th Street), a town house that has remained in the Tibbs family for five generations.

Poets who made their home in the area include Sterling Brown (2464 Sixth Street NW, between Howard Place and Fairmont Street), Paul Laurence Dunbar (321 U Street NW, between Third and Fourth Streets), and Langston Hughes, who lived at the 12th Street YMCA (1816 12th Street NW, between S and T Streets). Jean Toomer wrote his novel *Cane* while residing at 1341 U Street NW (between 13th

and 14th Streets). Other literati drawn to the area included novelist Zora Neale Hurston, historian and publisher Carter G. Woodson, and Howard University philosophy professor Alain Locke.

Robert Terrell, a lawyer and community leader, and his wife, Mary Church Terrell, civil and women's rights activist, lived at 1323 T Street Northwest (between 13th and 14th Streets) and at 1615 S Street Northwest (between 16th and 17th Streets). US Supreme Court Justice Thurgood Marshall once made his home in an apartment at the **Whitelaw Hotel** at 1839 13th Street Northwest (between S and T Streets). Congressman and clergyman Adam Clayton Powell resided at 8 Logan Circle NW. Dr. Charles Drew, a professor and the head of surgery at **Howard University Medical School**, whose plasma discoveries led to the development of blood banks, lived at 328 College Street NW (at Fourth Street).

Mary McLeod Bethune, educator and presidential adviser to FDR, resided at 1318 Vermont Avenue NW (between N Street and Logan Circle). The Victorian row house, now a small museum, is open to the public. The National Archives for Black Women's History, also housed here, includes Bethune's papers and those of the National Council of Negro Women (of which Bethune was both founder and president), and are available by appointment (673.2402).

In recent years, the **U Street/Cardozo Metro** stop, built in 1991, has increased accessibility to the U Street corridor. New restaurants and clubs, like **U-topia** (1418 U Street NW, between 14th and 15th Streets, 483.7669), the **9:30 Club** (815 V Street NW, at Ninth Street; 393.0930), and **Twins Jazz** (1344 U Street NW; 234.0072), have breathed new life into the area. The **Whitelaw Hotel**, designed by **Isaiah T. Hatton**, one of the first African-American architects, was restored in 1991 as an apartment building. The increasingly popular **Ben's Chili Bowl** (1213 U Street NW, between 12th and 13th Streets; 667.0909), in the building that once housed the Minnehaha silent-movie theater and later a pool hall, has become a neighborhood meeting spot and city landmark. Next door, the restored Lincoln Theatre reopened its doors to the public in 1994 and now draws theatergoers and music lovers to the area. As the song goes, here on U Street, almost a century later, "everything old is new again."

---

suicide by drinking her photography chemicals. **Stanford White** designed the grounds. Other local notables interred here are Julius Garfinckel, Henry Lansburg, and Montgomery Blair. Grounds open daily, 7:30AM-dusk. ♦ Webster St NW and Rock Creek Church Rd. 829.0585. Metro: Fort Totten

Within Rock Creek Cemetery:

ST. PAUL'S EPISCOPAL CHURCH

The first church in the area was built on this spot in 1775, 63 years after the congregation had first convened here. Of the **Delos H. Smith** original, only the brick walls remain, owing to a 1921 fire. The Federal splendor of the church—now reconstructed—is best exemplified by several excellent stained-glass windows. ◆ 726.2080. ♿

3 U.S. Soldiers and Airmen's Home (Old Soldiers' Home)

One of the oldest military retirement facilities in the country features a Norman-style fortress (constructed in the mid-1800s) complete with crenellated battlements. It reportedly was built with ransom money that General Winfield Scott exacted from Mexico City during the Mexican-American War in the 1840s. ◆ 3700 N Capitol St (between Irving St NW and Harewood Rd NW). Metro: Fort Totten

4 All Souls Unitarian Church

James Gibb's design for London's St. Martin-in-the-Fields (on Trafalgar Square) has been much copied, but seldom as successfully. Hailed by critics as one of the best re-creations, this church was built in 1924 by the architectural firm **Coolidge and Shattuck**. Following the Unitarian tradition, its simple interior is devoid of religious icons. ◆ 1500 Harvard St NW (at 16th St). 332.5266. ♿ www.all-souls.org. Metro: Columbia Heights

5 Meridian Hill Park (Malcolm X Park)

The southern end of this 12-acre green space is a spectacular sight during warm months. Completed in 1936, "a water staircase," formed by 13 terraced waterfalls, flows down to a large pool; nearby, an even larger lily pond surrounded by benches beckons. Though neighbors have been largely successful in ridding the park of undesirable characters, it's still best to visit during the day. ◆ Bounded by 15th and 16th Sts NW and by W and Euclid Sts NW. Metro: U St/Cardozo

6 Howard University

Founded in 1867 and named for General Oliver O. Howard, one of the school's founders and head of the Freedmen's Bureau, it is one of the more prestigious universities in the nation, with about 10,000 students in schools that include medicine, law, and theology. Among the school's alumni are the late Supreme Court Justice Thurgood Marshall, former Atlanta mayor Andrew Young, actress-dancer Debbie Allen, and author Zora Neale Hurston. The **Founders Library** (806.7250) on the south side of the quadrangle contains black history exhibitions and the **Moorland-Spingarn Research Center** (806.7240), one

of the largest collections of African-American history and culture in the world. ◆ Tours: by appointment. 2400 Sixth St NW (at Howard Pl NW). Information, 806.6100; tours, 806.2755. ♿ www.howard.edu. Metro: Shaw/Howard University

---

Restaurants/Clubs: Red | **Hotels: Purple** | **Shops: Orange** | **Outdoors/Parks: Green** | **Sights/Culture: Blue**

OFF THE WALL

Sure, there's plenty of art located *inside* Washington buildings. But don't miss these works that are proudly displayed on the outside of local structures.

At 1200 U Street NW (on the side of the True Reformer's building), find a tribute to native son **Duke Ellington**. G. Byron Peck's 1997 mural shows Ellington looking over the neighborhood where he grew up and began his career as a jazz musician. The painting is based on a photo on the front of the Duke's autobiography, *Music Is My Mistress*.

Adams Morgan could be considered mural central. Two cows ride bikes along one wall of **City Bikes** (2501 Champlain Street NW). Another Peck mural at 1706

Columbia Road NW reflects the city's ethnic diversity, with images of three parrots (native to South America, Asia, and Africa), an Asian dragon, and African warriors. At 1728 Columbia Road NW, neighborhood teens painted a multicultural vignette adjacent to the neighborhood launderette. But the most controversial work of art has to be the buxom, red-headed babe depicted on the side of the bar **Madam's Organ**. Some find her too risqué; others consider the Madam to be a good representation of the neighborhood's fun-loving scene.

Another glamorous gal also occupies prime real estate in the city. In **Woodley Park**, a larger-than-life Marilyn Monroe looks seductively down Connecticut Avenue.

Within Howard University:

HOWARD UNIVERSITY GALLERY OF ART

Renowned for its dedication to the arts, this gallery holds Italian Renaissance paintings from the **Kress Collections** and a permanent display of African art, as well as works by outstanding African-American artists. Special exhibitions change regularly. ♦ M-F, 9:30AM-4:30PM; Sa, Su, 12:30PM-6PM. 2455 Sixth St NW. 806.7070. ♿

7 FLORIDA AVENUE GRILL

★★$ Down-home Southern cooking is served in this old-style diner. For breakfast, try the scrapple (a Philadelphia specialty), home fries, grits, and biscuits. For lunch or dinner, recommended dishes include the pan-fried chicken, spareribs, or ham hocks, all served with greens or cabbage, sweet potatoes, and beans or rice. The homemade corn muffins can't be beat. ♦ Southern ♦ Tu-Sa, breakfast, lunch, and dinner. 1100 Florida Ave NW (at 11th St). 265.1586. ♿. Metro: U St/Cardozo

8 9:30 CLUB

Named for its original location at 930 F Street, DC's pioneer live music club during the punk era now features top local and national bands—from grunge to glam—including the White Stripes, Paul Westerberg, and George Clinton. ♦ Cover. Hours vary; call ahead. 815 V St NW (at Ninth St). 393.0930. ♿. www.930.com. Metro: U St/Cardozo

9 NANA

This cheerful shop (named for the owner's granny) carries new clothing from Built by Wendy, Levi's, and other hipster brands plus vintage fashions from the 1940s through '80s. There's also a good selection of jewelry,

bags, and other accessories by names like Angela Adams and Lilian Hartman. ♦ M-Sa, noon-7PM; Su, noon-5PM. 1528 U St NW (between 15th and 16th Sts). 667.6955. www.nanadc.com. Metro: U St/Cardozo

10 WILD WOMEN WEAR RED

This brightly painted boutique deals in stylish but comfy women's shoes from names like Camper, Rocket Dog, and Lisa Nading. T-shirts, jewelry, and hats are also sold amid walls decorated with posters of fearless females like Indira Gandhi. ♦ M-Sa, 11AM-7PM; Su, 11AM-5PM. 1512 U St NW (between 15th and 16th Sts). 387.5700. www.wildwomenwearred.com. Metro: U St/Cardozo

10 CAKELOVE

This bakery serves all kinds of treats, but, as the name would suggest, the cakes are the real stars here. Lawyer-turned-baker Warren Errol Brown creates delicious concoctions like Heavenly Hazey (layers of chocolate butter cake, hazelnut chiffon torte, hazelnut meringue, and chocolate custard buttercream) and Susie's a Pink Lady (fresh raspberries, yellow sponge cake, raspberry liqueur, and pink buttercream frosting). He also operates the **Love Café** nearby (1501 U St, 588.7100), a pleasant spot for a cup of coffee and slice of cake. ♦ M-F, 8AM-8PM; Sa, 10AM-6PM; Su, noon-5PM. 1506 U St NW (at 15th St). 588.7100. www.cakelove.com. Metro: U St/Cardozo

11 U-TOPIA

★$$ It's more the atmosphere than the food that makes this stalwart of the new U Street scene worth trying. Live music accompanies an eclectic menu that ranges from lamb couscous to New York sirloin. Other draws include works by local artists on the walls and good martinis. ♦ International ♦ M-F, lunch and dinner; Sa, dinner; Su, brunch and dinner. 1418 U St NW (between 14th and 15th Sts). 483.7669. &. Metro: U St/Cardozo

12 TWINS JAZZ

It's not just a clever name. Twin sisters run this intimate, upstairs club on U Street. Live musicians, from David "Fathead" Newman to Alex Hutchinson, perform nightly, while the kitchen serves American, Ethiopian, and Caribbean cuisine. ♦ Tu-Su. 1344 U St NW (between 13th and 14th Sts). 234.0072. www.twinsjazz.com. Metro: U Street/Cardozo

12 CRÈME CAFÉ LOUNGE

★★★$$ A restaurant of this quality is a surprise find in this rather mixed area. It features a small and understated dining area, and although the menu is limited, it is likely to feature such enticing and interesting dishes as shrimp and grits, meat and Potatoes Americana, and the Nine-Dollar Hot Dog. The wine list is heavy on reds, but also features a variety of sparkling wines. ♦ Modern American ♦ M-Sa, 10AM-8PM. 1322 U Street NW. 234.1884. Metro: U St/Cardozo

13 LINCOLN THEATRE

Following the example set by the **Warner Theatre** located Downtown, this veteran venue for theater, stage shows, and movies has been restored to its original luster. Back in the 1920s and '30s, the theater was an important cultural magnet for the area's flourishing African-American community. Over the years, however, it fell into disrepair, and it finally was shuttered in the 1970s. Today, concerts by the **Count Basie Orchestra**, gospel musicals, and mini film festivals have transformed the theater into the showplace it originally was intended to be. ♦ 1215 U St NW (between 12th and 13th Sts). Box office, 328.6000; tickets, 432.SEAT. &. www.lovethelincoln.org. Metro: U St/Cardozo

13 BEN'S CHILI BOWL

★$ Check out this hole-in-the-wall café that opened in 1958 and is a long-favored (and late-night) hangout of **Howard University** students, civil rights leaders, and musicians. Bill Cosby has been known to stop by when he's in town. The chili dogs are world famous and the chili ranges from reasonably mild to eye-tearingly hot and spicy. ♦ American ♦ No credit cards accepted. M-Sa, breakfast, lunch, and dinner; Su, lunch and dinner. 1213 U St NW (between 12th and 13th Sts). 667.0909. www.benschilibowl.com. Metro: U St/Cardozo

13 THE ISLANDER CARIBBEAN RESTAURANT & LOUNGE

★★★$$ For over 30 years, this attractive place has brought the color and authentic Caribbean ambience of the islands of Trinidad and Tobago to U Street. In a bright and airy dining area, with jazz music on weekends, you can sample the flavor of the islands in such typical dishes as channa, callaloo, exotic mango wings, red snapper, and pineapple shrimp. ♦ Caribbean ♦ Tu-Sa, lunch and dinner; Su, brunch. 1201 U St NW. 234.4971. Metro: U St/Cardozo

14 BOHEMIAN CAVERNS

This famous establishment closed early in 2006. It will be replaced by **Mahogany at Bohemian Caverns**. They promise to continue the traditions first established here in the 1920s. ♦ 2001 11th St NW (at U St). www.mahoganydc.com. Metro: U Street/Cardozo

15 AFRICAN-AMERICAN CIVIL WAR MEMORIAL (SPIRIT OF FREEDOM)

Dedicated in 1998, this memorial honors the 202,145 black soldiers and their 7,000 white officers who served the Union during the Civil War. The Ed Hamilton sculpture *Spirit of Freedom* features a bronze statue of black soldiers before three low semicircular granite walls that bear 166 stainless-steel plaques arranged by regiment with the names of all soldiers in the US Colored Troops. The $2.6 million monument stands in a small park in the Shaw neighborhood, which is named for Robert Gould Shaw, the white commander of the all-black 54th Massachusetts regiment (made famous by the 1989 film *Glory* starring Morgan Freeman and Denzel Washington). A few doors down on U Street, the **African-American Civil War Museum** (1200 U St) displays photos, documents, and artifacts and features a database for looking up soldiers by regiment. ♦ Museum: M-F, 10AM-5PM; Sa, 10AM-2PM. Vermont Ave NW and U St. 667.2667. &. www.afroamcivilwar.org. Metro: U St/Cardozo

16 LEDROIT PARK

In the 1870s, architect **James McGill** designed 64 homes in the picturesque Romantic Revival style, with patterned slate roofs. Fifty or so remain, most of them on the 400 block of U Street and the 500 block of T Street. By 1920 LeDroit Park had become the

LADIES FIRST

While the nation's attention generally focuses on the chief of state, several first ladies have captured their fair share of both press headlines and the public's imagination. Whether owing to a striking fashion sense or a radical political stance—or even just for speaking up when women generally didn't—the White House wives have left their individual marks on both the capital and the country.

1797–1801 Wife of one president and mother of another, **Abigail Smith Adams** rarely stifled a political opinion, freely discussing current events with her typically male dinner guests. Despite her keen intellect, Abigail remains best known for stringing clotheslines through a vacant room in the White House.

1809–1817 While journalists continually tried to rename her Dorothea, **Mrs. James Madison** insisted her name was just plain Dolley. She furthered the Adams style of drawing-room diplomacy well past her days as first lady, for her White House successors—as well as their husbands—sought her social and political opinions until her death in 1849. Always a style-setter, Dolley's trademark was a turban decorated with flowers and feathers.

1845–1849 At 41, the popular **Sarah Childress Polk** took her religion and her new role as first lady seriously, gaining great respect for her conservative standards. The Polks banned dancing and drinking at the White House—the first considered frivolous, the second somewhat sinful. On inauguration night, when the Polks arrived for the celebration, the dancing came to a halt. Following the first couple's 2-hour stay, the music and dancing resumed.

1877–1881 The first president's wife with a college degree, **Lucy Ware Webb Hayes** was an alumna of Wesleyan Female College in Cincinnati, Ohio. Referred to as "Lemonade Lucy" because she forbade even wine to be served at the White House, she brought the Easter Egg Roll to the White House grounds when children were banned from the Capitol lawns.

1885–1889 and 1893–1897 The only first lady to be married in the White House was **Frances Folsom Cleveland**. The president insisted on a small private ceremony inside, but crowds were allowed to peek through the windows.

1889–1893 While replacing a china closet, **Caroline Lavinia Scott Harrison** became interested in the bits and pieces of dinnerware she found, and began a White House collection of past presidents' china. She also served as the first president-general of the newly formed Daughters of the American Revolution.

1909–1913 Not a woman to hide in her husband's shadow, **Helen Herron Taft** set a precedent by riding beside the president in the inaugural procession down Pennsylvania Avenue to the White House. She ignored other conventions as well—allowing her cow, named Mooly-Wolly, to graze the White House lawn, and introducing musicales at state dinners. She also suggested placing cherry trees around the Tidal Basin.

1915–1921 The second wife of President Woodrow Wilson, **Edith Bolling Galt Wilson** proved invaluable to him and to the nation when his health was failing. She allowed few to bother Wilson during his illness, serving

---

premier address for middle-class African-Americans and a center for their businesses and culture. The neighborhood is now a historic district. ♦ Bounded by Second, Fifth, and Elm Sts NW and by Rhode Island and Florida Aves NW. Metro: Shaw/Howard University

17 CAFE SAINT-EX

★★$$ Named after aviator and *The Little Prince* author Antoine de Saint-Exupéry, this newish bistro boasts golden brick walls, a pressed tin ceiling, and aviation-related photos and artifacts. On the menu is American bistro-style fare like a wild mushroom and leek tart, herb-crusted pork loin chop, and mussels in garlic broth. Downstairs, the airplane hangar–inspired **Gate 54** lounge draws urban hipsters for DJ-spun electronica, jazz, funk, and lounge music. ♦ American ♦ M-Th, dinner, bar till 2AM; F, dinner, bar till 3AM; Sa, brunch and dinner, bar till 3AM; Su, brunch and dinner, bar till 2AM. 1847 14th St NW

(at T St). 265.7839. ♿. www.saint-ex.com. Metro: U St/Cardozo

18 GO MAMA GO

On U Street, this eclectic shop offers Asian and other worldly goods like Japanese dinnerware, ceramic giftware (sake sets, tea sets, etc.), Furoshiki (rayon crepe squares that can be used as wall hangings or as scarves), and two-panel Japanese Noren curtains. ♦ M, noon-7PM; Tu-Sa, 11AM-7PM; Su, noon-5PM. 1809 14th St NW (between S and T Sts). 299.0850. www.gomamago.com. Metro: U St/Cardozo

18 BLACK CAT

Indie rockers (from Phantom Planet and Ani DiFranco to Sleater-Kinney and Yo La Tengo) and their fans flock to this club that opened in 1993 and in 2001 moved to a bigger space up the street. Buy tickets in advance at the club's box office (8PM-midnight; cash only) or through Ticketmaster (202/432-SEAT; www.ticketmaster.com). The (no cover) **Red Room Bar** offers Belgian beers, pool tables,

as a de facto president, sending news and policy decisions from him to his administration.

1933-1945 Often criticized and always controversial, **Anna Eleanor Roosevelt** traveled 38,000 miles in her initial year as first lady and kept up the pace throughout her tenure. Known as the "First Lady of the World," Eleanor Roosevelt spoke her mind freely in her syndicated column *My Day*, on radio broadcasts, and in special press conferences for women reporters.

1961-1963 Setting the fashion trends for the 1960s, **Jacqueline Lee Bouvier Kennedy** was the first of the first ladies to appoint a personal dress designer. Women all over the world wore copies of her suit dresses and pillbox hats. Jackie Kennedy also brought culture to the mansion by inviting distinguished guests to perform and be honored.

1974-1977 Known for speaking out on social issues, **Elizabeth "Betty" Bloomer Ford** brought new candor to her office. She helped open up the issues of breast cancer and chemical dependency for public discussion.

1981-1989 The only first lady to hold the office after a film career, **Nancy Davis Reagan** decided to do something with her influence halfway through her husband's administration. She began a personal campaign to educate the country's youth about the dangers of drug abuse, making frequent television appearances and imploring youngsters to "Just Say No" to drugs. Her opinionated nature was one cause of friction between herself and Raisa Gorbachev during a visit to Russia, when she criticized her Soviet counterpart for discounting the religious content of several paintings during a tour.

1989-1993 Known even before her arrival at the White House as the "Silver Fox," **Barbara Pierce Bush** impressed many detractors by demonstrating a self-mocking sense of humor during her first address as first lady. Criticized before the election for her dowdy style—fake pearls and matronly dresses—she paused during her speech to model her latest unremarkable outfit. During George Bush's presidency, she established her own cause: improving literacy in America.

1993-2001 Though other first ladies throughout history may have been equally powerful, only lawyer and activist **Hillary Rodham Clinton** was handed the massive—and daunting—job of trying to reform the national health-care system (because of federal nepotism laws, a volunteer position). Following—and despite—the debacle, the first lady focused her energies on the running of the White House. In fact, it was at her urging that smoking was officially banned there. In November of 2000, she became the only first lady to win a seat in the US Senate and now serves as the junior senator from New York.

2001-2006 It would be hard to find as strong a contrast as there is between **Laura Lane Welch Bush** and her predecessor, Hillary Rodham Clinton. Less flamboyant, but a very strong character, Laura Bush is credited with encouraging her husband to make the decision to stop drinking and change the course of his life in the 1980s. By profession, she is a librarian and has championed educational causes and women's health matters, and started the National Book Festival.

and food by Food for Thought, a longtime neighborhood vegan-vegetarian restaurant that closed in 1999. ◆ Cover. Hours vary; call ahead. 1811 14th St NW (between S and T Sts). 667.7960. www.blackcatdc.com. Metro: U St/Cardozo

18 PULP

Hipper-than-Hallmark cards and pop culture–inspired wrapping paper are just some of the merchandise at this cool stationery store. It's also a great place to pick up gifts, from votive holders shaped like Chinese food take-out boxes to clever calendars. The store holds frequent showings of works by local artists. ◆ M-F, 11AM-7PM; Sa, 10AM-7PM; Su, noon-5PM. 1803 14th St NW (between S and T Sts). 462.7857. www.pulpdc.com. Metro: U St/Cardozo. Also at 303 Pennsylvania Ave SE. 543.1924. Metro: Capitol South

19 TEMPLE OF THE SCOTTISH RITE

In designing this temple, architect **John Russell Pope** was inspired by the Tomb of Mausolus at Halicarnassus in Turkey, one of the Seven Ancient Wonders of the World. He based the proportions of the 1915 building on numbers significant to Masonic mysticism, and it reflects an array of styles, from Egyptian to Roman. The two huge sphinxes that guard the entrance to the shrine, each cut from a solid block of limestone, were sculpted by Alexander Weinman. The temple is now the headquarters of the Supreme Council of the Southern Jurisdiction of the 33rd Degree of the Ancient and Accepted Scottish Rite of Freemasonry. ◆ M-F; closed holidays; groups of 25 or more by special arrangement. Tours: 8AM-2PM. 1733 16th St NW (at S St). 232.8155. www.dcsr.org. Metro: Dupont Cir

Restaurants/Clubs: Red | **Hotels: Purple** | **Shops: Orange** | **Outdoors/Parks: Green** | **Sights/Culture: Blue**

20 RICE

★★$$ At this stylish new Thai restaurant, dark woods and an exposed brick wall set the scene for a menu of both traditional dishes (pad Thai, curries) and contemporary spins on classics (spaghetti with herbs, Thai anchovies, and bacon). A $9 lunch menu is offered daily. ♦ Thai ♦ Daily, lunch and dinner. 1608 14th St NW (between Q and Corcoran Sts). 234.2400. &. www.simplyhomedc.com. Metro: Dupont Cir

21 LOGAN TAVERN

★★$$ Blue wainscoting and black-and-white photos of local landmarks cover the walls at this casual neighborhood spot. A diverse crowd (gays, straights, Gen X-ers, empty nesters) shows up for comfort food with Asian twists (think wasabi-crusted meat loaf, roasted pork loin in sweet Asian mustard). Mismatched plates and cutlery reflect the neighborhood's eclectic vibe. ♦ American ♦ M-Th, dinner; F, lunch and dinner; Sa, Su, brunch and dinner. 1423 P St NW (between 14th and 15th Sts). 332.3710. &. www.logantavern.com. Metro: Dupont Cir

22 STUDIO THEATRE

Half a dozen professional productions a year draw on American and European contemporary works, including such recent hits as Kenneth Lonergan's *Lobby Hero* and *Master Harold and the Boys*. ♦ Studio box office during performance weeks: M, Tu, 10AM-6PM; W-Sa, 10AM-9PM; Su, noon-8PM. During nonperformance weeks: M-F, 10AM-6PM. 1333 P St NW (at 14th St). Information, 232.7267; box office, 332.3300. &. www.studiotheatre.org. Metro: Dupont Cir, U St/Cardozo

22 VIRIDIAN

★★★★$$$ Found in the heart of the old auto row, and right next to the Studio Theatre, the style and décor of this restaurant is reflective of the fact that it used to be a Cadillac dealership. It opened in November 2005 with an array of art for sale and video art screened onto the wall behind the large bar. This place has quickly gained itself a fine reputation. Using only the freshest local seasonal produce, dishes such as Parisian-style gnocchi with mushrooms, fava beans, and spring garlic; soft-shell crab sautéed with buttered ramps; and yellow curry vinaigrette grace the menu. ♦ Contemporary American ♦ Tu-F, lunch and dinner; Sa, Su, brunch. 1515 14th St NW. 234.1400. Metros: Dupont Cir, U St/Cardozo

23 LOGAN CIRCLE

The Victorian and Richardsonian town houses built here between 1875 and 1900 made Logan Circle one of DC's most fashionable addresses. During the early 1900s, the area's racial makeup shifted, and by 1940 the city's most prominent black politicians and other social leaders were living here. Neglect, in the decades that followed, took its toll on the neighborhood, but determined preservationists have restored many of the circle's buildings. The area still has some problems, so it may be best to visit during the daytime. ♦ Metro: Mt. Vernon Sq/UDC, Shaw/Howard University

24 GRACE REFORMED CHURCH

Teddy Roosevelt laid the cornerstone for this church, built in 1903 and designed by **Abner Ritcher**. Presidents Eisenhower and Nixon worshiped here as well. ♦ 1405 15th St NW (between Rhode Island Ave and P St). 387.3131. &. Metro: Dupont Cir

25 IRVINE CONTEMPORARY ART

This gallery represents and exhibits established and emerging artists from the US, Europe, Latin America, and Asia, including John Gasper, Philip Knoll, and Robert Rauschenberg, and specializes in contemporary paintings and works on paper. ♦ Tu-Sa, 10AM-6PM and by appointment. 1412 14th St NW. 332.8767. www.irvinecontemporary.com. Metro: U St/Cardozo

26 MARY MCLEOD BETHUNE COUNCIL HOUSE

Born in South Carolina in 1875, Mary McLeod Bethune was the fifteenth of 17 siblings born to former slaves. She rose to prominence in the field of education as a founder of Bethune-Cookman College in Daytona Beach, Florida. Under Calvin Coolidge and Herbert Hoover, she worked for the National Child Welfare Commission. In 1935 Bethune was named special adviser on minority affairs to the Roosevelt administration and in 1936 as director of the Division of Negro Affairs in the National Youth Administration. She organized African-American officials into the "Black Cabinet," which lobbied for a fair share in New Deal programs, and founded the National Council of Negro Women. This Victorian town house, which served as the council's headquarters between 1943 and 1966, is now a center for black women's history and a National Historic Site. ♦ Free. M-Sa. 1318 Vermont Ave NW (between N St and Logan Cir). 673.2402. www.nps.gov/mamc. Metro: McPherson Sq

27 DC GUESTHOUSE

$$$ Once the site of a funeral home and, later, an art gallery, this spacious Victorian rowhouse-turned-B&B boasts six guest rooms and common areas decorated in a modern, eclectic style that mixes everything from Asian antiques to pieces picked up at discount stores. Amenities include in-room satellite TVs and DVD players, a business center, and

off-street parking. Friendly owners and a convenient location (close to the Washington Convention Center, 14th Street shopping district) add to the appeal. ♦ 1337 10th St NW (between N and O Sts). 332.2502; fax 332.6013. www.dcguesthouse.com. Metro: Mount Vernon Sq

28 SCOTT CIRCLE

General Winfield Scott, whose likeness was sculpted in 1874 by Henry Kirk Brown, rides through the circle, and a statue of Daniel Webster, sculpted in 1900 by Gaetano Trentanove, stands in the small triangular park just to the west. At 1 Scott Circle are the **General Scott Apartments**, designed in 1942 by **Robert O. Scholz**. One of the city's last and best Art Moderne buildings, it also was the first to have central air conditioning. Also of interest, at the end of Embassy Row, in front of Australia's bland modern embassy (1601 Massachusetts Ave NW), note the stylized bronze kangaroo and the emu holding the Australian seal. ♦ Metro: Farragut N, Dupont Cir

29 DOUBLETREE HOTEL, WASHINGTON, DC

$$$ After a spell as the Washington Terrace Hotel, and just a few blocks from the White House, this is once again a Doubletree Hotel. A brand-new boutique-style hotel that seeks to set the standard for such places in DC, it has 220 rooms, including 9 very spacious suites, and corporate-level floors with customized décor and state-of-the-art facilities. ♦ 1515 Rhode Island Ave NW (between 15th St and Scott Cir). 232.7000; fax 332.8436. www.doubletreewashington.com Metros: Farragut N, Dupont Cir

Within the Doubletree Hotel:

15 RIA

★★$$$ A dark wood bar (which serves peach juleps, cherry sidecar martinis, and other such libations), fireplace, and silk drapery-covered walls evoke a retro nightclub feel at this restaurant. The Southern-inspired menu features dishes like blue cheese-crusted sirloin and maple chili-rubbed salmon. It also offers room service for those staying at the hotel. ♦ M-Sa, breakfast, lunch, and dinner; Su, breakfast, brunch, and dinner. Reservations recommended. 742.0015. &. www.15ria.com

30 HOTEL HELIX

$$$ This 178-room, pop culture–obsessed boutique hotel—which includes 18 large suites and 12 specialty rooms—features rooms outfitted with faux-fur bedspreads, platform beds, Pucci-inspired curtains, flat-screen TVs, and lime-green minibars stocked with Altoids and Pop Rocks. Bathrooms sport orange porcelain and stainless-steel sinks. Amenities include room service, in-room spa services, a complimentary Bubbly Hour, a 24-hour exercise room, parking, and concierge service. ♦ 1430 Rhode Island Ave NW (between 14th and 15th Sts). 462.9001, 800/706.1202; fax 332.3519. &. www.hotelhelix.com. Metro: McPherson Sq

31 LUTHER PLACE MEMORIAL CHURCH

This post–Civil War–era house of worship designed by architect **Judson York** is a soaring Gothic Revival structure of red sandstone that provides a fitting balance to the **National City Christian Church** (see below) nearby. ♦ 1226 Vermont Ave NW (between Thomas Cir and N St). 667.1377. &. Metro: McPherson Sq

32 NATIONAL CITY CHRISTIAN CHURCH

The larger-than-life scale of this colonial-style church, designed by **John Russell Pope**, is heightened by its position atop a small knoll. Its perch, coupled with the elegant steeple, makes the church one of the highest buildings in town. Presidents James Garfield and Lyndon Johnson prayed here. ♦ 5 Thomas Cir (between 14th St and Massachusetts Ave). 232.0323. &. www.natcitycc.org. Metro: McPherson Sq

33 WASHINGTON PLAZA

$$$ Rooms and common areas were recently remodeled at this contemporary nine-story hotel. In the expansive lobby find Bauhaus Barcelona chairs and other Art Deco touches. Many of the 340 guest rooms boast views of the outdoor pool. Amenities include in-room movies, 24-hour room service, same-day valet service, an exercise facility, and a gift shop. **No. 10 Thomas Circle** serves American cuisine made with local ingredients; the menu changes daily. The **International** bar is a chic spot for a martini. There's also a seasonal poolside bar. Pets are welcome with advance notice and a refundable $50 deposit at check-in. Children under 18 stay free. ♦ 10 Thomas Cir NW (at M St). 842.1300, 800/424.1140; fax 371.9602. &. www.washingtonplazahotel.com. Metro: McPherson Sq

34 THOMAS CIRCLE

In the center of this busy roundabout stands a sculpture of Major General George H. Thomas, created in 1879 by John Quincy Adams Ward. The statue of the man known as the "Rock of Chickamauga" surveys Downtown DC to the south. ♦ Metro: McPherson Sq

---

Restaurants/Clubs: Red | Hotels: Purple | Shops: Orange | Outdoors/Parks: Green | Sights/Culture: Blue

DUPONT CIRCLE/ADAMS MORGAN

A frequent criticism hurled at the nation's capital is that it lacks "real" neighborhoods—areas of ethnic and economic diversity with friendly cafés, restaurants, bookstores, markets, galleries, and clubs grouped within convenient walking distance. Although this characterization may be somewhat true, there is an area that *does* fit that description: Dupont Circle/Adams Morgan.

East of **Rock Creek Park**, between **Columbia Road** (to the north) and **M Street** (to the south), the urban hiker will discover a section of DC where gleaming office towers give way to rows of brick town houses and stately prewar buildings. Elegant restaurants drawing the power elite sit next to low-rent cafés and funky bars. Vibrant art galleries line leafy **R Street** and a variety of bookstores (some with cozy cafés) cater to all kinds of tastes.

During the 1950s and 1960s, the fountain at Dupont Circle was the center of much "hanging out," which occasionally included people demonstrating against society's various ills. Today, the circle, with its benches and chessboard tables, attracts an eclectic—if less politically minded—crowd, from suited corporate types to spandex-ed bike messengers.

Adams Morgan (north of Dupont Circle) was also once the scene of political activity, but of a different sort. Once known as **Lanier Heights**, the neighborhood gained its current name in the 1950s: After the Supreme Court voted to integrate public schools in *Brown v. the Board of Education of Topeka*, two elementary schools, Adams (white) and Morgan (black), were merged as a symbol of hope. This auspicious union set the tone for what is now the only truly integrated neighborhood in DC.

The gentrification of Adams Morgan began in the 1970s, when urban pioneers, seeking to buy cheap and renovate, took advantage of the incredibly low prices of the area's historic homes. Although many of its black residents moved out around this time, the neighborhood was saved from homogeneity by successive waves of immigration—especially from South American and African countries. During the 1970s and 1980s, the neighborhood also experienced an influx of gay residents, who helped fuel the local club scene. Because of this rich cultural mix, Adams Morgan's restaurants, clubs, and shops reflect a diversity unmatched by any other Washington neighborhood, making it a popular weekend destination for tourists and Washingtonians alike.

Unfortunately, the transit system planners didn't anticipate the area's popularity, and it is a bit of a hike to and from the closest **Metro** stations, **Dupont Circle** and **Woodley Park-Zoo**. Parking can be a major problem here too. But despite transportation woes, most people consider these the city's cutting-edge neighborhoods—and Washington's most authentic neighborhood experience.

1 MAMA AYESHA'S RESTAURANT ROOM

★★$ Formerly called the **Calvert Cafe**, this inexpensive Middle Eastern spot was renamed and renovated after the death of its longtime proprietor. Mama Ayesha's family—still at the helm and serving such veterans as *baba ghannouj*, hummus, and stuffed grape leaves—has added an outdoor café. For a real bargain, make a meal out of appetizers. ◆ Middle Eastern ◆ Daily, lunch and dinner. 1967 Calvert St NW (between Adams Mill Rd and Woodley Pl). 232.5431. &. Metro: Woodley Park-Zoo

2 CHIEF IKE'S MAMBO ROOM

★$ Popular with the twentysomething crowd, this casual bar-restaurant features live blues and alternative rock bands during the week and dancing on weekends. Belly up to the bar and try the Jell-O shooters. ◆ American ◆ M-Th, 4PM-2AM; F, 4PM-3AM; Sa, 6PM-3AM. 1725 Columbia Rd NW (between Quarry and Ontario Rds). 332.2211. www.chefikes.com. &. Metro: Woodley Park-Zoo

3 CITY BIKES

Two former bicycle messengers founded this impressive store, which sells mountain, touring, and hybrid bikes. The service is great too. ♦ M-W and F, Sa, 10AM-7PM; Th, 10AM-9PM; Su, noon-5PM. 2501 Champlain St NW (at Euclid St). 265.1564. ♿. www.citybikes.com. Metro: Woodley Park-Zoo

3 CHURRERIA MADRID

★★$ Washington's first churreria shop has been in existence since 1973, and it's another restaurant whose specialty is Spanish cuisine, offering a wide selection of dishes such as *callos à la Madrileña* (tripe with pigs' trotters, Spanish sausage, and chickpeas), and *pulpo à la Gallega* (octopus Galician style), as well as Spanish subs. The El Toro bar has a daily happy hour from 5PM-7PM. ♦ Tu-Su, lunch and dinner. 2505 Champlain St NW (at Euclid St). 483.4441. Metro: Woodley Park-Zoo

4 INTER-AMERICAN DEFENSE BOARD

This 1906 building by **George Oakley Totten Jr.** is also known as the "Pink Palace." It's a Gothic version of the Ducal Palace in Venice, Italy (note the windows), but the massing is somewhat awkward. ♦ 2600 16th St NW (at Euclid St). Metros: Woodley Park-Zoo, U St/Cardozo

5 CASHION'S EAT PLACE

★★★$$$ At this casual New American eatery, owner-chef Ann Cashion takes success personally: She handwrites the frequently changing menu, adorns the walls with personal photos, and injects her impeccable taste into the culinary selections. Always fresh and adventurous, her specialty dishes might include lamb seared with eggplant and garlic or duck breast with sour cherries. ♦ American ♦ Tu-Sa, dinner; Su, brunch and dinner. 1819 Columbia Rd NW (between Mintwood Pl and Biltmore St). 797.1819. www.cashionseatplace.com. Metro: Woodley Park-Zoo

5 PERRY'S

★★$$ Brightly colored and imaginatively arranged sushi is served here, along with other tempting offerings. The atmosphere is stylish, and the pleasant rooftop deck always draws crowds. The popular Sunday drag brunch draws a lively mix of gay and straight locals. ♦ Japanese/American ♦ Daily, dinner.

1811 Columbia Rd NW (between Mintwood Pl and Biltmore St). 234.6218. www.perrysadamsmorgan.com. Metro: Woodley Park-Zoo

6 MIXTEC

★★$ Ebullient owner Pepe Montesinos offers spit-roasted chicken and freshly squeezed fruit drinks on his extensive menu of Mexican specialties—grilled pork, soft tacos, burritos, and the like. The food—always fresh—is an excellent value. ♦ Mexican ♦ Daily, lunch and dinner. 1792 Columbia Rd NW (at 18th St). 332.1011. Metro: Woodley Park-Zoo

7 EL RINCON ESPAÑOL

★★★$$$ Established in 1977, this delightful restaurant is very close to City Bikes, and serves traditional Spanish favorites such as *gambas al ajillo*, *chuletas de cerdo*, and *zarzuelas de mariscos*, along with a variety of paellas and a fine selection of Mexican and Latin American cuisine. ♦ Tu-Su, lunch and dinner 1826 Columbia Rd NW (between Belmont Rd and 18th St). 265.4943. Metro: Woodley Park-Zoo

8 SAKI

★$$ As its name suggests, this mod restaurant/lounge serves sake by the shot, carafe, or bottle. It also offers a menu of sushi and fusion fare like Asian lamb chops and garlic shrimp. In the lounge area, patrons mingle amid the Space Age-y décor and changing colored lights and nightly DJs play cutting-edge music from Europe, Latin America, and Asia. ♦ Asian ♦ Su-Th, dinner, bar till 2AM; F, Sa, dinner, bar till 3AM. 2477 18th St NW (between Kalorama and Columbia Rds). 232.5005. ♿. www.sakidc.com. Metro: Woodley Park-Zoo

8 MISS PIXIE'S FURNISHINGS & WHATNOT

Resembling a favorite aunt's attic, this wonderful little antiques shop is run by Pixie Windsor, who often bakes cookies for her customers. Furniture, books, glassware, oddball art, and other reasonably priced goods fill one and a half stories. ♦ Th, noon-9PM; F-Su, noon-7PM. 2473 18th St NW (between Kalorama and Columbia Rds). 232.8171. www.misspixies.com. Metro: Woodley Park-Zoo.

8 TRYST

★★★$$ This hip coffee bar attracts a mix of twenty-somethings, students, politicos, and writers. The furniture—circa 1950—is arranged living room-style, and in warm weather, French doors open to the street. Beyond superb coffee, light and

homey fare—including bowls of cereal, muffins, and cookies—plus beer and wine are served. ◆ American ◆ M-Sa, 6:30AM-2AM; Su, 7AM-2AM. 2459 18th St NW (between Kalorama and Columbia Rds). 232.5500; fax 232.5508. www.trystdc.com. ♿. Metro: Woodley Park-Zoo

8 THE DINER

★★$ In a former auto parts store, this popular 24-hour spot serves up omelettes, pancakes, burgers, and comfort food like meat loaf and mac and cheese at a retro counter or booths. ◆ Daily, 24 hours. 2453 18th St NW (between Kalorama and Columbia Rds). 232.8800. Metro: Woodley Park-Zoo

9 KALORAMA GUEST HOUSE

$ For budget-minded travelers, these four Victorian town houses (three at Adams Morgan, one in Woodley Park) are a fine choice. The rooms are charmingly outfitted with such details as brass beds, thick comforters, and late-Victorian antiques. Only about half of the rooms have private baths, however, and there's no restaurant. ◆ 1854 Mintwood Pl NW (between Columbia Rd and 19th St). 667.6369. Metro: Woodley Park-Zoo. Also at 2700 Cathedral Ave NW (at 27th St). 328.0860. www.kaloramaguesthouse.com. Metro: Woodley Park-Zoo

10 BEDROCK BILLIARDS

Several years ago, this was one of the only decent pool halls in Washington. It's got more competition now, and with only seven tables available there's often a wait, but it has terrific atmosphere, beer, munchies—and board games like Scrabble and Battleship to divert you. No one under 21 allowed. ◆ M-Th, 4PM-2AM; F, 4PM-3AM; Sa, 1PM-3AM; Su, 1PM-2AM. 1841 Columbia Rd NW (between Mintwood Pl and Biltmore St). 667.7665. www.bedrockbilliards.com. Metro: Woodley Park-Zoo

10 FLEET FEET

If you're craving exercise while vacationing but left your gear at home, this place is for you. A neighborhood institution (formerly across the street), the little store carries all kinds of athletic shoes and workout wear and has a knowledgeable staff. ◆ M-F, 10AM-8PM; Sa, 10AM-7PM; Su, noon-4PM. 1841 Columbia Rd NW (between Mintwood Pl and Biltmore St). 387.3888. ♿. www.fleetfeet.com. Metro: Woodley Park-Zoo

10 MANTIS

★★$$ Floor-to-ceiling windows provide views of the happening neighborhood at this intimate white-walled lounge. Sleek silver stools surround a dark wood bar, and an outdoor patio provides additional seating options in warm weather. Urbanites come here to sip martinis and share Asian small plates, then head to the basement area where they groove to DJ-spun tunes. ◆ Su-Th, dinner, bar till 1:30AM; F, Sa, dinner, bar till 2:30AM. 1847 Columbia Rd NW (at Mintwood Pl). 667.2400. Metro: Woodley Park-Zoo

11 MESKEREM

★★$ Sit at a woven-straw table and dine on specialties such as *kitfo* (a spicy steak tartare) and shrimp *watt* (shrimp cooked in fiery spices). When the balcony is open, diners sit Ethiopian style—atop leather cushions on the floor. ◆ Ethiopian ◆ Daily, lunch and dinner. Reservations recommended on weekends. 2434 18th St NW (between Belmont and Columbia Rds). 462.4100. www.meskeremonline.com. ♿. Metro: Woodley Park-Zoo

11 THE REEF

You might say there's something fishy about this place. There's a theme, but it's subtle enough that it works. Tanks of tropical fish separate the booths, the walls are painted ocean blue, and faux coral columns rise up from behind the bar. Floor-to-ceiling windows provide great views of all the action down on 18th Street. (The bar's on the second floor.) ◆ M-Th, 4PM-2AM; F, Sa, 5PM-3AM; Su, 11AM-3PM and 4PM-2AM. 2446 18th St NW. 518.3800. Metro: Woodley Park-Zoo (between Belmont and Columbia Rds)

12 SHAKE YOUR BOOTY

This chic shop, unmissable with its bright pink coloring, blends high fashion with superb craftsmanship in its unique selection of shoes, bags, and jewelry. European imports and cutting-edge American styles round out the stock. ◆ M-F, noon-8PM; Sa, noon-9PM; Su, noon-6PM. 2439 18th St NW (between Kalorama and Columbia Rds). 518.8205. Metro: Woodley Park-Zoo

12 LA FOURCHETTE

★★$$ Graced with tasteful floor-to-ceiling murals of French café scenes, this bistro serves such daily specials as bouillabaisse, duck, rabbit, and lobster with beurre blanc and a julienne of vegetables. ◆ French ◆ M-F, lunch and dinner; Sa, Su, brunch and dinner. 2429 18th St NW (between Kalorama and Columbia Rds). 332.3077. ♿. Metro: Woodley Park-Zoo

ALTERNATIVE AVENUES

Yes, DC has lots of lawyers and politicians and other folks who tend to lean toward the conservative. But it also has an active gay community, supported by a host of bars, restaurants, shops, and organizations. Just don't expect flamboyance and flash. Like the rest of the city, DC's gay residents also tend to be on the conservative side.

The epicenter of DC gay life is **Dupont Circle**. Around the 17th Street corridor, bars like **Chaos**, **30 Degrees**, and **J.R.'s** always have something going on—a dance party, drag bingo, cabaret shows, and the like. To prepare for a night on the town, male fashion plates shop at **Universal Gear** for the latest looks by Jocko, Energie, and French Connection. On Connecticut Avenue NW, **Lambda Rising** offers a wide selection of gay and lesbian books; the lounge **Gazuza** offers excellent people watching from a second-story outdoor patio.

There's always a scene in funky **Adams Morgan**, but on Sundays **Perry's** kicks things up a notch with its popular drag brunch. While diners feast on a traditional buffet brunch, drag queen performers take to the stage, grabbing a microphone for a little karaoke. It's quite a show.

Gays and lesbians from all over the country (and sometimes the world) meet in DC several times a year for special annual events. In late January, the **Centaur Motorcycle Club** (388.1010; www.centaurmc.org) sponsors the **Mid-Atlantic Leather Weekend**, which features a bevy of parties, dances, and brunches; ditto for the 3-day **Cherry**, run by the Cherry Fund (489.4209; www.cherryfund.com), in late April.

Every Memorial Day weekend, about 10,000 black lesbians and gay men flock to the nation's capital for **Black Lesbian and Gay Pride Day** (866/942.5473; www.dcblackpride.org), the largest event of its kind. What began as a 1-day affair has now become 4 days of festivities with parties, a film festival, a wellness expo, and other events.

For almost 30 years the **Capital Pride Festival** (661.7026; www.capitalpride.org) has celebrated gay, lesbian, and transgender life. Every June, a week of concerts and events (often benefiting area AIDS organizations such as the **Whitman-Walker Clinic**) culminates with a parade down Pennsylvania Avenue NW and a street festival with vendors and performers.

The full-length **Reel Affirmations Film Festival** (986.1119; www.reelaffirmations.org) takes place in October; **AIDS Walk Washington, DC** (332.9255; www.aidswalkwashington.org) is held in late September or early October.

Before you travel to DC, there are plenty of places you can go to find out about dining, shopping, and special events. For more than 30 years the **Washington Blade** (www.washblade.com) has served as the local gay community's source of weekly news. The paper provides the lowdown on everything from arts and entertainment to local and national issues.

And the **Washington, DC Convention & Tourism Corporation** publishes an informative Gay and Lesbian Travelers Guide. To obtain a copy, call 789.7000 or visit www.washington.org.

13 LEFTBANK

★★$ In the former **Cities** restaurant space, owner Sahir Erozan has opened this "wired bistro lounge" that boasts mod, minimalist décor, roving bartenders who mix drinks tableside, a high-tech sound-and-light system, and a high-speed wireless Internet network. The well-priced fusion menu includes everything from buffalo burgers and roasted lobster Parmesan to sushi and scallop ceviche. ♦ Daily, breakfast, lunch, and dinner; bar till 2AM Su-Th, till 3AM F, Sa. 2424 18th St NW (between Belmont and Columbia Rds). 464.2100. ঙ. Metro: Woodley Park-Zoo

13 FELIX RESTAURANT AND BAR

★★★$$$ This hopping establishment combines a cool dancing spot with a restaurant serving modern American cuisine. House specialties include the Friday "Kosher style" dinner with matzoh ball soup and beef brisket. On other nights, the grilled pork chop and

fettuccine with mushrooms, tomato, and shaved Parmesan are good bets. Save room for a brownie with ice cream and whipped cream, or grilled banana with caramel. Then burn it off with late-evening dancing to live jazz or swing bands. Felix extended into the building next door, opening **The Spy Lounge** (2408 18th Street NW). A smallish space with white walls and funky couches serves as the setting for DJ-spun tunes. ♦ American ♦ Daily, dinner. 2406 18th St NW (between Belmont and Columbia Rds). 483.3549. ঙ. www.thefelix.com. Metro: Woodley Park-Zoo

13 PRINCE CAFÉ

★★★$ This is a trendy lounge with a wide variety of Mediterranean, Indian, Pakistani, and tandoori cuisine at very reasonable prices. It also offers over 30 different tobacco flavors to select from and a delightful streetside patio. With very late hours, it is a favorite spot for night dwellers. Don't be surprised when you find no alcohol on the menu—a religious policy of the owners. ◆ Su-W, 11AM-3AM; Th-Sa, 11AM-5AM. 2400 18th St NW (at Belmont Rd). 667.1200. www.cafeprince.com. Metro: Woodley Park-Zoo

14 TOLEDO LOUNGE

★$ This down-home spot decorated with vintage American signs and murals done in the style of Works Project Administration artists draws low-key beer lovers. On the menu, find basic bar food like burgers, sandwiches, and salads. ◆ American ◆ Daily, dinner. 2435 18th St NW (between Kalorama and Columbia Rds). 986.5416. Metro: Woodley Park-Zoo

15 GRILL FROM IPANEMA

★★$$ There's a lot to enjoy about this popular restaurant. The Brazilian fish dishes are excellently prepared; try the fresh seafood stews, marinated grilled fish, or *feijoada* (black-bean stew). The tropical drinks taste great, but they pack quite a punch; stand forewarned, or you might find it difficult to stand at all. After 11PM, this spot is jumpin'. ◆ Brazilian ◆ M-F, dinner; Sa, Su, lunch and dinner. 1858 Columbia Rd NW (at Kalorama Rd). 986.0757. Metro: Woodley Park-Zoo

16 BRASS KNOB ARCHITECTURAL ANTIQUES

Architectural leftovers from old American homes fill this two-story shop. Among the minute details are a wide assortment of doorknobs, house letters, and mailboxes, but it's the chandeliers—from Victorian to 1950s models—that shine here. ◆ M-Sa, 10:30AM-6PM; Su, noon-5PM. 2311 18th St NW (between Kalorama and Columbia Rds). 332.3370. www.thebrassknob.com. Metro: Woodley Park-Zoo

17 MERIDIAN HOUSE

John Russell Pope built this limestone-faced, Louis XVI-style town house for Irwin Boyle Laughlin, a former ambassador to Spain and member of the Pittsburgh steel family. The entrance hall, loggia, and dining room are particularly impressive. Since 1960, the mansion has been home to the **Meridian International Center**, a nonprofit foundation that promotes international understanding through exhibits, concerts, and other cultural events, as well as tours and seminars for thousands of visitors to the US each year. ◆ 1630 Crescent Pl NW (between 16th and 17th Sts). 667.6800. ⑤. www.meridian.org. Metro: U St/Cardozo

Next door to the Meridian House:

WHITE-MEYER HOUSE

Another **John Russell Pope** creation, this Georgian-style mansion was constructed in 1912 for Ambassador Henry White, an American diplomat; the **Meridian International Center** annexed it in 1987. Together, this and the **Meridian House** form a block-long international campus. Most Meridian art exhibits are at the White-Meyer House. Free. W-Su, 2-5PM. ◆ 1624 Crescent Pl NW. 667.6800. www.meridian.org

18 THE LINDENS

Designed in 1754 for **Robert Hooper**, this New England–style Georgian house is, in fact, the oldest in Washington. But it didn't have a DC address until the mid-1930s, when it was disassembled and moved from its original spot in Danvers, Massachusetts. So, according to how you phrase it, the runner-up, Georgetown's **Old Stone House**, could get the title on a technicality. ◆ 2401 Kalorama Rd NW (at Kalorama Cir). Metro: Dupont Cir

19 TAFT BRIDGE INN

$$ This Georgian-style bed-and-breakfast is a charming alternative to cookie-cutter grand hotels. Each of the 12 guest rooms is individually decorated with antiques. Six rooms have private baths, four have fireplaces. Guests also have use of a paneled drawing room, porticoed porch, and garden. Amenities include laundry and housekeeping services, parking, and complimentary breakfast. ◆ 2007 Wyoming Ave NW (between 20th St and Connecticut Ave). 387.2007, fax 387.5019. www.taftbridgeinn.com. Metros: Dupont Cir, Woodley Park-Zoo

20 ADDISU GEBEYA

Wander in here for a taste of Ethiopia. Exotic spices, such as *awaze*, *mitmita*, and *berbere*, as well as the popular *injera* (foamy-textured round bread), are sold here. Books and CDs are also available. ◆ Daily, 9AM-9PM. 2202 18th St NW (between Wyoming Ave and Kalorama Rd). 986.6013. Metros: Dupont Cir, Woodley Park-Zoo

21 SKYNEAR AND COMPANY

Find here a collection of hand-painted furniture pieces, elaborate birdcages, leopard-print chairs and sculptures, animal statues, and other assorted household furnishings in a variety of funky, ornate, even neoclassical styles. Some of the stuff's really weird; some of it, truly beautiful. ◆ M-Sa, 11AM-7PM; Su, noon-6PM. 2122 18th St NW. 797.7160.

Restaurants/Clubs: Red | Hotels: Purple | Shops: Orange | Outdoors/Parks: Green | Sights/Culture: Blue

www.skynearonline.com. &. Metros: Dupont Cir, Woodley Park-Zoo

22 ISLAMIC CENTER

A collaborative effort by the various Islamic nations that maintain embassies in Washington, this cultural and religious center is one of the most interesting sights in town. The white limestone building is filled with fine craftworks by Middle Eastern artisans, including an ebony pulpit inlaid with ivory, stained-glass windows, and Persian carpets. The mosque, in the center of a courtyard, faces Mecca, and a 160-foot minaret rises above the complex. Among the most active in the country, the congregation comprises Muslims from more than 40 countries. The center publishes informative literature and conducts lectures; a bookstore is on the premises. Tours may be arranged by request. ♦ 2551 Massachusetts Ave NW (at Belmont Rd). 332.8343. &. Metro: Dupont Cir

23 JURYS NORMANDY INN

$$ Visiting French officials appreciate the charm of this 75-room hotel, with its pleasant patio and Tuesday evening wine-and-cheese receptions. The hotel was remodeled in 1993, but there is no restaurant. No-smoking rooms are available, and children under 12 stay free. ♦ 2118 Wyoming Ave NW (between Connecticut Ave and 23rd St). 483.1350, 800/424.3729; fax 387.8241. &. Metro: Dupont Cir

24 EL TAMARINDO

★$ There's nothing fancy here, just good Mexican and Salvadoran food, cold beer, and tables that can seat large parties. Not on the tourist circuit, this spot attracts a local crowd. ♦ Mexican/Salvadoran ♦ Daily, lunch and dinner. 1785 Florida Ave NW (between U and California Sts). 328.3660. &. Metro: Dupont Cir. Also at 7333 Georgia Ave NW (at Geranium St). 291.0525. &. Metro: Takoma

25 CHI-CHA LOUNGE

★★$ One of DC's hippest bars, this U Street spot serves Andean cuisine and drinks in eclectically decorated rooms. DJs spin tunes on weekends; on weeknights, find live bands playing everything from Latin jazz to Chilean folk music. ♦ South American ♦ Daily, dinner. 1624 U St NW (between 16th and 17th Sts). 234.8400; www.latinconcepts.com. Metro: U St/Cardozo

25 STETSON'S

★$ The closest thing in DC to a real live Texas bar, this local hangout is the place for burgers, enchiladas, and the like. There's a pool table upstairs. ♦ Tex-Mex ♦ Daily, dinner. 1610 U St NW (between New Hampshire Ave and 17th St). 667.6295. Metros: Dupont Cir, U St/Cardozo

26 JAPANESE EMBASSY

With its iron gates and austere courtyard, the original chancery building, built in 1932, manages to look at once neo-Georgian and Japanese. Although the embassy isn't open to the public, a branch of it, the **Japan Information and Culture Center** (1155 21st St NW, between L and M Sts; 238.6949) hosts art shows, lectures, and musical performances. ♦ 2520 Massachusetts Ave NW (between Sheridan Cir and Waterside Dr). Metro: Dupont Cir

27 COURTYARD WASHINGTON NORTHWEST

$$$$ Here the lobby sports an old English look with dark woods and chandeliers. This well-situated hotel offers 147 rooms, room service, an outdoor swimming pool, an exercise room, off-street parking, and a dining room. ♦ 1900 Connecticut Ave NW (at Leroy Pl). 332.9300, 800/321.2211; fax 328.7039. &. Metro: Dupont Cir

28 HILTON WASHINGTON

$$$$ Still remembered primarily as the place where John Hinckley shot Ronald Reagan in 1981, this huge property is always filled with conventioneers. A multilingual staff, several restaurants and lounges, a poolside bar, and an exercise room are among the amenities offered here. The lighted tennis courts and Olympic-size outdoor pool are open to hotel guests and health club members. No-smoking rooms are available, and children under 18 stay free. ♦ 1919 Connecticut Ave NW (at Columbia Rd). 483.3000, 800/HILTONS; fax 232.0438. www.hilton.com. Metro: Dupont Cir

29 GUBI XI

Abstract sculptor David Smith used steel, nickel, and chrome to fashion this powerful and startling work. Standing 11 feet tall, these squares and rectangles of gleaming

THE BEST

Betsy Fisher

Owner, Betsy Fisher Boutique

My small daughters and I attend the **Dupont Circle Sunday Farmer's Market** religiously, drawn by the enchanting makeover of a quotidian urban corner into a community bound by appreciation of earth's abundance and the skill of the artisans who offer cheeses, soaps, goat-hair yarn, exquisite bouquets, pies, and sorbets. After filling our bags, we plop on the curb to listen to Andean music or dance to the fiddle and banjo. The girls consider the morning perfect if we stop at **Firehook Bakery** on 20th Street NW for cinnamon coffee cake before wading into the crowds. The Firehook bread selection has no equal.

Because I shop for a living, filling my store, **Betsy Fisher**, with a unique blend of contemporary clothes, shoes, and accessories, it takes atmosphere and selection to get me to shop for pleasure. I head to **Miss Pixie's** when I'm in Adams Morgan to browse through two floors of her fabulous finds of furniture and knickknacks. We once discovered a bag of small vintage hats, just right for the girls' dress-up fests.

The **U Street** corridor near 15th Street NW requires consecutive stops at **Wild Women Wear Red**, to savor the selection of stylish shoes; **Habitat**, for pieces for the home or unusual jewelry at great prices; and **Cakelove**, where choosing between a cupcake and a slice of one of the specialty cakes can mean getting both.

The whole family takes advantage of the **Rock Creek Park Nature Center**, which offers a program almost daily, including kid-friendly lectures in the small planetarium and hikes throughout the enormous and beautiful park. We use the **Horse Center** for riding lessons and pony rides and sometimes just to visit and pat the horses.

My husband's and my favorite mellow date is a walk that starts in **Cleveland Park**, making sure to amble around 33rd Place NW, where we ogle the ornate Victorian homes. We stroll down Newark to Connecticut Avenue and head south, passing the **Zoo** entrance on our way to Calvert Street, where we head to Adams Morgan for a tryst at **Tryst**, an iconic coffee shop, and then down to 17th Street, where we stop at **Restorations** to see nifty furniture. By then we're ready for something serious to eat, and we head to **Johnny's Half Shell** or **Cashion's Eat Place**, where the ambience and quality of food make the prices worthwhile.

---

metal—perched above a reflecting pool—seem to hold the force of gravity at bay. ◆ Universal North Bldg, 1875 Connecticut Ave NW (between Florida Ave and T St). Metro: Dupont Cir

30 LAURIOL PLAZA

★★$$ The Spanish fare at this modern, airy—if sometimes noisy—café is taking on something of a Tex-Mex accent. The fajitas are wonderful, but don't overlook some of the best Spanish offerings, including roast pork and garlic chicken. When it's warm, dine on the sidewalk terrace or rooftop. ◆ Spanish/ Tex-Mex ◆ Daily, lunch and dinner. 1835 18th St NW (between S and Swann Sts). 387.0035. www.lauriolplaza.com. ᕕ. Metro: Dupont Cir

31 WOODROW WILSON HOUSE

Wilson's onetime home now serves as DC's only presidential museum. His distinguished career—as author, college professor, president of Princeton University, governor of New Jersey, and twenty-eighth US president—is covered in exhibitions and photographs. Objects from the **White House**, memorabilia, gifts from heads of state, and 1920s furnishings are also on view. The museum sponsors special events, including walking tours of the surrounding Kalorama neighborhood, a Christmas open house 1920s style, and Veterans Day services. The Georgian

Revival house was built in 1915 by **Waddy B. Wood**. ◆ Admission. Tu-Su, 10AM-4PM. 2340 S St NW (between Phelps Pl and 24th St). 387.4062. ᕕ. www.woodrowwilsonhouse.org. Metro: Dupont Cir

THE TEXTILE MUSEUM

32 TEXTILE MUSEUM

In 1896, George H. Myers purchased an Oriental rug for his college room and began a lifelong fascination with the art of textiles. In 1925, he turned his home and rich collection—by then consisting of more than 16,000 textiles and rugs—into this privately endowed showcase. The articles on display come from all over the world—the Mediterranean, North Africa, the Near and Far East, and Central and South America. His collection is now housed in a 1912 building designed by **John Russell Pope** and an adjoining 1908 building by **Waddy B. Wood**. The museum's 18,000-book resource library on textiles is open between 10AM and 2PM Wednesday through Friday and between

---

Restaurants/Clubs: Red | Hotels: Purple | Shops: Orange | Outdoors/Parks: Green | Sights/Culture: Blue

10AM and 4PM Saturday. The gift shop, housed in Myers's old library, offers textiles, publications, and more. Call for information on special exhibitions, lectures, and workshops. ♦ Donation. M-Sa, 10AM-5PM; Su, 1-5PM. 2320 S St NW (between Phelps Pl and 24th St). 667.0441. ♿. www.textilemuseum.org. Metro: Dupont Cir

33 DECATUR TERRACE

Marking the terminus of 22nd Street is a delightful staircase and fountain. ♦ Decatur Pl NW (between Florida and Massachusetts Aves). Metro: Dupont Cir

34 FRIENDS MEETING HOUSE OF WASHINGTON

Designed in 1930 by **Walter H. Price**, this simple, slate-roofed stone building, reminiscent of a country cottage, eloquently embodies the Quakers' disdain for ostentation. President Herbert Hoover and his wife worshiped here. ♦ 2111 Florida Ave NW (between Decatur and Phelps Pls). 483.3310. ♿. Metro: Dupont Cir

35 RUTH'S CHRIS STEAKHOUSE

★★$$$ Carnivore heaven, this dining room gives its chief rivals—**The Palm** and **Morton's of Chicago**—some serious competition. The prices here are a bit more reasonable; the atmosphere, less exclusive and clubby. ♦ Steak house ♦ Daily, dinner. 1801 Connecticut Ave NW (at S St). 797.0033. ♿. www.ruthschris.com. Metro: Dupont Cir. Also at 2231 Crystal Dr (at S 23rd St), Arlington, Virginia. 703/979.7275. ♿. Metro: Crystal City; 7315 Wisconsin Ave, Bethesda, Maryland. 301/652.7877. Metro: Bethesda; and 724 Ninth St NW. 393.4488. Metro: Gallery Pl/Chinatown

The Newsroom

35 THE NEWSROOM

In a town of diplomats, politicians, and media junkies, this shop's comprehensive collection of out-of-town and foreign newspapers and magazines is a local necessity. ♦ Daily, 7AM-9PM. 1803 Connecticut Ave NW (at S St). 332.1489. ♿. Metro: Dupont Cir

When he was called a "two-faced man" in a debate with Stephen A. Douglas, future president Abraham Lincoln replied, "If I had another face, do you think I would wear this one?"

36 CONNER CONTEMPORARY ART

With an emphasis on photography, sculpture, and digital media, this second-floor gallery represents artists like Jasper Johns, Annie Leibovitz, and Robert Rauschenberg. ♦ Tu-Sa, 11AM-6PM; Su, M, by appt. 1730 Connecticut Ave NW (between R and S Sts). 588.8750. www.connercontemporary.com. Metro: Dupont Cir

37 GINZA

Futons, kimonos, shoji screens, lamps, jewelry, porcelain, and other typically graceful Japanese crafts are sold here. ♦ M-F, 11AM-7PM; Sa, 11AM-7:30PM; Su, noon-6PM. 1721 Connecticut Ave NW (between R and S Sts). 331.7991. ♿. Metro: Dupont Cir

37 CITY LIGHTS OF CHINA

★★★$$ Although it looks unassuming, this place just may be the best Chinese eatery in town. The ingredients are always fresh, the portions are large, and the preparation (especially of shrimp and scallops) is expert. The always perfect Peking duck, eggplant with garlic, and salt-baked shrimp are standouts on a huge menu. ♦ Chinese ♦ Daily, lunch and dinner. Reservations recommended. 1731 Connecticut Ave NW (between R and S Sts). 265.6688. www.citylightsofchina.com. Metro: Dupont Cir. Also at 4820 Bethesda Ave, Bethesda, Maryland. 301/913.9501. Metro: Bethesda

38 GEOFFREY DINER GALLERY

This is one of the city's top showcases for furniture and artwork in the American and English Arts and Crafts style, which was popular at the turn of the 19th century. You might find an exhibit of exquisite Tiffany lamps or furnishings by the famous California designers Greene & Greene. ♦ By appointment only. 1730 21st St NW (between R St and Florida Ave). 483.5005. www.dinergallery.com. Metro: Dupont Cir

39 RESTAURANT NORA

★★★$$$ The US's first organically certified restaurant serves high-quality American cuisine—homegrown herbs, organic vegetables, and additive-free meats—in a lovely, country-style dining room and a glass-enclosed courtyard. The menu changes daily; try the rockfish with lobster mashed potatoes or pork with cumin if available. Although it's a

THE BEST

Allan Stypeck

President, Second Story Books, Inc., and Senior Appraiser, American Society of Appraisers

Take in the mosaics and murals with literary themes and domed reading room inside the **Library of Congress**'s rococo **Jefferson Building**. Just one block up on First Street, enjoy a good lunch and great desserts in the **US Supreme Court**'s public dining area.

Detour off the beaten path to the **Mexican Cultural Center** (adjacent to the embassy on 16th Street) for murals, paintings, and sculptures set in a beautiful interior.

For exquisite textiles from everywhere in the world other than North America and Western Europe, visit the **Textile Museum** on S Street NW (great gift shop). It is located in **Kalorama**, a neighborhood dotted with

majestic embassy residences and great for quiet strolls. Just east on S Street are steps leading down the hill past a secluded lion's-head fountain. Around the corner is the **Phillips Collection** of Impressionist Art (cozy lunchroom in basement), and directly across **Massachusetts Avenue** is the **Anderson House/Society of the Cincinnati** museum and library. This imposing mansion is an impressive repository of military history with special emphasis on the Revolutionary War. Take a moment to contemplate the tranquil, if out-of-place, Buddhist garden in the back.

In upper **Georgetown**, visit the **Pre-Columbian Collection** at **Dumbarton Oaks**. Nearby on **Wisconsin Avenue**, **Germaine's** has great Vietnamese food.

Canoe or kayak on the **Potomac**, change into clean clothes, and walk across **MacArthur Boulevard** for a memorable yet pricey lunch or dinner on the patio of **Old Angler's Inn**.

favorite among the famous, from the *Washington Post*'s Ben Bradlee to former President Clinton, the atmosphere and service remain decidedly democratic with a small *d*. ♦ American ♦ M-Sa, dinner. Reservations recommended. 2132 Florida Ave NW (at R St). 462.5143. www.noras.com. Metro: Dupont Cir

40 ODÉON

★$$ The portions are large and the pasta is well prepared at this funky restaurant. The drawback is that the tables are too close together. On weekends, when the restaurant gets crowded, you may be an unwilling eavesdropper on the dinner conversations around you. ♦ Italian ♦ M-F, lunch and dinner; Sa, Su, brunch and dinner. 1714 Connecticut Ave NW (between R and S Sts). 328.6228 Metro: Dupont Cir

40 TEAISM

★$ Stark, yet serene, this two-level teahouse serves all types of teas—black, oolong, green, and more. The iced mint tea is a bracing refresher on a hot day. Also available are

Japanese bento box assortments, kabobs, ostrich and veggie burgers, curries, and desserts. ♦ International ♦ Daily, breakfast, lunch, and dinner. 2009 R St NW (at Connecticut Ave). 667.3827. www.teaism.com. Metro: Dupont Cir. Also at 800 Connecticut Ave NW. 835.2233. Metro: Farragut W; and at 400 8th St NW. 638.6010. Metro: Gallery Pl

41 LA TOMATE

★$$ Indulge in fresh, well-prepared Italian food at reasonable prices. The huge windows are ideal for people watching, and tables are set outdoors for alfresco summer dining. ♦ Italian ♦ Daily, lunch and dinner. 1701 Connecticut Ave NW (at R St). 667.5505. www.latomatebistro.com. ♿. Metro: Dupont Cir

42 STUDIO GALLERY

About 40 years old, Studio Gallery is the longest-running artist-owned gallery in DC. It showcases works by established and emerging artists. An outdoor sculpture garden shows off pieces by resident artists. ♦ W-Sa, 11AM-5PM; Su, 1-5PM. 2108 R St NW (between 21st St and Florida Ave). 232.8734. www.studiogallerydc.com. Metro: Dupont Cir

42 FONDO DEL SOL VISUAL ARTS CENTER

This center showcases works by Latin American, Native American, Caribbean, and African-American artists. Video presentations

---

Restaurants/Clubs: Red | Hotels: Purple | Shops: Orange | Outdoors/Parks: Green | Sights/Culture: Blue

FABULOUS FREEBIES

A bonanza for the budget-conscious, Washington's **Smithsonian** museums (16 in all) and the **National Zoo** offer free admission. As if that weren't enough, the city abounds with free cultural entertainment. If you have time, here are more options—all on the house.

The **Library of Congress** (707.5502; see page 27) gives free classical recitals between October and May, with top-notch participants, including the Juilliard String Quartet. Tickets are free but must be obtained via Ticketmaster (432.7828).

Most Monday nights in fall and spring, the **National Theatre** (628.6161; see page 93) presents free one-act plays, local bands, and other musical performances. Children's entertainment usually appears Saturday mornings.

Between October and June, the **National Gallery of Art** (see page 42) holds free Sunday evening concerts (737.4215), some commemorating exhibits, in the

West Garden Court. Admission is first come, first served. All year long, the museum presents free classic films (842.6799) on Saturday and Sunday afternoons in its large, plush theater in the **East Building**.

DC satisfies even the most hardcore film buff. Free classic feature films are shown most weekday evenings at 7PM at the Library of Congress's **Mary Pickford Theater** (707.5677; see page 27) in the **James Madison Memorial Building**. The movies are first-rate.

The **Kennedy Center**'s (467.4600) **Millennium Stage** offers free performances daily at 6PM, everything from Irish bands to jazz trios.

The **Hirshhorn Museum** (see page 47) shows free in-dependent films and art documentaries. Call for schedule.

---

accompany the exhibits. ♦ W-Sa, 12:30PM-5:30PM. 2112 R St NW (between 21st St and Florida Ave). 483.2777. ♿. Metro: Dupont Cir

42 BURDICK GALLERY

This gallery specializes in high-quality Inuit sculpture and works on paper. ♦ Tu-F, 11AM-5PM; Sa, 11AM-5:30PM. 2114 R St NW (between 21st and 22nd Sts). 986.5682. www.burdickgallery.com. Metro: Dupont Cir

43 AFFRICA

Traditional African art—masks, figures, pottery, textiles, and beadwork—is the focus of this gallery. ♦ Tu, 2PM-6PM; W-Sa, noon-6PM and by appointment. 2010½ R St NW (between Connecticut Ave and 21st St). 745.7272. www.affrica.com. Metro: Dupont Cir

43 MARSHA MATEYKA GALLERY

L.C. Armstrong, Aline Feldman, Jae Ko, and William T. Wiley are some of the artists repre-sented in this space, where contemporary American and European paintings, sculpture, and works on paper are on display. ♦ W-Sa, 11AM-5PM, and by appointment. 2012 R St NW (between Connecticut Ave and 21st St). 328.0088. www.marshamateykagallery.com. Metro: Dupont Cir

43 SETTE OSTERIA

★★$ Neighborhood denizens flock to this newish spot with an open kitchen for pizza

cooked in wood-burning ovens and house-made pastas like gnocchi with tomato, mozzarella, and basil. The bar buzzes with activity; an outdoor patio packs 'em in during the summer. *Sette* is Italian for seven, the traditional "lucky" number. ♦ Italian ♦ Daily, lunch and dinner. 1666 Connecticut Ave NW (between Q and R Sts). 483.3070. www.setteosteria.com. Metro: Dupont Cir

National Museum of American Jewish Military History

44 NATIONAL MUSEUM OF AMERICAN JEWISH MILITARY HISTORY

It shouldn't come as any surprise in a city with so many statues, memorials, and museums dedicated to the military to find this specialized (but thoroughly fascinating) institution. World War II is understandably emphasized, although exhibits on other fronts have been about Desert Storm and the role of Jewish women in the military. ♦ Free. M-F, 9AM-5PM; Su, by appointment. 1811 R St NW (between 18th and 19th Sts).

265.6280. www.nmajmh.org.
Metro: Dupont Cir

45 BELMONT HOUSE (EASTERN STAR TEMPLE)

Architects **Sanson & Trumbauer** are responsible for this 1909 Gallic Romantic building built for New York Congressman Perry Belmont, a member of the Belmont Race Track family. The wedge-shaped lot dictated the structure's shape; its opulent interiors, complete with Louis Tiffany glass, brought the total construction cost to $1.5 million. Much of the original owner's art collection remains in the house, though it now belongs to the Order of the Eastern Star, a Masonic organization, which bought it in 1935 for a paltry $100,000. The building is closed to the public. ◆ 1618 New Hampshire Ave NW (between Corcoran and R Sts). 667.4737. www.easternstar.org. Metro: Dupont Cir

46 SHERIDAN CIRCLE

The statues of Union general Philip H. Sheridan and his favorite horse, Rienzi, were sculpted in 1908 by Gutzon Borglum, creator of Mount Rushmore. Along the outside curb in the southeast quadrant sits a small memorial to Chilean ambassador Orlando Letelier and aide Ronni Karpen Moffitt, who were killed here in 1976 when a remote-controlled bomb blew up their car—a crime for which Chilean secret police and army officials were eventually held responsible. ◆ Massachusetts Ave, R and 23rd Sts NW. Metro: Dupont Cir

47 COSMOS CLUB (TOWNSEND MANSION)

A railway baron's wife commissioned this palace, designed at the turn of the 19th century by the architectural firm **Carrère and Hastings**. Its façade is perhaps the city's most ostentatious. Today, it's the home of a private club for achievers in the arts, politics, and science. A good-ol'-boy holdout, the club finally got around to admitting female members in 1988. ◆ 2121 Massachusetts Ave NW (between Q St and Florida Ave). 387.7783. www.cosmo-club.org. ㅎ. Metro: Dupont Cir

48 PHILLIPS COLLECTION

In 1921, when Duncan and Marjorie Phillips opened two rooms of their four-story brownstone to the public, they created the first American museum of modern art. Duncan had already amassed an exemplary collection, starting with American Impressionists and

expanding into the French Impressionists and Post-Impressionists. Eventually, the Phillipses' holdings spanned not only European and American Modernism but also precursors of Modernism, such as Goya, El Greco, and Delacroix. Today, this jewel of a museum preserves a private-home atmosphere, and art lovers can stroll through the rooms or take advantage of the many couches and chairs to rest and admire the paintings. Art students posted in each room can answer any questions.

Works by such artists as Degas, Monet, Van Gogh, Cézanne, Bonnard, Klee, O'Keeffe, Braque, Rothko, and Renoir fill most of the Phillipses' original home and an adjoining building (added in 1960). Following the Phillipses' wishes, the museum sponsors publications, loans to other museums, and hosts special exhibitions. The museum's most well-known painting is Renoir's *Luncheon of the Boating Party*. The restored **Goh Annex**, which doubled the facility's exhibition space, allows the permanent collection to remain on view during temporary shows. A new education center was inaugurated in late 2005. The firm **Hornblower & Marshall** designed the original building in 1897. It was remodeled in 1915 by **McKim, Mead, and White** and restored in 1984 by **Arthur Cotton Moore Associates**.

Gallery talks take place at 2PM the first Thursday of each month. Sunday-afternoon concerts are given at 5PM, September through May. A gift shop and café are on the premises. ◆ Admission varies depending on temporary exhibits. Tu-Sa, 10AM-5PM; Th, until 8:30PM; Su, noon-7PM (noon-5PM during the summer). Call to arrange group tours a month in advance. 1600 21st St NW (at Q St). 387.2151. ㅎ. www.phillipscollection.org. Metro: Dupont Cir

48 BURTON MARINKOVICH FINE ART

The gallery's collection includes prints, drawings, and paintings by modern and contemporary artists like Georges Braque, Alexander Calder, Joan Miró, and Kiki Smith. ◆ Tu-Sa, 11AM-6PM, and by appointment. 1506 21st St NW. 296.6563. www.burtonmarinkovich.com. Metro: Dupont Cir

49 ETRUSCO

★★$$ This popular Italian eatery features well-known local chef Francisco Ricchi's Tuscan specialties like osso buco, stuffed pastas, and grilled fish. ◆ Italian ◆ M-Sa, dinner. Reservations recommended. 1606 20th St NW (between Q St and Hillyer Pl). 667.0047. Metro: Dupont Cir

49 CHILDE HAROLD

★$ Country star Emmylou Harris performed at this local bar and DC institution before hitting the big time. Live music is featured on Friday and Saturday nights, and you can get burgers downstairs and more formal fare upstairs. The patio is pleasant in warm weather, and there's a private room for parties. ♦ American ♦ M-F, lunch and dinner; Sa, Su, brunch and dinner. 1610 20th St NW (between Q St and Hillyer Pl). 483.6700. www.childeharold.com. ﺝ. Metro: Dupont Cir

49 TABLETOP

Specializing in "functional objects for all surfaces," this cool shop stocks sculptural vases, colorful pillows, sleek shelves, and other minimalist, Space Age-y home accessories. It also carries women's accessories, including Angela Adams handbags and funky jewelry by owner Daphne Olive. ♦ M-Sa, noon-8PM; Su, noon-6PM. 1608 20th St NW (at Q St). 387.7117. www.tabletopdc.com. Metro: Dupont Cir

50 KATHLEEN EWING GALLERY

Specializing in 19th- and 20th-century masterwork photography, this newly expanded gallery holds special exhibitions and represents about 50 American and European photographers. ♦ W-Sa, noon-5PM and by appointment. 1609 Connecticut Ave NW (between Q and 20th Sts). 328.0955. www.kathleenewinggallery.com. Metro: Dupont Cir

50 GAZUZA

Fashionable patrons (gay and straight) come here for martinis and good people watching from the seasonal outdoor patio. Not surprising, because the bar's name means "lust or hunger" in Castilian Spanish. Inside, artsy photos hang on the wall, and comfy chairs are decorated in a terry cloth–like fabric. ♦ M-Th, 5PM-2AM; F, 5PM-3AM; Sa, 6PM-3AM; Su, 6PM-2AM. Upstairs at 1629

The Columbia Heights neighborhood near Adams Morgan originally had streets named for major universities: Yale, Harvard, Princeton, Columbia, and Dartmouth. In the early 1900s, when the city began alphabetizing streets, *Yale* was changed to *Fairmont*, *Princeton* to *Girard*, and *Dartmouth* to *Lamont*. *Harvard* fit into the grid and was retained, *Princeton* was changed from *Street* to *Place*, and *Columbia Street* became *Columbia Road*, a major thoroughfare.

Connecticut Ave NW (between Q and R Sts). 667.5500. Metro: Dupont Cir

51 MELODY RECORDS

A welcome relief from the chains, this connoisseur's shop stocks all manner of CDs and tapes, from rock, blues, and jazz to reggae and vocals. If you can't find it here, they'll special order it for you. ♦ Su-Th, 10AM-10PM; F, Sa, 10AM-11PM. 1623 Connecticut Ave NW (between Q and 20th Sts). 232.4002. ﺝ. www.melodyrecords.com. Metro: Dupont Cir

51 REINCARNATIONS

Opulent accessories for the home, including well-crafted furniture and a wild array of shower curtains, occupy this four-story town house. Despite the tony location, prices here are reasonable. ♦ Tu-Su, 11AM-8PM. 1606 17th St NW (between Q and Corcoran Sts). 319.1606. Metro: Dupont Cir

51 ST. LUKE'S GALLERY

Located in a town house near Dupont Circle, St. Luke's features European Old Master paintings, 16th- to 19th-century watercolors, and Piranesi etchings. ♦ Call for hours. 1715 Q St NW (between 17th and 18th Sts). 328.2424. Metro: Dupont Cir

52 UNIVERSAL GEAR

Style-conscious men shop here for clothes and accessories—socks, belts, and watches. ♦ Su-Th, 11AM-10PM; F, Sa, 11AM-midnight. 1601 17th St NW (at Q St). 319.0136. ﺝ. www.universalgear.com. Metro: Dupont Cir

53 FOX & HOUNDS LOUNGE

Don't let the fancy word *lounge* fool you: This is a basic, no-frills neighborhood bar serving generous drinks at good prices. It's connected to **Trio Restaurant** next door (see below), the kitchen of which supplies the bar food. ♦ Su-Th, 11:30AM-1:30AM; F, Sa, 11:30AM-2:30AM. 1533 17th St NW (between P and Q Sts). 232.6307. ﺝ. Metro: Dupont Cir

53 TRIO RESTAURANT

★$ Long before 17th Street became Restaurant Row, this was a comfortable local favorite for meat loaf, waffles, and other hearty, diner-style fare. Eat on the outdoor patio in fair weather. ♦ American ♦ Daily, breakfast, lunch, and dinner. 1537 17th St NW (at Q St). 232.6305. ﺝ. Metro: Dupont Cir

53 LE PIGALLE

★★★★$$$ Newly opened in May 2006, this bright and cheerful restaurant is a welcome addition to the Washington scene. Naturally, the cuisine here is French, but with a twist in the flavors. This can be experienced in the *côtes d'agneau grillées, pomme au four, fenouil confit* (grilled lamb chop, baked potato, fennel confit, and balsamic sauce), and the *coquille Saint Jacques gratinée au four* (baked scallops in béchamel sauce, with mushrooms, leeks, and shallot confit). ♦ Tu-Su, lunch and dinner. 1527 17th St NW. 332.6767. Metro: Dupont Cir

54 BUFFALO BRIDGE

Spanning **Rock Creek Park**, this impressive structure, open to cars and pedestrians alike, sports aqueduct-like arches and four handsome buffalo sculpted by A. Phimister Proctor. From Rock Creek Parkway, you can see the Indian heads (in full war bonnet) that support the arches. The bridge was designed in 1914 by **Glenn** and **Bedford Brown**. ♦ 23rd and Q Sts NW. Metro: Dupont Cir

55 ANDERSON HOUSE/SOCIETY OF THE CINCINNATI

In 1783, a group of US Revolutionary War officers facing demobilization proposed forming an elite organization (the **Society of the Cincinnati**) to preserve their camaraderie. The group survived, though at the time it was regarded as undemocratic, even potentially conspiratorial. George Washington's membership, however, helped it withstand attacks. The name derives from that of Lucius Quinctius Cincinnatus, a Roman leader whose life Washington's paralleled. (The city of Cincinnati, Ohio, was named by a member of the society.) Membership is limited to male descendants—usually firstborn—of those original officers or officers who died while in service. The French even have a chapter, owing to the role they played in the Revolution. Behind the stately Palladian façade of the society's headquarters is one of the city's finest town houses, whose opulent interiors contain artistic treasures from the US, Europe, and Asia, including society portraits by such famous American painters as Gilbert Stuart, John Trumbull, Daniel Huntington, and Cecilia Beaux. The **Society of the Cincinnati Library** of reference works on the American Revolution is open to the public. ♦ Free. Tu-Sa, 1-4PM. 2118 Massachusetts Ave NW (at Q St). 785.2040. ⅊. Metro: Dupont Cir

56 BRICKSKELLER

★$ Beer mavens worldwide rave about this place because it gives them exactly what they want: more than 1,000 brands of beer in a basement pub conducive to heavy drinking. The menu features food from all 50 states,

from buffalo burgers to pierogies. ♦ American ♦ M-F, lunch and dinner; Sa, Su, dinner. 1523 22nd St NW (between P and Q Sts). 293.1885. ⅊. www.thebrickskeller.com. Metro: Dupont Cir

57 THE WESTIN EMBASSY ROW

$$$$ Despite several name changes in recent years—from **Ritz-Carlton** to **Luxury Collection** to **Westin**—this property has remained a constant class act. (It was also the childhood home of former vice president Al Gore during the 1950s, when his father was US senator.) American antiques and reproductions decorate these 206 rooms: Such niceties as hand-carved mahogany headboards and embroidered English chintz bedspreads are the norm. Valet parking, concierge service, a fitness facility, and 24-hour room service are among the hotel's many extras. The marvelously intimate alcoves in the **Fairfax Lounge** are perfect venues for cocktails, light lunches, and afternoon tea. The more formal **Fairfax Restaurant** serves three meals daily. No-smoking rooms are available, and children under 12 stay free. ♦ 2100 Massachusetts Ave NW (at 21st St). 293.2100; 888/625.5144; fax 293.0641. ⅊. Metro: Dupont Cir

58 RAKU

★★$ This self-proclaimed Asian diner serves mainly Japanese and Chinese fusion fare with fast service. Especially good for lunch, it turns out a fine yakatori. ♦ Asian ♦ Daily, lunch and dinner. 1900 Q St NW (at 19th St). 265.7258. ⅊. Metro: Dupont Cir. Also at 7240 Woodmont Ave (between Bethesda Ave and Elm St), Bethesda, Maryland. 301/718.8680. Metro: Bethesda

59 BEADAZZLED

Besides affordable jewelry, this friendly store sells glass, wood, and metal beads in all shapes and sizes; jewelry-making tools; stringing materials; and books on how to put it all together to make a masterpiece. It also offers classes on everything from macramé to chain mail jewelry. ♦ M-Sa, 10AM-8PM; Su, 11AM-6PM. 1507 Connecticut Ave NW (between Dupont Cir and Q St). 265.2323. ⅊. www.beadazzled.net. Metro: Dupont Cir. Also at Tysons Corner Center, McLean, Virginia. 703/848.2323

59 KRAMERBOOKS & AFTERWORDS CAFÉ

★$$ Kramerbooks specializes in hardcovers and paperbacks, a little pasta, and a split of wine. The extensive selection of books fills two rooms that are connected to afterwords, a

---

Restaurants/Clubs: Red | **Hotels: Purple** | Shops: Orange | **Outdoors/Parks: Green** | Sights/Culture: Blue

cozy café that offers live music Wednesday through Saturday evenings. Known as a pickup joint for the literati, it's open 24 hours on weekends. ♦ American ♦ Daily, breakfast, lunch, and dinner. 1517 Connecticut Ave NW (between Dupont Cir and Q St). Bookstore, 387.1400; café, 387.3825. ♿. www.kramers.com. Metro: Dupont Cir

60 JURYS WASHINGTON HOTEL

$$$$ The former **Dupont Plaza** has adopted an Art Deco look with an elegant Irish accent. The 314-room property's stone-framed lobby features sculptures imported from Ireland and Celtic-style latticework. All guest rooms have been refurbished and come with high-speed Internet access and minibars; the presidential suite offers a galley kitchen, Jacuzzi, and incredible views of Dupont Circle and Downtown. Along with Irish hospitality at its best, the hotel offers 24-hour room service, a small fitness room, laundry and dry-cleaning services, and no-smoking rooms. Stylish **Dupont Grille** serves American cuisine; **Biddy Mulligan's** offers traditional Irish food and drink. Children under 17 stay free. ♦ 1500 New Hampshire Ave NW (at Dupont Cir). 483.6000; fax 328.3265. ♿. www.jurysdoyle.com. Metro: Dupont Cir

61 WASHINGTON CLUB (PATTERSON HOUSE)

Designed by **Stanford White** at the turn of the 19th century, this wedge-shaped building fronts Dupont Circle. A gleaming-white Italian palazzo, it now houses a women's club and is not open to the public. ♦ 15 Dupont Cir NW (between P St and New Hampshire Ave). 483.9200. Metro: Dupont Cir

62 J.R.'s

A lively gay crowd gathers at this bar, thanks in large part to the DJs, who are continuously pumping out popular dance tunes. Appetizers and sandwiches are available, and there's never a cover charge. ♦ M-Th, 2PM-2AM; F, 2PM-3AM; Sa, 1PM-3AM; Su, 1PM-2AM. 1519 17th St NW (between P and Q Sts). 328.0090. www.jrswdc.com. Metro: Dupont Cir

63 CAFÉ LUNA

★$ A pleasant casual atmosphere reigns in this lower-level restaurant, which serves excellent sandwiches, pasta, and pizza. ♦ American/Italian ♦ M-F, breakfast, lunch, and dinner; Sa, Su, brunch and dinner. 1633 P St NW (between 16th and 17th Sts). 387.4005. ♿. www.skewers-cafeluna.com. Metro: Dupont Cir

63 SKEWERS

★★$ Exotically decorated with Middle Eastern fabric hanging from the ceiling, and walls painted in peacock blue, mint green, and red, this place is located directly upstairs from **Café Luna** (see above). Order any of the delicious kabobs—all served with saffron rice or homemade pasta and a skewer of fresh vegetables crowned with almonds and raisins. ♦ Middle Eastern ♦ Daily, lunch and dinner. Reservations recommended. 1633 P St NW (between 16th and 17th Sts) 387.7400. www.skewers-cafeluna.com. Metro: Dupont Cir

63 BUA

★★$$ Delicious Thai food, a comfortable setting, and a caliber of service usually found at more expensive restaurants combine to make a pleasurable dining experience. ♦ Thai ♦ Daily, lunch and dinner. Reservations recommended. 1635 P St NW (between 16th and 17th Sts). 265.0828. ♿. Metro: Dupont Cir

64 WASHINGTON FOUNDRY UNITED METHODIST CHURCH

Built in 1904 by **Appleton P. Clark**, it has fan vaults of rusticated gray granite that are characteristic of High Gothic Revival; the low dome contributes to this building's renowned acoustics. The church is named for Georgetown foundry owner Henry Foxhall, who established it. ♦ 1500 16th St NW (at P St). 332.4010. www.foundryumc.org. ♿. Metro: Dupont Cir

65 HOTEL PALOMAR

$$$$ The latest in a line of luxury boutique hotels by Kimpton, the Palomar has a great location west of Dupont Circle near Rock Creek Park. Its 335 spacious rooms and suites were inspired by the modern elegance of 1930s French Moderne designers. It features in-room service, the Women In Touch program, Wi-Fi, and even special packages for your dog or cat. ♦ 2121 P Street NW (between 21st and 22nd Sts). 448.1800; fax 448.1801. www.hotelpalomar-dc.com. Metro: Dupont Cir

Within the Palomar Hotel:

URBANNA

★★★$$$ This upscale restaurant has specialties from Northern Italy, the South of France, Greece, and Spain, including pizzas from their wood-burning oven. It also boasts an extensive collection of international red and white wines, with an entire wall of the restaurant dedicated to storing them. ♦ Mediterranean ♦ Daily, lunch and dinner. 956.6651

66 OBELISK

★★★★$$$$ This Italian dining room serves innovative fare as starkly elegant as the setting. The prix-fixe menu changes daily, but past gems have included ravioli with eggplant in a light tomato sauce, grilled veal medallions served with morels, and duck breast served in a simple thyme–duck stock. The items on the well-selected wine list are reasonably priced and the waiters are extremely knowledgeable. ♦ Italian ♦ Tu-Sa, dinner. Reservations recommended. 2029 P St NW (between 20th and 21st Sts). 872.1180. Metro: Dupont Cir

66 PIZZERIA PARADISO

★★$ Although it shares **Obelisk**'s address, this place is miles apart in ambience. Gourmet pizza is what this place does and does well. It isn't cheap—a 12-inch cheese pizza runs about $13—but the crusts are remarkably flavorful, the toppings fresh and abundant. Be warned, though: Long lines form here on weekends. ♦ Italian ♦ Daily, lunch and dinner. 2029 P St NW (between 20th and 21st Sts). 223.1245. Metro: Dupont Cir. Also at 3282 M St. 337.1245

67 BLAINE MANSION

A three-time presidential hopeful during the late 1800s, James Blaine used to occupy this Victorian fortress (now used as office space), designed by **John Fraser** in 1881. ♦ 2000 Massachusetts Ave NW (at 20th St). Metro: Dupont Cir

68 RESIDENCE INN WASHINGTON, DC/DUPONT CIRCLE

$$$$ This 10-floor property near Embassy Row offers underground parking, a complimentary breakfast buffet, an exercise room, and child care and room service. Every room has a full kitchen. ♦ 2120 P St NW (between 21st and 22nd Sts). 466.6800; fax 466.9630. Metro: Dupont Cir. 800/331.3131

68 MIMI'S AMERICAN BISTRO

★★$$ At this lively spot, the servers don't just bring the food; they also break out into song. But in between numbers, ask them to bring you the rack of lamb or rainbow trout. ♦ American ♦ M-F, lunch and dinner; Sa, Su, brunch and dinner. 2120 P St NW (between 21st and 22nd Sts). 464.6464. ♿. www.mimisdc.com. Metro: Dupont Cir

69 CAFE JAPONE

★$ If you've never tried sumo-video sushi, or sushi pizza, this is the place to do so. But beware the lackluster service. Tuesday night is comedy night here. ♦ Japanese ♦ Daily, dinner. Reservations recommended. 2032 P St NW (between Hopkins and 21st Sts). 223.1573. www.cafejapone.com. Metro: Dupont Cir

70 SECOND STORY BOOKS

DC's leading source for used books is lined with floor-to-ceiling shelves of old, rare, and out-of-print editions—all at reasonable prices. A search service and appraisals are also available. ♦ Daily, 10AM-10PM. 2000 P St NW (at 20th St). 659.8884. ♿. www.secondstorybooks.com. Metro: Dupont Cir. Also at 12160 Parklawn Dr (at Wilkins Ave), Rockville, Maryland. 301/770.0477

70 JOHNNY'S HALF SHELL

★★$$ Owned by Ann Cashion (of Adams Morgan's **Cashion's Eat Place**), this casual but bustling spot serves dependable seafood dishes like seafood gumbo, oyster or shrimp po' boy sandwiches, and grilled rockfish at small tables or a backroom bar. ♦ Seafood ♦ M-Sa, lunch and dinner. 2002 P St NW (between 20th and Hopkins Sts). 296.2021. Metro: Dupont Cir

70 AL TIRAMISÙ

★★$$ Though the food is quite good, the real charm here is the ebullient, familial atmosphere enhanced by chef Luigi Diotaiuti. As testimony to his skill, Diotaiuti is routinely asked to cater Italian Cultural Institute functions. Try homemade gnocchi, grilled Portobello mushrooms, carpaccio, or spinach-ricotta *agnolotti* (half-moon ravioli). ♦ Italian ♦ M-F, lunch and dinner; Sa, Su, dinner. 2014 P St NW (between 20th and Hopkins Sts). 467.4466. www.altiramisu.com. Metro: Dupont Cir

70 PESCE

★★$$$ In a town filled with steak houses, this small, casual seafood spot is a welcome alternative. The colorful Mediterranean menu changes daily but always features tastefully presented fish dishes. Pan-seared baby

Restaurants/Clubs: Red | **Hotels: Purple** | **Shops: Orange** | **Outdoors/Parks: Green** | **Sights/Culture: Blue**

125

flounder is a sure bet. There's also a well-stocked market on the premises. ♦ Seafood ♦ M-F, lunch and dinner; Sa, Su, dinner. 2016 P St NW (at Hopkins St). 466.FISH. &. www.pescebistro.com. Metro: Dupont Cir

70 SALA THAI

★★$ Splendidly authentic Thai food, right down to the ultrasweet iced tea, is served in a cool, neon-lit basement room. You won't go wrong with the *pad thai* (stir-fried noodles). This place is a gem, particularly at lunchtime, when the service is more consistently attentive and the noise level more bearable. ♦ Thai ♦ Daily, lunch and dinner. 2016 P St NW (at Hopkins St). 872.1144. &. Metro: Dupont Cir. Also at 2900 N 10th St, Arlington, Virginia. 703/465.2900. &. Metro: Clarendon; 3507 Connecticut Ave NW. 237.2777. Metro: Cleveland Park; and 4828 Cordell Ave, Bethesda, Maryland. 301/654.4676. Metro: Bethesda

71 DUPONT CIRCLE

A bronze statue of Civil War Admiral Samuel Francis du Pont used to adorn the circle, but the du Pont family whisked the statue away to Delaware and replaced it with this graceful marble fountain. The figures below its basin represent the wind, the sea, and the stars. Dupont Circle's benches and lawn are popular venues for political demonstrations, chess matches, and just hanging out. ♦ Metro: Dupont Cir

72 EURAM BUILDING

Designed in 1971 by **Hartman-Cox**, this is one of Washington's more imaginative contemporary buildings. Its eight slick stories of brick, glass, and prestressed concrete surround an inner courtyard. ♦ 21 Dupont Cir NW (between 19th St and New Hampshire Ave). &. Metro: Dupont Cir

73 LAWSON'S GOURMET

Shop here for great finds in take-out food, from salads and breads to pastries. Catering and delivery services also are offered. ♦ M-F, 7:30AM-5:30PM. 1350 Connecticut Ave NW (at Dupont Cir). 775.0400. &. Metro: Dupont Cir. Also at various locations throughout the city.

73 PROPER TOPPER

All kinds of hats—from berets and fedoras to dress hats and straw boaters—fill this chic shop. There are toppers for men, women, and children. The store also sells stylish jewelry and scarves and hip gifts (candles, note cards, etc.). ♦ M-F, 10AM-8PM; Sa, 10AM-7PM; Su, noon-6PM. 1350 Connecticut Ave NW (at Dupont Cir). 842.3055. www.propertopper.com. Metro: Dupont Cir. Also at 3213 P St NW. 333.6200

74 THE BIG HUNT

★$ There's nothing particularly fancy about this bar-restaurant, but the food is better than at most such places, and there are lots of beers on tap. The service is casual but prompt; the jukebox, outstanding. There's a private room for parties. ♦ American ♦ M-Th, 4PM-2AM; F, 4PM-3AM; Sa, 5PM-3AM; Su, 5PM-2AM. 1345 Connecticut Ave NW (between N St and Dupont Cir). 785.2333. &. Metro: Dupont Cir

75 NATIONAL TRUST FOR HISTORIC PRESERVATION (MCCORMICK BUILDING)

The **McCormick Building** was once the most opulent apartment house in DC. Each of its floors contained one 11,000-square-foot apartment, in which notables, among them Andrew Mellon, dwelled. Designed by **Jules Henri de Sibour** and considered the best of his many DC works (which include the former **Canadian Chancery** nearby), the building lends a Parisian flair to the neighborhood. It is now the headquarters for the nonprofit National Trust for Historic Preservation, which labors hard to save other special buildings. ♦ M-F. 1785 Massachusetts Ave NW (between 17th and 18th Sts). 588.6000. &. Metro: Dupont Cir

76 THE MANSION ON "O" STREET

$$$$ This hotel, consisting of three town houses that have been re-formed and connected, is unquestionably the most unusual and eclectic in Washington. In fact, from the outside you wouldn't even know it is a hotel. Inside it is an amazing collection of styles and décor that reflects the vivid imagination and character of its owner, Ms. H.H. Leonards. Reservations taken only by fax or e-mail. ♦ 2020 O Street NW (between 20th and 21st Sts). Fax 659.0547. E-mail hotel@omansion.com. Metro: Dupont Cir

77 THE BREWMASTER'S CASTLE

Christian Heurich was a German immigrant who achieved tremendous wealth in the beer industry (today's Foggy Bottom brand) during the 19th century. His legacy to Washington is this turreted, 31-room Romanesque Revival mansion, considered

THE BEST

Jackie Serwer

Chief curator, Corcoran Gallery of Art

My favorite neighborhood restaurant is **Colorado Kitchen**, 5515 Colorado Avenue NW, just off 14th Street (202/545.8280). The food is prepared with flair and originality, yet it always has a homey, earthy quality. The décor is homey as well—1950s-style Formica tables and chairs, red bandannas instead of cloth napkins, and kooky salt and pepper shakers on every table.

The best old-fashioned pizza can be found at **AV Ristorante**. It has been a great place for real pizza (in contrast to the manufactured, delivery kind) for many decades. I particularly like its white pizza—a delicious, yeasty crust topped with herbs and cheese.

For Sunday brunch, try the Gospel Brunch at the **Corcoran Gallery of Art** every Sunday from 11AM to 2PM. Several local groups alternate performances. The music provides the perfect accompaniment to a bountiful offering of breakfast/lunch dishes, served buffet style, as well as on-demand, fresh waffles and custom omelettes. Then, on a full stomach, you can enjoy a leisurely stroll through the current special exhibitions and the Corcoran's glorious 19th-century American collection.

The best ice cream can be found at **Larry's Homemade Ice Cream** on Connecticut Avenue just above Dupont Circle. Larry is not known for being warm and fuzzy, but the ice cream is a dream. Recently, he named a flavor in honor of former President Bill Clinton. He calls it "Libido."

For a serious Italian meal, try **Giovanni Trattu**, hidden away in the middle of downtown at 1823 Jefferson Place NW. The salads (try the tomato carpaccio) and pastas (like a deliciously rich gnocchi with a pesto cream sauce) are particularly outstanding.

Julia's Empanadas (3 locations: 1221 Connecticut Ave NW; 2452 18th St NW; 1000 Vermont Ave) is a great choice for a meal on the run. The empanadas are baked rather than fried, but they don't lose any of their robust taste.

Don't miss the student performances at Georgetown's **Duke Ellington School of the Arts**. Drama, musical theater, dance, and the Show Choir programs during the school year, performed in the school's professional theater, are among the neighborhood's unexpected treats.

Catholic University Summer Opera (June-July) at the **Hartke Theater** offers brilliant performances of both classics and lesser-known works at very reasonable prices.

My favorite old-fashioned movie theater is the **Avalon** on upper Connecticut Avenue NW. Recently restored to its 1920s glory, it offers two different films, usually one of which is an art film.

Authors' talks at **Politics and Prose** are very popular with the locals. Literary celebrities as well as politicians and political journalists draw enthusiastic audiences that insist on a spirited dialogue.

If you're looking for a bit of old Washington off the beaten track, **Oak Hill Cemetery** is a great place to visit. The beautiful grounds include the graves of many prominent 19th-century residents, including the Corcoran family mausoleum designed by Thomas U. Walter, one of the architects of the U.S. Capitol, and a Gothic chapel designed by James Renwick, architect of the Smithsonian Castle and St. Patrick's Cathedral in New York.

The best nighttime stroll would have to be a walk through the **FDR Memorial**, beautifully lit after dark.

America's most intact late-Victorian house. Many of the rooms still contain their original furnishings. There's a pleasant Victorian garden behind the house, where nearby office workers often spend their lunch hours. The property once served as home to the Historical Society of Washington, DC, but is now owned by the Heurich House Foundation, formed by two of Christian Heurich's grandchildren. ◆ Donation. Tours, W-F, 11:30AM and 1PM; Sa, 11:30AM, 1PM, and 2:30PM; Su, 1PM and 2:30 PM. Garden, M-F, 10AM-4PM spring through fall. 1307 New Hampshire Ave NW (between 20th St and Dupont Cir). 429.1894. ৬. www.brewmasterscastle.com. Metro: Dupont Cir

78 FIRST BAPTIST CHURCH

Designed in 1955 by **Harold E. Wagoner**, the massing of this neo-Gothic church, reminiscent of the work of **Frank Lloyd Wright**, playfully leads the eye upward toward a steeple that isn't there. ◆ 1328 16th St NW (entrance on O St). 387.2206. ৬. www.firstbaptistdc.org. Metro: Dupont Cir

79 HOTEL ROUGE

$$$$ One of Washington's newest boutique hotels, Hotel Rouge offers 137 guest rooms with stylish touches like flat-screen TVs, floor-to-ceiling red faux leather headboards, and crimson velvet drapes. Amenities include weekday happy hours, 24-hour room service,

---

Restaurants/Clubs: **Red** | Hotels: **Purple** | Shops: Orange | Outdoors/Parks: Green | Sights/Culture: Blue

WANDERING WASHINGTON'S LITERARY LANES

Washington's primary concern may be government, but its literary dimension—past and present—also holds a place of prominence. Book lovers can enjoy a truly capital experience by following the footsteps of legendary writers where they worked and played. Some sites have since been replaced or are still private residences, leaving your imagination to create images from the past. Other sites, like the **Library of Congress** and the **Hay-Adams Hotel**, invite you in for a novel experience.

Among the literary greats who resided in upper northwest Washington was Randall Jarrell, who lived at 3916 Jenifer Street Northwest (between 39th Street and Reno Road) while poetry consultant to the Library of Congress between 1956 and 1958. Some in the neighborhood gained a reputation for hosting literary salons or throwing grand bashes. Classical scholar Edith Hamilton, author of *The Greek Way*, entertained in grand style at 2448 Massachusetts Avenue Northwest (between Sheridan Circle and Waterside Drive). The renowned columnist and founder of the *New Republic* magazine, Walter Lippmann, held an annual New Year's Eve party at 3525 Woodley Road Northwest (between 35th and 36th Streets).

No Washington neighborhood is richer in literary history than **Georgetown**. Francis Scott Key, author of the "Star Spangled Banner," lived at 3518 M Street, but his home was torn down to make way for the **Key Bridge** (named in his honor). Louisa May Alcott resided at 30th

and M Streets (now a gas station) while working at the Union Hotel Hospital during the Civil War. She moved away after contracting a case of typhoid and pneumonia, but not before acquiring the material for *Hospital Sketches*. Sinclair Lewis, Nobel Prize–winner and author of many satirical novels, including *Main Street* and *Babbitt*, lived at 3028 Q Street (between 30th and 31st Streets). Nearby 3106 P Street (between 31st Street and Wisconsin Avenue) was home to Pulitzer Prize–winner Katherine Anne Porter, author of acclaimed short stories and the novel *Ship of Fools*. Poet and librarian of Congress Archibald MacLeish resided at 1520 33rd Street (between P Street and Volta Place). Columnist Drew Pearson, whose daily column was titled "Washington Merry-Go-Round," made his home at 2820 Dumbarton Street (between 28th and 29th Streets).

Not every writer's footsteps can be traced to Georgetown, however. Clare Boothe Luce—playwright, magazine editor (for *Vogue* and *Vanity Fair*), and congresswoman—lived first at the grand Wardman Park apartment building, now part of the **Marriott Wardman Park Hotel** (2660 Woodley Road NW, between Connecticut Avenue and 29th Street), and then at the former **Watergate Hotel** (2650 Virginia Avenue NW, between New Hampshire Avenue and Rock Creek and Potomac Parkway).

In the early 1960s, Tom Wolfe, author of *Bonfire of the Vanities* and *A Man in Full*, paid $85 a month for a one-

and an on-site fitness center. ♦ 1315 16th St NW. 232.8000; fax 667.9827. www.rougehotel.com. Metro: Dupont Cir

Within Hotel Rouge:

BAR ROUGE

★$ A soundtrack of liquid lounge and acid jazz sets the scene for trendy cocktails, and lots of lounging on leather and mohair-covered furniture. The extensive wine list changes often. ♦ Daily, breakfast, lunch, and dinner. 939.6422

80 HOTEL MADERA

$$$$ This boutique hotel's 82 rooms feature headboards with mohair padding, quilted bedspreads, "grass cloth" wallpaper, and minibars stocked with martini kits. Amenities include high-speed Internet access, concierge service, an evening wine hour, valet parking, and a DVD and CD library. ♦ 1310 New Hampshire Ave NW (at N St). 296.7600, 800/430.1202; fax 293.2476. &. www.hotelmadera.com. Metro: Dupont Cir

Within Hotel Madera:

FIREFLY

★★$$ A floor-to-ceiling birchlike "Firefly Tree," hung with lanterns and lit by candles, serves as the focal point of this neighborhood bistro. In the kitchen, partially concealed behind a rustic stone wall, chefs turn out modern American cuisine like roasted Amish chicken with red chili gravy, braised short ribs, and risotto with roasted onion vinaigrette and buffalo mozzarella. The backlit amber glass bar is a nice place for a cocktail or a glass of wine. ♦ American ♦ M-F, breakfast, lunch, and dinner; Sa, Su, breakfast, brunch, and dinner. 861.1310. &

81 OLSSON'S BOOKS & RECORDS

One of DC's best haunts for bibliophiles, this top-flight, full-service book shop also offers a wide selection of pop, jazz, country, blues, and classical CDs and cassettes. ♦ M-W, 10AM-10PM; Th-Sa, 10AM-10:30PM; Su, noon-8PM. 1307 19th St NW (between N St and Dupont Cir). 785.1133. &

bedroom apartment at 1343 Connecticut Avenue NW (between N Street and Dupont Circle). Frances Hodgson Burnett, beloved children's book author of *Little Lord Fauntleroy* and *The Secret Garden*, gained a reputation as a scintillating hostess of literary salons in her mansion at 1770 Massachusetts Avenue Northwest (between 17th and 18th Streets; it's since been torn down to make way for the Brookings Institution). Her husband, Dr. Swan Burnett, operated on James Thurber after he suffered an eye injury. (James Thurber was the writer and *New Yorker* cartoonist who immortalized the secret life of Walter Mitty.) As a child, Thurber and his family spent their winters at 2031 I Street NW (between 20th and 21st Streets), on the same street where the poet Stephen Vincent Benét grew up.

Among the African-American writers who took up residence near **Howard University** were Paul Laurence Dunbar (at 321 U Street NW, between Third and Fourth Streets), Jean Toomer (at 1341 U Street NW, between 13th and 14th Streets), and Langston Hughes (at the 12th Street YMCA, 1816 12th Street NW, between S and T Streets). One of the world's best African-American collections is at the **Moorland-Spingarn Research Center** (806.7240) at Howard University.

Walt Whitman came to Washington during the Civil War to care for his brother and wounded soldiers. He took rooms at numerous boardinghouses, including downtown at 1407 L Street NW (between 14th Street and Vermont Avenue). He was fired from his job at the Department of the Interior after his supervisor discovered *Leaves of Grass* in his desk drawer.

Every literary tour of Washington should include a stop at the **Hay-Adams Hotel** (800 16th Street NW, at H Street, 638.6600), once home to America's greatest man of letters, Henry Adams, author of *The Education of Henry Adams*. He and good friend John Hay—also an author, President Abraham Lincoln's private secretary, and secretary of state to Presidents William McKinley and Theodore Roosevelt—built adjoining houses across from **Lafayette Square**. The twin houses were taken down in 1927 and replaced by the elegant hotel now standing (see page 80). The **Willard Hotel** (1401 Pennsylvania Avenue NW; 628.9100) also has its place in literary history. Julia Ward Howe wrote "The Battle Hymn of the Republic" as a guest. Nathaniel Hawthorne took up residence while reporting on the Civil War for *Atlantic Monthly*. Mark Twain dined there, and Emily Dickinson once visited.

Neighboring **Chinatown** is home to DC's main public library. An austere building of steel and glass, the **Martin Luther King Jr. Memorial Library** (901 G Street NW, at Ninth Street; 727.0321) was designed by **Mies van der Rohe**.

To the northeast Marjorie Kinan Rawlings, author of the children's classic *The Yearling*, grew up at 1221 Newton Street NE (between 13th and 12th Streets) and attended Western High School (now the Duke Ellington School for the Performing Arts).

www.olssons.com. Metro: Dupont Cir. Also at numerous other locations throughout the area

800/775.1202, 393.3000; fax 785.9581. www.topazhotel.com. Metro: Dupont Cir, Farragut N

Within the Topaz Hotel:

TOPAZ BAR

★★$ This hip hangout for hotel guests and local Gen-Xers boasts sapphire velvet-covered settees, funky colored lights, and cool tunes. Fashionable patrons mix and mingle here while sipping specialty cocktails. ♦ American ♦ Daily, breakfast and dinner. 393.3000

82 TOPAZ HOTEL

$$$$ This boutique hotel's 99 rooms give off an exotic vibe with green-striped walls, richly colored fabrics, and silk taffeta draperies. Amenities like yoga mats, New Age CDs, and personalized horoscope wake-up calls aim to soothe the mind and body. ♦ 1733 N St NW (between 17th and 18th Sts).

82 TABARD INN

$$ A haven for Anglophiles, this friendly bed-and-breakfast might be mistaken for a place right out of the English countryside, thanks to its rustic but comfy furnishings and dark paneled walls. It has 40 rooms, many with fireplaces, and a restaurant (see page 130). Guests often congregate in the

Restaurants/Clubs: Red | Hotels: Purple | Shops: Orange | Outdoors/Parks: Green | Sights/Culture: Blue

large first-floor parlor and cocktail lounge. Most of the staff has been here for many years, adding to the inn's familial air. ♦ 1739 N St NW (between 17th and 18th Sts). 785.1277; fax 785.6173. &. www.tabardinn.com. Metro: Dupont Cir

Within the Tabard Inn:

TABARD INN RESTAURANT

★★$$$ The casual, bustling dining room decorated with folk art is a local favorite for Sunday brunch. It features a changing, seasonal menu of healthful, inventive dishes: lavish salads, fish with crisp vegetable garnishes, and free-range chicken. Save room for the homemade desserts. There's garden dining in warm weather. The adjoining bar—more like a living room, really—is a romantic place for a drink in the winter, when the fireplace blazes. ♦ American ♦ M-Sa, breakfast, lunch, and dinner; Su, breakfast, brunch, and dinner. Reservations recommended. 331.8528. &

83 BETSY FISHER

A standout among Washington's often staid clothiers, this small boutique carries the creations of designers like Debra de Roo and Nanette Lepore. ♦ M-W, 10AM-7PM; Th, F, 10AM-9PM; Sa, 10AM-6PM; Su, noon-4PM. 1224 Connecticut Ave NW (between Jefferson Pl and N St). 785.1975. &. www.betsyfisher.com. Metro: Dupont Cir

84 I RICCHI

★★★$$$$ This Tuscan eatery's high ceilings, large columns, and golden, mural-decorated stucco walls help create an enchanting dining experience. Changing seasonal menus feature a selection of pastas, risottos, and grilled meats and fish. The homemade bread is delicious. ♦ Italian ♦ M-F, lunch and dinner; Sa, dinner. Reservations recommended. 1220 19th St NW (between M and N Sts). 835.0459. &. www.iricchi.net. Metro: Dupont Cir

85 SAM & HARRY'S

★★★$$$ This steak house is giving **Morton's of Chicago** in Georgetown a run for its money. The beef is superb, and the chicken, fish, and other dishes are more than adequate. The service is outstanding, and the dining room—outfitted in dark wood and brass—

manages to be comfortable and classy. Another plus: It has one of the nicest bars around. ♦ Steak house ♦ M-F, lunch and dinner; Sa, dinner. 1200 19th St NW (at M St). 296.4333. &. www.samandharrys.com. Metro: Dupont Cir. Also at 8240 Leesburg Pike, Vienna, Virginia. 703/448.0088

86 THE PALM

★★$$$$ Since 1972 regular patrons, including high-powered lobbyists and sports figures, prize this institution's clubhouse atmosphere and steak-and-potatoes fare. The lobster is also superb. Caricatures of famous personages dominate the walls. ♦ American ♦ M-F, lunch and dinner; Sa, Su, dinner. Reservations required. 1225 19th St NW (at Jefferson Pl). 293.9091. &. www.thepalm.com. Metro: Dupont Cir. Also at 1750 Tysons Blvd, McLean, Virginia. 703/917.0200

86 C.F. FOLKS

★$ This is perhaps the city's best carryout joint; its menu ranges from Mexican to French, and its clientele is a bipartisan blend of messengers and lobbyists. Arrive either early or late to avoid the worst of the lunch crush. If the few sidewalk tables are occupied, take your lunch to Dupont Circle and watch the people parade. ♦ M-F, lunch. 1225 19th St NW (at Jefferson Pl). 293.0162. www.cffolksrestaurant.com. &. Metro: Dupont Cir

87 DAILY GRILL

★★$$ Harking back to American grills of the 1920s, this casual eatery sports simple black booths and burnished wood. Best bets from the enormous menu include Manhattan clam chowder, blackened chicken sandwich, Cobb salad, and strawberry shortcake. ♦ American ♦ M-Sa, lunch and dinner; Su, brunch and dinner. 1200 18th St NW (at M St). 822.5282. www.dailygrill.com. Metro: Dupont Cir. Also at 1310 Wisconsin Ave NW (between N and O Sts). 337.4900; and one Bethesda Metro Center, Bethesda, Maryland. 301/656.6100. &. Metro: Bethesda

88 SIGN OF THE WHALE

★★$ This old-fashioned neighborhood pub has been here since 1981 and is now rather incongruous in an area that is becoming increasingly upmarket. Nevertheless, this is part of its attraction, whether you visit for a refreshing beer or partake of its wholesome pub food, including a vast selection of half-price Whaleburgers on Monday and Sunday nights. It also claims to have DC's biggest and best Bloody Mary bar at $9.95 unlimited. ♦ Daily, 11:30AM-2AM. 1825 M St NW (between 18th and 19th Sts). 785.1110. Metro: Farragut N

88 DRAGONFLY

Sushi and cocktails help draw an international crowd to this glamorous lounge near Dupont Circle. It's one of the city's most stylish spots, with funky bar stools and an all-white décor. Dress to impress, or the bouncers may not let you in. ◆ M-Th, 5:30PM-2AM; F, 5:30PM-3AM; Sa, 7PM-3AM; Su, 7PM-2AM. 1215 Connecticut Ave NW. 331.1775. Metro: Dupont Cir

88 MCCXXIII

★★$$$ This upscale, three-level club draws visiting celebs and international types. Velvet couches stand ready for lounging; tall, illuminated columns provide flattering mood lighting. For dinner, try the lamb tenderloin or the ahi tuna; wash it down with a champagne cocktail, then head out onto the dance floor. ◆ American ◆ Tu, 7PM-2AM; W, Th, 6PM-2AM; F, 5PM-3AM; Sa, 7PM-3AM; Su, 8PM-2AM. Reservations suggested. 1223 Connecticut Ave NW. 822.1800. ♿. www.1223.com. Metro: Dupont Cir

89 ST. MATTHEW'S CATHEDRAL

John F. Kennedy worshiped in this late-19th-century church, and his funeral Mass was said here; an inscription marks the spot on the altar where his casket rested. The dome, reminiscent of the Cathedral of Santa Maria del Fiore in Florence, Italy, and the simple brick geometries of the exterior give no hint of the florid interior, with its fine mosaic work. Architect **C. Grant la Farge** is responsible for its design. The church honors the patron saint of civil servants and serves as the seat of the Archbishop of Washington. ◆ 1725 Rhode Island Ave NW (between 17th St and Connecticut Ave). 347.3215. ♿.

When the 14-story Cairo apartment building (still standing on Q Street NW, near 17th Street) was built in 1894, it exceeded the reach of Washington's municipal firefighting equipment. It also exceeded the height of the Capitol building. Soon after, Congress passed a law that no building would exceed 130 feet, abolishing the city's skyscraper potential.

www.stmatthewscathedral.org. Metro: Farragut N

89 LONGFELLOW BUILDING

DC's first modern "glass-box" structure, it was built in 1940-1941 by **William Lescaze**, who also designed the Swiss Embassy. ◆ 1741 Rhode Island Ave NW (between 17th St and Connecticut Ave). Metro: Farragut N

90 CHARLES SUMNER SCHOOL MUSEUM AND ARCHIVES

Built in 1872 by **Adolph Cluss** and named for abolitionist senator **Charles Sumner,** this historic redbrick building served as one of DC's first schools for black children. It has since been renovated and now houses the archives of all of DC's public schools, plus revolving exhibitions on local history and culture. ◆ Free. M-F, 10AM-5PM; Sa, 10AM-4PM. 1201 17th St NW (at M St). 442.6046. ♿. Metros: Farragut N; Farragut W

91 JEFFERSON HOTEL

$$$$ With the feel of an elegant British estate, this hostelry run by Loews offers 67 rooms and 33 suites. Original documents signed by Thomas Jefferson are on view in the restaurant. Rooms are outfitted with antiques and reproduction furniture; some have canopy beds and fireplaces. Amenities include 24-hour concierge and room service and valet parking. Children under 18 stay free. ◆ 1200 16th St NW (at M St). 347.2200, 800/23LOEWS; fax 331.7982. ♿. www.thejeffersondc.com. Metros: Farragut N, Farragut W

Within the Jefferson Hotel:

JEFFERSON RESTAURANT

★★★$$$ A wood-burning fireplace, Federal-period furnishings and artwork, and lots of nooks and crannies make this a cozy spot. The kitchen here is far more adventurous than at most hotel restaurants, with such dishes as Chilean bass with mushroom purée, smoked tomato, and ricotta gnocchi; and pan-roasted sturgeon with lentils. ◆ American ◆ Daily, breakfast, lunch, and dinner. Reservations advised. 347.2200

Restaurants/Clubs: Red | **Hotels: Purple** | Shops: Orange | **Outdoors/Parks: Green** | Sights/Culture: Blue

GEORGETOWN

Next to **Capitol Hill**, Georgetown is Washington's best-known neighborhood; after **Dupont Circle/Adams Morgan**, it's DC's hippest, and it is certainly among the city's wealthiest. Georgetown's popularity is not hard to understand—its tree-lined streets and historic town houses give it a fetching elegance, whereas the country's oldest Catholic institution of higher learning lends it the zesty atmosphere of a college town.

Georgetown was founded in 1751, 40 years before DC; owing to its choice location on the **Potomac River**, it briefly prospered as a major international port. There's little evidence of that now, however; the waterfront, which once contained warehouses and ramshackle docks, is marred by an elevated freeway, the **Whitehurst**, which carries commuters to and from suburban Maryland and Virginia. Although Georgetown was the terminus of the **Chesapeake and Ohio Canal (C&O Canal)**, the area failed to catch on with real-estate speculators. When the B&O Railroad put the canal out of business, Georgetown fared even worse. It became part of the District of Columbia in 1871; in reality, it functioned as a poor relative to Washington.

In the early 20th century, Georgetown was rediscovered. Urban pioneers were looking for cheap housing, of which there was plenty in crumbling Georgetown. By the 1950s, when Congressman John F. Kennedy set up house in the area (at 3271 P Street, then at 3307 N Street) to prepare for a run at larger quarters down on **Pennsylvania Avenue**, Georgetown's Cinderella-like transformation was complete. The prices of modest 19th-

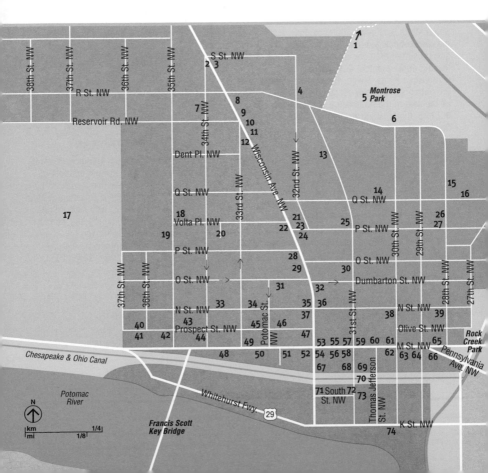

century homes had already skyrocketed into the six figures, with larger ones exceeding the million-dollar mark.

During the Kennedy and Johnson years, and even into the Nixon era, no Washington neighborhood was hotter for shopping, dining, and club-hopping. Along Georgetown's two main arteries, **M Street** and **Wisconsin Avenue**, establishments sprang up, flourished, and often disappeared, to be quickly replaced by others eager for a fashionable address.

Today, Georgetown still boasts some of the best shopping in town. Eateries are plentiful, and thanks to the large college student population, many of them are quite affordable. Finding a parking spot can be virtually impossible, though. (Garage rates are very steep too.) It's a 15-minute walk from the nearest **Metro** stop (**Foggy Bottom/GWU**), but the **Georgetown Metro Connection** (298.9222; www.georgetowndc.com), a new shuttle service, transports passengers from the **Dupont Circle**, Foggy Bottom/GWU, and **Rosslyn** Metro stations. Exploring by foot may be the best option—and there's no better way to savor the quaint cobblestone streets. Try not to miss the **Washington Harbour** complex, with its restaurants, shops, and lovely waterfront promenade. It allows visitors a chance to sit and observe the tranquil yet powerful Potomac River.

1 DUMBARTON OAKS PARK

These 27 acres of natural woodlands are particularly well known for their profusion of spring wildflowers. The fact that they are only accessible by foot—via **Lovers Lane** off 31st and R Streets—helps keep them unspoiled. The land was given to the city by Robert and Mildred Bliss, who once lived next door at Dumbarton Oaks. ♦ Closed in winter. 31st and R Sts NW. 895.6000

2 CAFÉ DIVAN

★★$$ Located in upper Georgetown, in a corner building shaped like a piece of cheese, this modern restaurant offers Turkish cuisine with a fine selection of appetizers; sandwiches, including vegetarian ones; entrées, and wood-burning oven specials. You can even create your own pizzas. ♦ Turkish ♦ Daily, lunch and dinner. 1834 Wisconsin Ave NW (at 34th St). 338.1747. www.cafedivan.com

2 GEORGETOWN HILL INN

$$$$ This luxury hotel in a prestigious location in upper Georgetown, and connected to the Turkish restaurant **Café Divan**, is one of DC's more modern and sumptuous hotels. Exquisitely furnished, the suites include full kitchens, Jacuzzi tubs, plasma TVs with cable service, and high-speed wireless Internet. ♦ 1832 Wisconsin Ave NW (at 34th St). 298.6021. www.georgetownhillinn.com

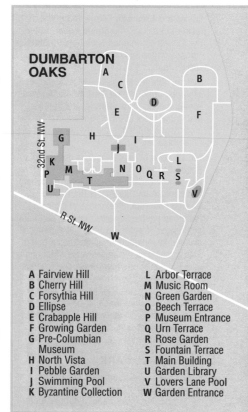

DUMBARTON OAKS

A Fairview Hill
B Cherry Hill
C Forsythia Hill
D Ellipse
E Crabapple Hill
F Growing Garden
G Pre-Columbian Museum
H North Vista
I Pebble Garden
J Swimming Pool
K Byzantine Collection
L Arbor Terrace
M Music Room
N Green Garden
O Beech Terrace
P Museum Entrance
Q Urn Terrace
R Rose Garden
S Fountain Terrace
T Main Building
U Garden Library
V Lovers Lane Pool
W Garden Entrance

Restaurants/Clubs: Red | Hotels: Purple | Shops: Orange | Outdoors/Parks: Green | Sights/Culture: Blue

3 MILLER AND ARNEY ANTIQUES, INC.

Eighteenth- and 19th-century American and European antiques, as well as lamps, rugs, and accessories, can be found here. ◆ M-Sa, 9:30AM-5:30PM. 1737 Wisconsin Ave NW (at S St). 338.2369. ৬. www.millerarney.com

4 DUMBARTON OAKS

Famous for its enchanting gardens and world-class museums of Byzantine and pre-Columbian art, this estate was originally part of the Port of Georgetown land grant made by Queen Anne in 1702. Former ambassador Robert Woods Bliss purchased the property in 1920, and he and his wife, Mildred, began assembling the present museum collection. In 1963 **Philip Johnson** designed a small museum (a group of eight domed glass cylinders) to house the **Pre-Columbian Collection**. The intricate objects designed by Aztecs, Mayans, and other peoples include gold necklaces and jade figurines. The adjacent **Byzantine Collection** displays mosaics, sculpture, ivories, and other medieval items. The restored 1801 mansion is filled with European art and architectural treasures; the **Music Room**, where the Blisses entertained such noted friends as composer Igor Stravinsky, contains El Greco's *The Visitation*.

Several libraries house books reserved for scholars, although the **Rare Books Room** is sometimes open for viewing. The libraries hold more than 150,000 books on landscape gardening and Byzantine and pre-Columbian art.

The 10 acres of formal gardens designed by Beatrix Farrand and Mrs. Bliss are a wonderland of manicured walkways, terraces, arbors, and pools. A favorite spot is the **Pebble Garden Fountain**, an expanse of intricately patterned pebble mosaics that sparkle through a thin layer of water in spring and summer. A graceful Italianate fountain features a pair of putti romping on seahorses while water springs from the hands of a third. ◆ Gardens: admission 15 Mar-Oct; free Nov-14 Mar. Tu-Su, 2-6PM, 15 Mar-Oct; 2-5PM, Nov-14 Mar. Museum: Donation. Tu-Su, 2-5PM. 1703 32nd St NW (between R and S Sts). Information, 339.6401; tours, 339.6409. www.doaks.org

5 MONTROSE PARK

⊕ This small, quiet, woodland-hugging park has tennis courts, a playground, picnic areas, and walking trails. **Lovers Lane**, a cobblestone walking path, forms the western border, separating Montrose and **Dumbarton Oaks** estate (see above). Tennis courts are available on a first-come, first-served basis. ◆ 30th and R Sts NW. 895.6000. ৬

6 BEALL HOUSE

George Washington's great-nephew, Colonel George Corbin Washington, and his bride, Elizabeth Beall, were given this house as a wedding gift by her father. The original Georgian structure, built in 1784, has been much altered. The building is now a private residence. ◆ 2920 R St NW (between 28th and 32nd Sts)

6 OAK HILL CEMETERY

⊕ Such notables as John Howard Paine (author of "Home, Sweet Home") and statesmen Edwin M. Stanton, James G. Blaine, and Dean Acheson are buried in this cemetery, given to the city by William Wilson Corcoran. The **1849 Gatehouse** and the simple Gothic Revival chapel, built in 1850 by **James Renwick**, are architecturally noteworthy. ◆ M-F, 10AM-4PM. 30th and R Sts NW. 337.2835

7 MACKALL-WORTHINGTON HOUSE

Built in 1820 by **Leonard Mackall**, this large, Federal-style house was once the focal point of the neighborhood it occupies. The incongruous mansard roof was added later. A private residence, it is not open to the public. ◆ 1686 34th St NW (between Reservoir Rd and R St)

8 A MANO

Glimmers of Provence and Tuscany suffuse this shop where majolica and faïence tableware and garden pots, fine linens, and imported silver abound. ◆ M-Sa, 10AM-6PM; Su, noon-5PM. 1677 Wisconsin Ave NW (between Q and R Sts). 298.7200

8 CARLING NICHOLS

This small boutique sells high-end 18th- and 19th-century Chinese antiques like desks, tables, and chairs. ◆ Tu-Su, noon-5PM; M by appointment. 1675 Wisconsin Ave NW (between Reservoir Rd NW and R St). 338.5600

pâtisserie poupon
tradition française

9 PÂTISSERIE POUPON

Artistic pastries and chocolate are created at this authentic Parisian patisserie. Whether for tea or lunch, customers are tempted by sweets, salad platters, huge baguette sandwiches, and superb coffee. ◆ Tu-Sa, 8AM-6:30PM; Su, 8AM-4PM. 1645

Wisconsin Ave NW (between Q and R Sts). 342.3248

9 MARSTON LUCE

Eighteenth- and 19th-century French painted furniture and folk art are sold here. ♦ Tu-Sa, 11AM-5PM. 1651 Wisconsin Ave NW (between Q St and Reservoir Rd). 333.6800. ♿

10 SASSANOVA

Imelda Marcos, eat your heart out. Run by a pair of New York City transplants, this fashionable boutique with a leopard-print carpet carries women's shoes from Hollywould, Terre Peck, Cynthia Rowley, and other high-style lines not found many places around DC. There's also a nice selection of jewelry, handbags, and gift items like photo albums and note cards. ♦ Tu-Sa, 10AM-6PM; Su, noon-5PM. 1641 Wisconsin Ave NW (between Q St and Reservoir Rd). 471.4400. www.sassanova.com

11 SUGAR

In a sweet, white-walled space, racks hold floaty tops, girly dresses, and slim-fitting pants by names like Nanette Lepore, Beth Bowley, Hype, and Tibi. Other finds include accessories like delicate drop earrings, necklaces, and purses. ♦ M-W, F, Sa, 10:30AM-6PM; Th, 10:30AM-7PM; Su, noon-5PM. 1633 Wisconsin Ave NW (between Q St and Reservoir Rd). 333.5331. www.sugardc.com

11 SPACE

Lucite chairs, patent leather pillows, bright colored rugs, and Asian screens are just some of the goods you'll find at this shop that fills two floors of a former row house. ♦ Tu-Sa, 10AM-6PM; Su, noon-6PM. 1625 Wisconsin Ave NW (between Q St and Reservoir Rd). 333.0140. www.space-dc.com

12 URBAN CHIC

Super-stylish mannequins stand in the windows of this new women's boutique, hinting at the celeb-worthy clothes inside. The roster of designers featured reads like something out of In Style—Blue Cult, Catherine Malandrino, Rock & Republic, Shoshanna, Three Dots. Clotheshorses could do some serious damage here. ♦ Tu-Sa, 10:30AM-7PM; Su, noon-5PM. 1626 Wisconsin Ave NW (between Q St and Reservoir Rd). 338.5398. www.urbanchic-dc.com

13 TUDOR PLACE

Martha Washington's granddaughter, Martha Parke Custis, and her husband, Thomas Peter,

were the original occupants of this house, completed in 1816 by architect **Dr. William Thornton**. Their descendants lived here until 1983. Between 1805 and 1816, wings were added to the original pavilion; the entire structure is now open to the public as a historic house, with period furnishings and formal gardens. Breathtaking candlelight tours are given during the Christmas season. ♦ Admission. Tours: Tu-F, 10AM, 11:30AM, 1PM, 2:30PM; Sa, 10AM-3PM, on the hour; Su, noon-3PM, on the hour. Closed Jan. 1644 31st St NW (between Q and R Sts). 965.0400. ♿ www.tudorplace.org

14 COOKE'S ROW

Although Georgetown is perhaps best known for its Federal-style buildings, these mid-Victorian charmers offer a welcome twist on the row-house theme. Built in 1868 by **Starkweather & Plowman**, each of the four villas has more than 4,000 square feet of space and its own side yard. The exterior details—bay windows, dormers, porches—give each building its own character: The outer two are in the Second Empire style; the middle two are Italianate. Inside, however, these four private residences have exactly the same floor plan. ♦ 3007-29 Q St NW (between 30th and 31st Sts)

15 EVERMAY

In 1801, when it was built by **Nicholas King**, this was considered the most elegant house in the city—and that was back when opulence was the neighborhood norm. Now available for weddings and other events, it has been restored to its former extravagance and features a garden of Southern favorites such as azaleas, magnolias, and boxwood. ♦ 1623 28th St NW (between Q and R Sts). www.evermay.org

16 DUMBARTON HOUSE

Known until 1932 as **Belle Vue**, this is a typical early-19th-century Georgian home complete with oval rooms, ornate mantels, and breezy hallways. **Benjamin Latrobe** installed the rear bays. The house is now owned by the National Society of the Colonial Dames of America, which has maintained the Federal furnishings, including Hepplewhite and Sheraton pieces, and fine collections of silver and textiles. Tours Tu-Sa, 10:15AM, 11:15AM, 12:15PM, and 1:15PM. ♦ Donation. Tu-Sa. 2715 Q St NW (between 27th and 28th Sts). 337.2288. ♿ www.dumbartonhouse.org

17 GEORGETOWN UNIVERSITY

Founded by Father John Carroll in 1789, the country's first Roman Catholic university has

Restaurants/Clubs: Red | Hotels: Purple | Shops: Orange | Outdoors/Parks: Green | Sights/Culture: Blue

always been open to "students of every religious profession" and today its students hail from 130 countries around the world. But even if you haven't come for an education, its shady cobblestoned streets make for a pleasant walk.

The **Old North Building** was the original structure, finished in 1792. The fortresslike **Healy Building**, built in 1879 by **Smithmeyer and Pelz**, is a grim German Gothic affair topped with an amazing spire. (The best view of the school's famous spires is to be had across the river in Arlington.) The building was named for the Reverend Patrick Healy, the country's first black person to earn a doctorate.

The university's highly regarded **School of Medicine** sponsors a 609-bed hospital. Other colleges include schools of arts and sciences, nursing, and business administration. **GU**'s location in the nation's capital is one reason it includes the country's first and largest foreign service program.

Campus tours are offered weekdays and Saturday mornings; call the admissions office for more information. ♦ 37th and O Sts NW. Information, 687.0100; admissions and tours, 687.3600. ♿ www.georgetown.edu

18 VOLTA BUREAU

Built in 1893 by **Peabody & Stearns**, this strange amalgam of early Roman temple and institution is home to the **Alexander Graham Bell Association for the Deaf and Hard of Hearing**. Bell funded the building with money he received from his work on the phonograph, and there's a small monument to him inside. ♦ 3417 Volta Pl NW (at 35th St). 337.5221. ♿

19 CONVENT OF THE VISITATION

After a near-disastrous fire in 1993 destroyed much of Visitation School, the convent and school were rebuilt and expanded. The convent's three buildings—an 1820 Federal-style chapel, a Gothic monastery, and an ornate Victorian school building dating from 1872—represent a merry pastiche of 19th-century tastes. ♦ 35th St NW (between P St and Reservoir Rd)

20 POMANDER WALK

Renovation in the 1950s changed this from a blighted alley to a charming set of private residences.

21 HUGO BOSS

Elegant men's suits, casual sportswear, accessories, and other items by the German designer fill this shop. ♦ M-Sa, 11AM-7:30PM; Su, noon-5PM. 1517 Wisconsin Ave NW (between P and Q Sts). 625.BOSS

22 THE PHOENIX

This boutique offers women's clothing and a quality collection of handcrafted items from Mexico: wedding dresses, contemporary silver jewelry, candelabras, and pottery. ♦ M-Sa, 10AM-6PM; Su, 1-6PM. 1514 Wisconsin Ave NW (between P St and Volta Pl). 338.4404. www.thephoenixdc.com. ♿

22 CAFÉ BONAPARTE

★$ It's not Paris, but it's close. This charming café serves crepes, gourmet coffees, soups, pastries, and other French-style fare. Right in the heart of Wisconsin Avenue's shopping zone, it's a good place to stop for lunch or an afternoon snack. ♦ French ♦ M-F, breakfast, lunch, and dinner; Sa, Su, brunch and dinner. 1522 Wisconsin Ave NW (between P St and Volta Pl). 333.8830. www.cafebonaparte.com

23 PROPER TOPPER

All kinds of hats—from berets and fedoras to dress hats and straw boaters—fill this chic shop. There are toppers for men, women, and children. The store also sells stylish jewelry and scarves and hip gifts (candles, note cards, etc.). Don't miss the pleasant garden behind the shop. ♦ M-F, 10AM-6PM; Sa, 10AM-7PM; Su, 11AM-6PM. 3213 P St NW (between 32nd St and Wisconsin Ave). 333.6200. www.propertopper.com. Also at 1350 Connecticut Ave NW. 842.3055. Metro: Dupont Cir

24 APPALACHIAN SPRING

Fine country-style American crafts, including pottery, quilts, and jewelry, are sold here. ♦ M-F, 10AM-8PM; Sa, 10AM-6PM; Su, noon-6PM. 1415 Wisconsin Ave NW (between O and P Sts). 337.5780. ♿

24 THOMAS SWEET ICE CREAM

Bon Appetit has named this old-fashioned ice-cream parlor "among the ten best in America." Fine coffee, bagels, soup, and homemade sandwiches are also among the offerings. ♦ M-Th, 8AM-midnight; F, Sa, 8AM-1AM; Su, 9AM-midnight. 3214 P St NW (at Wisconsin Ave). 337.0616

25 THE RALLS COLLECTION

A Sothebys.com associate, this gallery specializes in contemporary photography, paintings, and sculpture by artists like Tom Baril, Annie Leibovitz, and Michael Kenna. ♦

Tu-Sa, 11AM-4PM and by appointment. 1516 31st NW (between P and Q Sts). 342.1754. www.rallscollection.com

26 Miller House

This New England clapboard-style house is set in the midst of the city's original neighborhood. The portico hints at the Greek Revival styles that gained popularity soon after it was built in 1840. It's now a private residence. ♦ 1524 28th St NW (between P and Q Sts)

27 Reuben Daw's Fence

Made in the 1860s of musket barrels from the 1848 Mexican-American War, this fence encloses three houses on P Street and a pair on 28th Street. ♦ 2803 P St NW (at 28th St)

28 Just Paper & Tea

Handmade gift wrap, faux-finishing supplies, tea in bulk, unusual pens, and creative cards are just some of the wonderful miscellany that fill this shop. ♦ Tu-Sa, 10AM-5PM. 3232 P St NW (at Wisconsin Ave). 333.9141

28 Yiro

This is one of the most unusual stores in DC, offering organic clothing and accessories for newborns to 8-year-olds. Organic comfort products for body and bath for expectant and new mothers is also a specialty here. ♦ M-F, 10AM-7PM; Sa, 10AM-6PM; Su, 11AM-5PM. 3236 P St NW (at Wisconsin Ave). 338.9476. www.yirostores.com

29 Commander Salamander

The source for all things fabulous: myriad articles of black clothing, sequins, rhinestone sunglasses, and the latest in hairspray colors. The funky-punky clientele alone is worth seeing. ♦ M-Th, 10AM-9PM; F, Sa, 10AM-10PM; Su, 11AM-7PM. 1420 Wisconsin Ave NW (between O and P Sts). 337.2265. &

30 Christ Church, Georgetown

Built in 1886 by **Henry Law**, this scaled-down Gothic cathedral features an unusual gabled tower. Although it's too small to be really awe-inspiring, it fits neatly into the neighborhood. This is actually the third building on the site; the parish was founded in 1817. The chapel and its garden, adjacent to the west of the church, were added in 1968. The chapel was designed by **Philip Ives**, and the garden landscape design was by Peter G. Rolland. Francis Scott Key was a

member of the Episcopal congregation. ♦ 3116 O St NW (between 31st St and Wisconsin Ave). 333.6677. www.christchurchgeorgetown.org. &

31 Susquehanna Antiques

American and English antiques of the 18th and 19th centuries, plus some 19th- and 20th-century paintings, can be found here. ♦ M-F, 10AM-6PM; Sa, 10AM-5PM. 3216 O St (between Wisconsin Ave and Potomac St). 333.1511. &. www.susquehannaantiques.com

31 St. John's Episcopal Church, Georgetown Parish

The second-oldest Episcopal church in DC was built in 1809 by **Dr. William Thornton** and renovated in 1870 by **Starkweather & Plowman**. Like Thornton's design for the **Capitol**, this Georgian edifice was drastically altered in the renovation. ♦ Services: Su, 9AM and 11AM. 3240 O St NW (at Potomac St). 338.1796. &

32 Five Guys

★★$ This popular local burger chain took over the space once occupied by **Au Pied de Cochon**, a notorious spy site. But today there's nothing sneaky going on here, just great ground beef burgers (repeatedly voted the area's best by *Washingtonian* magazine readers) and fresh-cut spicy fries. ♦ American ♦ Su-Th, 11AM-midnight; F, Sa, 11AM-4AM. 1335 Wisconsin Ave NW (at Dumbarton St). 337.0400. www.fiveguys.com. Also at 808 H St NW (at 8th St). 393.2900. Metro: Gallery Pl/Chinatown; 2301 Georgia Ave NW (at Bryant St). 986.2235

32 Betsey Johnson

A bevy of zebra skirts, crushed-velvet dresses, fleecy coats with that destroyed-by-the-dry-cleaner look, and plaid everything is displayed in this ultrahip shop. If this is your thing (and your wallet allows), go ahead and pounce. ♦ M-F, 11AM-7PM; Sa, 11AM-8PM; Su, noon-6PM. 1319 Wisconsin Ave NW (between N and Dumbarton Sts). 338.4090. www.betseyjohnson.com

33 Cox's Row

Built around 1817 by **John Cox**, this is often acclaimed as the finest series of Federal row houses in Georgetown. Some of the middle houses were remodeled during the Victorian era; the end houses remain as they were originally built. All are private residences now.

Restaurants/Clubs: Red | Hotels: Purple | Shops: Orange | Outdoors/Parks: Green | Sights/Culture: Blue

THE BEST

Nora Pouillon

Executive Chef and Owner,
Restaurant Nora and Asia Nora

Attending the Sunday-morning farmer's market at **Dupont Circle**—wonderful farmers selling fresh, seasonal produce—a great "village" atmosphere right in the heart of DC.

Going to the **East Wing** of the **National Gallery of Art**, where there are always interesting exhibits.

Also, the **Museum of Natural History, Freer Gallery**, and **Holocaust Museum**, along with so many of the other great museums in DC.

Bicycle riding along the paths of the canal.

Dinner at **Nora**'s—of course!

Rollerblading, skating, and biking along **Beach Drive** when it is closed.

Visiting the memorials at night—the **Lincoln** and **Vietnam Veterans** in particular—and sitting on the steps of the **Jefferson** overlooking the **Tidal Basin** across to the **White House**.

In spring, definitely check out the fantastic cherry blossoms around the Tidal Basin and drive through the dogwood trees and azaleas in the **Kenwood** neighborhood of **Bethesda**, Maryland.

Check out what is on at the **Kennedy Center**.

Take tea at the **Four Seasons Hotel** in Georgetown.

For nightlife, go to the **9:30 Club**, where there are always good bands/music.

Shop in **Georgetown Park**—stop at Dean & DeLuca for coffee or lunch, and don't forget to wander around the store and enjoy their fantastic selection of produce.

Rent a boat on the **Potomac** and go across to **Roosevelt Island**.

Step back into history and visit **Mount Vernon**. Scour the antiques shops on **Wisconsin Avenue**.

Visit the **Washington National Cathedral**.

Go for a drink at the top of the **Hotel Washington** on 15th Street.

Ice skating in front of the **Willard Hotel**.

Dining at **Asia Nora** too!

Driving out to the eastern shore and visiting **St. Michaels** and **Tilghman Island**—perfect for antiquing.

♦ 3327-39 N St NW (between 33rd and 34th Sts)

34 SMITH ROW

These five Federal houses, side by side, are nearly identical in construction. Built in 1815 by **Walter** and **Clement Smith**, all are now private residences. ♦ 3255-63 N St NW (between Potomac and 33rd Sts)

35 THE GEORGETOWN INN

$$$$ This recently refurbished 96-room hotel, one in a series of restored 18th-century buildings, features traditional décor and fine antiques throughout. Amenities include a restaurant (see below), small health club, room service, and valet parking. ♦ 1310 Wisconsin Ave NW (between N and O Sts). 333.8900, 800/424.2979; fax 333.8308. &. www.georgetowncollection.com

Within the Georgetown Inn:

DAILY GRILL

★★$$ Harking back to American grills of the 1920s, this casual eatery sports simple black booths, burnished wood, and black-and-white photos of Georgetown. Best bets from the enormous menu include Manhattan clam chowder, blackened chicken sandwich, Cobb salad, and strawberry shortcake. ♦ American ♦

Daily, breakfast, lunch, and dinner. 337.4900. &. www.dailygrill.com. Also at 1200 18th St NW (at M St). 822.5282 Metro: Farragut W

36 PAOLO'S

★★$$ This bar-restaurant fills the narrow site with a pleasing sense of space and style. The service here is both brisk and friendly, and the pasta, salads, and fish of the day stand out on the modern menu. ♦ Italian ♦ Daily, lunch and dinner. 1303 Wisconsin Ave NW (between N and Dumbarton Sts). 333.7353. &. www.paolosristorante.com

36 RANDOM HARVEST

The owners of this shop have gleaned objects from many a tasteful household. The stock includes handsome antique furniture, rugs, maps, frames, and mirrors as well as elegant new fabrics. ♦ M-Th, Sa, 11AM-6PM; F, 11AM-8PM; Su, noon-6PM. 1313 Wisconsin Ave NW (between N and Dumbarton Sts). 333.5569. Also at 7766 Woodmont Ave (between Old Georgetown Rd and Cheltenham Dr), Bethesda, Maryland. 301/280.2777. Metro: Bethesda; and at 810 King St (at Columbus St), Alexandria, Virginia. 703/548.8820. www.randomharvesthome.com. Metro: King St

37 MARTIN'S TAVERN

★★$$ The oldest tavern in Georgetown is warm, classy, and quieter than most other Irish pubs. Tiffany lamps and gold-framed paintings give the place a clubby feeling. The conservative clientele comes for the crab cakes or the excellent lamb chops. Especially charming around Christmas, the dining room is overtaken with extravagant decorations and holly, and a big red bow wraps the façade. ◆ Irish/American ◆M-F, breakfast, lunch, and dinner; Sa, Su, brunch and dinner. 1264 Wisconsin Ave NW (at N St). 333.7370. www.martins-tavern.com. 占

38 LAIRD MANSION (LAIRD-DUNLOP HOUSE)

Built in 1799, this was originally the home of tobacco merchant John Laird. Robert Todd Lincoln, son of the sixteenth president, also once owned this Federal-period mansion, now a private residence. ◆ 3014 N St NW (between 30th and 31st Sts)

39 SUSAN DECATUR HOUSE

After Commodore Stephen Decatur, the dashing naval hero of the War of 1812, was killed in a duel, his widow moved to this stately Federal-style house. Built in 1813 by **John Stull Williams**, it is now a private residence. ◆ 2812 N St NW (between 28th and 29th Sts)

40 1789

★★★$$$ Tucked in a town house, this restaurant offers impeccable service and a lavishly intimate Federal-style décor. Limoges china, American antiques, and a blazing fireplace in winter add to the enchanting mood. The menu is American, with chef Ris Lacoste often focusing on seafood. Crab cakes are a good starter, followed by the excellent rack of lamb in rosemary-Shiraz sauce. A pre-theater menu ($30) is served weekdays after 6:45PM. There's free valet parking. ◆ American ◆ Daily, dinner. Jacket required. Reservations recommended. 1226 36th St NW (at Prospect St). 965.1789. 占. www.1789restaurant.com

41 3600 PROSPECT STREET NORTHWEST

Scenes in *The Exorcist* were filmed at this redbrick building owned by **Georgetown University**. It was modified for the movie, but you can still walk down the steep steps (to M St) where the title character met his fate. ◆ Between 35th and 37th Sts

42 PROSPECT HOUSE

The view (or prospect) of the Potomac commanded from this sharply detailed Federal house by **James M. Lingan** is the basis for the name. Built in 1788, the house is now a private residence. ◆ 3508 Prospect St NW (between 35th and 37th Sts)

43 QUALITY HILL

The entire neighborhood may once have been called Quality Hill after its many fine homes; somehow, this 18th-century house by **John Thomson Mason** (the nephew of George Mason) was the sole inheritor of the nickname. It is now a private residence. ◆ 3425 Prospect St NW (between 34th and 35th Sts)

44 STODDERT HOUSE

This large, rangy, and ornate Federal town house was built in 1787 by owner and architect **Benjamin Stoddert**, who called it **Halcyon House**. Although the north façade has been completely redesigned, the south side and garden of this private residence remain as they were more than 2 centuries ago. ◆ 3400 Prospect St NW (at 34th St)

45 BOOEYMONGER

★★$ Huge sandwiches to eat in or take out are the specialty at this small café. Also try its locally famous cinnamon coffee. ◆ American ◆ Daily, breakfast, lunch, and dinner. 3265 Prospect St NW (at Potomac St). 333.4810. www.booeymonger.com. 占

46 MORTON'S OF CHICAGO

★★★$$$$ A favorite of Capitol Hill power-brokers, this macho steak house makes a show of parading its raw beef before customers to demonstrate the meat's quality and freshness. In truth, the steaks, which are shipped in from Chicago, are widely considered the best around. Be prepared, however, to pay dearly: These magnificent slabs of meat command hefty prices. ◆ Steak house ◆ Daily, dinner. Reservations recommended. 3251 Prospect St NW (between Wisconsin Ave and Potomac St). 342.6258. 占. www.mortons.com. Also at 1050 Connecticut Ave NW. 955.5997; and at 8075 Leesburg Pike (at Old Gallows Rd), Vienna, Virginia. 703/883.0800. 占

46 CAFE MILANO

★★$$$ Haute cuisine and haute couture combine to make this café a people-watcher's paradise. The "show" is good, and the fare is fresh and delicate; good choices include the house-made pastas and any of the enormous salads with shaved Parmesan. The café has a

---

Restaurants/Clubs: Red | Hotels: Purple | Shops: Orange | Outdoors/Parks: Green | Sights/Culture: Blue

very pleasant, and large, open-air terrace. ♦ Italian ♦ M-Sa, lunch and dinner; Su, brunch and dinner. 3251 Prospect St NW (between Wisconsin Ave and Potomac St). 333.6183. &. www.cafemilanodc.com

47 RESTORATION HARDWARE

This California-based outlet is not your father's hardware store. Occupying the old **Key Theater** (pictures of the much-loved Key hang in the windows), this shop carries furniture, house-wares, hardware, and offbeat items that invoke an earlier era—including the Slinky, rubber gardening boots, and cocktail shakers. ♦ M-Sa, 10AM-8PM; Su, 11AM-6PM. 1222 Wisconsin Ave NW (between M and Prospect Sts). 625.2771. &. www.restorationhardware.com. Also at 614 King St, Alexandria, Virginia. 703/299.6220. Metro: King St

48 LIGNE ROSET

Behind a Victorian exterior, a modern world awaits. A skylit shop is filled with sleek, contemporary sofas, tables, and beds. ♦ M-Sa, 11AM-6PM; Su, noon-5PM. 3306 M St NW. 333.6390. www.ligne-roset-usa.com

48 HOLLIS & KNIGHT

An eclectic array of furniture, rugs, lamps, home accessories, and antiques (some of it not carried anywhere else in DC) fills this two-level, 10,000-square-foot space near the Key Bridge. ♦ Tu-Sa, 10AM-6PM; Su, M, noon-5PM. 3320 M St NW. 333.6999. www.hollisandknight.com

49 ADITI

★★★$ This may not be the plushest Indian restaurant in town, but it's certainly one of the best, with complex curries, tandoori chicken, stir-fried lamb, and vegetarian selections that are just as satisfying as the meat dishes. ♦ Indian ♦ Daily, lunch and dinner. 3299 M St NW (at 33rd St). 625.6825. &

50 DEAN & DELUCA GEORGETOWN

New York's acclaimed food market has a Washington outpost in a former Victorian market in the heart of Georgetown, right next door to **The Shops at Georgetown Park** (see opposite). Shopping here is a twofold experi-ence: First your eyes pop at the vast selection of coffees, fresh pastas, deli items, fresh fish and meats, and gourmet nibblings; then your eyes pop again at the price of such quality. Careful shopping does yield some relative bargains. ♦ Daily, 10AM-8PM. 3276 M St NW (between Warehouse Pl and 33rd St). 342.2500. &. www.deandeluca.com

Within Dean & DeLuca Georgetown:

DEAN & DELUCA CAFÉ

★★★$ Take a load off with a cup of espresso or a sandwich. As with the food emporium, if

you order carefully, the bill won't dent your wallet too severely. ♦ Café ♦ Daily, breakfast, lunch, and dinner. 342.2500. &. Also at 1299 Pennsylvania Ave NW (at 13th St). 628.8155. &. Metros: Federal Triangle, Metro Center

51 CLYDE'S

★★$$ Almost 40 years old and nicely reno-vated in 1996, this archetypal fern bar has matured nicely, thank you. It's the place's classics that bring people back: the quintessential cozy-pub décor, good thick burgers, excellent crab cakes, and brunch—still among the best omelettes and Bloody Marys around. ♦ American ♦ M-F, lunch and dinner; Sa, Su, brunch and dinner. 3236 M St NW (between Wisconsin Ave and Warehouse Pl). 333.9180. &. www.clydes.com. Also at 70 Wisconsin Cir (between Western and Wisconsin Aves), Chevy Chase, Maryland. 301/951.9600

52 J. PAUL'S

★$$ The under-30 preppy crowd bellies up to the bar, while the dining room features decent bar food such as fresh seafood, pasta, burgers, chicken, and ribs. Check out the "meet market" at the bar through the large picture windows. ♦ American ♦ M-Sa, lunch and dinner; Su, brunch and dinner. 3218 M St NW (between Wisconsin Ave and Ware-house Pl). 333.3450. &. www.j-pauls.com

52 THE SHOPS AT GEORGETOWN PARK

Billed as the world's first shopping park, it is the only such commercial venture that overlaps a national park—the historic **C&O Canal** (see page 144), which has supported Georgetown trade since 1831. It was certainly the first DC shopping mall to capture the attention of well-heeled shoppers and reverse the retail traffic pattern back into Northwest Washington. Even Bill Clinton did some Christmas shopping here while he resided at 1600 Pennsylvania Avenue.

Built in 1981 behind a preserved and recon-structed century-old façade in the heart of commercial Georgetown, the mall boasts a magnificent Victorian interior. Its three levels of brass-and-iron-railed mezzanine shopping encircle a grand atrium and an indoor garden that flourishes under the skylight roof. All the details, from the brass-and-glass elevators to regular performances of classical music, give **Georgetown Park** an aura of sophistication (the prices do too).

Among the mall's tony fashion boutiques are **H&M** (298.6792) for men and women and **Monsoon** (338.6174) and **Arden B** (965.2655) for women. For gifts, try **Caswell-Massey** (965.3224) for upscale soaps and bath products and **Chesapeake Knife and Tool Co.** (338.5700) for cutlery, hunting and collectors' knives, and accessories. Shoppers get up to 2 hours of discounted parking with a $10 purchase, validated at the concierge center. ♦ Mall: M-Sa, 10AM-9PM; Su, noon-6PM. Individual store hours may vary. 3222 M St NW (between Wisconsin Ave and Warehouse Pl). 298.5577. www.shopsatgeorgetownpark.com

53 OLD GLORY ALL AMERICAN BARBECUE

★$$ Reveling in the flag, Elvis, Patsy Cline, and everything else that makes our country unique, this place has a noisy downstairs bar with TVs blaring the day's big sporting event and an upstairs dining room that is a little calmer. There's a choice of several sauces for your ribs. It's not as good as Mama's home cookin', though. ♦ Barbecue ♦ M-Sa, lunch and dinner; Su, brunch and dinner. 3139 M St NW (between 31st St and Wisconsin Ave). 337.3406. www.oldglorybbq.com

54 NATHAN'S

★★$$ Pin-striped politicos, lobbyists, and business people gravitate toward this clubby bar that has a quality view of the passing sidewalk crowd. In addition to a lively bar scene, this place has surprisingly good food (handmade pasta, fresh seafood). For brunch, try one of the five versions of eggs Benedict. ♦ American ♦ M-F, lunch and dinner; Sa, Su, brunch and dinner. Reservations recommended. 3150 M St NW (at Wisconsin Ave). 338.2000. ⑤. www.nathanslunch.com

54 GEORGETOWN TOBACCO

Native Washingtonian David Berkebile has supplied the city with smokes since 1964, and is ever popular with celebrities and politicians. ♦ M-Sa, 10AM-9PM; Su, noon-8PM. 3144 M St NW (between 31st and

Wisconsin Ave). 338.5100. ⑤. www.gttobacco.com. Also at Tyson's Corner Center, 1961 Chain Bridge Rd (between I-495 and International Dr), McLean, Virginia. 703/893.3366

55 MIE N YU

★★$$$ Over-the-top décor sets the scene at this newish restaurant and lounge. Several dining areas boast exotic accents like plush daybeds, fabric-covered walls, ornate ottomans, and crystal chandeliers. Both the design and the menu of contemporary American cuisine are influenced by the cultures and tastes of Asia, North Africa, and the Mediterranean. Think coffee-dusted grouper, Shanghai shrimp, and braised lamb shank. ♦ American ♦ M, Tu, dinner; W-Sa, lunch and dinner; Su, brunch and dinner. 3125 M St NW (between 31st St and Wisconsin Ave). 333.6122. www.mienyu.com

56 BISTRO FRANÇAIS

★★★$$ Francophiles will delight in the authentic bistro fare prepared in a romantic wood- and mirror-paneled restaurant. This café is great for after the theater, and it stays open to the wee hours. ♦ French ♦ Daily, lunch, dinner, and late-night meals. 3128 M St NW (between 31st St and Wisconsin Ave). 338.3830. www.bistrofrancaisdc.com. ⑤

57 URBAN OUTFITTERS

This is the source for dorm-room furnishings, trendy women's clothing by Free People and Lux, retro men's fashions, jewelry and accessories, and just about every other necessity for the **Georgetown University** set. ♦ M-Sa, 10AM-10PM; Su, 11AM-8PM. 3111 M St NW (between 31st St and Wisconsin Ave). 342.1012. ⑤. www.urbanoutfitters.com

58 MR. SMITH'S

★$ Fresh-fruit daiquiris and the garden patio are the big advertised draws for this casual

Thomas Twining, writing in 1795, describes Georgetown as "a small but neat town . . . the road from Virginia and the Southern States, crossing the Potomac here, already gives an air of prosperity to this little town, and assures its future importance, whatever may be the fate of the projected metropolis."

—*The Architecture of Washington*, American Institute of Architects

Restaurants/Clubs: **Red** | Hotels: **Purple** | Shops: **Orange** | Outdoors/Parks: **Green** | Sights/Culture: **Blue**

restaurant, but the piano bar in the front room also packs them in. Good burgers and sandwiches round out the fun. ♦ American ♦ Daily, lunch and dinner. 3104 M St NW (between 31st St and Wisconsin Ave). 333.3104. ♿

59 SMITH & HAWKEN

This gardeners' paradise occupies the second floor of a 200-year-old brick building. (Look for the shovel on the door.) Inside, find tools, seeds, pots, books, and other items useful for sprucing up outdoor spaces. ♦ M-W, 10AM-6PM; Th, F, 10AM-8PM; Sa, 10AM-7PM; Su, 11AM-5PM. 1209 31st St NW (between M and N Sts). 965.2680. www.smithandhawken.com

59 THE WASHINGTON POST OFFICE, GEORGETOWN BRANCH

In 1857 **Ammi Young** designed this timelessly simple composition of heavy plain stone walls, acclaimed as one of the best Italianate Federal buildings ever built. Stunningly renovated in 1997, it's worth a look. ♦ 1215 31st St NW (between M and N Sts). ♿

60 LOUGHBORO-PATTERSON HOUSE

An authentic Federal-period restoration, the house is made more interesting by a single delicate dormer in the roofline. It was built in 1806 and restored by **Macomber & Peter** 58 years later. It is used by the Junior League. ♦ 3037-41 M St NW (between 30th and 31st Sts)

60 OLD STONE HOUSE

This little cottage is believed to be the oldest structure built in DC. The house, a National Park Service site, is furnished in 18th-century style, and its old-fashioned gardens with fruit trees and masses of blooms are a welcome respite from the bustle of M Street. ♦ Free. House: Sa, Su, noon-5PM. Garden: daily, 9AM-4PM. 3051 M St NW (between 30th and 31st Sts). 426.6851. ♿ www.nps.gov/rocr/oldstonehouse

60 MISS SAIGON

★★$ Noodle soup with roasted quail, crisp spring rolls, and caramel salmon with black

The first known play produced in Washington was performed in Georgetown in 1790. McGrath's Company of Comedians presented *The Beggar's Opera*.

Mount Zion United Methodist Church at 1334 29th Street Northwest is reportedly the oldest black congregation in the District of Columbia, with records that go back to 1816. Before the Civil War, it was a station on the Underground Railroad.

pepper are some of the exotic specialties at this pretty pink-and-green restaurant, decorated with potted trees. The place is often packed. In warm months there's intimate seating on the adjacent patio. ♦ Vietnamese ♦ Daily, lunch and dinner. Reservations recommended on weekends. 3057 M St NW (between 30th and 31st Sts). 333.5545

60 BLUEMERCURY

The finest beauty, bath, and hair products (from Diptyque to Nars) are sold in this whimsical boutique. Patrons can sit at luxurious vanity tables and dab away with makeup samples. ♦ M-Sa, 10AM-8PM; Su, noon-6PM. 3059 M St NW (between 30th and 31st Sts). 965.1300. www.bluemercury.com. Also at 1619 Connecticut Ave NW (between Q and R Sts). 462.1300. Metro: Dupont Cir

61 GARRETT'S

★$ Upstairs in the dining room, the fare is pretty standard—burgers, pasta—but the downstairs bar is a popular neighborhood pub. On summer nights, there can be a lengthy wait to get in on either floor. ♦ American ♦ Daily, lunch and dinner. 3003 M St NW (between 30th and 31st Sts). 333.1033. www.garrettsdc.com

62 THE LATHAM HOTEL

$$$$ An offshoot of the Philadelphia original, this hotel offers 143 rooms, a rooftop pool, genuine elegance, and a prime location. Many of the rooms have great views of the C&O Canal. ♦ 3000 M St NW (at 30th St). 726.5000, 800/368.5922; fax 337.4250. ♿. www.georgetowncollection.com

Within the Latham Hotel:

CITRONELLE

★★★★$$$$ One of Washington's finest restaurants brings a little bit of L.A. to the capital city; the "French, California style" cuisine is both creative and aesthetically pleasing, and the open kitchen allows diners to watch the chef at work. Chef Michel Richard changes the menu frequently, but when available, the rack of lamb or Greek swordfish are musts. The restaurant's design is nearly as fine as its food: A lounge overlooks the sunken dining area, which is studded with plants and artwork. Besides the main room, there are two smaller dining rooms—one lined with glassed-in wine racks, and the other, an indoor garden. ♦ French ♦ Daily, breakfast and dinner. Jacket required. Reservations recommended. 625.2150. ♿. www.georgetowncollection.com

63 VIETNAM GEORGETOWN

★★$ One of the pioneers among Washington-area Vietnamese restaurants, it's still a great place for a quick, cheap meal. Try the spring rolls or the fragrant beef noodle soup; in warm weather, ask for a table on the patio. ♦ Vietnamese ♦ Daily, lunch and dinner. 2934 M St NW (between 29th and 30th Sts). 337.4536. ♿

64 AMERICAN STUDIO

This store showcases works by contemporary American ceramists and jewelers, as well as elegant housewares. Just call it Wedding Gift Central. ♦ M-Sa, 11AM-6PM; Su, 1-5PM. 2906 M St NW (between 29th and 30th Sts). 965.3273. ♿

INDESCRIBABLY DELICIOUS

65 ZED'S ETHIOPIAN CUISINE

★★$$ Excellent *watts* and *alitchas* (spicy sweet stews) and some of the best *injera* (a soft bread used in place of utensils) in DC can be found here. ♦ Ethiopian ♦ Daily, lunch and dinner. Reservations recommended for six people or more. 1201 28th St NW (at M St). 333.4710. ♿. www.zeds.net

66 THE FOUR SEASONS HOTEL

$$$$ Luxurious, elegant, and relaxed, this is a favorite resort of celebrities, including Tom Hanks, James Taylor, and Bonnie Raitt. Many of the 257 rooms overlook the historic **C&O Canal** or **Rock Creek Park**. Amenities include an elegant dining room (see below), a multilingual staff, 24-hour concierge and room service, a pool, a top-notch health club and spa, and valet parking. The **Garden Terrace** lounge overlooking Rock Creek, with its soft flowered sofas, piano, and profusion of greenery, is one of the city's best cocktail-hour rendezvous spots: A pleasureful afternoon tea is served here daily; and a light menu is available throughout the day. Children under 18 stay free. ♦ 2800 Pennsylvania Ave NW (between Rock Creek and Potomac Pkwy and M St). 342.0444, 800/332.3442; fax 944.2076. www.fourseasons.com

Within the Four Seasons Hotel:

SEASONS

★★★$$$$ The hotel's ultraposh dining room, with its floor-to-ceiling windows and slate floors, offers stylish fare in a stunning setting. Superb choices include honey-thyme roast chicken, and risotto. Ask to see the wine list, which has won awards from *Wine Spec-*

tator. Top the meal off with vanilla crème brûlée or the velvet chocolate pyramid. ♦ American ♦ M-Sa, breakfast, lunch, and dinner; Su, breakfast, brunch, and dinner. Reservations recommended. 342.0444. ♿

66 LORENZO

This boutique carries men's designer clothing (and a few women's items) direct from Italy—at prices that have so many zeros tacked on they seem to be quoted in lire. ♦ M-Sa, 11AM-7PM; Su, by appointment. 2812 Pennsylvania Ave NW. 965.6149

66 ANIMATION SENSATIONS

Original cartoon art—sketches, paintings, and animation cels—from *Peter Pan*, *Pinocchio*, *The Road Runner*, *Bugs Bunny*, and hundreds of other productions—can be found here. A host of studios, including Disney, Warner Brothers, and Hanna-Barbera, are represented. ♦ M-Sa, 10AM-6PM; Su, noon-5PM. 2902½ M St NW (between 28th and 29th Sts). 338.1097. www.animationsensations.com

67 FILOMENA RISTORANTE

★$$ A huge and noisy basement-level space with a tiled floor and lots of hanging greenery, this restaurant is filled with trendy types gobbling up pasta and veal, seafood, and chicken dishes. ♦ Italian ♦ M-Sa, lunch and dinner; Su, brunch and dinner. Reservations recommended. 1063 Wisconsin Ave NW (between the Chesapeake and Ohio Canal and M St). 338.8800. www.filomenadc.com

67 BLUES ALLEY

★$$ Since 1965, jazz fans have come to this intimate nightspot to hear such stars as Charlie Byrd, Maynard Ferguson, and Nancy Wilson. To complement the music, there's a menu of New Orleans–style dishes as well as seafood and steaks. Dinner guests are given preferential seating during the shows. Those who want to enjoy the music and the candlelight ambience without eating will have to pay a cover charge. The club is set on a small alley officially named in its honor in 1982. ♦ Southern ♦ Cover. Dinner.

Shows M-Th; Su, 8PM, 10PM; F, Sa, 8PM, 10PM, and sometimes midnight. Box office: daily, noon-10:30PM. Reservations recommended; required for certain shows. 1073 Wisconsin Ave NW (between the Chesapeake and Ohio Canal and M St). Main entrance on Blues Alley. 337.4141. www.bluesalley.com

68 Sea Catch

★★$$$ During warmer months, diners can enjoy crab cakes, poached lobster linguine, and Louisiana seafood gumbo at outdoor tables overlooking the **C&O Canal**. When it's cold outside, roaring fireplaces keep things cozy inside the brick-walled dining room. ◆ Seafood ◆ M-Sa, lunch and dinner. 1054 31st St NW (between South and M Sts). 337.8855. www.seacatchrestaurant.com

68 Parish Gallery

Part of the **Canal Square** complex, this gallery focuses on contemporary visual arts by artists from Africa and the African diaspora. Artists represented include David Boothman, Richard Mayhew, and Patricia Underwood. ◆ Tu-Sa, noon-6PM. 1054 31st St NW (between South and M Sts). 944.2310. www.parishgallery.com

69 Paper Moon

★$$ The neon-lit, sleek-style dining room is often noisy with a young international crowd who want to see and be seen in the wide-open dining room. The menu features good pasta served in enormous bowls, plus pizzas and salads. ◆ Italian ◆ Daily, lunch and dinner. Reservations recommended. 1073 31st St NW (between the Chesapeake and Ohio Canal and M St). 965.6666

One of the most distinctive elements of Washington Harbour's Postmodern architecture is a series of large lampposts that line the property's riverfront. The "lampposts" are actually pylons supporting an electronic floodgate that can be raised when the Potomac threatens.

The only two American presidents to be buried in Arlington Cemetery are John F. Kennedy and William Howard Taft.

The highest-ranking KGB agent to defect from the Soviet Union, Vitaly Yurchenko, escaped from his CIA handlers while dining at former restaurant Au Pied de Cochon to defect back to the Soviet Union. Soon after, the Georgetown restaurant introduced the "Yurchenko shooter," a drink of Stolichnaya and Grand Marnier.

70 Chesapeake and Ohio Canal

Historically, this is one of the last and best preserved of the great canals that helped move goods westward in the late 18th and early 19th centuries. An engineering marvel, the canal employs 74 locks and the 3,100-foot-long **Paw Taw Tunnel** carved through the stone mountains of western Maryland. The C&O extends just over 184 miles, from Georgetown to Cumberland, Maryland, where the Allegheny Mountains interrupted its intended meeting with the Ohio River.

The precursor of the C&O, the **Potowmack Canal** was the brainchild of George Washington: He invested $10,000 in the Potowmack Canal Company—stocks that were eventually left to endow **George Washington University**—and supervised much of the work. John Quincy Adams broke ground for the larger canal on 4 July 1828, and for several decades mule-drawn canal clippers slowly carried lumber, coal, whiskey, and grain from the West along the C&O. By the end of the 19th century, the railroad had stolen most of the canal's customers, and by 1924, the C&O was obsolete. The best-preserved portion of the canal is the 22-mile stretch from Georgetown to Seneca, Maryland, although you can hike or bike the old **Towpath** for the canal's entire length.

The National Park Service sponsors guided hikes and maintains campsites. The timberland nestled along the waterway and its rich wildlife make it an idyllic spot for outdoor activities, such as rock climbing (by permit) on its rugged overhangs, hiking, biking, canoeing, boating, and, in winter, ice-skating. There are even some old gold mines, battle sites, and cabins along the route.

From April through mid-September, catch the *Georgetown* at the dock at Thomas Jefferson Street in Georgetown (653.5190), the mule-drawn canal boat replica, run by operators in full period attire. For biking along the towpath, bikes can be rented at **Thompson Boat Center**, 2900 Virginia Avenue Northwest, at Rock Creek and Potomac Parkway (333.9543; www.thompsonboatcenter.com); **Revolution Cycles**, 3411 M Street Northwest, at the foot of the Key Bridge (965.3601; www.revolutioncycles.com); and **Fletcher's Boat House**, 4940 Canal Road Northwest (just north of Reservoir Road), 3 miles west of Georgetown (244.0461; www.fletchersboathouse.com). ◆ Admission for park and boat rides. *Georgetown* departures W-Su; schedule times vary; call ahead. C&O headquarters: 1850 Dual Hwy, suite 100, Hagerstown, Maryland. 301/739.4200; recording, 301/299.2026. www.nps.gov/choh. Georgetown Visitors' Center: 1057 Thomas Jefferson St NW (between K and M Sts). 653.5190

71 GRACE EPISCOPAL CHURCH

This early Gothic Revival stone church was established in 1866 as a mission to the boaters on the **Chesapeake and Ohio Canal** (see page 144). ♦ 1041 Wisconsin Ave NW (between South St and the Chesapeake and Ohio Canal). 333.7100. &. www.gracedc.org

72 RITZ-CARLTON, GEORGETOWN

$$$$ Located on the site of Georgetown's historic incinerator building and within walking distance to stores, restaurants, and the Georgetown waterfront, this new 86-room luxury hotel offers rooms and suites outfitted with feather duvets, goose-down pillows, and oversized marble baths. Amenities include 24-hour room service, twice-daily house-keeping, high-speed Internet access, and DVD players. There's an on-site fitness center as well as a spa offering facials, massages, and other services. **Fahrenheit Restaurant** on the top floor of the building serves regional American cuisine; the **Degrees Bar & Lounge** is an elegant spot for a martini or glass of wine. ♦ 3100 South St NW (at 31st St). 912.4100, 800/241.3333; fax 912.4199. &. www.ritz-carlton.com

73 CAFÉ LA RUCHE

★★★$$ A sophisticated renovation has given this café, a favorite among French nationals in Washington, a much sleeker look. Moss-green banquettes, late-18th-century framed French posters, and Parisian street signs only add to the appeal. Renowned for its fresh-fruit tarts, chocolate mousse, and luscious cakes, this restaurant balances the sweet stuff with huge salads, rich slices of zucchini pie and quiche, and low-priced daily specials, such as mussels, grilled chicken with garlic, and trout amandine. There's outdoor dining in warm weather. ♦ French ♦ M-F, lunch and dinner; Sa, Su, brunch and dinner. 1039 31st St NW (between K St and the Chesapeake and Ohio Canal). 965.2684. &. www.cafelaruche.com

74 WASHINGTON HARBOUR

After a cement factory occupied this river-front site for years, the Fine Arts Commission recommended that a park be built to replace it. Instead **Arthur Cotton Moore**'s bombastic mixed-use development was built in 1986. Though some may criticize its somewhat clunky flamboyance, it redeems itself by providing a boardwalk promenade with panoramic views of the river, a popular spot in fine weather. Also here are restaurants offering indoor and outdoor seating, a few shops, and an office complex. Boats docked at the boardwalk are available for sightseeing tours downriver to the **Mall** or **Old Town Alexandria** and back. ♦ 3000 K St NW (at 30th St). &

At Washington Harbour:

SEQUOIA

★★$$ The terrace tables of this harborside restaurant are arguably among the best places in town to catch the sunset on a warm evening. An immense interior dining room is for the see-and-be-seen crowd, although the view is difficult to upstage. The extensive menu of contemporary American cuisine includes seafood dishes, steak, and pork. ♦ American ♦ Daily, lunch and dinner. 944.4200. &

TONY AND JOE'S SEAFOOD PLACE

★$$$ Fish it is, served simply and fresh in a casual and comfortable dining room or at outdoor, waterside tables. ♦ Seafood ♦ Daily, lunch and dinner. 944.4545. &. www.tonyandjoes.com

The Whitehurst Freeway, the elevated roadway that provides a canopy over K Street along Georgetown's waterfront, was completed in 1949. The firm that handled the job, Alexander and Repass, was unusual for the time, because Alexander was black and Repass white, and Washington was very much a segregated city. The men had been friends since 1910, when they were teammates on the University of Iowa football team. Their company also completed the Tidal Basin project.

Restaurants/Clubs: Red | Hotels: Purple | Shops: Orange | Outdoors/Parks: Green | Sights/Culture: Blue

UPPER NORTHWEST

Woodley Park, Tenleytown, Cleveland Park, Spring Valley, Friendship Heights, and **Chevy Chase/DC** are all mini-neighborhoods in the triangle-shaped area known as **Upper Northwest**. Possessing a definite suburban feel, this is where many of Washington's loveliest homes and some of its finest shops can be found. **American**

MARYLAND

Davenport St. NW
Chesapeake St. NW
Brandywine St. NW
Albemarle St. NW
Yuma St. NW
Warren St. NW
Van Ness St. NW

River Rd. NW
41st St. NW
Nebraska Ave. NW

1 2
3 4
5
6 7
8

M Tenleytown/AU

Tenley Circle

International Dr. NW

9

SPRING VALLEY

49th St. NW
48th St. NW
46th St. NW
44th St. NW
42nd St. NW

38th St. NW
37th St. NW
36th St. NW
Reno Rd. NW

Upton St. NW
Tilden St. NW

Wesley Circle

University Ave. NW

Upton St. NW

13

Wisconsin Ave. NW

12
Tilder St.

Quebec St. NW

Ward Circle

Rodman St. NW
Quebec St. NW

15

16
Glover Archbold Park

Ordway St.
17
18
Newark St. NW

Dalecarlia Pkwy. NW

Rockwood Pkwy. NW
Loughboro Rd. NW

Embassy Park Dr. NW

Massachusetts Ave. NW

New Mexico Ave. NW

Idaho Ave. NW

26
27 CLEVELAND PARK
Woodley Rd. NW

25

Lowell St. NW
Klingle St. NW

Macomb St. NW
MacArthur Blvd. NW

Cathedral Ave. NW

Arizona Ave. NW

29
Battery Kemble Park

Hawthorne St. NW

Cathedral Ave. NW

30

34th St. NW

Sherrier Pl. NW

Garfield St. NW

44th St. NW

Garfield St. NW

33

Potomac Ave. NW

Chain Bridge Rd. NW

49th St. NW
Dexter St. NW

Fulton St. NW
Tunlaw Rd.

32
Dana Pl.

48th St. NW

Foxhall Rd. NW

42nd St. NW

Calvert St. NW

Edmunds St. NW
Davis St.
39

40 41
Hall Pl.

Observatory La.
42

Benton St. NW

W St. NW

45 V St. NW

W St. NW

Wisconsin Ave. NW

Dumbarton Oaks Par

46

Whitehaven Pkwy.

47

Reservoir Rd. NW

MacArthur Blvd. NW

Foxhall Rd. NW

Glover Archbold Park

37th St. NW

T St. NW

R St. NW

Reservoir Rd. NW

Georgetown Reservoir

Canal Rd. NW

Georgetown University

35th St. NW
34th St. NW
33rd St. NW

N St.
M St.

VIRGINIA

N

km
mi
1/4   1/2   1/2   1

Potomac River

Francis Scott Key Bridge

University is here, as is the **US Naval Observatory**, site of the vice president's residence. Nearby, on one of Washington's highest elevations, sits the magnificent **National Cathedral**. The area's two main commercial thoroughfares, **Wisconsin** and **Connecticut Avenues**, are lined with some of the city's finest historic apartment buildings, particularly along Connecticut north of the **National Zoo**. Upper Northwest's third "Main Street," **Massachusetts Avenue**, is lined with embassies both magnificent and modest. Adding to the refined atmosphere is the Cleveland Park area, between the **Cathedral** and Connecticut Avenue. Cleveland Park takes its name from President Grover Cleveland, who, in the late 19th century, led an exodus of Washingtonians here to escape Downtown's steamy summer humidity, which was especially suffocating in the low-lying **Mall** area near the **Potomac**. The higher ground and leafy shade trees in this area provided respite and a site for luxurious mansions, one of which— **Hillwood**, owned by cereal heiress Marjorie Merriweather Post—now serves as a museum.

Washington's most far-flung neighborhood, Upper Northwest offers the quiet of suburbia within city limits and rewards the casual stroller with yet another view of our multifaceted national home. But unless you're driving, reaching certain spots in this tranquil refuge can be time-consuming: As some places are far from any **Metrorail** stop, the slower **Metrobus** is your only option.

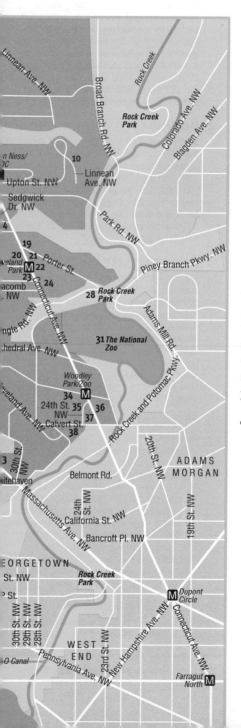

1 BOOEYMONGER

★★$ Overstuffed sandwiches—from a Reuben to the Veggie Special—are the forte of this casual restaurant. The brownies are divine. ♦ American ♦ Daily, breakfast, lunch, and dinner. 5252 Wisconsin Ave NW (between Harrison and Jenifer Sts). 686.5805. www.booeymonger.com. ♿ Metro: Friendship Heights

1 MAZZA GALLERIE

Neiman Marcus (966.9700) anchors this high-fashion mall. Among the two dozen or so other stores are **Filene's Basement** (966.0208) for budget shopping; **Williams-Sonoma** (237.1602) for fine housewares; and **Pampillonia Jewelers** (263.6305) for bangles and baubles. A recent, large-scale renovation converted the entire third floor into an upscale multiplex cinema. ◆ M-F, 10AM-8PM; Sa, 10AM-7PM; Su, 10AM-5PM. 5300 Wisconsin Ave NW (at Jenifer St). 966.6114. ⚹. www.mazzagallerie.com. Metro: Friendship Heights

1 SYLENE

This unique store, close to Tiffany's, Brooks Brothers, and Saks Fifth Avenue, located in an up-market shopping district, offers the widest array of lingerie in the DC area. Owned and operated by two sisters for more than 30 years, it has everything a woman needs. They also donate to women's shelters and other charitable groups. ◆ M-Sa, 10AM-6PM. 4407 S Park Ave (at Wisconsin Ave). 301/654.4200. www.sylenedc.com. Metro: Friendship Heights

2 ROCHE BOBOIS

Extremely elegant (and expensive) European furniture is sold at this shrine to interior decoration. ◆ M-W, F, Sa, 10AM-6PM; Th, 10AM-8PM. 5301 Wisconsin Ave NW (at Jenifer St). 686.5667. ⚹. www.roche-bobois.com. ⚹. Metro: Friendship Heights

2 CHEVY CHASE PAVILION

More subdued and low-key than most malls, this one has two dozen stores and restaurants on three levels that surround a skylit atrium; the whole place is decorated in cool green, gold, and cream. Giant palm trees line the requisite fast-food establishments on the bottom floor. Stores include **Pottery Barn** (244.9330) for housewares and **Georgette Klinger** (686.8880) for facials, manicures, and pedicures. ◆ M-Sa, 10AM-8PM; Su, noon-5PM. 5345 Wisconsin Ave NW (between Jenifer St and Western Ave). 686.5335. www.ccpavilion.com. Metro: Friendship Heights

Within Chevy Chase Pavilion:

THE CHEESECAKE FACTORY

★$$ This bustling California import specializes in cheesecakes, of course (more than 30 flavors). Before you indulge in dessert, peruse the extensive menu, which offers a dizzying variety of entrées. You may want to share the huge portions. Good bets are the crab cakes and fried calamari. Long waits for a table are

common. ◆ American ◆ M-Sa, lunch and dinner; Su, brunch and dinner. 364.0500. ⚹. www.thecheesecakefactory.com. Also at 2900 Wilson Blvd, Arlington, Virginia. 703/294.9966. Metro: Clarendon

2 EMBASSY SUITES HOTEL AT CHEVY CHASE PAVILION

$$$$ Located right above **Chevy Chase Pavilion** (see left), this all-suite hotel offers 198 suites with kitchenettes; a health club with an indoor pool, sauna, and Jacuzzi; and meeting rooms. All rates include complimentary breakfast and cocktails. Children under 19 stay free. ◆ 4300 Military Rd NW (at 43rd St). 362.9300, 800/EMBASSY; fax 686.3405. ⚹. Metro: Friendship Heights

2 BAMBULE

★★$$ Around 40 kinds of tapas are served at this attractive spot, which offers seasonal outdoor seating, flamenco dancers on Thursdays, and live "Gypsy-rumba" music Fridays and Saturdays. Roughly translated, the name means "How's it going?" ◆ Spanish ◆ M-Sa, lunch and dinner; Su, brunch and dinner. 5225 Wisconsin Ave NW. 966.0300. Metro: Friendship Heights

3 AMERICAN CITY DINER

★$ This re-creation of a 1950s diner is authentic down to the Coke machine, tabletop jukeboxes, and the menu, which includes the inevitable burgers, chili dogs, and milk shakes. Free movies with free popcorn are shown some nights on a heated, covered deck. ◆ American ◆ M-Th, Su, breakfast, lunch, and dinner; F, Sa, 24 hours. 5532 Connecticut Ave NW (at Morrison St). 244.1949. ⚹. www.americancitydiner.com. Metro: Friendship Heights

3 MAGRUDER'S

This gourmet food store, part of a local chain, is famous for its produce. Though not as roomy as suburban locations, it offers a better selection than most grocers in the area. There's parking in the rear. ◆ Daily. 5626 Connecticut Ave NW (at Northampton St). 244.7800. ⚹. www.magruders.com. Metro: Friendship Heights. Also at 3527 Connecticut Ave NW. 237.2531. Metro: Cleveland Park; 7010 Columbia Pike, Annandale, Virginia. 703/941.8864. ⚹; and 205 N Washington St (at Beall Ave), Rockville, Maryland. 301/424.1098. ⚹. Metro: Rockville

4 POLITICS AND PROSE

This full-service bookstore specializes in, but isn't limited to, the books and interests of local authors, be they public policy or fiction. Great book-signing parties are held here. Comfortable furniture for browsers is a nice

The first movie at the Uptown Theater on Connecticut Avenue Northwest was *Cain and Mabel*, with Marion Davies and Clark Gable. The Uptown still hosts Washington premieres with Hollywood stars at the openings. Locals know to look for the crisscrossed spotlights that illuminate the night sky—and the stretch limos that block the avenue.

touch. A pleasant coffee bar addition in the lower level serves pastries and light lunches. Parking in the rear. ♦ M-Th, 9AM-10PM; F, Sa, 9AM-11PM; Su, 10AM-8PM. 5015 Connecticut Ave NW (between Fessenden St and Nebraska Ave). 364.1919. &. www.politics-prose.com. Metro: Tenleytown/AU

4 MARVELOUS MARKET

With the best bread south of New York, this bakery also offers sandwiches and the usual assortment of coffees and light snack foods. ♦ M-Sa, 7:30AM-8PM; Su, 8AM-7PM. 5035 Connecticut Ave NW (between Fessenden St and Nebraska Ave). 686.4040. &. www.marvelousmarket.com. Metro: Tenleytown/AU. Also at 1511 Connecticut Ave NW (between Dupont Cir and Q St). 332.3690. &. Metro: Dupont Cir; 3217 P St NW. 333.2591; and 4832 Bethesda Ave (between Woodmont Ave and Arlington Rd), Bethesda, Maryland. 301/986.0555. &. Metro: Bethesda

5 YUSAKU

★$$ Sushi, tempura, and other Japanese favorites are served in an airy dining room and sidewalk café. ♦ Japanese ♦ M-F, lunch and dinner; Sa, Su, dinner. 4712 Wisconsin Ave NW (between Chesapeake and 42nd Sts). 363.4453. www.yosakusushi.com. &. Metro: Tenleytown/AU

6 MORTY'S

★★$$ Appearing like a mirage to homesick New Yorkers, this deli doles out potato pancakes, blintzes, lox and bagels, and matzoh ball soup. It also has an interesting array of photographs on the walls. ♦ Jewish ♦ Daily, 8AM-9PM. 4620 Wisconsin Ave NW (between Brandywine and Chesapeake Sts). 686.1989. &. Metro: Tenleytown/AU

7 DANCING CRAB & MALT SHOP

★$$ Crabs are the order of the day. Grab a mallet and a pitcher of beer, and go to it. Dress in keeping with the casual atmosphere—the tablecloths are brown paper; the napkins, paper towels. ♦ Seafood ♦ M-Sa, lunch and dinner; Su, dinner. Reservations recommended. 4611 Wisconsin Ave NW (between 41st and Davenport Sts). 244.1882. www.dancingcrab.com. Metro: Tenleytown/AU

8 GUAPO'S

★$$ **American University** students and neighborhood locals head here for reasonably priced fajitas and margaritas. House specialties include mesquite-grilled pork ribs and jumbo shrimp sautéed with fresh garlic and Spanish onions. ♦ Mexican ♦ Daily, lunch and dinner. 4515 Wisconsin Ave NW. 686.3588. www.guaposrestaurant.com. Metro: Tenleytown. Also at 4038 S 28th St, Arlington, Virginia. 703/671.1701; and 8130 Wisconsin Ave, Bethesda, Maryland. 301/656.0888 Metro: Bethesda

9 UNIVERSITY OF THE DISTRICT OF COLUMBIA (UDC)

Chartered in 1974, UDC is a commuter school, with most of its students attending part time. The 10-building complex at the urban **Van Ness** campus houses the colleges of liberal arts, law, business, and engineering, as well as a 1,000-seat auditorium, a physical activities center, outdoor tennis courts, an FM radio station (**WDCU**), a cable TV station, and an athletic field. ♦ 4200 Connecticut Ave NW (at Van Ness St). 274.5000. &. www.udc.edu. Metro: Van Ness/UDC

10 HILLWOOD

There are plenty of good reasons to visit the estate of the late Marjorie Merriweather Post, cereal heiress and longtime cornerstone of DC—and American—society. A recent renovation here improved climate conditions for art preservation, returned the gardens to their 1950s (during Mrs. Post's lifetime) appearance, and added a new visitors' center that includes a theater, reservations office, and museum shop. The house, a 40-room redbrick Georgian mansion designed by **John M. Deibert**, dates from 1926, when it was a showpiece of Gatsby-esque formality. The estate was purchased by Post in 1955, and under her direction it surpassed its earlier opulence. A 2-year renovation by **Alexander McIlvaine** included the addition of a third story to the structure. The heiress's staff included a chef, a butler, a footman, and a resident curator. The last is a clue to the estate's raison d'être: Every bit a museum even while it was a residence, the place displayed an excellent and eccentric collection of French and Imperial Russian art. Included are gilded icons and ecclesiastical vestments, portraiture and folk art, Fabergé eggs, gold and silver crafts, and fine porcelain, including pieces commissioned by Catherine the Great. (Post had traveled with one of her husbands, an ambassador to the Soviet Union, on the eve of World War II.) Fine French furniture and tapestries fill the house.

Outside, on the 25-acre estate, are formal Japanese and French gardens, a one-room Russian dacha (summerhouse), and a **Rose Garden** (created by Perry Wheeler,

---

Restaurants/Clubs: Red | Hotels: Purple | Shops: Orange | Outdoors/Parks: Green | Sights/Culture: Blue

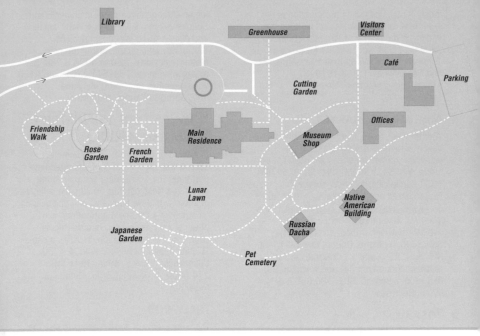

who also designed the famous Rose Garden at the White House), exhibiting thousands of varieties of flora. Within the greenhouses alone flourish 2,000 orchid plants. Finally, to the southeast, over the treetops of **Rock Creek Park** (see page 154), is a stunning view of the **Washington Monument**. Self-guided and docent-led tours are offered, featuring a film on the history of Hillwood narrated by Post's daughter, Dina Merrill Hartley.

Reservations are required several weeks in advance for house tours; a refundable reservation deposit is also required. Children under 6 are not allowed on the mansion tour. An on-the-premises café serves light fare and a proper tea with scones. ♦ Admission (refundable reservation deposit). Tu-Sa, 10AM-5PM (closed Jan). Tours: Tu-Sa, 9:30AM (self-guided), 12:30PM (docent-led), 2:30PM (self-guided); reservations required several weeks in advance. Café: Tu-Sa. 4155 Linnean Ave NW (just north of Upton St). 686.5807. www.hillwoodmuseum.org. Metro: Van Ness/UDC (a 20-minute walk)

11 KUWAITI EMBASSY, CULTURAL DIVISION

This gracefully balanced cube artfully plays with the Islamic motif of rotated squares. Note how the square tinted windows are cut diagonally by steel tubes. It was designed in 1982 by the architectural firm **Skidmore, Owings & Merrill**. ♦ 3500 International Dr NW (just south of Van Ness St). 364.2100. www.kuwaitculture.com. Metro: Van Ness/UDC

12 THE INTELSAT BUILDING

A silvery spaceship, improbably located on a bustling commercial strip, houses the United Nations of satellite communications. Octagonal office "pods," protected from the sun by louvers of photogray glass, and cylindrical stair towers faced in glass brick are clustered around four top-lit atria. **John Andrews** laid out the complex with the local architectural firm of **VVKF** to create an energy-efficient working environment. Existing trees were preserved, but the building makes no attempt to hide itself from public gaze. ♦ 3400 International Dr NW (south of Van Ness St). ৬. Metro: Van Ness/UDC

13 CAFÉ OLÉ

★★★$$ Mezze (small portions) of French, Italian, North African, and other cuisines are the specialty at this simple, modern eatery. The vast menu offers round-the-world tasting with such superb dishes as chicken Provençal and *polenta tartufo* (grilled mushrooms mixed with caramelized onions and garlic). Year-round outdoor dining is available on the enclosed patio. ♦ International ♦ M-F, lunch and dinner; Sa, Su, brunch and dinner. 4000 Wisconsin Ave NW (between Rodman and Van Ness Sts). 244.1330. www.cafeoledc.com. ৬. Metro: Tenleytown/AU

THE BEST

Sherri Dalphonse

Senior Editor, *Washingtonian* magazine

Marveling at the view from the rooftop café of the **Hotel Washington**.

Taking an early-morning ride on one of the many bike paths in Virginia, especially the **Mount Vernon Trail** along the **Potomac River** and the **W&OD Trail** through the countryside.

Seeing a movie in the restored splendor of the **Uptown Theater**.

Getting a half-price ticket 90 minutes before any play (that's not sold out) at **Arena Stage**.

Wandering about the **National Zoo** on a warm spring day, stopping to see the exotic Komodo dragons and to watch the orangutans on their high-wire act.

Catching dinner and a show in **Adams Morgan**: Start with wonderful Ethiopian food at **Meskerem**, then head to **Café Toulouse** for live jazz.

Going to the **National Building Museum**, which is in a grand space and has a terrific gift shop.

Seeing the azaleas in bloom at the **US National Arboretum**.

Taking visitors to the **Einstein** statue on **Constitution Avenue**.

Idling away some time at **Kramerbooks & afterwords café**, a bookstore-and-café that has a wonderful selection of books and a good brunch—and it's open 24 hours on weekends.

14 SEDGWICK GARDENS

This is the highlight of several blocks of subdued Art Deco apartments along this stretch of Connecticut Avenue. Architect **Mihran Mesrobian** animated the building's expanse of brick with rich detailing, giving the private residence a splendid porte cochere. ♦ 3726 Connecticut Ave NW (between Rodman St and Sedgwick Dr). Metros: Cleveland Park, Van Ness/UDC

15 AMERICAN UNIVERSITY (AU)

This Methodist-affiliated university is one of the area's leading educational and cultural forces. Among the colleges attended by approximately 11,000 students are arts and sciences, law, communication, public affairs, and international service. FM radio station **WAMU** broadcasts National Public Radio, bluegrass, and locally produced public-affairs programs. **Hurst Hall**, the oldest building on the 84-acre campus, dates back to 1896. The public is welcome to attend performances at the **Harold and Sylvia Greenberg Theatre** or music and sports events in **Bender Arena**. **Watkins Art Gallery** hosts undergraduate and graduate exhibitions. Call for more information. ♦ Appointments requested for guided campus tours, but walk-in tours are available. 4400 Massachusetts Ave NW (between Ward and Wesley Cirs). 885.1000; tours, 885.6000. &. www.american.edu. Metro: Tenleytown/AU

16 GLOVER ARCHBOLD PARK

When you tire of the bustle around the monuments and museums, this is the perfect escape: 183 acres of deliciously unkempt park and a sanctuary for local wildlife. Paths wind through the park, crossing Foundry Branch Creek. The 3.1-mile nature trail is smooth enough for jogging. ♦ Van Ness St NW (between Wisconsin and Nebraska Aves). 895.6000. Metro: Tenleytown/AU

17 WINTHROP FAULKNER HOUSES

Three mid-20th-century houses by **Winthrop Faulkner** fit into their surroundings by using the vernacular of their older neighbors. All are now private residences. ♦ 3530 Ordway St NW (between 34th Pl and 36th St). Metro: Cleveland Park

18 ROSEDALE

This genteel and breezy 18th-century clapboard house was built by **Uriah Forrest** as a country home before the city grew to surround it. Once owned by the Youth for Understanding organization—an international exchange program for high school students—the 6.5 acres of land were recently sold to several different people. More than 3 acres were sold to a group of 80 families for the new nonprofit Rosedale Conservancy, which will continue to maintain the land as open space with public access. The remaining 3 or so acres were sold to a developer and home builder, while the farmhouse itself was purchased by a lawyer who plans to live in it. ♦ 3501 Newark St NW (between 34th Pl and 36th St).

19 PALENA

★★★$$$$ Former White House chef Frank Ruta and pastry whiz Ann Amernick (whose bakery is down the street) run this elegant restaurant. The changing menu features classic

Restaurants/Clubs: Red | **Hotels: Purple** | **Shops: Orange** | **Outdoors/Parks: Green** | **Sights/Culture: Blue**

151

dishes, cheeses, and, of course, Amernick's pastries. A café area offers less expensive menu options. ♦ American ♦ Tu-Sa, dinner. Café: M-Sa, dinner. 3529 Connecticut Ave NW. 537.9250. www.palenarestaurant.com. Metro: Cleveland Park

20 IVY'S PLACE

★★$ Indonesian and Thai specialties such as stuffed squid and shrimp with broccoli are served here. It's a good place for a bite after a movie at the nearby **Uptown Theater** (see opposite). ♦ Indonesian/Thai ♦ Tu-Sa, lunch and dinner; Su, dinner. 3520 Connecticut Ave NW (between Ordway and Porter Sts). 363.7802. www.ivysplacethairestaurant.com. Metro: Cleveland Park

20 INDIQUE

★★$$ This stylish, two-level restaurant serves inventive (its name is a mixture of "India" and "unique") small plates and platters like shrimp Varuval, *dosas*, and fresh fish wrapped in a banana leaf with ginger, tomato, and spices. Unusual cocktails include a margarita spiked with tamarind. ♦ Indian ♦ Daily, lunch and dinner. 3512-14 Connecticut Ave NW (between Ordway and Porter Sts). 244.6600. ♿. Metro: Cleveland Park

21 WHATSA BAGEL

Where New York bagel aficionados go when they want the real thing. Quite simply, this place features the best bagels in town. ♦ Daily, breakfast and lunch. 3513 Connecticut Avenue NW (between Ordway and Porter Sts). 966.8990. Metro: Cleveland Park

21 SALA THAI

★★$ Splendidly authentic Thai food, right down to the ultrasweet iced tea, is served at the newest outpost of this local favorite. You won't go wrong with the *pad thai* (stir-fried noodles). ♦ Thai ♦ Daily, lunch and dinner. 3507 Connecticut Ave NW (between Ordway and Porter Sts). 237.2777. www.salathaidc.com. Metro: Cleveland Park. Also at 2016 P St NW (at Hopkins St). 872.1144. ♿. Metro: Dupont Cir; and 2900 N 10th St, Arlington, Virginia. 703/465.2900. ♿. Metro: Clarendon. Also at 4828 Cordell Ave, Bethesda, Maryland. 301/654.4676. Metro: Bethesda

22 YES! ORGANIC MARKET

Organic fruits and vegetables, bulk grains and spices, fresh milk and yogurt, and organic

One of the most coveted Washington invitations is to the June Garden Party, held annually at the British Embassy in honor of the queen's birthday.

toiletries are on hand here. ♦ M-Sa, 8AM-9PM; Su, 9AM-7PM. 3425 Connecticut Ave NW (between Macomb and Ordway Sts). 363.1559. Metro: Cleveland Park

22 FIREHOOK BAKERY AND COFFEE HOUSE

Formerly home to an Italian restaurant, this bakery-café inherited a lovely outdoor garden, complete with grape arbor and fountains—the perfect setting for lunch after a trip to the zoo. The sandwiches are enormous and the pastries tasty, but the real specialty here is fresh bread, baked daily, including Cuban, pumpkin, and ciabatta. ♦ American ♦ Daily, breakfast, lunch, and dinner. 3411 Connecticut Ave NW (between Macomb and Ordway Sts). 362.2253. ♿. www.firehook.com. Metro: Cleveland Park. Also at numerous other locations in the city

22 AROMA

This stylin' little Cleveland Park bar features retro Scandinavian furniture and cool DJ-spun tunes, perfect for lounging. Order one of the bar's quirky cocktails like a Nuts & Berries or Tropico Martini. ♦ Su-Th, 6PM-2AM; F, Sa, 6PM-3AM. 3417 Connecticut Ave NW (between Macomb and Ordway Sts). 202/244.7995. Metro: Cleveland Park. www.thearomaco.com

23 UPTOWN THEATER

This much-beloved, 840-seat Art Deco theater was built in 1936, then renovated in 1996. With its wide screen and capacious balcony, it's considered DC's best movie theater. Spotlights crisscrossing the night sky signal the occasional Hollywood openings held here, complete with celebrities and stretch limos. In recent years, *Black Hawk Down* with Josh Hartnett and *Ali* with Will Smith had premieres here. ♦ 3426 Connecticut Ave NW (between Newark and Ordway Sts). 966.5400. Metro: Cleveland Park

23 IRELAND'S FOUR PROVINCES

★$ Gaelic music, from local Irish musicians, is the big draw, but don't overlook the Harp and Guinness on tap, shepherd's pie, and other authentic touches in this cavernous club. There's a sidewalk café for warm-weather dining. ♦ Irish ♦ Daily, dinner. 3412 Connecticut Ave NW (between Newark and Ordway Sts). 244.0860. www.irelandsfourprovinces.com. Metro: Cleveland Park. Also at 105 W Broad St, Falls Church, Virginia. 703/534.8999

24 SPICES

★★$ A strong performer in the crowded Cleveland Park restaurant scene is this lovely all-Asian spot, serving Chinese, Malaysian, Korean, and Vietnamese cuisine. Start with the

Korean spring onion–cake appetizer. Follow up with Thai shrimp or ginger salad. ♦ Asian ♦ M-Sa, lunch and dinner; Su, dinner. 3333 Connecticut Ave NW (between Macomb and Ordway Sts). 686.3833. Metro: Cleveland Park

24 LAVANDOU

★★★$$ Cleveland Park's best bistro has ultracozy surroundings, dotted with paintings of the Provençal landscape and dried-flower arrangements. Don't be discouraged by the inevitable wait for a table—your patience will be rewarded with excellent Provençal cooking and attentive service. The soups—*pistou*, especially—and stews (either beef or lamb) are wonderful. ♦ French ♦ M-F, lunch and dinner; Sa, Su, dinner. Reservations recommended. 3321 Connecticut Ave NW (between Macomb and Ordway Sts). 966.3003. www.lavandourestaurant.net. Metro: Cleveland Park

24 NANNY O'BRIEN'S

★$ Drop by this friendly neighborhood pub for the burgers, Irish stew, a pint of Guinness, and live music. Some of the region's best Irish musicians gather informally for Monday-night *seisuins*; folk, bluegrass, or Irish bands perform Wednesday through Sunday. ♦ Irish/American ♦ Daily, dinner. 3319 Connecticut Ave NW (between Macomb and Ordway Sts). 686.9189. Metro: Cleveland Park

24 ARDEO

★★$$ This sophisticated little spot, with open windows and a rooftop patio, offers dishes like sautéed halibut, maple-brined pork chops, salmon, and rack of lamb. After dinner, head next door to **Bardeo** (see below) for a glass of wine. ♦ American ♦ M-Sa, dinner; Su, brunch and dinner. 3311 Connecticut Ave NW (between Macomb and Ordway Sts). 244.6750. Metro: Cleveland Park

24 BARDEO

★★$ This stylish new wine bar offers a good selection of wines by the glass, bottle, or flute, as well as a menu of small plates like venison skewers and diver scallops. ♦ American ♦ Daily, dinner. 3309 Connecticut Ave NW (between Macomb and Ordway Sts). 244.6550. Metro: Cleveland Park

25 BALDUCCI'S

This comprehensive gourmet food store has prime meats (the aged fillets are unmatched), freshly baked pastries and bread, produce from around the world, hundreds of varieties of cheese, fresh seafood, wines, and prepared entrées ready to take home and serve. It's not cheap, but the quality is generally worth the price. ♦ M-Sa, 8AM-9PM; Su, 8AM-8PM. 3201 New Mexico Ave NW (between Cathedral Ave and Embassy Park Dr). 363.5800. ♿. www.balduccis.com. Metro: Tenleytown/AU. Also at numerous locations throughout the area

25 CHEF GEOFF'S

★★$$ Geoffrey Tracy, a graduate of **Georgetown University**, runs this neighborhood spot frequented by **American University** students and professors and local families. On the menu, find entrées like pan-roasted duck, cumin-crusted salmon, and hazelnut chicken ravioli, as well as sandwiches and pizza. Go early to take advantage of the sunset specials offered from 4-6:30PM; you get a choice of starter, entrée, and dessert for $19.95. ♦ American ♦ M-Sa, lunch and dinner; Su, brunch and dinner. 3201 New Mexico Ave NW (between Cathedral Ave and Embassy Park Dr). 237.7800. www.chefgeoff.com Also at 13th St NW (between E and F Sts). 464.4461. Metro: Metro Center

26 CACTUS CANTINA

★★$$ A long wait for a table at dinnertime is always a possibility, but you can while the time away with a margarita at the bar and whet your appetite for the delicious grilled quail, spareribs, or beef fajitas to come. The portions are generous. ♦ Tex-Mex ♦ M-Sa, lunch and dinner; Su, brunch and dinner. 3300 Wisconsin Ave NW (at Macomb St). 686.7222. www.cactuscantina.com. ♿. Metro: Cleveland Park

26 TWO AMYS

★★$$ Named for the wives of Peter Pastan (the owner of Dupont Circle's **Obelisk**) and his business partner Tim Giamette, this family-friendly spot serves Neapolitan pizzas cooked in 650-degree ovens. Save room for the good desserts like almond cake and orange sorbet. ♦ Italian ♦ Tu-Su, lunch and dinner; M, dinner. 3715 Macomb St NW (at Wisconsin Ave). 885.5700. Metro: Tenleytown

27 CAFE DELUXE

★★★$$ A hit since it opened its French doors in 1995, this brasserie and bar offers surprisingly good fare: tuna burger with ginger mayo, Greek feta cheese salad, ever-popular meat loaf, and excellent daily soups. A victim of its own success, there's often an hour-plus wait on weekends—especially for the outdoor patio. ♦ American ♦ M-Sa, lunch and dinner; Su, brunch and dinner. 3228 Wisconsin Ave NW (between Woodley Rd and Macomb St). 686.2233. ♿. www.cafedeluxe.com. Metro:

Restaurants/Clubs: Red | **Hotels: Purple** | **Shops: Orange** | **Outdoors/Parks: Green** | **Sights/Culture: Blue**

Cleveland Park. Also at 4910 Elm St, Bethesda, Maryland. 301/656.3131. Metro: Bethesda; and 1800 International Dr, McLean, Virginia. 703/761.0600

28 ROCK CREEK PARK

In 1890 President Benjamin Harrison signed Congress's million-dollar endowment mandating the preservation of this rugged 1,754-acre stretch, once the home of Algonquin Indians. Over the centuries it has nurtured bear, elk, and even bison; early settlers tapped the creek's swift waters to power their grist- and sawmills. Later, the woodlands served as a retreat for harried leaders such as Teddy Roosevelt.

The park still stubbornly maintains its sense of ruggedness as it winds for miles along Rock Creek (see map on p. 155). Wildlife and wildflowers are abundant here, and you can still see the occasional deer and perhaps even a fox. Nature lovers haunt the place, searching for thrushes, chickadees, and ducks. Several links in the capital's chain of defenses against the Confederate Army, including **Fort DeRussy** and **Fort Stevens**, are still in evidence. (If all this seems too idyllic to be true, you're right— it is. Unfortunately, Rock Creek's waters are sour with pollution, and many of the fish have died. Fishing, swimming, and wading are prohibited.)

The park's bike path–footpath begins along the **Potomac**, just below the **Kennedy Center**, and winds along the creek and beside park roads. Sites near the route include the **Watergate** complex and the **National Zoo**, where the hilly terrain is a pleasant challenge for running enthusiasts. The path ends behind **Hillwood**, a 6-mile trek from the **Mall**. ♦ Free. Daily, dawn to dusk. Information, 895.6000 or 895.6070. www.nps.gov/rocr. Metros: Foggy Bottom/GWU, Dupont Cir, Woodley Park/Zoo, Cleveland Park, Van Ness/UDC, Takoma, Silver Spring

Within Rock Creek Park:

ROCK CREEK NATURE CENTER

This National Park Service facility is the place to stop first to orient yourself within the park. It's especially great for kids, who can view wild-animal exhibitions or watch the workings of a beehive behind glass. The center also offers nature films, planetarium shows, and guided hikes. ♦ Free. W-Su, 9AM-5PM. 5200 Glover Rd NW (just south of Military Rd). 895.6070. &

BICYCLE PATH

It runs from the **Lincoln Memorial** into Maryland and connects via the Memorial Bridge to the Mount Vernon bike trail in Virginia. Beach Drive, between Broad Branch and Military

Roads, is closed to cars between 7AM Saturday and 7PM Sunday.

ROCK CREEK GOLF COURSE

This 18-hole public course has a clubhouse where clubs and carts are available for rental: it also has lockers and a snack bar. ♦ Fee. Daily, dawn-dusk. Joyce Rd NW (between 16th St and Beach Dr). 882.7332

CARTER BARRON AMPHITHEATRE

Operated by the National Park Service, this open-air performance venue (seating 4,000) holds a yearly summer festival that showcases live pop, rock, and jazz bands. Free Shakespeare productions, courtesy of Downtown's **Shakespeare Theatre**, and free concerts by the National Symphony Orchestra are also held here. ♦ 16th St and Colorado Ave NW. 426.0486. &

PICNIC AREAS

Thirty of them are scattered throughout the park, and some can accommodate groups of up to 75. Advance reservations are required year-round and must be made in person. ♦ 673.7646

PLAYGROUNDS

The large playing field at 16th and Kennedy Streets NW includes soccer, football, volleyball, and field hockey areas. Some can be reserved through the **DC Department of Parks and Recreation**. ♦ 673.7449

ROCK CREEK PARK HORSE CENTER

Located near the **Nature Center** (see left), it offers guided trail rides. Riding lessons include special classes for the disabled. Children under 12 may not go on trail rides; however, pony rides are available weekends by appointment. ♦ Admission. Trail rides: Tu-Th, 3PM; Sa, Su, noon, 1:30PM, 3PM. Prepaid reservations accepted. 5100 Glover Rd NW (south of Military Rd). 362.0117. &. www.rockcreekhorsecenter.com

ROCK CREEK TENNIS CENTER

The center features 15 soft-surface (open April through mid-November) and 10 hard-surface courts (open year-round). Reservations must be made through **Guest Services, Inc.** (722.5949). Six soft-surface courts off Park Road, just east of **Pierce Mill**, are open May through September. Go to the courts to make reservations in person through the **Washington Area Tennis Patrons**. ♦ 16th and Kennedy Sts NW. 722.5949. www.rockcreektennis.com

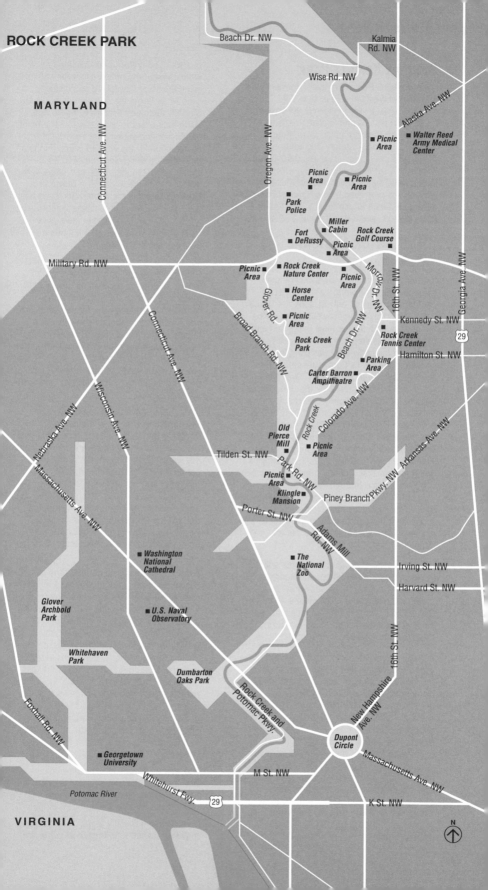

29 BATTERY KEMBLE PARK

Named after Governor Kemble, a former president of West Point Foundry in Cold Spring, New York, this pocket of green is the ideal spot for summer picnics and Frisbee tosses. In winter, when there's enough snow, it turns into great sledding territory. The south end of the jogging path connects to the **C&O Canal Towpath**. A small cannon battery, which was once part of the capital's chain of Civil War defenses, is preserved by the National Park Service. ◆ Chain Bridge Rd NW, MacArthur Blvd, 49th St, and Nebraska Ave. 282.1063

30 WASHINGTON NATIONAL CATHEDRAL

If America were to have an official national cathedral, this, the world's sixth-largest cathedral—in the US, only St. John the Divine in New York City is larger—would certainly be the one. Indeed, it is so large that if laid on its side the Washington Monument would fit inside! No federal money was used in its creation, but citizens from every part of the country have contributed funds. Over the years, it has been the site for the burial services of famous Americans, such as Presidents Woodrow Wilson and Dwight Eisenhower and Generals Omar Bradley and Douglas MacArthur. Services for the men and women killed in Vietnam were held here, as were prayer services for the Iranian hostages and a memorial service for Commerce Secretary Ron Brown. Although the cathedral is the seat of the Washington Episcopal Diocese, it has maintained the ecumenical stance of its founders. It has no standing congregation but opens its doors to worshipers of all denominations.

In 1893 Congress created the Protestant Episcopal Cathedral Foundation, and Henry Yates Satterlee—Washington's first bishop—began securing the land and raising funds, a mission that would last a lifetime. Two architects were hired, **George Bodley** of Britain and **Henry Vaughan**, an American.

Although they had to exchange drawings across the Atlantic, the design was completed in only 13 months. No less important was the hiring of the George A. Fuller Company as chief contractor, which it remained until 1980. Over the years the company maintained a staff of technicians able to build with limestone in the stone-on-stone Gothic style of the 14th century. For most of the 20th century (it was begun in 1907; construction was completed in 1990), the cathedral grew slowly in size and splendor until the limestone towers of this Gothic cathedral (formally the **Cathedral Church of St. Peter and St. Paul**) rose high on **Mount Saint Alban**, above the treetops of Upper Northwest.

In 1907, Teddy Roosevelt officiated at groundbreaking ceremonies for the cathedral, using the silver trowel George Washington used when laying the cornerstone of the **US Capitol**. Architects **Frohman, Robb, and Little** took over the project in 1921, refining the design and supervising every facet of construction for the next 23 years. (Frohman remained on the project until 1972.) The church is built in the shape of a cross, with twin towers in the west and a **Gloria in Excelsis Tower** in the center. (Its top marks the highest point in Washington.) Ninety-six angels, each with a different face, pose in a frieze around the tower, which holds a 10-bell peal and a 53-bell carillon.

As you tour the cathedral, remember that in Gothic architecture, structure and symbol merge. The design must communicate as much as the hymnals, but often without words, so look closely for the narratives and references in the intricate carvings and luminous windows. Enter the cathedral at the north or south transept, or through the doors at the west end. When entering from the west, you will find yourself in the narthex (enclosed porch). Inlaid into the mosaic floor are the 50 state seals.

In the nave above the **Warren Bay** is the **Space Window**, which commemorates the scientists and astronauts of *Apollo XI*. (Moon rock retrieved on that mission is embedded in the glass.) Farther down is **Wilson Bay**, containing the tomb of Woodrow Wilson, the only president buried in the District of Columbia. A crusader's sword on the sarcophagus symbolizes Wilson's quest for peace through the League of Nations. Look for a thistle (representing his Scottish heritage) and for the seal of Princeton University (Wilson was once its president).

A few steps toward the center of the cathedral should place you in the crossing, a magnificent space where the transepts bisect the nave. Four massive stone piers soar 98 feet to meet the vaulted ceiling. The pulpit is made of stones from Canterbury Cathedral. It was here that Martin Luther King Jr. delivered his last Sunday sermon before his assassination in Memphis, Tennessee. Don't miss the charming **Children's Chapel**, where everything is scaled down, designed to delight a child. The windows tell the stories of Samuel and David as boys, and the kneelers are embroidered with all manner of baby animals—pets as well as wild beasts.

N.C. Wyeth, the father of Andrew Wyeth, designed the altar panel in the **Holy Spirit Chapel**, where golden-haloed angels sing the praises of God on a piercing field of blue.

If you've been walking along the aisles, now might be a good time to step closer to the center and admire the nave. Part of the genius of Gothic architecture was the flying buttress, which, by taking the weight of the roof from the walls, allowed the walls to be opened with stained-glass windows. Scores of windows on either side of the nave depict biblical themes as well as artists who have glorified God in their works: Dante, Milton, Bach, and Christopher Wren.

Turn toward the western end of the cathedral to view the dazzling **West Rose Window**, designed by Rowan LeCompte. The fiery wheel (more than 25 feet in diameter) burns with kaleidoscopic color, particularly as it catches the last rays of a setting sun.

On the lower floor, or crypt, are four more chapels, burial vaults, a gift shop–bookstore (with excellent cathedral guides), and a visitors' lounge.

Before leaving, you might want to take the elevator at the west end of the main level to the **Pilgrim Observation Gallery**. Located in the twin towers, the gallery's 70 windows command a panoramic view of Washington, Maryland, and Virginia, as well as a bird's-eye look at some of the cathedral's exterior carvings.

The cathedral's close (grounds) is a 57-acre plot that includes three schools, a college of preachers, and some delightful gardens. A stroll here can be a restful way to end an afternoon of sightseeing. Leave the building from the south transept or west doors and go to the **Herb Cottage**, where sachets, herbs, honeys, and herb vinegars are for sale. Outside, a small garden is redolent with the scent of rosemary, mint, and other herbs. Continue south through a Norman arch to enter one of the city's loveliest garden spaces, the **Bishop's Garden**. Actually several gardens, it includes a rose garden, a medieval herb garden, boxwood, magnolias, and the **Shadow House**, a small medieval stone gazebo that's cool in the summer and dry in the rain—a perfect resting spot.

A bit farther down the hill is Herbert Hazeltine's statue of George Washington, a bronze of the young lieutenant general astride a graceful, well-muscled horse—according to rumor, the spitting image of the famous racehorse Man O' War. In the style of the ancient Egyptians, the horse's eyes are made of glass.

You might also take a walk on the **Woodland Path**, maintained by local garden clubs. It starts at a Japanese footbridge and makes its way up a wooded hill planted with wildflowers. The **Cathedral Greenhouse** southeast of the church raises rare herbs; if you're interested, be sure to request a catalog of the ones on sale.

The **Summer Music Festival** is a series of free outdoor concerts featuring multifaith music ranging in style from choral to gospel and bluegrass. The dramatic Christmas Eve service, complete with hymns and 12-foot trees, draws crowds, especially when the first family is in attendance. The carillon is played every Saturday afternoon, and organ recitals follow Evensong on most Sundays; call for more information.

The cathedral is served by most of the Massachusetts Avenue and Wisconsin Avenue buses. A $3 donation is requested for tours, which take about 30 to 45 minutes and leave continuously from the west entrance except during services. ♦ Donation. Cathedral: M-F, 10AM-5:30PM and tours 10AM-11:30AM, 12:45PM-3:30PM; Sa, 10AM-4:30PM and tours 10AM-11:30AM, 12:45-3:30PM; Su, 8AM-6PM and tours 12:45PM-2:30PM; nave later, M-F, May-Aug. Services: M-F, 7:30AM, noon, 2:30PM, 5:30PM; Su, 8AM, 9AM, 10AM, 11AM, 4PM, 6:30PM; no 10AM service during July and Aug. Chapel of the Good Shepherd: daily, 6AM-9:30PM. Pilgrim Observation Gallery: M-Sa, 10AM-4PM. Tours: daily. Wisconsin Ave NW (between Massachusetts Ave and Woodley Rd). Information, 537.6200; 24-hour recording, 364.6616. ₺. www.cathedral.org/cathedral

31 THE NATIONAL ZOO

Established in 1889 and placed under the direction of the **Smithsonian Institution** 1 year later, the zoo moved from the **Mall** to Rock Creek Valley when William Temple Hornaday, the Smithsonian's chief taxidermist, persuaded Congress to provide funds to establish a site to protect the American bison from extinction. When you enter the 163-acre zoo (see map page 158), follow **Olmsted Walk**, the main pedestrian pathway. Along the walk you'll find **Gibbon Ridge**, the **Great Ape House**, and invertebrate exhibitions. A circular walkway overlooks the great cats—full-maned lions and a rare blue-eyed white tiger, plus leopards and cheetahs.

In the **Reptile Discovery Center** is a collection of some 70 species of amphibians and reptiles, from the smallest snakes to the venomous king cobras, giant pythons, and anacondas. Designed in 1931 by **Albert Harris**, the building is an Italian Romanesque–style structure. Its stone corbels are carved with intricate reptilian heads, and its columns rest on carved stone turtles.

Outside the Reptile Discovery Center, 550-pound Aldabra tortoises wander in the summer months. Crocodiles bathe in shallow pools—indoors in winter, outdoors in summer.

Restaurants/Clubs: Red | Hotels: Purple | Shops: Orange | Outdoors/Parks: Green | Sights/Culture: Blue

SMITHSONIAN NATIONAL ZOOLOGICAL PARK

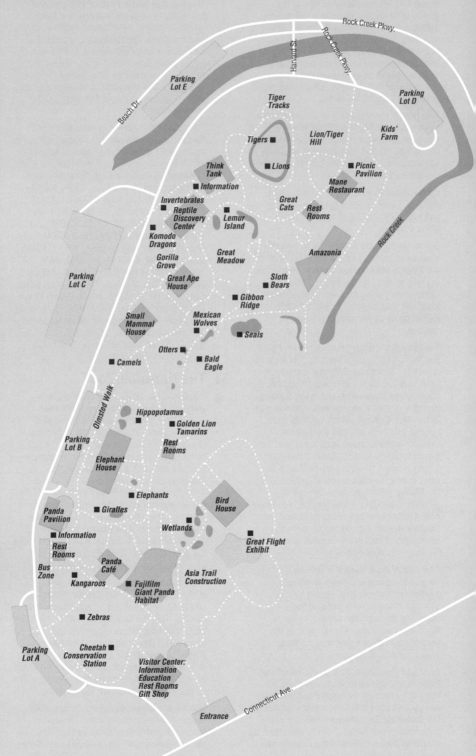

N

Rock Creek Pkwy.

Harvard St.

Rock Creek Pkwy.

Beach Dr.

Parking Lot E

Parking Lot D

Tiger Tracks

Kids' Farm

Tigers ■

Lion/Tiger Hill

■ Lions

Picnic Pavilion ■

Think Tank

■ Information

Great Cats

Mane Restaurant

Invertebrates ■

Reptile Discovery Center

■ Lemur Island

Rest Rooms ■

Komodo Dragons ■

Gorilla Grove

Great Meadow

Amazonia

Great Ape House

Sloth Bears ■

Parking Lot C

Rock Creek

■ Gibbon Ridge

Small Mammal House

Mexican Wolves

Otters ■

■ Seals

Camels ■

■ Bald Eagle

Olmsted Walk

Hippopotamus ●

■ Golden Lion Tamarins

Rest Rooms

Parking Lot B

Elephant House

■ Elephants

Bird House

Panda Pavilion

■ Giraffes

Wetlands

Great Flight Exhibit ■

■ Information

Rest Rooms ■

Panda Café

Asia Trail Construction

Bus Zone

■ Kangaroos

■ Fujifilm Giant Panda Habitat

■ Zebras

Parking Lot A

Cheetah ■ Conservation Station

Visitor Center: Information Education Rest Rooms Gift Shop

Entrance

Connecticut Ave.

Also watch for the giant Komodo dragon lizards and alligators. The *Invertebrate Exhibit*, behind the reptile building, includes octopuses, crabs, spiders, and microscopic organisms. The **Great Ape House** gives you and the apes a perfect look at one another. A family of lowland gorillas watches visitors from indoors and out. The building, specially designed for apes, features sculptured steel-frame trees. All of the Great Ape House orangutans were born in zoos. Their housing is carefully constructed, as orangutans like to unbolt things and take them apart.

The **Small Mammal House**'s exotic creatures include golden lion tamarins—small, blond, monkeylike creatures—fennec foxes, and Asiatic small-clawed otters. Going from the extra small to the extra large, the **Elephant House** guides you to elephants, hippos, and giraffes. Favorites include the versatile-trunked Asiatic elephants and the two pygmy hippos.

Giant pandas Tian Tian (his name means More and More) and Mei Xiang (Beautiful Fragrance) came from China in 2000, and produced an offspring, Tai-Shan (Peaceful Mountain) on July 9, 2005, and, naturally, these draw the biggest crowds. In September 2006, they moved into the **Fujifilm Giant Panda Habitat**, a customized state-of-the-art living area.

Kangaroos, cheetahs, and zebras roam near the zoo's entrance. The **Bird House** has about 480 birds comprising about 120 species, from the seldom-seen kiwi to the endangered Bali mynah. Special features include the **Indoor Flight Room** and the outdoor *Great Flight Exhibit*. Along the **Valley Trail** are otters, gray seals, sea lions, beavers, and Mexican wolves. At the **Think Tank** near the Great Ape House, visitors can watch orangutans studying language and even using computers.

The zoo also runs a 3,200-acre preserve near Front Royal, Virginia, for the study of endangered species. Parking is accessible from Connecticut Avenue NW, Rock Creek Parkway, and Harvard Street and Adams Mill Road NW. Lots often fill by 10AM on busy days, and parking on nearby side streets is limited. The zoo also can be reached from the bike path in **Rock Creek Park** (see page 154). No bicycle riding is allowed within the zoo, however. Gifts are available at shops at the **Panda Plaza**, the **Visitors' Center**, and **Lion/Tiger Hill**. ♦ Grounds: daily, 6AM-8PM Apr-Oct; 6AM-6PM Nov-Mar. Buildings: daily, 10AM-6PM Apr-Oct; 10AM-4:30PM Nov-Mar. 3001 Connecticut Ave NW (between Hawthorne and Macomb Sts). 673.4800. www.natzoo.si.edu. Metros: Woodley Park-Zoo, Cleveland Park

32 LISTRANI'S

★$ This neighborhood café features good pizzas and pasta and offers free home delivery within a limited area. ♦ Italian ♦ Daily, lunch and dinner. 5100 MacArthur Blvd NW (at Dana Pl). 363.0619. www.listranis.com. Metro: Woodley Park-Zoo

33 SAINT SOPHIA GREEK ORTHODOX CATHEDRAL

DC's Greek Orthodox congregation meets in this magnificent Byzantine-inspired building, which was designed in 1956 by **Archie Protopappas**. The mosaics are definitely worth seeing. ♦ Office: M-Sa; services: Su, 10AM. Tours: by appointment. 36th St NW and Massachusetts Ave. 333.4730. www.saintsophiawashington.org. Metro: Woodley Park-Zoo

34 MARRIOTT WARDMAN PARK

$$$$ Almost a city in itself, this vast 1,190-room and 145-suite hotel is usually filled with visiting executives taking advantage of the exhibition, meeting, and banquet rooms and ballrooms. Escapes from the workaday world include two huge outdoor swimming pools (open 15 May-15 Oct), barbershops, a jeweler, and 16 acres of landscaped gardens. Culinary pleasures range from seafood and brick-oven pizzas at **Perle's** to coffee drinks at **Starbucks**. Amenities include multilingual concierge service, no-smoking rooms, exercise facilities, a post office, and a gift shop–newsstand. ♦ 2660 Woodley Rd NW (between Connecticut Ave and 29th St). 328.2000, 800/228.9290; fax 234.0015. www.marriott.com. ♿. Metro: Woodley Park-Zoo

35 MURPHY'S OF DC

★$ Along with pints of Guinness and Harp, this casual spot serves standard pub fare like burgers and sandwiches. There's outdoor seating and live Irish music Tuesday through Saturday. ♦ Irish ♦ M-Sa, lunch and dinner; Su, brunch and dinner. 2609 24th St NW (between Calvert and Garfield Sts). 462.7171. Metro: Woodley Park-Zoo

36 PETIT PLATS

★★$$ This charming French restaurant, tucked away in a turn-of-the-19th-century Victorian brownstone, specializes in traditional bistro fare like shrimp flambé, rack of lamb with potatoes au gratin, and beef medallions in red-wine mushroom sauce. For dessert, try the crème brûlée. ♦ French ♦ M-F, lunch and dinner; Sa, Su, brunch and dinner. 2653 Connecticut Ave NW (between Calvert St and

---

Restaurants/Clubs: **Red** | Hotels: **Purple** | Shops: **Orange** | Outdoors/Parks: **Green** | Sights/Culture: **Blue**

Woodley Rd). 518.0018. Metro: Woodley Park-Zoo

36 LEBANESE TAVERNA

★★$$ Feast on traditional three-course meals or graze on *mezza*—the Lebanese version of tapas. Chicken *shawarma*, Lebanese pizzas, and beef and lamb sausages are good choices at this popular spot. ♦ Lebanese ♦ M-Sa, lunch and dinner; Su, dinner. 2641 Connecticut Ave NW (between Calvert St and Woodley Rd). 265.8681. www.lebanesetaverna.com. &. Metro: Woodley Park-Zoo

37 JANDARA

★★$$ Despite having new owners, the former **Thai Taste** has retained its chef and menu. This revamped Art Deco diner offers an intricate menu complemented by an attentive, extremely helpful staff. The chicken satay; *yum nua* (salad with beef and spicy sauce); rockfish grilled in banana leaves; and deep-fried flounder with basil, garlic, and chili are particularly worth trying. ♦ Thai ♦ Daily, lunch and dinner. 2606 Connecticut Ave NW (between Calvert and 24th Sts). 387.8876. &. Metro: Woodley Park-Zoo

37 NEW HEIGHTS

★★★$$$ Chef Arthur Rivaldo's seasonal menus feature seafood, beef, and chicken specialties like sesame-seared bluefin tuna. Overlooking Rock Creek, the dining room is a knockout, decorated with American Crafts furniture. ♦ New American ♦ M-Sa, dinner; Su, brunch and dinner. Reservations recommended. 2317 Calvert St NW (between Connecticut Ave and 24th St). 234.4110. www.newheightsrestaurant.com. Metro: Woodley Park-Zoo

38 OMNI SHOREHAM HOTEL

$$$$ This historic hotel—designed in 1929 by **Harry Bralove** and set in 11 acres of its own grounds—has been the site of many presidential inaugurations, from Franklin Roosevelt's to Bill Clinton's. President Harry Truman held his private poker games in room D-406, and the 834-room hotel's luxurious ambience has attracted such luminaries as Clark Gable, Rudy Vallee, Marilyn Monroe, and Gary Cooper. Amenities include multilingual concierge services, massage services, an outdoor heated pool, and a fitness center. The hotel's dining room, **Roberts**, serves American Continental cuisine; the **Marquee Bar & Lounge** offers martinis and cigars in an Art Deco setting. ♦ 2500 Calvert St NW (between Connecticut Ave and 28th St). 234.0700, 800/THE OMNI; fax 265.7972. www.omnihotels.com. &. Metro: Woodley Park-Zoo

39 SAVOY SUITES

$$$$ Located right across the street from the **Russian Embassy**, this recently renovated, 150-room establishment offers suites with good views of the city, and Wi-Fi facilities too. There is a restaurant as well as a seasonal outdoor bar, **The Deck**, and some rooms include kitchens or Jacuzzis. Children under 18 stay free. ♦ 2505 Wisconsin Ave NW (between Calvert and Davis Sts). 337.9700; fax 337.3644. &. www.savoysuites.com

40 BUSARA

★★$$ Here you'll find Thai food filtered through a California sensibility: less heat, more vegetable dishes, less frying. Try the *pad thai* (stir-fried noodles), *larb gai* (minced chicken with lime and pepper), or shrimp bikini (fried shrimp spring roll). ♦ Thai ♦ Daily, lunch and dinner. 2340 Wisconsin Ave NW (between Hall Pl and Calvert St). 337.2340. &. www.busara.com

40 AUSTIN GRILL

★★★$ This jaunty restaurant is serious about the food; no fewer than three salsas are set on the table. A casual young crowd lines up here for the fajitas, enchiladas, BBQ ribs, and some of the best chili in DC. Afterward, cool off with a margarita. ♦ Tex-Mex ♦ Daily, lunch and dinner. 2404 Wisconsin Ave NW (between Hall Pl and Calvert St). 337.8080. www.austingrill.com. Also at several other locations throughout the area

40 GROG & TANKARD

Big with a very young (twenty something) crowd, this nightclub-bar features earsplitting live rock music every night, with an emphasis on local bands. ♦ M-Sa, 7PM-close; showtime between 8PM and 9PM. 2408 Wisconsin Ave NW (between Hall Pl and Calvert St). 333.3114. www.grogandtankard.com. &

40 ROCKLANDS

★★★$ Vegetarians, beware: This barbecue joint may turn you into carnivores. Pork, chicken, and fish are grilled over red oak and hickory and come with such tasty sides as tart potato salad, apple compote, minted cucumber salad, and mustard greens. The teal-blue-and-red diner décor, complete with stools along the counter, grows on you. ♦ Barbecue ♦ Daily, lunch and dinner. 2418 Wisconsin Ave NW (between Hall Pl and Calvert St). 333.2558. www.rocklands.com. Also at 4000 Fairfax Dr (at N Quincy St), Arlington, Virginia. 703/528.WOOD. Metros: Virginia Sq, Ballston

41 SUSHI-KO

★★★★$$ DC's first sushi bar is still its best. Now sporting a coppery red exterior, this great place prepares a vast range of top-quality fresh fish and seafood, as well as tempura and a few broiled dishes. The adventurous can try grilled baby octopus with mango and daikon salad. ♦ Japanese ♦ M, dinner; Tu-F, lunch and dinner; Sa, Su, dinner. 2309 Wisconsin Ave NW (between Observatory La and Calvert St). 333.4187. ♿

42 US NAVAL OBSERVATORY

This was originally the **Depot of Charts and Instruments**, located in Foggy Bottom and charged with caring for the navy's chronometers, charts, and other navigational equipment. The first astronomical involvement was for the testing of ship chronometers. **Observatory Circle** was created to distance the delicate instruments from the rumblings of city traffic. Collections include atomic clocks and a refractor telescope that was used in the 1877 discovery of the Martian moons. Free 90-minute observatory tours are offered on alternating Monday evenings, except federal holidays. Reservations must be made 4 to 6 weeks in advance by fax (762.1489) or online. ♦ Free. Tours: every other M, 8:30PM (gates open around 8PM). Valid ID required for entrance; parking outside grounds on Observatory Cir; enter at South Gate across from the New Zealand Embassy. Observatory Cir NW (off Massachusetts Ave). Recording, 762.1467; tour reservations, 762.1438. ♿ www.usno.navy.mil

On the grounds of the Naval Observatory:

VICE PRESIDENT'S HOUSE

In the early 1970s, Congress decided that too much money was being spent on security measures for the homes of US vice presidents. So in 1975, over protests by the navy, it co-opted this house, which for decades had been home to naval admirals. Despite the fact that it is located on a navy post, which makes it easy to defend, this large, sunny Victorian home with acres of lawn doesn't seem like a fortress at all. The residence is not open to the public.

43 KAHLIL GIBRAN MEMORIAL GARDEN

Directly across the street from the **British Embassy** (see opposite), this landscaped garden is dedicated not to a politician or military figure, but to the Lebanese-born poet and philosopher best known for his book *The Prophet*. A bronze bust of Gibran overlooks a small marble pool facing the street. Behind it, set in a grove of trees, is a fountain surrounded by a circle of stone benches inscribed with quotes from Gibran's inspirational writings, such as "We live only to discover beauty. All else is a form of waiting." ♦ Massachusetts Ave NW (between 30th and 34th Sts)

44 BRITISH EMBASSY

Edwin Lutyens's grandiose classicism glorified the British Raj in New Delhi; here, he created a country house in the style of Christopher Wren for British representatives. Back in the 1930s, they received hardship pay for enduring the rigors of Washington summers—but at least the building and its ample lawns reminded them of home. William McVey's statue of Winston Churchill stands with one foot on British soil and one foot on American soil. It's a nod to Churchill's British-born father and US-born mother as well as his honorary American citizenship. The 1997 death of Princess Diana had the embassy flooded with mourners and its steps laden with bouquets. ♦ 3100 Massachusetts Ave NW (between Whitehaven St and Observatory Cir). 462.1340. ♿

45 BLACKSALT RESTAURANT & FISH MARKET

★★★★$$$ This stylish and interesting place with ultramodern décor is an intriguing combination of a fish market, neat restaurant, and bar. The selection of fish and other seafood to eat here or at home is as good as, if not better than, anything found elsewhere. ♦ Seafood ♦ Tu-Su, dinner; Tu-Sa, lunch; Su, brunch. 4883 MacArthur Blvd (at V St). 342.9101. www.blacksaltrestaurant.com

46 ONCE IS NOT ENOUGH

Some of the secondhand clothing in this second-floor shop has never been worn—many items still have the original price tags. Well-to-do area residents bring their high-fashion Valentino, Ungaro, Chanel, and Donna Karan designer fashions here for consignment. ♦ M-Sa, 10AM-4:30PM. 4830 MacArthur Blvd NW (between Reservoir Rd and W St). 337.3072. ♿

47 EMBASSY OF THE FEDERAL REPUBLIC OF GERMANY

This construction cleverly fit a lot of working space into a narrow, sloping site. A white steel trellis lightens the bulk of the structure, built in 1964 by **Egon Eiermann**, and makes it compatible with the residential neighborhood. The cool, sophisticated design is vastly more imaginative than that of most Washington embassies. ♦ 4645 Reservoir Rd NW (between Foxhall Rd and 47th St). 298.4000

SUBURBAN MARYLAND

Although it has grown by leaps and bounds since the 1980s, suburban Maryland is for the most part resisting the kind of large-scale development that has obliterated much of the green from Northern Virginia's landscape. However, you may find this difficult to believe when traveling northwest from DC along **Interstate 270**. The extra lanes for express traffic cut through a long corridor of business parks and shopping centers, giving the impression that the entire state of Maryland has been completely paved over.

The diverse ways in which each suburb handles the area's growing population make for an interesting study in contrasts. **Bethesda** is now dominated by high-rise office buildings and apartments but has the biggest concentration of good restaurants outside DC, whereas **Potomac** and **Chevy Chase** remain largely residential. **Silver Spring**, undergoing a renaissance, struggles with redevelopment—many of its residents are

opposed to its becoming another Bethesda. **Glen Echo** and **Old Town Rockville** are still "undiscovered" and hope to remain so, although **Rockville** proper is already a nightmare of congestion. **Takoma Park**, more like a village than a suburb, maintains its strong sense of community, thanks to its residents, who fiercely resist unbridled development, whereas **Columbia**—a planned city begun in the 1960s for commuters to the equidistant cities of Washington and Baltimore—owes its very existence to the region's growth.

Area code 301 unless otherwise noted.

HOWARD COUNTY

Roughly midway between Washington and Baltimore, this suburb is home to people who commute to work in both cities. It includes **Savage**, **Jessup**, and **Ellicott City**, but its main claim to fame is **Columbia**, a planned community conceived in the 1960s.

1 CRAB SHANTY

★$$ Classic Maryland seafood, from steamed crabs to more formal grilled dishes, is served in this casual place. ♦ Seafood ♦ M-F, lunch and dinner; Sa, dinner; Su, brunch and dinner. 3410 Plumtree Dr (between Frederick Rd and Baltimore National Pike), Ellicott City. 410/465.9660. www.crabshanty.com. &

2 MERRIWEATHER POST PAVILION

Set in a 50-acre park, this outdoor amphitheater hosts major rock and pop concerts in the summer with lawn or pavilion seating; tickets are sold through major DC outlets. ♦ 10475 Little Patuxent Pkwy, Columbia. 410/715.5550. &. www.merriweathermusic.com

2 SHERATON COLUMBIA HOTEL

$$$$ This gracious 288-room hotel offers a fitness facility, outdoor pool, meeting rooms, and a restaurant and bar. Amenities include concierge service and room service. ♦ 10207 Wincopin Cir (just east of Little Patuxent Pkwy), Columbia. 410/730.3900, 800/638.2817; fax 410/730.1319. &

3 HILTON COLUMBIA

$$ This comfortable hotel has 152 rooms; an indoor pool, saunas, and Jacuzzi; meeting facilities; and a restaurant. ♦ 5485 Twin Knolls Rd (north of Thunder Hill Rd), Columbia. 410/997.1060, 800/HILTONS; fax 410/997.0169. &

4 KING'S CONTRIVANCE

★$$$ The historical country estate, on a 370-acre farm granted by one of the Lords of Baltimore in 1730, complements a seasonal menu of continental cuisine, such as duck and rockfish with crabmeat. Sample a dram or two from one of the most extensive selections of single-malt scotches in the Baltimore–Washington area. ♦ American ♦ M-F, lunch and dinner; Sa, Su, dinner. Reservations recommended. 10150 Shaker Dr (between Rte 32 and Rte 29), Columbia. 301/596.3455. www.thekingscontrivance.com

5 HOLIDAY INN COLUMBIA

$$ In addition to the 175 rooms here are meeting facilities, an outdoor pool, and an exercise room, as well as a restaurant and bar. No-smoking rooms are available, and children under 12 eat free. ♦ 7900 Washington Blvd (at Waterloo Rd), Columbia. 410/799.7500. 800/HOLIDAY; fax 410/799.1824. &

6 SAVAGE MILL

Built in 1822 to manufacture canvas for clipper ship sails, this factory complex, which ceased operations after World War II, has been transformed into a 12-building crafts center. Today it houses artist studios, specialty and antiques shops, and cafés. ♦ M-W, 10AM-6PM; Th-Sa, 10AM-9PM; Su, 11AM-6PM. Tours, M-F, 9:30AM-3PM (admission). 8600 Foundry St (between Gorman Rd and Washington St), Savage. 800/788.6455. www.savagemill.com

7 BLOB'S BAVARIAN BIERGARTEN

★$ Over 70 kinds of beer, sauerbraten, and live polka music draw families to this cavernous beer garden. ♦ German ♦ F-Su, dinner. 8024 Blob's Park Rd (south of Jessup Rd), Jessup. 410/799.0155. &. www.blobspark.com

ROCKVILLE

This town is the **Montgomery County** seat and, as such, the center of its municipal activity. **Rockville Pike**, the main commercial strip, is chockablock with shopping centers and is notorious for its traffic congestion. Little known even to most DC residents, **Old Town Rockville**

Restaurants/Clubs: Red | **Hotels: Purple** | **Shops: Orange** | **Outdoors/Parks: Green** | **Sights/Culture: Blue**

with its lovely Victorian architecture still has the quaint feel of a small town.

8 IL PIZZICO

★★$$ Simple but very good Italian fare, including homemade ravioli and veal dishes, is offered at this restaurant, whose name means "the pinch." On the walls, find hand-painted murals by local Italian artists. Lines form early, since the restaurant doesn't take reservations. ♦ Italian ♦ M-F, lunch and dinner; Sa, dinner. 15209 Frederick Rd (at E Gude Dr). 309.0610. &. www.ilpizzico.com

9 THAT'S AMORE

★★$$ The quantities of food served at this busy and fun restaurant are abundant. But refreshingly, the quality of the Southern Italian fare doesn't suffer. It's best to go with a big group and eat family style. ♦ Italian ♦ Daily, lunch and dinner. 15201 Shady Grove Rd (between W Gude Dr and I-270). 268.0682. &. www.thatsamore.com

10 BEALL-DAWSON HOUSE

Legend has it that Upton Beall (of the prominent colonial family of merchants and landowners) entertained General Marquis de Lafayette here. Now owned by the Montgomery County Historical Society, the house features furnishings dating from 1815 through the Victorian era. Also on the grounds is a small medical museum, the former office of Dr. Stonestreet, with medical implements from 1852-1903, and a gift shop. Dr. Stonestreet was the Beall family doctor and one of the first practicing MDs in Rockville. Tours are given on a walk-in basis; group tours can be arranged by appointment. ♦ Admission. Tu-Su, noon-4PM. 111 W Montgomery Ave (at N Adams St). 762.1492. www.montgomeryhistory.org. Metro: Rockville

10 TASTE OF SAIGON

★★★★$ This family-run Vietnamese place is one of the best values in the entire area. A very pleasing ambience, with murals of the homeland and lacquered chairs, complements such superb dishes as rockfish with black-bean sauce, caramel chicken, and Cornish hen stuffed with pork. ♦ Vietnamese ♦ Daily, lunch and dinner. Reservations recommended. 410 Hungerford Dr (at Beall Ave). 424.7222. www.tasteofsaigon.com. &. Metro: Rockville

11 ST. MARY'S CHURCH

Novelist F. Scott Fitzgerald and his wife, Zelda, are buried in the cemetery of this Roman Catholic church, built in 1817. The resting place may seem an unusual choice for the fast-living expatriate couple, but it makes

some sense, considering Zelda was born here in Rockville. ♦ 520 Veirs Mill Rd (between Stonestreet Ave and Hungerford Dr). 424.5550. &. www.stmarysrockville.org. Metro: Rockville

12 LEBANESE TAVERNA CAFÉ

★★$ Part of a popular local chain, this casual café opened in 2000. Eat in or take out items like falafel and chicken *shawarma*. Or, try the "Feast for Two" *mezza* platter, which features a variety of appetizers (many of which are vegetarian friendly). ♦ Middle Eastern ♦ Daily, lunch and dinner. Congressional Plaza, 1605 Rockville Pike. 468.9086

13 SEVEN SEAS

★★$ Here diners are sure their meal is fresh—they can see the live lobsters, crabs, and assorted fish swimming in the tanks at the restaurant's entrance. The tasty shrimp are served with the heads on; the deep-fried oysters and whole fish steamed with ginger and scallions are also excellent. Ask for the Chinese menu, which has English translations—it offers selections that the standard English menu doesn't. ♦ Chinese ♦ Daily, lunch and dinner. 1776 E Jefferson St (between Montrose Rd and Rollins Ave). 770.5020. www.sevenseasrestaurant.com. &

13 G STREET FABRICS

Despite the name, this shop is no longer located on G Street in Downtown Washington. Nevertheless, if you're in the market for fabrics, it's worth making a special trip here for designer textiles, a full bridal facility, and sewing classes. ♦ M-Sa, 10AM-9PM; Su, 11AM-6PM. 11854 Rockville Pike (at Montrose Rd). 231.8998. www.gstreetfabrics.com. &. Metro: White Flint

14 CABIN JOHN REGIONAL PARK

This 500-acre park is run by Montgomery County. Ice-skating, indoor and outdoor tennis courts, miniature train rides, and hiking trails attract lots of locals. The park also features a playground, picnic area, snack bar, and campground. ♦ Fee for ice-skating and train rides. Ice-skating rink: open year-round; call for hours. Train rides: daily, Apr-Sept. Tennis: daily. 7400 Tuckerman La (between Westlake Dr and Seven Locks Rd). Park, 495.2503; ice rink, 365.2246; train, 469.7835; tennis, 365.2440

WHEATON

The **Metro**'s **Red** line finally reached this suburb in late 1990. But despite the accessibility, this place has managed to remain fairly low-key, with plenty of mom-and-pop shops. A plethora of ethnic restaurants adds spice to the area, and the **Westfield Shoppingtown Wheaton** shopping mall (University Boulevard and Veirs Mill Road; 946.3200) offers almost everything else.

15 NATIONAL CAPITAL TROLLEY MUSEUM

Built as a replica of an old terminal, this trolley museum in **Northwest Branch Park** offers memorabilia from Austria, Germany, and DC. While you're there, take the 1.5-mile trolley ride though park grounds and visit the gift shop. ♦ Admission. Sa, Su, noon-5PM, Jan-Nov. Additional hours: Th, F, 10AM-2PM, 15 Mar-15 May; Th, F, 11AM-3PM, 15 June-15 Aug; Th, F, 10AM-2PM, 1 Oct-15 Nov. 1313 Bonifant Rd (between Carona Dr and Layhill Rd), Colesville, Maryland. 384.6088. www.dctrolley.org

16 BROOKSIDE GARDENS

Possibly the most beautiful outdoor spot in the area, this section of **Wheaton Regional Park** includes two conservatories, fountains, ponds, and 50 acres of green grass, trees, and meticulously landscaped gardens. Find answers to all of your questions about horticulture at the **Horticultural Reference Library** (M-F, 10AM-3PM) or stop by the **Visitors' Center**, daily, 9AM-5PM, for park information. ♦ Free. Gardens daily, sunrise to sunset. 1800 Glenallan Ave (between Kemp Mill and Randolph Rds). 962.1400. ⅃. www.brooksidegardens.org

17 GOOD FORTUNE

★★$ Excellent dim sum is why you should visit this nondescript but pleasant Chinese restaurant near the **Metro** stop. The large number of Chinese customers is a good endorsement. ♦ Chinese ♦ Daily, lunch and dinner. 2646 University Blvd W (between Georgia Ave and Veirs Mill Rd). 929.8818. ⅃. Metro: Wheaton

KENSINGTON

Pleasant and mostly residential, this community has some attractive, family-oriented neighborhoods. Because it's one of the few suburbs not directly accessible by **Metrorail** (although it's within easy bus or driving distance), it maintains a lower profile than some of its neighbors—and residents seem perfectly happy to keep it that way.

18 ANTIQUE ROW

One of the best places in the area for antiques and collectibles, these blocks boast more than 40 shops, offering a variety of styles, periods, and prices. Items range from Art Deco and railroad memorabilia to stained glass, folk art, and vintage clothing. ♦ Howard Ave (between Montgomery and Connecticut Aves)

19 TEMPLE OF THE CHURCH OF JESUS CHRIST OF LATTER-DAY SAINTS

This massive traffic-stopper stands on a 57-acre hill overlooking the Beltway. The $15 million building, designed by **Wilcox, Markham, Beecher & Fetzer** in 1974, is 248 feet long and 136 feet wide and stands 16 stories high. Built on a solid rock foundation, it is sheathed in 173,000 square feet of Alabama white marble, enough to cover three and a half football fields. Even the windows are made of marble (five eighths of an inch thick and translucent), casting an otherworldly light on the interior. The fortress is topped with six gold-plated steel spires, the highest of which supports a gold-leaf statue of the angel Moroni. Although passersby are welcome to admire the architecture and Irwin Nelson's landscape design, the temple is open to members only. Its many rooms, on nine levels, are reserved for important occasions, such as weddings and baptisms. A 30-minute tour guided by volunteers is offered to the public, however, and includes a stop at the **Visitors' Center**, where photographs, sculptures, and lifelike mannequins tell the story of Mormonism. ♦ Visitors' Center: daily, 10AM-9PM. 9900 Stoneybrook Dr (west of Capitol View Ave). 587.0144. ⅃.

SILVER SPRING

Originally this suburb's revitalization was patterned after Bethesda's, but heated controversy over the scope of the development has undercut the project's momentum. When the Mall of America developers proposed a shopping–entertainment facility, residents rejected the

THE ROVING CAPITAL

The Continental Congress first convened in 1774, and from then until 1800, when the country's legislative body moved into official headquarters in the District of Columbia, it resembled nothing so much as a band of nomads in knee breeches. During these years, the members met in eight cities, each having the right to call itself the capital—at least for a while. Congress was so transient that when a statue in honor of George Washington was proposed in 1783, Francis Hopkinson, a representative from Pennsylvania, suggested that it be mounted on wheels—the better to follow Congress in its wanderings.

Philadelphia was the capital more frequently than any other city, but in 1777, with the British closing in, Congress hightailed it to the town of Lancaster, Pennsylvania. From Lancaster, Congress moved across the Susquehanna River to York, where it remained until June 1778. The Articles of Confederation (the first constitution of the 13 American states) was passed there, and Benjamin Franklin had his press moved up so he could print a million dollars' worth of much-needed Continental money. Congress moved back to Philadelphia but was again threatened by the British and moved to Baltimore in 1779.

In 1783 the Revolutionary War ended, leaving the nation broke and the union tenuous. Congress once again was meeting in Philadelphia and might have remained there had a group of soldiers not invaded the city and rioted for back pay. Congress fled to Princeton, New Jersey, where it met in Nassau Hall (still part of Princeton University's campus and then the largest building in the country). However, there wasn't enough room in town for the growing bureaucracy, so the federal government moved on to **Annapolis**, Maryland,

where there was presumably more hotel space. In Annapolis, Congress decided that the new government needed its own city, but no one could agree on which one.

Every town in the country began lobbying to be named capital, including Trenton, New Jersey. (Congress met there briefly in 1784 before rejecting the proposal.) New York City became the capital in 1784, and 5 years later George Washington was inaugurated there. Later, in 1789, Congress moved back to Philadelphia and stayed put until 1800.

Debate on where to put the capital grew fierce. Northerners wanted it near a financial center, whereas agrarian Southerners feared the power of Northern financiers and special interests. A political compromise between Alexander Hamilton and Thomas Jefferson settled the issue in 1790. During the Revolutionary War, the South had managed to pay its soldiers, but the North had not. Led by Hamilton, the Northern states wanted Congress to absorb their debt. The South, led by Jefferson, opposed this. Finally the two men worked out a deal whereby the North was relieved of its debt and the South gained the prestige of a national capital.

Congress specified the size of the site, but the choice was left to George Washington, a former surveyor. Although hounded by land speculators, he made an independent choice: a diamond-shaped area where the **Potomac** and **Anacostia Rivers** merged. He hoped the Anacostia would provide a deep-water naval port, and that the Potomac would be a link to western provinces by way of the proposed **Potowmack Canal**. Perhaps it was no accident either that the capital would be an easy day's ride from Washington's home at **Mount Vernon**.

---

plan as incompatible with the scale of their neighborhood. But encouraging signs are emerging: The **American Film Institute**'s move into the Art Deco **Silver Theatre** could be the anchor that Silver Spring needs. A number of restaurants and small businesses have also persevered in the area, and some are worth seeking out.

20 HISTORIC ST. JOHN'S CHURCH AND CEMETERY

Jesuit churchman (and Georgetown University founder) John Carroll began a private Evangelist Mission chapel on this site in 1774 and served here until moving to Baltimore in 1786. Though the main church has since moved to a new location (10103 Georgia Ave), the "Old Church" still holds Masses, weddings, and funerals. The small frame building on the property is an exact reproduction of the Carroll Chapel, with all the original fixtures and sacred

vessels intact. Since 1977, the congregation of Our Lady of Poland has occupied the Old Church rectory and holds Polish-language masses here. ♦ 9700 Rosensteel Ave (at Forest Glen Rd). 681.7663. &. www.sjeparish.org. Metro: Forest Glen

21 PARKWAY DELI AND RESTAURANT

★★$ Regularly voted the best deli in the Washington area (admittedly, there isn't much competition in this category), this place offers big bowls of matzoh-ball soup, kosher sandwiches, and delicacies that include chopped chicken liver, herring, whitefish, and, of course, lox and bagels. ♦ Deli ♦ Daily, breakfast, lunch, and dinner. 8317 Grubb Rd (between Washington Ave and Colston Dr). 587.1427

22 HILTON SILVER SPRING

$$ In addition to newly refurbished rooms, this property offers **Capital Bleu**, serving American/French cuisine, and **Sergio's**, a Northern Italian dining room. It also features an exercise room and indoor pool. Children under 18 stay free. ♦ 8727 Colesville Rd (between Fenton and Spring Sts). 589.5200; fax 588.1841. www.hilton.com. Metro: Silver Spring

23 AMERICAN FILM INSTITUTE (AFI) SILVER THEATRE AND CULTURAL CENTER

The citizens of Montgomery County, Maryland, banded together with the American Film Institute to save the circa-1938 Silver Theatre from the wrecker's ball. That film house was not only stunningly restored, but two new state-of-the-art theaters with stadium seating were added to the complex. Now folks can take in both classic and recent movies at this cultural center that also hosts film festivals, educational programs, and other events. Also on-site: office and meeting space, a café, and reception and exhibit areas. Call for schedule. ♦ 8633 Colesville Rd (between Fenton St and Georgia Ave). 495.6720. &. www.afi.com/silver. Metro: Silver Spring

24 CHINA

★★★$ Although this comfortable, family-run restaurant specializes in elaborate banquets (a minimum of four guests; call at least 1 day in advance), feel free to wander in for an excellent meal of authentic lemon chicken, pan-fried dumplings, Hong Kong pork, and Szechuan beef. ♦ Chinese ♦ Daily, lunch and dinner.

8411 Georgia Ave (between Bonifant St and Wayne Ave). 585.2275. &. Metro: Silver Spring

25 CRISFIELD

★★★$$ Run continuously since 1945 by the Landis family, this place offers outstanding regional specialties. Chincoteague oysters, Maryland crabs (every which way but steamed), and fresh clams are offered on a menu that hasn't changed in 50 years. ♦ Seafood ♦ Tu-Su, lunch and dinner. 8012 Georgia Ave (between East-West Hwy and Blair Mill Rd). 589.1306. www.crisfieldseafoodrestaurant.com

POTOMAC

Probably the toniest of DC's Maryland suburbs, Potomac is home to diplomats, politicians, and celebrities. Drive northwest from the city on **River Road** and you'll soon be in horse country, where mansions set on vast grounds are visible from the road. Millions of dollars change hands when these estates are bought and sold.

26 NORMANDIE FARM

★★$$ Traditional French country cooking is served here in an almost rural setting, which also happens to be *très romantique*. Best known for its popovers, the restaurant offers other specialties as well, including beef Wellington and poached salmon. ♦ French ♦ Tu-Sa, lunch and dinner; Su, brunch and dinner. Reservations recommended. 10710 Falls Rd (between Glen Rd S and Eldwick Way). 983.8838. &

27 C&O CANAL NATIONAL HISTORICAL PARK

This park offers scenic overviews of the **Great Falls** of the Potomac, as well as access to the 184.5-mile C&O Canal, which is operated by the National Park Service; its paths are great for walks and bicycling. The cliffside **Billy Goat Trail**, overlooking scenic Mather Gorge, is not for the timid, however. ♦ Admission. Daily. 11710 MacArthur Blvd (west of Falls Rd). 299.3613. www.nps.gov/choh

Within C&O Canal National Historical Park:

GREAT FALLS TAVERN

Despite the name, this isn't a restaurant but a tiny museum with photographs and artifacts reflecting 19th-century life in this area of Maryland. ♦ Free, with park admission. Daily

28 OLD ANGLER'S INN

★★$$$ The Contemporary American cuisine and tasting menus at this romantic country

---

Restaurants/Clubs: Red | Hotels: Purple | Shops: Orange | Outdoors/Parks: Green | Sights/Culture: Blue

inn measure up to its fine Edwardian-style décor. However, the true magic is not in the food but in the atmosphere (many a marriage proposal has taken place here). Nothing beats a cup of hot chocolate next to the lounge's roaring fire or, in warm weather, dining on the terrace. ♦ American ♦ Tu-Su, lunch and dinner. Reservations recommended. 10801 MacArthur Blvd (between Brickyard and Falls Rds). 299.9097. www.oldanglersinn.com

BETHESDA

Virtually unrecognizable today to anyone who knew it as a quiet outpost, Bethesda has experienced some of the most phenomenal commercial growth of any local suburb. The transformation has been largely a successful one, with new office buildings balanced by an influx of restaurants and creative architecture. Although this growth has come at the expense of a good number of the mom-and-pop operations that had once given the area its character, it has also increased the number of diversions available here. At the **Bethesda Metro Center Plaza** (information, 652.4988; ice rink 656.0588) in front of the **Hyatt Regency**, dance concerts are offered in the summer every Friday evening, and in the winter, ice-skating (daily from Thanksgiving through early March).

29 WHITE FLINT MALL

Even the mannequins are perfectly coiffed and manicured at this three-tiered fashion mall, with an interior inset with rosewood and copper terrazzo floors. **Bloomingdale's** and **Lord & Taylor** are the big-leaguers anchoring about 100 smaller shops and fashion boutiques, as well as the **Cheesecake Factory**, **P.F. Chang's China Bistro**, **Dave & Busters**, and **Borders Books and Music**. ♦ M-Sa, 10AM-9:30PM; Su, noon-6PM. 11301 Rockville Pike (between Strathmore Ave and Nicholson La), North Bethesda. 468.5777. &. www.shopwhiteflint.com. Metro: White Flint

The longest escalator in the Western Hemisphere is at the Wheaton Metro stop. It is 230 feet long.

In 1792, a competition was announced for the design of the Capitol and the President's House. It read, in part, "A premium lot in the city of Washington . . . and $500 shall be given by the Commissioners of the Federal Buildings to the person who before the 15th of July 1792 shall produce to them the most approved plan for a Capitol to be executed in this city."
—*The Architecture of Washington,* American Institute of Architects

30 JEAN-MICHEL

★★$$$ Although located inside a suburban shopping center, this French restaurant can hold its own with many of the better ones in Downtown DC. And no wonder: It's run by Jean-Michel Farret (formerly of K Street's **Jean-Pierre**), whose highlights include osso buco with noodles in a light sauce, pan-fried salmon, and grilled Dover sole. ♦ French ♦ M-F, lunch and dinner; Sa, Su, dinner. Wildwood Shopping Center, 10223 Old Georgetown Rd (between Cheshire Dr and Democracy Blvd). 564.4910. &

31 BETHESDA MARRIOTT

$$$$ A step up from the usual suburban accommodations, this newly renovated 399-room and 8-suite hotel features a large outdoor swimming pool, an indoor pool, an exercise room, and lighted tennis courts. Two restaurants—Northern Italian and family-style American—provide a choice of prices and cuisines. For an extra treat, ask about the **Executive Kings** room, an upgraded minisuite. No-smoking rooms are available. ♦ 5151 Pooks Hill Rd (west of Rockville Pike). 897.9400, 800/228.9290; fax 897.0192. www.marriott.com. &

32 NATIONAL INSTITUTES OF HEALTH (NIH)

Part of the US Department of Health and Human Services, the National Institutes of Health (NIH) is the primary federal agency for conducting and supporting medical research. It employs more than 17,000 people, many of whom work here at NIH headquarters. Professionals affiliated with the medical sciences as well as interested laypersons are welcome to come to Building 45 for an eight-minute film and a 20-minute talk about the facility, offered Monday, Wednesday, and Friday at 11AM. In Building 38, the **National Library of Medicine** (NLM) (594.5983) is the world's largest research library in a single professional field. It also hosts changing exhibits. Library tours are given Monday through Friday at 1:30PM followed by gallery talks at 2PM. A photo ID is required to enter the NIH campus. ♦ NLM: M-W, F, 8:30AM-5PM; Th, 8:30AM-9PM; Sa, 8:30AM-12:30PM. 9000 Rockville Pike (between Woodmont Ave and Cedar La). 496.4000. &. www.nih.gov. Metro: Medical Center

33 FOUR POINTS BY SHERATON BETHESDA

$$$ At this completely no-smoking hotel, the 164 recently upgraded guest rooms feature free high-speed Internet access and in-room

movies. Amenities include an outdoor pool, free local shuttle service, a fitness facility, a car rental desk, and a restaurant/bar. ◆ 8400 Wisconsin Ave (at Chestnut St). 654.1000, 888/625.5144; fax 654.0751. ♿. www.starwood.com/fourpoints. Metro: Bethesda

34 STEAMERS

★★$ This restaurant looks like it would be at home on a tropical beach rather than located in suburban Maryland. Quintessentially a beach shack, it serves all the typical fare expected, including shrimp, lobster, mussels, and crabs, as well as sandwiches and burgers, appetizers, and a raw bar with specialty Steamers' Wraps. ◆ Seafood ◆ Daily, lunch and dinner. 4820 Auburn Ave (between Rugby and Norfolk Aves). 718.0661. www.steamersseafoodhouse.com. Metro: Bethesda

35 GRAPESEED

★★$$$ Part wine bar, part restaurant, where dishes like seared scallops, soft-shell crabs, or pan-roasted filet mignon are matched with suitable companion wines on the menu. The spot hosts wine tastings on Tuesdays. ◆ American ◆ Daily, dinner. 4865 Cordell Ave (between Norfolk and Woodmont Aves). 986.9592. www.grapeseedbistro.com. Metro: Bethesda

36 CALIFORNIA TORTILLA

★★$ This popular spot draws locals for huge, tasty burritos (blackened chicken Caesar, crunchy barbecue ranch chicken). It's often a fun scene here, with weekly specials and a Monday-night "wheel of fortune" that offers a chance to win discounts or free desserts. ◆ Mexican ◆ Daily, lunch and dinner. 4862 Cordell Ave (between Norfolk and Woodmont Aves). 654.8226. www.californiatortilla.com. Metro: Bethesda. Also at several other locations throughout the area

37 IMAGINATION STAGE

The largest multidisciplinary theater arts organization for young people in the region, Imagination Stage offers a season of professional shows for families as well as classes and school outreach programs. The company dates from 1979; it moved to this new theater in Bethesda in 2003. Recent shows have included *Bunnicula*, *Charlotte's Web*, and *James and the Giant Peach*. In 2005 it received two Helen Hayes Awards nominations. ◆ Box office: M-F, 10AM-4PM; Sa, Su, 11AM-4PM. 4908 Auburn Ave (between Old

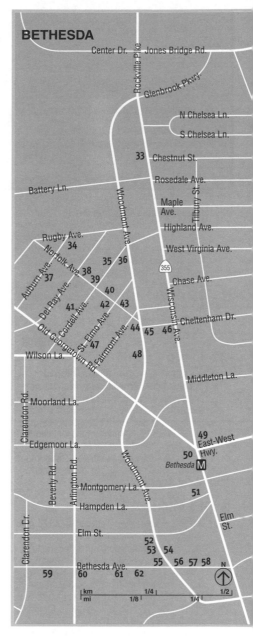

BETHESDA

Georgetown Rd and Norfolk Ave). 280.1660. ♿. www.imaginationstage.org. Metro: Bethesda

38 BACCHUS OF LEBANON

★★$$ A larger outpost of the DC restaurant, this branch serves the same excellent hummus, lamb- or chicken-topped pilafs,

---

Restaurants/Clubs: Red | Hotels: Purple | Shops: Orange | Outdoors/Parks: Green | Sights/Culture: Blue

THE BEST

Michael Kahn
Artistic Director, the Shakespeare Theatre

Take a walk through the **Capitol Hill** district, lovely small houses and gardens. Visit **Eastern Market**, a covered food market that has open stalls on Saturdays and a huge flea market on Sundays. Be sure to have a breakfast of pancakes or a lunch of crab cakes or soft-shell crab sandwiches from the food stand in the corner.

Hire a bicycle and ride through **Rock Creek Park**. Pack a picnic and eat by a stream or under the trees. If it's

summer, see a free performance at the **Shakespeare Theatre** *Free For All* at the **Carter Barron Amphitheater** or a concert by the **National Symphony Orchestra**.

Get off the **Metro** at the **National Archives** and stroll through the many art galleries of the **Penn Quarter** district in Downtown DC. Stand on the map of the world at the **Naval Memorial** and move around on it to measure how far you have traveled in your life. Have a meal of tapas at **Jaleo** in the **Lansburg** building and then see a great classic play at the Shakespeare Theatre next door.

---

stuffed eggplant, and *lahm mechwi* (lamb shish kebab). The appetizers are so good you may want to order a *mezza*, which is a feast of three or four of them. ◆ Lebanese ◆ M-F, lunch and dinner; Sa, Su, dinner. 7945 Norfolk Ave (between Cordell and Del Ray Aves). 657.1722. ৬. Metro: Bethesda. Also at 1827 Jefferson Pl NW (between Connecticut Ave and 19th St), DC. 202/785.0734. Metros: Dupont Cir, Farragut N. www.bacchusrestaurant.com

39 CESCO

★★$$$ Chef Francesco Ricchi (also of Dupont Circle's **Etrusco**) prepares Tuscan specialties here, such as veal-stuffed tortellini, grilled lamb T-bone chops, and a risotto of the day. There's seasonal outdoor dining and a good wine list too. ◆ Italian ◆ Tu-F, lunch and dinner; Sa-M, dinner. 4871 Cordell Ave (between Norfolk and Woodmont Aves). 654.8333. www.cescotrattoria.com. Metro: Bethesda

40 LA MICHE

★★$$$ French country cuisine is served here in a gracious farmhouse setting replete with lace curtains and fresh flowers. The menu offers generous portions of such favorites as rack of lamb, Dover sole, and roasted Long Island duckling. ◆ French ◆ M, Sa, dinner; Tu-F, lunch and dinner; Su, brunch and dinner. 7905 Norfolk Ave (between St. Elmo and Cordell Aves). 986.0707. www.bethesdalamiche.com. Metro: Bethesda

41 TRAGARA

★★$$$ Winner of DiRoNA (Distinguished Restaurants of North America) and *Wine Spectator* awards, this upscale, family-owned spot serves Northern Italian dishes like osso buco, lobster, and pastas. It's a good place for special occasions, and there's complimentary valet parking in the evenings. ◆ Italian ◆ M-F, lunch and dinner; Sa, Su, dinner. 4935 Cordell Ave (between Old Georgetown Rd and Norfolk Ave).

951.4935. www.tagara.com. ৬. Metro: Bethesda

42 ROCK BOTTOM RESTAURANT & BREWERY

★★$ This is one of the better examples of a brewpub. Besides an interesting selection of home-brewed ales, the dishes here are more imaginative than might be expected. There is also an Especially Healthy selection. ◆ American ◆ Daily, lunch and dinner. 7900 Norfolk Ave (at St. Elmo Ave). 652.1311. www.rockbottom.com. Metro: Bethesda

43 DESIGN WITHIN REACH

This purveyor of modern furnishings recently opened shop here in a 2,200-square-foot former diner. Original Art Deco details include a curved interior wall and numerous windows that provide natural light. Furnishings are displayed gallery-style and include pieces for the office, bedroom, dining room, and patio by designers like George Nelson and Philippe Starck as well as lighting and floor coverings. ◆ M-F, 11AM-7PM; Sa, 10AM-6PM; Su, noon-6PM. 4828 St. Elmo Ave (at Norfolk Ave). 215.7200. www.dwr.com. Metro: Bethesda. Also at 3307 Cady's Alley NW (at 33rd and M Sts), DC. 202/339.0890

44 FOONG LIN

★★$$ The menu, which includes Cantonese, Szechuan, Hunan, and Peking dishes, changes daily. Peking chicken, crispy rockfish, steamed oysters, and General Tso's chicken are just a few of the offerings. ♦ Chinese ♦ Daily, lunch and dinner. 7710 Norfolk Ave (between Woodmont and Fairmont Aves). 656.3427. www.foonglin.com. &. Metro: Bethesda

45 TASTEE DINER

★$ This popular spot is the genuine article, replete with wood paneling and chrome throughout. The food is exactly what you'd expect: meat loaf and mashed potatoes, thick shakes, homemade pies and cakes—in other words, all of your classic diner favorites. However, you may have to wait for seating. ♦ American ♦ Daily, 24 hours. 7731 Woodmont Ave (between Old Georgetown Rd and Cheltenham Dr). 652.3970. www.tasteediner.com. &. Metro: Bethesda. Also at 8601 Cameron St (between Wayne Ave and Colesville Rd), Silver Spring, Maryland. 589.8171. &. Metro: Silver Spring; and 118 Washington Blvd (between Little Montgomery and Main Sts), Laurel, Maryland. 953.7567. &

46 TAKO GRILL

★★$$ For most people Japanese food means sushi, teriyaki, and tempura, all of which are served here, but the specialty at Tako's is *robatayaki*—grilled meats and fish. You can make a meal of a host of small dishes priced as low as $2 apiece. Look also for the Sake Bar. Though this popular restaurant is spacious, you still may have to wait. ♦ Japanese ♦ M-F, lunch and dinner; Sa, Su, dinner. 7756 Wisconsin Ave (at Cheltenham Dr). 652.7030. www.takogrill.com. Metro: Bethesda

47 DAISY TOO

The sister store to Adams Morgan's **Daisy**, this sunny shop carries women's fashions by Frankie B, Diane von Furstenberg, Tracy Reese, and other designers. In the back of the store, find **Zelaya**, a hip shoe boutique that sells footwear in a variety of styles and prices. ♦ M-W, F, Sa, 10AM-6PM; Th, 10AM-8PM; Su, noon-5PM. 4940 St. Elmo Ave (between Old Georgetown Rd and Norfolk Ave). 656.2280. www.daisyclothing.com. Metro: Bethesda. Also at 1814 Adams Mill Rd NW (between Columbia Rd and Lanier Pl), DC. 202/797.1777. Metro: Woodley Park-Zoo/Adams Morgan

48 BLACK'S BAR AND KITCHEN

★★★$$$ This much-praised spot serves Jeff Black's Gulf Coast–style dishes in a stylish dining room or on a two-level deck. The menu features mainly seafood (mahimahi, salmon,

halibut), but there are choices for meat-eaters as well. The bar area serves as a popular meeting place for Bethesda Gen-Xers. ♦ American ♦ M-F, lunch and dinner; Sa, Su, dinner. 7750 Woodmont Ave (between Old Georgetown Rd and Cheltenham Dr). 652.6278. www.blacksbarandkitchen.com. &. Metro: Bethesda

49 ROUND HOUSE THEATRE

Contemporary plays, musicals, and classics are offered at this new 347-seat theater across from the Bethesda Metro. The longtime company's five-play season runs from September to June. If you're under 28 years of age, tickets are half-price. ♦ Shows: W-Su. Box office: M-F, noon-5PM. 7501 Wisconsin Ave (at East-West Hwy). 240/644.1100. &. www.round-house.org. Metro: Bethesda

50 HYATT REGENCY BETHESDA

$$$$ An elegant 390-room hotel right at Bethesda's **Metro** stop, it has an indoor pool, an exercise area, and the **Daily Grill**, a casual restaurant with an American menu. No-smoking rooms are available, and children under 18 stay free. ♦ One Bethesda Metro Center, Wisconsin Ave and Old Georgetown Rd. 657.1234, 800/233.1234; fax 657.6453. www.bethesda.hyatt.com. &. Metro: Bethesda

51 PINES OF ROME

★$ Popular with families, this casual restaurant is known for its white pizza (a fontina pie flavored with garlic), which makes a good appetizer. Entrées include mussels in marinara sauce and stewed octopus. ♦ Italian ♦ Daily, lunch and dinner. 4709 Hampden La (between Wisconsin and Woodmont Aves). 657.8775. &. Metro: Bethesda

52 AUSTIN GRILL

★★★$ Families and young professionals pack this casual restaurant for margaritas, fajitas, enchiladas, and some of the area's best chili. ♦ Tex-Mex ♦ Daily, lunch and dinner. 7278 Woodmont Ave (at Elm St). 656.1366. www.austingrill.com. Metro: Bethesda. Also at several other locations throughout the area

53 LEVANTE'S

★★$$ This high-style, chrome-and-tile restaurant has been a hit since it opened in 1998. The Eastern Mediterranean menu fuses Greek, Italian, and Middle Eastern fare in its salads, pita-wrapped sandwiches, and brick-oven pizzas. ♦ Eastern Mediterranean ♦ Daily, lunch and dinner. 7262 Woodmont Ave (between Bethesda Ave and Elm St). 657.2441. &. www.levantes.com. Metro: Bethesda

Restaurants/Clubs: Red | Hotels: Purple | Shops: Orange | Outdoors/Parks: Green | Sights/Culture: Blue

The Best

Maura McCarthy

Entertainment Guide editor, washingtonpost.com

There's no better refuge from DC's notorious humidity than the city's oases of green. The **National Arboretum**, off the beaten tourist path, offers acres of foliage including a bonsai museum, a springtime burst of cherry blossoms, and an autumn light show of colorful leaves. Sunk below the National Mall, the **Hirshhorn Museum**'s sculpture garden is a peaceful Eden graced with world-renowned modern sculpture. Across the Mall, the **National Gallery of Art**'s sculpture garden offers more 20th-century masterpieces and a lush fountain that morphs into the city's most scenic ice rink in colder months. Nearby is my beloved **Teaism**, where you can stock up on teas, baked treats, and healthy meals should the picnic mood strike you.

Over the years, DC has yielded its fare share of colorful boutiques. Along 14th and U Streets, local shops market trendy clothing and home accessories. Upper Wisconsin Avenue in Georgetown yields darling shoes, gifts, and hyper-preppy apparel. From there, bags in hand, I plop down for the perfect sweet at nearby **Patisserie Poupon** or an ice-cream cone at **Isee Icy** or **Thomas Sweet**.

On weekend mornings, the stalls of **Eastern Market** beckon with old-time prints, homemade jewelry, and crafts. For classic breakfast fare, brave the bustling counter of its **Market Lunch** or, for something quieter, brunch at nearby **Montmartre** for some of Capitol Hill's best people-watching.

DC is weighty with words, and not just from its politicos. I'm overwhelmed each time I glimpse some of our nation's most treasured documents inside the **National Archives**. On the Hill, the halls of the **Library of Congress** are some of the handsomest in Washington, dripping with neoclassical style and inspiring quotes. And the Library's monumental reading room contains some of the city's finest murals. And who'd believe the largest repository of Shakespearean works outside of England would be just around the corner at the **Folger Shakespeare Library**?

54 Tickled Pink

This bright, colorful store deals in dresses, capri pants, and other beachy apparel for girls and women by Lilly Pulitzer. ♦ M-Sa, 10AM-6PM; Su, noon-5PM. 7259 Woodmont Ave (between Bethesda Ave and Elm St). 913.9191. Metro: Bethesda. Also at 103 S Asaph St, Alexandria, Virginia. 703/518.5459. www.tickledpinkapparel.com. Metro: King St

54 Jaleo

★★$$ With Spanish tapas meant for sharing and pitchers of sangria, this spot serves as a popular place for large groups. Flamenco dancers perform for diners on some nights; otherwise, Spanish tunes help set a festive mood. ♦ Spanish ♦ M-Su, lunch and dinner; Su, brunch. 7271 Woodmont Ave (between Bethesda Ave and Elm St). 913.0003. ♿. Metro: Bethesda. Also at 480 7th St NW, Washington, DC. 202/628.7949. Metro: Gallery Pl

55 Barnes & Noble

This bright, airy megastore offers a huge selection of books, plenty of comfortable seats in which to enjoy them, and a **Starbucks** to keep you from dozing off. The fountain in front of the store has become a popular neighborhood hangout. ♦ Daily, 9AM-11PM. 4801 Bethesda Ave (at Woodmont Ave). 986.1761. ♿. Metro: Bethesda

56 Mon Ami Gabi

★★$$ The newest location of this small chain of French brasseries occupies prime real estate in the heart of Bethesda. The menu features French classics like steak *au poivre*, mussels marinière, and trout Grenobloise. ♦ French ♦ M-F, lunch and dinner; Sa, Su, brunch and dinner. 7239 Woodmont Ave (between Bethesda Ave and Elm St). 654.1234. www.monamigabi.com. Metro: Bethesda

THYME SQUARE

57 Thyme Square

★★★$$ This eatery pays homage to its star dishes with colorful murals of vegetables on ochre walls. A delightful choice of mainly vegetarian dishes (many made with local organic ingredients) includes wild mushroom and spinach lasagna, curry roasted vegetables on Israeli couscous, and several wood-oven pizzas. Pasta with lemon prawns and chicken Havana style are among the better nonveggie choices. Have a fresh juice concoction made to order. ♦ American ♦ Daily, lunch and dinner. 4735

Bethesda Ave (between Wisconsin and Woodmont Aves). 657.9077. &. Metro: Bethesda

58 GEORGETOWN BOOK SHOP

One of Bethesda's best secondhand-book stores, this shop specializes in history—particularly military and Soviet. But a good variety of other items, including pre-1945 magazines and posters, is also available. ◆ Daily, 10AM-6PM. 4710 Bethesda Ave (at Willow La). 907.6923. www.georgetownbookshop.com. &. Metro: Bethesda

59 BETHESDA CRAB HOUSE

★★★$$ Fresh, perfectly cooked crabs are served in a setting that focuses on the business at hand: The tables are covered with newspapers, and utensils consist of a wooden mallet and a small knife. An outdoor patio adds to the fun. Be sure to call ahead and arrive on time—the crab supply may be limited. ◆ Seafood ◆ Daily, lunch and dinner. Reservations recommended. 4958 Bethesda Ave (between Arlington Rd and Clarendon Dr). 652.3382. &. Metro: Bethesda

60 RIO GRANDE CAFE

★★$$ This bustling Tex-Mex joint recently moved to bigger digs decorated in earth tones, colorful tilework, and south-of-the-border–style furnishings and accents. The menu offers standard Southwest favorites—from tortillas and sizzling fajitas to chiles rellenos and potent, icy margaritas. ◆ Tex-Mex ◆ Daily, lunch and dinner. 4870 Bethesda Ave (at Arlington Rd). 656.2981. &. Metro: Bethesda. Also at 4301 Fairfax Dr (at N Taylor St), Arlington, Virginia. 703/528.3131. &. Metro: Ballston

61 THE PAPERY OF BETHESDA

This new shop offers a solution to all your stationery needs. Note cards from Crane's, Laura Stoddart, and Roger la Borde fill tables at the front of the store. Toward the back, find elegant wrapping paper, photo albums, and greeting cards. ◆ M-Sa, 10AM-9PM; Su, noon-5PM. 4852 Bethesda Ave (between Woodmont Ave and Arlington Rd). 240/497.1420. Metro: Bethesda

62 CITY LIGHTS OF CHINA

★★★$$ This new branch of the longtime Dupont Circle favorite **China Village Restaurant** offers large portions made with fresh ingredients and skilled preparation. Menu highlights include Peking duck, eggplant with garlic, and salt-baked shrimp. ◆ Chinese ◆

Daily, lunch and dinner. 4820 Bethesda Ave (between Woodmont Ave and Arlington Rd). 913.9501. www.citylightsofchina.com. Metro: Bethesda. Also at 1731 Connecticut Ave NW (between R and S Sts), Washington, DC. 202/265.6688. Metro: Dupont Cir

63 GLEN ECHO

Nestled off **MacArthur Boulevard**, this tiny incorporated town is an enclave of narrow, tree-lined streets and an eclectic mix of houses. It has a loyal community of residents proud to be in on a well-kept secret.

Within Glen Echo:

GLEN ECHO PARK

Built in 1891, this park originally provided a base for the then-emerging Chautauqua movement, which offered education and entertainment for adults in a summer-camp environment. The park's next life, a 70-year incarnation as an amusement park, is better remembered. Declared a National Park Service site in 1971, the park includes artist studios, classroom space, children's theater performances, and a wonderful recently renovated Spanish ballroom. The folk, big-band, and ballroom dances that normally take place there are being held in the bumper car pavilion. Call ahead for schedule information. Young and old alike still take turns on the renovated **Dentzel Carousel** (installed in 1921), which boasts its original 256-pipe Wurlitzer organ; rides cost 75 cents. ◆ Free. Daily, 9AM-5PM. Carousel: W, Th, Sa, Su, May-Aug; Sa, Su, only in Sept. 7300 MacArthur Blvd (at Oxford Rd). 492.6229. www.nps.gov/glec

Within Glen Echo Park:

DISCOVERY CREEK CHILDREN'S MUSEUM

This Washington-based museum offers programs in a historic stable at Glen Echo and in a nearby one-room former schoolhouse. Through innovative art projects, nature and history are brought to life for children (best suited for ages 6–11). ◆ Admission. Sa, Su, 10AM-3PM. Reservations required for some activities. 202/337.5111. www.discoverycreek.org

CLARA BARTON NATIONAL HISTORIC SITE

In 1897, 75-year-old Clara Barton, founder of the American Red Cross, moved to the **Glen Echo House**, originally built as a warehouse for the organization's supplies. After

---

Restaurants/Clubs: Red | Hotels: Purple | Shops: Orange | Outdoors/Parks: Green | Sights/Culture: Blue

removing some of the 72 concealed closets, deep enough to store wheelchairs, the indefatigable Barton expanded the house to 36 rooms. Her personal effects and furniture remain as they were during her last years. Tours are given on the hour 10AM-4PM. ♦ Free. Daily. 5801 Oxford Rd (south of MacArthur Blvd). 320-1410. &. www.nps.gov/clba

CHEVY CHASE

Centered around **Chevy Chase Circle** (the intersection of Connecticut and Western Avenues), this suburb straddles both Montgomery County and DC, but the town of Chevy Chase proper sits squarely on the Maryland side. The site of two of Washington's most exclusive country clubs, **Chevy Chase Club** and **Columbia Country Club**, it offers real estate as pricey as Potomac's—the per capita income in the 20815 ZIP code is one of the highest in the country—but with more history behind it. Chevy Chase predates Potomac by several decades.

Chevy Chase has its own mini "Fifth Avenue" enclosed within a two-block stretch of **Wisconsin Avenue** (between Willard and Dorset Avenues). Among the high-toned names to be found there are **Tiffany and Co., Gianni Versace, Cartier, Brooks Brothers**, and **Gucci**.

64 AUDUBON NATURALIST SOCIETY

The society makes its home in a Georgian mansion designed in 1928 by **John Russell Pope**, the architect of the **Jefferson Memorial**. Located on 40 acres of wildlife sanctuary, the estate, known as **Woodend**, is traversed by a three-quarter-mile nature trail. Self-guided tours are available daily. ♦ Free. Daily. 8940 Jones Mill Rd (between Jones Bridge Rd and Woodhollow Dr). 652.9188. www.audubonnaturalist.org

In 1883, developer Benjamin Franklin Gilbert bought a 90-acre parcel of land that straddled both the District of Columbia and Maryland. He named his new suburb Takoma Park: *Takoma* is an Indian word meaning "high up, near heaven," and at the time the area had an abundance of trees and two healthful natural springs.

65 LEMON DROP

This quaint little shop has a unique variety of high-quality children's clothes and accessories. For women's clothes, visit the **Lemon Twist** next door. ♦ M-Sa, 10AM-6PM; Su, noon-5PM. 8534 Connecticut Ave (at Manor Rd). 656.1357

66 CLYDE'S OF CHEVY CHASE

★★$$ This popular restaurant celebrates the 1920s and 1930s age of elegant travel with a re-creation Orient Express room and displays of model planes and ships. Adding to the fun, an electric train chugs along the ceiling. The innovative menu changes often, with burgers and rotisserie chicken consistent favorites. Desserts, especially chocolate bread pudding and cappuccino custard, are sinfully good. ♦ American ♦ Daily, lunch and dinner. Reservations recommended. 70 Wisconsin Cir (between Western and Wisconsin Aves). 951.9600. &. www.clydes.com. Metro: Friendship Heights. Also at various locations throughout the area

TAKOMA PARK

Founded more than a hundred years ago, this unique spot has retained a strong sense of its past (see the meticulously renovated Victorians) while distinguishing itself through civic and political activism. (The city has designated itself a nuclear-free zone and a sanctuary for non-American refugees.) The ethnic diversity and rejuvenated **Old Town** business district make this pretty town, nicknamed Azalea City, well worth a visit.

67 EVERYDAY GOURMET

★★$ Homemade breads, pastries, and luscious desserts, plus sandwiches, salads, and entrées, can be consumed on the spot or carried out. Catering is available too. ♦ American ♦ M-Sa, breakfast, lunch, and dinner; Su; breakfast and lunch. 6923 Laurel Ave (just south of Carroll Ave). 270.2270. &. Metro: Takoma

67 HOUSE OF MUSICAL TRADITIONS

Area musicians and music lovers flock to this shop that sells, rents, and repairs all kinds of musical instruments—from harmonicas and tambourines to concertinas, hammered dulcimers, drums, guitars, and banjos. It also stocks CDs by local artists and a wide selection of books on topics like folk and klezmer music. ♦ Tu-Sa, 11AM-7PM; Su, M, 11AM-5PM. 7040 Carroll Ave (between Tulip and Willow Aves). 270.9090. www.hmtrad.com. Metro: Takoma

Prince George's County

Covering a large area east of DC, from **Laurel** to the **Potomac River**, Maryland's second-largest county is the most populous jurisdiction in the Washington area. Already, more than 775,000 residents call it home, and the community of rolling hills is still growing. Prince George's also claims some historic firsts: Captain John Smith landed here in 1608, and the first American airport was built in **College Park** in 1908— Wilbur and Orville Wright were teachers here. NASA's **Goddard Space Flight Center** is here in **Greenbelt** (one of the country's first planned communities, dating from the 1930s), and so the pioneering tradition continues.

68 Ledo

★$ The many pizza variations served here are the ticket at this long-standing hangout. ♦ Italian ♦ M-Th, breakfast, lunch, and dinner; F-Su, lunch and dinner. 2420 University Blvd E (between West Park Dr and 24th Ave), Hyattsville. 422.8622. ♿. Also at numerous other locations throughout the area

69 University of Maryland

The main campus of this coeducational state-supported facility has more than 35,000 students and 3,600 faculty members. It's also home to the Maryland Terrapins, the 2002 NCAA National Champion men's basketball team. Its physics, mathematics, and computer science departments are highly regarded among the country's public universities. Free walking tours are given by the admissions office Monday through Friday. ♦ Baltimore Ave and Regents Dr, College Park. Main campus, 405.1000; admissions office, 314.8385. ♿. www.umd.edu. Metro: College Park/University of Maryland

69 College Park Aviation Museum

An affiliate of the **Smithsonian Institution**, this 27,000-square-foot facility is located on the grounds of the world's oldest continuously operating airport. Animatronics and interactive exhibits highlight important moments in aviation history. There are nearly a dozen aircraft on display (some original, some reproduction), including a 1924 Berliner helicopter and 1941 Stearman. During warmer months, visitors can picnic at outdoor tables overlooking the airport's runway. ♦ Admission. Daily, 10AM-5PM.

1985 Corporal Frank Scott Dr (off Paint Branch Pkwy). 864.6029. www.pgparks.com. Metro: College Park

70 Recreational Equipment Inc. (REI)

This indispensable cooperative for backpackers, climbers, and other outdoors types gives members a substantial year-end rebate on purchases. Fortunately, you don't have to be a member to take advantage of the reasonable prices offered here. Watch for end-of-season sales. ♦ M-F, 10AM-9PM; Sa, 10AM-8PM; Su, 11AM-7PM. 9801 Rhode Island Ave (at Muskogee St), College Park. 982.9681. www.rei.com. ♿. Metro: Greenbelt. Also at 3509 Carlin Springs Rd (at Leesburg Pike), Baileys Crossroads, Virginia. 703/379.9400. ♿

71 Old Greenbelt Theatre

Nestled in an Art Deco shopping center, this little gem of a movie theater has defied the multiplexes and stayed in business, attracting a loyal following for its mostly art-house fare (low-budget independent and foreign films). ♦ 129 Centerway Rd (at Crescent Rd), Greenbelt. 474.9744. www.pgtheatres.com

72 Greenbelt Park

Only 12 miles from Downtown DC, this pine forest is a haven for deer, red fox, and gray squirrel. The streams are filled with small fish, and the air is fragrant with the scent of flowers. Nine miles of walking trails and a number of camping facilities and picnic areas dot the 1,176 acres. ♦ Free. Daily. Administrative offices, M-F. 6565 Greenbelt Rd (between Baltimore Washington Pkwy and Kenilworth Ave), Greenbelt. 344.3944. www.nps.gov/gree

73 Goddard Space Flight Center

Named after Dr. Robert H. Goddard ("The Father of American Rocketry"), NASA's Goddard Space Flight Center is home to the world's largest collection of scientists and engineers dedicated to exploring Earth from space. The research facility and museum offer special programs, events, and lectures that highlight the center's work. Two gallery spaces house exhibits on subjects like the Hubble telescope and the Gemini spacecraft. Model rocket launches are held on the first Sunday of the month at 1PM (weather permitting).

Restaurants/Clubs: Red | Hotels: Purple | Shops: Orange | Outdoors/Parks: Green | Sights/Culture: Blue

◆ Free. Tu-F, 9AM-5PM; Sa, Su, noon-4PM. 8800 Greenbelt Rd, Greenbelt. 286.2000. &. www.nasa.gov/goddard

74 MARIETTA HOUSE

Follow Route 193 east from the Goddard Space Center, and little before Route 450 on the right you will find this Federal-style brick house dating from 1813. Originally part of a 650-acre estate, it was the plantation home of Gabriel Duvall, 1752-1844, who dedicated his life to public service. Duvall was an Associate Justice on the US Supreme Court for 23 years. In the 1830s a two-story addition was added, and the house remained in the Duvall family until 1902. The décor and furniture reflect the three generations of the family's occupancy. ◆ Admission. Tours: F, 11AM-3PM; Sa, Su, noon-4PM. 5626 Bell Station Rd (at Glenn Dale Blvd), Glenn Dale. 464.5291

75 94TH AERO SQUADRON RESTAURANT

★★★$$ Undoubtedly the quaintest restaurant in the area. Several real aircraft sit outside a building resembling a 1919 French farmhouse, and the ambience inside takes you back into another world that existed decades ago, down to big-band music from the '30s and '40s and World War II radio news broadcasts. The food is scrumptious, and the Sunday brunch is especially popular. ◆ American ◆ Daily, dinner; M-Sa, lunch; Su, brunch. 5240 Paint Branch Pkwy (between Corp. Frank Scott Dr and Riverside Ave), College Park. 699.9400; fax 779.2305

76 PRINCE GEORGE'S PUBLICK PLAYHOUSE

Housed in a renovated Art Deco movie theater, this performing arts center hosts dance, music, and theatrical events, with special attention to ethnic artists. ◆ Shows: F-Su. Box office: M-F, 10AM-4PM and 1 hour before performances. 5445

The Gridiron Club is a venerable Washington institution, limited to 50 Washington press correspondents. Their annual Gridiron Dinner presents skits lampooning current affairs and politicians. The president is always invited and usually attends.

The Secret Service has code names for each president. President Nixon was known as Searchlight, President Carter as Dixon, and President Ford as Passkey.

Landover Rd (at 55th Ave), Cheverly. 277.1710

77 FEDEX FIELD

The new home of the beloved Washington Redskins football team opened with great fanfare in 1997. This 80,000-seat arena—including 280 luxury suites, a 14,000-square-foot locker room, and 3.5 miles of concourse railings—makes their former home, **RFK Stadium**, seem cozy by comparison. The grass field is kept from freezing by underground pipes; giant (24-by-32-foot) video screens run replays and highlights in each end zone; and 38 concession stands sell everything from pizza and hot dogs to Mexican food and desserts. The difficulty is in actually getting tickets for a game. The **Redskins** have been sold out for years and have thousands on their season-ticket waiting list—despite their glorious new stadium. For those who do score a ticket, allow plenty of time to compensate for often-heavy traffic. Shuttle buses (fee) run constantly from the **Addison Road**, **Cheverly**, and **Landover** Metro stations (a 10- to 15-minute ride). ◆ Box office and information office: M-F. Arena Dr (off Lottsford Rd), Landover. Information, 276.6000; ticket office, 276.6050. &. Metros: Cheverly, Landover

78 SIX FLAGS AMERICA

Formerly known as **Adventure World**, this amusement park is now filled with even more rides, shows, concessions, and attractions guaranteed to drive youngsters wild and parents crazy. Assorted water slides, an innovative children's pool, and **Monsoon Lagoon**, one of the country's largest wave pools, provide big splashes of fun. There are various shows and special events each weekend and sometimes during the week. Though this one suffers in comparison to **Kings Dominion** 2 hours south, it's still the biggest theme park in the DC area. ◆ Admission. Weekends, 1 May-Memorial Day and Oct; daily, Memorial Day–Labor Day. 13710 Central Ave (between Church and Enterprise Rds), Largo. 249.1500.www.sixflags.com

79 WATKINS REGIONAL PARK

Inside this 850-acre park, the authentic hand-carved, hand-painted, turn-of-the-19th-century carousel is worth seeing. The park also has train rides, miniature golf, hiking and biking trails, indoor and outdoor tennis courts, and a snack bar. ◆ Free (fee for some activities). Daily (some activities are seasonal). 301 Watkins Park Dr (between Largo Rd and Central Ave), Largo. 218.6700

80 OXON COVE PARK AND OXON HILL FARM

City folks can get a taste of country life at this working farm, where rural charms abound. Farm animals provide plenty of diversions for wide-eyed urban kids, who can watch as the cows are milked and the fields plowed. Family activities include hayrides and special events, such as a cornhusk doll-making workshop and "Jimmy Crack Corn," at which you can help shuck, shell, and grind corn for poultry feed. A forest, an orchard, and a vegetable garden complete the rustic picture. The park is administered by the National Park Service. ♦ Free. Daily, 8AM-4:30PM. 6411 Oxon Hill Rd (just west of Indian Head Hwy), Forest Heights. 839.1176. www.nps.gov/oxhi

81 ROSECROFT RACEWAY

Enjoy the excitement of nighttime harness racing, and the view, from the raceway's restaurant. ♦ Admission. Post time: Th-Sa, 7:20PM. 6336 Rosecroft Dr (south of Brinkley Rd), Fort Washington. Restaurant reservations, 567.4045; raceway information, 567.4000. www.rosecroft.com

82 FORT WASHINGTON

Built on this site to replace the original fort (destroyed in 1814), the present structure was manned as a river defense post, at times by as many as 350 soldiers. High brick and stone walls enclose the 3-acre fort; the entrance has a drawbridge suspended over a dry moat to prevent enemy attacks. Lethal bombardments could be delivered from three levels: the ramparts, the casement positions, and the water battery (designed by **Pierre Charles L'Enfant**), which is placed 60 feet below the main fort. Volunteer guides in period costume give musket demonstrations during the summer. Several trails lead to picnic areas in the 341-acre historical park surrounding the fort. ♦ Admission. Daily. Tours: M-F. 13551 Fort Washington Rd, Fort Washington. 763.4600. www.nps.gov/fowa

83 NATIONAL COLONIAL FARM

This working re-creation of an 18th-century tobacco farm offers a fascinating glimpse into colonial life in southern Maryland. Farm work and crafts are demonstrated. The grounds are managed by the National Park Service. Tours are available through the **Visitors' Center**. ♦ Admission. Park: daily, dawn to dusk. Visitors' Center: Tu-Su, 10AM-4PM. 3400 Bryan Point Rd (at Cactus Hill Rd), Accokeek. 283.2113. ♿

"Note that the city of Washington is always referred to as the capital spelled with an *al*, as in accumulated wealth or excess of assets over liabilities. The building occupied by the Congress of the United States and the surrounding Hill are always referred to as the Capitol with *ol* and an upper case initial. That is, the Capitol building is always spelled with a capital C but the capital city is spelled without." Is that clear?

—E.J. Applewhite,
Washington Itself

ALEXANDRIA

Alexandria was established in 1749, serving for many years as a principal colonial port, and during the late 18th century as a vital social and political center. George Washington was a native son, as were Revolutionary War heroes General Henry "Light Horse Harry" Lee and his son, General Robert E. Lee, the commander in chief of the Confederate army. Fortunately, several generations of residents and city leaders have preserved the rich past in dozens of historic buildings.

Old Town served as the merchant district for the old seaport and is still a lively shopping and entertainment center. **King Street,** the main east–west drag, is a browser's paradise, lined with shops selling clothing, crafts, housewares, and gifts. And this is *the* place for antique hunting; no section of DC has the wealth of antiques shops that fill the western stretch of King Street. **Prince** and **Queen Streets,** east of **Washington Street,** are lined with unusually handsome early 19th-century row houses, and a riverfront park offers a retreat from the bustle of commerce. Old Town has for some years presented parking challenges similar to those found in Georgetown and Adams Morgan. Our advice: Find a garage and spend a little money for peace of mind, or take the **Metro** to King Street. On the weekends, a free shuttle bus (370.3274) runs between the Metro and the waterfront along King Street.

Though Alexandria proper extends far west and south of Old Town, the outer areas contain more modern (and, many say, less interesting) homes and businesses. For many years, this city has served as both a bedroom community for Washington and a place with its own distinctive identity as the unofficial capital of Northern Virginia.

Area code 703 unless otherwise noted.

1 FIVE GUYS

★★$ For generations raised on fast-food hamburgers, the freshly ground beef versions at these hole-in-the-wall carryouts will come as a shock. For the rest of us, it's instant (and delicious) nostalgia. The fresh-cut spicy fries are wonderful too. ♦ Daily, 11AM–10PM. 4626 King St (between Beauregard St and Dawes Ave). 671.1606. &. www.fiveguys.com. &. Metro: King St

2 R.T.'s

★★$$ Even before the Clintons and Gores stopped here on their way to see Jerry Jeff Walker at the neighboring **Birchmere** (see opposite), this bar-restaurant had a loyal following. An appetizer of Jack Daniel's shrimp is the best way to dive into a meal of

New Orleans–style seafood. The portions are generous, the prices are reasonable, and everyone seems to be having a great time. The original artwork on the walls is by Brian McCall. ♦ Cajun/seafood ♦ M-Sa, lunch and dinner; Su, dinner. 3804 Mt. Vernon Ave (at Russell Rd). 684.6010

2 BIRCHMERE

Although recently expanded, this is still a small venue for some big musical talent, from folk and bluegrass to light rock. The food isn't much, so eat elsewhere, especially if you have to arrive early for a big-name act. Recent acts have included Issac Hayes, Hot Rize, and the Commitments. ♦ Hours for performances vary. 3701 Mt. Vernon Ave (at Bruce St). 549.7500. &. www.birchmere.com

3 FORT WARD MUSEUM AND HISTORIC SITE

The fifth-largest Civil War fortification protecting Washington was reconstructed with the help of photographs by Mathew Brady and dedicated in 1964. The museum, which features a collection of 2,000 Civil War items, is located in a 45-acre city park with picnic facilities and an

At a White House dinner honoring Nobel Prize winners, John F. Kennedy remarked, "I think this is the most extraordinary collection of talent, of human knowledge, that has ever been collected together at the White House—with the possible exception of when Thomas Jefferson dined alone."

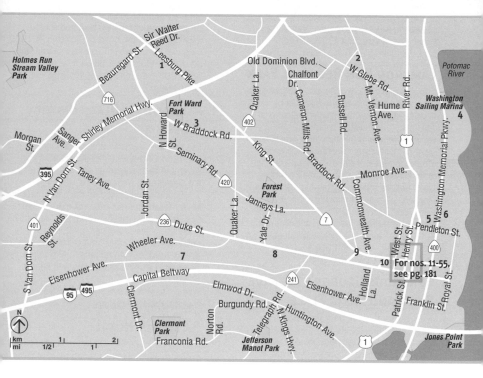

outdoor amphitheater. ◆ Free. Museum: Tu-Sa, 9AM-4PM; Su, noon-5PM; park: daily, 9AM-sunset. 4301 W Braddock Rd (between Marlboro Dr and N Van Dorn St). 838.4848. ಠ. www.fortward.org

4 WASHINGTON SAILING MARINA

Sailboat rentals and sailing lessons are available here; bicycles can be rented to ride along the Mount Vernon path on the banks of the Potomac, one of the prettiest riding routes in the area. **Spinnaker N' Spoke** sells gifts and boating equipment. ◆ Daily; hours for boat rental vary. 1 Marina Dr (east of George Washington Memorial Pkwy). 548.9027. ಠ. www.washingtonsailingmarina.com

At the Washington Sailing Marina:

INDIGO LANDING

★★★$$$ This building, which once housed the Potowmack Landing restaurant, has the best views of the river in DC. You can also enjoy watching planes take off and land at nearby Reagan National Airport. The menu might include dishes like shrimp and grits, fried skate wing, and cornbread-dusted crab cakes, as well as their signature dish, Indigo's Seafood Tower, featuring an amazing array of

seafood. It comes in two sizes, Short Tower at $50 and Tall Tower at $65. ◆ American ◆ Daily, lunch and dinner. 1 Marina Drive. 548.0001. www.indigolanding.com

5 BEST WESTERN OLD COLONY INN

$$ Here's a moderately priced 49-room inn on the edge of Old Town that shuttles guests to the subway, **National Airport**, or Old Town's shopping district. Amenities include a gift shop, complimentary breakfast, free parking, and laundry service. No-smoking rooms are available. Children under 19 stay free. ◆ 1101 N Washington St (at First St). 739.2222, 800/528.1234; fax 549.2568. ಠ. Metro: Braddock Rd

6 EXECUTIVE CLUB SUITES

$$$$ Suites only (80 of them) are offered in this pretty Georgian-style building. There's a health club (with Universal weights, treadmills, and bicycles), an outdoor swimming pool, and complimentary continental breakfasts. A free shuttle service takes you to **National Airport** and, in the evening, to Old Town. ◆ 610 Bashford La (at E Abingdon Dr). 877/316.CLUB; fax 548.0266. www.dcexeclub.com. Metro: Braddock Rd. Also

---

Restaurants/Clubs: Red | Hotels: Purple | Shops: Orange | Outdoors/Parks: Green | Sights/Culture: Blue

at 108 S Courthouse Rd (between S Second St and Walter Reed Dr), Arlington. 522.2582. Metro: Courthouse; and 1730 Arlington Blvd, Arlington. 525.2582. Metro: Rosslyn

7 CAMERON RUN REGIONAL PARK

If you're in DC in July or August, you'll need to escape the brutal heat and humidity by ducking inside air-conditioned museums or staying in a hotel with a swimming pool. Or you can venture to this nifty park, which has a wave pool, four-story water slides, a water playground for kids (inhabited by an oversize foam alligator, snake, and turtle), a batting cage, and 18 challenging and imaginatively landscaped holes of miniature golf. ♦ Admission. Pool: daily, Memorial Day–Labor Day. Golf and batting cages: daily, mid-Mar–Oct. 4001 Eisenhower Ave (between Bluestone Rd and Clermont Ave). 960.0767. www.nvrpa.org/cameron.html

8 GENEROUS GEORGE'S POSITIVE PIZZA AND PASTA PLACE

★★$ If your favorite part of a pizza is the crust, you'll like the doughy pies served here. Toppings range from basic to elaborate. All pasta dishes are served in generous portions on a pizza crust with mozzarella cheese. The restaurant can get crowded and noisy, but it's a good place to take young children. ♦ Italian ♦ Daily, lunch and dinner. 3006 Duke St (between Roth and Sweeley Sts). 370.4303. www.generousgeorges.com. ᕃ. Metro: King St

9 GEORGE WASHINGTON MASONIC NATIONAL MEMORIAL

The distinctive 333-foot tower atop this memorial to George Washington is visible from many parts of Alexandria. Inside are a museum with some of Washington's personal effects, a replica of the room he presided over when he was Master of the Alexandria Masonic Lodge, and an elevator, rising at a 7.5-degree incline, that takes you to the ninth-floor observation deck with a superb view of Alexandria. Tours daily, 9:30AM, 11AM, 1PM, 2:15PM, 3:30PM. ♦ Free. Daily, 9AM–4PM. King St and Callahan Dr. 683.2007. ᕃ. www.gwmemorial.org. Metro: King St

10 EMBASSY SUITES HOTEL

$$$$ Directly across from the **King Street Metro**, this 268-suite hotel has an indoor

pool, an exercise room, and free cocktails and cooked-to-order breakfasts. A free shuttle takes guests to the heart of Old Town. ♦ 1900 Diagonal Rd (between Reinekers La and Duke St). 684.5900, 800/EMBASSY; fax 684.1403. www.embassysuites.com. ᕃ. Metro: King St

11 ALEXANDRIA BLACK HISTORY MUSEUM

The City of Alexandria built the Robert Robinson Library in 1940 after five African-American men staged a "sit-down strike" at the segregated Queen Street Library in 1939. Robinson served as the city's main library for African-Americans until desegregation in the early 1960s. Today, it's home to a museum, where paintings, photos, documents, and other artifacts tell the history of African-Americans in Alexandria. The center also holds lectures and special programs. ♦ Free. Tu-Sa, 10AM-4PM. 902 Wythe St (at N Alfred St). 838.4356. www.alexblackhistory.org

12 RADISSON HOTEL

$$$ This 253-room establishment offers an exercise room, outdoor rooftop pool, and shuttle service to **National Airport**. Its restaurant **Chequers** serves standard American fare, from beer-battered onion rings and burgers to chops and steaks. ♦ 901 N Fairfax St. 683.6000, 800/333.3333; fax 683.7597. www.radisson.com

13 DANIEL DONNELLY

The specialty here is 20th-century modern designer furniture and lighting by, among others, Charles Eames, George Nelson, and Gilbert Rohde. Browse through the shop's collection of modern furniture reference books. ♦ M-F, 11AM-6PM. Sa, Su, noon-6PM; 520 N Fayette St (between Oronoco and Pendleton Sts). 549.4672. ᕃ. www.danieldonnelly.com. Metro: Braddock Rd

14 LEE-FENDALL HOUSE

Philip Richard Fendall, cousin of Henry "Light Horse Harry" Lee, built this Greek Revival house in 1785. The Lee family lived in the house between 1785 and 1903. (According to legend, it was here that "Light Horse Harry" authored a farewell address to George Washington.) Between 1937 and 1969, it was the home of labor leader John L. Lewis. Today, the house is interpreted as a Lee family home circa 1850-1870 with heirlooms and period pieces. Tours are available on a walk-in basis, although it's wise to check as sometimes it is closed for private events, and it will undergo an extensive restoration. ♦ Admission. Tu-Sa, 10AM-4PM; Su, 1-4PM. 614 Oronoco St

Virginia just ain't what it used to be. Under its first charter in 1606, the colony extended west all the way to the Pacific Ocean.

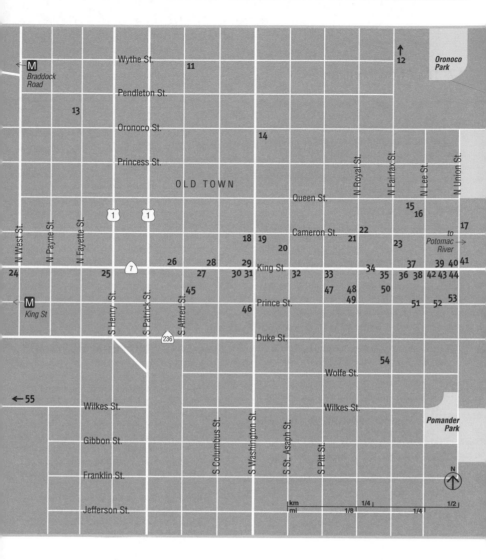

(between N St. Asaph and N Washington Sts). 548.1789. Metro: King St. www.leefendallhouse.org

15 BILBO BAGGINS

★$$ The quality of both food—mainly pastas, seafood, and chicken—and service can be spotty, but this cute restaurant has Alexandria's best wine bar. Many Alexandrians come here for Sunday brunch and the unbeatable raisin bread. ◆ Continental ◆ M-Sa, lunch and dinner; Su, brunch and dinner. Reservations recommended. 208 Queen St (between N Lee and N Fairfax Sts). 683.0300. www.bilbobaggins.net. ⛬. Metro: Braddock Rd

16 LA BERGERIE

★★★$$$ Located on the second floor of the old Crilley Warehouse, this neighborhood mainstay serves such Basque specialties as baked onion soup, duck confit, and crème brûlée. The real charm is in the handsome setting: leather banquettes, exposed brick, and chandeliers. ◆ French ◆ M-Sa, lunch and dinner; Su, dinner. Reservations required on

Restaurants/Clubs: Red | Hotels: Purple | Shops: Orange | Outdoors/Parks: Green | Sights/Culture: Blue

Sa. 218 N Lee St (between Cameron and Queen Sts). 683.1007. &. www.labergerie.com. Metro: King St

17 THE FOOD PAVILION

Located next to the **Torpedo Factory Art Center** and boasting an appropriately industrial décor, this pavilion houses food concessions selling inexpensive Chinese, Italian, deli, and Mexican fare. Kids will like the giant gumball machine, and there's outdoor seating facing the river. ♦ Daily, 10:30AM-10PM. 5 Cameron St (east of N Union St). Metro: King St

18 CHRIST CHURCH

George Washington paid 36 pounds and 20 shillings for his pew as a vestryman in this 18th-century colonial Georgian-style church. Built in 1767 and originally called the Church in the Woods, it's the oldest continually active Episcopal church in the nation. The church was occupied by Union troops throughout the Civil War, and much of the building, inside and out, is original. Incumbent presidents are invited to attend services on the Sunday closest to Washington's birthday. Shortly after Pearl Harbor, Franklin D. Roosevelt and Winston Churchill attended services here together. Robert E. Lee, a parishioner, worshiped here from the age of 4 until the beginning of the Civil War. Plaques mark the pews where the Washington and Lee families sat. ♦ Services: Su, 8AM, 9AM, 11:15 AM, 5PM. Tours: M-Sa, 9AM-4PM; Su, 2-4PM. 118 N Washington St (between King and Cameron Sts). 549.1450. &. www.historicchristchurch.org. Metros: Braddock Rd, King St

19 LE REFUGE

★★$$$ A cozy, candlelit spot, it offers French-country dishes, including cassoulet, bouillabaisse, cold salmon, and other seasonal favorites. ♦ French ♦ M-Sa, lunch and dinner. 127 N Washington St (between King and Cameron Sts). 548.4661. &. Metros: Braddock Rd, King St. www.lerefugealexandria.com

> Visitors come to Washington "not to see some Claghorn on Capitol Hill or to tut-tut at the hard streets where the city's poor live, not to count the ways the Government falls short of the Founding Fathers' ideals, but to pay homage to the ideas themselves, to keep the ideals alive and try to imbue the kids with them."
>
> —R.W. Apple,
> the *New York Times*,
> 11 December 1998

20 SILVERMAN GALLERIES, INC.

This shop offers one of the area's largest collections of 18th- through 20th-century jewelry—diamonds are a specialty. Also, 18th- and 19th-century American and European furniture, silver, porcelain, and various decorative arts and furnishings are available. ♦ Sa, 11AM-5PM; most Th by appointment. 110 N St. Asaph St (between King and Cameron Sts). 836.5363. &. www.silvermangalleries.com. Metro: King St

20 KING STREET BLUES

★$ The "comfort" food may not be inspired (meat loaf and mashed potatoes, homemade desserts), but this is a fun bar, decorated with neon lights and artsy murals. There's live music some nights. The owners aren't singing the blues, however; the joint is packed on weekends. ♦ American ♦ M-Sa, lunch and dinner; Su, brunch and dinner. 112 N St. Asaph St (between King and Cameron Sts). 836.8800. www.kingstreetblues.com. Metro: King St

21 GADSBY'S TAVERN MUSEUM

Between 1797 and 1799, John Gadsby, the proprietor, hosted annual balls in George Washington's honor. Today, the tavern still celebrates his birthday with a traditional Birthnight Ball. The inn has been completely restored, to the point of acquiring period china and silverware, although the original ballroom interior is now at the Metropolitan Museum of Art. What you see here is a reproduction. ♦ Admission. Museum hours: Nov-Mar, W-Sa, 11AM-4PM and Su, 1PM-4PM; Apr-Oct, Tu-Sa, 10AM-5PM and Su, M, 1PM-5PM. 134 N Royal St (between King and Cameron Sts). 838.4242. &. www.gadsbystavern.org. Metro: King St

21 GADSBY'S TAVERN

★$$ This 200-year-old restaurant serves game pie, prime rib, seafood, trifle, and "drunken" gingerbread. There's entertainment some nights, including 200-year-old "news of the day" Wednesday through Saturday. ♦ American ♦ M-Sa, lunch and dinner; Su, brunch and dinner. 138 N Royal St (at Cameron St). 548.1288. &. Metro: King St. www.gadsbystavern.org

22 GOSSYPIA

Wedding dresses, tea-length dresses, and other unusual women's clothing, jewelry, and accessories from South America and Asia can be found here. ♦ M-W, F, Sa, 10AM-6PM; Th, 11AM-7PM; Su, noon-5PM. 325 Cameron St (at N Royal St). 836.6969. Metros: Braddock Rd, King St. www.gossypia.com

THE BEST

Anthony Pitch

Founder of Anecdotal History Tours and Author of *The Burning of Washington: The British Invasion of 1814*

Everyone correctly anticipates that the observation level near the top of the **Washington Monument** will offer panoramic views over downtown Washington, DC, the **Pentagon**, the **Lincoln** and **Jefferson Memorials**, **Reagan National Airport**, and other sites across the **Potomac River** into Virginia. Less well known are the spectacular views offered from a number of other easily accessible vantage points.

Walk up the steps leading up to the west front of the **Capitol** and you will come to the promenade level above the area where presidents from Ronald Reagan on have been inaugurated. From here you will get a breathtaking view down the **Mall** and **Pennsylvania Avenue**.

Another place from which to look down on the nation's capital is in front of the **Custis-Lee Mansion**, once home to Robert E. Lee, on the heights of **Arlington National Cemetery**. The mansion looks down in a straight line over the grave of President John F. Kennedy, **Memorial Bridge**, and beyond to the Lincoln Memorial. The view from here is so stupendous that the remains of 18th-century city planner Pierre L'Enfant were reinterred here in 1909, giving him posthumous recognition and honor that eluded him during his lifetime.

Another choice location to experience the spaciousness of Washington is atop the **Old Post Office Tower** at the corner of 12th Street and Pennsylvania Avenue. An elevator ride to the 12th floor of the tower brings you to a landing high above the city's landmarks. When you descend 71 steps down a spiral staircase, you will come to the 10th-floor repository of the 10 bells given by the British Ditchley Foundation as a Bicentennial gift to the US Congress.

23 CARLYLE HOUSE

Built 1751-1753 by city founder John Carlyle to resemble a Scottish manor house, this great Georgian-Palladian home was Alexandria's first stone building. The mansion is decorated with authentic 18th-century furnishings. This is where General Edward Braddock and five colonial governors planned the initial campaigns of the French and Indian War. Behind the house, find a pleasant 18th-century-style garden with boxwood parterres. Guided tours are offered. ♦ Admission. Tu-Sa, 10AM-4PM; Su, noon-4PM (last tour at 4PM, Nov-Mar). 121 N Fairfax St (between King and Cameron Sts). 549.2997. ⚬. www.carlylehouse.org. Metro: King St

24 HARD TIMES CAFE

★★$ This is chili heaven, with Cincinnati-style, vegetarian, and Texas-style among the options. You'll find cheap but good eats, with large portions. There is a great jukebox for fans of classic country music. ♦ American ♦ Daily, lunch and dinner. 1404 King St (between S West and S Peyton Sts). 837.0050. www.hardtimes.com. Metro: King St. Also at 3028 Wilson Blvd (between N Garfield and N Highland Sts), Arlington. 528.2233. ⚬. Metro: Clarendon; and 428 Elden St (between Herndon Pkwy and Grant St), Herndon, Virginia. 318.8941. ⚬

LE GAULOIS

25 LE GAULOIS

★★★$$ When the block on which it sat—on Pennsylvania Avenue downtown—was razed in the name of progress, this popular bistro relocated to Alexandria, but it still serves first-rate French food at bargain prices. Its signature wintertime dish, the *pot au feu gaulois*—a dinner of boiled beef, chicken, oxtail, and vegetables—is a perennial winner, but it's hard to go wrong with anything here, including the quenelles (pike dumplings in lobster sauce). ♦ French ♦ Daily, lunch and dinner. Reservations recommended. 1106 King St (between S Henry and S Fayette Sts). 739.9494. ⚬. Metro: King St

25 VERMILLION

★★$$ Opened in 2003, this place has established itself as a genuine neighborhood restaurant and bar. The style is casual and elegant, with a menu that features dishes such as roast Alaskan halibut fillet and saffron fettuccini. ♦ Contemporary American ♦ M-F, lunch; daily, dinner; Sa, Su, brunch. 1120

Restaurants/Clubs: Red | Hotels: Purple | Shops: Orange | Outdoors/Parks: Green | Sights/Culture: Blue

King St (between S Henry and S Fayette Sts). 684.9669. Metro: King St

26 MAJESTIC CAFÉ

★★★$$ A neon sign points the way to this restored Art Deco–era landmark. On the menu, find international cuisine like braised rabbit leg, chicken breast with cornbread dressing, spoonbread, and top-notch buttermilk pie. ◆ American ◆ Tu-Sa, lunch and dinner; Su, brunch and dinner. 911 King St. 837.9117. &. Metro: King St. www.majesticcafe.com

27 RANDOM HARVEST

The owners of this shop have gleaned objects from many a tasteful household: Three floors contain handsome antique furniture, rugs, lamps, frames, and mirrors, as well as elegant new fabrics. ◆ M-Th, Sa, 11AM-6PM; F, 11AM-8PM; Su, noon-6PM. 810 King St (between S Columbus and S Alfred Sts). 548.8820. www.randomharvesthome.com. Metro: King St. Also at 1313 Wisconsin Ave NW (between N and Dumbarton Sts), DC. 333.1202

27 TAVERNA CRETEKOU

★★$$ This picturesque little restaurant has a vine-covered courtyard in back. The grilled lamb, perfectly trimmed and seasoned with a lemon–herb mixture, is recommended, as are the appetizers and homemade desserts. It's authentically rowdy on Saturday nights, when the waiters may spontaneously dance or burst into song. ◆ Greek ◆ Tu-Sa, lunch and dinner; Su, brunch and dinner. Reservations recommended. 818 King St (between S Columbus and S Alfred Sts). 548.8688. &. Metro: King St. www.tavernacretekou.com

28 SOUTH AUSTIN GRILL

★★★$$ A spin-off of the popular **Austin Grill** in DC, this restaurant offers the same mouthwatering Tex-Mex favorites—and the same long lines during peak hours. But the fajitas

and margaritas, among other specialties, make it well worth the wait. The colorful dining room includes huge copper sculptures of animals and an eclectic array of tiles laid into the floor. ◆ Tex-Mex ◆ Daily, lunch and dinner. 801 King St (at N Columbus St). 684.8969. &. www.austingrill.com. Metro: King St

29 MURPHY'S IRISH RESTAURANT & PUB

★$ On Sundays, this lively gathering spot offers an inexpensive Irish country breakfast, and it's always a good choice for dependable pub fare. Live entertainment starts nightly at 8:30PM. ◆ Irish/American ◆ M-Sa, lunch and dinner; Su, brunch and dinner. 713 King St (between N Washington and N Columbus Sts). 548.1717. &. www.murphyspub.com. Metro: King St

30 GERANIO

★★$$ This comfortable, rustic trattoria serves classic homemade pastas, like *agnolotti* stuffed with Portobello mushrooms, and such seafood specialties as grilled shrimp over creamy polenta. It can be especially romantic on a cold night with a warm fire. ◆ Northern Italian ◆ M-F, lunch and dinner; Sa, Su, dinner. Reservations recommended. 722 King St (between S Washington and S Columbus Sts). 548.0088. &. Metro: King St

31 LAS TAPAS

★★★$$ An interesting restaurant for those who like Spanish food and culture. It claims to offer the largest selection of tapas in the metropolitan area, with over 62 varieties. These include perennial favorites like *jamón Serrano* and *queso Manchego*, and the signature dishes for dinner are paella Valenciana and marinera. Expect authentic flamenco performances on Tuesday and Thursday, and Spanish guitar music Wednesday, Friday, and Saturday. ◆ Spanish ◆ Daily, lunch and dinner. 710-714 King St (between S Washington and S Columbus Sts). 836.4000. www.lastapas.us. Metro: King St

32 TICKLED PINK

This bright, colorful store deals in dresses, capri pants, and other beachy apparel for girls and women by Lilly Pulitzer. ◆ M-Sa, 10AM-6PM; Su, noon-5PM. 103 S St. Asaph St. 703/518.5459. Metro: King St. Also at 7259 Woodmont Ave, Bethesda, Maryland. 301/913.9191. Metro: Bethesda. www.tickledpinkapparel.com

33 HOLIDAY INN OF OLD TOWN

$$$ You wouldn't guess that there is a modern 227-room hotel behind these colonial brick

THE BEST

E. David Luria

Freelance photographer and director of Washington Photo Safari

You can capture the power of motherhood with your camera at *Motherland*, a statue commemorating the Red Cross's response to Armenia's devastating 1988 earthquake, located in front of the **American Red Cross** headquarters at 17th and D Streets NW. It's a statue of an Armenian peasant woman clutching her son during the earthquake. Get in close with your camera in the morning light to photograph the right side of her face, next to the baby, and notice the protective and caring look in her right eye. Now move over to her left side and photograph her face again. Notice that her left eye is half-closed in anger over the fact that her home collapsed because the builder never put enough metal rebars into the cement structure. If it's raining, you'll see tears running down her cheeks. It's a great picture for a Mother's Day gift!

There is one spot in the DC area where you can get "The Big Three" monuments (the **Lincoln Memorial**, the **Washington Monument**, and the **U.S. Capitol**) all neatly aligned in your camera viewfinder. Go to the stone plaza in front of the Netherlands Carillon, near the Marine Corps Memorial in Arlington, Virginia, for a postcard-perfect view in the late afternoon sun. On full-moon nights, this is also the place to go to capture the moon rising above the Capitol.

If you don't mind getting up REAL early (about one hour before sunrise), you can always get a lovely view of mist on the **Potomac River** between the Kennedy Center and the Arlington Memorial Bridge, along Rock Creek Parkway. Then walk over the bridge and capture early morning views of the Rosslyn skyline. With luck, there will be crew teams training in their shells on the Potomac, which is always a good picture. While you're in the neighborhood, walk over to the **Lincoln Memorial** and photograph Mr. Lincoln in his chair one hour after sunrise, just as the sun lights up the whole statue. Work quickly, because as the sun rises past the memorial's roofline, the statue retreats into the shade.

walls. Among the amenities are a restaurant that offers a great champagne brunch on Sunday, a large indoor swimming pool, and shuttle service to **National Airport** and the **Metro** on request. Small pets stay free. ♦ 480 King St (at S Pitt St). 549.6080, 800/HOLIDAY; fax 684.6508. ♿. Metro: King St

34 MARKET SQUARE/CITY HALL

Established in 1749, this is the nation's oldest operating farmers' market. The U-shaped Victorian building with a central courtyard was erected in the 1870s, and in 1962 the court-yard was filled in by an addition to the building. But the farmers' market goes on, set up in arcades on the south plaza of **City Hall** each Saturday. Among the many offerings are salt-cured meats, produce, homemade baked goods, flowers, and handmade crafts. ♦ Sa, 5:30AM-9AM. King St (between Fairfax and Royal Sts). ♿. Metro: King St

35 STABLER-LEADBEATER APOTHECARY

Patrons such as Martha Washington and Robert E. Lee once frequented this pharmacy, which first opened its doors in 1792. On sale here now are old medical books and remedy bottles, T-shirts imprinted with the Stabler-Leadbeater Apothecary label, games, and some collectibles. Adjoining the shop is a tiny museum, with the original apothecary furnish-ings. On display are antique medical objects, pill rollers, mortars and pestles, old potions, and vintage bottles. ♦ Admission to museum. M-Sa, 10AM-4PM; Su, 1-5PM. 105-07 S Fairfax St (between Prince and King Sts). 836.3713. www.apothecary.org. Metro: King St. www.apothecarymuseum.org

36 WAREHOUSE BAR & GRILL

★$$ Winners at this spiffy, popular place are the crab cakes and the 20-ounce T-bone. ♦ American ♦ M-Sa, lunch and dinner; Su, brunch and dinner. Reservations recommended. 214 King St (between S Lee and S Fairfax Sts). 683.6868. ♿. Metro: King St. www.warehousebarandgrill.com

37 RAMSAY HOUSE/ALEXANDRIA CONVENTION AND VISITORS' BUREAU

An Alexandria founder, William Ramsay, shipped his house down the Potomac River and hauled it in one piece to its proper lot here. Ramsay, a merchant trader, later added a small office and otherwise expanded the house. None of his personal belongings remain, however, save for a couple of letters from his children. Several rooms have been rebuilt to accommodate the **Alexandria Convention and Visitors' Bureau**, which provides free maps, hotel and group tour reservations, and lists of shops and restaurants in the area. ♦ Free. Daily. 221 King St (at N Fairfax St). 838.5005; 800/388.9119. www.funside.com

38 THE TROPHY ROOM

Even if you weren't planning on buying anything in this store, it is highly unlikely you will leave without something from its eclectic display of goods, particularly the large range of ORVIS products. This place deserves a visit. The owners are hunters and fishermen, and the trophies lining the wall give it its name. ♦ M, Tu, Th-Sa, 11AM-7PM; W, 2PM-7PM; Su, noon-5PM. 210 King St (between S Lee and S Fairfax Sts). 837.8215. www.trophyroomonline.com. Metro: King St

39 LANDINI BROTHERS

★★$$ At times, this restaurant seems to be a little bit of everything—power lunch spot for local politicians and business bigwigs, watering hole, rest stop for shoppers and tourists (it's smack-dab on Old Town's main drag). But the food is fine—especially the calamari and homemade pasta dishes—and the quiet, softly lit atmosphere is conducive to conversation and relaxation. ♦ Italian ♦ M-Sa, lunch and dinner; Su, dinner. 115 King St (between N Union and N Lee Sts). 836.8404. &. www.landinibrothers.com. Metro: King St

40 THE FISH MARKET

★$$ This bustling chowder and seafood house has several cozy dining rooms rigged with nautical décor and a popular upstairs piano bar. ♦ Seafood ♦ Daily, lunch and dinner. 107 King St (between N Union and N Lee Sts). 836.5676. www.thefishmarketoldtown.com. Metro: King St

41 TORPEDO FACTORY ART CENTER

Works by some 165 artists—including photographers, jewelers, sculptors, painters, and textile designers—are displayed in six galleries and 84 studios within this converted munitions factory, which during World War II was a major producer of naval torpedoes and parts. Although everything is for sale, the artists (many of whom work in the studios on the premises) are more interested in explaining than hawking their works. ♦ Free. Daily, 10AM-5PM. 105 N Union St (between King and Cameron Sts). 838.4565. &. www.torpedofactory.org. Metro: King St

Within the Torpedo Factory Art Center:

ALEXANDRIA ARCHAEOLOGY MUSEUM

Since 1961 the city of Alexandria has conducted its own excavations, unearthing everything from 10,000-year-old artifacts to 20th-century objects. The museum documents digs' progress and findings. ♦ Free. Tu-F, 10AM-3PM; Sa, 10AM-5PM; Su, 1-5PM. Third floor. 838.4399. &

42 RUGS TO RICHES

This "shabby chic" paradise is filled with beds, environmentally conscious chairs by Lee Industry Furniture, lamps, aromatherapy candles, home accessories, and, of course, a large selection of rugs. ♦ M-F, 10AM-8PM; Sa, 9AM-8PM; Su, noon-6PM. 116 King St (between Union and Lee Sts). 739.4662. www.rugstoriches.com. Metro: King St

43 BIRD-IN-THE-CAGE ANTIQUES

This shop sells a hodgepodge of antique wedding gowns, vintage jackets, books, glassware, political buttons, quilts, dolls, and more. ♦ Daily, 10AM-9PM. 110 King St (between S Union and S Lee Sts). 549.5114. www.birdinthecage.com. Metro: King St

44 BEN & JERRY'S

If you scream for ice cream, here's the scoop: This outpost is said to be the highest-volume link in the long chain. So if plain vanilla just won't do, stop in for some Cherry Garcia or Wavy Gravy. ♦ Daily. 103 S Union St (between Prince and King Sts). 684.8866. &. Metro: King St. Also at various locations throughout the region

Virginia was the tenth of the original 13 states to ratify the Constitution.

The Russians did it with marble; we did it with shadows.

—Harry Weese,
Metro system architect

45 MORRISON HOUSE

$$$$ Most of the 45 rooms and suites in this Colonial-style mansion have four-poster beds, brass chandeliers and sconces, and fireplaces. Tea is served every afternoon in the parlor. Amenities include a multilingual staff, concierge and valet service, indoor valet parking, and babysitting. ◆ 116 S Alfred St (between Prince and King Sts). 838.8000, 866/834.6628; fax 684.6283. &. www.morrisonhouse.com. &. Metro: King St

Within the Morrison House:

THE GRILLE

★★ $$$ Overseen by Vienna-born executive chef Robert Ulrich, this elegant spot—formerly **Elysium**—boasts three dining areas and a menu that spotlights fresh, regional ingredients ranging from wild-game fish to free-range fowl. Finish off the meal with crème brûlée or a cheese plate. ◆ American ◆ Daily, dinner. Reservations recommended. 838.8000. &

46 THE LYCEUM

This two-story Greek Revival–style brick-and-stucco building documents Alexandria's history with memorabilia, photographs, video presentations, antiques displays, and changing exhibits. The 1839 building served as a hospital during the Civil War; it was restored in 1974 by Carrol Curtice. ◆ Free. M-Sa, 10AM-5PM; Su, 1PM-5PM. 201 S Washington St (at Prince St). 838.4994. &. Metro: King St

47 RESTAURANT EVE

★★$$$ Husband-and-wife team Cathal and Meshelle Armstrong run this new spot (formerly **Santa Fe East**) named after their daughter. In the 34-seat Tasting Room, guests choose from five- or nine-course prix-fixe tasting menus of "modern American cooking with classical French influences." In the Bistro and Lounge areas, skylights, chandeliers, and fireplaces set the scene for entrées like braised veal short ribs and salt-baked prawns. The wine list features 100 bottles, and innovative cocktails include "The New Age Gibson." ◆ Modern American ◆ M-F, lunch and dinner; Sa, dinner. Reservations recommended. 110 S Pitt St (between Prince and King Sts). 706.0450. &. www.restauranteve.com. Metro: King St

48 SHOE HIVE

In-the-know fashionistas head to this cozy shop—formerly **Hysteria**—for ultrastylish flats, heels, slingbacks, and boots from designers like Bettye Muller, Hollywould, Marc Jacobs, and Sigerson Morrison. ◆ M-Sa, 11AM-6PM; Su, noon-6PM. 115 S Royal St (between Prince and King Sts). 548.7105. http://theshoehive.com. Metro: King St

49 BRITISH CONNECTION & TEA COSY

A taste of England comes to Old Town in this tearoom, where you'll find all the right stuff: teas, biscuits, sweets, kippers, and Scottish meat pies. The scones with Devon cream and jam are as authentic as they get this side of the Atlantic. In the back, a shop sells jolly good provisions and wares. ◆ Tu, noon-5PM; W-Su, 10AM-5PM. 119 S Royal St (between Prince and King Sts). 836.8181. &. Metro: King St

50 HYSTERIA

Boasting lime-green walls, this stylish shop (which recently moved into bigger digs) stocks fashion-forward clothing by names like Trina Turk, Milly, Chaiken, and Petit Bateau. Known for its customer service and good selection of merchandise, the boutique also offers jewelry, handbags, and other accessories. ◆ M-Sa, 11AM-6PM; Su, noon-6PM. 125 S Fairfax St (between Prince and King Sts). 548.1615. www.shophysteria.com. Metro: King St

51 GENTRY ROW

The houses on this mid-18th-century block form a collage of characteristic Georgian themes. All residences are private, except for the Greek Revival–style Athenaeum. ◆ Prince St (between S Lee and S Fairfax Sts). Metro: King St

For generations, the work of Italian and Italian-American stone carvers has adorned Washington's most famous buildings, with the National Cathedral being perhaps their most impressive. Though they usually re-created figures from sculptors' plastic models, the carvers were given free rein with some of the gargoyles and grotesques found in the niches of the cathedral. With binoculars, a careful viewer can see cats, an owl, a beast with four arms, the head of a horse, a hoofed beast with bells (symbolic of the cathedral bell ringers), and a drunk stone carver, chisel and mallet in hand.

Restaurants/Clubs: Red | Hotels: Purple | Shops: Orange | Outdoors/Parks: Green | Sights/Culture: Blue

THE BEST

Ann Cashion

Chef and Proprietor, Cashion's Eat Place

Of course, if you visit Washington, you can spend all your time on or in the vicinity of the **Mall**. Between the various museums of the **Smithsonian**, the national monuments, the **White House**, the **Capitol**, and the federal bureaus and agencies, there's enough to keep a tourist going for weeks. You really can't do it all, but personal favorites of mine in and around the Mall are:

- The **National Air and Space Museum** . . . which, contrary to popular wisdom, is not just for kids. It speaks eloquently, I think, to those of us who lived through the infancy of NASA and the space program. Stand beside the *Mercury* and *Gemini* capsules and weep at the courage and patriotism of men who were propelled into the great unknown in these tiny, fragile cones of rivets and corrugated metal. Be sure to catch a movie in the **IMAX Theater**; I like *To Fly* best of all.

- Visit the **Reading Room** at the **Library of Congress**.

- Don't miss the **Vietnam Veterans Memorial**, somber and understated, the only war memorial with which I am familiar that quantifies and makes concrete the magnitude of the sacrifice that war extracts from a nation.

If you have the time and inclination to go beyond the Mall and experience the city that a resident like myself enjoys on a daily basis, here are some suggestions:

- Stroll through residential **Georgetown**, where you'll discover block after block of beautifully maintained mansions, town houses, and tiny row houses from the 19th century. Tour the grounds of the **Dumbarton Oaks Library**.

- Experience the **Potomac**. Rent a canoe at **Jack's Boat House**. Paddle downstream to get a unique view of the monuments. Stop for refreshment at the grand terraced bar at **Sequoia**. Or paddle upstream for more of a "wilderness" experience. You are likely to see herons gliding gracefully just above the river's surface.

- Drive out to **Great Falls**, where the national kayaking team practices.

- Tour the **Washington National Cathedral**; learn the story behind its gargoyles. Admire the herb garden.

- Visit the **Phillips Collection**, which houses a remarkable array of Impressionist and post-Impressionist works, including Renoir's *Luncheon of the Boating Party*. Lunch around the corner at **Teaism** with its astonishing variety of teas and delicious light meals and snacks.

- While in **Dupont Circle**, browse the galleries that feature the work of contemporary area artists. Enjoy the remarkable number of thriving independent bookstores that the neighborhood supports. Visit **Melody Record Shop**.

- Go to **Glen Echo Park**, formerly the city's largest amusement park. Ride the old carousel. On weekends join hundreds of area residents who swing-dance to live bands in the historic, Mission-style **Spanish Ballroom**.

- Ride the **Washington Metro**, a truly elegant and comfortable public transit system.

- Absolutely reserve an evening for live music. Besides **Blues Alley**, excellent venues include the **Birchmere** in **Alexandria** for bluegrass and country/folk artists of national prominence and the **9:30 Club** for new music and contemporary rock.

- Attend a performance at the **Shakespeare Theatre**, where there's not a bad seat in the house from which to experience director Michael Kahn's brilliant and provocative productions. Tapas next door at **Jaleo** before or after the show.

On Gentry Row:

ATHENAEUM

This impressive example of 19th-century Greek Revival architecture, originally the **Bank of Old Dominion**, was purchased a century later by the Northern Virginia Fine Arts Association for use as an art gallery and cultural activities center. Guest curators stage original exhibitions of paintings, photographs, or crafts often done by local artists. The organization also hosts lectures, readings, performances, and workshops. In addition, the Athenaeum is home to the Alexandria Ballet, a small professional organization that specializes in ballets for kids. ◆ Free for exhibits; admission for ballet. W-F, 11AM-3PM; Sa, 1-3PM; Su, 1-4PM. 201 Prince St (at S Lee St). 548.0035

52 CAPTAINS' ROW

The early-19th-century cobblestone walk from the waterfront up Prince Street is known for its charming homes, all private, built by sea captains. The rooflines, proportions, materials, and trim of these houses vary wildly, reflecting the independent spirits of their original owners. ◆ Prince St (between S Union and S Lee Sts)

53 UNION STREET PUBLIC HOUSE

★★$$ Located down near the river, and behind an attractive façade of 200-year-old bricks, this

Boyhood Home of Robert E. Lee

place has been an Alexandria favorite for the last 20 years. Expect to find an enticing array of beers, as well as a good selection of pub grub. ♦ American ♦ Daily, 11AM-2AM. 121 South Union St (between Prince and King Sts). 548.1785. www.unionstreetpublichouse.com. Metro: King St

53 CHRISTMAS ATTIC

This festive shop occupies two floors of an 18th-century former tobacco warehouse. The walls are covered with ornaments by Christopher Radko, Byers' Choice carolers, nutcrackers, and other such holiday necessities. ♦ Daily; hours vary by season. 125 S Union St. 548.2829. www.christmasattic.com. Metro: King St

54 OLD PRESBYTERIAN MEETING HOUSE

The Scottish Presbyterians of Alexandria established this brick church in 1774.

George Washington's funeral services, canceled at **Christ Church** because of muddy streets, were held here in December 1799, and the bell tolled nonstop for 4 days thereafter. The church was struck by lightning and burned in 1835; the following year it was rebuilt as a Greek Revival–style sanctuary. A weathered tombstone in the cemetery honors the Unknown Soldier of the American Revolution. ♦ M-F, 8:30AM-4:30PM. Services: Su, 8:30AM, 11AM, Sept-May; Su, 10AM, June-Aug. 321 S Fairfax St (between Wolfe and Duke Sts). 549.6670. www.opmh.org. Metro: King St

55 ALEXANDRIA NATIONAL CEMETERY

One of 12 sites selected by President Abraham Lincoln in 1862 to serve as military burial grounds, this cemetery holds 3,500 graves of Civil War soldiers, including members of the US Colored Troops. ♦ 1450 Wilkes St

---

Restaurants/Clubs: Red | Hotels: Purple | Shops: Orange | Outdoors/Parks: Green | Sights/Culture: Blue

ARLINGTON

Situated directly across the **Potomac River** from the capital, **Arlington** was originally part of the District of Columbia. In 1847, on what some call one of Washington's saddest days, the 25.7-square-mile parcel was ceded back to Virginia; the federal government couldn't imagine having a need for all that extra space. Today, Arlington is a booming suburban community containing many federal offices and monuments, including **Arlington National Cemetery**, the **Pentagon**, the **Iwo Jima Memorial**, and the **Netherlands Carillon**. **Ronald Reagan National Airport** (formerly **Washington National Airport**) stands on a landfill just south of the Pentagon, providing convenient access to the city for tourists and, perhaps more important, members of Congress who keep voting down bills to relocate it.

This small county also contains the concrete high-rise office and hotel complexes of **Rosslyn**, **Pentagon City**, and **Crystal City**, which, because they have much taller buildings, seem to look more like cities than Downtown DC. However, while DC is still pulsing after dark with restaurant- and theatergoers, the streets in these mini-cities seem to roll up after rush hour. Other neighborhoods in Arlington are home to a lively immigrant community, where ethnic stores and restaurants bustle with activity. Ongoing development around the **Metro** stations at **Courthouse**, **Clarendon**, **Virginia Square**, and **Ballston** is transforming the faces of these once-sleepy communities with new shops, restaurants, hotels, and high-rise apartment buildings, drawing an influx of young professionals.

Area code 703 unless otherwise noted

1 KEY BRIDGE MARRIOTT

$$$$ Amenities in this recently renovated 582-room hotel include indoor and outdoor swimming pools, exercise facilities, two restaurants (one offers a spectacular panoramic view of DC), and a lounge. ◆ 1401 Lee Hwy (between Francis Scott Key Bridge and N Oak St). 524.6400, 800/228.9290; fax 524.8964. www.marriott.com. ᕃ. Metro: Rosslyn

2 HOLIDAY INN ROSSLYN

$$$ Located at Key Bridge, this 307-room hotel is a short walk to Georgetown and close to major highways. Decorated in a modern contemporary style, the hotel offers a rooftop restaurant, a fitness facility and indoor swimming pool, and dry cleaning and laundry service. A room on one of the top floors will assure you a breathtaking view. There's Wi-Fi, and children under 19 stay free. ◆ 1900 N

During the Civil War, Theodore Roosevelt Island was taken over by the Union Army to house the First US Colored Troops, a black unit.

Fort Myer Dr (between Key Blvd and Lee Hwy). 807.2000, 800/465.4329; fax 522.8864. www.holiday-inn.com. ᕃ. Metro: Rosslyn

2 CONTINENTAL MODERN POOL LOUNGE

★$ Retro rules at this welcome addition to Rosslyn's somewhat lacking nightlife scene. Bright colors (think aqua, orange) cover the walls, spaghetti lights purchased on eBay hang from the ceiling, a tiki bar occupies a back corner, and eight purple-felt-covered pool tables fill the center of the space. Women play pool for free all day and night on Mondays, and happy-hour specials are offered Monday through Saturday. The menu features a good selection of appetizers, salads, and sandwiches. ◆ American ◆ M-F, lunch and dinner; Sa, Su, dinner; bar daily till 2AM. 1911 Fort Myer Dr N (at 19th St N). 465.7675. ᕃ. www.modernpoollounge.com. Metro: Rosslyn

3 THEODORE ROOSEVELT ISLAND NATIONAL MEMORIAL

◉ In the Potomac River, between the Roosevelt and Key Bridges, lie these gentle marshlands

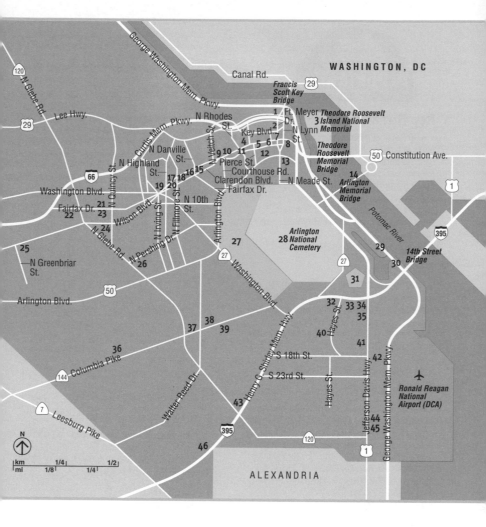

honoring the twenty-sixth president. The island's 91 acres allow red-tailed hawks, red and gray foxes, and marsh wrens to roam freely, along with groundhogs, great owls, and wood ducks. Old sycamore, oak, hickory, and dogwood trees shade the 2.5 miles of nature trails. Paul Manship's 18-foot-tall bronze memorial statue of Roosevelt stands in front of four granite tablets, each inscribed with his thoughts on nature and the state. The parking lot and pedestrian bridge to the island are accessible from the northbound lanes of the George Washington Parkway. The island can also be reached by canoe from **Thompson Boat Center** (202/333.9543) in DC. Nature walks are available. ♦ Free. Daily, dawn to dusk. George Washington Memorial Pkwy (between Custis Memorial Pkwy and Francis Scott Key Bridge). 289.2500. www.nps.gov/this

4 VILLAGE BISTRO

★★$$ This charming little spot manages to feel French while offering something for everyone. The casual, high-ceilinged room is simple and bright. If you pick one of the day's seafood specials or a veal or chicken dish, you probably can't go wrong. The numerous vegetables and side dishes, neglected in so many other restaurants, can be real show-stoppers here. ♦ American/continental ♦ M-F, lunch and dinner; Sa, Su, dinner. 1723 Wilson Blvd (between N Quinn and Rhodes Sts). 522.0284. ᯤ. Metro: Court House. www.villagebistro.com

---

Restaurants/Clubs: Red | Hotels: Purple | Shops: Orange | Outdoors/Parks: Green | Sights/Culture: Blue

5 RED HOT & BLUE

★★$$ Political gossip mixes with rhythm-and-blues selections from the jukebox at this upscale barbecue joint. Try one of several microbrews on tap with hickory-smoked pork ribs, beef brisket, or a pulled pork sandwich. Photos of blues artists and celebrity customers adorn the walls. ♦ Southern ♦ Daily, lunch and dinner. 1600 Wilson Blvd (at N Pierce St). 276.7427. &. www.redhotandblue.com. Metro: Rosslyn

5 CAFÉ ASIA

★$ Located in a former bank, this stylish spot features a 320-seat dining area, lounge, and sushi bar. The menu offers a wide range of well-priced Asian dishes (tempura, curries, teriyakis) and sushi. ♦ Asian ♦ Daily, lunch and dinner. 1550 Wilson Blvd (between Oak and Pierce Sts). 741.0870. www.cafeasia.com. Metro: Rosslyn

6 COURTYARD ROSSLYN

$$$ Within walking distance of the **Iwo Jima Memorial**, this hotel has been recently renovated. It includes 144 rooms and 18 suites, and features an on-site restaurant, indoor pool, and an exercise room. It offers shuttle service to the **Rosslyn Metro**. ♦ 1533 Clarendon Blvd (between Nash and Pierce Sts). 528.2222; fax 528.1027. www.marriott.com. Metro: Rosslyn

6 RESIDENCE INN ARLINGTON/ROSSLYN

$$$$ This long-term-stay property offers 176 suites with fully equipped kitchens, free high-speed Internet, an exercise room, same-day valet service, and a complimentary breakfast buffet. ♦ 1651 N Oak St (at 17th St). 812.8400; fax 812.8516. www.residenceinn.com. Metro: Rosslyn

7 TOM SARRIS' ORLEANS HOUSE

★★$$ Bringing New Orleans style—signature black wrought-iron balconies and all—to Virginia, this restaurant is best known for its huge portions of prime rib and fully stocked

salad bar. Seafood and other grilled meat entrées also come in hearty portions. ♦ American ♦ M-F, lunch and dinner; Sa, Su, dinner. 1213 Wilson Blvd (between N Lynn St and Fort Myer Dr). 524.2929. Metro: Rosslyn

7 HYATT ARLINGTON

$$$$ This 304-room European-style hotel is convenient to both the **Iwo Jima Memorial** and **Arlington National Cemetery**. It's also a quick walk across Key Bridge to Georgetown. Catering to individuals rather than conventioneers, the hotel provides complimentary high-speed Internet, a fitness facility, in-house movies, **Mezza 9** (a restaurant serving Mediterranean cuisine), and a lounge. Discount rates and free parking on weekends. Children under 18 stay free. ♦ 1325 Wilson Blvd (between Fort Myer Dr and N Nash St). 525.1234; 800/233.1234; fax 908.4790. &. www.hyattarlington.com. Metro: Rosslyn

7 BEST WESTERN KEY BRIDGE

$$$ Just over the river from Georgetown, this 11-story hotel features 178 recently refurbished guest rooms, complimentary continental breakfast, parking garage, meeting facilities, outdoor pool, gift shop, and exercise and game rooms. Top-floor rooms offer good views of DC. Children 17 and under stay free. ♦ 1850 N Fort Meyer Dr (at Key Blvd). 522.0400; fax 524.5275. Metro: Rosslyn

8 CHEVY CHASE BANK

It is rather difficult to miss this bank, at 1100 Wilson Boulevard, as it has a Times Square–style ticker tape and large TV telling you all the latest news.

9 OLSSON'S

This much-loved local independent bookseller carries fiction and nonfiction titles as well as a wide range of CDs. Throughout the store, find helpful staff members' recommendations. Call to ask about upcoming author readings. Café with sandwiches, coffee, desserts. ♦ Daily. 2111 Wilson Blvd (at Veitch St). Books, 525.4227; music, 525.3507. www.olssons.com. Metro: Courthouse. Also at 1735 N Lynn St. 812.2103. Metro: Rosslyn; and Reagan National Airport, Terminal C. 417.1087. Metro: Reagan National Airport

10 GUA-RAPO

This hip lounge takes its name from a Latin American juice squeezed from sugarcane.

Considered an aphrodisiac, the juice is featured in the bar's signature fruity drinks. Downstairs, find a glowing blue bar and tables for dining on Nuevo Latino cuisine. Upstairs is a lounge with stylish armchairs and live music some nights. ◆ Daily, 5PM-1:30AM. Latin American ◆ 2039 Wilson Blvd (at Courthouse Rd). 528.6500. Metro: Courthouse

11 RHODESIDE GRILL

★$$ This casual spot serves sandwiches, burgers, and entrées at indoor or streetside tables (weather permitting). The main-level bar area can get loud and boisterous; a lower-level bar with pool tables and darts plays host to live bands some nights. ◆ American ◆ M-Sa, lunch and dinner; Su, brunch and dinner. 1836 Wilson Blvd (at Rhodes St). 243.0145. www.rhodesidegrill.com

12 QUALITY INN IWO JIMA

$$ Just over two blocks from the Metro, this 141-room brick hotel has an indoor-outdoor pool, restaurant, and exercise room. Close by the **Iwo Jima Memorial**, the gift shop features World War II memorabilia and the front desk sports more of the same. Occasional specials drop this hotel into the one-dollar-sign ($) range. Children under 18 stay free. ◆ 1501 Arlington Blvd (between Fort Myer Dr and N Pierce St). 524.5000. 800/221.2222; fax 522.5484. ಈ. Metro: Rosslyn

13 UNITED STATES MARINE CORPS WAR MEMORIAL

More popularly known as the **Iwo Jima Memorial**, this is Felix W. de Weldon's re-creation of Joe Rosenthal's Pulitzer Prize–winning photograph. Five marines and a sailor raise the American flag on Mount Suribachi, Iwo Jima. The 78-foot-high, 100-ton sculpture represents the World War II battle site where more than 5,000 marines died but is dedicated to all marines who have died in service since 1775. A cloth flag flies 24 hours a day as a result of a presidential proclamation on 12 June 1961. ◆ N Meade St (south of Arlington Blvd). 289.2500. www.nps.gov/gwmp/usmc.htm. Metros: Rosslyn, Arlington Cemetery

On the Marine Corps War Memorial grounds:

SUNSET PARADE

This takes place on Tuesdays at 7PM during the summer and features the **Marine Silent Drill Team** and the **Drum and Bugle Corps**. ◆ Free. No reservations necessary. Information, 202/433.6060

13 NETHERLANDS CARILLON

This gift from the Netherlands to the United States was officially presented on 5 May 1960, the fifteenth anniversary of the liberation of the Netherlands from the Nazis. It was completely renovated and dedicated on Friday, 5 May 1995, the fiftieth anniversary of the liberation of the Netherlands. Within the 127-feet-tall tower there are 50 stationary bells—the largest weighs 12,654 pounds and the smallest just 35 pounds—with a range of two notes in more than four octaves. ◆ Free. Daily. Concerts: Sa, 2PM, May, Sept; Sa, 6PM, June-Aug. Adjacent to the United States Marine Corps War Memorial. 289.2550. www.nps.gov/gwmp/carillon.htm

14 ARLINGTON MEMORIAL BRIDGE

Although a bridge had been planned at this location for years, it took a massive traffic jam on Armistice Day 1921 to get one built. A long, low series of arches spans the Potomac with architectural firm **McKim, Mead, and White**'s usual Beaux Arts flair in the form of flamboyant equestrian statues. ◆ Metro: Arlington Cemetery

15 ISPIRATO

Owner Lilian Wibisono fills this small space with mod vases by designers like Jonathan Adler, funky patterned pillows, and other cool gift items as well as her colorful Pop Art-y paintings. ◆ Tu-Sa, 11AM-8PM; Su, noon-4PM. 2620 Wilson Blvd (between N Cleveland and N Edgewood Sts). 875.8182. www.ispirato.com

15 SHOEFLY

Affordable, trendy shoes by brands like XOXO and Farylrobin line the shelves at this funky shop, which also offers handbags and jewelry. ◆ Tu-Sa, 11AM-7PM, Su, noon-4PM. 2618 Wilson Blvd (between N Cleveland and N Edgewood Sts). 243.6490. Metro: Clarendon

16 IOTA CLUB AND CAFÉ

★$$ One side is a long, narrow restaurant with eclectic American cuisine. On the other side is a bar that hosts local and national acts, from singer-songwriters to indie bands. Cover charge to enter club side; when bands are performing, the music can be heard from the restaurant side. ◆ American ◆ Daily, lunch and dinner. 2832 Wilson Blvd (between Danville and Fillmore Sts). 522.8340. www.iotaclubandcafe.com. Metro: Clarendon

Restaurants/Clubs: Red | Hotels: Purple | Shops: Orange | Outdoors/Parks: Green | Sights/Culture: Blue

PILLARS OF STRENGTH

Egyptians created the first obelisks, using pairs of the graceful geometric figures to adorn the doorways of temples. The tall, slender, four-sided pillars were most often carved of red granite and honored Ra, the Egyptian sun god. Traditionally, an obelisk was designed so that its height equaled 10 times the width of its flat bottom. The stone column usually sat on a circular base and tapered to a point or pyramid.

Several Egyptian obelisks have survived the ages, including those at the Great Temple at Karnak in Thebes. During the period of European colonialism, several of these Egyptian treasures were moved to Europe and the US. The obelisk at Paris's Place de la Concorde once stood at Luxor. Twin obelisks, each known as Cleopatra's Needle, have been separated: One now stands at London's Embankment, the other in New York City's Central Park.

Of course, the **Washington Monument** is obelisk-shaped and follows the Egyptian formula for such a pillar's height. But the fact that it isn't a single, solid stone—a monolith—keeps it from being a true obelisk.

17 FACCIA LUNA

★★$$ A neighborhood favorite since 1992, Faccia Luna dishes out delicious pizza, calzones, grinders, and pasta dishes. It's part of a small, local chain run by two Penn State fraternity brothers, with additional locations in Alexandria; Washington, DC; and State College, Pennsylvania. ♦ Italian ♦ Daily, lunch and dinner. 2909 Wilson Blvd. 276.3099. www.faccialuna.com. Metro: Clarendon. Also at 823 S Washington St, Alexandria, Virginia. 838.5998

18 MARKET COMMON CLARENDON

Spanning several buildings along bustling Clarendon Boulevard, this new multi-use facility has livened up the neighborhood's retail scene. Both national chains, such as **Crate & Barrel** (890.2300) and **Williams-Sonoma** (248.8150), and local retailers, including **All About Jane** (243.4424) and **South Moon Under** (807.4083), are represented. Also find a variety of restaurants, including **The Cheesecake Factory** (294.9966) and **Harry's Tap Room** (778.7788). ♦ Daily (hours vary by store/restaurant). Clarendon Blvd (between N Edgewood and N Garfield Sts). Metro: Clarendon

In case of nuclear attack, federal officials would head to underground bomb shelters in the Virginia countryside. According to *Washingtonian* magazine, the bunker at Mount Weather has streets, sidewalks, and a small underground lake. The shelter designated for the Federal Reserve Board chairperson is equipped with electronic banking equipment and, reportedly, about a trillion dollars in cash.

18 WHITLOW'S ON WILSON

★$$ This local restaurant-bar is popular with the weekend brunch and beer-drinking crowds. Originally located in downtown DC, the bar relocated to Arlington in 1992. The menu features good burgers, (half-price on Mondays), sandwiches, and down-home entrées like meat loaf, grilled pork chops, and roast turkey with stuffing. ♦ American ♦ M-F, lunch and dinner; Sa, Su, brunch and dinner. 2854 Wilson Blvd (at Fillmore St). 276.9693. www.whitlows.com. Metro: Clarendon

19 HUNAN NUMBER ONE

★★$$ The best dishes are Cantonese offerings such as sizzling black-pepper steak, steamed shrimp in a lotus leaf with black-bean-and-garlic sauce, and fillets of flounder with asparagus. But perhaps the best reason to stop here is the dim sum—served daily between 11AM and 3PM. ♦ Chinese ♦ Daily, lunch and dinner. 3033 Wilson Blvd (between N Garfield and N Highland Sts). 528.1177. Metro: Clarendon

19 NAM VIET

★★$ Stop in for crispy rolls, orange beef, and other spicy Vietnamese dishes. ♦ Vietnamese ♦ Daily, lunch and dinner. 1127 N Hudson St (between Wilson Blvd and N 13th St). 522.7110. ♿. Metro: Clarendon. www.namviet1.com

19 CLARENDON BALLROOM

Once a carpet store, this bar draws well-dressed Gen-Xers for dancing to live bands or DJs or drinking on a seasonal rooftop deck. The swanky ballroom is also available for private events. ♦ W, 5PM-midnight (rooftop only); Th, F, 5:30PM-2AM. 3185 Wilson Blvd (at Washington Blvd).

469.2244. www.clarendonballroom.com. Metro: Clarendon

20 HARD TIMES CAFE

★★$ This honky-tonk saloon specializes in hearty chili (vegetarian too) and ice-cold long-necks. But before you settle into one of the wooden booths with a beer and some grub, make sure you play your favorites on the country-western jukebox. ♦ American ♦ Daily, lunch and dinner. 3028 Wilson Blvd (between N Garfield and N Highland Sts). 528.2233. Metro: Clarendon. Also at 1404 King St (between S West and S Peyton Sts), Alexandria. 837.0050. &. Metro: King St; and 428 Elden St (between Herndon Pkwy and Grant St), Herndon, Virginia. 318.8941. &. www.hardtimes.com

20 CLARENDON GRILL

★$$ Though a fixture on the Clarendon scene for several years now, the décor at this restaurant-bar is still purposely "under construction" (blueprints beneath glass table-tops, scaffolding on the ceiling). On weekend nights, young residents cram the bar area and outdoor patio (during warm weather) for microbrews and live music. The menu features burgers, sandwiches, and entrées. ♦ American ♦ Daily, lunch and dinner. 1101 N Highland St (between Clarendon Blvd and 10th St). 524.7455. www.cgrill.com. Metro: Clarendon

21 FOOD FACTORY

★$ Bare-bones but cheap—everything in this Middle Eastern cafeteria is less than $10. The kabobs are the best choices. No alcohol is served. ♦ Middle Eastern ♦ Daily, lunch and dinner. 4221 Fairfax Dr (between N Stafford and N Stuart Sts) 527.2279. &. Metro: Ballston

21 UNCLE JULIO'S RIO GRANDE CAFE

★★★$$ Excellent Tex-Mex staples (enchiladas, tacos, and—most popular—fajitas), as well as such surprises as frogs'

legs, are served in a fun, lively setting. The hour-plus wait for a table is easily soothed by the swirled margaritas. ♦ Tex-Mex ♦ Daily, lunch and dinner. 4301 Fairfax Dr (at N Taylor St). 528.3131. &. Metro: Ballston

22 HOLIDAY INN ARLINGTON AT BALLSTON

$$ The main features of this 221-room hotel are the large meeting rooms, complete with state-of-the-art video equipment, and an outdoor swimming pool. The lobby and the **Lacy Station Dining Car Restaurant**, where kids eat free, are decked out in the style of an old railroad depot, on which the restaurant was built. Extras include a fitness facility, a nearby jogging trail, and a free shuttle to local restaurants, shopping, and the **Metro**. ♦ 4610 N Fairfax Dr (between N Glebe Rd and N Buchanan St). 243.9800, 800/HOLIDAY; fax 527.2677. &. Metro: Ballston. www.holiday-inn.com

23 HILTON ARLINGTON AND TOWERS

$$$$ Directly over the **Ballston Metro** stop, this 209-room hotel has a restaurant, a bar, and privileges at the downstairs health club, which features a lap pool and a whirlpool. Rooms on the top floor—the concierge floor—are larger and include hors d'oeuvres and continental breakfast. ♦ 950 N Stafford St (at Fairfax Dr). 528.6000, 800/HILTONS; fax 812.5127. &. Metro: Ballston

24 BALLSTON COMMON MALL

Though **Ballston Common** has seen better days, this enclosed mall still features numerous shopping spots. Included are **Hecht's** department store; **B. Dalton Bookseller**, **Victoria's Secret**, and a raft of other chain stores; a 12-screen movie theater with stadium seating; and a food court with about 15 choices. ♦ M-Sa, 10AM-9PM; Su, noon-6PM. 4238 Wilson Blvd (between N Randolph St and N Glebe Rd). 243.8088. &. www.ballston-common.com. Metro: Ballston

Within Ballston Common:

ROCK BOTTOM BREWERY

★$$ This popular local branch of the national brewpub chain lures area young professionals with hearty salads and sandwich platters, good happy-hour specials, and house-made brews like

---

Restaurants/Clubs: Red | **Hotels: Purple** | **Shops: Orange** | **Outdoors/Parks: Green** | **Sights/Culture: Blue**

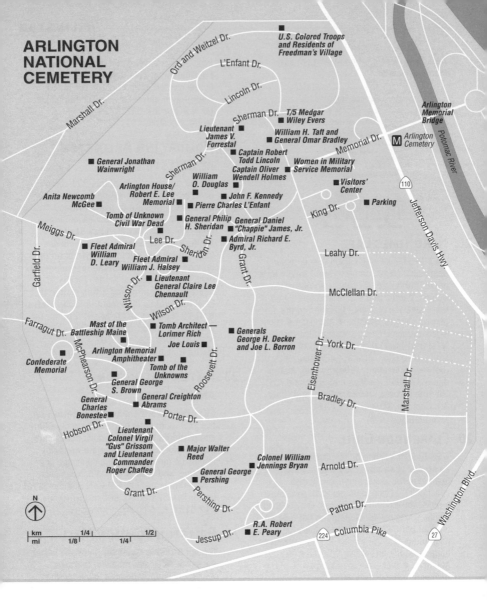

ARLINGTON NATIONAL CEMETERY

U.S. Colored Troops and Residents of Freedman's Village

Ord and Weitzel Dr.

L'Enfant Dr.

Lincoln Dr.

Marshall Dr.

Sherman Dr. T/5 Medgar
Wiley Evers

Arlington Memorial Bridge

Potomac River

Lieutenant James V. Forrestal

William H. Taft and General Omar Bradley

Memorial Dr.

Ⓜ Arlington Cemetery

General Jonathan Wainwright

Captain Robert Todd Lincoln
Captain Oliver Wendell Holmes

Women in Military Service Memorial

Sherman Dr.

Arlington House/ Robert E. Lee Memorial

William O. Douglas

Visitors' Center

Anita Newcomb McGee

John F. Kennedy
Pierre Charles L'Enfant

110

Parking

King Dr.

Tomb of Unknown Civil War Dead

General Philip H. Sheridan

General Daniel "Chappie" James, Jr.

Meiggs Dr.

Lee Dr.

Sheridan Dr.

Admiral Richard E. Byrd, Jr.

Leahy Dr.

Jefferson Davis Hwy.

Garfield Dr.

Fleet Admiral William D. Leary

Fleet Admiral William J. Halsey

Wilson Dr.

Grant Dr.

Lieutenant General Claire Lee Chennault

McClellan Dr.

Wilson Dr.

Farragut Dr.

Mast of the Battleship Maine

Tomb Architect — Lorimer Rich

Joe Louis

Generals George H. Decker and Joe L. Borron

York Dr.

McPherson Dr.

Arlington Memorial Amphitheater

Tomb of the Unknowns

Roosevelt Dr.

Eisenhower Dr.

Confederate Memorial

General George S. Brown

General Creighton Abrams

Bradley Dr.

Marshall Dr.

General Charles Bonestee

Porter Dr.

Hobson Dr.

Lieutenant Colonel Virgil "Gus" Grissom and Lieutenant Commander Roger Chaffee

Major Walter Reed

Colonel William Jennings Bryan

Arnold Dr.

General George Pershing

Pershing Dr.

Grant Dr.

R.A. Robert
E. Peary

Patton Dr.

Washington Blvd

N

Jessup Dr.

224 Columbia Pike

27

| km | 1/4 | 1/2 |
| mi | 1/8 | 1/4 |

Potomac Pale Ale and Spout Run Porter. Offers live music some nights. ♦ American ♦ Daily, lunch and dinner. Street level. 516.7688. www.rockbottom.com

25 LAYALINA

★★$$ This friendly, homey Middle Eastern eatery serves such Syrian specialties as stuffed grape leaves with lemon, *soujok* (hot sausage), and *fattoush* salad. The *mezze* combination, which serves two to three, and vegetarian sampler are good introductions to the menu. ♦ Syrian ♦ Tu-Su, lunch and dinner. 5216 Wilson Blvd (between N Frederick and N Greenbrier Sts). 525.1170. www.layalinarestaurant.com. Metro: Ballston

A Taste of Italy
PINES OF ITALY
Ristorante Italiano
Southern Italian Cuisine

26 PINES OF ITALY

★★$ Neighborhood Italian at its simple, casual best: good fried zucchini, fried arti-choke hearts, homemade pasta, and white pizza. If you're on a budget, ask for the prices of the specials before ordering—they can be relatively high. ♦ Italian ♦ Daily, lunch and dinner. 237 N Glebe Rd (between Piedmont St and N Pershing Dr). 524.4969. &

27 FORT MYER

Neat brick barracks house troops, chiefs of staff, a clinic, and a firehouse. Its **Parade Ground** nearby has held demonstrations of aviation history's bests, including the Wright brothers' first military aircraft test flight in 1908. ♦ Arlington Blvd (between Washington Blvd and N 10th St). 545.6700. &. www.fmmc.army.mil. Metro: Court House

28 ARLINGTON NATIONAL CEMETERY

Just over the **Arlington Memorial Bridge**, 612 acres of rolling hills dotted with simple head-stones give silent testimony to US military sacrifice. The quarter of a million soldiers buried here have served in every major military action, from the Revolutionary, Civil, and Spanish-American Wars and the two World Wars to the Korean, Vietnam, and Persian Gulf conflicts and now the Iraq War. In 1868 General John Logan set aside 30 May to decorate Civil War graves in a service held at the portico of **Arlington House**. Thus began an annual day of tribute—Memorial Day. Space at the cemetery, reserved for officers and enlis-tees of the US military and government employees and their spouses, is expected to run out around 2030, so certain requirements for interment have been set: The deceased must have been on active duty, a 20-year veteran, or the recipient of a high honor such as the Purple Heart. After parking your car in the parking lot (no cars are allowed on the cemetery grounds), start your visit at the nearby **Visitors' Center**, an imposing modern building with a giant skydome designed in 1989 by **Frances Lethbridge** and **Patricia Schiffelbein**. It houses the main information offices (where you can obtain a map of the grounds), a bookstore, and the **Tourmobile** station (202/554.5100). Guided tours aboard the Tourmobile stop at various monuments and points of interest. ♦ Free, but nominal parking fee. Daily. Memorial Dr and Jefferson Davis Hwy. 607.8000. www.arlingtoncemetery.org. Metro: Arlington Cemetery

Within Arlington National Cemetery:

WOMEN IN MILITARY SERVICE MEMORIAL

Dedicated 18 October 1997, this is the first national memorial to honor US servicewomen. Located at the ceremonial entrance of the main gateway to **Arlington National Cemetery**, the museum and educational center includes a hall of honor, four exhibit alcoves, and a 196-seat theater. A computerized database allows visitors to access photos and the military histo-ries of registered servicewomen.

JOHN F. KENNEDY'S GRAVE

This memorial, designed by John Carl Warnecke, is marked by an eternal flame and paved with Cape Cod granite. The simple marble terrace yields a panoramic view of the city; one low wall reminds visitors of Kennedy's power with words, showing an inscription from his inaugural address. Jacqueline Kennedy Onassis is buried beside him. Nearby in a grassy plot is Robert F. Kennedy's grave, marked by a white cross. An adjacent granite wall and fountain memorialize the words of the late attorney general and senator.

TOMB OF PIERRE CHARLES L'ENFANT

The grave of the designer of DC's city grid lies on a hillside overlooking Washington, just in front of **Arlington House**. His original plan is carved on the tomb.

ARLINGTON HOUSE/ ROBERT E. LEE MEMORIAL

The story of this house is really the story of two great Virginia families—the Washingtons and the Lees—and their struggle to hold on to this 1,100-acre estate, which overlooks the Potomac River and is now part of **Arlington National Cemetery**.

John Parke Custis, Martha Washington's son, purchased the land in 1778. In 1802 his son, artist George Washington Parke Custis (the adopted grandson of George and Martha), started building the Greek Revival mansion and, in turn, passed it along to his daughter Mary Anna Randolph Custis, who married Lieutenant Robert E. Lee in 1831. The house took its more common name, the **Custis-Lee Mansion**, from this famous marriage. The house is preserved as a memorial to Robert E. Lee, a man highly regarded by both sides in the Civil War. It was here, in 1861, that Lee learned of Virginia's secession from the Union and decided to resign his commission in the US Army to serve his native state. "My affections and attachments are more strongly placed here," he once wrote of the house, "than at any other place in the world."

Mrs. Lee left the estate when the Union Army crossed the Potomac during the Civil War. In 1864 the federal government claimed legal title to the land for unpaid taxes that had been questionably imposed during the war.

Complaining of unconstitutional seizure, George Washington Custis Lee sued for the return of the property in 1873. Later, in 1882, the Supreme Court ordered that the house be returned to Lee's son, George Washington Custis Lee. Because of its condition, however, he was unable to live in the house, and he sold it back to the government for $150,000. Congress approved the restoration of the ransacked house in 1925, and the estate was taken over by the federal government in 1933.

Thanks to extensive research and curatorial zeal, the house has largely been restored to its 1861 appearance. Each room has a few pieces of the Lee family's furniture, artwork, and housewares; others are period pieces. A portion of the double parlor set has survived and now furnishes the **White Parlor**; the violin given to Robert E. Lee's father-in-law by George Washington is also on display here. The bedchamber in which Lee resigned his commission in the US Army contains his original bedstead and writing chair. The dining room is furnished with original china, silver, and glassware. Copies of many of the paint-ings that once hung here—among them, an 1830 Italian Madonna by William George Williams—decorate the house. Original artworks include George Washington Parke Custis's *Battle of Monmouth*, which was intended for the **Capitol** but is now on display in the **Morning Room**, and the 1831 portrait of Mary Anna Randolph Custis by August Herview, painted shortly before her wedding to Lee, which is in the family parlor. Both floors of the house are open, as are the flower garden and a museum that traces Robert E. Lee's life and includes many objects he used. This glimpse into the lifestyle of pre–Civil War Southern gentility is a must for DC visitors. Tours are self-guided. ◆ Free. Daily. 235.1530

TOMB OF THE UNKNOWNS

Also known as the **Tomb of the Unknown Soldier**, this memorial remains the focus of sentiment and ceremony at the cemetery. Cut from white marble, it is decorated by sculpted wreaths and three figures representing Valor, Victory, and Peace. The inscription on the back panel reads, "Here Rests in Honored Glory an American Soldier Known But to God." Entombed in the monument are four crypts,

Warships at sea, traditionally, fired salutes of seven guns—because of that number's symbolic significance in the Bible as representing completeness. Three signified perfection, and as there were not the same problems storing gunpowder on land, batteries fired three guns for each one fired at sea. Thus the 21-gun salute (7 × 3) has become the highest international salute to high-ranking dignitaries and members of the military.

three of which hold the remains of unknown US servicemen, one each from World War I, World War II, and the Korean War. After much controversy, the Vietnam War crypt was disturbed in 1998 when the remains of First Lieutenant Michael Blassie were identified through DNA testing, subsequently disinterred, and moved to his family's cemetery in St. Louis.

At all times, a soldier from the "Old Guard" of the Third US Infantry protects the tomb, performing the impressive and solemn Changing of the Guard ceremony every 30 minutes in the summer and each hour in the winter. This routine of heel-clicking, rifle maneuvers, and salutes takes place on a 63-foot walkway that is covered in exactly 21 paces, followed by a heel-clicking turn to face the Tomb for 21 seconds; then another 21-second walk is taken after a turn and 21-second wait. (The **Iran Rescue Mission Monument**, marking the aborted rescue mission of American hostages in 1980, and the **Space Shuttle *Challenger* Memorial**, created in memory of the seven astronauts on board the doomed shuttle, are located near the tomb.)

ARLINGTON MEMORIAL AMPHITHEATER

The 1920 memorial by **Carrère and Hastings** is dedicated to the army, navy, and marine corps. Finished in white Vermont marble, the 5,500-seat amphitheater is reminiscent of Greek and Roman theaters. Memorial Day and Veterans Day services, and the Easter Sunrise Service, are held there.

USS *MAINE* MEMORIAL

The mast—its tower still in place—was raised in 1912 from the ship, which sank in 1898 in Havana Harbor. It is set in a granite base inscribed with the names of the 260 men who died in the mysterious explosion that preceded the Spanish-American War.

CONFEDERATE MEMORIAL

Erected in 1912 by the United Daughters of the Confederacy, Moses Ezekiel's Baroque bronze monument honors the soldiers of the short-lived Confederate States of America. A female figure in the center stands for the "South in Peace," and a frieze on the base portrays the sons and daughters of the South coming to the aid of their "fallen mother." President Woodrow Wilson dedicated the statue.

AIR FORCE MEMORIAL

Up until October 2006, the air force had been the only branch of the service that did not have a memorial in DC. Now, though, the more than 54,000 airmen and women who have died in combat are honored by three stainless-steel spires soaring to a height of 270 feet in a spectacular representation of the precision "bomb burst" maneuver performed by the US Air Force Thunderbird Demonstration team. Embedded beneath them is the famous air force "Star," and leading up to it is a Runway to Glory with two granite inscription walls and a Glass Contemplation Wall, all protected at the entrance by a bronze Honor Guard statue by Zenos Frudakis. ♦ 703.247.5808. www.airforcememorial.org

29 LYNDON BAINES JOHNSON MEMORIAL GROVE

At the south end of **Lady Bird Johnson Park** stretch 15 acres of pines, flowering dogwoods, and daffodils planted to commemorate the thirty-sixth president and his first lady. The memorial site, marked by a large Texas pink-granite monolith, is surrounded by stones inscribed with quotations by Johnson. A picnic in the park brings you frighteningly close to the planes landing at nearby **Reagan National Airport**. ♦ Free. Daily during daylight hours. George Washington Memorial Pkwy (between Henry G. Shirley Memorial Hwy and Washington Blvd). 289.2500. www.nps.gov/lyba

30 NAVY AND MARINE MEMORIAL

This is a simple, graceful representation of seven seagulls in flight, sculpted in 1930 by Ernesto Begni dei Piatti. ♦ George Washington Memorial Pkwy (just north of I-395)

31 PENTAGON

One of the world's largest office buildings, this five-sided structure has three times the floor space of the Empire State Building. The headquarters of the Department of Defense covers 29 acres, with a 5-acre courtyard at its center. There are 17.5 miles of corridors, yet no office is more than 7 minutes from any other. Built during World War II, the structure took only 16 months to complete, and was one of the targets of the 9/11 attacks. Public tours are offered only to school and other organized groups. ♦ Jefferson Davis and Henry G. Shirley Memorial Hwys. Tour info: 697.1776. ♿. Metro: Pentagon

32 THE FASHION CENTRE AT PENTAGON CITY

One of Washington's most elegant malls is also one of the few with its own **Metro** stop. Some of the 170 shops and restaurants

under the stunning glass atrium include **Nordstrom**, **Macy's**, **J. Crew**, **Crate & Barrel**, **BCBG**, **Sephora**, and **L'Occitaine**; there are also seven restaurants and a large food court on the lower level. ♦ M-Sa, 10AM-9:30PM; Su, 11AM-6PM. S Hayes and S 15th Sts. 415.2400. www.fashioncentrepentagon.com. Metro: Pentagon City

32 RITZ-CARLTON PENTAGON CITY

$$$$ This plush 366-room hotel features a complete fitness center with indoor lap pool, steam and sauna rooms, and massage services; afternoon tea to the strains of classical music; valet parking, concierge, babysitting, and round-the-clock room service; plus the **Grill** restaurant (notorious as the site where Monica Lewinsky blabbed to Linda Tripp) and nighttime entertainment. A gracious environment, the décor includes Oriental rugs, gilt mirrors, fine oil paintings, antiques, and freshly cut flowers in porcelain vases. Guests on the top two floors have access to a cozy little club that features five food presentations daily (from a continental breakfast to dessert and after-dinner drinks), a friendly concierge who aims to please, and a terrific view. As an added bonus, the hotel is connected to the **Fashion Centre at Pentagon City**. Discounted weekend rates are available. An extensive renovation, begun in late 2006, will make this an even more luxurious destination. ♦ 1250 S Hayes St (between S 15th St and Army Navy Dr). 415.5000, 800/241.3333; fax 415.5061. ♿. Metro: Pentagon City. www.ritz-carlton.com

32 PENTAGON ROW

Next to the **Fashion Centre at Pentagon City**, find this new mixed-use area, with apartments on upper levels and stores and restaurants on the street level. Shops include national chains like **Bed Bath & Beyond** and **Chico's** and local sellers like women's clothing boutique **What's In** (414.3353). Restaurants offer a variety of cuisines, from Irish to Thai. ♦ S Joyce St and Army Navy Dr. 418.6692. www.pentagon-row.com. Metro: Pentagon City

Within Pentagon Row:

ARLINGTON COUNTY VISITORS' CENTER

This is the place to go for information about sights and attractions, restaurants, and lodging in Arlington County. The center also provides info on things to do and see in Washington, DC. ♦ Daily, 9AM-5PM. 1301 S Joyce St. 800/677.6267. www.stayarlington.com

---

Restaurants/Clubs: Red | **Hotels: Purple** | **Shops: Orange** | **Outdoors/Parks: Green** | **Sights/Culture: Blue**

33 PENTAGON CENTRE

For an alternative to the higher prices and smaller stores of the **Fashion Centre at Pentagon City**, try this collection of super-stores and reasonably priced restaurants across the street. (One of the escalators from the **Pentagon City Metro** exit leaves you right at its door.) Stroll through **Marshalls** for discounted fashions, **Best Buy** (414.7090) for home electronics and CDs, **Linens 'n Things** (413.0993) for house-wares, and **Borders Books and Music** (418.0166) for a large selection of reading and listening matter. Of the restaurants, the best is **Chevy's** (413.8700), whose friendly staff members serve better-than-average Mexican food in a barn of a room. ♦ M-Sa, 10AM-9PM; Su, 11AM-7PM; restaurants open later. 1201 S Hayes St (at S 12th St). Metro: Pentagon City

34 DOUBLETREE HOTEL CRYSTAL CITY—NATIONAL AIRPORT

$$$ Conveniently located near the **Pentagon City** shopping complex and its **Metro** stop, this 631-room high-rise includes 152 suites with balconies and 24-hour housekeeping. Rooms on the upper floors offer spectacular views of the Potomac River and the Washington skyline. Two restaurants, **Skydome Lounge** (a rooftop, revolving lounge), a health club, an enclosed rooftop swimming pool, and shuttle service to **Pentagon City** and **Reagan National Airport** are among the amenities offered. ♦ 300 Army Navy Dr (at Jefferson Davis Hwy). 416.4100, 800.222.8733; fax 416.4126. www.doubletree.com. &. Metro: Pentagon City

35 EMBASSY SUITES CRYSTAL CITY–NATIONAL AIRPORT

$$$ This upscale all-suite newly renovated property has 267 suites, all outfitted with the comforts of home: hair dryers, microwaves, irons and ironing boards, VCRs, and voice mail. The hotel also has a tropical atrium, meeting facilities, a fitness center (with indoor swimming pool), and complimentary parking and shuttle service. Guests receive a complimentary breakfast. ♦ 1300 Jefferson Davis Hwy (between S 15th and S 12th Sts). 979.9799, 800/EMBASSY; fax 920.5947. &. Metros: Pentagon City, Crystal City

The Potomac River was known as Co-hon-go-roo-ta to the indigenous people, Espiritu Santo to the Spanish, and the Elizabeth to the English.

36 ATLACATL II

★★$ Recommended Mexican and Salvadoran specialties at this place include fried yucca, *pupusas* (corn tortillas filled with pork and cheese), and tamales. ♦ Mexican/Salvadoran ♦ Daily, lunch and dinner. 4701 Columbia Pike (at S Buchanan St). 920.3680. &

37 MATUBA

★★$$ Excellent sushi, tempura, and teriyaki are the specialties of this friendly spot. For a great bargain stop in on Monday, when the sushi is sold for $1 apiece. ♦ Japanese ♦ M-F, lunch and dinner; Sa, Su, dinner. Reservations recommended. 2915 Columbia Pike (between Walter Reed Dr and S Garfield St). 521.2811. &

37 ARLINGTON CINEMA 'N' DRAFTHOUSE

This big old movie theater serves beer, wine, pizzas, and snacks while showing second-run movies. Relax in the comfy sofas and chairs. It's very popular with residents of the nearby military installations. You must be 21 to enter. ♦ No credit cards accepted. Daily. 2903 Columbia Pike (at Walter Reed Dr). 486.2345. www.arlingtondrafthouse.com. &

38 ATILLA'S

★★$ You can tell that this small pastel-colored restaurant and carryout place is something of a local institution because it's almost always packed. Choose from two menus: Indian and Middle Eastern. The housemade pita and hummus are as good as any in the area, and, best of all, the first round is set upon your table without charge for your munching pleasure. ♦ Indian/Middle Eastern ♦ Daily, lunch and dinner. Reservations recommended. 2705 Columbia Pike (between S Adams St and Walter Reed Dr). 920.4900. &

39 BOB & EDITH'S DINER

★$ A bona fide old-fashioned diner—counter, booths, Formica aplenty—it's a local favorite and your best bet for eggs and hash browns at 3AM. ♦ American ♦ Daily, 24 hours. 2310 Columbia Pike (between S Wayne and S Barton Sts). 920.6103

40 WOO LAE OAK

★★$$ Decorated with ancient ceramics, this restaurant specializes in Korean barbecue (which you cook on the grill built into your table). You can't go wrong with the dumpling and noodle dishes or hot pots of vegetables in spicy sauce. ♦ Korean ♦ Daily, lunch and dinner. Reservations recommended. 1500 Joyce St (between S 16th St and Army Navy Dr). 521.3706. &. Metro: Pentagon City

41 CRYSTAL GATEWAY MARRIOTT

$$$$ This second—and larger (615 rooms and 82 suites)—Marriott fixture is also connected to the **Underground** shops and subway line and is an easy 5-minute drive to **Reagan National Airport**. Amenities include a six-story sunlit atrium, indoor and outdoor swimming pools, a health club, concierge service, four restaurants, and a free shuttle to the airport. Rooms are done up in yellow, blue, and burgundy; the concierge-level rooms are the nicest. ♦ 1700 Jefferson Davis Hwy (between S 18th and S 15th Sts). 920.3230, 800/228.9290; fax 271.5212. www.marriott.com. ♿. Metro: Crystal City

42 CRYSTAL CITY SHOPS

Beneath an area of glass-and-concrete highrises that shoot out of the flatlands near **Reagan National Airport**, this gem of a small mall contains some 200 shops, services, and dining establishments. Winding cobblestone walkways and twisting alleys connect to the **Metro** and the two **Marriott** hotels. Stores include the **Crystal Boutique** (415.1400), for designer women's fashions, and **Signature Leather & Travelware** (413.4171), with a variety of luggage sets and rolling bags. ♦ M-Sa; Su, some shops open. 1600 Crystal Sq Arcade (between S 23rd and S 18th Sts). 922.4636. www.thecrystalcityshops.com. Metro: Crystal City

42 CRYSTAL CITY MARRIOTT AT REAGAN NATIONAL AIRPORT

$$$$ This hotel is connected to the **Crystal City Underground** shops and the **Metro** station, and it's less than 1 mile from **Reagan National Airport** (a shuttle service runs every 15 minutes between 6:05AM and 11PM). The 333-room and 10-suite hotel has a restaurant and lounge, a health club (with an indoor swimming pool, whirlpool, and sauna), and meeting facilities. The lobby and rooms are decorated in blue, burgundy, and yellow. ♦ 1999 Jefferson Davis Hwy (at S 20th St). 413.5500, 800/228.9290; fax 413.0192. www.marriott.com. ♿. Metro: Crystal City

43 ECONO LODGE

$ This 161-room hotel features an outdoor swimming pool, meeting rooms, a restaurant, and free morning and late-afternoon shuttle service to **Reagan National Airport** and the **Pentagon Metro**. Children under 19 stay free. ♦ 2485 S Glebe Rd (at Henry G. Shirley Memorial Hwy). 979.4100, 877/424.6423; fax 979.6120. ♿. www.econolodge.com

44 HYATT REGENCY CRYSTAL CITY AT REAGAN NATIONAL AIRPORT

$$$$ The big, shiny 685-room hostelry offers all you'd expect from a Hyatt, plus the convenience of its location near **Reagan National Airport**. Amenities include two restaurants (one with a lovely view across the Potomac), lounge, health club (with a whirlpool), outdoor swimming pool, and shuttle service to the airport and **Crystal City**. The hotel also offers special weekend packages and meeting facilities. ♦ 2799 Jefferson Davis Hwy (at Crystal Dr). 418.1234, 800/223.1234; fax 418.1289. ♿

45 COURTYARD ARLINGTON CRYSTAL CITY/REAGAN NATIONAL AIRPORT

$$$ Located near **Reagan National Airport** and **Pentagon City** and **Crystal City** shops and restaurants, this 268-room and 4-suite hotel features an on-site restaurant, indoor pool, exercise room, and Alamo rental car desk. ♦ 2899 Jefferson Davis Hwy. 549.3434, 800/321.2211; fax 549.7440. www.marriott.com. Metro: Crystal City

46 BISTRO BISTRO

★★★$$ Here's one of the area's most pleasant and imaginative restaurants and watering spots. The bi-level dining room is casually elegant with marble-top tables, a large dark wood bar, floor-to-ceiling windows, and murals on the walls. Oyster stew, fried calamari with three dipping sauces, pizza, and roast chicken with mashed potatoes are among the hits. And don't pass up the crème brûlée. The fare, invariably good, often verges on great. An added bonus: a terrific (and reasonably priced) selection of single-malt scotches. ♦ American ♦ M-Sa, lunch and dinner; Su, brunch and dinner. Reservations recommended. 4021 S 28th St (between S Quincy and S Randolph Sts). 379.0300. ♿

46 CARLYLE

★★★$$ This two-level restaurant has a lot going for it, from the striking Art Deco posters on the walls to the no-smoking-anywhere policy, but head upstairs if you want to relax—the bar downstairs is boisterous and noisy. The two menus aren't identical, but they overlap in all the right places. The kitchen particularly shines when it comes to grilling and smoking, so fish (particularly salmon) and chicken are nearly always perfect. ♦ American ♦ M-Sa, lunch and dinner; Su, brunch and dinner. 4000 S 28th St (at S Quincy St). 931.0777. ♿

Restaurants/Clubs: Red | Hotels: Purple | Shops: Orange | Outdoors/Parks: Green | Sights/Culture: Blue

Much of the DC area's wealth is concentrated across the **Potomac River**, within the rapidly growing Northern Virginia suburbs. The region's prosperity is readily evident in the enormous **Tysons Corner** complex of malls and office buildings, as well as in the paralyzing rush-hour traffic. Other shops and some of the area's best ethnic kitchens can be found on **Route 7**, the main thoroughfare between **Falls Church** and **Baileys Crossroads**. Beneath all the hustle and newness, however, lies the subtle dignity of the Old Dominion in the shape of such gracious colonial mansions as **Mount Vernon**, such Civil War battlefields as **Manassas**, and the rolling green **Hunt Country** to the west. Even some of the newness has its own charm, particularly in the planned community of **Reston**, with its million-dollar residences. Rural Virginia, just an hour's drive from Downtown Washington, remains remarkably similar to the pastoral ideal so admired by Thomas Jefferson.

Area code 703 unless otherwise noted.

1 ALGONKIAN REGIONAL PARK

This 511-acre park overlooks the Potomac and features an 18-hole golf course, vacation cottages, miniature golf, a swimming pool, boat launching ramp, walking trail, and picnic areas. ♦ Fee for boat launch, golf, and pool. 47001 Fairway Dr (at Cascades Pkwy), Sterling. 450.4655. &. www.nvrpa.org

2 L'AUBERGE CHEZ FRANÇOIS

★★★★$$$$ Fresh country cooking is served in a magical sylvan setting at this country inn. Large bay windows overlook the garden and, inside, three fireplaces and white stucco walls with exposed beams lend warmth and coziness. Chef and owner François Haeringer turns out such delicacies as *choucroute garni*, a collection of sausages and duck with sautéed foie gras, as well as bouillabaisse and chateaubriand. Reservations required; book up to 4 weeks in advance, especially for weekends. The terrace is perfect for alfresco dining on a warm evening. ♦ French ♦ Tu-Su, dinner. 332 Springvale Rd (between Georgetown Pike and Beach Mill Rd), Great Falls. 759.3800. &. www.laubergechezfrancois.com

3 GREAT FALLS PARK

The best view of the imposing 76-foot-high waterfall on the Potomac River is from the Virginia side. During full spring floods, the volume of water surpasses that of Niagara Falls: 480,000 cubic feet per second. To watch kayakers at the base of the falls, head for an **Observation Deck**.

Swamps and a forest along the Potomac's banks offer spectacular displays of wildflowers in their seasonal blooms. Bird-watchers claim that this park—a migration stop for many birds—provides one of the East Coast's best vantage points; even bald eagles have been spotted here. Natural pools along the river attract deer, foxes, muskrats, beavers, opossums, and rabbits. An excellent system of hiking trails leads you through the woods and along the river, and picnic areas are located throughout the park. (No open fires, please.) At the **Visitors' Center**, rotating exhibitions about nature, conservation, and safety are offered; the helpful staff answers questions and will direct you to the season's special vistas.

In the late 1700s George Washington came here to oversee the building of the **Potowmack Canal**, a bypass of the falls and other unnavigable parts of the river. Locks 1 through 5 and part of the canal are still visible, and the National Park Service works constantly to prevent further deterioration. Ruins of the canal are located southeast of the Visitors' Center. Also visible are a chimney, a spring house, and other remnants of Matildaville, the city founded by Henry "Light Horse Harry" Lee in honor of his first wife.

Note: This area is a beautiful yet extremely dangerous section of the river; currents are swift and the rock faces are sheer. Everyone is urged to stay off the rocks near the river and out of the water near the falls. Drownings occur several times yearly when the swift current pulls careless climbers and waders into the torrent. Parents: Watch your children!

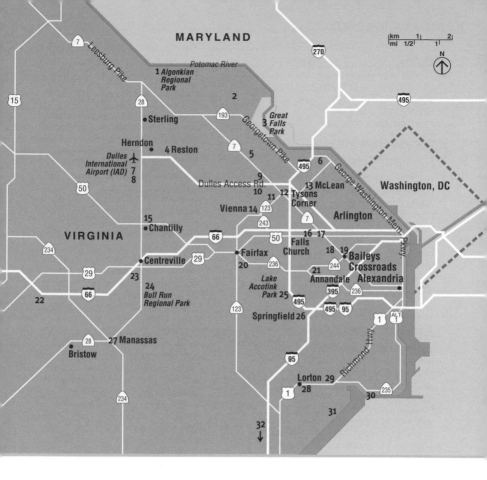

Experienced rock climbers with proper equipment can register at the Visitors' Center.

Take Route 193, Exit 44 from the Beltway; the park entrance is 4.5 miles west; the Visitors' Center is a quarter mile past the entrance on the right. ♦ Admission. Daily, 7AM to dusk. 9200 Old Dominion Dr (at Georgetown Pike), McLean. 285.2965. www.nps.gov/grfa

4 RESTON

Envisioned by Robert E. Simon in the mid-1950s and begun in 1962, this is one of the nation's few remarkable "new towns." (Simon's initials form the basis of the city's name.) It is conveniently located between Downtown DC and **Washington–Dulles International Airport** and is a completely planned city, covering more than 7,000 acres.

More than 1,000 acres of land is open and/or public space. Homes are arranged in small neighborhood clusters, which are distributed evenly throughout the city. Recreational amenities include golf courses, pools, ballparks, tennis courts, bridle paths, and a **Nature Center**. This picture of suburban serenity also has been very successful in attracting companies like Oracle, Accenture, and BAE Systems as well as the US Geological Survey.

Development is supervised by Terrabrook, which coordinates the design and construction of homes (ranging from small apartments to town houses and minimansions, of varied quality and styles), schools, business complexes, and shopping centers. Away from the central core, the landscaping far outshines the architecture.

In Reston:

RESTON TOWN CENTER

This outdoor shopping mall—framed by sleek office buildings, a **Hyatt** hotel, and parking lots—has brick-and-marble walkways open only to pedestrian traffic. Among the upscale stores are **Appalachian Spring** (American crafts), **Ann Taylor**, **Talbots**, **The Gap**, and

---

Gap Kids. Most of the restaurants in the complex offer alfresco dining, and a pavilion serves as a venue for summer concerts and winter ice-skating. ♦ 11921 Freedom Dr (off Reston Pkwy). 263.8520. www.restontowncenter.com

5 COLVIN RUN MILL HISTORIC SITE

This 19th-century gristmill still grinds grain. Throughout the year, special weekend events include an Easter egg hunt, Civil War reenactments, puppet shows, and concerts. Call for schedule. ♦ Admission for mill tour. M, W-Su, 11AM-5PM; Jan and Feb, 11AM-4PM. 10017 Colvin Run Rd (between Leesburg Pike and Walker Rd), Great Falls. 759.2771. &. www.co.fairfax.va.us/parks/crm

6 CLAUDE MOORE COLONIAL FARM AT TURKEY RUN

You can take an amazing look at an authentic pre–Revolutionary War farm, including a costumed "family" (acting courtesy of staff members) that uses reproductions of period tools to perform household chores and farm work that vary with the seasons (spinning, churning, breaking flax, cultivating, and harvesting). There are lots of chances throughout the year for visitors to "help" with farm chores. ♦ Admission. W-Su, 10AM-4:30PM, Apr–mid-Dec; closed on rainy days. 6310 Georgetown Pike (between Dolley Madison Blvd and Balls Hill Rd), McLean. 442.7557. &. www.1771.org

7 WASHINGTON DULLES AIRPORT MARRIOTT

$$$$ This is the closest hotel to the airport, with indoor-outdoor pools, a Jacuzzi, a health club, outdoor tennis courts, and a picnic pavilion. The 368 rooms are typical Marriott, done in neutral beige and forest green with dark wood furniture. The hotel's dining room, called the **Oakleaf Restaurant**, serves continental fare for dinner; the **Lobby Lounge** offers an American menu for lunch and dinner. ♦ 45020 Aviation Dr (at Dulles Access Rd), Dulles. 471.9500, 800/228.9290; fax 661.8714. www.marriott.com

7 HOLIDAY INN DULLES AIRPORT

$$$ The Holiday Inn at this convenient airport location offers 297 rooms and boasts an impressive array of extras. The indoor pool, sauna, whirlpool, and lounge make these accommodations pleasant for business travelers and others. ♦ 1000 Sully Rd (at Dulles Access Rd), Sterling.

471.7411, 800/HOLIDAY; fax 834.7558. www.hidullesairport.com

8 STEVEN F. UDVAR-HAZY CENTER

In order to better showcase its vast collection of historically significant air- and spacecraft, the **National Air and Space Museum** built this massive new companion facility on the grounds of **Dulles International Airport**. In an aviation hangar that's 10 stories high and the length of three football fields, it displays 80-plus aircraft (with more than 100 yet to come), including the *Enola Gay*, an Air France Concorde, and an F-4 Phantom. Some of the planes sit on the floor. Others hang from the rafters, positioned near elevated walkways so that visitors can get a closer look at them. It's a striking museum, and it's worth seeing even if you're not "an airplane person." The **James S. McDonnell Space Hangar** houses the space shuttle *Enterprise* (sister ship of the *Columbia*) as well as out-of-this-world artifacts like astronaut uniforms and equipment. Also on view throughout the facility: engines, rockets, satellites, and models. From the 164-foot **Donald D. Engen Observation Tower**, visitors can watch modern-day aircraft come in for a landing at Dulles Airport and learn about air traffic control. There's also an IMAX theater that boasts a six-story screen. While the museum is free, there's a $12 charge to park on site. If you don't have a car, take the shuttle that connects the Hazy Center to the Air and Space Museum on the National Mall. It runs approximately every hour and a half from 9AM to 5PM and costs $7. ♦ Free. Daily, 10AM-5:30PM. 14390 Air and Space Museum Pkwy (just off Route 28), Chantilly. 202/633.1000. &. www.nasm.si.edu

WOLF TRAP FOUNDATION
FOR THE PERFORMING ARTS

9 WOLF TRAP NATIONAL PARK FOR THE PERFORMING ARTS

Situated on 117 acres of woodland, this concert-arts facility has brought the best of the performing arts to Virginia. The Wolf Trap Foundation presents events ranging from the **National Symphony Orchestra** to folksingers, **Riverdance**, and a variety of comedians. The concert hall, called the **Filene Center**, comprises a stage, a lofty tower, and a soaring, open-sided wood canopy that shelters 3,868 seats built into a natural slope. Higher up there's unprotected lawn seating for 3,160 more. The romantic setting is matched by fine acoustics. ◆ Tickets required for performances. Filene Center box office: daily. 1645 Trap Rd (between Dulles Access Rd and Leesburg Pike). General information, 255.1900; ticket information, 255.1868. www.wolftrap.org

Within Wolf Trap Farm Park:

THE BARNS OF WOLF TRAP

During off-season, when the weather's too chilly, this intimate concert stage housed in two restored barns, just down the road from **Filene Center**, offers an intriguing blend of folk, international, bluegrass, and pop music. It is also the home of the **Wolf Trap Opera** company. There's not a bad seat in the house, and beer and wine are available. ◆ 1635 Wolf Trap Rd. Information, 938.2404, tickets, 218.6500. ㅊ

10 MEADOWLARK BOTANICAL GARDENS

Just 5 miles from Tysons' high-tech towers is this 100-acre oasis of woods and gardens, including three lakes and a gazebo. Swimming and boating are not allowed. ◆ Admission. Hours vary by season. 9750 Meadowlark Gardens Ct (off Beulah Rd). 255.3631. www.nvrpa.org

WU'S GARDEN RESTAURANT

PEKING DUCK

Famous Peking Szechuan Cuisine

鲁园饭店

11 WU'S GARDEN RESTAURANT

★★$ Among the ordinary restaurants in the Vienna area, this comfortable Chinese dining place stands out. Enjoy exceptionally good Mandarin cuisine amid rosewood partitions and Oriental décor. Try the shrimp imperial or the sesame beef. ◆ Chinese ◆ Daily, lunch and dinner. 418 Maple Ave E (between East St NE and Beulah Rd), Vienna. 281.4410. ㅊ

12 TYSONS CORNER

The largest of the suburban cities that have developed around DC, this one is known primarily for two things: high-rise office towers and shopping malls. In fact, the area has so much office space that only about a dozen other downtowns in the US have more. That, plus two megamalls and assorted strip malls on Routes 7 and 123, can bring traffic to a standstill. But the area does have hidden charms, including a quiet park and the **Wolf Trap National Park for the Performing Arts.**

In Tysons Corner:

TYSONS CORNER MARRIOTT HOTEL

$$$$ Adjacent to the shopping center, this 390-room hotel matches the surrounding area—pleasant suburbia with a touch of class. The traditional rooms are done in forest green and blond wood. In addition to such regular amenities as free parking, cable TV, and room service, the hostelry sports a health club, complete with an indoor swimming pool, whirlpool, sauna, and exercise room with locker facilities. **Shula's Steak House** offers steaks and other dishes fit for those with large appetites. ◆ 8028 Leesburg Pike (between I-495 and Gallows Rd). 734.3200, 800/228.9290; fax 734.5763. ㅊ

TYSONS CORNER CENTER

The original Tysons Corner mall offers more than 250 stores aimed at a middle-income clientele. Major department stores are **Bloomingdale's**, **Hecht's**, and **Nordstrom**; fashionistas will find plenty of places to put their credit cards to use. Dining options include the **Rainforest Café**, a marvel with waterfalls, live birds and tropical fish, rainfall, and simulated thunder and lightning. ◆ M-Sa, 10AM-9:30PM; Su, 11AM-6PM. 1961 Chain Bridge Rd (between I-495 and International Dr). 893.9400. ㅊ. www.shoptysons.com

12 TYSONS GALLERIA

More upscale than the megamall across the street, this specialty mall has about 100 stores of its own, including **Macy's**, **Saks Fifth Avenue**, **Neiman Marcus**, and more one-of-a-kind boutiques. ◆ M-Sa, 10AM-9PM; Su, noon-6PM. 2001 International Dr (between Chain Bridge Rd and Westpark Dr). 827.7700. ㅊ. www.tysonsgalleria.com

12 FAIRFAX SQUARE

Across from **Tysons Corner Center**, this complex gives spendthrifts even more reasons to shop. The chic—and by no means cheap—retailers include **Tiffany & Co.**, **Gucci**, **Hermès**, and **Louis Vuitton**. ◆ Daily. 8045-75

Restaurants/Clubs: Red | Hotels: Purple | Shops: Orange | Outdoors/Parks: Green | Sights/Culture: Blue

Leesburg Pike (at Old Gallows Rd). 391.8644. www.theshopsatfairfaxsquare.com Within Fairfax Square:

Morton's of Chicago

★★$$$ Set on the basement level with a clubby mahogany interior, this well-known restaurant features prints by LeRoy Neiman. Everything on the menu is huge, including the house specialty: "The Porterhouse" is a 24-ounce half fillet and half New York strip, served with a 16-ounce baked potato. ◆ Steak house ◆ M-F, lunch and dinner; Sa, Su, dinner. Reservations recommended. 883.0800. Also at 11956 Market St, Reston. 796.0128; 3251 Prospect St NW (between Wisconsin Ave and Potomac St), Washington, DC. 202/342.6258. ♿; and 1050 Connecticut Ave NW, Washington, DC. 202/955.5997. www.mortons.com

12 Clyde's of Tysons Corner

★★$$ Classier than the Georgetown original, this popular outpost serves equally reliable burgers and salads, as well as seafood. Choose from four dining rooms, each with a different theme: The **Palm Terrace** boasts a 75-foot mural of nymphs and satyrs; the **Cafe** style is Art Nouveau; a seashore motif appropriately dominates the **Oyster Bar**; and the **Grill** is done in Art Deco. ◆ American ◆ M-Sa, lunch and dinner; Su, brunch and dinner. 8332 Leesburg Pike (between Gallows and Chain Bridge Rds). 734.1901. ♿. www.clydes.com. Also at 3236 M St NW (between Wisconsin Ave and Warehouse Pl), Washington, DC. 202/333.9180; and 11905 Market St (at Bluemont Way), Reston, Virginia. 787.6601

12 Embassy Suites Hotel Tysons Corner

$$$ A stone's throw from **Tysons Corner Center**, this large and glitzy hotel has 234 two-room suites and an indoor swimming pool, sauna, and Jacuzzi. Amenities include complimentary breakfast and shuttle service within a 3-mile radius. ◆ 8517 Leesburg Pike (between Chain Bridge and Dulles Access Rds). 883.0707, 800/EMBASSY; fax 760.9842. ♿. www.embassysuites.com

12 Colvin Run Tavern

★★★$$$ Robert Kinkead's (of the popular **Kinkead's** in Foggy Bottom) elegant **Tysons Corner** outpost serves contemporary

> As President Ford led Queen Elizabeth to the White House dance floor, the US Marine Band struck up "The Lady Is a Tramp."

American fare like pepper-and-spice-seared rare tuna mignon; cornmeal-crusted flounder with tasso ham, crayfish, and garlic lemon butter; and breast of magret duck with foie gras. There's complimentary valet parking during dinner. ◆ American ◆ M-F, lunch and dinner; Sa, Su, dinner. Reservations recommended. 8045 Leesburg Pike (in Fairfax Sq behind Tiffany's). 356.9500. ♿. www.kinkead.com

12 Courtyard Tysons Corner Fairfax

$$$ This 229-room high-rise hotel offers a swimming pool, whirlpool, bath in select king rooms, free high-speed and Wi-Fi Internet, a fitness area, and two restaurants. Amenities include a weekday shuttle to **Tysons Corner Center** and **Tysons Galleria**, laundry service, and complimentary parking. ◆ 1960-A Chain Bridge Rd (at International Dr). 790.0207; fax 790.0308. www.marriott.com

Within the Courtyard Tysons Corner Fairfax:

Fleming's Prime Steakhouse & Wine Bar

★★$$$ This high-ceilinged space with an exhibition kitchen serves its famous aged beef as well as swordfish, lobster, and veal chops. Living up to the wine-bar portion of its name, it also offers a 100-by-the-glass wine list. ◆ Steak house ◆ Daily, dinner. 442.8384. ♿. www.flemingssteakhouse.com

12 Ritz-Carlton

$$$$ This 398-room luxury property including 50 suites and 34 Club Level rooms offers amenities like twice-daily housekeeping service, high-speed Internet access, and 24-hour room service. There's also a spa, fitness center, and pool. Reserving a room on the **Ritz-Carlton Club** level gets you a separate lounge, concierge, and five complimentary food and beverage presentations throughout the day and evening. ◆ 1700 Tysons Blvd (off International Dr). 506.4300; fax 506.2694. www.ritz-carlton.com

Within the Ritz-Carlton:

Maestro

★★★★$$$$ Excellent traditional and contemporary Italian cuisine is prepared here by chef Fabio Trabocchi in an open kitchen. Try one of the special tasting menus (three-, five-, or seven-course), which highlight seasonal ingredients. The top-notch wine list contains almost 500 wines. ◆ Italian ◆ M, breakfast; Tu-F, breakfast and dinner; Sa, dinner; Su, brunch. Reservations suggested. 821.1515

VANTAGE POINTS

For a glorious view of Washington, especially at dusk, visit the **Iwo Jima Memorial**, just across the **Potomac River** in **Arlington**. After you've inspected this huge bronze statue, which commemorates the raising of the American flag over Mount Suribachi during World War II, enjoy the twinkling displays of the **Lincoln** and **Jefferson Memorials**, the **Washington Monument**, and the **Capitol** in the distance.

In warm weather, relax with a cool drink at the **Sky Terrace**, the canopied rooftop of the **Hotel Washington** in **Downtown DC**. From there you can take in the **Treasury Building** and the **White House** or contemplate the view south toward the **Mall** and the banks of the Potomac.

If you're visiting the nation's capital on the holiday weekends of Memorial Day, the Fourth of July, or Labor Day, pack a picnic supper and head for the west lawn of the US Capitol grounds (between the Capitol building and its reflecting pool), where the **National Symphony Orchestra** offers a free, first-class performance. The wonderful music enhances the twilight scene as you gaze down the Mall toward the Washington Monument and the Lincoln Memorial. (Check local newspapers for programs.)

Thrusting 555 feet into the sky, the Washington Monument is the city's highest and most spectacular viewing station (you can see to distant horizons from the top). But if vertigo is your middle name, the view from the obelisk's base is perfectly fine. (Tickets required; see page 46.)

Heading south on **16th Street NW** toward Downtown DC, pause at the top of **Meridian Hill Park**. The sight of the **White House** directly ahead and the Washington Monument and Jefferson Memorial beyond is a dramatic reminder of the city's historical and political importance.

From the **Clocktower Pavilion** at the **Old Post Office** (315 feet), you can see Downtown DC and the monuments. Victorian brass fittings, red oak woodwork, and frosted glass decorate the atrium of the Old Post Office, and the Capitol looks especially magnificent from this lovely spot.

Take the elevator up to the roof terrace of the **John F. Kennedy Center for the Performing Arts** for a panorama of the city and the Potomac. You can also enjoy the view while dining at the **Roof Terrace Restaurant**.

The Potomac looks glorious up close too. In the light of day, sit on its banks in **East and West Potomac Park**; the prime stretch is from just south of the Lincoln Memorial to Hains Point.

Due west of DC, across **Arlington Memorial Bridge**, is **Arlington House** (also called the **Custis-Lee House**). From its portico on the bluff, you can look across the Potomac directly to the Lincoln Memorial. Below lie the graves of President John Kennedy (marked by an eternal flame), wife Jacqueline, and his brother Robert. **Arlington National Cemetery**, carved from the plantation that Robert E. Lee's family abandoned during the Civil War, stretches through the hills around the mansion.

From the **Pilgrim's Observation Gallery** of **Washington National Cathedral** in **Upper Northwest**, you can survey **Wisconsin Avenue** down into **Georgetown** and beyond to Northern Virginia. Turn in the other direction, and you'll see suburban Maryland. Crowning the highest hill in the District, the cathedral's tower, accessible by elevator, provides a vista like no other in the city.

To gain a perspective on **Old Town Alexandria**, venture to the top of the city's **George Washington Masonic National Memorial**. Its observation deck, more than 300 feet high, furnishes a breathtaking, and sometimes windy, view of Alexandria. On a clear day, you can see into Washington.

For a trip through time, pause on the grounds of **Mount Vernon** in Northern Virginia. From here, it's easy to imagine the way the Potomac River and the surrounding countryside looked in George Washington's time. (Every effort is being made to keep the scenery free of suburban sprawl.) With nothing but trees, water, and sky in all directions, it's among the area's best vistas.

Restaurants/Clubs: Red | Hotels: Purple | Shops: Orange | Outdoors/Parks: Green | Sights/Culture: Blue

12 e-Citi Restaurant & Bar

★★$$ Looking for Mr. Right? *Washingtonian* magazine named this techie hangout the most likely place to meet a millionaire. But if you're just going for dinner, you'll find dishes like crab cakes, tuna steak, and New York strip on the menu. ♦ American ♦ M-Sa, dinner. 1524 Spring Hill Rd (entrance at 8300 Tyco Rd, off Rte 7). 760.9000. www.eciticafe.com

13 McLean

This wealthy suburb, best known as the home of the Central Intelligence Agency, offers a few tourist stops and several fine restaurants. Its town center is relatively small and can be navigated on foot. Most of its businesses and homes seem to have sprung up in the last 25 years, so it offers more Southern hospitality than historic charm.

13 Taste of Saigon

★★★★$ A lengthy menu offers items like caramel chicken, deep-fried whole fish, and coconut milk-based curries at this pleasant spot that's often rated a best bargain by *Washingtonian* magazine. ♦ Vietnamese ♦ Daily, lunch and dinner. 8201 Greensboro Dr, McLean. 790.0700. ♿. Also at 410 Hungerford Dr (at Beall Ave), Rockville, Maryland. 301/424.7222. www.tasteofsaigon.com

Nizam's Restaurant

14 Nizam's

★★★$$$ From suburbia to Istanbul: Middle Eastern delicacies, including *doner kebab* (grilled lamb, pita bread, and yogurt sauce) and *manti* (ground lamb with a tomato sauce and yogurt), are served in romantic settings on two floors in this elegant restaurant. ♦ Turkish ♦ Tu-F, lunch and dinner; Sa, Su, dinner. Reservations recommended. 523 Maple Ave W (at Nutley St NW), Vienna. 938.8948. ♿

15 Sully Historic Site

Between 1794 and 1799 Richard Bland Lee—uncle of General Robert E. Lee and Northern Virginia's first representative to Congress—built this plantation, which is furnished with Federal-period antiques. Tours, given on the hour, include the smokehouse and stone dairy. ♦ Admission. M, W-Su, 11AM-4PM (11AM-3PM Jan-Feb). 3601 Sully Rd (between Hwy 50 and Wall Rd), Chantilly. 437.1794. www.co.fairfax.va.us/parks/sully

16 National Memorial Park

This vast cemetery is noted for its gardens and sculptured fountains. The **Fountain of Faith**, the centerpiece of the grounds, was created by Swedish sculptor Carl Milles. Thirty-seven graceful bronze figures—each with a face depicting one of the sculptor's friends—seem to hover in a spray of water. ♦ 7482 Lee Hwy (between S West St and Hollywood Rd), Falls Church. 560.4400

17 Falls Church

The original wooden church was completed in 1734 near a road leading to the Potomac waterfalls. In 1769, a new structure was built on the same site. The church served as a recruiting station during the Revolutionary War, a federal hospital during the Civil War, and later as a stable. It was completely renovated in 1959. ♦ M-F. Services (Episcopal): W, noon; Su, 8AM and noon. 115 E Fairfax St (between E Broad and S Washington Sts), Falls Church. 532.7600. ♿. www.thefallschurch.org

17 Haandi

★★★$$ If you like pink, this is the place: walls, tablecloths, nearly everything is pink. And if you don't—well, the lamb vindaloo and *makhini* (chicken in a tomato-based curry sauce) more than compensate. The menu also offers kabobs, tandoor-cooked dishes, delicious mango chutney, and other Indian favorites. ♦ Indian ♦ Daily, lunch and dinner. 1222 W Broad St (at Haycock Rd), Falls Church. 533.3501. ♿. www.haandi.com. Also at 4904 Fairmont Ave, Bethesda, Maryland. 301/718.0121. Metro: Bethesda

17 Bangkok Blues

★★$ This fun Falls Church spot serves up not only good Thai food (curries, drunken noodles, *pad thai*) but also nightly live music that ranges from jazz to blues to swing. There's also a kids' menu with standard American fare (burgers, fries) if Mom and Dad want something exotic but Junior doesn't. ♦ Thai ♦ Tu-Su, dinner. 926 W Broad St (between N Spring and N West Sts), Falls Church. 534.0095. www.bangkokbluesrestaurant.com

17 Panjshir

★★$$ This cozy place serves up top-notch *aushak* (a ravioli-like creation stuffed with scallions and topped with meat sauce and yogurt), kabobs (beef, chicken, and lamb), and a nice selection of Afghan vegetarian dishes. Ornate mirrors add to the charm. ♦ Afghan ♦ M-Sa, lunch and dinner. Reservations recommended for groups. 924 W Broad St (between N Spring and N West Sts), Falls Church. 536.4566

18 PEKING GOURMET INN

★★★$$ George Bush Sr.'s favorite Chinese restaurant (when he was president) was equipped with a bulletproof window. Many political photos, of the Republican bent, still grace one wall. Three generations of the Tsui family provide dedicated service and a consistently high standard of classic dishes in a handsome Oriental setting. The Peking duck is unusually crisp and fat-free; other specials include pork with garlic sprouts, Szechuan beef proper, Hong Kong–style fresh lobster, and Jou-Yen shrimp. Surprisingly inexpensive, this place is even worth a wait on the weekends. ♦ Chinese ♦ Daily, lunch and dinner. Reservations recommended. 6029 Leesburg Pike (at Glen Carlyn Dr), Falls Church. 671.8088. ♿. www.pekinggourmet.com

19 FORTUNE

★★$$ Despite the European décor, this spacious, comfortable restaurant sticks with Chinese tradition where it matters—the menu. Dim sum is served from rolling tea carts during lunch. The regular menu offers beautifully prepared seafood specialties (try the steamed flounder or crabs with ginger and onions), along with meat and noodle dishes. On Saturday and Sunday afternoons, the restaurant is packed with Chinese families. ♦ Chinese ♦ Daily, lunch and dinner. 6249 Seven Corners Center (on Arlington Blvd), Falls Church. 538.3333. ♿

19 DUANGRAT'S

★★★$ Recently voted "Top Thai Restaurant" by *Zagat Survey*, this spot offers superb Thai specialties. Good choices include beef satay, *pad thai* (stir-fried noodles), beef or chicken with basil, and the Happy Family jambalaya (seafood and chicken in green-curry fried rice). On Friday and Saturday nights, Thai dancers perform in the upstairs dining room. If you want to re-create your favorite dish, try the Thai grocery store a few doors down, which is owned by the same folks. ♦ Thai ♦ Daily, lunch and dinner. 5878 Leesburg Pike (at Glen Forest Dr), Falls Church. 820.5775

20 GEORGE MASON UNIVERSITY

A branch of the **University of Virginia** until 1972, the university enrolls about 28,000 students. Its major emphases are the humanities, public policy, and high technology. The **Recreation Sports Complex**, commonly known as the **Field House**, boasts basketball, tennis, and volleyball courts; a 200-meter indoor track; and archery and fencing facilities. Concerts, dance, and theater fill the university's **Center for the Arts**. The **Patriot Center** hosts concerts as well as sporting events. Tickets are sold through **Ticketmaster** outlets for the Patriot Center, through Tickets.com for Center for the Arts. ♦ Patriot Center box office: M-Sa. 4400 University Dr (off Rte 123), Fairfax. University information, 993.1000; Patriot Center box office, 993.3000; Center for the Arts, 993.8888; Ticketmaster, 202/397.7328, 573.7328, Tickets.com, 218.6500. www.gmu.edu

21 DUCK CHANG'S

★★$ Peking duck is the specialty of this modest neighborhood establishment since 1975, and nobody does it better. ♦ Chinese ♦ Tu-Su, lunch and dinner. 4427 John Marr Dr (between Little River Tpke and Columbia Pike), Annandale. 941.9400. www.duckchangs.com

22 NISSAN PAVILION AT STONE RIDGE

The area's newest and most elaborate outdoor concert facility opened in May 1995 to rave reviews for its state-of-the-art presentation. Seating over 21,000 between its covered pavilion and gently sloping lawn, the concert venue offers an advantage over its two competitors (**Wolf Trap Farm Park** and **Merriweather Post Pavilion**): Giant video screens give even back-row patrons a good view of the stage. The schedule emphasizes popular rock and country music acts. Beware the long lines to get out of the parking lot after concerts. ♦ Wellington Rd (off Hwy 29), Bristow. Information, 754.6400; tickets, 573.SEAT. ♿. www.nissanpavilion.com

23 SWEETWATER TAVERN

★★$$ Part of the Great American Restaurants chain, this brewpub offers baby back ribs, chicken tenders, crab cakes, jambalaya pasta (sausage, shrimp, and chicken in a spicy sauce) . . . and, of course, the requisite home brew. ♦ American ♦ Daily, lunch and dinner. 14250 Sweetwater La (off Multiplex Dr), Centreville. 449.1100. ♿. Also at 45980 Waterview Plaza, Sterling. 571/434.6500; 3066 Gatehouse Plaza, Falls Church. 645.8100

24 BULL RUN REGIONAL PARK

Ⓟ These several thousand acres include 150 campsites, a swimming pool, miniature golf,

Restaurants/Clubs: Red | **Hotels: Purple** | **Shops: Orange** | **Outdoors/Parks: Green** | **Sights/Culture: Blue**

209

THE BEST

Rick Mollineaux

Publisher, *WHERE Magazine*

Take a 20-minute drive up the George Washington Parkway to **Great Falls** and see the beautiful scenery where the Potomac takes its biggest drop. Think Colorado River with lush greenery. Go on the Virginia side for best view of the falls; if you're athletic, head to the Maryland side and hike the **Billy Goat Trail**.

Come back into the city, park the car, and walk or take the Metro for the rest of your trip. Venture off the **Mall** into the neighborhoods. Take the red line to the **Dupont Circle** north exit (Q Street) and look up as you ride one of the longest escalators from one of the deepest stations and pop out in the middle of vibrant Dupont Circle. With its many art galleries, restaurants, and interesting shops, like **Beadazzled**, with beads from all over the world, this neighborhood has it all. If it's a nice afternoon, sit in the circle and watch as office workers, visitors, and residents relax and people-watch.

Later, take in a live performance at a large venue like the **Kennedy Center**, **National Theatre**, or **Warner Theatre**, or see a play in more intimate surroundings at the **Arena Stage**, **Source Theatre**, or **Studio Theatre**. Surround yourself in history at **Ford's Theatre**, or experience one of the finest classical theaters in the country, the **Shakespeare Theatre**.

Pick up a copy of *WHERE Magazine* to check out the city's many restaurants. There are many that I love, but three that I go to most often are **I Ricchi**, an award-winning Northern Italian restaurant just south of Dupont Circle; **Oceanaire**, for fresh seafood downtown; and **Mimi's**, just west of Dupont Circle, for the boisterous crowd and singing waiters.

Most of all, though, walk and walk some more. Take in the buildings, the people, and the beauty and realize that you are in the center of the capital of the free world.

---

a skeet and trap range, a clay-target range, indoor archery, picnic areas, nature trails, and an amphitheater for concerts. There are dog shows in the spring and fall, a yearly country jamboree in June, and a craft show in September. From late November through early January, the Bull Run Festival of Lights—2 miles of colored-light displays—dazzles visitors, and the holiday fair in early December features carolers, craftspeople, and Santa himself. ♦ Admission. Mid-Jan through Nov. 7700 Bull Run Dr (off Rte 28), Centreville. 631.0550, Miracle of Lights, 709.KIDS. www.nvrpa.org

25 LAKE ACCOTINK PARK

Meandering through 493 acres of a landscaped park area, Accotink Creek flows into a pretty lake. A historical 4-mile hiking trail follows along the **Old Alexandria Railroad**, whose tracks once ran through the park. Canoes, paddleboats, and rowboats can be rented at the marina facility, which also operates a miniature golf course and a seasonal concession stand. There are playgrounds, baseball fields, and a carousel, and fishing is permitted (with a license). ♦ Daily; call for marina hours. 7500 Accotink Park Rd (between Old Keene Mill and Braddock Rds), Springfield. 569.3464. www.co.fairfax.va.us/parks/accotink

26 TALBOTS OUTLET

You'll save money but still look soigné at this outlet store, a popular purveyor of the town-and-country look. ♦ M-F, 10AM-9PM; Sa, 10AM-6PM; Su, noon-5PM. 6825 Bland St, Springfield. 644.5115

27 MANASSAS

Although the town didn't exist when the famous battle took place, it boasts a pretty Victorian-era downtown with a courthouse built in 1892 and a bank built 4 years later. It's a pleasant surprise in the midst of booming suburbia. A few years ago, locals interested in preserving the tranquillity of this area took on and defeated the folks from Walt Disney who wanted to erect a theme park devoted to American history.

In Manassas:

THE MANASSAS MUSEUM

MANASSAS MUSEUM

Here you can see displays of the history of Manassas as well as of the entire Piedmont region, including Civil War and railroad memorabilia. There are quilts and other textiles, agricultural implements, and a section devoted to African-American history. The museum provides maps for walking, driving, and architectural tours of downtown and the surrounding area. There's also a gift shop. ♦ Admission. Tu-Su, 10AM-5PM. 9101 Prince William St (at Main St). 368.1873. ♿ www.manassasmuseum.org

Woodlawn Plantation

Carmello's & Little Portugal

★$$ This Northern Italian and Portuguese restaurant spices up the traditionals: chicken, seafood, and veal dishes. The Mediterranean décor creates an elegant yet casual atmosphere. ◆ Italian/Portuguese ◆ M-F, lunch and dinner; Sa, Su, dinner. Reservations recommended. 9108 Center St (at Battle St). 368.5522. www.carmellos.com

28 Pohick Church

George Washington and George Mason were on the select building committee that influenced the design of this 18th-century country church. The simple block of brick is set off with handsome quoins and pediments of Aquila Creek stone cut from Washington's own quarries. ◆ Services (Episcopal) Su, 7:45AM, 9AM, 11:15AM, Sept-May; Su, 8AM, 10AM, June-Aug. 9301 Richmond Hwy (between Gunston Rd and Mt Vernon Memorial Hwy), Lorton. 339.6572. www.pohick.org

29 Woodlawn Plantation

This estate was bequeathed by George Washington to his adopted granddaughter, Nelly Custis Lewis, and his nephew, Lawrence Lewis. The late-Georgian Federal-style mansion is architecturally more coherent and impressive than **Mount Vernon** (3 miles to the east), and its rooms and restored formal gardens (managed by the National Trust for Historic Preservation)

are well worth the trip. Guided tours are given every half hour. ◆ Admission. Daily, 10AM-5PM, Mar-Dec. 9000 Richmond Hwy (at Mt Vernon Memorial Hwy), Mt Vernon. 780.4000. www.woodlawn1805.org

At Woodlawn Plantation:

Pope-Leighey House

Originally located in Falls Church, this early 1940s house by **Frank Lloyd Wright** was rescued from destruction in 1965, when it was moved to **Woodlawn Plantation** and donated to the National Trust for Historic Preservation. Built of cypress, brick, and glass, the house contains features that were uncommon in their time: heated concrete floors, a flat roof, and windows vital to the structural integrity of the wall. This is a rare example of what Wright called Usonian architecture—well-designed housing for moderate-income families. Guided tours are given every half hour. ◆ Admission. Daily, 10AM-5PM, Mar-Dec

30 Mount Vernon

Though today's presidential home is characterized by privacy and security—sliding iron gates, video cameras, and guard posts—no such security was needed in the early days of the Republic. What presidential homes then had in common were wheat and tobacco fields, mills, smokehouses, and stables. In a time of broad personal mastery, a gifted leader was often able to administer a nation, lead troops in battle, design a building, and

---

Restaurants/Clubs: **Red** | Hotels: **Purple** | Shops: **Orange** | Outdoors/Parks: **Green** | Sights/Culture: **Blue**

Mount Vernon

CHRIS MIDDOUR

run a profitable farm. George Washington exemplified this spirit, and his estate is its testimony. He lived here between 1754 and his death in 1799.

In its prime, the plantation comprised nearly 8,000 acres divided into five working farms, and it was self-sufficient in almost every way. There were orchards, a gristmill, and facilities for making textiles and leather goods. "No estate in America is more pleasantly situated than this," Washington wrote, but the proprietor was allowed little time here. First there was the French and Indian War and then the Revolutionary War, which kept Washington away for 8 years. When he returned, he was determined to become a successful planter, experimenting with crop rotation and comparing notes with like-minded growers. His harvests were good, and he even won a "premium for raising the largest jackass" from the Agricultural Society of South Carolina. But only 4 years later, he went to Philadelphia as a delegate to the Constitutional Convention and then served two terms as president. Finally, in 1797, he returned home, where he lived contentedly until his death 2 years later.

The current estate, a more manageable 400-plus acres, is probably the best-preserved 18th-century plantation in the country, and in the summer thousands of people visit it daily. The best strategy is to arrive early and tour the mansion before seeing the outbuildings and grounds. The inside of the white Georgian mansion has been lovingly restored: All wallpaper, drapery, and upholstery are exact replicas, and the walls were repainted with the original colors. Note the Palladian window in the large dining room and the harpsichord Washington imported for his step-granddaughter,

Nelly, in the **Little Parlor**. Upstairs, the master bedroom holds a trunk Washington carried with him during the Revolutionary War, as well as the bed in which he died. (Washington—who stood more than 6 feet 2 inches—had the extra-long bed made to order.)

Visitors have access to many of the outbuildings, including the spinning room and open-hearth kitchen house. (In days when fires were common and virtually unstoppable, the kitchen was often set apart from the main house.) Be sure to visit the coach house, where a rare 18th-century coach is on display. In the reconstructed greenhouse and slave quarters is a fascinating exhibition about archaeology at the estate. (Ongoing digs take place on the premises.) And up on a hill, where the hundreds of slaves who lived and worked here are buried in unmarked graves, stands a stone memorial in their honor.

On either side of the gracious bowling green are period gardens with flowers, vegetables, and boxwood hedges. Note the partially submerged walls called ha-has that separate tended lawns and gardens from pasture. It's a pleasant walk down to the family vaults where George and his wife, Martha, are buried. Check out a new addition to the grounds: a reconstruction of a 16-sided barn that once stood about 3 miles from the house. The working unit at the **Pioneer Farmer** site demonstrates Washington's method of separating grain from chaff. Also new: **George Washington's Gristmill**, a reconstruction of where the first president turned wheat grown on the farm into flour (separate admission).

A pleasant way to get to Mount Vernon is on one of the **Spirit Cruises**, sailing from DC, time and season permitting (www.spiritofwashington.com). Plan to spend about 2 hours touring the grounds; tours of the mansion are self-guided, but there are also several special tours—offered at no extra charge, and with no reservations required—that take in the gardens and an overview of the slaves' living quarters and working conditions. Call ahead for tour schedule. There's a gift shop, and outside the gates is a restaurant and food court. Parking is free. ◆ Admission. Daily. George Washington Memorial Pkwy and Mt Vernon Memorial Hwy. 780.2000. www.mountvernon.org

31 GUNSTON HALL

This was the home of George Mason, a Virginia farmer who authored the Virginia Declaration of Rights in 1776 and helped to frame the Bill of Rights. The Georgian-style home, replete with 18th-century English and American furnishings, overlooks the Potomac River. **William Buckland**, a joiner-turned-architect, designed the sumptuous Palladian drawing room and Chinese Chippendale dining room, as well as the two distinctive porches (one Gothic, the other 18th-century-style). Equally glorious are the boxwood gardens behind the house. Occasionally there are special events—costumed guides cooking in the restored kitchen, for example. Tours of the house, outbuildings, gardens, and other areas of the plantation offered daily. ◆ Admission. Daily, 9:30AM-5PM. 10709 Gunston Rd

(southeast of Hwy 1), Mason Neck. 550.9220. www.gunstonhall.org

31 POHICK BAY REGIONAL PARK

This water-oriented park (Pohick is Algonquin for "water place") has 150 campsites, an 18-hole golf course, miniature golf, Frisbee golf, sailboat and paddleboat rentals, a swimming pool, and nature trails. ◆ Admission. 6501 Pohick Bay Dr, Lorton. 339.6104. www.nvrpa.org

32 POTOMAC MILLS MALL

One of the world's largest discount and outlet centers, **Potomac Mills** contains more than 220 stores, including **IKEA**, a Swedish furniture store, and outlets for such major designers and retailers as **Nordstrom**, **Saks Fifth Avenue**, **Eddie Bauer**, **L.L. Bean**, **Brooks Brothers**, and **Nine West**. Weekend shoppers are advised to arrive early; the crowds can be overwhelming. There are many food vendors (the IKEA restaurant is terrific), as well as an 18-theater cinema. Drive south on I-95 and take the exit marked **Potomac Mills**. ◆ M-Sa, 10AM-9:30PM; Su, 11AM-7PM. 2700 Potomac Mills Cir (south of Prince William Pkwy), Dale City. Information, 643.1770. www.potomac-mills.com

---

Restaurants/Clubs: Red | **Hotels: Purple** | **Shops: Orange** | **Outdoors/Parks: Green** | **Sights/Culture: Blue**

213

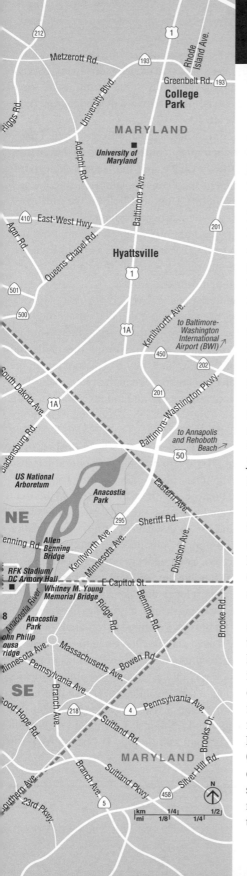

GAY WASHINGTON, DC

The majestic nation's capital on the Potomac and Anacostia Rivers—museums, monuments, stately buildings and mansions—also offers a diverse menu of restaurants, culture, and nightlife—including a very active gay scene. For all its problems, it can still be said that the **District** (as locals call it) can be a great place to visit, live, and play. Say what you will about the legacy of Marion Barry: His liberal city hall often went out of its way to please its many gay constituents, stopping by local nightspots and sending officials to gay fund-raisers. The local police are another story, however; in 1998 officers harassed patrons of gay nightspots by taking down license plate numbers and threatening blackmail. Even worse is the federal government, which besides being the largest tenant in the District also controls the purse strings here and hobbles the city council and mayor on gay, AIDS, and abortion issues. On the political scene, homosexuals may be just one of a multitude of lobbies and pressure groups, but the alphabet soup of groups in DC rivals those in New York, San Francisco, and Chicago: everything from the quixotic Log Cabin Republicans (who caused a mini-brouhaha in 1996 when Bob Dole rejected, then accepted their campaign contribution) to the World Congress of Gay and Lesbian Jewish Organizations.

But when wandering Washington's attractive neighborhoods—whether tranquil and genteel like **Georgetown** or hopping and edgy like **Adams Morgan**—it's easy to tune all that out. Architecturally one of the top cities in the country, DC is far more than the austere Greek Revival monuments to bureaucracy lining the **Federal Triangle**. Owing in part to **Pierre Charles L'Enfant**, the Frenchman who designed the capital city in 1792, its leafy squares and avenues have a distinctly European flavor. The buildings that line them, though, run the gamut of periods and

215

styles—colonial, Italianate, Gothic, and minimalist glass-and-steel—often cheek by jowl.

In these 67 square miles, the population of nearly 600,000 is even more diverse. Sixty-five percent is African-American, but you'd never know it by strolling in some neighborhoods, which are entirely peopled by an ethnic patchwork of groups from Asia, Africa, Europe, Latin America, and the Caribbean.

You'll find gays and lesbians too, in burgeoning numbers. The Georgetown, **Foggy Bottom**, and **Capitol Hill** neighborhoods have their queer contingents, as do the suburbs of **Arlington** in **Virginia** and **Silver Spring**, **Chevy Chase**, and **Bethesda** in **Maryland**. But the single gayest zone in the city also happens to be among its most attractive and diverse. The historic dozen or so blocks surrounding **Dupont Circle** in the northwest quadrant are home to a potpourri of old money, new politicos, embassies, avant-garde types, Supreme Court justices, and lots of gay folks—among them a few luminaries like lesbian writer and socialite Natalie Barney, pioneering homophile activist Frank Kameny, and queer congressmen Gerry Studds and Bob Bauman. It's so out around here, in fact, that the Circle has been dubbed the Fruit Loop and Bouffant Circle.

Radiating from the Circle, **Connecticut Avenue** is lined with a plethora of art galleries, trendy coffee shops and restaurants, bookstores both gay and not, and gourmet food and wine shops, most of which cater (consciously or otherwise) to the tastes of the gay urban professional. Nearby **P Street** was ground zero of queer nightlife during the 1970s and 1980s, and it still holds its own. To the north of Dupont Circle lie Adams Morgan and the burgeoning **U Street** corridor. Something of a dicey neighborhood in the 1990s, these days it's got a trendy flavor not unlike New York's East Village or San Francisco's SoMa. With funky shopping and some first-rate eateries, it's a roost for an ever-growing community of alternative homos, urban pioneers, and more than a few curious college kids. Bordering Adams Morgan and **Rock Creek Park**, nearby **Mount Pleasant** has been dubbed Dyke Heights by nesting lesbians, and the lovely though still crime-troubled Capitol Hill is also home to a growing number of lesbian and gay families—pitter-patter of little feet and all.

But without a doubt, the very nerve center of homosexual DC in the 1990s is **17th Street** between P and S Streets N. This strip of gayware boutiques, sidewalk cafés, cruise bars, galleries, and java joints is the stomping ground for an assortment of boybabes, lipstick lesbians, heavy-metal homos, drag queens, and guppie suits deconstructing this year's House appropriations bill over a frothy cappuccino. You'll quickly notice that the overall tone in this town is more buttoned down than flamboyant; out and proud is okay, but flaming and loud just isn't the norm. Fortunately, most locals are open and visitor-friendly; a few flaunt a degree of attitude more associated with big-league gay scenes like New York and South Beach. Just recently, to provide room for the new Washington Nationals' stadium, some of the clubs in the southeast down by the Anacostia River have had to be closed.

This conservative (small c) but varied mélange—plus a horde of college kids from big-name area schools—feeds a steady stream of new gay clubs, restaurants, and businesses that keeps the city fresh and hip. It's part of what makes Washington, DC, an interesting hybrid: a clean, friendly homo haven coexisting with a federal government that just doesn't get it. Some online resources for the gay and lesbian scene are the *Washington Blade* (www.washblade.com; www.metroweekly.com) and the Gay & Lesbian Activists Alliance (www.glaa.org).

Symbols

♂ predominantly/exclusively gay-male–oriented

♀ predominantly/exclusively lesbian-oriented

♂
♀ predominantly/exclusively gay-oriented, with a male and female clientele

1 LATHAM HOTEL

$$$$ Historic Georgetown is not a particularly gay area despite its busy M Street bar and restaurant corridor. But it can be a fun and certainly attractive place to stay, and this redbrick offshoot of the original Philadelphia Latham offers genuine elegance, a prime location, a rooftop pool, and 143 well-equipped rooms, many with great views of the old **C&O Canal**. Also within is one of Washington's finest restaurants, **Citronelle** (625.2150), serving creative French cuisine by way of California. ♦ 3000 M St NW (at 30th St). 726.5000, 800/528.4261; fax 342.1800. www.georgetowncollection.com. &

2 HUNG JURY

♀ Odd name for a dyke club (it's a leftover from the previous establishment), but this place, mere blocks from the **White House**, has been hopping with a diverse group of women since 1980. The copper-green–walled room holds a pool table and a good-size dance floor, from which issues a fun mix of tunes; for the hungry, light food is served on the order of burgers and fries. By day, it's just another eatery for Downtown office drones. On Friday and Saturday nights, when the **Jury** is in session, you must be or be accompanied by a woman to enter. ♦ Cover. F, Sa, 8:30PM-3AM. 1819 H St NW (between 18th and 19th Sts). 785.8181. &

3 LAFAYETTE PARK

It was here, just north of the **White House**, in this park designed by **Pierre Charles L'Enfant** as part of **President's Park**, that laborers camped and bricks were dried during the construction of the president's residence. During the 1960s, the park was often the scene of antiwar and other demonstrations—but for at least a century, the place has also been a gay cruising ground. No fewer than 18 men were arrested for engaging in oral sex here in 1892; over 1,000 gays a year were nabbed for solicitation during the 1950s; and in 1963 a NASA employee named Clifford Norton was fired after he was caught cruising here (his case

ended up in a DC Court of Appeals, which in 1969 banned firings on grounds of homosexuality, unless it could be proved to directly affect job performance). Fittingly, among the statues in the park is one (at the northwest corner) of Baron Wilhelm von Steuben, the Prussian general who led American Revolutionary troops at Valley Forge—always accompanied by his 18-year-old "translator," who it seems spoke not a word of English. A scene on the base of the statue depicts the old goat giving a nude youth "military instruction"; seen from a certain angle, he appears to be grabbing the lad's crotch (a sculptor's inside joke?). ♦ Bounded by Madison and Jackson Pls NW and by Pennsylvania Ave and H St NW

4 TWO QUAIL

★★$$ Creative (if uneven) New American cuisine is served in three intimate rooms, all quirkily furnished with mismatched chairs and silverware. Highlights include grilled tuna, rainbow trout stuffed with spinach or crabmeat, and sublime Key lime cheesecake. ♦ Nouvelle American ♦ M-F, lunch and dinner; Sa, Su, dinner. Reservations recommended. 320 Massachusetts Ave NE (between Third and Fourth Sts). 543.8030. www.twoquail.com. &

4 CAFE BERLIN

★★$$ Dine inside or out on stick-to-your-ribs delights such as sauerbraten with potato dumplings and red cabbage. The best choices on the huge dessert menu are apple strudel, the Black Forest cake, and linzer torte. ♦ German ♦ M-Sa, lunch and dinner; Su, dinner. Reservations recommended. 322 Massachusetts Ave NE (between Third and Fourth Sts). 543.7656. www.cafeberlindc.com. &

5 REMINGTON'S

♂ DC's only full-time gay country-western dance spot is popular as an after-work watering hole for Capitol Hill staffers and Library of Congress types. It's rather gentrified, with exposed brick walls, gleaming wood floors, and comfy sofas, but when the locals hit the dance floor, it's a rootin', tootin' party. ♦ M-Th, Su, 4PM-2AM; F, Sa, 4PM-3AM. 639 Pennsylvania Ave SE (between Sixth and Seventh Sts). 543.3113. www.remingtonwdc.com. &

6 PHASE 1

♀ Wood-paneled, rustic, and generally no-nonsense, this sapphic saloon—Washington's oldest lesbian bar—tends to draw a butcher bunch than Downtown's **Hung Jury** (see left).

Restaurants/Clubs: **Red** | Hotels: **Purple** | Shops: **Orange** | Outdoors/Parks: **Green** | Sights/Culture: **Blue**

GAYE OLDE TIMES ON THE POTOMAC

Homo politicus has, of course, inhabited our fair capital since the first cornerstones were laid in a Maryland swamp. Alexander Hamilton, the first secretary of the Treasury, wrote touching love letters to one of George Washington's young lieutenants. As for the White House, the first queen to check in may not have been England's current Queen Mum but Pennsylvania's James Buchanan, the "bachelor" president of the years 1857-1861. His ever-so-close relationship with Alabama senator William Rufus De Vane King led sharp tongues all over the capital to dub him Miss Nancy and Aunt Fancy.

Over the years, though, press and politicos conspired to sweep this sort of thing under the rug, so that most of the public never heard the real poop on the likes of J. Edgar Hoover, Roy Cohn, and Reagan faves Terry Dolan and Carl "Spitz" Channell. Once in a while, though, peeps of pederasty did surface, as when Franklin Roosevelt refused to fire his undersecretary of state, Sumner Welles, over rumors that the fellow was *comme ça*. (After all, he didn't leave his wife, Eleanor, over her relationship with Lenora Hickok.) But FDR eventually caved in to pressure and asked for Welles's resignation.

The occasional sex scandals that did pop up were mostly the province of heterosexuals. (Remember Wilbur Mills and Fanne Fox?) A notable exception was Lyndon Johnson aide Walter Jenkins, who was caught having man-to-man sex in a YMCA and hounded from office. But it took a string of gay scandals to pry open Congress's closet door. In 1977 a fire at DC's **Follies** porn theater killed eight people—but among those who escaped was Representative Jon Hinson (Democrat, Mississippi). In 1979 conservative congressman Robert Bauman (Republican, Maryland) was collared for doing the nasty with a young man at a DC gay bar and bathhouse called **Chesapeake House**, and 4 years later, liberal Representative Gerry Studds (Democrat, Massachusetts) declared that he was gay after being censured for hanky panky with a male page. Bauman was run out of town and wrote his memoirs, whereas Studds is still serving in Congress, and didn't. Then, in the mid-1980s, another Massachusetts Democrat, Representative Barney Frank, also came out, and was embroiled in his own scandal when it was found that his "housekeeper" was a call boy who was running a male escort service out of Frank's apartment. Frank also rode out the scandal and has gone on to make his mark in Congress in many ways—not least of all by, in 1987, threatening to out closeted GOP congressmen if their party insisted on restoring sexual orientation as grounds for denying government security clearance.

Since then, gays and lesbians (such as Roberta Achtenburg, undersecretary of housing in the early part of the first Clinton administration) have grown more visible, as in the Clinton executive branch, and Congress has become openly gayer in dribs and drabs—even on the gay-hostile Republican side of the aisle. In 1994 Representative Steve Gunderson (Republican, Wisconsin) came out, 3 years after an activist tried to out him with publicity. In 1996 two Republican congressmen who voted for the so-called Defense of Marriage Act were threatened with outing; Jim Kolbe of Arizona subsequently outed himself (and was reelected shortly thereafter).

Not surprisingly, most politicians are still not brave enough to unseal their closets, so that speculation on some folks—however widespread—remains just that. Don't ask, don't tell, indeed.

The women come to shoot pool and catch **Redskins** games on the big-screen TV over a cold brew. There are tables and chairs and a small dance floor too. ♦ Cover, F, Sa. M-Th, Su, 7PM-2AM; F, Sa, 7PM-3AM. 525 Eighth St SE (between E and G Sts). 544.6831. www.phase1dc.com. ♿

7 ELAN

♀ From sophisticated to sizzling, this incredibly popular women's bar draws the femmes fatales to a warm environment of antique mirrors, comfy couches, and candlelight. Call, or check out their web site, for their constantly evolving repertory of theme parties; at press time, Wednesdays were quiet, with no DJ and no cover; Thursdays featured "Ginger's Tea" for tea dancing; "Phat Fridays" got phatter at 9PM; and just about anything could happen on weekends. If you're looking for Ms. Right or just Ms. Right Now, you just might find her here, but just in case you don't, there's an awful lot of other stuff to do, and on-street parking too. ♦ Cover most nights. M, W, Th, 8PM-2AM; F, Sa, 10PM-3AM. 1129 Pennsylvania Ave SE (at 12th St). 544.6406. www.elandcusa.com

8 HISTORIC CONGRESSIONAL CEMETERY

Opened in 1807, the 32.5-acre site now holds some 60,000 souls, among them Civil War photographer Mathew Brady, bandleader John Philip Sousa, and 19th-century statesman Henry Clay. But no grave site is more visited than the elegant black marble slab resting under a cherry tree down the hill from the chapel. Identifying the occupant as

"A Gay Vietnam Veteran," the inscription continues, "When I was in the military I was given a medal for killing two men, and discharged for loving one." The case of air force sergeant Leonard Matlovich made the cover of *Time* when he was cashiered for coming out in 1975; he won reinstatement in 1980 but didn't go back into the service, and he died of AIDS on 22 June 1988. Look closer: There's a plaque honoring him signed by President George Bush. Ironically, a dozen stones away is FBI Director J. Edgar Hoover; nearby, his boyfriend and fellow G-man Clyde Tolson rests under a pink headstone. (So *that's* what the G stands for!) ♦ Daily, dawn to dusk. Office open M, W, F, 10AM–2PM; Sa, 9AM–1PM. 1801 E St SE (at 18th St). 543.0539. &

9 BACHELOR'S MILL

♂ Looking for the hottest African-American men? This is the place you'll find them. Known for its strong drinks and its hard men, this bar will rock you out. The neighborhood isn't the greatest—locals may offer to "watch" your car for you—but don't let that put you off. This is a scene not to be missed. ♦ M-Th, 5PM–2AM; F, 5PM–3AM; Sa, 5PM–4AM. 1104 8th St SE (at L St). 544.1931

10 EDGE

♂ Formerly the **Lost and Found**, this mostly gay
♀ dance spot has no less than four dance floors (one outdoors) pulsing with the latest hi-NRG vibrations. Distractions from the beat include a sexy shower show and a cozy lounge with a fireplace. The crowd varies from night to night, with Monday heavy on African-Americans and Thursday drawing women. Straights take over 2 nights a week, so call ahead. ♦ Cover. M-Th, Su, 9PM–2AM; F, Sa, 9PM–3AM. 52 L St SE (at Half St). 488.1200. www.edgewet.com. &

11 PERRY'S

★★$$ Imaginatively wrapped sushi is part of the menu here, which borrows from Japanese, Chinese, and Mexican culinary traditions, among others. The stylish atmosphere is usually better than the food, but on weekends there's a fun drag brunch, and the rooftop deck has the best view of any restaurant in the city. For the privilege of sitting outside, though, you have to shell out a minimum of at least $10 per person, drinks not included. ♦ International ♦ M-Sa, dinner; Su, brunch and dinner. 1811 Columbia Rd NW (between Mintwood Pl and Biltmore St). 234.6218. www.perrysadamsmorgan.com

12 KALORAMA GUEST HOUSE

$ For budget-minded travelers, these gay-friendly lodgings occupying four Victorian town houses are a fine choice. The charming rooms are outfitted with brass beds, thick comforters, and late-Victorian antiques, and the low rates include continental breakfast, sherry in the evening, use of the laundry room, and local telephone calls. Only 12 of the 31 units have private baths, however, and there's no on-premises food service. ♦ 1854 Mintwood Pl NW (between Columbia Rd and 19th St). 667.6369. www.kaloramaguesthouse.com

13 RESULTS

When several gay partners opened DC's biggest and hottest gym in early 1997 in a former Chrysler showroom, it made a queen-sized splash, for sure. With three floors, 14-foot ceilings, huge windows all around, a special women's fitness area, artfully placed mirrors, oodles of free weights, and the most advanced cardio- and strength-training machines on the market, this place is mega in every sense of the word—including the way cute clientele. There's also a pro shop, a rooftop sundeck, a dry sauna, and a café serving such light fare as salads, sandwiches, and protein shakes. Best of all, you don't have to miss *Oprah*, as you can tune your Walkman to one of the many TV monitors. ♦ M-F, 6AM–11PM; Sa, Su, 8AM–10PM. 1612 U St NW (between New Hampshire Ave and 17th St). 518.0001. www.resultsthegym.com

14 WASHINGTON SPORTS CLUB

The white, bright local branch of the national health club chain is a longtime homo favorite. There are three levels and 20,000 square feet of everything it takes to work that body— Hammer Strength, Cybex, and Nautilus machines; free weights aplenty; cardio contraptions; and aerobics classes. ♦ M-Th, 6AM–11PM; F, 6AM–10PM; Sa, Su, 8:30AM–8:30PM. 1835 Connecticut Ave NW (between Florida Ave and T St). 332.0100. www.mysportsclub.com

15 STRAITS OF MALAYA

★★$$ In good weather, the rooftop deck and sidewalk café are wonderful places to savor delicacies from Malaysia and Singapore in a relaxed, attractive setting. Try the tasty *pohpia* (stir-fried shredded leeks, bean sprouts, and chicken wrapped in pancakes), or the curried Chinese eggplant, vegetarian-style or with

---

Restaurants/Clubs: Red | Hotels: Purple | Shops: Orange | Outdoors/Parks: Green | Sights/Culture: Blue

meat. ◆ Malaysian ◆ M-F, lunch and dinner; Sa, Su, dinner. Reservations recommended. 1836 18th St NW (between Swann and T Sts). 483.1483. www.straitsofmalaya.com. ㅊ

16 FOOD FOR THOUGHT

★$ Sometimes this vegetarian eatery really does live up to its nickname, Food for Lesbians, with a boho, earthy-crunchy atmosphere and service that can be casual to the point of nonexistent. But what the heck, the eats are good (and cheap) and it's where the girls are. ◆ Health food/American ◆ Daily, lunch and dinner. 1738 Connecticut Ave NW (between R and S Sts). 797.1095. ㅊ

17 THE LEATHER RACK

Perched above the fast-foodish **China Café**, this shop appeals to leather, Western, and bondage buffs with a wide selection of accessories, from well-priced jeans and boots for beginners to galvanized iron cages for old pros. Some of the goods defy description, but the helpful staff will be more than happy to answer all your questions. For those still confused about that old color-coded hanky bit, pick up the handy-dandy chart-*cum*-business card. ◆ Daily, 10AM-11PM. 1723 Connecticut Ave NW (between R and S Sts), second floor. 797.7401. www.theleatherrack.com

18 RESTAURANT NORA

★★★$$$ Chef-owner Nora Pouillon serves prime-quality American cuisine—organic vegetables and meats, homegrown herbs—in a lovely country-style dining room and a glass-enclosed courtyard that's a favorite of Bill Clinton and granola dykes alike. ◆ American ◆ M-Sa, dinner. Reservations recommended. 2132 Florida Ave NW (at R St). 462.5143. www.noras.com. ㅊ

19 PLEASURE PLACE

Tucked beneath the stoop of a handsome town house, this is a more attractive, polite breed of sex shop. The usual range of erotic paraphernalia, gay and straight—from condoms to blue movies—is on display, in addition to feather boas, "do-me" clubwear, and tongue-in-cheek fare like cream-filled "chocolate willies." Check out the leather-and-latex room in the rear. ◆ M-Tu, 10AM-10PM; W-Sa, 10AM-midnight; Su, noon-7PM. 1710 Connecticut Ave NW (between R and S Sts). 483.3297. Also at 1063 Wisconsin Ave NW (between the C&O Canal and M St). 333.8570, 800/386.2386

20 THE CARLYLE SUITES

$$ Close to the 17th Street scene, this former apartment building has been turned into a charming Art Deco hotel popular with gay and straight visitors alike. The Deco touch is more evident inside than out, with a tasteful lobby and a mauve-and-gray color scheme; the 170 comfortable suites have kitchenettes, and some offer views of DC landmarks. For eats, gay entrepreneur Randy Sullivan (who founded the popular **Randy's** on 17th Street) serves up continental fare at his more "grown up" **Randolph's Grill** right here on the premises. Ask about the economical weekend packages available year-round. Also here is the **Wave**, a gay-popular martini bar also owned by Sullivan. ◆ 1731 New Hampshire Ave NW (between R and S Sts). 234.3200, 800/964.5377; fax 387.0085. www.carlylesuites.com. ㅊ

21 WILLIAM LEWIS HOUSE

$ After 15 years fixing up a 1904 Edwardian town house in a slightly down-and-out area near Logan Circle, David Holder and Theron White furnished it with family heirlooms and opened it to guests. A homey turn-of-the-19th-century atmosphere—not to mention the love and hard work of the gay proprietors—radiates through the four rooms and the period parlor and dining room. Other extras include beds with feather mattresses, direct-dial phones with answering machines, a garden with hot tub, and continental breakfast on weekdays; the bathrooms, however, are shared. David and Theron are warm and friendly hosts, and once Winston, their old Staffordshire, gets to know you, he's just a doll. ◆ 1309 R St NW (between 13th and 14th Sts). 462.7574, 800/465.7574. www.wlewishous.com

22 DUPONT ITALIAN KITCHEN

★$ Dubbed DIK by members of the local tribe, this gay-popular standby serves up old Italian standards on the order of chicken *francese*, pizza, and pasta. The décor is strictly dropped ceilings and hanging plants, but the big streetside windows and fair-weather outdoor seating are half the fun here, if not more. ◆ Italian ◆ M-F, lunch and dinner; Sa, Su, brunch and dinner. 1635 17th St NW (at R St). 329.3222. www.dupontitaliankitchen.com

Above Dupont Italian Kitchen:

DIK BAR

♂♀ The clientele at this bar (formerly Windows) is usually between 35 to 50, though some younger admirers are found here too. There's cabaret on Thursday nights, and the first Monday of every month is a singers' showcase night. ◆ Daily, 4PM to late. 328.0100

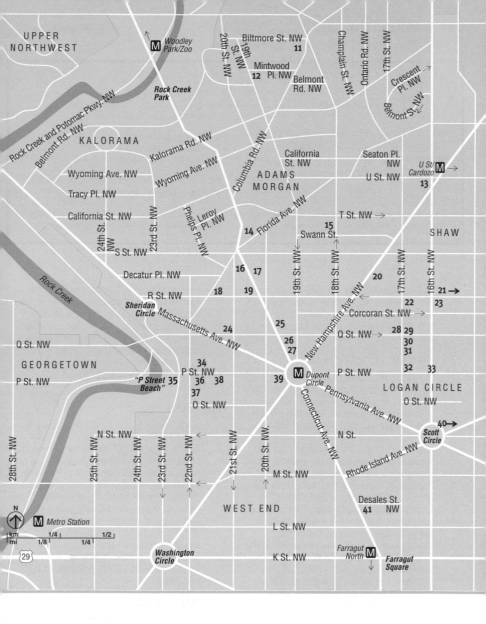

22 COBALT 30 DEGREES

♂ This upstairs lounge draws a predominantly gay clientele with a clever martini menu featuring drinks like the Just Jack (Jack Daniel's and sweet vermouth) and Mommie Dearest Cosmo. ◆ M-Th, 5PM-2AM; F, 5PM-3AM; Sa, noon-3AM; Su, noon-2AM. 1639 R St NW (at 17th St). 462.6569. Metro: Dupont Cir

22 CHAOS

♂ There's always lots happening at this popular gay bar—like drag bingo on Tuesdays, Latin tunes and dancing on Thursdays, and a drag cabaret on Saturdays. ◆ Tu-Sa, dinner; Su, brunch and dinner. 1603 17th St NW. 232.4141. www.chaosdc.com. Metro: Dupont Cir

23 THE EMBASSY INN

$$ Built in 1910 as an apartment house, this inn offers a good balance of charm, convenience, and price. Its 38 smallish rooms are comfortable and have the usual amenities; the elegant lobby is a pleasant setting for complimentary evening sherry and munchies. A block north, a somewhat larger sister

---

Restaurants/Clubs: Red | Hotels: Purple | Shops: Orange | Outdoors/Parks: Green | Sights/Culture: Blue

THE BEST

Jane Troxell

Owner, Lammas Women's Books & More

· Living in the hometown of Sweet Honey in the Rock, a singing group internationally known but DC-based.

· Sharing a quiet late-night conversation at the **Reflecting Pool** in the lap of the **Capitol** building.

· **Black Gay Pride Day**, Memorial Day weekend— my absolute favorite day of the year. It always

rains, but everyone shows up, lovely and loving anyway.

· Poring through all the international magazines at the **News Room** on **Connecticut Avenue**.

· Shopping at **Eastern Market** on Saturday and **Takoma Park** fresh market on Sunday.

· The rooftop at **Perry's**—vegetarian sushi for two and the relaxed atmosphere of straights, gays, and anybody in between at twilight.

· Any moment spent on the Castro-like **17th Street**, **Lammas Women's Books**' new home.

property, the **Windsor Inn** (667.0300), has similarly equipped suites at comparable rates. ♦ 1627 16th St NW (between Corcoran and R Sts). 234.7800, 800/423.9111; fax 234.3309

24 PHILLIPS COLLECTION

In 1921, industrialist Duncan Phillips turned his four-story brownstone mansion into the capital's first museum of modern art. The collection today includes American and French Impressionists, post-Impressionists, and Modernists, along with precursors such as Goya, El Greco, and Delacroix. Gay and bisexual artists are amply represented among the 2,500 works here: Charles Demuth, Marsden Hartley, David Hockney, and Georgia O'Keeffe, to name but a few. There's a gift shop and café on the premises, and the concert series is a great way to spend Sunday afternoons September through May. ♦ Admission varies depending on temporary exhibits. Tu, W, F, Sa; Th, 10AM-8:30PM; Su, noon-7PM. Call to arrange group tours a month in advance. 1600 21st St NW (at Q St). 387.2151. www.phillipscollection.org. ♿

25 LAMBDA RISING

♂ For 2 decades, DC's only gay and lesbian bookstore, today the flagship of a mini-empire
♀ (with outlets in Baltimore and the gayish resort of Rehoboth Beach, Delaware—see page 223), is one of the country's foremost homo lit shops. There are titles on every

conceivable topic, T-shirts, and assorted knickknacks; the magazine racks in the rear are sometimes cruisier than the **Circle** bar down the street. It's also a good spot to get clued in on what's happening on the local club scene. ♦ Daily, 10AM-midnight. 1625 Connecticut Ave NW (between Q and R Sts). 462.6969, 800/621.6969. www.lamdarising.com. ♿

26 RAKU

★★$ Hungry queers have been among the many flocking to this upscale pan-Asian eatery where noodle dishes from various countries mingle with dumplings, spring rolls, meat and seafood skewers, and exotica like caramelized squid in soy ginger glaze and Thai curry shark fillets. It's all served in a no-smoking Japaneseoid dining room with bamboo and verdigris accents, faux rice-paper ceilings, and an open kitchen; strangely, though, there's nary a shard of *raku* pottery in sight. ♦ Pan-Asian ♦ Daily, lunch and dinner. 1900 Q St NW (at 19th St). 265.7258. ♿

27 STARBUCKS

The small, piece-of-pie-shaped Dupont Circle branch may or may not be the gayest **Starbucks** in the country, but it is the highest-grossing. Finding a seat, therefore, is usually futile, but pretty views of the Circle and the fun, cruisy crowd compensate. (This is one of the prime see-and-be-seen gay landmarks.) ♦ M-Th, 6:30AM-11PM; F, 6:30AM-midnight; Sa, 7AM-midnight; Su, 7AM-11PM. 1501 Connecticut Ave NW (at Dupont Cir). 588.1280. ♿

27 KRAMERBOOKS & AFTERWORDS CAFÉ

★$$ Specializing in popular hardcovers and paperbacks (including plenty of gay titles), this trendy bookstore had a café years before it was fashionable. Today, the crowds are just

REHOBOTH BEACH, DELAWARE

When homos from Washington (and elsewhere in the mid-Atlantic region) want to hit the sand, they head by the thousands for the small Delaware shore town of Rehoboth Beach. As a gay-popular (though far from entirely gay) resort, it's closer to the laid-back, down-home feel of Provincetown or Saugatuck than the attitudinal trendiness of South Beach or Fire Island, with quiet lanes and fine old homes alongside T-shirt shops and a honky-tonk shopping district and board-walk area.

Though it's common for groups to take a house for the summer, Fire Island–style, there are also dozens of hostelries that cater mostly to same-sexers, including the well-run, 17-room **Silver Lake** ($$; 133 Silver Lake Drive, off Robinson Drive, between Park Avenue and Route 1; 302/226.2115, 800/842.2115; fax 302/226.2732), with its white columns and lake and ocean views; and the lesbian-oriented **Sand in My Shoes** ($$; Canal and Sixth Streets; 302/226.2006, 800/231.5856), with 12 rooms and a hot tub. Then, of course, there's the **Renegade** ($$; 4274 Route 1, at Country Club Rd; 302/227.1222; fax 227.4281), a gay resort well away from downtown and the beach, with 20 motel-like rooms, 8 cottages, a pool, and a highly hopping nightclub.

The beach, of course, is the raison d'être of Rehoboth. The guys mostly head for the stretch of sand—universally known as Poodle Beach—near the boardwalk at the foot of Queen Street (honest). Because it's in town, though, you've got to keep those trunks on. Dykes, on the other hand, tend to cluster on an out-of-the-way strand on the North Shore which has been ever so wittily dubbed Dinah Shores.

Off the sand, there are plenty of gay cafés and coffee-houses to snag a pastry, sandwich, and steaming hot caffeine, including **Coffee Mill** (★★$; 127 Rehoboth Mews, between Rehoboth and Baltimore Avenues, 227.7530). The shopping can be fun too, at shops

like **Lambda Rising** bookstore (39 Baltimore Avenue, between First and Second Streets; 302/227.6969). Summer's gay restaurant scene hops with more than two dozen great venues in town, many of which cross-pollinate chefs and waiters with Washington eateries. From the traditional surf 'n' turf of gay-owned **Mano's Restaurant** (★★$$; 10 Wilmington Avenue, between the boardwalk and First Street; 302/227.6707) to eclectic multiculti fare and a great Sunday brunch at **Back Porch** (★★$$$$; 59 Rehoboth Avenue, between the boardwalk and First Street; 302/227.3674), Rehoboth has most of the popular culinary bases covered. Other gay faves include the eclectic **Cloud 9** (★★$$$; 234 Rehoboth Avenue, between Bayard and Scarborough Avenues; 302/226.1999) and **Celsius** (★★★$$$; 50C Wilmington Avenue, between First Street and Bayard Avenue; 302/227.5767). For a top-notch experience, there's the **Blue Moon** restaurant and bar (★★★$$$; 35 Baltimore Avenue, between First and Second Streets; 302/227.6515), with a menu full of imaginative fare with Asian touches.

For the happy hour and after-dinner scenes, check out the (mostly male) crowd at the **Blue Moon** or **Cloud 9**. If you haven't read about or gotten an invitation to one of the many house bashes, head over to the gay dance club in town, **Renegade** (4274 Route 1, at Country Club Road; 227.4713), which besides a disco also has a video bar and a country-western area. You can get clued in on local social happenings by asking at Lambda Rising or checking the local gay rags, the *Rehoboth Beach Gazette, Letters from Camp Rehoboth*, and the *Underground*.

Rehoboth Beach is about 3 hours (120 miles) east of Washington, DC, by car on **Highway 50** and **Route 404**; 120 miles from Philadelphia; and 200 miles south of New York City. The nearest airport is at **Ocean City, Maryland** (410/213.2471), about a 40-minute drive. Further information is available from the local chamber of commerce (302/227.6181).

---

as thick in the glassed-in patio out back, and weekend brunch is especially popular—though any time is right for a little quiche and a split of wine. The desserts are uneven, though, and the prices relatively steep. Known as a pickup spot both gay and straight, it's open 24 hours on weekends, and there's live music of various types Wednesday through Saturday evenings. ♦ American ♦ Daily, breakfast, lunch, and

dinner. 1517 Connecticut Ave NW (between Dupont Cir and Q St). 387.3825. www.kramers.com. ♿

28 MERCURY GRILL

★★$$ With a tasteful blue-and-white dining room set in a 19th-century town house, this small gay eatery (which started out in the seaside getaway of Rehoboth Beach,

---

Restaurants/Clubs: Red | Hotels: Purple | Shops: Orange | Outdoors/Parks: Green | Sights/Culture: Blue

Delaware) has a lot going for it: attentive service, chef Tony Romano's artfully presented quality food, and a streetside patio that rocks on summer evenings. Entrées like cornmeal-crusted salmon or grilled veggies on a tortilla with Monterey Jack and avocado crème fraiche are light yet filling. ♦ New American ♦ M-Sa, dinner; Su, brunch and dinner. 1602 17th St NW (between Q and Corcoran Sts). 667.5937

29 ANNIE'S PARAMOUNT STEAKHOUSE

★$ To Hades with Lean Cuisine! An older (and often heftier) set of queens digs with gusto into the big burgers, prime rib, and pot roast at this surf-and-turf eatery. There are a couple of Levantine and Greek touches on the menu, but mostly this is old-fashioned comfort cooking the way it used to be, before we knew about calories and cholesterol. It also makes a great weekend standby for brunch around the clock. ♦ American ♦ M-Th, lunch and dinner; F, Su, open 24 hours. 1609 17th St NW (between Q and Corcoran Sts). 232.0395. &

29 LAMMAS WOMEN'S BOOKS & MORE

♀ Long the unofficial nerve center of the DC lesbian-feminist community, this shop holds an extensive selection of sapphic books, magazines, and CDs, along with an excellent self-help and recovery section. The staff is also happy to fill visitors in on local lesbo happenings, social and otherwise. ♦ M-Th, 11AM-10PM; F, Sa, 11AM-midnight; Su, 11AM-8PM. 1607 17th St NW (between Q and Corcoran Sts). 775.8218, 800/955.2662. &

In January 1993 the first-ever gay and lesbian Inaugural Ball was held at the National Press Club. Melissa Etheridge, k.d. lang, and more than 1,000 hopeful others heard a video from Bill Clinton promising, "I have a vision, and you're part of it." Gays wore T-shirts with sayings like "Due to the change in the administration, the light at the end of the tunnel will be turned back on." Unfortunately, as with many political promises, Clinton's weren't fulfilled. His backing down on gays in the military and his signing of the Defense of Marriage Act disappointed the gay and lesbian community. And although gay and lesbian balls and benefits marked Clinton's second inauguration, they had a markedly less exuberant mood.

29 UNIVERSAL GEAR

♂ Gay fashion victims browse for jeans, sportswear, swim togs, and big-name underwear under unflattering fluorescent lighting and a tangle of exposed wires and pipes. This is, after all, one of the few outlets in straitlaced DC for slutty and slinky clubbing threads of the type that abound in the gay ghettos of South Beach or Chelsea. ♦ Su-Th, 11AM-10PM; F, Sa, 11AM-midnight. 1601 17th St NW (at Q St). 319.0136. www.universalgear.com. &

30 TRIO RESTAURANT

★$ A local favorite for diner-style fare since 1948, this comfortable dive was tarted up with speckled pink walls when 17th Street went queer. It has since attracted a considerable homo crowd who love the retro-camp value of the place and the old-time waitresses—one of whom, a certain Margo, served as the model for ventriloquist Wayland Flowers's character Madame. ♦ American ♦ Daily, breakfast, lunch, and dinner. 1537 17th St NW (at Q St). 232.6305

31 PEPPER'S

★★$ Bright red and blue walls, leopard-skin banquettes, and tabletops splashed with rivulets of color set the tone for the Sybil-style (i.e., multipersonality) menu here, careening from Tex-Mex (steak burrito) to Thai (green-chili fried noodles) to Jamaican (jerk chicken). Or try a crossbreed, like the jerk chicken fajitas; either way, most of it's good, and the price is right. Another fun option is to hang with the festive mixed gang at the bar. Outdoor seating is accessible by wheelchair. ♦ International ♦ Daily, lunch and dinner. Bar: M-Th, Su, 11:30AM-2AM; F, Sa, 11:30AM-3AM. No reservations. 1527 17th St NW (between P and Q Sts). 328.8193

31 J.R.'S

♂ The DC branch of the Texas-based minichain of stand-and-model bars does a good job of packing in the after-work and after-school bunch (especially for the popular cheapo vodka nights). The place looks like a gentrified saloon, with exposed brick and a high tin ceiling. If the downstairs gets too tight, head up to the mezzanine, with its pool table, for a bird's-eye view. ♦ M-Th, 2PM-2AM; F, 2PM-3AM; Sa, 1PM-3AM; Su, 1PM-2AM. 1519 17th St NW (between P and Q Sts). 328.0090. www.jrswdc.com

32 CAFÉ LUNA

★$ Dubbed Café Gay by 17th Street habitués, its great menu offers competent salads, sandwiches, pizza, and pasta to an

THE BEST

Candace Gingrich

Spokesperson, Field Organizer, and author of *The Accidental Activist* for the Human Rights Campaign

- **17th Street**: the soul of **Dupont Circle**. Sit outside at one of the many restaurants and eat, drink, and person-watch. I strongly suggest the margaritas at **Sol**. Stop in at **Lammas Women's Bookstore**, one of the area's oldest and best literary havens. If you happen to be in town on a Wednesday, and you happen to be a lesbian, stop in at **Trumpets** for ladies' night. Or if you're around on a Sunday, brunch is mandatory—Trumpets has one of the best around.

- **Dupont Circle**: Folks gather all around the circle park to play chess, read, lay out, and watch the tourists driving in a traffic circle for the first time (sheer comedy, except when they wreck). Travel north on **Connecticut Street** for more great eats and shopping. **Kramerbooks and afterwords** has two of my favorites—books and food. My partner, Kris, raves over the chicken potpie with cornbread crust (I'd rave too if I weren't a vegetarian!); my fave is the B-52 Coffee drink. Excellent desserts too. Continue up Connecticut to **Lamdba Rising**, one of the most complete queer bookstores I've ever been in. If all this has you thirsty, stop in **The Circle**, one of the most diverse bars around. One other favorite on Connecticut is **Food for Thought** (also known as Food for Lesbians), a haven for vegetarians that also accommodates carnivores. With live folk music weekly (Shawn Colvin and Mary Chapin Carpenter played here way back when), it is one of the only "crunchy-granola" type places in the District.

- **Adams Morgan**: One of Dupont's sister neighborhoods, Adams Morgan holds culinary delights from all over the world. My favorite is all-American, though—**Perry's** on **Columbia Road**. Perry's rooftop is perfect for nice weather with a view and a breeze always blowing. If dining inside, request a sofa table. After dinner, go a few doors down the street to **Bedrock Billiards**. The regulation-size tables and well-kept equipment would please any pool player, but there's more—an eclectic jukebox and Guinness on tap.

- **Washington Furies Ruggerfest**: At the end of March and into early April, the **Furies** host the largest women's rugby tournament on the East Coast. Held at **Anacostia Park**, the tourney brings 12 to 16 highly competitive teams to DC.

- A good way to see the city is by boat. I suggest visiting **Thompson's** or **Fletcher's Boat House** to rent a canoe and paddle around the **Potomac**.

- To truly appreciate a city, one must *walk*. The turn-of-the-19th-century architecture should not be missed. If you'd rather not walk, the world-famous **DC Metro** is the best way to go—clean, reliable, and reasonable. If you have a car, you must drive the length of **16th Street**, which goes from the **White House** to the **Maryland** suburbs. Drive slowly and enjoy more beautiful homes, as well as the largest variety of houses of worship anywhere. Lastly, you must visit the **US Capitol** and lobby your representative or senator on the issue of your choice.

---

exceedingly queer—and generally cute—local clientele. There are plenty of choices for vegetarians too, along with fat-free dishes for waist-watchers. Weekend brunch is especially popular, though breakfast fare is served all day amid cheesy fake brick walls. ♦ American/Italian ♦ M-F, breakfast, lunch, and dinner; Sa, brunch and dinner until 2AM; Su, brunch and dinner. 1633 P St NW (between 16th and 17th Sts). 387.4005. www.skewers-cafeluna.com

33 CLUB CHAOS

★★$$ Set below street level, this stylish gay restaurant and bar yearns for hipness yet still manages a comfy feel. After work especially, guys and gals of various ages mix easily at the front Drama Lounge, with its campy cocktails. Toward the back, the warm dining room is awash in nifty touches like sponge-painted tables and sheet-metal menus—a fitting setting for the tasty array of New American creations with influences ranging from Mobile to Marrakesh. The Sunday brunch is upscale and popular. ♦ Continental ♦ M-Sa, dinner; Su, brunch and dinner. Bar daily, 3PM-2AM. 1603 P St NW (between 16th and 17th Sts). 232.4141. www.chaosdc.com

34 THE FIREPLACE

♂ A warm fire visible from the street through the glass-backed fireplace draws in a fun mix of local boys, especially for happy hour on cold winter nights. Downstairs, large video screens predominate, whereas the upstairs feels cruisier and more boho, with exposed-brick walls and splattered paint. ♦ M-Th, 1PM-2AM; F, Sa, 1PM-3AM; Su, 1PM-2AM. 2161 P St NW (at 22nd St). 293.1293. ♿

Restaurants/Clubs: Red | Hotels: Purple | Shops: Orange | Outdoors/Parks: Green | Sights/Culture: Blue

THE BEST

Susan Stamberg
Special Correspondent, National Public Radio

Union Station: The ultimate gateway, a place to visit, arrive, and depart. Built in 1907 in the heyday of rail travel, it was grand. . . . By the time I moved here in the 1960s, Union Station had become just a serviceable transportation spot. The best thing about it was the throat-catching sight of the **Capitol** building as you walked out the station's front door. In the 1970s, Union Station sat and rotted. "That white elephant on Massachusetts Avenue," we called it. By 1981, it was closed.

Then, in the fall of 1988, after a $181 million renovation, it reopened, not just as a train station, but as a lively social center on **Capitol Hill**, a place to shop, eat, see a movie, meet a friend, and listen to what Washington writer Marita Golden once described as the "cacophony of good times": fountains, pianists, plus the always haunting sounds of the trains and the announcements of arrivals and departures.

The entrance hall is really the most spectacular part of Union Station, an enormous vaulted ceiling with geometric patterns and gold centers to each of the patterns. . . . The special thing about the Roman warrior statues is that each one carries a shield, a big, long thing that goes from about waist length down to the ground and rests between their feet. Apparently some delicate-minded souls, around 1907 when **Daniel Burnham** did the design for Union Station, felt it would be unseemly for the scantily clad Roman soldiers to be seen frontally, so the shield was designed in order to give them the proper cover-up.

Eastern Market: The next place is Eastern Market at 7th and C Streets SE . . . the only remaining farmers' market of three that were in the original plan that **Pierre L'Enfant** did for the City of Washington. It was built in 1873, just after the Civil War when the city was really booming; the population doubled at that point. So there were all kinds of public works projects, and Eastern Market is one of them. And this is the only

building from that post–Civil War period that still survives on Capitol Hill. Suspended signs list the various vendors' names and what they sell: Smithfield Hams, that's a local favorite—we are near Virginia and Maryland, remember—slab bacon, smoked sausage. Down the line in the produce section, there are stalls jammed with deep-purple eggplant, oranges, and honey tangerines. You can work up an appetite there. Eastern Market is on the National Register of Historic Places, and there's continual talk about restoring it, and what that might cost. Meantime, the old farmers' market just keeps going. Some of the vendors have been here for decades.

Washington Harbour: Fantastic. In **Georgetown** at the southern end of Wisconsin Avenue just at the edge of the **Potomac River**, Washington Harbour is glitzy, a complex of fountains, terraced steps banked with flowers in most seasons, restaurants, a few shops, and luxury condominiums, really luxury—$440-a-square-foot luxury. But you don't have to be rich to come here just to hang out, have a cup of coffee, check out the view.

In summer, Washington Harbour becomes our Venice, I think, and the river is our Grand Canal. All the fountains are going. The water's jammed with motorboats, canoes, mini-yachts. Across the Potomac, people are fishing on the Virginia shore. Washington Harbour has given us back our waterfront.

Rock Creek Cemetery: The cemetery was established in 1719 in a corner of Northwest Washington off North Capitol Street. And there's an incredible sculpture there. It's absolute. It's like the visualization of silence and peacefulness: in a grove of holly, a seated bronze figure larger than life, a woman shrouded in drapery, one hand at her chin, her eyes closed in reflection. She has a noble strength. Augustus Saint-Gaudens made this statue for Henry Adams, writer, historian, descendant of presidents, to mark the grave of his wife, Clover. She died in 1885. In 1918 it became Adams's burial place too. Eleanor Roosevelt came often during her White House years to take refuge in the serenity of this figure of repose.

35 ROCK CREEK PARK/ "P STREET BEACH"

Part of a winding, 4-mile stretch of meadows, woods, pathways, and the eponymous Rock Creek, the narrow segment of park west of Dupont Circle below the P Street bridge is a haven for sunbathers on warm days. The neighborhood being what it is, many of said sunbathers are gay, making for a fun, cruisy atmosphere. Rumor has it that heavier-duty cruising goes on in the nearby wooded area at night, especially after the bars close—at your own risk, of course. ◆ At P St NW. Park information, 282.1063

36 SOHO TEA & COFFEE

★★$ All right, so it's not quite SoHo in New York, but this coffeehouse is plenty funky for DC, and lots more interesting than **Starbucks**. Among the young, attractive java junkies here (both gay and not), alternative types and students predominate, with lots of piercings and laptops in evidence. That, plus the great windows overlooking the street scene and the local art (for sale) on the walls, makes this an interesting spot for the nonboozy set. The offerings range from insipid (watery hot chocolate) to tasty (sandwiches, quiches, cakes, and cookies). Jazz brunches, open-mike nights, and drag shows liven things up,

THE BEST

David B. Mixner
Writer and Activist

- A quiet walk in **Arlington National Cemetery**.
- Drinks at **Trumpets** after a day's work to exchange information with political gays and lesbians.
- Sitting on the west side of the **US Capitol** overlooking the **Mall**.
- Going to the **Kennedy Center**, especially if it is an opening night—all Washington is in the audience.
- Going to the **Human Rights Campaign Black Tie Dinner** in the fall with hundreds of others.
- Spending an afternoon "hanging" on **Dupont Circle** and visiting the local gay and lesbian shops, restaurants, and bookstores.
- Going to Sunday-morning services at the **National Cathedral**.
- Visiting John Kennedy's grave site to remember better times.
- Visiting the **US Memorial Holocaust Museum** to remember where intolerance takes us as a people.
- Taking a walk on the beautiful and quiet **Roosevelt Island**.
- Walking around gay and lesbian bars at midnight in the **P Street–17th Street** area and watching people.
- Afternoon tea at the **Four Seasons Hotel**.
- Taking the basement passage underneath the US Capitol from the Senate side to the House side—it makes you feel like a real insider!
- Watching from the south side of the **White House** as the presidential helicopter lands or takes off.

and the Internet terminal's a great way to keep up with your e-mail back home. Smoking is allowed but usually not overwhelming. ◆ Coffeehouse ◆ M-Tu, 6AM-2AM; W-Su, 6AM-4AM. 2150 P St NW (between 21st and 22nd Sts). 463.7646. ㅤ&

37 APEX

♂ This used to be Badlands, but it still holds its own with a young, cute bunch of guys. As always, the flavor here is basically white college boy, leavened of late with some Latinos and Asians. When the dance-floor action gets too hot, repair to the small lounge area on the way to the rear video bar; upstairs, a laid-back lounge annex with a pool table offers a quieter option. The throng burgeons for Tuesday night's half-price drinks, Thursday's college night (free admission with a student ID), Saturday is Liquid Ladies night, and any night for the after-hours scene. Last call is at 2AM on any given night; after-hours fun then continues until closing. ◆ Cover F, Sa after 10PM, Su after 4PM. Tu, Th, 9PM-3AM; F, Sa, 9PM-4AM. 1415 22nd St NW (between O and P Sts). 296.0505. www.apex-dc.com

38 OMEGA DC

♂
♀ Tucked in the alley behind **Escándalo!**, the former **Fraternity House** underwent a major overhaul in 1997. Gone is the dance floor, but the spiffed-up lower level now sports a more mod look and attracts more women than it used to. The upstairs is still a bit seedy, with pool tables and a darkish room showing porn films (women tend to steer clear). Both levels play music videos: progres-sive and retro below, dance and high-energy above. There are popular pool tournaments on Wednesday, but Thursday's drag karaoke may offer the best time of all to a friendly crowd of all ages and races. ◆ M-Th, Su, 4PM-2AM; F, 4PM-3AM; Sa, 8PM-3AM. 2122 P St NW (entrance off P St, between 21st and 22nd Sts). 223.4917. www.omegadc.com

39 DUPONT CIRCLE

Ⓟ Named after Civil War admiral Samuel DuPont, this compact park gives the area its name. The figures on the graceful marble fountain at its center were carved by Daniel Chester French, who created the **Lincoln Memorial**. The benches and lawn all around are popular venues for political demonstrations, chess matches, jam sessions, cruising, shirtless tanning, and plain old hanging out. Just don't hang out after dark, when the place attracts a less than salubrious element. ◆ At the intersection of Massachusetts, Connecticut, and New Hampshire Aves NW

40 THE CREW CLUB

♂ A gym, it calls itself, and a "naturalist preserve"—but at the bottom (so to speak) it's a bathhouse, and the cleanest and best in DC. The main floor houses a battleship-gray warren of "dressing rooms," along with a comfy and capacious TV lounge, a smaller porn-video room, a billiards room, vending machines, and a gym area. Downstairs is a chain-link maze draped in camouflage for voyeurs, exhibitionists, and group scenes. The guys here are mostly in their twenties and thirties, and range from average to deeelicious. ◆ Daily, 24 hours. 1321 14th St NW (between N St and

Restaurants/Clubs: Red | Hotels: Purple | Shops: Orange | Outdoors/Parks: Green | Sights/Culture: Blue

Rhode Island Ave). 319.1333.
www.crewclub.net

41 RENAISSANCE MAYFLOWER

$$$$ Serving Washington's glitterati with elegance and style for over half a century, this 657-room hotel is one of the most luxurious and historic lodgings in DC. The centrally located brick-and-limestone Beaux Arts building has a block-long lobby accented with Italian marble, brilliant chandeliers, and ornate ceilings. The **Grand Ballroom** is truly grand, with terraces, balconies, and bas-reliefs reminiscent of Wedgwood porcelain topped by a 21-foot ceiling. The **Café Promenade**, set in a light and airy atrium, serves Mediterranean fare daily; homosexual (and homophobic) FBI director J. Edgar Hoover lunched with his lovebunny Clyde Tolson here every day. The clubby **Town and Country Lounge** offers a buffet lunch and is reputed to serve the best martinis in town. Splendid rooms and suites—all top-of-the-line, some no-smoking, some with wet bars, and some furnished by Henredon—help justify the price tag. Concierge service, 24-hour room service, and valet parking are also available. ◆ 1127 Connecticut Ave NW (at Desales St). 347.3000, 800/468.3571; fax 776.9182. www.renaissancemayflower.com. ♿

42 DC EAGLE

♂ On a suitably grungy block, this big, three-floor ex-warehouse packs in everything from boy-next-door types to big, bearded, and pierced leather daddies (especially on weekends, and for special events like the "Mr. DC Eagle" contest). On the whole, though, Levi's outnumber chaps, and the average age is above 30. The main bar is quite a sight, with a mean motorcycle and machine gears hanging overhead; the warm-weather patio out back can get mighty frisky indeed. ◆ M-Th, 6PM-2AM; F, Sa, noon-3AM; Su, noon-2AM. 639 New York Ave NW (between Sixth and Seventh Sts). 347.6025. www.dceagle.com. ♿

43 NATIONAL MUSEUM OF WOMEN IN THE ARTS (NMWA)

Art collector Wilhelmina Holladay founded this unique museum in 1981 to promote the work of female artists; in 1987 the collection and library moved to its present 1907 Renaissance Revival home, and a new wing was opened in March of 1997. The growing collection includes the work of such well-known lesbian/bisexual artists as Georgia O'Keeffe, Frida Kahlo, and French painter Rosa Bonheur. ◆ Donation. M-Sa; Su, noon-5PM. Group tours by appointment.

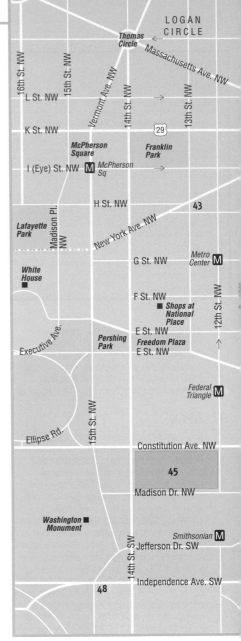

1250 New York Ave NW (at 13th St). 783.5000. www.nmwa.org. ♿

44 DONALD W. REYNOLDS CENTER FOR AMERICAN ART AND PORTRAITURE

During its 92-year stint as the US Patent Office, this building held archives of American ingenuity. Now the arched and pillared marble hallways that **Robert Mills** designed in the mid-1800s contain a wealth

M St. NW Ⓜ *Mt. Vernon Sq/UDC*

New York Ave. NW

L St. NW

42

K St. NW

Greyhound Station ■

Mt. Vernon Square

Massachusetts Ave. NW

I (Eye) St. NW

N Capitol St.

1st St. NE

2nd St. NE

I (Eye) St. NW

H St. NW

New Jersey Ave. NW

H St. NW

8th St. NW

Ⓜ *Gallery Place/ Chinatown*

G St. NW

G St. NW

44

F St. NW

4th St. NW

3rd St. NW

395

Ⓜ *Union Station*

■ **Union Station**

Shakespeare Theatre ■

6th St. NW

5th St. NW

E St. NW

Ⓜ

■ **Judiciary Square**

Judiciary Sq

2nd St. NW

1st St. NW

10th St. NW

9th St. NW

7th St. NW

Indiana Ave. NW

D St. NW

Pennsylvania Ave. NW

C St. NW

Ⓜ *Archives/ Navy Memorial*

Marshall Park

Louisiana Ave. NW

Delaware Ave. NE

Constitution Ave. NW

46

Reflecting Pool

47

E Capitol St.

Mall

4th St. SW

Smithsonian

49

Ⓜ *L'Enfant Plaza*

■ **Air and Space Museum**

Maryland Ave. SW

Ⓜ *Federal Center SW*

1st St. SW

Metro Station Ⓜ

N ↑

km
mi

1/4

1/8

1/2

1/4

of American artistic talent. The building is a century-old replica of the Parthenon rendered in Virginia freestone. During the Civil War, it served as a temporary barracks, hospital, and morgue. Clara Barton and Walt Whitman ministered to the wounded here. After an extensive renovation, this beautiful building was reopened on schedule on 1 July 2006 as the Donald W. Reynolds Center, which houses both the **National**

Portrait Gallery and the **Smithsonian American Art Museum.**

Most visitors to the National Portrait Gallery find it both humbling and inspiring to stand face-to-face with so much greatness. The gallery is filled with images of George Washington—including the famous "Lansdowne" version—that many Americans first see on their schoolroom walls, as well

Restaurants/Clubs: **Red** | Hotels: **Purple** | Shops: **Orange** | Outdoors/Parks: **Green** | Sights/Culture: **Blue**

as portraits of explorers, military heroes, Hollywood moguls, composers, and prizefighters. Among the colorful figures immortalized on canvas are Babe Ruth, Butch Cassidy, and the Sundance Kid. The federal government unintentionally began this collection in 1857 when it commissioned a series of presidential portraits. The permanent collection now totals 18,600 objects, including paintings, sculptures, etchings, photographs, and drawings. Works by John Singleton Copley, John Singer Sargent, Thomas Sully, Augustus Saint-Gaudens, and Charles Willson Peale, among other artists, can be found here.

The Smithsonian American Art Museum collection includes more than 39,000 pieces, including works by Edward Hopper, Andrew Wyeth, Winslow Homer, Mary Cassatt, Jacob Lawrence, and Benjamin West. There are selections of Hiram Powers's sculpture, oils by Albert Pinkham Ryder, New Deal art, and landscapes and frontier lifestyle depicted by Thomas Moran and Albert Bierstadt. The museum also has folk art, a large collection of miniatures, a 140,000-volume library, and a collection of daguerreotypes and photos dating back to 1839. A branch of the museum, the **Renwick Gallery** (see page 85), located in a separate building diagonally across from the White House, exhibits American crafts and decorative arts. ♦ Free. Daily, 11:30AM–7PM. F St NW (between Seventh and Ninth Sts). Information, 633.1000. &. www.npg.si.edu or www.americanart.si.edu. Metro: Gallery Pl/Chinatown

45 NATIONAL MUSEUM OF AMERICAN HISTORY

Closed for renovations until 2008. ♦ Free. Daily, 10AM–5:30PM. Tours: Tu-F, 10:15AM and 1PM; Sa, 10:15AM. Constitution Ave NW (between 12th and 14th Sts). 633.1000. &

46 NATIONAL GALLERY OF ART

One of the world's most exceptional collections of European and American painting, sculpture, and graphic art dating from the Middle Ages to the present is housed in two structures that are works of art in

themselves. The neoclassical **West Building**, built in 1941 and devoted to pre-20th century art, holds precious canvases by Titian, Rembrandt, El Greco, Monet, and Cézanne, along with works by famous homosexuals like Leonardo da Vinci (whose *Ginevra de' Benci* is currently his only painting on permanent display outside Europe). Among the 20th-century treasures of the **East Building**, contemplate the queer genius of Andy Warhol and Robert Rauschenberg. ♦ Free. Daily. Tours meet at the main-floor entrance of the West Building M-Sa at 10:30AM, 12:30PM, and 2:30PM and on Su at 12:30PM, 2:30PM, and 4:30PM and at the East Building M-Sa at 11:30AM and 1:30PM and on Su at 11:30AM, 1:30PM, and 3:30PM. West Bldg: Constitution Ave NW (between Fourth and Seventh Sts). East Bldg: Fourth St NW (between Madison Dr and Constitution Ave). 737.4215. www.nga.gov. &

47 CAPITOL

Since the cornerstone was laid in 1793, this building has seen a lot of action—much of it having a far-reaching effect on the gay and lesbian community. Most recently, it was here that the Defense of Marriage Act passed in 1996 to forestall same-sex unions after it appeared that Hawaii might legalize them, and it was also here that the ENDA bill banning discrimination in employment went down in defeat. Sit in the **Visitors' Galleries** or to find out what's on the agenda, call the switchboard or check the *Washington Post*. This is a fascinating place to visit. Be sure to see the **Rotunda** and **Statuary Hall**, with their artwork, and the **Old Senate Chamber**, the **President's Room**, and the **Old Supreme Court Chamber**. Tours of the Capitol are given Monday through Saturday between 9AM and 4:30PM; they last 30 minutes. Beginning at 8:15AM, free, timed, same-day tour tickets are given out on a first-come, first-served basis at the **Capitol Guide Service kiosk** located southwest of the Capitol near the intersection of First Street SW and Independence Avenue. Ticket holders then proceed to the South Visitor Screening Facility, and from there to the Capitol tour. Write your senator or representative in advance to arrange a VIP tour. The address for senators is **Senate Office Building**, Washington, DC 20510; for representatives, it's **House Office Building**, Washington, DC 20515. Foreign visitors can enter by showing a passport. ♦ Daily, 9AM–8PM, Memorial Day–Labor Day; daily, Labor Day–Memorial Day. East Front entrance at Capitol Plaza (between Independence Ave SE and Constitution Ave NE). 225.6827. &

I have nothing against gays. We had plenty of them in my administration.

—Richard Nixon, quoted in the *New Yorker*, July 1996

48 UNITED STATES HOLOCAUST MEMORIAL MUSEUM

Honoring *all* victims of the Holocaust—Jewish, Gypsy, disabled, mentally handicapped, and homosexual—one of the most moving memorials in Washington opened in May 1993 in a structure that reveals the intelligence and creativity of architect **James Ingo Freed** in every detail: from light fixtures that resemble watchtower spotlights to exits that look like prison doors.

At the start of the tour, visitors receive a card with information on a particular Holocaust victim, thus establishing a bond with a historical individual. Keep an eye open as you move through the exhibits for memorabilia such as the ID cards of pink triangle–wearing inmates. Don't miss the "Homosexuals in the Holocaust" account, and save time for the last exhibit, an hour-long film called *Testimony* in which survivors, including gays, deliver haunting accounts of the horror. Other gay testimonies, in print and on video, are available at the museum's library; check out *Homosexuals*, a booklet on gays in the Holocaust. There's also a computer learning center where databases enable everyone, regardless of computer literacy, to conduct research. After your visit, stop in the **Hall of Remembrance**, a good place to reflect on the experience.

Owing to the volume of visitors, (free) tickets are required for the permanent exhibition. You can call any Ticketmaster outlet, but the company will levy a service charge. A limited number of same-day tickets are available at the museum beginning at 10AM; get there early. ◆ Free, with ticket. Daily, 10AM–5:30PM. 100 Raoul Wallenberg Pl SW (between Maine and Independence Aves). 488.0400. www.ushmm.org. &

49 HIRSHHORN MUSEUM AND SCULPTURE GARDEN

For the modern art enthusiast, this doughnut-shaped building with its neat sculpture garden is the stuff of dreams; for the gay person, it's also a wonderful chance to discover the work of queers like David Hockney, Jasper Johns, Francis Bacon, and Andy Warhol. The gayest painting in the collection, though, is Larry Rivers's 1964 *The Greatest Homosexual*, a portrait of Napoléon Bonaparte. Check out the cafeteria and nifty museum shop. ◆ 1 Sept-31 May, M-F, 10:30AM and noon; Sa, Su, noon and 2PM; 1 June-31 Aug, M-F, noon; Sa, Su, noon and 2PM. Outdoor cafeteria hours vary seasonally; call for schedule. Independence Ave and Seventh St SW. Information, 633.1000; special tours, film and lecture schedule, 633.1618. www.hirshhorn.si.edu. &

Restaurants/Clubs: Red | Hotels: Purple | Shops: Orange | Outdoors/Parks: Green | Sights/Culture: Blue

1607 The first permanent English settlement is founded at Jamestown, Virginia.

1608 Captain John Smith sails up the **Potomac** to where Algonquin-speaking Indians live. Henry Fleete, a British fur trader, is the first European known to visit the area. He's captured by Indians and held prisoner for several years.

1662 The Maryland Colony is divided into large plantations. The first land patent on the future site of the District is granted.

1749 The city of **Alexandria** is laid out along the northern edge of the Virginia Colony.

1751 The Maryland Assembly establishes **Georgetown** along the southern border of the colony.

1765 The **Old Stone House** is built on what is now **M Street** in Georgetown.

1783 The US and Britain sign a peace treaty ending the American Revolution. Congress meets in Philadelphia to discuss the future of the newly independent colonies. There is no president, no money, and no strong unifying interest now that the war is over. Unpaid soldiers march on Congress to demand back pay. The legislatures discuss the possibility of establishing a federal capital where they could conduct the business of government without fear of intimidation. Several ideas are discussed but no agreement is reached, because of conflicting interests between Northern and Southern delegates.

1787 The Constitutional Convention meets in Philadelphia and frames the federal constitution. It provides for the selection of a tract of land, not to exceed 10 square miles, on which to build the federal capital.

1788 Virginia and Maryland offer parcels of territory for the establishment of a federal district.

1789 The US Constitution is ratified. George Washington is elected the first US president.

1790 The nation's capital is moved to Philadelphia. A political compromise is reached to build the federal capital on the Potomac River. Congress authorizes George Washington to choose the exact site on a federal territory and he selects an area that includes Georgetown on the north and Alexandria on the south. He envisions the growth of a great commercial port city on the Potomac, much like New York on the Hudson or Philadelphia on the Delaware.

1791 Washington appoints Andrew Ellicott to survey the area and **Pierre Charles L'Enfant**, a French military engineer who served in the Continental Army, to draw up plans for the city, to be known as the Territory of Columbia. Work is slow and difficult. The terrain is swampy, there is little infrastructure, and there is no place for workers or government officials to live. As a result, there is constant agitation in the press and in Congress to relocate to more civilized surroundings.

1792 Influenced by the Baroque landscape architecture of Paris and Versailles and envisioning a vast country with an enormous population, L'Enfant's plans for the capital reflect a sense of grandeur and scale. His design calls for a broad mile-long road (now **Pennsylvania Avenue**) to connect the **Capitol** with the **President's House** (the Executive Mansion). Public buildings are to be set widely apart on broad open roads. L'Enfant is soon dismissed from the job because he is late completing the plans and is unable to work with the commissioners overseeing the building of the city. His plan, though not followed in its entirety, nonetheless serves as the blueprint for Washington, DC. The cornerstone is laid for the **White House**.

1793 Washington lays the cornerstone of the **Capitol** building designed by **Dr. William Thornton**.

1800 Inadequate finances lead to delays in finishing the government buildings. When John Adams and other officials of the federal government move into the District, the White House, designed by **James Hoban**, is still under construction and only one wing of the Capitol is complete. Despite its incomplete state, the District becomes the nation's capital.

1801 Congress formally designates as federal territory the District of Columbia, which includes the town of Alexandria on the Virginia side of the Potomac.

1802 The City of Washington is incorporated with an elected council and a mayor appointed by the president. City population: 3,000.

1808 Construction begins on the **Washington Canal** along current-day **Constitution Avenue**.

1810 Population: 24,000.

1812-1814 Barely 25 years after the American Revolution, the former colonies are again pitted against England in the War of 1812. British armies under Admiral George Cockburn invade the District and burn the Capitol, the White House, and other public buildings. The image of Washington as the nation's capital is actually strengthened by its destruction. Although the city is devastated, it rebuilds within 5 years. The **Library of Congress** is burned and its collection of 3,000 books destroyed. Thomas Jefferson sells his personal collection of 6,500 volumes to Congress to start a new library. Today, the Library of Congress holds over 90 million items and is the largest in the world.

1815 President Madison signs the Treaty of Ghent, ending the War of 1812. Washington Canal is finished, running along what is now Constitution Avenue.

1820 Congress votes to give Washington residents the right to vote for a mayor and city council. However, the power of self-government is extremely limited. The population reaches 33,039.

1829 James Smithson, a British professor of chemistry at Oxford, dies. Although he had never visited the US, he greatly admired the new nation and leaves his considerable fortune to the US government to establish an institute for research and public education in Washington. His only stipulation is that his name be on the institute. It takes more than a decade for Congress to act on Smithson's wish. Today, the **Smithsonian** is the largest museum complex in the world.

1842 Although Washington has recovered from the destruction of the British invasion in 1814, the city remains a bit rough around the edges. English author Charles Dickens describes it as a "monument raised to a deceased project," consisting of "spacious avenues that begin in nothing and lead nowhere."

1846 Although Virginia donated land for the District in 1788, its citizens change their minds and ask for it back. The District territory south of the Potomac is returned to Virginia, reducing the capital by one third of its original size. Alexandria, Virginia, becomes an independent city again.

1848 The cornerstone is laid for the **Washington Monument**.

1850 Congress abolishes slave trade in the District, though owning slaves remains legal.

1855 The Smithsonian's first building, the **Castle**, designed by **James Renwick**, is completed.

1860 City population: 75,000.

1861 Abraham Lincoln is sworn in as the sixteenth president. When the Civil War breaks out, the population of the city explodes with an influx of Union soldiers, workers, and escaped slaves. An all-out effort is made to protect Washington from Confederate troops, many of which are billeted dangerously close to the capital. Government buildings are converted to hospitals and barracks for Union soldiers. A network of forts is erected around the city's southern perimeter.

1862 Congress frees all slaves in the District.

1863 President Abraham Lincoln issues the Emancipation Proclamation. **Ford's Theatre** opens.

1864 The war gets dangerously close to the District. Confederate General Jubal Early threatens to overrun the city but is defeated at nearby Fort Stevens. The Confederacy never again comes close to capturing the Union capital.

1865 End of the Civil War. Confederate General Robert E. Lee surrenders to Union General Grant at Appomattox. Five days later, President Lincoln is assassinated at Ford's Theatre.

1867 Congress gives Washington residents the right to vote. **Howard University**, the capital's first black university, is chartered by Congress.

1870 Spurred by an influx during the Civil War, Washington's population nearly doubles to about 132,000.

1871 Congress creates a territorial government for the District. All local officials are appointed by the president.

1874 The territorial form of government is abandoned. Congress resumes direct control of the District. A panel of three commissioners appointed by the president runs the city. Voting rights for Washington residents are stripped. The city's first art museum, the **Corcoran Gallery**, opens on Pennsylvania Avenue.

1880 The construction of streetcar lines hastens the growth of outlying areas. The population reaches about 178,000.

1885 Nearly 100 years after Congress passed a resolution to build a monument to the hero of the American Revolution, the Washington Monument is completed.

1890 **Rock Creek Park** and **Potomac Park** are established. The cornerstone of the Library of Congress is laid. The population reaches about 230,000.

1895 Washington annexes Georgetown.

1897 The first permanent Library of Congress building opens. (Previously, the Library had been housed within the congressional complex.)

1900 Washington celebrates its centennial. The population reaches about 279,000.

1902 The McMillan Commission is established to ensure that construction in Washington remains true to L'Enfant's original plans: There is to be an emphasis on wide avenues and open spaces punctuated by great monuments.

1907 **Union Station** is completed. President Roosevelt lays the cornerstone for the **National Cathedral**.

1912 First Lady Helen Taft and Japan's Viscountess Chinda (wife of the Japanese ambassador) plant the first of two cherry trees as Japan's gift to Washington; the total gift is 3,020 trees.

1914 Construction begins on a memorial to Lincoln.

1917 As the nation enters World War I, Washington experiences a construction boom. Rows of buildings, intended to be temporary, are erected around the **Mall**. (So much for L'Enfant's plan for wide-open spaces.)

1918 By the end of World War I, Washington's population has reached nearly 400,000.

1922 The **Lincoln Memorial**, designed by Henry Bacon, is dedicated. Black officials are segregated at opening ceremonies.

1926 The National Capital Parks and Planning Commission is established. The Public Buildings Act leads to the construction of many federal buildings.

1931 The nation is in the midst of the Great Depression. Marchers demonstrate in Washington, seeking relief from economic hardship.

1932 The election of Franklin D. Roosevelt and the launching of the New Deal results in an explosion in the size of the federal government; new buildings change the Washington landscape. Over 17,000 army veterans march on Washington demanding back pay.

1937 Congress grants a charter to establish a **National Gallery of Art**. Andrew Mellon, the financier, donates a building to house the museum.

1940 The District's population soars to about 663,000, spurred by New Deal programs and black migration from the South.

1941 The National Gallery of Art opens.

1943 The **Jefferson Memorial** is dedicated, and the **Pentagon** is completed.

1950 During the Korean War, the population of Washington peaks at approximately 802,000.

1960 The District's population drops for the first time, to about 764,000.

1961 John F. Kennedy is inaugurated the thirty-fourth president. Congress ratifies the twenty-third amendment to the Constitution, giving Washington residents the right to vote in presidential, not local, elections.

1963 Civil rights leader Martin Luther King Jr. leads 200,000 demonstrators in a "March on Washington for Jobs and Freedom." King delivers his "I Have a Dream" speech on the steps of the Lincoln Memorial. John F. Kennedy is assassinated in Dallas and buried in **Arlington National Cemetery**.

1964 The **Capital Beltway** is completed.

1967 Congress reorganizes the District's government. The three-commissioner system is replaced with a mayor, an assistant commissioner, and a city council, all appointed by the president. Although pressure grows for self-rule, it remains elusive.

1968 Race riots rock the city following the assassination of Martin Luther King Jr. Twelve people are killed, and property damage costs $24 million.

1970 Anti–Vietnam War demonstrations in The Mall reach enormous proportions. District residents are given the right to elect one nonvoting delegate to the House of Representatives. Population: about 757,000.

1971 The **John F. Kennedy Center for the Performing Arts** opens.

1973 Limited local self-rule is achieved. Residents of the District are given the right to vote for their local leaders. Congress reserves the right to veto any action that threatens the federal interest. Moreover, the city budget must be reviewed and enacted by Congress.

1975 Walter Washington is the first popularly elected mayor of Washington, DC.

1976 The US celebrates its bicentennial. The modernistic Washington subway system, called the **Metro**, begins operation.

1978 The **East Building** of the National Gallery, designed by **I.M. Pei**, opens.

1979 Continuing in a long tradition of civil protest, farmers demonstrate for farm relief in Washington.

1980 Washington's population falls to approximately 638,000.

1982 Amid controversy, the **Vietnam War Memorial**, designed by Maya Ying Lin, is built. Known as The Wall, it contains the names of all US casualties in Vietnam. Contrary to expectations, the popular reaction is clear, powerful, and favorable. It becomes one of the most visited Washington attractions.

1984 The **Washington Convention Center** opens.

1987 Opening of the **Smithsonian Quadrangle**.

1990 The National Cathedral, begun in 1907, is finally completed.

1992 Near the Vietnam War Memorial, the **Women's Memorial**, Glenna Goodacre's bronze sculpture of three uniformed women tending a wounded male soldier, is dedicated; it honors the estimated 10,000 women who served in the war. William Jefferson Clinton, Democratic governor of Arkansas, is elected the forty-first president of the US.

1995 Pennsylvania Avenue closes to motorists between 15th and 17th Streets to protect the White House from terrorist attacks.

1997 Washington's first memorial to Franklin D. Roosevelt is dedicated. The **Women in Military Service Memorial** opens, honoring women who serve in the US armed forces.

1998 Anthony Williams is elected mayor, ending nearly 2 decades of local rule by former mayor Marion Barry.

1999 Bill Clinton becomes the second US president ever to be impeached by the House of Representatives; like Andrew Johnson before him, Clinton is found not guilty (of high crimes and misdemeanors) by the Senate.

2000 George W. Bush defeats Al Gore in a highly contested presidential election that's eventually decided by the Supreme Court.

2001 On September 11, terrorists fly American Airlines Flight 77 into the Pentagon, destroying a significant portion of the building and killing 125 people. That same day, two other planes destroy the World Trade Center, killing nearly 3,000 people, and a third crashes in rural Pennsylvania in the worst terrorist attack in American history.

2003 Ranking as the largest building in DC, the city's new 2.3-million-square-foot convention center opens, offering more than 700,000 square feet of exhibit space and more than 100,000 square feet of meeting space.

2004 The long-awaited **National World War II Memorial** opens just west of the Washington Monument. It was dedicated with great fanfare during Memorial Day Weekend 2004, with President George W. Bush, Bob Dole, and Tom Hanks participating in the opening ceremonies.

2005 On July 9, after a long wait, Tian Tian and Mei Xiang, the Giant Pandas at the National Zoo, finally produce their first offspring, Tai Shan.

2006 On November 13, President George W. Bush dedicates a memorial to Dr. Martin Luther King Jr. where a monument will be built on a 4-acre site near the Lincoln Memorial and close to the location where Dr. King delivered his famous "I Have a Dream" speech in 1963. The construction is expected to be completed in 2008.

INDEX

H

M

RESTAURANTS

Only restaurants with star ratings are listed below. All restaurants are listed alphabetically in the main (preceding) index. Always call in advance to ensure a restaurant has not closed, changed its hours, or booked its tables for a private party. The restaurant price ratings are based on the average cost of an entrée for one person, excluding tax and tip.

★★★★ An Extraordinary Experience
  ★★★ Excellent
    ★★ Very Good
      ★ Good

$$$$ Big Bucks ($31 and up)
 $$$ Expensive ($21-$30)
  $$ Reasonable ($13-$20)
   $ The Price is Right (less than $12)

HOTELS

The hotels listed below are grouped according to their price ratings; they are also listed in the main index. The hotel price ratings reflect the base price of a standard room for two people for one night during the peak season.

$$$$ Big Bucks ($200 and up)
$$$ Expensive ($150-$200)
$$ Reasonable ($100-$150)
$ The Price is Right (less than $100)

$$$$

$

FEATURES

$$$

BESTS

$$

MAPS

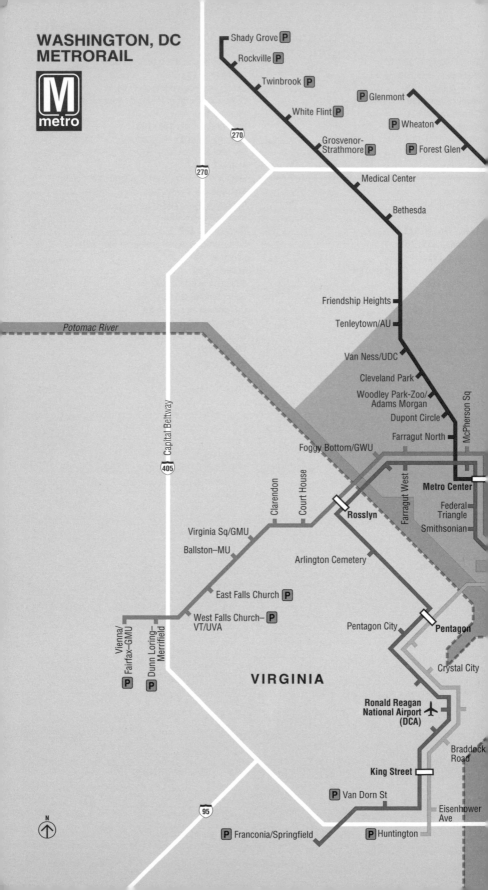